CW01498217

Mexico

Mexico
A History

PAUL GILLINGHAM

ALLEN LANE
an imprint of
PENGUIN BOOKS

ALLEN LANE

UK | USA | Canada | Ireland | Australia
India | New Zealand | South Africa

Allen Lane is part of the Penguin Random House group of companies whose addresses can be found at global.penguinrandomhouse.com.

Penguin Random House UK
One Embassy Gardens, 8 Viaduct Gardens, London SW11 7BW

penguin.co.uk

First published in the United States of America by Atlantic Monthly Press, an imprint of Grove Atlantic 2025
First published in Great Britain by Allen Lane 2025
001

Printed and bound in Great Britain by Clays Ltd, Elcograf S.p.A.

The authorized representative in the EEA is Penguin Random House Ireland, Morrison Chambers, 32 Nassau Street, Dublin D02 YH68

A CIP catalogue record for this book is available from the British Library

ISBN: 978-0-241-38604-0

Penguin Random House is committed to a sustainable future for our business, our readers and our planet. This book is made from Forest Stewardship Council® certified paper.

For Snježana, who makes so much possible.

History is nothing more than a dream. Those who made it dreamed things that never happened; those who study it dream of things past; those who teach it dream that they own the truth.

Rodolfo Usigli, El Gesticulador

Contents

Mexico

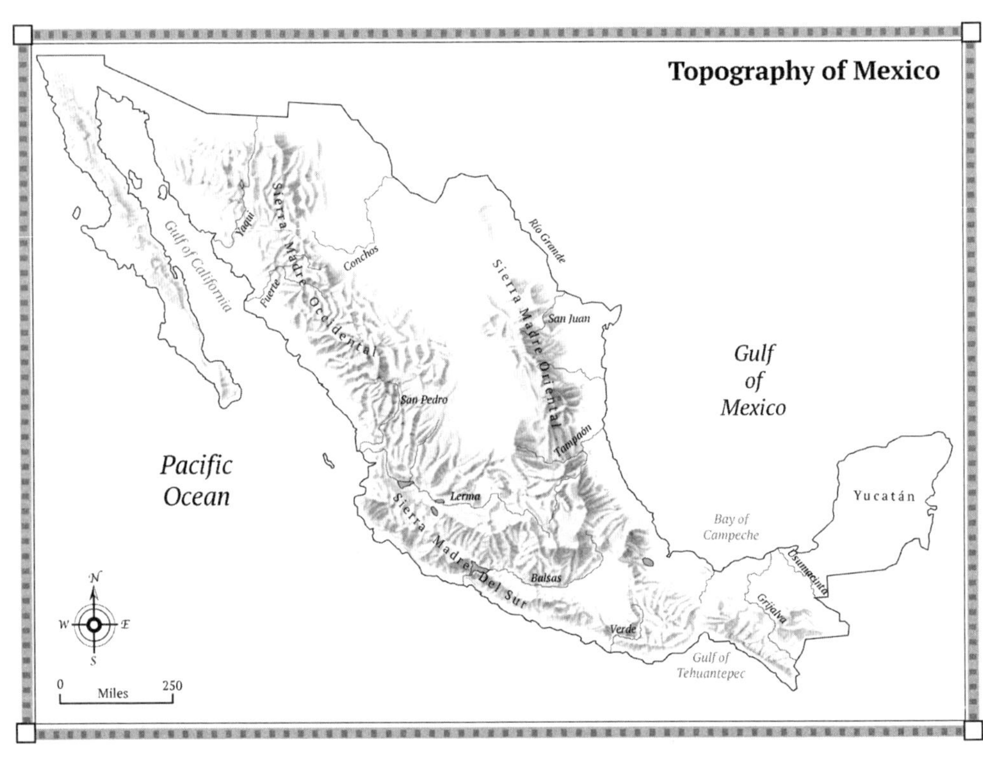
Topography of Mexico
Gulf of California
Yaqui
Sierra Madre Occidental
Fuerte
Conchos
Río Grande
Sierra Madre Oriental
San Juan
San Pedro
Tampaón
Gulf of Mexico
Pacific Ocean
Lerma
Sierra Madre Del Sur
Balsas
Bay of Campeche
Yucatán
Usumacinta
Grijalva
Verde
Gulf of Tehuantepec
N
W
E
S
0
Miles
250

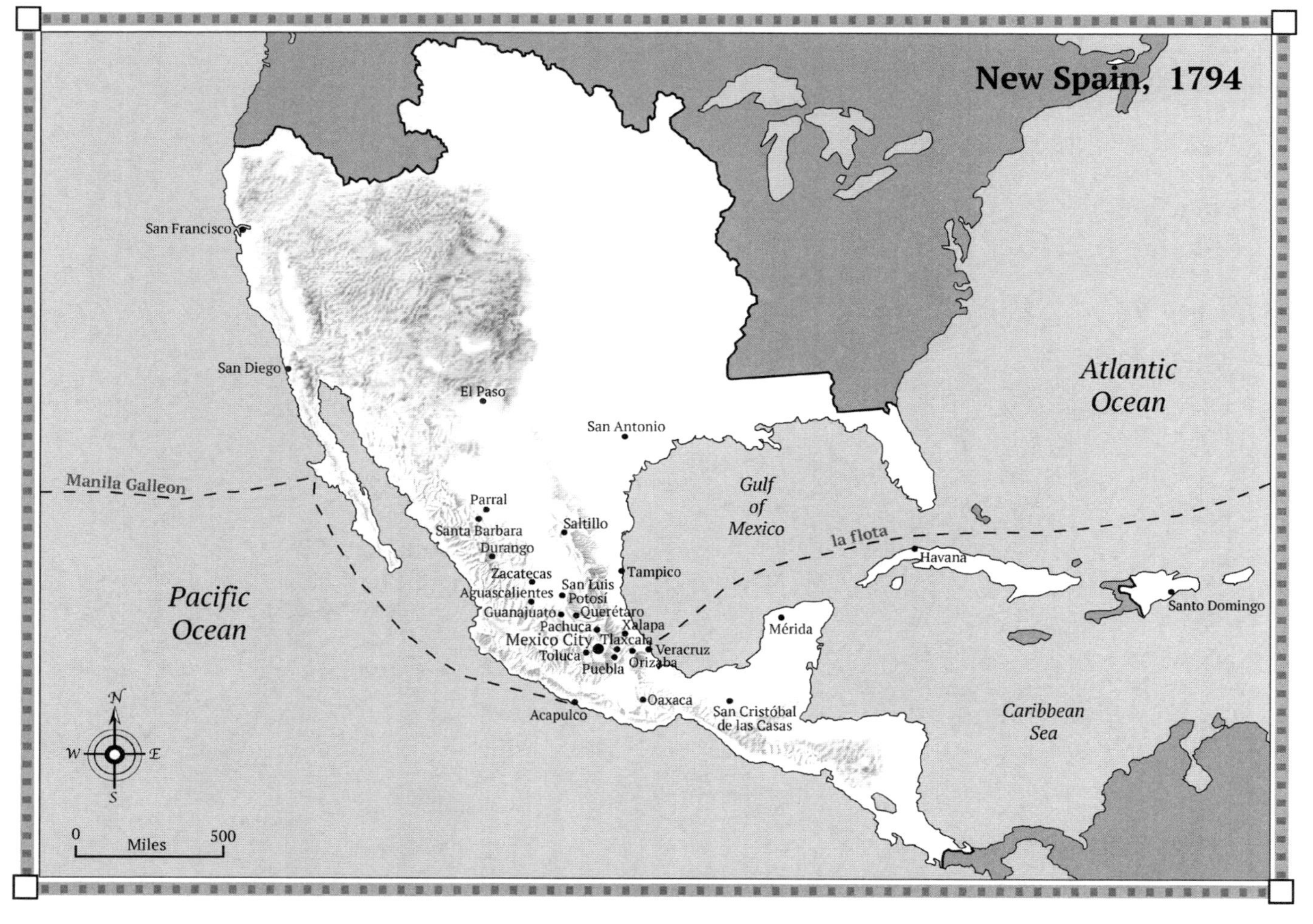

New Spain, 1794
Atlantic Ocean
Pacific Ocean
Gulf of Mexico
Caribbean Sea
Manila Galleon
la flota
San Francisco
San Diego
El Paso
San Antonio
Parral
Santa Barbara
Saltillo
Durango
Zacatecas
Tampico
San Luis Potosí
Aguascalientes
Guanajuato
Querétaro
Pachuca
Xalapa
Mexico City
Tlaxcala
Veracruz
Toluca
Puebla
Orizaba
Oaxaca
Acapulco
San Cristóbal de las Casas
Mérida
Havana
Santo Domingo
N
W
E
S
0
Miles
500

Indigenous Mexico, 1821
Comanche raiding trails, 18/19th Century
Pima Alto
Apache
Ópata
Seri
O'odham
Pima Bajo
Rarámuri
Concho
Toboso
Cochimí
Yaqui
Mayo
Cahita
Coahuilteco
Tepehuano
Irritila
Tebaca
Acaxee
Guaycura
Sabaibo
Xixime
Tamaulipeco
Gulf of Mexico
Guachichil
Pericú
Pisones
Zacateco
Cora
Pame
Tepecano
Huasteco
Chichimeca
Otomí
Maya
Totonaco
Nahua
Mazahua
Purépecha
Nahua
Popoloco
Pacific Ocean
Chontal
Mixteco
Mixe
Zoque
Tzeltal
Tzotzil
Amuzgo
Zapoteco
Nahua
N
W
E
S
0
Miles
250

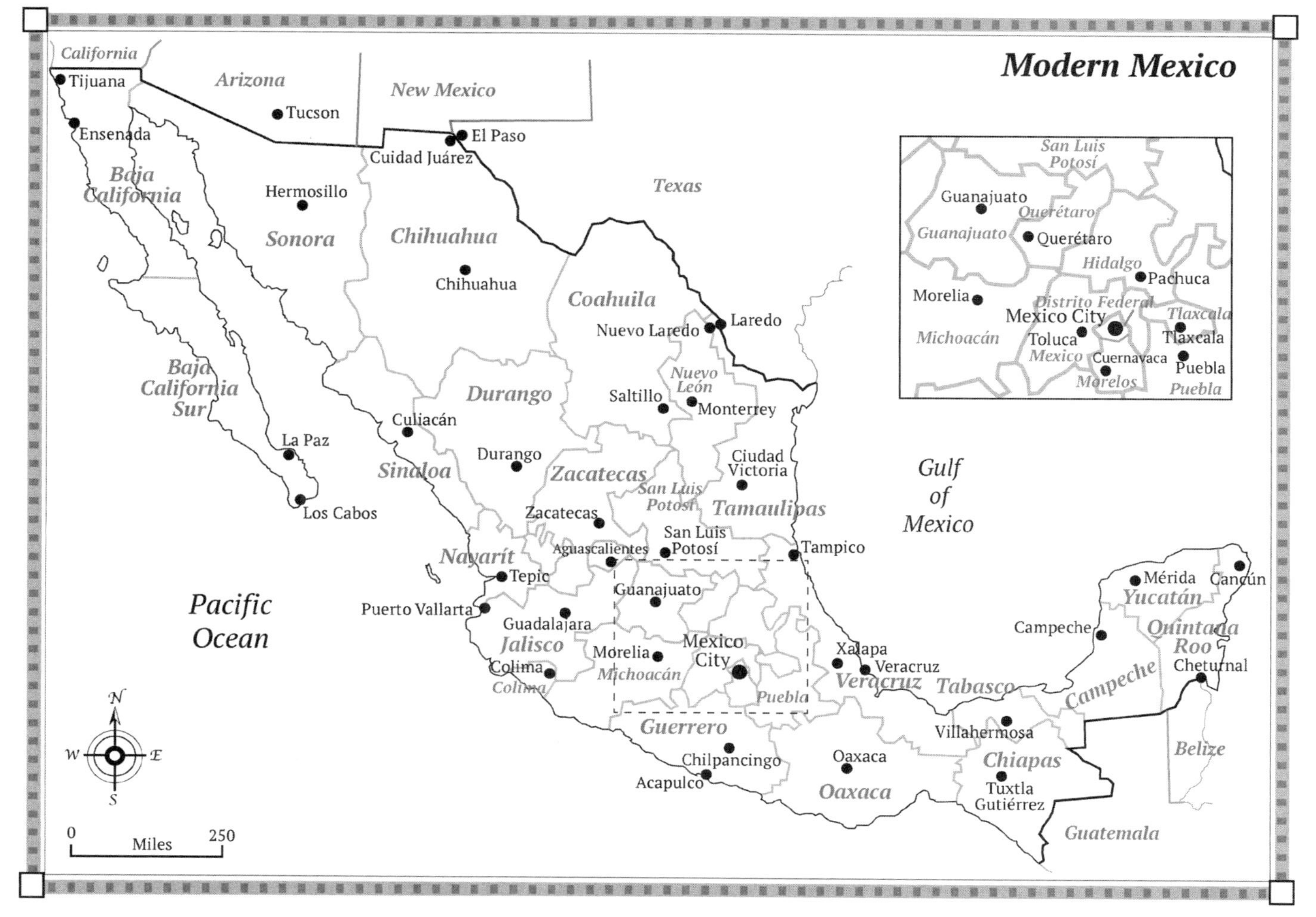

Modern Mexico
California
Tijuana
Ensenada
Arizona
Tucson
New Mexico
El Paso
Cuidad Juárez
Texas
Baja California
Hermosillo
Sonora
Chihuahua
Chihuahua
Coahuila
Nuevo Laredo
Laredo
Baja California Sur
Nuevo León
Saltillo
Monterrey
Durango
Culiacán
La Paz
Durango
Sinaloa
Zacatecas
Ciudad Victoria
San Luis Potosí
Tamaulipas
Los Cabos
Zacatecas
San Luis Potosí
Aguascalientes
Tampico
Nayarít
Tepic
Gulf of Mexico
Pacific Ocean
Puerto Vallarta
Guanajuato
Guadalajara
Jalisco
Morelia
Mexico City
Michoacán
Colima
Colima
Puebla
Xalapa
Veracruz
Veracruz
Tabasco
Guerrero
Chilpancingo
Acapulco
Oaxaca
Oaxaca
Villahermosa
Chiapas
Tuxtla Gutiérrez
Guatemala
Belize
Campeche
Campeche
Chetumal
Quintana Roo
Mérida
Yucatán
Cancún
San Luis Potosí
Guanajuato
Querétaro
Guanajuato
Querétaro
Hidalgo
Pachuca
Morelia
Distrito Federal
Mexico City
Tlaxcala
Michoacán
Toluca
Tlaxcala
Mexico
Cuernavaca
Puebla
Morelos
Puebla
N
W
E
S
0
Miles
250

Introduction

In 1534, or maybe 1535, the Spaniards found him among the dead, far to the south in Honduras. He was dark-skinned, pierced, and tattooed, and he had led the Maya people of Chetumal to war for two decades. But he was also in his own way white, a fellow Spaniard called Gonzalo Guerrero, and his three children, born of marriage with a Maya woman, might be seen as the first Mexicans.[1]

The history of Mexico, understood as the country and people that grew from such first contacts, began with that Spaniard in 1511, when his caravel foundered on a reef called Los Alacranes, the Scorpions, about seventy miles north of the Yucatán Peninsula. Seventeen men and two women made it off the wreck and rowed toward the nearest land, pushed by the westward ocean current and the prevailing northerlies. After some two weeks in a small boat without food or water, ten made it to shore. The nearest Maya captured the survivors and sacrificed half of them; another three died, of exhaustion, starvation, and grief, according to one chronicler; two endured, the sailor Gonzalo Guerrero and the friar Jerónimo de Aguilar. Both came from the southern Spanish province of Andalusia, like so many others in the New World, and like so many others in the New World both had been born poor. Aguilar came from Écija, a barren town on the Río Tinto; Guerrero came from Niebla, close to Columbus's port of Palos, a place impoverished enough to have known famine and cannibalism. After their capture both Aguilar and Guerrero learned Chontal Maya and were accepted into Maya society. But thereafter their stories diverged radically.[2]

Aguilar became a slave who literally counted the days—he ended up off by three—and who according to his own, probably unreliable story rejected paganism and women and consoled himself with a prayer book.[3] Guerrero, on the other hand, became a military advisor to the lord of Chetumal, the cacique Na Chan Can, and "taught the Indians to fight, showing them how to make barricades and bastions . . . and by living as an Indian gained a great reputation."[4] He married the cacique's daughter. When the Spanish landed on the coast in 1519 Jerónimo de Aguilar escaped to their camp in a loincloth and a canoe, falling to his knees, croaking, "God and Santa María and Seville."[5] By then his Spanish had degenerated to near-pidgin, but even so he became the expedition's first translator, putting across the diplomacy and menace of the early days of the Spanish landing. By contrast the aptly named Guerrero, "warrior," told the Maya from the outset that they had to make war on the Europeans, and led by example until he died fighting. In 1527 the Spanish tried to lure him back with a letter reminding him he was a fellow Christian and telling him of his "great opportunity to serve God and the Emperor, Our Lord, in the pacification and baptism of these people." Guerrero wrote back with the assurance that he did "remember God." "The Spaniards," he said, "will find in me a very good friend."[6] It was a very Mexican irony. He fought on against his countrymen, first in Yucatán and later in Central America, for the rest of his life.

Improbable stories of meetings across oceans hardly start with the Spaniards in the New World. In the Dark Ages the *Navigatio Sancti Brendani Abbatis* told of how Saint Brendan had set off around 500 CE from Ireland to find the Promised Land of the Saints, which he did, returning with accounts of a green and pleasant land somewhere across the open ocean. In 922 the Baghdadi envoy Ibn Fadlān traveled to the Upper Volga River, where he met some Vikings, recording with ethnographic neutrality their gruesome human sacrifices; less than a century later other Vikings actually made it to the Americas, where they established a short-lived hamlet at L'Anse aux Meadows in grim Newfoundland. By the end of the Middle Ages ships were bigger and navigation better; at the start of the fifteenth century the Chinese Muslim Zheng He took large fleets as far as the Horn of Africa and Zanzibar, conquering Sri Lanka and Sumatra en route. And in the early sixteenth century the Portuguese progress in the Far East mirrored that of the Spanish in the Americas even down to the year. When the Spanish took Cuba in 1511, the Portuguese took Malacca; as Hernán Cortés settled in central Mexico in January 1520, his forgotten Portuguese equivalent, Tomé Pires, was setting off from the port of Guangdong to Beijing.[7]

The difference between these voyages, though, was not that the Spanish won and the Portuguese lost, with the Chinese executing Pires. It was that in the sixteenth century the Spanish were not just explorers, like their Old World forebears. In Mexico they were sometimes raiders, sometimes traders, but above all they were settlers. Individuals might dream of making a fortune and going home to lord it in Spanish society, Iberian nabobs, but collectively the Spanish were colonists from their first landing onward, coming to the New World to found towns and stay. And this was the meeting of two long-separated worlds. The fossil record and genetic analyses establish that ten or so species made it across the Atlantic before the Spanish, including the ancestors of all American rodents and monkeys. An iguana had crossed the Pacific.[8] Yet they made next to no impact on human culture. The two worlds remained radically different in everything from biota—the Indians[9] had no livestock to speak of, the Europeans no tomatoes or potatoes—to urban planning. Mexican urbanites had invented public toilets and highly sophisticated hydraulic engineering, but neither steel nor the wheel.

But alongside the striking differences came multiple similarities. Both the Spanish and the Aztec empires were patchworks of quite different societies, stitched together in a very recent past. The Iberians were historically divided between two mutually hostile religions, Christianity and Islam; two different language groups, Semitic (Arabic), and Indo-European (Castilian, Catalan, and Portuguese); and the language isolate Basque, unrelated to any other tongue on Earth. Politically they lived in a loose confederation of medieval kingdoms, three of which—Portugal, Castile, and Aragon—preserved their own monarchies as the sixteenth century began. Half the peninsula, the South and East, was culturally and economically embedded in the Mediterranean world; the other half, the West and Northwest, was committed to the fast-growing Atlantic world, with its fisheries, northern markets, and possibilities in Africa and beyond. The entire assemblage was knit together mythically by the centuries of war that drove the Muslim armies, once dominant, back to the south, and politically by the central kingdom of Castile, whose warlords controlled the production and exchange of wool and wheat, Europe's two main commodities. Modern Spain was born only at the end of the fifteenth century, when Castile absorbed its junior partners Valencia, Catalonia, and Aragon and seized Granada, the last Muslim stronghold. Only then was the modern Spanish language formalized with its first book of grammar. The country's very name, *España*, was first written on a map decades after the conquest of Mexico, at about the same time as people there began to call themselves Mexicans.[10]

The Aztec Empire was likewise a recent creation, also dating from the turn of the sixteenth century. Its center lay in the high Valley of Mexico and the city of Tenochtitlán, whose hundreds of thousands of inhabitants made it one of the world's largest; it had absorbed its own junior partners, the neighboring kingdoms of Texcoco and Tlatelolco, at more or less the same time as the Spanish did theirs. The Aztecs, or Mexica as they more often called themselves, had migrated over generations from the dry Northwest into the temperate central highlands, drawn by the wealth and sophistication of the Nahua cities there and the maize that underlay it all. Outclassed by better-funded and -organized armies, in the thirteenth century the Mexica settled the swamplands of the large central valley and set out to climb from mercenaries to rulers. Two centuries later, their meritocratic flair for dynastic intrigue, engineering, and warfare had brought them dominance over the Valley of Mexico. With that dominance came access to the tax revenues and military resources of the culturally homogenous peoples who surrounded the valley for hundreds of miles, spoke versions of the same Nahua language and believed in the same gods of their own classical antiquity. All of those resources—cultural, economic, and military—became raw materials for dramatic expansion.

Thus, in terms of the basic structures of history, mythos, and politics, the Mexica and the Spanish were in some ways poised to understand each other. Both kingdoms were products of a long march south from a harsh North; both were militarized theocracies, their leaders proclaiming manifest destinies. Both had warrior saints as their intercessors with the divine, Huitzilopochtli for the Mexica and Saint James for the Spanish. Both saw themselves as being caught between barbarians of mountains and drylands—the Chichimeca to the north of the Aztec capital, the Berbers of the Atlas Mountains and the Sahara to the south of Spain—and civilized neighbors too powerful to crush: the Maya for the Mexica, the French and the Ottomans for the Spanish. And in stitching together their empires, both combined elegant centers with piratical frontiers, marriages of nobility and extortion that meant not any single political system but rather a series of defensible strongholds, claims to new ownership, domination of some but not all the people of the new territories.

The meeting of the two places in that first contact between the Maya and the two shipwrecked sailors could be straitjacketed into many meanings. The encounter of the two worlds was bound to happen, and what happened next was not the story of great men or—in the case of Malintzin, an indigenous power behind the conquistador's throne—great women. Yet the lives of those first two people on the coast of Yucatán, the priest Aguilar and the sailor Guerrero, were apt symbols of much to come: the cosmopolitan and the parochial, the violent and the tolerant, the inevitable and the improbable, the many Mexicos. Above all, their stories evoke an unprecedentedly hybrid place. In its first centuries Mexico was more profoundly, globally hybrid than anywhere else in the prior history of the world, a meeting of hundreds of indigenous peoples with Iberians, with West Africans as numerous as those Iberians for the first century, with half-forgotten Asians who arrived as slaves and melted into local societies. Colonial authorities from the start tried to prevent this promiscuity, at times violent, at times free; everyday people felt differently and ignored them. By the seventeenth century Mexico had become what the United States aspired to be at the end of the twentieth century: not *e pluribus unum*, but out of very, very many a smaller number of multicultural groups whose members could sometimes move from one to another and who, despite their cultured and legislated differences, were all acknowledged to be fully human.

This was not the beginnings of a deliberately chosen, progressive mingling of races, in Spanish *mestizaje*. The claim that to be Mexican is to be mestizo is a modern nationalist claim that has propped up an intolerant liberalism, authoritarianism, and even ethnocide. Those who hawked mestizaje were often disingenuous: While twentieth-century political and intellectual elites boasted of a post-racial Mexico, they secretly aimed to whiten its population with racist immigration policies.[11] Dozens of indigenous societies wanted little to do with such people and fought to remain autonomous for centuries. To some influential thinkers, a "deep Mexico" persisted, *México profundo*, where a broad swathe of the rural and urban poor hung on against the odds to an unacknowledged pre-Hispanic civilization.[12] Yet while mestizaje is an ambiguous and loaded ideology, it is also an incontestable sociological reality, because Mexico for centuries was the world's greatest melting pot, in some ways its center, the crossroads of an empire that at its peak stretched from Sicily to southern China and from the Netherlands to West Africa.

This book aims to tell that story from the early sixteenth to the early twenty-first century, with all the predictable caveats. It is a history simultaneously comprehensive and partial, one that seeks to identify the most important phenomena that shaped Mexican lives and then explore them in greater depth. It intersperses chapters that narrate the outlines of a period with chapters that take different perspectives on that same time, aspiring to "a series of [stories] with sliding panels . . . like some medieval palimpsest where different sorts of truth are thrown down one upon the other, the one obliterating or perhaps supplementing another."[13] The approach of circling the same history from different viewpoints does not mean a loss of causation, however, and I have tried to preserve a hierarchy of the reasons why things happened when they did. I have also tried to avoid our enormous condescension toward the past, recognizing not just differences but also parallels between the history of Mexico and the histories of closer times and places. Mexico has always contained multitudes.[14]

Part One

Inconclusive Conquest

1519–c. 1650

Chapter One

Invasion and Civil War

The numbers in what we call the conquest of Mexico, like the stories, tend not to add up. Most of the invading Spanish were semiliterate; their numbers were often based on enemy estimates or "body counts," which are always questionable, whether the source is Julius Caesar on the conquest of Gaul or General Westmoreland on the conquest of Vietnam.[1]

To make matters worse, the Spanish had a flair for melodrama—the conquistadors were passionate about amateur dramatics and put on plays wherever they went[2]—and good reason to exaggerate the odds they faced and the slaughter they perpetrated. So, whether in the florid prose of their letters and chronicles or in the wooden boasting of *probanzas*, self-aggrandizing catalogues of services rendered, the Spanish were strategically innumerate.[3] In a series of casual asides, they did however include one critical dataset: the vast numbers of indigenous warriors who fought by their side in the wars against the Mexica and the peoples beyond the Valley of Mexico. Figures vary from account to account, but the order of magnitude is always the same: thousands for expeditions to the coasts, deserts, and forests; tens of thousands at the beginning of the siege of Tenochtitlán, the Mexica capital; hundreds of thousands by its end. The conclusion is inescapable: It was not the Spanish but the indigenous peoples of central Mexico who destroyed the Mexica Empire, and the conflict itself was not so much foreign conquest as vicious civil war.

The Mexica, like all empire builders, told stories of manifest destiny. They had been guided to their home on the Valley of Mexico's central lake by a prophecy, they said, in which an eagle ate a snake while perched on a cactus. They also told the Spaniards they had been in this promised land for millennia. Yet in reality theirs was a young state, and their island had initially been a wasteland refuge from more powerful and hostile neighbors. The Mexica had been subordinate to the neighboring city-state of Azcapotzalco until 1428, and only took firm control over the central valley in the second half of the fifteenth century, a few decades before the Spanish arrived in 1519. Their first major war of the sixteenth century was against Atlixco, a town just the other side of Popocatépetl, the volcano that rises high above the valley rim. By then, their territories stretched as far east as the Gulf Coast and nearly as far south as Guatemala. But it was a patchwork empire made up of recently conquered and recalcitrant city-states.

By the time the Spanish arrived it had also reached something like its natural limits, which were far narrower than those of modern Mexico. The Mexica Empire enveloped but did not conquer the kingdoms of the Purépecha of Michoacán and the Zapotecs of Oaxaca, whose accomplished militaries and forbidding mountains preserved their independence during the rise of the central powers. In 1478 some twenty thousand imperial troops died in the last campaign against the Purépecha.[4] Not far to the north were the drylands, where paltry resources and decentralized, mobile, dangerous peoples—the Pames, Guamares, Zacatecos, and Guachichiles, all barbarians to metropolitan eyes—militated against expeditions into what the Mexica called the Great Chichimeca. In the highlands to the east of the Valley of Mexico the small but bellicose city-state of Tlaxcala was still, by the skin of its teeth, free. Mountains did not guarantee survival against Mexica conquest, but when combined with sophisticated enemy states they made the effort of establishing direct rule unappealing.

Above all, the Mexica had yet to push into the lands of the other great sedentary civilization of the time, the Maya. In 1519 the conquest of the Yucatán Peninsula and the country stretching into modern Guatemala was their ultimate strategic goal. It had been done before, in the fourth century, when the central empire of Teotihuacán forcibly installed its ruler in the wealthiest city-state, Tikal.[5] There was compelling reason for such tricky expansionism: The southern city-states, politically divided but culturally quite homogenous, controlled the lucrative trade routes into Central America and beyond. Jade, feathers, shells, dyes, cacao, and gold were all superb commodities in the indigenous value system, combining portability with low volume and high value; their commerce was the Indian equivalent of the European spice trade. The Maya of the time were some six centuries past their own golden age, the classical period of wealth when major cities such as Tikal housed tens of thousands of people and some of the most sophisticated intellectual, military, and material cultures in the world. Those metropolises collapsed toward the end of the first millennium CE, victims of overpopulation and climate change, severe droughts and tropical storms that devastated southern Mexico and the Caribbean.[6] Yet however many centuries past their prime, the Maya of the sixteenth century remained notably accomplished traders and warriors, ensconced in readily defended forest and highland, and they kept the Aztecs confined to the north with a chain of garrisons beyond which only their traders, the *pochteca*, could go.

So in 1519 a joined-up Mexica state did not stretch as far south as Yucatán or all that far north of its capital; it did not even encompass all of the central highlands. The empire was, like its European contemporaries, a mafia state, demanding privileges and tribute in exchange for peace, and the Mexica had built it with mafia-like ruthlessness and theatrical violence, leaving behind lurid stories of gambling, murder, and human sacrifice on an industrial scale.[7] They were consequently loathed by many of those recently conquered, which makes it unsurprising that so many of their subjects seized the opportunity to rebel when the Spanish landed.

It was not the first Spanish expedition to the North American mainland. The first one reached Yucatán in 1517, a crew of 110 optimists without the necessary funds for even decent water barrels. They came back, according to one pithy sixteenth-century summary, with nothing but wounds.[8] Neither was it the second; that one mapped some of the coast but lost its way in 1518. This was the third expedition, an operation on a grander scale, which set out from Cuba in 1519 under Hernán Cortés. Extraordinary in some ways, Cortés was in many others typical of the first generation of Spanish in the New World. He came from Medellín, a poor place in the southwestern province of Extremadura. He belonged to the impoverished ranks of the lower Spanish nobility: His father, Martín, was a knight of the Order of

Alcántara who chose the wrong side in rebelling against Queen Isabella but survived to tell the tale, or more probably not to tell it. His mother, Catalina, was also from a good family, but without the dowry that would have made them more than the provincial worthies they were, owners of a mill, an apiary, and a small vineyard. Cortés was certainly not upwardly mobile: A small-town refugee, he dropped out of the renowned university in Salamanca without a degree, went back home to live with his parents, fought with them, and slept around. And he was relatively young, twenty-two when he first traveled to the Indies, and only thirty-four when he sailed toward Yucatán.[9]

Twelve years in the Americas marked him. Cortés's first steps came as a settler on Hispaniola, the island at the center of Spanish hopes for wealth from the Indies. Cortés had subsequently been useful to the veteran leader Diego Velázquez in the conquest of Cuba, and he was rewarded with land, Indian slaves, and a series of plum jobs, including a stint as the governor's secretary and culminating with the mayoralty of the capital, Santiago de Baracoa. According to the myth that Cortés co-authored, he was a brilliant maverick from early on: seducing the wrong woman, being jailed when he dumped her, seducing the governor—platonically—and ending up the natural choice for the next major expedition. According to critics then and now, he was nothing of the sort. His main talents were survival and mythmaking. He was jailed not for sexual swagger but rather for petty crookedness, lifting some of Velázquez's papers. He was, according to his greatest critic of the time, "an ordinary man . . . very bowed and humble, like the very lowliest crony that Diego Velázquez might wish to favor."[10] But if that governor was at all competent, and he was, then he would not have appointed an incompetent mediocrity to be his captain on an important and time-sensitive expedition. (Unless he was a relative, in which case in that time and place all bets were off.) And when Cortés lobbied for the job of commanding the third expedition to the mainland, Velázquez gave it to him.

Cortés's mandate was, however, limited. He was authorized to look for the earlier Spanish mission, to trade for gold with the Indians, and to promote their conversion to Christianity. He was quite explicitly not to be his own man, authorized neither to make war nor to settle. Yet Cortés immediately prepared to do just that. He raised extensive loans to equip ten ships, arm and train 450 men—nearly a quarter of the male Spanish population of Cuba—and buy himself the sort of clothes he believed any great captain should sport; velvet and gold featured heavily.[11] All this unsettled Velázquez. Suspecting—rightly—that Cortés was once more acting the crook, plotting to usurp the new lands and profits, he changed his mind and tried to arrest him. When Cortés found out, he left the island in a hurry and with a flourish, allegedly telling the dithering Velázquez that "these and like things have to be done not mulled over."[12] If he actually said this, the cheek was typical, and so too was his luck. In March 1519, Cortés landed at Cozumel and picked up Jerónimo de Aguilar, the Spaniard who had been shipwrecked there and whom the Maya had captured and enslaved. That meeting alone gave Cortés a translator and valuable intelligence about the Maya. But Cortés's real stroke of luck came shortly afterward, when the Potonchan Maya gave him twenty teenage girls, one of them a slave called Malintzin.

Malintzin was actually Mexica, not Maya, taken before puberty by slave traders from her home on the Gulf Coast in Veracruz—either kidnapped or bought, accounts differ—and rowed down the coast to be sold on. She was beautiful and bilingual in Nahuatl, the language of central Mexico, and the Maya language of the South; she rapidly became fluent in Spanish as well. She became Cortés's concubine, and a key source of local knowledge and advice throughout the war. In the codices, the indigenous pictogram histories, she appears over and over again next to him, for good or bad, whispering in his ear, fleeing an Indian attack, looking on as he has a mastiff tear a chained native priest to pieces, lecturing a cacique. In the images of some postconquest documents, like the *Codex Durán* (1579) or the *Lienzo de Tlaxcala* (1585), her body language and expressions are masterful enough to call into question who was actually making policy, captive or captor.

Malintzin had very little check on what she said to each side in those early days before the Spanish had learned anything beyond crude Nahuatl. At one stage their words passed through three different interpreters and four languages: Spanish to Maya to Nahuatl to Totonac. As a result the Spanish hadn't a clue what Malintzin was telling the indigenous people they met. Neither do we know much about what she said, felt, and did beyond the outlines of a short obituary. Malintzin was born at the turn of the sixteenth century; picked up by Cortés in

Malintzin and Cortés have an animated discussion at Veracruz, 1519.
Codex Durán (1579).

1519; discarded by him in the mid-1520s after bearing his firstborn son, Martín, who was later legitimized by the pope; married off to another conquistador, Juan Jaramillo; and rewarded for her services with a grant of estates in Olutla, her hometown; she had a daughter, María, with Jaramillo in 1526; parted from her firstborn forever when he was sent to Spain at the age of six; and died in early 1529. Her enemies accused her of assorted sins, like money laundering for Cortés, notorious promiscuity, and equally notorious dishonesty in manipulating both sides. One thing is clear: Cortés's manipulation of indigenous politics, maybe his very survival, is unthinkable without her.[13]

Yet there was more than luck or judgment at work. People had been crisscrossing the Caribbean for centuries, and the Spaniards had been doing so for decades. Cortés benefited greatly from the fact that his was the fourth, not first, contact with the indigenous mainlanders. Even his predecessors had been greeted with cries of "Castilian" when they first landed. The peoples of Mexico knew something earthly was in the offing before Cortés turned up: A Maya canoe met with Columbus in 1502, a Spanish ship was wrecked off Yucatán in 1511, and European clothes and books had already washed up on Gulf shores.[14] So while Cortés was dismissive of the Spaniards he brought with him—"of low manner and type, and dissolute with assorted vices and sins"[15]—several of his captains had been to Mexico before him, and they were extremely useful because of that. Men like Pedro de Alvarado, Alonso de Ávila, Francisco de Montejo, Bernardino Vásquez de Tapia, and Bernal Díaz del Castillo had the experience Cortés lacked, and provided him with intelligence, confidence, and advice. (Alvarado may have paid for one of the bigger ships into the bargain.)[16] Writing decades later, Díaz carefully deflated the myth of Cortés the brilliant individualist:

> And as among us there were such excellent sons, gentlemen and soldiers of such valour and good judgement, Cortés neither said nor did anything without first seeking our very well-considered counsel and agreement.[17]

Most important of all, the earlier contacts provided him with his critical first interpreter, the bilingual Spaniard Aguilar. He could translate Spanish into Maya; Malintzin could translate that Maya into Nahuatl; and Cortés, consequently, could from the very start communicate with the people he planned to overpower. These linguistic and cultural tools in hand, Cortés wielded them with distinctive guile to manage his own first contacts with the indigenous world. He worked hard to charm and terrify the Indians, encouraging them to believe that both his guns and his horses were hostile living beings, controlled by his goodwill alone. In April 1519, he moved up the coast to central Mexico, where he founded the Villa Rica de la Vera Cruz, the Rich Town of the True Cross, later just Veracruz; established good relations with the local people, the Cempoalans; and sent messengers directly to Spain to ask for the royal appointment that would establish his independence from Governor Velázquez in Cuba, entitling him to the leader's share of any profits. He also received the first messengers from the Mexica capital, Tenochtitlán, and began planning his march there. Finally, he rounded off his coup by beaching and derigging—not burning—his boats, making hasty retreat to the Caribbean islands impossible, and so encouraging his faction-ridden expedition to follow him up into the highlands.[18]

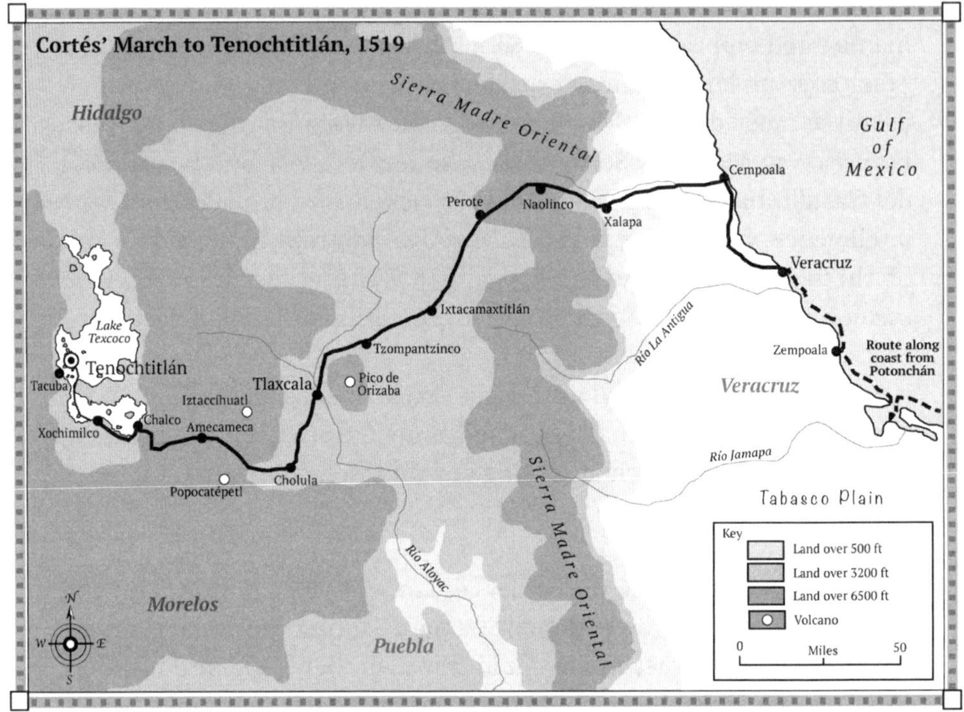

A depiction of one of the many route maps re-creating Cortés's march to Tenochtitlán, 1519.

After it was all over, indigenous historians and informants recounted how the Cortés expedition had been prefigured for nearly twenty years by auguries of disaster. The emperor Ahuitzótl had allegedly died after banging his head on the lintel of his bedroom, a suspicious story. (He was held responsible for a failure in the city's water management system, which led to a catastrophic flood: reason enough for discrete murder.) Legend held that the Valley of Mexico had hosted multiple supernatural phenomena. Comets, solar eclipses, temple fires, inexplicable storms, and a string of zoological freaks abounded. A mysterious woman, *la llorona*, prowled the city by night wailing: "O my sons! We are about to perish." Most striking of all, Cortés was reported by these later writers as fulfilling a central Mexica myth, the return of Quetzalcóatl, the feathered serpent god. The Spaniard was white and bearded and came from the East, bringing with him bewildering technological superiority. Quetzalcóatl, similarly white and bearded, had disappeared to the East on a raft after his fall from grace, an indigenous Prometheus who was now honoring his vow to return and reclaim his birthright.[19]

These reports were clearly nonsense. Even in his own writing Cortés never claimed to have been taken for the god Quetzalcóatl, and so this particular form of European megalomania does not seem to have had him in its grasp. Neither are the Nahua of the 1520s or 1530s reported as identifying him with Quetzalcóatl.[20] The first written version of the story appeared in 1555, in an unpublished draft of a history written by the Franciscan friar Bernardino de Sahagún and some ten *tlacuiloani*, indigenous scribes, and so the earliest record came a generation after the events were supposed to have happened.[21] This begs the question of why the sons and grandsons of the defeated should subscribe to the myth while the Europeans did not. But there were good political reasons for the conflicting versions. It was not at all in Cortés's interest to portray himself to the Spanish emperor as a rival theocrat, nor to give the first missionaries room to see him as a heretic. For the Mexica, by contrast, a story of supernatural advantage would help them live with the indignity of defeat by old neighbors and enemies as well as pleasing the Franciscans, with their party line of a divinely justified conquest. The nameless Nahua who collaborated with Franciscan authors had tactical and emotional reasons to shape stories of magic and loss to their teachers' taste.[22]

Yet neither is it impossible that the Spanish collectively were briefly seen as gods. In Mexico their initial identification as one more group of shape-shifting divinities would have made perfectly good sense. The Mexica Empire was a world where multiple unpredictable and violent gods were empirically established and ever-present, a cosmology rather like that of the Old Testament, with God the capo, Archangel Michael the consigliere, and Saint James the soldier, turning up to help the Spanish when things got tough. The Spanish certainly hoped to be seen as gods, and tried to foster the impression. When Cortés first sent an emissary to the Totonacs he chose a battered and ancient-looking

Basque soldier, telling him, "When they see your ugly face they'll certainly take you for one of their idols."[23] Yet there is so little firsthand information about the war that it isn't even clear what Cortés himself looked like: strong-jawed leader to some, syphilitic dwarf to others.[24] If the argument over the question of Spanish divinity in Mexica eyes establishes anything beyond reasonable doubt, it is how the weakness of the chief historical sources—all either geriatric, geographically or historically removed, self-interested, or some combination thereof—allows each age to reinvent the story of the war to its own taste.

Only a handful of Spanish participants in the war with the Mexica wrote books about it: Cortés, in five letters to his emperor; the "Anonymous Conquistador"; Francisco de Aguilar; and Bernal Díaz. The paucity and unreliability are striking. Bernal Díaz wrote the best of them, the revealingly named *True History of the Conquest of Mexico*, in old age and in disgust at other authors' mendaciousness. Yet even he was currying favor at court and lying about how much of the war he had seen. Aguilar was even older than Díaz when he wrote his account: He was in his eighties, the conquest sixty years in his past. The influential Francisco López de Gómara was Cortés's chaplain and never went to the Americas; his *Historia general de las Indias*, paid for by Cortés's son, was written in Spain with the conquistador peering over his shoulder.[25] The Franciscan Toribio de Benavente, whom the Mexica nicknamed Motolinía, "the Poor Man," hadn't witnessed the wars, and his *Historia de los indios de la Nueva España* was a social history. Motolinía's main concerns were the before and after; the war's narrative interested him much less. The Dominican Bartolomé de las Casas had been in the region and knew some of the conquistadors, but he was more concerned with indicting them than with footnoting his sources. (The title of his work, *Brevísima relación de la destrucción de las Indias*, says it all.) That Cortés is an unreliable narrator goes without saying. But aside from a scattering of terse mentions in private letters, his first three letters to Charles V were the first widely read versions of the war for Tenochtitlán, and their heroic narrative and persuasive prose poisoned the well for almost all successive accounts.

As for the written indigenous accounts, most came from several generations after conquest. Some of the canonical indigenous historians, like Hernando de Alvarado Tezozómoc, Domingo de San Antón Muñón Chimalpahin Quauhtlehuanitzin, and Fernando de Alva Ixtlilxóchitl, took a step forward in professionalism by specifying their sources. Yet like the Europeans they borrowed from each other (and from the slippery Gómara) and in the main wrote in the early seventeenth century, long after events. Chimalpahín's closest personal link to the war was his grandfather, who at best experienced it as an infant. Some Nahua writers had their own axes to grind for self-advancement. Ixtlilxóchitl self-identified as indigenous (despite a Spanish father) and over the years became increasingly dismissive of European historians: "Having considered," he wrote, "the varied and contrary presentations of the [European] authors who have treated the history of New Spain, I did not want to follow any of them."[26] But he was the great-great-grandson of the king of Texcoco, which made him distant in time but also self-interested in the present in stressing the importance of the Texcocans. Some of the first European historians valued early indigenous sources above Spanish letters, reports, and chronicles. Writing in the 1570s, the Franciscan Diego Durán explicitly chose to believe painted Mexica codices over Spanish books. Yet Indian and Spanish accounts shared some of the same weaknesses.[27]

The second big story of the war for Tenochtitlán is dodgy too: that the Mexica leader Montezuma II, shocked by the Spaniards' unearthly gifts, suffered a nervous breakdown in the face of their advance and surrendered to them at the gates of his city. According to the first indigenous accounts, Montezuma, the *tlatoani*—emperor, literally "he who speaks"—was remembered as doing next to nothing bar hand-wringing in the face of the Spanish coalition-building and steady advance. As they later told it, "He conceived within himself a feeling that great ills were coming upon him and his kingdom, and not just he, but all those who knew of these tidings, began to fear mightily."[28] But such a lurch into ineffectuality would have been a surprising shift in character for a forceful, effective, and absolutist ruler. He began his rule by executing all his predecessor's bureaucrats and replacing them with nobles. He went on to enforce draconian protocol in his relations with the Mexica. It was forbidden to look directly at his face, or to wear shoes or anything but the coarsest clothing in his presence. When he proceeded through the streets, everyone was to bow before him.[29]

This authoritarianism was more than a question of style. Montezuma lived up to the literal meaning of his name, "the man who is angered," by repeated use of arbitrary terror as an instrument of government. His people, he explained to Cortés, "did not like being treated with love but with fear."[30] His people weren't so sure. Indigenous informants of the priestly Spanish historians Sahagún and Motolinía repeatedly condemned Montezuma as extraordinarily cruel. Yet Montezuma cannot be painted as weak or incompetent until 1519, when, confronted with the growing Spanish threat, he eschewed the strategy of total war that the Maya had (rightly) advocated. The Spanish, whatever else they might have been, were clearly obsessed with meeting the emperor in person; they insisted on it from the first encounter. And they had magical allies in the form of cavalry and cannon, which the indigenous peoples initially believed (and were consistently encouraged to believe by Cortés) to be sentient and intrinsically hostile. But they were also killable, as battles with other indigenous peoples had proven, and they weren't all that numerous. There was strategic logic behind Montezuma's policy of wait and see, gathering intelligence, shadowing the Spanish, watching as they were battered in the first major fighting of the expedition, perhaps considering their quest for his city the path into his trap.

But the Spaniards' battering had been salutary and in the long run critical. They had begun recruiting indigenous soldiers on the coast: Cortés marched up toward Tenochtitlán in company with two thousand Cempoalan warriors. In September 1519 they reached the frontiers of Tlaxcala, the kingdom that had used its uneven mountainland and powerful military to retain a tenuous independence from the Mexica empire. Bloody enmity helped Tlaxcalans to hold together as a unique polity that welded four of the usually individualist city-states, in Nahua *altepeme*, into a province with a deliberative assembly; they were—as generations of Mexica had realized—formidable opponents.[31] The Tlaxcalans' first reaction to the newcomers was to fight. In the first battle, with his habitual mixture of overstating the odds and understating the costs, Cortés told his emperor that he had faced a hundred thousand Tlaxcalan warriors and battled

> all day, until an hour before sunset, when they withdrew; and with half a dozen cannon, five or six muskets and forty crossbowmen,

> and the thirteen horsemen I had left, I did them great harm, suffering in return only the labor and weariness of fighting and hunger. And it seemed that God fought for us, because among such a multitude of people so spirited and masterful in fighting and with so many different weapons to attack us we got off very lightly.[32]

In reality the conflict between the Spanish and Montezuma's longstanding enemies in the treacherous highlands was devastating for both sides. Two major battles and assorted skirmishes left Cortés with only half of his total force alive and in fighting condition, perhaps as few as 350 foot soldiers and horsemen.

The war ended after eighteen days, however, with the Tlaxcalans convinced of both the threat and the utility of the invaders. They had been divided since the beginning between a hawkish party led by Xicotencatl the Younger from the altepetl of Tizatlán, captain-general of the army, and doves led by Maxixcatzin from the less bellicose altepetl of Ocotelulco, who stressed the military and mercantile advantages of joining the Spanish. Their numerous casualties and the arrival of a delegation to the foreigners from the Mexica, who hoped to egg on the mutual slaughter, led to the doves winning the debate. The four altepeme agreed to ally themselves with Cortés and sent an army of six thousand to join the invasion of the Valley of Mexico (they offered tens of thousands more, but the Spanish, understandably wary, politely declined).[33] The extent of Tlaxcalan influence over the unknowing Spanish was made immediately clear when they diverted the march to Cholula, a city of their bitter enemies, which was out of their way. There they duped Cortés into launching an exemplary massacre, telling him a story of an impending ambush, which probably never existed but served as a casus belli for sacking the city.[34] It was the first demonstration of the intruders' potential for urban warfare, and it was clearly troubling for Montezuma. For all their losses—of both soldiers and autonomy—the Spaniards had fought the Mexicas' old enemies to a standstill and then converted them to allies, leveraging an expedition of hundreds into an army of thousands.

According to the Nahua accounts from a generation later, Montezuma reasoned that the only viable defense against such aliens was counter-magic. Yet when he unleashed his necromancers in a last-ditch attempt to keep Cortés out of his city, they were derailed by a drunk from Chalco who prophesied divine abandonment and fiery destruction. The story is one more in Sahagún's chronicle of doom foretold and psychological collapse; coming from long after the fact, it is similarly dubious. On the other hand, the revisionist idea that Montezuma set out to collect the Europeans, one more species for his extensive zoo, is also inherently dubious.[35] Cortés's men may have totaled a quarter of one percent of the city's population, but letting them into its heart out of ethnographic curiosity was the equivalent, in relative terms, of letting four thousand heavily armed alien troops into today's Manhattan on a whimsy. Since we are left with nothing but unreliable accounts, speculation on the basis of Montezuma's previous astute war-making is perhaps best. His appreciation of the military capabilities of the Spanish was on the rise. To fight them would mean engaging them on the city outskirts, ravaging the lakeside towns critical for his people's food supply. If, as the Spanish maintained, they were simply after high-up encounters and gold, then meeting some of their demands and manipulating them into going away, or maybe even turning them against their Tlaxcalan allies, was a subtler stratagem. So the most likely explanation is that the tlatoani opted for diplomacy backed by force. Both curious and wary, on November 8, 1519, he invited the Spanish into his island city and put them up in his father's palace.

The palace was built of basalt, limestone, and the red lava rock the Mexica called *tezontle*, which littered the valley floor. Three great volcanic eruptions, the oldest dating back twenty-six million years, had created a deep basin; over geologic time, smaller eruptions part-filled it with lava and ash, and a million or so years ago came the water. When humans arrived from the north about twelve thousand years ago they found that springs, seasonal runoff from the valley slopes, and rivers draining from the west formed marshlands and a large salty lake.[36] These people were few and the wetlands inhospitable, and consequently the first indigenous nomads stayed on the rich soils of the lakeside, surrounded by the sheltering valley rim and the threat of its two live volcanoes, the southern peaks of Popocatépetl and Iztaccíhuatl. It was a good place to live, and about a thousand years BCE they settled in villages that grew into towns that grew into cities. When the Aztecs arrived from the far northwest in the thirteenth century, the only land left was wetland. Over the next three hundred years they moved mud and rock to form a firm central island, and built giant causeways that both connected the growing city to the lakeshore and helped manage the great seasonal floods. The solid causeways also dealt with the problem of drinking water, separating salt- from freshwater lakes, while the Mexicas' skill in terraforming allowed them to create rafts of floating gardens, the *chinampas*, to provide food. The story of Tenochtitlán was a story of volcanoes and men moving mud on a massive scale.

Even before they got to Tenochtitlán, the Spanish were groping for parallels for the indigenous cities they found along the way. The higher they climbed up toward the central valley, the harder it became for them to conceive the new world they were encountering. The Anonymous Conquistador thought Tlaxcala quite like Granada, the capital of Muslim Iberia, only bigger.[37] To Bernal Díaz the white walls and high towers of Cholula made it look like Valladolid, the medieval capital of Spain.[38] Cortés ran out of comparisons of place and turned to the rhetoric of numbers, telling Carlos V that Cholula had 20,000 houses and some 430 mosques, which would have made it bigger than almost every European city of that time.[39] When the Spanish crossed the valley rim and saw the Mexican capital, there was only one comparison left—Venice—and calling Tenochtitlán an American Venice quickly became a trope. It was not just a question of water management; *la Serenissima Repubblica* was by far the most populous, powerful, and sophisticated European city-state of its time.

Marching into Tenochtitlán, seeing the buildings rise up out of the water, was "to see things never before heard of nor seen nor even dreamed." When they settled in town the wonder continued. Montezuma's palace was duly large and opulent, stuffed with valuables, staffed by hundreds, and home to a zoo and an aviary. Above all it was the everyday city that struck Díaz. The marketplace was vast, packed, and organized; he "had never seen such a thing before." The array of food, clothes, commodities, and luxuries was beyond words: "If I describe everything in detail I shall never be done." He tried hard, cataloguing for over a page (he didn't have enough space for more, he said) the many slaves, textiles, wild and domestic animals and their hides, building materials, paper, dyes, pottery, knives, axes, and gold measured in goose quills. Climbing to the top of the main temple he saw the straight, paved roads; the canals with their myriad canoes; the bridges and causeways; the aqueduct bringing fresh water down from Chapultepec, the "Hill of the Grasshopper"; the pyramids, squares, courtyards, and orderly houses. From three miles away he could still hear the murmur of the buyers and sellers in the great market. Even the best-traveled of the Spanish said they "had never seen a market so well laid out, so large, so orderly, and so full of people."[40]

Perhaps that was no wonder, because the Spanish who were there were a mixture of provincials and yokels (leavened by a couple of Venetian solders whose names never made it into history).[41] None of the leaders came from Valladolid or Barcelona. There was only one Madrileño. Cortés had lived briefly in Salamanca, a university town with a great plaza, but like his captain, Gonzalo de Sandoval, he was a small-town boy: Medellín had a couple of thousand inhabitants. Bernal Díaz came from Medina del Campo, whose medieval fairs made it a center for wool trading and banking, but it was still at heart a market town. Badajoz and Baeza, home respectively to Alvarado and Cristóbal de Olid, were first and foremost military bases, strategically important, massively fortified, but otherwise small and higgledy-piggledy. None of these bore comparison to the size, complexity, and sophistication of Tenochtitlán. Iberians had lived in sedentary settlements three thousand years longer than the indigenous peoples they were encountering, and they had learned the use of iron, wheels, pulleys, and the Roman arch.[42] But the Mexica, who lacked all those inventions, built a city beyond anything the Spanish had seen.

The first eight months in that city, from November 1519 to June 1520, were surreal even by the standards of such expeditions, which their participants conceptualized in terms of medieval stories of adventure—chansons de geste, Spanish romances, and Christian crusades. (These stories were popular across the whole range of Spanish society: Bernal Díaz was fond of *Amadís of Gaul*, a 1508 blockbuster, while Queen Isabella preferred the *Legend of Lanzarote.*)[43] While the two sides exchanged labyrinthine courtesies, they plotted against each other in mutual ignorance, suspicion, and mistrust. Each was good at war;

both were afraid; neither was confident that it could win should the tense modus vivendi collapse. The Mexica were, said one of Sahagún's indigenous informants, "awaiting death, and they talked of this among themselves, saying, "What can we do? Go where we may, we shall be destroyed. Let us await death here.""[44] Meanwhile, the Spanish sized up the trap in which they found themselves: a small band of Europeans in the heart of an unknown and warlike society, whose vast army—according to the Tlaxcalans—aimed to eat them slow-cooked with salt, chili, and tomatoes.[45]

And so, with the improvisational thuggishness that underwrote much Spanish achievement, Cortés and his captains decided to kidnap Montezuma. They were not the first to use this strategy—the conquistadors of Panama and Nicaragua had captured native rulers to subdue their peoples—but they were undeniably the most ambitious and successful. The Spanish had been in the city for perhaps a week. On the pretext of a Mexica attack on his Veracruz encampment, Cortés and Malintzin visited Montezuma's palace and offered him the choice of imprisonment or summary death. It was one of several critical moments revealing Montezuma's helplessness: He went along with Cortés and the fiction that he was doing so freely. He became, at a stroke, a puppet and collaborator. He still legislated in petty affairs of the Mexica and had some freedom; the Spanish took him yachting and even allowed him to continue his human sacrifices. But that did not make him a free man; a European officer might have expected the same treatment (minus the human sacrifice) on parole. Montezuma's lack of real authority quickly became apparent when Cortés put him in chains and had the captains who had allegedly attacked Veracruz burned alive.

In the aftermath of that public execution Cortés offered the emperor the chance to return to his palace, but Montezuma refused—in fear, according to the chronicler Juan de Torquemada, of his own people.[46] Whether this is the case or whether, as Díaz claims, he recognized the speciousness of the offer, hardly matters. What is unimpeachable is that Montezuma's imprisonment revived dormant tensions among the Mexica. The tlatoani had great, divinely sanctioned, and customarily uncontested power, and Montezuma had been unusually violent in deploying it; but now opposition to his appeasement of the Spaniards crystallized in a hawkish faction of nobles and priests. At first, these hawks continued to pledge absolute loyalty to the sovereign, restricting themselves to urging war in their daily visits to Montezuma. But the tlatoani's acts of collaboration grew increasingly compromising. When the Spanish discovered the great treasure of Ahuitzótl concealed within their quarters, Montezuma did not just give it to them; he sent his silversmiths to help them melt it down. Provoked by the kidnapping and then the robbery, Cacamatzin, King of Texcoco, began organizing a surprise attack on the Spanish. Upon learning of the plan, Montezuma had the king arrested and handed over to Cortés, who garroted him. Although the emperor was a deeply religious high priest of the Mexica, he nevertheless allowed the Spanish to set up a chapel to the Virgin Mary in the Great Temple. The tlatoani was clearly eager for his jailers' approval and gave them gold as well as some of his mistresses. His jailers did not, however, respond in kind: One called him a dog, and another deliberately farted noisily while on guard. Cortés, though, continued to play Montezuma both metaphorically and literally, amusing him with frequent visits for games of *totoloque*, a form of toss ha'penny played with gold (at which Alvarado, characteristically enough, cheated).[47]

Finally, in the spring of 1520, the hawks gave Montezuma an ultimatum, couched in the language of divine command, to declare war on the Spanish. The emperor warned Cortés and temporized, negotiating time for the Spanish to build ships in which to depart. Whether they would have left is a moot point: Before the ships were completed, a fifth Spanish expedition landed on the coast. With at least eighteen ships, over a thousand men, and nearly a hundred horses, it far outnumbered that of Cortés, and it came to stay; the new arrivals brought with them large amounts of merchandise to sell to both Spaniards and Indians.[48] Dispatched by his powerful enemy Diego Velázquez, governor of Cuba, the new expedition was hostile to Cortés and established secret contact with Montezuma. But it was commanded by the uninspiring Pánfilo de Narváez. Gonzalo de Sandoval, one of Cortés's most politically gifted men, skillfully subverted Narváez's soldiers, winning over commanders and artillerymen, some of them his relatives, with gold and promises. At the end of May Cortés made a forced march to the coast, leaving Pedro de Alvarado and a small contingent in Tenochtitlán to guard Montezuma. When they reached the coast, Cortés and his men fell on the new arrivals by night and swiftly defeated them. There were very few casualties, and Cortés incorporated Narváez's men into his own expedition, trebling his forces. It should have been a moment of triumph and relief. Yet in keeping with the melodrama of the Spanish chronicles, Díaz tells us that "at the very moment of victory news came from Mexico that Pedro de Alvarado was besieged." The Mexica had finally gone to war.[49]

It was bound to happen. But it was no coincidence that the final rupture came in Cortés's absence. He was a gifted Machiavellian who had steadily increased his demands on the Mexica while maintaining an improbable peace. When he left for the coast, he handed over command to Alvarado, who had Cortesian pretensions, charm, and courage but few of the other abilities. As Cortés afterward recognized, it was a bad choice. The Mexica asked Alvarado's permission to celebrate the festival of Huitzilopochtli, the god of war, in the main temple. He gave permission and then, at the height of the celebration, launched a carefully planned attack that sealed the temple compound and turned it into a killing ground. There were hundreds, perhaps thousands, of dancers present; almost all were killed. An indigenous survivor left a graphic account:

> They surrounded those who were dancing, going among the cylindrical drums. They struck a drummer's arms; both of his hands were severed. Then they struck his neck; his head landed far away. Then they stabbed everyone with iron lances and struck them with iron swords. They struck some in the stomach, and then their intestines came spilling out. They split open the heads of some, they cut their skulls to pieces; their skulls were cut up into little bits. They hit some on the shoulders; their bodies broke open and ripped. Some they hacked on the calves, some on the thighs, some on their stomachs, and then all their entrails would spill out. And if someone tried to run it was useless; he just dragged his intestines along. There was a stench that smelled like sulphur.[50]

The motive is baffling; surviving explanations were penned a generation or more after the fact. The late sixteenth-century Codex Ramírez calls it robbery plain and simple, with Alvarado—covetous even by his peers' high standards—seduced by the Mexica nobles' jewelry. The seventeenth-century Texcocan historian Fernando de Alva Ixtlilxóchitl has a more complicated and convincing version, whereby the Tlaxcalans duped Alvarado into a preemptive and exemplary massacre with reports of a (nonexistent) Mexica conspiracy, much as they had done in Cholula. The Mexica had regularly sacrificed Tlaxcalans at this festival, and this was their revenge. It was one more chapter in their longstanding civil war.

A mob of Mexica immediately attacked the Spanish barracks and would have overrun them had Montezuma not ordered them to withdraw. At that point, his people still obeyed him. When Cortés reentered the city on June 24, bolstered by Narváez's men and another two thousand Tlaxcalans, he found the streets empty and the market closed, but the fighting paused. Cortés then compounded Alvarado's blunder by insulting Montezuma, the only possible mediator, and releasing his younger brother, Cuitláhuac, to negotiate with the nobility. Cuitláhuac was a hawk; predictably enough he never came back. Instead he became the new Mexica leader and launched a massive assault on the Spanish quarters. Cortés supposedly sent Montezuma onto a rooftop to urge a ceasefire that would let the Spanish leave in peace, but the crowd was having none of it; someone down below—according to the Codex Ramírez, his nephew Cuauhtémoc, soon to be emperor—denounced him as a scoundrel and a homosexual and the attack resumed. The Mexica rained darts and stones onto the roof, wounding Montezuma in the head, arm, and leg. He died the next day. It was "quite unexpected," said Díaz, one of several unexpected deaths of people close to Cortés. Montezuma had outlived his usefulness and might yet have mounted some opposition, and several indigenous historians either hint at or straightforwardly accuse the Spanish of his murder.[51] It is his most likely ending, placing him among the rest of the captive lords, stabbed to death in their chains.

Diplomacy in tatters, the only option left to the Spanish was retreat. Blas Botello Puerto de Plata, the expedition's soothsayer, foresaw annihilation if they did not leave immediately. This was not a prediction requiring second sight. They faced tens, possibly hundreds of thousands of Mexica warriors; they themselves numbered around fourteen hundred Spaniards and several thousand Tlaxcalans. On the night of July 1, 1520, they tried to sneak out of the city, carrying what treasure they could and a large portable bridge.

The bridge was vital, for the miles-long causeways leading across the lake out of Tenochtitlán were punctuated by canals, from which the Mexica had removed the bridges. The withdrawal began in a light rain, the column heading west along the Tacuba causeway. They managed to cross the first canal in safety, but a woman saw them and gave the alert and at the second canal the fighting started. The night collapsed into bloody chaos: The Spanish lost their bridge and retreat turned rout. At the canal of the Toltecs, attacked on both sides by canoes and harried by Mexica chasing them down the causeway, the panicking Spanish and Tlaxcalans were forced into the water and were either drowned—many had stuffed their clothes with roughcast bars of gold—or killed in such numbers that those running behind found the gap bridged by corpses. Some at the rear of the column were cut off and turned back into the city, where they made a last stand in their palace before the Mexica captured and sacrificed them. The luckier Spaniards on the lakeshore took a week to fight their way to the safe haven of Tlaxcala, where they took stock.

At this unlikely point, Cortés named the country he was losing. Earlier baptisms involved tediously literal Spanish descriptions, saints' names, or bastardized indigenous words: Puerto Rico, Rich Port, or Tierra Firme, the Mainland; Santo Domingo, for Saint Dominic; Cuba, from the corruption of a Taino noun meaning "great place." Cortés knew that he had taken a leap beyond these footholds and wanted Emperor Charles V to believe it so that he would send him a proper legal title and even reinforcements. So in October 1520 he wrote Charles a self-aggrandizing letter, toward the end of which he let the emperor know that

> from what I have seen and understood regarding the similarity that this entire land bears to Spain, as much in fertility as in grandeur and the cold weather and in many other things that make them comparable, it seemed that the most apt name for this happy land was that of the New Spain of the Ocean Sea, and consequently in the name of Your Majesty I gave it that name.

He hoped, he wrapped up, that His Majesty thought that was acceptable and would sign off on it.[52]

The report of a revolutionary future for Spanish power was also meant as distraction and consolation prize for the news of their lethal rout from Tenochtitlán. Cortés watered his defeat down, claiming that he had lost a mere 150 countrymen on that slaughterous night, which became known as the Night of Sorrow, the *Noche Triste.* But when he mustered his forces in late December there were only 590 men left, and that was after receiving at least 150 fresh troops in the autumn. He had had by all accounts a force of over 1,400 Spaniards before the outbreak of war; consequently, the Mexica probably killed some 900 Spanish that week.[53] As for his indigenous allies, they suffered even more; according to Ixtlilxóchitl some four thousand Tlaxcalans died in the retreat from Tenochtitlán.[54]

Yet any Mexica celebrations were short-lived. As the Spanish regrouped in the Tlaxcalan highlands, they gained a new, microbial ally in the form of smallpox. The disease seems to have been brought to Mexico with Narváez by a Black slave, Francisco Eguía; it broke out in Chalco at the end of September. Smallpox was fairly common in Europe, and though it was certainly dangerous to Europeans, the Spanish had a reasonable degree of resistance; the indigenous peoples of the Americas had none whatsoever. As a result, a Franciscan recorded, "among them the sickness and pestilence was so great throughout the land that in most provinces more than half the people died, and in the others little less."[55] This great dying weakened the Mexica armies; it also caused, within months, a generational shift in political leaders across central Mexico. In Cholula, Tlaxcala, and various other towns, it was Cortés who chose successors for the dead caciques, tightening his grip on the region. In Tenochtitlán it fell to the Mexica state council to choose a new leader, because among the dead was the short-lived emperor Cuitláhuac.

In his place the Mexica chose Cuauhtémoc, a talented and intransigent warrior in his mid-twenties. The high priests' traditional somber admonition to their new tlatoani must have rung particularly bleak:

> Perchance you will bear for a while the burden entrusted you, or perchance death will attack you and this your election to this kingdom will be but a dream . . . perchance other kings who despise you

> will wage war on you, and you will be defeated and detested, or perchance God will permit that hunger and dearth fall upon your kingdom. What will you do if in your time your kingdom is destroyed, or our lord God unleashes his wrath upon you, sending plague? What will you do if in your time your kingdom is destroyed and your splendour becomes darkness?[56]

The Mexica's recent history had been disastrous, and Cortés was gathering allies among their neighbors—this was now a multinational coalition of indigenous peoples from both outside and inside the Valley of Mexico—to assault the city. So the new emperor continued his predecessor's preparations for war. He dispatched ambassadors to both subject peoples and sworn enemies, even the Tlaxcalans, offering new deals in return for support. He mustered troops and strengthened Tenochtitlán's fortifications, deepening canals, building walls, digging trenches, and planting stakes in the lakebed. A later chronicle has it that Cuauhtémoc met with Cortés before the siege began. This seems unlikely: Such an encounter would have fit too neatly into the Spanish trope of chivalric warfare to escape every Spanish contemporary's account. If it did happen it was not the emperor's idea; as Spanish soldiers reported learning from their Mexica prisoners, "Cuauhtémoc's intentions . . . were that they would never make peace, but either kill us or die to the last person."[57]

The siege began on May 13, 1521. The Spanish divided their forces to blockade the three main causeways into Tenochtitlán, and broke the pipes that brought fresh water from the springs at Chapultepec. Cortés initially followed a scorched-earth strategy, sallying daily down the causeways into the city, burning houses and defenses, and then retreating for the night. This was painfully slow; the Mexica had the manpower to rebuild their defenses; and the Spanish, sleeping in half-ruined huts, eating grasshoppers, oppressed by heavy rains and continuous fighting, grew impatient. The failure of their first plan seemed clear at the end of June, when Cuauhtémoc made simultaneous night attacks on the Spanish camps before launching a concentrated assault on Alvarado's troops on the western lakeshore. The Spanish, very nearly overrun, took heavy losses. In the aftermath they decided to end the war rapidly with a three-pronged attack on the center of Tenochtitlán. It turned out to be a disastrous idea: The Mexica lured Cortés's men deep into the city and ambushed them. In addition to the many deaths, the Mexica took sixty-six Spanish alive, once more at one of the bridges, and sacrificed them. The effect on Cortés was critical, and he decided to act on his earlier conclusion:

> Seeing that those of the city were rebellious and showing such determination to defend themselves or die, I gathered from them two things: first, that we would have little or none of the wealth that they had taken from us, and second, that they . . . were forcing us to destroy them utterly.[58]

Cuauhtémoc's leadership—sometimes fighting on the ground, sometimes directing operations from the top of one of the city's temples—worked well at first. His men nearly captured Cortés in the defeat at the bridge; in the aftermath, the combination of Mexica victory and subsequent propaganda briefly scared off many of Cortés's indigenous allies. The Mexica, sometimes portrayed as destined to lose because of their sheer incomprehension of their situation, were acutely aware of the novelty—and gravity—of confrontation with the Spanish. They fought with the characteristic sophistication of Mexica warfare, making use of spies, saboteurs, and complex ambushes. They adapted to the new weapons and tactics employed by the invaders. Warriors learned to run in zigzags to confuse the aim of bowmen and gunners, and to throw themselves to the ground and take cover from cannon. Indigenous armorers turned captured swords into scythes and lances; archers learned how to use crossbows.[59] Open spaces such as the market were strewn with boulders to hold up the cavalry. And yet for all that, the Mexica faced certain structural disadvantages that made defeat the most probable ending.

One disadvantage, the least important, was the gap in military technology. The Mexica fought with shield and *macquahuitl*, a wooden sword edged with obsidian blades; for projectiles they had *atlatls*, or spear-throwers, as well as bows and slingshots. They were mismatched against the Spaniards' early modern tools: steel swords and armor, early small arms called arquebuses, a handful of cannon. In addition to the weapons they imported, the Spanish fabricated more in the course of the war. A giant siege catapult fashioned by a veteran of the Italian wars was comically useless; gunpowder made with sulfur hauled up from the volcano Popocatepétl was not. Yet arquebuses were inaccurate and complicated to load; the few cannon were light. They were impressive as novelties but indecisive as weapons. The Spanish wrote them off as failures in more than one bout of heavy fighting.

As for steel, Spanish armor was hot and cumbersome, and overengineered for this sort of war anyway; most Spanish swapped it for the cotton armor of the Indies. Steel swords were better than anything indigenous, but while obsidian was fragile, it could also be sharpened enough to shave, or to cut open the chest of a human sacrifice. It scared the Spanish; the mysterious Anonymous Conquistador, after Cortés and Díaz the only soldier to write about the war, claimed that the shiny black stone

> cut like a blade from Tolosa. One day I saw an Indian fighting with a horseman, and the Indian gave his adversary's horse such a slash in the stomach that it opened all the way to the entrails. And that same day I saw another Indian deliver a cut to the neck of a different horse, with which he laid him dead at his feet.[60]

Gunpowder and steel, in short, were not the advantages they have been made out to be.

Transport was a different matter. Horses were extraordinarily difficult for enemies to deal with, and their value was such that Cortés, describing the death of a mare, expressed more grief than he did in describing many human deaths. When the astrologer Botello asked the spirits about the future, the first question he posed was whether he would survive the war; the second, "If they are going to kill me will they kill my horse too?"[61] The Spanish knew their steeds would be critical even before they left Cuba, and thirty years on Díaz could remember every one of the sixteen they shipped over ("a very fine chestnut mare, lively and fast . . . a dappled stallion, chiseled forelegs, well built . . . a very good stallion, quite a light chestnut in color and a good gallop").[62]

But it was the ships that were, as Cortés put it, "the key to the entire war": not the ships he left on the beach at Veracruz, but the brigantines he ordered built in the central highlands in early 1521, new hulls mounted with the rigging, sails, and fittings from his original flotilla.[63] These thirteen small ships, heavily manned and armed with cannon, gave Cortés control of the lake. The Mexica immediately realized their importance and repeatedly sent saboteurs to burn them. Once the brigantines were launched, the Mexica fleets of canoes were overpowered by these larger, faster, and more heavily armed vessels. In them, the Spanish could raid the outskirts of the city with relative impunity and move reinforcements and materiel quickly between their different camps. Most important of all, the brigantines converted Tenochtitlán's great defensive advantage, its vast natural moat, into a critical weakness. The city was densely populated and dependent on imported food. By patrolling the lake night and day, the Spanish cut the Mexica supply lines; by mid-July the city began to starve.

To attribute the Mexica's eventual defeat to this particular form of technological superiority would be, however, to miss the point. The blockade could never have worked without the support of the lakeside towns and villages, and the brigantines could never have been deployed without the manpower of the Tlaxcalans, who built the hulls and supplied eight thousand porters to carry them some fifty miles down to the lakeshore. The entire campaign is, in fact, unthinkable without Cortés's indigenous alliances, which began with the Tlaxcalans and steadily expanded until they formed a coalition encompassing almost all the central Mexican peoples. The Mexica empire-building of the preceding century had encompassed a systematic terrorism, involving not just conquest but also ongoing sacrifices of human tributes from the defeated. As Montezuma himself said, they had been ruled by fear. When the calculus of fear shifted in favor of the coalition, so did their loyalties. By the end of June 1521, the Mexica were under attack by over one hundred thousand indigenous troops, with more arriving as their erstwhile subjects deserted them.

Not just on the Gulf Coast or in the highlands did history weigh against the Mexica. Their closest neighbors were also quick to turn on them. Early in the siege Cuauhtémoc called for reinforcements from lakeside towns such as Mixcoac and Xochimilco; the latter sent boatloads of warriors into the city, where, instead of joining the defense, they robbed unprotected houses and carried off slaves; they then went over permanently to the Spanish, completing the capital's encirclement. Even within the closely allied cities of Tlatelolco and Texcoco there was endemic disunity, as the war fostered violent struggles for power. In Texcoco, prey to a violent dynastic dispute even before the Spanish arrived, Cacamatzin's successor, suspected of pro-Spanish sympathies, was assassinated by his younger brother. In Tenochtitlán, a purge of Montezuma's faction began with the new hawkish court hunting down his servants and pages and ended in the execution of any of the dead emperor's sons who came to hand. The bloody, Shakespearean strife peaked, according to a Tlatelolcan chronicler, immediately before the siege began; its effects were catastrophic.[64] While an intransigent Texcocan faction went to the defense of Tenochtitlán, the Spaniards' puppet sent seventy thousand Texcocan troops to support the coalition. "Your Majesty might well consider," Cortés wrote to his emperor, "how the people of Tenochtitlán would feel to see coming against them those whom they held to be vassals and friends, relatives and brothers, and even fathers and sons."[65] It was a literally fratricidal war.

It was also a total war. The Spanish were shocked at the intensity of the fighting, even in the dying days of the siege: "The arrows and darts were so thick," remembered one of Sahagún's interviewees, "that the whole sky seemed yellow." Their indigenous allies, Díaz reported grimly, "knew of nothing but killing," and the standard-bearers were changed daily, for they came off "so badly battered that no one could carry the standards into battle a second time." Yet while Spanish casualties were high, deaths were relatively low. The Mexica by contrast lost thousands. The first skirmish in Iztapalapa cost them an estimated six thousand dead. By mid-July the combination of bad water, hunger, and disease was killing the Mexica in the tens of thousands. When they began foraging on the city borderlands by night, Cortés planned a dawn ambush that killed and captured over eight hundred of those he described as the most miserable, mostly unarmed women and children. By the end of the siege, broad estimates of Mexica deaths from the fighting alone were upward of one hundred thousand. Such devastation was off the scale of contemporary European warfare. The Battle of Stoke of 1487, which effectively concluded England's century-long Wars of the Roses, was fought with a total of about four thousand casualties. The destruction of Tenochtitlán, for more than one chronicler, could only be compared with that of Jerusalem.

The siege was fought to the bitter end. By the last days of July the surviving Mexica were driven to a final stand in a small enclave in the north of the city. For weeks they had eaten whatever came to hand, and not much did: rats, lizards, worms, and marsh grass. They dug up roots and stripped the bark off trees. Running out of warriors, the Mexica armed the women and children and sent them out on the rooftops to fight. Streets and houses filled with corpses; it was impossible to avoid treading on them. A contemporary elegy gives some of the horror of the last days:

> Worms swarm through the streets and squares,
> And the walls are splattered with our brains.
> Red run the waters, red as if dyed;
> And when we drink of them,
> It is as though we drank
> Salt water.[66]

On August 12, after waiting two days for Cuauhtémoc to come to peace talks, Cortés launched a final attack on the almost defenseless Mexica. His forces killed and captured thousands, possibly tens of thousands. "The screaming and weeping of the women and children were so great," wrote Cortés, "that there was no one whose heart it would not break." Yet they still refused to surrender. On August 13 the Spanish stormed the last stronghold. Cuauhtémoc either tried to escape to the reed beds in a canoe or came out to surrender, depending on whom you choose to believe. The last tlatoani was taken back to Tlatelolco, where he met Cortés and said, weeping,

> Lord Malintzin, I have assuredly done my duty in defense of my city and vassals, and I can do no more. I am brought by force into your presence and beneath your power. Take the dagger you have in your belt, and strike me dead immediately.[67]

Good though they were, these were not his last words; Cortés gave Cuauhtémoc fulsome praise and empty reassurances and hanged him four years later. Perhaps the last word belongs instead, as it often does, to the soldier-chronicler Bernal Díaz, who paints night falling on the ruins of the greatest city in the Americas and ends by observing quietly that "it rained and thundered that evening, and the lightning flashed, and up to midnight heavier rain fell than usual."[68]

Except this was not actually Díaz's last word. He went on at length to relate the dystopian aftermath of the city's destruction. He did so because he was a lot more concerned with politics than with narrative symmetry; he was writing from old age in Guatemala, as one of the many conquistadors for whom victory did remarkably little. His book was not aimed at literary immortality but at a far-off king who he hoped might yet reward his services. That urgent drive to persuade helped shape his extraordinary authorial voice, a voice with the apparent candor of a simple soldier, a sixteenth-century grunt, whose bluff, self-deprecating confessions of fear and ignorance were meant to carry greater weight than his contemporaries' more florid prose.

The king probably never read it. Philip II and his predecessor Charles V overlooked many similar—and shorter—claims from the Spanish who had fought in Mexico, and indeed overlooked the country itself. There is not a single mention of Mexico, the New World, or the Indies in Charles's memoirs, which he dictated in the early 1550s; his was still the world of the Mediterranean. Neither is there any mention of Cortés, whom he once asked for a personal loan to make war on the French, whom he granted the license to conquer China, and who after returning from Mexico joined him in a disastrous attempt to attack the rather different infidels of North Africa. The victory in Tenochtitlán had turned sour almost immediately. Most of the Mexica gold disappeared in the war, and after two and a half years of hardship, uncertainty, and often mortal danger, the ordinary foot soldier was allotted fifty or sixty pesos in the division of the treasure—about what each had paid for his sword or crossbow in the first place.[69] Even some of the most important conquistadors got next to nothing: The carpenter

Martín López, who built the small ships vital to success in the siege, ended up with nothing more than half a small farm. The Spanish fell out over this lack of spoils, both with the king's treasurer, who accused them of tax evasion, and with each other. Critics of Cortés used everything from graffiti to a series of rebellions in Michoacán, Honduras, and finally Tenochtitlán itself to express their dissatisfaction. In Tenochtitlán, now renamed Mexico City, Cortés's faction was toppled in an opportunistic coup while he was off marching against other rebels. He led expeditions in all directions, intending in part to stabilize the new regime in Mexico City by despatching rivals across the continent. Instead Cortés found his adversaries taking a leaf out of his own book and trying to escape his authority as quickly as possible.

Not that escapology did those other conquistadors much good. The main expeditions of the next twenty years were more disastrous than fruitful. Cristóbal de Olid was defeated in the North, rebelled in Honduras, and was garroted by his own men. Unaware that Olid was already dead, Cortés himself set off to capture the traitor and lost most of his men and treasure en route; by 1526 he was asking his family for money.[70] Francisco de Montejo made more lasting inroads into a family fortune, marrying a rich widow to fund his expeditions to Yucatán and leaving her bankrupt; his will shows him bankrupt too at the end, an impoverished nobleman pawning his valuables for medicine.[71] Pánfilo Narváez, having failed to defeat Cortés, failed to survive his 1527 expedition to Florida. His lieutenant, Álvar Núñez Cabeza de Vaca, spent the next seven years trekking westward across the continent to end up on the Pacific Coast with three other survivors, gathering nothing but a beard, a reputation as a holy man, and a thousand indigenous followers. Cabeza de Vaca's next expedition, to Argentina, was even less successful from a personal viewpoint; he was toppled, poisoned—saving himself, he recorded, with "oil and a fragment of unicorn"—and disowned by the king.[72] Cortés lost two of the four ships he dispatched on his first two expeditions up the coast to Baja California, neither of which led to lucre or settlement. The roguish Pedro de Alvarado was in some ways the most successful, getting to the highlands of Guatemala, playing different Maya states against each other, and establishing his own fief. Yet none of Alvarado's conquests up to that point had been particularly profitable; so he headed first to Peru, where he was paid to go away, and then back to Mexico to gather ships and sail for the Spice Islands. He never reached them, dying instead in the frontier wars of the North.

These wars were the greatest obstacle to Spanish expansion. Their enemies were small groups of indigenous nomadic and seminomadic tribes, generically lumped together as Chichimeca, the Nahua word for "barbarians," who met Spanish expansion and slave raiding with able and persistent guerrilla warfare. Their ambushes and hit-and-run raids cut roads and turned everywhere outside of the main towns and forts into war zones. Horror stories returned to Mexico City of human sacrifice, mutilation, scalping and baby-eating.[73] The wars ran from the 1550s to the 1580s and were partly settled in the end with an insecure frontier of forts and missions, priestly diplomacy, and a long-term policy of sticks and carrots—raids, trades, and bribes. These became even more necessary when the Apache, Ute, and Comanche adopted horses and guns and turned into exceptional irregular cavalry. Against rivals like these, wholesale Spanish colonization failed completely.

It was not just territorial failure that made the idea of a completed conquest a fantasy; it was also the manpower used in the successes. Spanish expeditions continued to rely on Indian armies. Having leaned on Tlaxcalans, Otomí, and Huejotzincans to topple the Mexica, the Spanish then sent them west against the Purépecha, north against the Chichimeca, and south against the Zapotecs, Mixe, and Chinantec in the rugged sierra of Oaxaca. Both the winners and losers of the war for Teotihuacán joined in: The defeated Mexica manned the expeditions to the south, were critical for Cortés's survival in Tabasco, formed the vanguard for Montejo in Yucatán, and constituted the overwhelming majority of Alvarado's troops in Guatemala. The Spanish won the great Mixton War of the early 1540s, a major conflict that spread from the Pacific Coast lowlands up into the mountains of western Mexico, thanks to an army of thirty thousand central highlanders.[74] Some, the porters called *auxiliares* or *naborías*, served, in effect, as the wheels of the supply trains. Many others were Indian conquistadors—soldiers, not slaves, not even second-class citizens. In Michoacán the nobility noted that the Mexica were willing troops, who "did not come resentfully" but without compulsion, dressed in their traditional finery.[75] In the far north, Tlaxcalan troops came on horses, armed with guns, and bearing the distinguishing Spanish title of "don."[76] Alvarado even took a detachment of Maya warriors with him to Peru, where (after eating "countless native people," wrote the chronicler) they froze to death in the high mountain passes of the Andes.[77] Across the Pacific, the small Spanish garrison in Manila held out against a determined Chinese pirate fleet in 1575 thanks only to their Filipino auxiliaries, who outnumbered the Spaniards ten to one.[78]

And Indians did not just defeat the Spaniards' enemies on the expanding frontiers but also settled them, founding Tlaxcalan, Mexica, and Otomí colonies from Coahuila to the Maya highlands of Guatemala. Small Tlaxcalan territories grew up across large swathes of the North: San Luis Potosí, Sonora, Coahuila, and much later Texas and even Florida.[79] In Coahuila Tlaxcalans founded a town called Nueva Tlaxcala and sent out Tlaxcalan militias to defend the frontier across the seventeenth and eighteenth centuries.[80] Indigenous garrisons anchored Spanish expansion into the dangerous mountains of northern Oaxaca, fighting off local attacks year after year.[81] At times the Indians on the peripheries used the Spanish, as in Chiapas, where the Zinacantecos joined Bernal Díaz to capture Chamula, the capital of their neighbors and enemies.[82] Some became important leaders in their own right: Before a tardy baptism, Don Fernando de Tapia, one of the founders of the city of Querétaro and an owner of vast cattle and wheat estates, had been Conín, Otomí trader and warrior. Others, like the surviving children of Montezuma, received titles and lands and colonized Spanish high society. Descendants of the royal families of Texcoco and Tenochtitlán continued in positions of power in those cities for decades, gradually intermarrying with Spaniards. At a lower level, the majority of Indians across Mexico continued to be ruled directly by other Indians until well into the seventeenth century. Many villages were dominated by the same noble families at the end as at the beginning of colonial rule.[83]

Thus, while capturing the Valley of Mexico was shockingly quick, capturing the rest of what became Mexico was grindingly slow. It took nearly a century of exploring, raiding, and civil war for the Spanish to achieve anything approaching stable dominion. Until then they controlled most of the central highlands and mere islands of rule elsewhere. Within their territories there persisted islands of a different sort of rule, most notably Tlaxcala, for centuries a law unto itself. Further afield, expansion was a stop-and-start enterprise, with retreats as well as advances on the frontiers: The capital of Tabasco had to move inland due to pirate attacks; eastern Yucatán was effectively abandoned to holdout Maya; and Aguascalientes, an important stop on the way north to the new silver mines, was founded and in short order virtually abandoned. Santa Bárbara, the first capital of Chihuahua, was abandoned twice. New Spain for its first century actually looked remarkably like the old empire, where the Mexica were, in one anthropologist's words, "little more than a band of pirates, sallying forth from their great city to loot and plunder and to submit vast areas to tribute payment, without altering the essential social constitution of their victims."[84] The Spanish, in reality, never completed their conquest. In the mountains along the Pacific Coast, Nayarit remained a formally independent kingdom until 1722.[85] In the South, large swathes of the Maya lands remained functionally independent until the mid-nineteenth century. So did most of the North, where the desert ran into the Great Plains and the Mexicans after Independence actually lost ground to the indigenous nations. In the Northwest, the last flickers of an independent Yaqui nation were only extinguished with air raids and poison gas in 1929.[86] In Chiapas indigenous rebels maintain to this day the autonomous fiefdom they made in the Zapatista rising of 1994. 1521 was by no means the end of the conquest of Mexico. It was the end of the beginning.

Chapter Two

The Quick and the Dead

Even the Spanish on the ground had until the 1550s little idea of what it was they were actually conquering, and not all that much more for the next century or so. That was natural enough: New Spain stretched from Oregon to Texas to Guatemala and across the Pacific to the Philippines, on the enduringly haphazard maps of the time at least, and exactly what lay within those fantastical and hypothetical outlines was often unknown. Legends of distant cities of almost vulgar wealth, virgin metropolises of desert or rainforest, drew Spaniards north into California and south toward the Amazon. These optimists left remarkably sketchy accounts of the actual landscapes and animals of the New World, but at times they went into quite detailed visions of the cities that somewhere, over the next horizon, punctuated the inconvenience of nature.[1] Some of those accounts were hearsay, possibly malicious, possibly clever ways of ridding their authors of unwelcome visitors, possibly practical jokes practiced by Indians on gullible Europeans. Others were either mendacious or delusional; one friar wrote breathlessly of the "beautiful city" of Cíbola that he had positively seen with his own eyes, with a skyline of ten-story buildings, "larger than the city of Mexico," lurking somewhere in the wastelands of the North.[2] Beyond the mountains to the west lived a queen who owned huge silver mines, wrote one judge home, a "*señora de la plata*," gossiped a merchant, who was already in league with Cortés.[3] On the thin limestone soils of Yucatán, one upwardly mobile conquistador informed the king, there were "very large and beautiful cities," where he had "found many signs of gold." He had in reality spent the first months of his expedition in huts on a beach, and marching inland found wattle-and-daub towns and hunger.[4] New Spain in its entirety was unknowable, and parts of it unthinkable, "outside the imagination of men" for one royal chronicler.[5] That did not stop the Spanish from trying.

The land that ended up being Mexico stretched for over a thousand miles on either side of the Tropic of Cancer, passing through seven climate zones, and climbing from the shores of a sea and two oceans up to peaks of eighteen thousand feet in the volcanic highlands. In the far Northwest, beyond Spanish colonization for centuries to come, a pocket of Mediterranean-like weather gave way to hot desert surrounding the Sea of Cortés. Moving east, the land rose into the Sierra Madre, the geological continuation of the long spine of the Rockies, where temperatures fell and rain returned, bringing with it the forestlands of pine, juniper, and oak of Sonora, Sinaloa, Durango, and western Chihuahua. On the other side of the watershed the land fell off and the rain ran out and the climate became arid or desert all the way to the Gulf Coast, grasslands giving way to mesquite and cactus. Moving southward across the Tropic, the coasts turned to savanna with a band of monsoon wetlands in Tabasco and Campeche and a swathe of rainforest that stretched from the Isthmus of Tehuantepec down into Central America. In the center the land rose over seven thousand feet into a cold, semi-arid plateau, the altiplano, punctuated by the watery Valley of Mexico, before descending again into the subtropical highlands of Morelos.

With the partial exception of the altiplano, the coasts and more inhabitable parts of the South were precisely the types of environment that produced, according to Enlightenment thinkers, dark-skinned peoples with incurable sloth, mental weakness, and barbarism. The Spanish didn't need the climatic determinism of contemporary philosophy to feel justified and confident colonizers; they had centuries of success in campaigns against Muslims on the Iberian Peninsula, and more recently in North Africa, to provide models of strategy and legalism. They thought with labels and comparisons from those wars: Cortés compared Tlaxcala to Granada, Coronado compared the northerners to Turks, others dubbed the Chichimeca "al-arabs." This was unsurprising given the frontier backgrounds of so many, even some of the poshest: The first viceroy, Antonio de Mendoza, was the

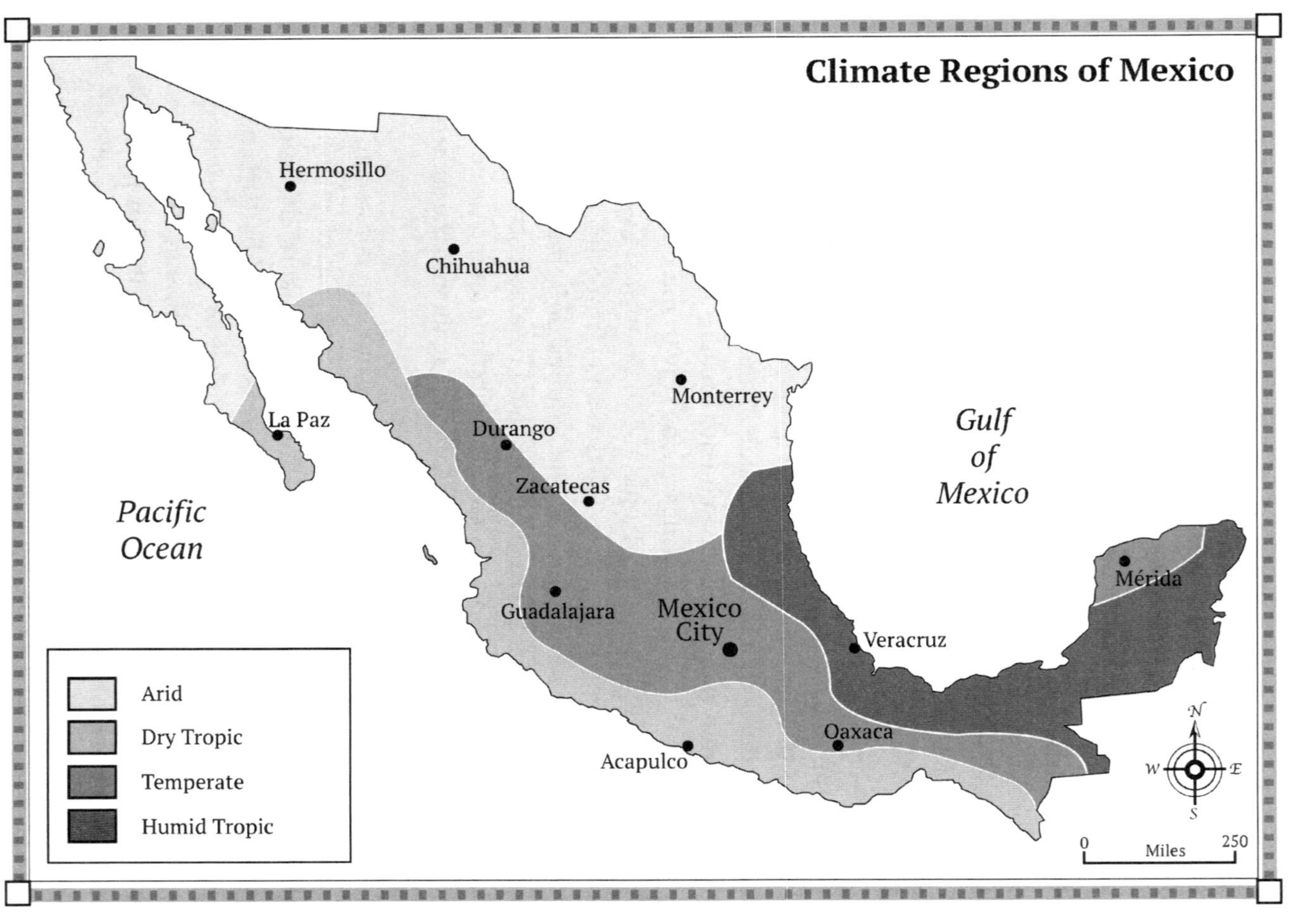

Hydrographic map of Mexico.

son of the Count of Tendilla, the man responsible for administering Granada after its fall in 1492.[6] Mexico provided a new frontier for very old wars. In the words of Fray Gómara, one of the more jihadi-like Spaniards of the time—albeit an absentee jihadi, a chronicler of Mexico who never actually went there—"The conquests of the Indians began once those of the Moors were over, because Spaniards have always waged war on infidels."[7]

In considering those infidels, prejudice collided with confusion, imagination, and theology. The people of the Americas couldn't, they reasoned, have sprung from nowhere, raising serious problems with both Old and New Testaments. It was hard to know which of Noah's sons had made it from Mount Ararat to Mexico—Japheth, not having much of a story to that date, was a clear favorite—and why the Son of God subsequently spiritually wrote off such a large portion of humanity. Neither did the urban sophistication of the center and Southeast of Mexico square with barbarian origins. It followed, naturally, that the New World had thinkable origins in the Old. The Maya worshipped their Great Tree of the World; it was shaped like a cross; quod erat demonstrandum. Quetzalcóatl, the pale, bearded god who came from the East to bring civilization to central Mexico, was clearly Saint Thomas, the apostle who vanished after the Crucifixion; the *Acta Thomae* said he had gone to preach "beyond the Ganges." The Christian origins of the Indians might be even more recent, the work of seven bishops who fled the Muslim invasion of Spain in the Dark Ages.

For others (including the Protestants of New England) the indigenous city dwellers had claims to the legitimating ancestry of classical antiquity: Carthaginians, Egyptians, or one of the ten lost tribes of Israel.[8] Some Indians staked the claim themselves: In 1554 the Maya of Quiché wrote down an origin myth in which their ancestors "came from over there, where the sun rises, descendants of Israel."[9] The ancestry was self-evident, there for all to see in pyramids and skin color. In 1626 an Italian, Lorenzo Pignoria, drew on the *Codex Ríos* and artefacts in his friends' private collections to argue that the Egyptians had lent the Mexica both their cosmology and their writing.[10] Centuries later the search for links continued, at times flatteringly reversed to give the New World the prize of originality. For a Victorian scientist it was the Maya who brought civilization to Egypt, and for

Mormons the great eschatological battle between Good and Evil had been fought in Chiapas or Veracruz. (Good lost, until Joseph Smith turned up thousands of miles north and thousands of years later.)[11] The question of Mexican origins, whether geographical or spiritual, ran unresolved for centuries.

Uncertainty had important consequences, legal in the short term and philosophical in the long term. The extent of barbarism of the indigenous peoples helped determine to what extent their rule from Europe might be considered legitimate. The philosopher Juan Ginés de Sepúlveda, enlisted to defend the morality of Spanish rule, did not (as commonly believed) question the Indians' humanity; that had been definitively settled by the papal bull *Sublimis Deus* in 1537. On the contrary, he argued with clear humanism, they were rational yet without civilization and precisely for that reason subject to natural law. Their practices and above all institutions broke natural law through human sacrifice, laying them open to just war and Christian rule. This doctrine went back to Saint Augustine and was well within the intellectual mainstream of the time: In England Thomas More advanced a more extremist version, arguing that a mere failure to cultivate fertile land legitimized a just war against such idlers.[12]

But how much human sacrifice Indians actually practiced and what it meant was debatable. For Bartolomé de las Casas, the Dominican friar who defended the rights of the conquered, human sacrifice had been cynically exaggerated for political gain.[13] For Juan de Torquemada, on the other hand, it was slaughter on an industrial scale, with one emperor alone—"very affable and a friend to doing well by all"—offering up 72,344 captives over four days.[14] From the archaeological record it seems that Las Casas was closer to the truth, with skulls recovered from Tenochtitlán's main temple numbering in the hundreds rather than tens of thousands, although the frequency of killings increased markedly under Montezuma, and the remains could perfectly well have been interred elsewhere. A later nationalist defended the practice of showily pulling a beating heart from under a rib cage as an overenthusiastic take on the Eucharist; for one eminent historian it was a good way of buying off the masses with scarce protein, a search for political stability through "meat and circuses."[15] Beyond the normative—and people who firebomb Dresden or drop atomic bombs on Hiroshima probably shouldn't cast too many stones—the issue of human sacrifice forms part of a broader analytical problem, that of life and death before the Spanish arrived.

Spanish manuscripts of the conquest clearly left something to be desired in their reliability. Abbé Raynal, a French intellectual of the eighteenth century, sneered in the second edition of his *Histoire philosophique des deux Indes* (1774) at the scribblings of "barbarous soldiers, greedy merchants, and missionaries."[16] Even the collection of those were incomplete, decimated by the vagaries of censorship, low print runs, and dangerous times. The Spanish were by no means disinterested: As early as 1615 Fray Torquemada drew on indigenous sources to hypothesize the Bering Strait migration. Nor were they intellectual chauvinists, automatically dismissing the truth value of indigenous writings even if they were pictographic. Fray Durán privileged native over Spanish accounts of the stoning of Montezuma.[17] But there were not very many writers, and some books that might have been canonical simply disappeared. In short, while we have some idea of pre-Hispanic beliefs in philosophy and the afterlife thanks to a handful of surviving manuscripts and ethnographically inclined churchmen, we don't know how many people were sharing those beliefs. This in turn matters because it means we then can't know exactly how many people died in the apocalyptic century that followed, which has opened space for questioning just how apocalyptic that first century of Spanish presence actually was.

Estimates of pre-Hispanic populations vary hugely, even in the legible cities of the center. At one end of the scale demographers once suggested that up to twenty-five million people lived in the Valley of Mexico in 1519, nearly as many as do today; more recent numbers run as low as 350 thousand. (Low is a relative term in a world with only about two hundred thousand Parisians, fifty thousand Londoners, and fifteen thousand Lenape Indians in New York.)[18] Further north the dry environs of Zacatecas may have been home to between 90 and 120 thousand people; the desert lands of Chihuahua and Durango, perhaps 350 thousand; the rainforests of the Yucatán Peninsula, perhaps as many as 800 thousand.[19] The total numbers of the dead are unknowable. The question has been debated for centuries; the nineteenth-century polymath Alexander von Humboldt thought the devastation much exaggerated. Some current scholars would agree with him; most lean toward the apocalyptic firsthand accounts of Indians, conquistadors, and missionaries.[20] As early as 1542 there were reportedly only 250 thousand Maya left, a dying-off of perhaps two-thirds of the population, although it is difficult to see how such a huge count could be made in the very first days of Spanish settlement. By later and more accurate counts, Mexico City's population shrank to about fifty thousand by the end of the first century of Spanish contact; in fertile Morelos twenty thousand were left from some ninety thousand; in the Mixteca Alta of Oaxaca 350 thousand gave way to thirty-five thousand; in far-off Tabasco only five thousand people were left, a reduction of up to 95 percent. The tropical lowlands may have been in the long run the most dangerous places, but the peoples of the highlands suffered at least 50 percent decline in population, and most probably the population of central Mexico fell by some three-quarters in less than a hundred years.[21] No single epidemic caused this, but rather the cumulative impact of successive waves and a wide range of sicknesses acting in complex, lethal ways. Faced with this scale, exactitude is redundant; the basic order of magnitude is beyond appeal. Indians died in vast numbers. As the young died, they never had the chance to have children and replace their vanishing forebears, and their populations collapsed.

For skeptics about the massive mortality of the sixteenth century there is a simple rebuttal: comparative epidemiology. In the early modern period, the first arrival of any particularly aggressive microbe anywhere in the world brought death on an epic scale. The smallpox virus took a third of Icelanders between 1707 and 1709.[22] The bacterium *Yersinia pestis*—the Black Death—killed between a third and a half of the population across fourteenth-century Europe, and in Spain it started an epidemic cycle that by 1500 had reduced the population by two-thirds. Most of Iberia's demographic recovery across the following century was wiped out by the plague's return in 1599.[23] Another new bacterial disease, cholera, killed a quarter of a million Spaniards in 1854.[24] Europeans in the New World of the sixteenth century were by no means exempt from fatal disease; a judge writing home in 1529 offered "infinite thanks" to heaven for his survival, explaining that "God greatly blesses those to whom he gives health in this land, because many die at the moment they take a fever, as happened to many who came in the last fleet, and it is the greatest pity in the world."[25]

Yet mass fatalities among the indigenous peoples were far greater because they stemmed from several epidemics simultaneously hitting a dense population for the first time. Even after a certain level of immunity to the more everyday pathogens emerged in the seventeenth century, the inhabitants of the New World remained vulnerable to the great killers. The Spanish brought with them to the Americas the novel germs of smallpox, typhoid, measles, mumps, rubella, flu, malaria, yellow fever, salmonella, and the common cold; at the most they took syphilis back home, and that is still debated.[26] The extraordinary imbalance of this exchange of diseases stemmed from the microbial parochialism of the Americas. For millennia Europeans, Asians, and Africans suffered the attacks of regularly evolving pathogens that crossed the species barrier from the domestic animals with which they lived in close proximity, returning in mutated guise; the microbes then traveled great distances at great speed along global trade routes that stretched from Beijing to Dublin, Zanzibar to Norway. Such shifting long-range infections favored the development of immunities that, combined with a greater genetic diversity, made Old World populations more resistant to both existing and emergent strains of disease. Before 1492 Indians had neither domestic animals (barring turkeys) nor contact with the rest of the world on any scale, and thus no significant resistance.

It took four to six generations for their society to acquire much immunity; in the interim they were brutally culled. There were regional epidemics every few years throughout the sixteenth century. Measles swept Chiapas in 1539; mumps spread out from Chalco in 1550; yellow fever struck Veracruz in 1556; typhus broke out in the Valley of Mexico in 1576; measles, scarlet fever, and chicken pox together roiled the central highlands in 1588.[27] Above all, three great epidemics stretched across all of New Spain in the sixteenth century: in 1520 smallpox, and in 1545 and again in 1575 an illness that the Nahua called *matlazahuatl* or *cocoliztli*, "pestilence," a mysterious disease identified only recently as an enteric fever, cousin to typhoid.[28] Later precise death counts are eloquent proof of that bacterium's enduringly lethal nature: As late as 1736 an outbreak of cocoliztli in Mexico City killed 40,157 out of a population of less than 100,000.[29]

At the outset all the new diseases were mysterious to the indigenous peoples. The smallpox virus could be transmitted by droplets and contact with scabs or pus; at times it was airborne, riding throughout enclosed spaces on particles of dust. Being coughed or sneezed upon, touching a carrier or the dead, brushing against scabs or pus in clothes or blankets, or even just sharing a room could all pass it on. As it was also waterborne, the fact that Indians bathed more regularly than the Spanish only increased the transmission rate, as one friar observed, better hygiene counterintuitively causing greater disease.[30] Smallpox was consequently contagious enough to run far ahead of major Spanish settlement, breaking out among the Maya as early as 1517 and subsequently across and beyond New Spain, wiping out towns as far away as the northern Amazon and killing Huayna Capac, a major indigenous leader in the Andes, before the conquistador Francisco Pizarro had even arrived.[31]

The virus was also a trickster, which increased its mobility: Symptoms only appeared twelve or so days after it was contracted, they were initially quite mild—headaches, fever, and nausea—and they often went away for a while. The infected, effectively asymptomatic, might not even realize they had the disease until they entered its second, often fatal phase. Lesions turned into pustules that spread across the skin and affected the internal organs as well. The body reacted with fever and shedding skin, opening a new front of vulnerability to other pathogens such as measles, what the Nahua called the "little plague" that followed the great one.[32] After two weeks the pustules and blisters turned to scabs, in which the virus could survive for weeks, and which fell off to infect others. Indians were three times as likely to die from smallpox as Europeans were.[33] The first epidemic began in September 1520 and lasted for years; it killed, survivors remembered, "infinite numbers."[34]

The typhoid-like cocoliztli came subsequently in two great waves, crushing the first two postconquest generations. Its symptoms were equally dire, and it was undoubtedly greater, the two epidemics combined, in total mortality. Like smallpox, the pathogen could move unseen through asymptomatic carriers. Unlike smallpox, onset was fast: The victims quickly developed high fever and extreme pain, bled from

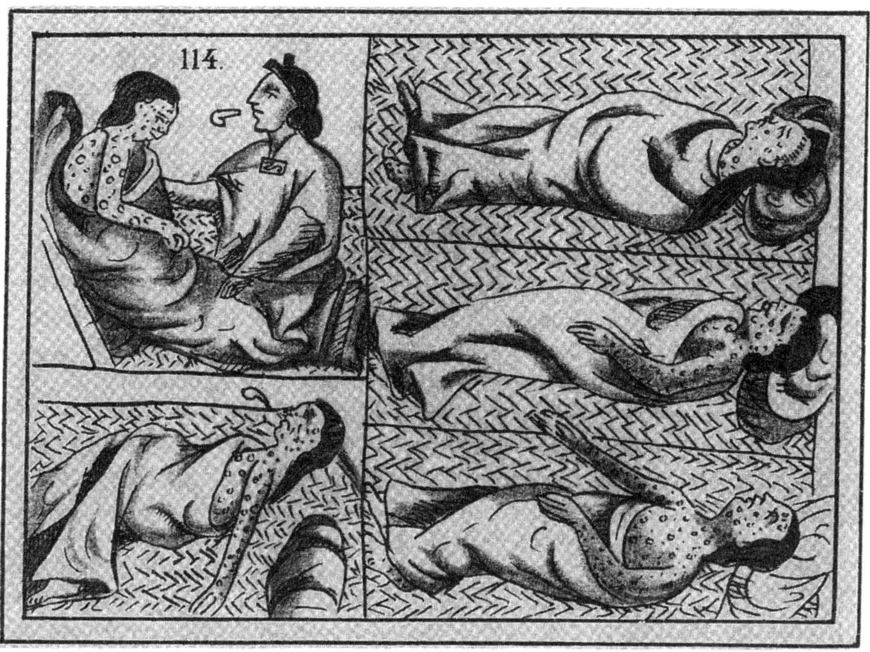

The symptoms and progression of smallpox. Florentine Codex Book XII (1576).

their eyes, mouths, and anuses, contracted jaundice as organs began failing, and died within a week. Cocoliztli struck everywhere—the early ethnographer Fray Bernardino de Sahagún contracted it, and it killed Fray Agustín de Deza—but indigenous deaths were again of a different order of magnitude. Before the first outbreak ended, the Bishop of Mexico counted eighty thousand deaths; between the two outbreaks the population of Mexico City halved, and that of Texcoco fell from fifteen thousand to six hundred.[35] The Bishop of Oaxaca estimated that 90 percent of his flock died in the twenty years between 1534 and 1554.[36] Torquemada, who lived through the second epidemic, recorded the carnage: "In the cities and large towns, big ditches were dug, and from morning to sunset the priests did nothing else but carry the dead bodies and throw them into the ditches."[37] Europeans faced with similar plagues traditionally fled the towns—the Spanish medieval epigram held that one should *"huir luego, lejos y largo rato,"* flee fast, far away, and for a long time—but the Spanish instead clustered the Indians in larger, more readily taxed and proselytized settlements, a policy called *congregación*, which only increased transmission rates. There were few safe places anyway, and villages to the north of Mexico City turned to ghost towns, where the newly introduced sheep grazed among the ruins, while the disease spread across the entire colony from Sinaloa to Guatemala.[38]

There were three contemporary antidotes to epidemic disease; none worked very well. The indigenous drew on an extensive pharmacopeia and a long history of specialization in medical practices that the people of central Mexico called *tiçiyotl*. These ranged from diagnosis by the descrying of patterns in fire and maize kernels, through palmistry, through observing the effects of tobacco or peyote on the sufferer, to the straightforward observation of symptoms. Conclusions reached, healers prescribed the appropriate parts of plants or animals. Women in childbirth, for example, would receive from female doctors herbs called *tiçitl* and, should labor prove difficult, ground opossum tails.[39] Indigenous treatments were often empirically based, and assorted herbs, roots, leaves, and tree bark all exercised demonstrable physiological impacts; one friar approvingly noted how "experienced native doctors" cured the Spanish of some diseases that left their own doctors perplexed.[40] The newcomers recognized the power of these treatments early on and set out to collect them and the associated medical knowledge, assembling a bilingual catalogue of botanicals, the Codex Cruz-Badiano, in 1552. For all the strategic vagueness of their Indian informants (worried, and with some justification, about being arrested by the Church's demonologists), the Spanish identified many new drugs: for purgatives alone multiple wild herbs, such as *chichicpatl, cacalosuchitl,* and *mecasuchil*, whose Nahuatl names the friars duly learned. The white jalap was such an effective laxative that they exported it back to Spain, whence it spread across Europe.[41] Spanish medical antidotes to mass dying, by contrast, were often positively harmful, and applying purgatives or bleeding, staple treatments, only increased death rates among their fast-fading patients. But very few Spanish treated Indians anyway, so the question was largely moot.[42]

Both indigenous and Spanish antidotes layered the medical with the supernatural; the third approach, however, was straightforwardly religious, when indigenous and Spanish alike eschewed terrestrial theories of causation and treatment in favor of the divine. Indian authorities might prescribe, with increasing secretiveness, traditional appeasements (though rarely human sacrifice); the Spanish organized vigils and processions of saints and virgins, marching doggedly behind their churchmen, mixing the infected with the uninfected. Nobody's gods seemed impressed. Cocoliztli's origin was not just a medical but also a spiritual mystery. The God of the Old Testament had punished sinners by killing them on a massive scale, the friar Andrés de Olmos told his indigenous flock, taking 94,900 Jews' lives in revenge for a single rape.[43] For one missionary, such logic was hard to take, and when the cocoliztli arrived and "God . . . began to depopulate New Spain of Indians," the Creator's rationale was hard to see in "his secret judgements." The whiff of doubt—how could a good Lord permit such suffering?—is distinct.[44]

The only mitigation, in the absence of medicine, lay in the social distancing of quarantine, whether individual or collective, through cordons sanitaires or hospitalization. This was understood but undoable on a sufficient scale. At the end of the sixteenth century, after the three great plagues, there were still only one hundred hospitals in all of New Spain, and those that existed were not necessarily top of the list for community funding.[45] The 1561 accounts for Santa Catalina Texupa in Oaxaca record 150 pesos going to the hospital, while 281 went on "a white damask cloak, with dark blue and red velvet all along its border and one cloth that is adorned with red taffeta for the lord bishop."[46] So the sick stayed at home, killing whole families, or were abandoned. As fields were left untended, harvests failed and villages began to starve. In one of the few native accounts of the dying, the Florentine Codex registers a possible witness's testimony: "The pustules that covered people caused great desolation; very many people died of them, and many just starved to death; starvation reigned, and no one took care of others any longer."[47]

In some places the universal basic of a decorous burial or cremation broke down, and the survivors, faced with the danger of infection and the omnipresent smell of rotting corpses, simply knocked the houses down to cover the dead.[48] It was a social revolution of sorts: Mass dying had occurred before the conquest, through the failure of maize harvests—caused visibly enough by native locusts, drought, flooding, and even, in the highlands, occasional snowstorms—but never through such invisible agents of disease, and the new dying caused in some places a breakdown of the old social norms.[49] It also undermined the new norms: As the Dominican Agustín Dávila Padilla put it lugubriously after the 1576 Mexico City epidemic, "The common enemy of the souls waged his war, as always, and while the monks called for patience, the devil provoked rage and despair. A number of Indians thus lost their souls, as well as their bodies. They would flare up in a furious rage at being so trampled by Death, while disease did not touch the Spanish."[50] For the Indians, another friar said, it was indeed very different: "They died in heaps, like bedbugs."[51]

Alien microbes were the main but not the only destroyers of Indians. The same friar, Motolinía, produced a graphic catalogue of what he called the nine other plagues that devastated the Mexican altiplano, describing not just the stricken towns and villages but also the mines and the city streets suffused with the stench of decay. His plagues were phrased in the metaphors of the Old Testament—the stories from Exodus of the pharoah's cursed Egypt, the Israelites' worship of the golden calf, the destruction of Jerusalem—and the surreal visions of the Book of Revelations. The besieged Tenochtitlán, he wrote, was filled with "vile spirits who emerged from the mouth of the dragon and of the Beast in the form of frogs, when the sixth Angel poured out his vial or cup into the River Euphrates."[52] One of the more literal plagues was the starvation that followed that siege, a product of fields burnt or never sown. The majority of Motolinía's tragedies, however, were tales of destruction caused by forced labor and ethnic cleansing. Enslaved provincials were driven to the city in herds like metaphorical sheep. Some were forced out by real sheep, a source of destruction vast enough to earn its own classification as a plague.

The introduction of sheep on a commercial scale anywhere tends to exact a high human cost, whether through ecological degradation or the seizure of common lands or smallholdings. English and Lowland Scottish sheep farmers, for example, eradicated the Scottish peasantry of the mountains and western isles in a campaign of ethnic cleansing known as the Highland Clearances. Thomas More, in *Utopia*—a book read by some of the Spanish upper classes—wrote of sheep eating men. (One of his readers, Viceroy Mendoza, was also responsible for introducing Merino sheep to Mexico, so the warning clearly didn't stick.) In Mexico the clearing of villages for sheep was more complex and less deliberate; but it was possible at all because of laws that favored pastoralists greatly, allowing them, for example, to graze all unfenced lands. In a land without fences the consequences for indigenous maizefields were foreseeable but ignored.[53]

Outside the rangelands, Motolinía wrote, Spanish peasants-turned-lords became overseers of the new estates and, together with their Black slaves-turned-foremen, set out to extort more from the indigenous peasantry than it could bear.[54] The discovery that some Spaniards had received gold offerings from indigenous communities led other Spaniards to overestimate the amount of that metal still to be uncovered. They tried, fruitlessly, through jail and torture to get the rest; when the Indians were unable to pay, they sold their lands and their sons in an endless running to stand still. Gold that wasn't to be found could always be dug up, it was vainly hoped, and Indians who were forced down the barren mines were killed by rockfalls; others died of exhaustion or hunger carrying food to the diggers. The rebirth of Tenochtitlán as Mexico City likewise brought death, as demolition brought buildings down on some of the builders while others fell from the heights. The war had brought devastation on the grandest of scales. But Spanish violence did not end with the scorched-earth taking of Tenochtitlán; it endured on both petty and massive levels, with the purpose of driving, particularly in the first two generations, work and extortion.

The Spanish had long deployed exemplary, performative violence in Iberia as they fought their way south over the centuries of the *Reconquista*, the war to take the peninsula back from the Muslims. They did the same in the Americas; at an early stage in the march to Tenochtitlán Cortés cut off the hands of fifty Tlaxcalan emissaries and "stage[d] a bloody massacre of the most public possible kind in order to terrorize" the citizens of Cholula. (Not just terrifying them, but also stiffening the resolve of his own men with "the therapeutic effects of a good massacre.")[55] Everday behavior was infused with casual brutality: As refugees streamed out of Tenochtitlán in 1521—"men, women and children, so thin, yellow, dirty and stinking that it was pitiful to see them"—they were strip-searched by the Spanish, who "looked everywhere, ripping the clothes off women to search between their legs, in their mouths and in their hair."[56] That records speak of abortion, along with suicide, as one more reason for population decline is unsurprising. In addition to sexual violence, the Spanish used beating, whipping, torture, and deadly inventions that ranged from the strict choreography of hanging or burning in the auto-da-fé to the bloody free-for-all of throwing to the dogs, an end common enough to have its own verb, *aperrear*. In Yucatán, the soldiers cut off women's breasts or hanged them with their infants dangling from their feet.[57] The most egregious practitioner of mass violence, Nuño de Guzmán, took villages' food stocks before burning the houses and torturing, enslaving, or killing their inhabitants. Even would-be allies, like the welcoming cacique of Michoacán, were fair game; after receiving his food, gold, silver, and soldiers, Guzmán had him dragged behind a horse and then burned.

Yet such violence was egregious even to Spanish eyes, and Nuño de Guzmán was judged to have gone beyond the pale, recalled, and imprisoned. In 1549 he actually lost a lawsuit brought by two former Indian slaves and was ordered to pay them substantial damages.[58] The psychopathic Guzmán was not the only Spanish leader to be disciplined for violence against Indians, moreover. Among others the first Bishop of Mexico, Juan de Zumárraga, no less than the "Protector of the Indians," was demoted after burning a Texcocan nobleman for heresy in 1539.[59] But even after the historical rebuttal of the *leyenda negra*, the Protestant "Black Legend" of unremitting Catholic evil in the New World, a dog whistle keeps the idea of the legend alive in the use of the words "holocaust" and "genocide" to describe Spanish policy and actions.[60] The word, only coined in 1944, has unequalled resonance, but also a precise definition aimed at preserving both that resonance and its legal power. Article II of the 1948 UN Genocide Convention defines genocide as activities including killing, wounding, brutalizing, starving, and kidnapping people of a "national, ethnical, racial or religious group," all of which the Spanish did; but it critically specifies the violence be rooted in a blanket "intent to destroy" such a group.[61]

Aperreamiento (the method of execution by throwing to the dogs) as depicted in a Protestant propaganda woodcut. Theodor de Bry, *Brevísima Relación de la Destrucción de las Indias* (1598).

Such an intention was absent in Mexico, at least in sedentary Mexico (northern nomads were at times a different matter); the Spanish on the contrary aimed to preserve the pre-Hispanic cities and their populations as much as possible.

This was not out of Renaissance humanism or fear for their immortal souls—after all, God and some of his more important henchmen, such as Saint James, were on their side—but for straightforward economic reasons: After the disappointment of gold and before the promise of silver, Indians themselves were the main source of wealth (as laborers rather than chattel slaves, officially if not invariably). The main reward for the first generation of Spanish lay in the royal grant of Indians and their associated land in the *encomienda*, the commendation of a place's souls, land, and labor to a Spanish master. The indigenous peoples were, even Columbus had noted, "the greatest wealth" of his discoveries in the Americas.[62] So the great dying was a problem for the Spanish too, albeit one of business rather than existence.

Extracting wealth from human labor had not been the original aim of the Spanish; the Spanish had come to the Americas to take home the portable, enduring wealth of gold. There was a chronic shortage of gold in Europe at the time, and precious metals were at first the only means of buying their way homeward and upward in society. No other American commodity combined high value and low volume to make long-distance shipping particularly profitable. But there was also an obsessive undertone to the search that ran beyond the mere accumulation of wealth—the repeated use of the word "quest" in subsequent accounts may be revealing—and no shame in advertising it alongside the more selfless claims to extend the realm of kings, queens, and Christianity. Some sixty-five references to gold appear in Columbus's diary from his first outbound trip; he recruited sailors by promising a country whose houses were roofed with gold; and in his letter to the *reyes católicos*, the Catholic monarchs Ferdinand and Isabella, he promised them "as much gold as they have need of." It quite literally grew on trees.[63]

That letter had gone through twenty printed editions by the time Cortés was in his teens. He continued the tradition himself in the several editions of his letters that appeared in Spain in the first few years after the capture of Tenochtitlán.[64] His lesser contemporaries repeated the point ad nauseam in their unprinted letters home, with poignant appeals for relatives and friends to join them in places like Veracruz. The Mexica viewed the obsession with some puzzlement, as the Spanish explicitly communicated (in acts as well as words) the psychological edge to this particular form of the universal search for money. Cortés had, he told the first Indians he met on the coast, a "sickness that only gold can cure."[65] So, the Mexica observed, it seemed. As one man put it, talking to a friar long after the scant bullion was gone, "Like monkeys they grabbed the gold. It was as though their hearts were put to rest, brightened, renewed. For gold was what they greatly thirsted for; they were gluttonous for it, starved for it."[66]

The Mexica, regrettably, did not share the Spaniards' obsession. Their nobles and royal families were avid consumers of luxury goods who appreciated and amassed gold; the preconquest tax records of the *Matrícula de tributos* show an income of 270 bowls of gold dust a year, and as many golden discs.[67] But in the final analysis they valued other materials as much if not more. Bright-green feathers from the quetzal of the southern rainforests, jadeite from Nicaragua, turquoise from the American Southwest, the red *Spondylus* shells from the Pacific coast—these were all greatly valued, and of greater antiquity in their culture. The Maya bought gold ornaments from Veraguas in Panama—they have been found in the holy wells, the *cenotes*—and the Mexica merchants, the pochteca, had trade networks that reached as far as gold-rich Colombia; but the Mexica had only begun working gold on their own lands about 150 years before the Spanish arrived, and there was not all that much gold to be mined in the central highlands anyway.[68] They did not seem overly concerned with the matter, and threw much of what accumulated gold and treasure they had into the great lake, beyond recovery, in the last days of the siege. The Spaniards were left using the pre-Hispanic tax records of the *Matrícula de tributos* to collect indigenous valuables that they did not themselves value much ("They cared nothing for green-stone, precious feathers, or turquoise," another puzzled Mexica observed) and with them the more quotidian tax-in-kind of the ancien régime—copper axe-heads, hides, honey—while hoping for the second-best of a country estate and some Indians to cultivate it.[69] By 1524 the supply of such estates in central Mexico was more or less exhausted; those that could be granted to conquistadors had been.[70]

Some decided to look beyond country life. Cortés's followers did not originally come to the New World to be gentleman farmers; the overwhelming majority were not gentlemen at all, with only sixteen hidalgos among the first wave of colonists in arms. (The first wave of English conquistadors, arriving in Virginia in 1607, were distinctly posher, and after reinforcement had six times more gentlemen per capita than did their society back home.)[71] The Spanish had little intention of sweating, except perhaps in armor, aiming instead to win portable riches through feats of arms, or perhaps by just being in the right place at the right time, before returning home and joining the nobility there, where being a gentleman farmer was a different proposition. "I came here to get rich," Cortés is supposed to have bragged, "not to till the soil like a peasant."[72] Some conquistadors instead ended up working, and several became innkeepers, running hostels from huts with straw roofs on the road uphill from the coast to the city, servicing travelers with beds, fodder, and food. Not all were poor. Rodrigo Rangel, after failing to defeat the Zapotecs, went on to become alcalde of Veracruz and—drawing on experience as Cortés's chamberlain—set up an inn in Cholula.[73] The first hotel in Mexico City, founded in 1526 by Pedro Hernández Paniagua, offered not just beds but also "clean clothing . . . barbecued meat, stew, bread and water." It was clearly a hit, and his street in the south of the city rapidly filled up with competing establishments.[74] But even a successful career in hotel management was not a common aim, and the more ambitious captains took the more ambitious soldiers (and some, like Bernal Díaz, who grumbled all the way but had little choice in the matter) in search of new cities on the far side of new frontiers.

The Spanish were historically urbanites rather than countrymen. In these early years, though, they expanded across Mexico through raiding and plundering, and only established towns or forts in the more profitable areas, forming islands of rule that across centuries might join up in the metaphorical continent of a kingdom. This was what they called conquest: not the immediate, wholesale creation of new domains, but rather the carving out of corridors of tenuous rule between places of wealth—water sources, mines and their boomtowns—and places of security behind older borders. It was only a conquest in quotation marks, sneered Las Casas, "really and truly nothing more than a series of violent incursions."[75] Legally, the Spanish did it with *capitulaciones*, licenses from the king to explore, wage semiprivate war, and divvy up the resulting profits. Practically, they did it with the adventurous, the petty or would-be nobility, and the poor; foreign auxiliaries invariably outnumbered Spaniards. This was a standard model across the empire: In Europe, the Netherlands was held by small numbers of Spanish and numerous auxiliaries from Germany, Italy, Burgundy, Wallonia, and even Ireland, and the Spanish army that defeated the French in 1557 was only 10 percent Spanish.[76] In the Americas, Spanish expeditions were manned not by other Europeans but by hardened indigenous soldiers marching down from the center, and by mutually hostile neighbors seizing their chances to settle scores on the periphery.

In the first fifty years of contact the conquistadors and some latecomers set off in all directions: north, south, east, west, and beyond across the Pacific. Concerned about the threat posed by ambitious underlings, potential imitators of his own rebellion against Diego Velásquez, Cortés sent his captains out of the city in short order: the bellicose Cristóbal de Olid to the west, a more diplomatic Sandoval to the coast of Veracruz, the charismatic but cruel Pedro de Alvarado to the south. They were followed later by Francisco de Montejo to the South proper, Yucatán; Nuño de Guzmán to the west and up the coast, Francisco de Garay to the east, Hernando de Soto to the northeast, and Francisco Vázquez Coronado to the northwest.

There were some early successes, in Castilian terms. In Michoacán Olid gathered appreciable amounts of gold and silver from the Purépecha, again to the bewilderment of the locals ("They must eat it if they like it so much," observed their king wryly). On the Isthmus of Tehuantepec, the narrow waist of Mexico where Oaxaca meets Veracruz, a long tradition of goldwork in the highlands meant that Alvarado struck it comparatively lucky (though he later claimed that Cortés then robbed him). Sandoval discovered no gold but did found a major town on the Coatzacoalcos River, Espíritu Santo, and with it some of the first encomiendas outside of the central valley.[77] Montejo, on the other hand, retreated after five years of futile presence in Yucatán; more successful the second time around, in 1540 he divided much of the peninsula into encomiendas, built himself a palace in Mérida, and, finding that there was little future in export crops or cattle, ended up lording it over a frugal barter economy. He died, back in Spain, a bankrupt. After his early profits in Michoacán, Guzmán struggled up the Pacific Coast in the rainy season, bemoaning the hardship to his king:

> Only he who has traveled through those dank and shadowy jungles, across those plains whose mires are covered by high grasses that lend the earth a deceptive appearance of firmness, having to jump continually between fallen trees, black and rotting, wading constantly

> beneath torrential rains, can understand the miracle of energy and vigour that is necessary.[78]

At least he survived; in September 1530 a hurricane killed hundreds of his indigenous warriors and servants through drowning, disease, and starvation.[79] De Soto, magnificently rich from the conquest of Peru, landed in Florida in 1539, marched westward, and died. Vázquez Coronado married into one of the richest families in New Spain, set off to find the golden Seven Cities of Cíbola in New Mexico, and returned notably less rich. On their main front in the central North the Spanish ran into drylands and, from 1550 onward, dogged resistance from the more nomadic peoples there, the Pames, Guamares, Zacatecos, and Guachichiles, whom they followed the Mexica in lumping together as Chichimeca, barbarians. Elusive and talented warriors, they ended Spanish progress further north until the peace of the 1590s.

Cortés himself followed his lieutenants across New Spain in the early years: first south to Honduras to crush Olid's rebellion, four hundred strong and gallingly funded by his own cash, then back to Mexico City to crush a coup, then back to Spain to defend his actions since 1519, and finally, a decade after taking Tenochtitlán, to the northwest to launch an expedition that aimed to reach China. All of those voyages were failures of one sort or another, barring that first legal pilgrimage to Spain, from which he returned with royal favor, the title of Marqués de la Valle de Oaxaca, vast land grants, and the contract to colonize China. Cortés's earliest major sortie, the 1524 punitive expedition to Honduras, epitomized the blithe confidence with which the captains of the first generation of Spanish headed out of the city, their self-acknowledged ignorance of where they were going, and some of the consequences that hubris brought. In this case, four hundred Spaniards, three thousand Mexica, and a herd of pigs set out to march fifteen hundred miles to the southeast, much of it through unexplored swamplands. The difference between central Mexico and the southern Gulf Coast was quickly apparent: In one sixty-mile stretch they were forced to build close to one bridge for every mile they won. Their Maya guides vanished, leaving the expedition bereft of food and local knowledge.

The Spaniards, floundering along a dismal trail of deserted and burnt-out villages eastward across the Tabasco Plain, quickly began dying of hunger. Would-be reinforcements from Chiapas under Pedro de Alvarado ran into similar difficulties of terrain and never found them.[80] The Mexica turned to cannibalism, trapping local Indians—including, unfortunately, two of the guides—and roasting them. Some Spaniards took note. Cortés had brought along a band; they now split up for more than artistic differences, as "Medrano, flautist of the church of Toledo, [ate] the brains of Medina, trombonist, a native of Seville, and the tripe and brains of Bernaldo Caldera and a cousin of his, for they were dying of hunger." The survivors straggled into Honduras after six months to find that Olid had already been garroted by his own men and that the whole trip had been for nothing. Cortés tried three times to sail back against the prevailing winds to Veracruz, then spent three months convalescing in Guatemala.[81] Less than a hundred of his men, Mexica, Black, and Spanish, made it back to Mexico City.[82]

Turning to the ocean, and the dream of a sea road to China, he sent five separate expeditions over fifteen years to the north and west. The casualty rate as ever was high, with whole ships lost or disappeared, crews killed by indigenous attackers, captains toppled in bloody mutinies. The one he led personally to Baja California in 1535 ended in a profitless colony that folded within the year. The first flotilla he sent out into the Pacific was the most successful because one of the three ships, the *Florida*, actually made it to the Philippines. Yet Magellan had got there first, sailing around Cape Horn, and even had the Mexican route been a more useful prospect, it wouldn't have brought any advance at the time, as the Spanish—led by Cortés's cousin Álvaro de Saavedra—were unable to find favorable winds to return across the Pacific. They sailed perforce the longer way around, westward across the Indian Ocean and up the African Coast, and ended up in Spain seven years later. Futility, litigation, and disaster were close attendants on any expedition, whether by land or sea.[83] Francisco de Montejo—who had not bothered to take a translator on his first expedition south, despite the Mayas' fierce reputation—spent many of his last years in court fighting for ownership of the unpromising swamp that became Tabasco.[84] Such court cases were redolent of the unstable fortunes of the first generation of the conquistadors. Most died, many indigent, before the silver boom of the 1550s, when the discovery of massive deposits in the north of Mexico revolutionized the entire world's economy.

Even Cortés, Marquis del Valle de Oaxaca, overlord of twenty-three thousand Indians, wealthy enough at one stage to cast a cannon in silver for his king and later to lend him money, ended up with financial problems. On his deathbed in Seville in 1547, scarred and almost literally toothless, down to a solitary incisor, he pawned treasures to pay the bills. He wrote to the king begging his help; the prime minister jotted "not to be answered" on the letter. Cortés probably feared hell, trying to buy his way out in his will by telling his executor to make reparations to any Indians he might have harmed, return them their lands, and even pay them for their past work. Conquistadors were lucky just to survive past 1521; about two-thirds of them died in the war.[85] The luckiest ended up with encomiendas where they successfully grew wheat or herded sheep. Some made a killing in trading slaves, first indigenous and later African. It was eloquent of the conquistadors' disappointed prospects, however, that one of the most successful, Pedro de Alvarado, ended up trying his luck a couple of thousand miles further south in the war for the Inca Empire before returning to die at war in the North. The Spanish traveled light on their way from Spain, the islands, and finally Mexico City. Those who made it home came home relatively light too.

Chapter Three

Life in the Beginnings of the New World

The Spanish footprints were in some ways also light, particularly in the first fifty years. The friars built missions, some almost castle-like, while Spanish viceroys, governors, and town councils took up residence in the great houses of the towns. But the indigenous nobility still exercised political power, and not just on the frontiers. Mexico City, Texcoco, Tlaxcala, and Oaxaca were all administered by the old royal lineages. The division of society by race was in its infancy, and the children of the conquistadors, half Spanish and half indigenous, enjoyed much the same civil rights and status as anyone else. In the wilder places people hadn't realized that the new religion condemned the old religion to death. Finally, the environmental impact of the miners who clear-cut forests or the sheep that transformed arable land into desert was only just gathering force; and was localized at that.[1]

Yet the Spanish also brought mass dying, alien overlords, revolutionary technology, and a wholly new cosmology. To emphasize continuity in indigenous lives seems counterintuitive. But indigenous people across Mexico did continue to live, in most cases, in the same places and with the same daily rhythms as before; to survive on the corn they themselves grew; to speak their own languages, perhaps using no more everyday Spanish words than we do; to trade the same things, in the same markets, run by the same old bureaucrats; to pay tribute to their own lords, the caciques, as they had always done; to watch, at times, the same foreign foot soldiers as previous generations had watched march through their towns and villages. The majority of newcomers were old and comprehensible rivals, such as the diverse Maya communities of the South, some enemies for centuries, or the far-ranging troops of the Nahua, the ethnicity that encompassed all the people of the central highlands, whether Mexica, Tlaxcalteca, or anyone else. As for the minority of newcomers who spearheaded the invasion, the conquistadors, they generally kept going, and a century after first contact, over half the entire Spanish population remained clustered in ten cities.[2] The names they gave those cities' barrios were revealing in their nostalgia: Triana, one of Seville's main neighborhoods, a bustling place of sailors, Roma, and flamenco singers, was transplanted from the banks of the Río Guadalquivir to the dusty way station of Aguascalientes. New Spain was very new, and not very Spanish.

So indigenous continuity was in part a straightforward matter of Spanish numbers. In Yucatán in 1550 the new town of Valladolid (not to be confused with an equally new Valladolid in Michoacán, or another one in Peru, and certainly not with the Spanish city frequented by the king) was home to 45 Spaniards; the new Salamanca, 15 or 20.[3] Even Zacatecas, the mining town at the center of the silver boom, housed only 160 Spaniards.[4] Eighty years later there were a mere 250 Spaniards in the new capital of New Mexico, Santa Fe.[5] The cost-benefit ratio was clearly against settlement in much of the country. Sixty years of warfare (1541 to c. 1600) against seminomadic peoples and the high costs of exploration left Spaniards chary above all of the desert North, which for more than a century was thought of as an ocean, the wagon trains that crossed it actually called flotillas.[6] The farther one got from the central highlands, the lower were the foreign populations and the greater the continuities. Yet even in the Nahua homelands the Spanish presence stayed low and overwhelmingly concentrated in Mexico City, home to half the encomenderos in New Spain and, by 1574, a third of the entire population of the colony.[7]

Spaniards were outnumbered not just by indigenous peoples but also in some places by Africans, and not just in the more predictable places such as the plantations of the tropical coasts. The largest foreign group in the sheep-rearing country of the Valle del Mezquital just north of Mexico City was made up of Africans from Senegambia, Guinea, and the mouth of the Congo River, brought across the Atlantic in the first forced migration of the modern slave trade. In the cities the numerous

Black domestic servants were status symbols, markers of the wealth, exoticism, and possibly sophistication of the new ruling classes; in Mexico City there was roughly one Black for every two Spaniards.[8] And in some places, such as the independent province of Tlaxcala and the utopian religious communities of Michoacán, Spanish settlers were from the start quite effectively excluded by Spanish authorities. In 1563 the exclusion, on paper at least, became universal when Philip II issued a decree that banned any and all Spaniards or even mestizos, the children of mixed Indian-Spanish unions, from living in indigenous villages.[9] For the first generation after the Spanish invasion, despite all the political revolutions, wars, epidemics, and priestly instructions for fundamental change, not much actually did change in how the Nahua thought about, survived, and organized their lives.[10]

Religion was one area of life where the foreigners offered the prospect of immediate and fundamental change, however. Cortés had brought two holy men with him, the friar Bartolomé de Olmedo and the priest Juan Díaz; in keeping with the pattern to come, the missionary did almost all the work. Between 1519 and the early 1570s the Church in Mexico remained largely in the hands of the first monastic orders. Friars were technically designated "regular clergy," which was wholly apt; the so-called secular clergy of parish priests wasn't much use. (The first viceroy told his successor that "they are disasters, in it for what they can get, and were it not for His Majesty's orders and [the need] for baptism, the Indians would be better off without them.")[11] The first mission was of twelve friars from the Franciscan Order, who made a carefully choreographed landing at Veracruz in May 1524 and then proceeded in a slow climb to Mexico City. The great and universal change that these foreigners brought was, amid the ubiquity of epidemic death, the potential for joy or horror in the afterlife. It was this absolute guarantee of the eternal, and its extremist sticks-and-carrots nature, that lay at the center of Christianity's cultural revolution.

Ideas of what came after death for the people of pre-Hispanic Mexico varied significantly but lacked much promise or punishment. A handful of the Mexica dead, either men who died in battle or women who died giving birth, became hummingbirds and ascended to join the sun. Most people ended up in Mictlan, the underworld kingdom of the dead, a gloomy place that lacked charm but also torment, and which was also temporary. Maya beliefs were essentially the same (although at least one of their death gods had a clear sense of humor that came through in paintings and sculpture).[12] Like the Mexica, they believed that in the end the dead just disappeared; the Maya great beyond was actually called Xibalbá, the "place of those who have vanished."[13] A Catholic eternal afterlife, graded by virtue, an existence of either great pleasure or nightmarish pain, consequently had the power to revolutionize life. The first period of Catholic life in Mexico, 1524 to 1572, defined by the first and last arrivals of the various missionary orders, was all about that power.

Christianity's new belief system of death as the regulator for life was at the outset largely lost in translation, the friars who hawked it seen as a handful of voluble, barely comprehensible eccentrics who provoked pity rather than awe. Tlaxcala, as the great ally of the Spanish, drew most of the attention of the churchmen; ten out of the first twelve Franciscans set up shop there. The Tlaxcalan historian Diego Muñoz Camargo described what they did next:

> As they did not know the language, they only said that in hell (gesturing with the hand to show that it lay under the ground) there was fire and toads and snakes. That said, they then raised their eyes to heaven, saying that a single God was up in the sky, and likewise pointing with their hand. They used to say this in the markets, and anywhere there was a meeting or gathering of the people . . . and when they were preaching such things the lords and *caciques* used to say "What's up with these miserable wretches? See if they are hungry, and if they need anything give them some food." And others said "These men must be ill or mad."[14]

This early evangelization had something of the quality of Speakers' Corner, a small patch of London's Hyde Park where traditionally anything could be said without legal consequence. It met a tolerance that some friars tested to its limits; Fray Jacobo de Testera illustrated the sufferings of hell by setting fires into which he threw live cats and dogs.[15] For the Nahua, accustomed to human sacrifice as the price of continued human survival, this must have seemed a provocative blasphemy.

That the Europeans—by no means all were Spanish—were insane was a common indigenous conclusion at first contact. Another Franciscan, Alonso de Benavides, was told in a pueblo in New Mexico, "You Spaniards and Christians are lunatics. You act like crazy people, and you want to teach us to be crazy too."[16] A more considered rejection occurred in the first formal encounter of the twelve friars with the Mexicas' religious leaders, whose theological debate was recorded in the *Libro de los Coloquios*. The indigenous priests, having laid out the risks of their defiance—"perhaps we are just going to our perdition, to our destruction"—then laid out their understanding of the fundament of Christianity, a single deity who came to Earth in human form. They then refused to accept it, at least as a sole truth, in unambiguous terms:

> Consider calmly and peacefully, our lords, what is necessary. We cannot be calm and we definitely do not believe what you are saying, we do not take it as true, even should you take offence . . . do with us what you will.[17]

The European insistence on an exclusive monotheism, a single path to Rome, was wholly alien to inclusive polytheists. One relativist Texcocan observed that the different monastic orders had different ways of dressing, praying, and teaching, and wondered why, since each of these ways was apparently good, the different way of indigenous religion should be any less tolerated. "Each person," he said, "should live in the law they wish."[18]

Yet the first generation of friars were driven men. They believed the mass conversion of the indigenous peoples to be a moral imperative, and one that needed acting upon to save an entire continent's souls in light of both current epidemics and a looming apocalypse. Further north, the later settlers of New England were largely indifferent to the spiritual health of the natives, the Puritans seeing them as more God's concern than theirs; if He wanted them to be citizens in their "city upon a hill" then he would doubtless make the necessary arrangements.[19] In Mexico, by contrast, the Franciscans saw themselves as the only

A Franciscan in the early years preaches to the many. "To the senses the heavenly gifts are adapted." Diego Valadés, *Rhetórica christiana* (1579).

barriers between hundreds of thousands of innocents and the fires of hell. And so they began an extraordinary decade or so of urgent proselytization, individual men walking across much of Mexico south of the drylands to perform the sacraments, and above all baptism, on an industrial scale.

The numbers were remarkable. In central Mexico Motolinía estimated that he had at times baptized two or three thousand a day; his superior, Martín de Valencia, claimed that the average friar converted about a hundred thousand in his first seven years. One friar in Yucatán allegedly processed five thousand Maya in a single day. By 1536 Motolinía believed that some four million indigenous people had been baptized. Even as the number of friars grew, the same superficiality born of exigency endured. It was, one sacrilegious rancher opined, about as meaningful as baptizing mules.[20] Confession, the individual sacrament key to avoiding at the very least purgatory, was generally communal and so meaningless. Indians attained absolution by merely turning up at mass and getting ticked off a roll call.[21] As for the final sacrament, extreme unction, it was an insurance policy out of reach for all but a very select few of the moribund. The friars felt, however, that they had won; in 1570 their own history concluded that "nowhere else in the world has the Devil been defeated and overthrown so quickly and comprehensively as in New Spain."[22]

Some indigenous people may have opted for the new religion following the cold logic of Pascal's wager: The consequences of belief, if God did not exist, were a lot less woeful than the consequences of disbelief if he did. They also appreciated the empirical heft of victory. The Spanish had hammered home the religious side of the invasion in Cortés's flag, emblazoned with a cross and the Latin motto FRIENDS, LET US FOLLOW THE CROSS AND, IF WE HAVE FAITH, LET US CONQUER UNDER THIS BANNER. Saint James, invoked by their war cry "Santiago, Santiago!," was clearly more effective than his Mexica equivalent, the warrior god Huitzilopochtli. And there was eloquence in Spanish behavior once battles were won, destroying some indigenous temples, putting up crosses on the summits of others, preaching to the uncomprehending townsfolk, saying daily masses.[23] In Mesoamerican warfare, sweeping military success was a compelling theological argument all by itself. The Maya glyph for a captured city was a temple in flames; the Mexica would haul off the patron saint of their victims' cities to imprisonment in the "god captive house" in Tenochtitlán.[24] As the friars asked the Mexica caciques at one of their first meetings, "If your gods were the true gods, if they were really the Giver of Life, why have they despised your people? Why have they mocked them? Why have they no compassion for those who are their creation?"[25] (They seem to have glossed over, at this stage, the theological safety valve of a perfect God ruling an imperfect world, or the roundabout rewards of martyrdom, with all the room for random pain that those lines of argument opened up.) The Christian God was a compassionate one, for believers at least.

For unbelievers, though, only an angry Old Testament God and his hell existed, and as time passed the friars became more convincing in their depictions. The second Spanish play written in Mexico, the 1531 work of the talented linguist Fray Andrés de Olmos, was entitled *The Final Judgement*; its message, conveyed in Nahuatl by eight hundred indigenous actors, was self-explanatory. The amateur directors staged the inferno with shocking realism in another play, in the course of which impious drunkards and women who practice abortion interrupt Saint Francis, who is quite naturally preaching to the birds, and as a consequence are dragged to hell by obedient demons. The stage-set fires were graphically real: As Motolinía described it,

> Hell had a secret door by which all those who were within could emerge, and as soon as they had come out it was set on fire, and it burned so fiercely that it seemed no one had escaped, and that everyone, demons and the damned, was burning; and all the souls and devils groaned and screamed, which filled with horror and fright even those who knew that no one was [really] burning.[26]

Other productions carried more positive messages, promoting the inevitability and righteousness of Christian victory across the globe, a victory in which the indigenous were participants. (The Maya were, one friar wrote, "actors who perform with great skill," who learned fast to mimic Europeans.)[27] To celebrate Corpus Christi in 1539, for example, fifteen hundred Indian extras were marshalled to reenact the retaking of Jerusalem from the Moors, complete with fake blood encased in cannon balls and a flying Archangel Michael dangling from a rope. In the dramatic lead came the Spanish army; in its wake a Mexican army, in which Tlaxcalan and Mexica soldiers headed a column representing all the main ethnic groups of the Indies. An audience led by impersonators of the Pope and his cardinals looked on as, in a triumphal ending, many of the defeated extras were baptized.[28]

This was not the only big production of 1539: It was preceded at Easter by *The Fall of Our First Fathers*, whose lavish production (including scores of the parrots so valued by the Indians) and tragic climax reduced the audience to tears.[29] Such plays, watched by thousands, were part of the friars' broader intellectual assault on the old religion, using all means possible to instruct and entertain their would-be flocks and smooth their passage out of paganism. The missionaries invested huge efforts in language learning, producing well over one hundred books to enable their evangelization in the first fifty years. Some were grammars and vocabularies, others translations of Holy Scripture, the catechisms, sacraments, lives of the saints, and cut-and-paste sermons that allowed newcomers to get to work without delay. The first generations of missions covered most of the major language groups: Nahuatl, Otomí, Purépecha, Huaxtec, Matlatzinca, Totonac, Chichimeca, Tlapanec, Ocuiltec, Chontal, Zoque, and Zapotec. They were tackled by some formidable linguists—Fray Francisco de Toral preached in two languages every Sunday, Fray Olmos reputedly spoke as many as ten—with local knowledge and painstaking ambition. Fray Benito Fernández, for example, produced two different editions of the *Doctrina Mixteca* within two months in order to accommodate that language's two very different dialects.[30] Such complications could be bypassed, it was suggested, by promoting Nahua as a lingua franca for all Mexico; such a strategy would be just a continuation of the cultural imperialism of the previous overlords, the Mexica, who had done much the same.

Twinned with the proselytization came wide-ranging (at least in theory) censorship. A royal decree of 1531 banned the trashy romances beloved of the conquistadors and the rest of Spain, potboilers such as *Amadís of Gaul*, "so that the Indians who may know how to write should not take them up, thus abandoning books of good and healthy doctrine." Once the Inquisition arrived it was easier for the authorities to exclude such stuff; their representatives, theological customs officers, would be the first to board arriving ships.[31] In 1605 they confiscated the first two copies of *Don Quijote* to arrive in Mexico (despite its satirizing of *Amadís of Gaul* et alia as "cursed books . . . which might well deserve to be burnt, just as much as if they were heretics").[32] *Quijote* nevertheless quickly topped the list of books sold in New Spain, because the books inquisitors really minded were the deliberate heresies of Erasmus, the Protestant Bible, and assorted works of magic.[33] Even works of good and healthy doctrine had their dangers, however, and their stories were doctored for the spiritual health of the indigenous. The prohibition of polygamy, the main target of the ecclesiastics, would have been weakened by the story of Abraham, whose wife instructs him to sleep with their servant Hagar so that they can have a child. The relevant passage from Genesis was cut.[34] Not that there were many bibles in New Spain to cut; the Church kept records of all the books that were exported, and between 1583 and 1584 these only register three copies of the Good Book crossing the Atlantic.[35]

The persuasive language of music offset the uncertainty of words. Indigenous converts sang in choirs and in time backed those choirs with their own orchestras of flutes, bugles, trumpets, oboes, clarinets, trombones, stringed instruments, and kettledrums, all of which they themselves made. In Michoacán the Franciscans taught the mystery of organ-making. (The instrument once finished was mysterious, too, as its compound name, *ehuatlapitzalhuehuetl*, "hide-wind-instrument-drum," showed.)[36] The people of the future Mexico had great appreciation for music before the conquest; the Spanish brought a technological revolution with their much greater range of instruments. Choirs were indigenous spiritual organizations as much as, perhaps more than, they were Spanish institutions. After a relatively short time, Nahua cantors, changed each year, were running their own choirs, performing the same repertoires as their counterparts in Europe and attaining the same level of skill—faster, said Spanish minstrels, than their own people, "picking up in two months what Spaniards could not in two years." Writing their own music was a natural next step. Singing and playing were more accessible than reading and writing and drew huge audiences: Fray Bartolomé de las Casas claimed to have entertained some eighty thousand spectators for his 1538 musical. For many, the musical presentations were also more convincing. As Bishop Zumárraga told the emperor Charles V, the Indians were "converted more by music than by preaching, and we see them coming from far off to hear it and they work to hear it and they work to learn it."[37]

Finally, as the bishop also reported, proselytization was backed by the violence of Kulturkampf, a continuous, no-holds-barred war on the indigenous religion that structured so much of daily life and thought in the old theocracies. As early as 1531, a mere three years into his ministry, Zumárraga claimed to have destroyed five hundred temples and some twenty thousand idols.[38] In 1562 Diego de Landa, another Franciscan, conducted a three-day auto da fé, the Christian ceremony of purification by fire, in the town of Maní in Yucatán. Like other urban societies of pre-Hispanic Mexico, the Maya remembered their culture, science, and history through codices, painted manuscripts made from the bark of the wild fig tree. These were complex books, painted in exacting detail by teams of scribes, showing astronomical calculations—at which the Maya were particularly accomplished—religious ceremonies, histories, and everyday activities like hunting and beekeeping. Some dated back several centuries. By the time Landa had finished, only three pre-Hispanic Maya codices remained in existence, their titles unknown, renamed for the European cities where they ended up: Paris, Dresden, and Madrid. All other apparent survivors have been proven fakes. The written world of an entire culture quite literally went up in smoke. The Maya, Landa observed, "regretted [it] to an amazing degree."[39]

The statistics of destruction were revolutionary, and so were the statistics of formal conversion. The numbers of friars, however, were paltry. The vanguards of the monastic orders arrived quickly: the Franciscans in 1524, Dominicans in 1526, Augustinians in 1533, and finally Jesuits in 1572. But the main hosts followed slowly. The first twelve Franciscans, the "Twelve Apostles" (and their imitators the first twelve Dominicans, and then the first twelve Augustinians) were quite self-consciously an American primitive Church, seeing in themselves the handful of Saint Peter's companions who founded the very first Church. A generation after first contact there were only some eight hundred missionaries to cover the entire territory. Moreover, they were overwhelmingly concentrated in the central highlands; not a single friar moved to Yucatán until 1545.[40] Casualty rates among lonely evangelizers in the strange country were appreciable. Two of the first three postconquest arrivals, the Flemish friars Johann van den Auwera and Johann Dekkers (in Spanish Fray Juan de Aora and Fray Juan de Tecto), sickened and died almost immediately during Cortés's disastrous march to Hibueras. Friars in central Mexico were generally safe from violent death, but like everyone else at the time they were taken in numbers by disease: Five of the first twelve Dominicans were dead within a year. "As I have told you before," the archbishop nagged Philip II, the Jesuits needed His Majesty to send more of their company to Mexico, because although five had come out with the 1577 fleet, four had already died.[41]

For those on expeditions or in missions in the northwest plains and Sierra Madre Occidental, it was a bloodier story, for Indians killed assorted religious pioneers there. But it was above all in the Center-North where friars met sticky and theatrical ends at the hands of the indigenous Mixton rebels of the early 1540s, whose war was strongly religious, their targets the friars' persons, properties, and symbols, their success promised by their own god Tecoroli. And not just the first wave of friars courted danger to its end. Even after a ragged sort of peace had come to the North, missionaries continued to die violently throughout much of the seventeenth century. All the missionaries on the 1581 expedition to New Mexico were killed; in Chihuahua the Tepehuan who rebelled in 1617 and 1618—inspired by the devil, according to a Franciscan chronicler—killed eight Jesuits; in 1631 the medicine men of Taos finally got rid of Fray Pedro de Miranda, whom they had been poisoning with urine and mouse meat in his tortillas; in 1632 the Zuni decapitated and scalped Friars Francisco de Letrado and Martín de Arvide; in 1695 the O'odham riddled the Jesuit Fray Francisco Saeta with arrows. It is unsurprising that convents and monasteries often resembled medieval castles. It is also unsurprising that deaths like those, married to the obstacles of transport, kept ecclesiastics thin on the ground.[42] As Philip II waspishly observed in 1561,

> We have been informed that monasteries are built very close together, because the religious prefer to establish themselves in the green lands near the city of Mexico, leaving stretches of twenty to thirty leagues untended, because the religious avoid the rough, poor, and hot regions.[43]

In this light, the numbers of indigenous converts who passed through a revolutionary spiritual transformation cannot have been anything like the reported numbers. The religious accounts of the first century were triumphalist, but they were always going to be. Motolinía's partisan account might stand in for many:

> For five years the Mexicans were very cold, due to either the demands of the Spanish and the construction of Mexico City, or because the elders among the Mexicans weren't all that warm towards us. After

> five years many of them awakened and built churches, and now they come to mass a lot every day and take the sacraments with devotion.[44]

Later indigenous historians had their own partisan motives, namely the strategic advantage in a Christian theocracy of being perceived as early adopters.[45] The friars had the best chance of molding the minds of the children of the elite whom they schooled, and they schooled anyone worth knowing, starting with the royals and caciques. In 1536 the Franciscans founded the College of Santa Cruz de Tlatelolco in Mexico City, where they instructed eighty adolescents from the main families of New Spain, the idea being that their acquired skills in Latin, Spanish, and theology would make them the cadre of the religious revolution.[46] They and their provincial peers were not just at intellectually malleable ages. For some, religious fervor was a route to power; others must have seen Christianity as an outlet for teenage rebellion against their parents. They were helped along by their radical teachers, the Franciscans, who urged them to burrow into the idolatry of their elders and even egged them on to violence. Enough of the young took their chance. Tlaxcalan students of the first postconquest cohort enthusiastically destroyed shrines and temples, and beat a pagan priest to death; later equivalents in New Mexico sacked whole villages of unbelievers.[47] It was a time of generational conflict and Maoist-style denunciation, even within families.

As in all history it is difficult to get inside the heads of the long dead. What the indigenous converts of the first decades thought of Christianity we can discern only through educated guesswork, founded on what religious education we know they could access and what can be glimpsed in snapshots of their subsequent knowledge and practice. The only two meaningful sacraments in the early years were marriage and baptism. Baptism was either a passive experience for the young or, for those who desired it, a yes-man's exercise for the old. Marriage was consequently the main focus of the churchmen, its prohibition of polygamy a social revolution, its ceremony a major test of at least some knowledge of Christian teachings. The locals fought back against monogamy. Why, some asked, should the men of their nobility forego multiple wives while the Spanish men did not? It was a fair point, and

Spanish bigamy became an obsession of authorities from Cortés to the Inquisition, but it did not prevent the exercise of great pressure on the indigenous. God despised lust, Fray Andrés de Olmos told his flock, punishing individuals with scorpions, disease, and deformation, and whole societies with annihilation; it was the main cause of the Flood, and later on some twenty-three thousand Moabites were wiped out for promiscuity.[48] The final judgement of that first Nahuatl play, *The Final Judgement*, went against a woman who had scorned marriage.[49]

On paper the results were notable, but once again dubious. Caciques were baptized promising monogamy and then kept their concubines anyway. Failed marriages continued for a long time to have happy endings in consensual divorce, enshrined in the serial monogamy of indigenous societies but strictly prohibited by Catholic doctrine. Everyday people got married in church and then went through the ceremony all over again, this time with the old rites and incantations and indigenous officiants.[50] A flood of marriages followed the first Mexica royal wedding of 1526, but the only religious requirement was for bride and groom to recite the Paternoster and the Nicene Creed, in Latin a combined total of 114 words. In a culture that relied heavily on memorization this was not much of a challenge.[51] Even for enthusiasts, phonetic translation of Latin words into indigenous pictograms didn't communicate much theological refinement. The Nahuatl words closest to *pater* and *noster* are *pantli* and *nochtli*, which mean "banner" and "cactus fruit" respectively, and so converts invoked Our Father via mental images of a flag and a prickly pear.[52]

Even the Virgin Mary, the most graspable of the new gods, was linguistically tricky; the closest Nahautl could get was the spinsterish "forever an unmarried daughter."[53] Nevertheless at the century's end, a cowboy hauled up before the Inquisition (on the grounds of demonic possession) could make the case for his Christian orthodoxy by crossing himself and reciting the Lord's Prayer and a Hail Mary, two very short prayers. Beyond that, his Nicene Creed had errors, and he didn't know the Ten Commandments, but he passed anyway. (Not that it did him much good; he was convicted of fraternizing with one of Lucifer's pages, flogged, and sent to the galleys.)[54] In the first half of the seventeenth century a rural priest found his flock steeped in everyday preconquest ritual, asking the old gods for success in everything from chopping wood to healing the sick. The coexistence of elements of Christianity and the old ways was the norm; in the first generation a majority of the baptized were à la carte Christians.

The farther from the center one went the more à la carte things got. In the South the early seventeenth-century Maya text *Chilam Balam* recounted the Maya creation story after a cursory Christian preface, continued with a death of Christ that was "resolutely Maya," and ended with a final reckoning in which Jesus rules over a purified world, the Spanish gone, the Maya nobility his disciples. Meanwhile in the North people in the Pueblo villages and California were burying idols beneath the altars of the new missions.[55] Some missionaries in a very distant past had winked at such transitional confusions: Nearly a millennium earlier Pope Gregory the Great had told his vanguard in England, "It is certainly impossible to eradicate all errors from obstinate minds at one stroke, and whoever wishes to climb to a mountain top climbs gradually step by step, and not in one leap." The first Anglo-Saxon converts, the pope said, should be allowed to keep their temples, dances, and feasting; the missionaries should just work to change which gods were to be propitiated.[56] The first missionaries in Mexico were not so patient but ended up in many places with similar results. Some of their worldlier successors, such as the Jesuits, positively encouraged mixed Nahua-Christian ceremonies.[57] The bar for even the formalities of religious belief remained low for some time, and with it doctrinal purity. Thus a certain syncretism endured, albeit with decaying power, for centuries.[58]

Such popular cosmopolitanism was helped along by surprising compatibilities of theology and practice. In the first place, the Franciscans were firm believers in the prophecies of the twelfth-century mystic Joachim of Fiore. He had preached that the world had three ages, and that at the end of the third the prophecies of the Book of Revelation would be made good: The Antichrist would appear and be defeated, and God would punish the wicked with morbidly inventive zeal and then bring the remainder of humanity into a new Heaven and a new Earth, a New Jerusalem. The guides to this time and place were, Joachim specified, to be missionaries, not priests. The story of the Apocalypse came wrapped in a baffling mysticism of symbols and catastrophes, and like any prophecy worth its salt, could be read in a host of different ways. But the Franciscans could clearly identify several of its main threads in Mexico, and believed that they were in that third stage, with the End of Times imminent.

The logic was sound. An Antichrist for revolutionary times had already appeared in Europe in the form of Martin Luther, but Satan more traditionally appeared as a snake, and across Mexico the slippery reptile was ubiquitous in statues of Quetzalcóatl, the feathered serpent. The New World was, of course, the fourth part of the Earth; the French pamphlet that invented the name America, the *Cosmographiae introductio*, explicitly said so in 1507.[59] And in one of the most famous passages of Revelation, Saint John is said to have

> looked, and beheld a pale horse: and his name that sat on him was Death, and Hell followed with him. And power was given unto them over the fourth part of the earth, to kill with sword, and with hunger, and with death, and with the beasts of the earth.[60]

A similar eschatology ran deep in Mesoamerican religion. The Mexica believed in Five Suns—five epochs, each of which ended in a different apocalyptic manner with the disappearance of the sun. Their current Fifth Sun was predestined to be the last and to end in earthquakes. So was the world of Revelation, with "a great earthquake" to strike after the Lamb of God opened the sixth seal followed by another at the hands of the seventh angel. The Mexica also believed in a sort of secondary Apocalypse, the possibility of the world descending into darkness at the end of each fifty-two-year cycle should the complex Fire Ceremony fail.[61] In Revelation the fifth angel makes the kingdom of the beast "full of darkness."[62] The coincidences were—for an open mind, emerging from medieval times—extraordinary.

Moreover, the missionaries talked of monotheism, a single God, but they then went on to explain how he was really one God in three: God the Father, God the Son, and God the Holy Spirit. Moreover, he enjoyed a substantial backing cast of saints with quite specific characteristics and duties. These could draw on their supernatural power to grant favors or condemn. This was, natives could only conclude, a somewhat confused but nonetheless functional polytheism, and as such wholly compatible with their own theologies. Multiple personality disorder was a characteristic of pre-Hispanic gods like Tetzcatlipoca, the Lord of the Smoking Mirror, who could bring either apocalyptic destruction or great favor on a whim. In times of drought the Mexica prayed to Tlaloc, the rain god, the Maya to Chaac; faced with the same catastrophe, priests paraded the images of each community's specific patron saint. The first churchmen matched saints with places in the early stages of evangelization, giving them pride of place in church altars, paintings, and names. At the very center, the indigenous zone of Mexico City was consecrated to Saint John, becoming San Juan Tenochtitlán, and within it the barrio of Tlatelolco to Saint James. In Tlaxcala the term in Nahuatl for a subject village became *santopan*, "the place where a saint lives." The first generation of saints were in general stern and somewhat distant figures, prone to standing in as God's deputies to put away sinners. They were often quite prickly: In Yucatán the faithful needed to wash the Virgin Mary's linens regularly if they wanted to avoid her ill humor.[63] But by the beginning of the seventeenth century they were also intimate allies, more approachable and straightforward supernatural managers of earthly success, and households in central Mexico generally had collections of several saints' images.[64]

The greatest intercessor of them all, the Virgin of Guadalupe, became popular at the turn of the seventeenth century, though she is held to have first manifested herself in 1531. The legend is poignant. Mary Mother of God appears three times to a humble, pious Nahua on a hill near Mexico City; rushing to Bishop Zumárraga, he is told not to make things up. When he returns to the hill, Mary appears to him again, throwing flowers into his cloak, the roughly woven *tilma*. She then magically paints an artistically superb self-portrait, one that mirrors the Mary of the Book of Revelation 12:1 into the bargain, depicting as it does "a woman clothed with the sun, and the moon under her feet, and upon her head a crown of twelve stars." The miracle convinces, and the brown Virgin becomes the first stop in everyman's pleading for divine intervention, good for anything and everything. She may really be a later creation of Spanish priests and creole nationalists, the cloak painted by the great indigenous artist Marcos Cipac de Aquino, the cult only pushed from the 1590s onward. She certainly only became a figure across Mexico after the publication of the Spanish priest Luis Lasso de la Vega's Nahuatl account of the miracle in 1649. A predecessor in Tlaxcala, the story a faithful parallel down even to the name of the Indian witness, had failed. But the Virgin of Guadalupe was powerful earlier on around Mexico City, quite possibly as a potent survivor of the old religion, the mother goddess Tonantzin adopting a new—but popularly grasped—form of indigenous sainthood.[65]

There were also marked parallels in devotional violence among Europeans and Nahua: self-mortification, death cults, and blood sacrifice. Cortés with typical pragmatism grasped the tactical possibilities of confusion from the start, whitewashing the blood-spattered walls of the first temple he came across, installing an altar and cross, giving the indigenous priests haircuts and reappointing them keepers of the retooled shrine. Self-mortification was a central practice among the elites of the Mexica theocracies, whose members used tools such as cactus thorns or stingray spines to donate blood to the gods.[66] The indigenous priests Cortés recruited didn't just have long hair ("so clotted and matted with blood that it could not be pulled apart") but also "their ears . . . cut to pieces as a sacrifice."[67] Christian holy men were prone to similar self-inflicted pains, following in the footsteps of Christ. Franciscan novices were instructed that the flesh "had to be tamed, punished . . . and repressed with devout and continuous prayer, with flagellations." Saint Francis had told his followers that they should positively long for a martyr's death; he himself got one, expiring after an illness that started when he received stigmata, mystic reincarnations of Christ's wounds on the Cross.[68]

Christians' ghoulish ideas of interior design also mirrored those of pre-Hispanic priests. Like their indigenous counterparts, friars surrounded themselves with the images and relics of the dead. Fray Diego de Magdalena notoriously carried around not just a skull but an entire taxidermized Indian while on mission among the Chichimeca.[69] Facing a real shortage of the relics still central to Catholicism, the Jesuits sent an ambassador to the graveyards of northern Spain to dig up some they could import. The few body parts that the Mexicans secured over the centuries were third-class—two heads of the Eleven Thousand Virgins, the cadaver of a nameless monk from Burgos—but were received with a reverence that their indigenous predecessors might have grasped reflexively. The chronicler Antonio de Robles had this to say about one of the outstanding days of 1672:

> Sunday 7 [August] - in the church of the Santísima Trinidad, the congregation of San Pedro celebrated a festival with a procession and mass that was sung by the Abbot Don Bartolomé de Quevedo, canon, in which the Licenciado Juan de Gárate delivered a sermon, to mark the enshrining of the distinguished relic that arrived in the last fleet, one of the two hundred martyrs of the Order of Saint Benedict.[70]

Blood sacrifice was also at the center of the belief and practice of the Catholic church, at least in indigenous eyes. The key symbol of Christianity was an instrument of torture, and Christ had enjoined his followers to eat his own body at Communion: This is my body, this is my blood. It was perhaps unsurprising that the First Provincial Council of Mexico in 1555 should ban Indians from possessing communion wafers, "because scandals and very suspicious things have followed from this."[71]

The problem, from the Spanish viewpoint, was a double ignorance. The indigenous people remained worryingly ignorant of much of the new faith; the Spanish friars were ignorant of much of the old. As Fray Bernardino de Sahagún put it, several decades after conversion began,

> The sins of idolatry and idolatrous rites and idolatrous superstitions and omens and abuses and idolatrous ceremonies are even now not wholly forgotten. To preach against these things, and even to know if they are there, it is necessary to know how they used them in the time of their idolatry. And through not knowing this they do many idolatrous things in our presence without us realizing.[72]

Sahagún ironically did more than any other Spaniard to preserve Nahua memories of their idolatrous past. He came to New Spain in 1529, a thirty-year-old Franciscan iconoclast from the University of Salamanca, convinced, as he wrote, that "you have to break and shatter into pieces their figurines, and you have to topple and break up all the demon's possessions and temples, and you have to burn all of their houses and estates and all of their sacrifices." He went as far as climbing the two great volcanoes on the rim of the Valley of Mexico, Popocatépetl and Ixtaccíhuatl, to search for hidden idols (and possibly for the metaphorical hell of it). Yet systematic extirpation of the old religion would be undoable, he wrote, without an understanding of its proponents' "spiritual sicknesses," and so he learned Nahuatl and together with twenty-two Nahua intellectuals and scribes, fluent in Latin and Spanish, pieced together the great ethnohistory of the Mexica, the *Historia general de las cosas de Nueva España*.[73]

It was a trilingual *magnum opus*: on the left side of each page Spanish text, on the right Nahuatl, and painted throughout the stunningly colored pictograms of pre-Hispanic codices; a symbol in form alone—in a further irony—of an emerging hybrid culture. The illustrations drew on the European uses of perspective in contemporary woodcuts, found in the better class of Bible, mixed with the visual language of indigenous glyphs for places, names, and speech. Time runs linear in the Spanish text describing the Conquest, but spirals in the paintings to place events inside the mythical circular cosmology of the Mexica. The ink is local; the paper, European. In a final irony, the *Historia general* became known as *The Florentine Codex* because in 1576 the Viceroy withdrew his support for the project, the Inquisition banned the book, and the only copy in existence was smuggled out to Italy by the Franciscan Rodrigo de Sequera. (Who left in such haste that the final volume's drawings cease to be colored and then run out completely.) Sequera presented the codex to Cardinal Medici, who retired to Florence and buried this sole survivor of decades of work in his great library. After Medici's death it lay there uncatalogued, unknown, until the end of the eighteenth century.[74]

In the absence of the sort of ethnohistorical detail that Sahagún sought, local authorities made it up as they went along. In the church built at Cuauhtinchán in the 1530s, they either missed the point or else tactfully overlooked ritual paintings of flowers, a jaguar, and an eagle.[75] In Tlaxcala, by contrast, the city government banned churchgoers from dancing around the cross with feathers; having feathers adorning the church at all, by 1550, was suspicious enough.[76] But churches were run by generally permanent indigenous staff, while the Spanish priests moved from place to place, and so such variants were perhaps unsurprising; the locals were, after all, quite often running the show. More substantially, indigenous builders put up churches and monasteries across Mexico on the sites and with the materials of the old religions. Sometimes the Spanish did this deliberately, first reconsecrating and later razing pyramids to raise up monasteries in their place. (At the beginning this was a local initiative, later confirmed and made total by order of the emperor.) They recycled even the stones with images. The symbolism of Mexico's first crude cathedral resting on the bas-reliefs of an Aztec temple was unmissable. In the greatest example of all, the Spanish built the basilica of the Virgin of Guadalupe on the hill of Tepeyac, a longstanding sanctuary for Mary's indigenous equivalent.[77]

At other times the recycling was certainly not a strategic choice. That Indians hid idols in or behind altars was a cliché with substance in fact. On a grander scale, the entire Franciscan monastery in Cholula was oriented to align with the rising sun on the spring equinox, an orientation common among the sun-worshipping ancients.[78] It was a massive demonstration of the most important characteristic of coexistence between Spaniards and Nahua, namely the indigenous ability to adopt European exteriors when unavoidable while preserving the main points of their own culture across multiple generations. That general principle stretched from feathers to bricks.

The Church tried to clamp down on those they believed were the more entrepreneurial or duplicitous of the native converts. The outraged Fray Diego de Valadés, defending his confrères' successes, argued that while it was natural that one or two might have slipped, the meeting of exceptional European clergy with willing indigenous minds had led the natives out of oppressive paganism and into the comparative freedom of the "gentle and light yoke of God."[79] Valadés, the first mestizo Franciscan, had an axe to grind, and skimmed over the fact that a substantial part of the strategy of conversion was neither gentle nor light. At the same time as the friars criticized the violence of the conquistadors, they were not above using it themselves, albeit to a lesser degree, across the entire territory. In New Mexico some Indians were brought to God when friars grabbed their testicles and twisted hard, clearly feeling that when they had them by the balls their hearts and minds would follow.[80] In Texcoco Bishop Zumárraga had Don

Carlos Chichimecatecuhtli, a pretender to the throne, burned alive for heresy in 1539; he had been keeping hold of idolatrous images (though none was ever found) and of his niece as a lover.[81] In Cuauhtinchán the Franciscans tolerated the syncretic church interior after hanging two pagan priests and the town cacique, Don Tomás Huilacapitzin, for alleged human sacrifice.[82]

Most significant of all, in Yucatán Fray Diego de Landa committed the greatest single act of priestly violence that New Spain ever saw. Landa, like Sahagún, was a highflier. He came from an old family from near Toledo, took orders with the Franciscans when young, and came to Mexico when he was twenty-five as part of their first mission to Yucatán. In 1561 the Franciscans elected him Provincial, their leader for the region, at the comparatively tender age of thirty-seven. His rapid ascent was partly due to his skill as a linguist and his ethnographic understanding of the Maya, amongst whom he lived for long periods, sleeping in their houses, appreciating their recipes, cuddling their "marvelously pretty and plump" babies, talking with their elders, even reading their books.[83] His own book, the *Relación de las cosas de Yucatán*, grew out of those close relationships; like Sahagún's it went unpublished until the nineteenth century, and like Sahagún's it became fundamental to what is known of the pre-Hispanic past. Landa's literary success also owes much to his literal destruction of almost all the competition: While the iconoclast Sahagún grew more convinced as he aged of the urgency of preserving Mexica history and culture, Landa took the opposite approach, and in 1562 he deployed his learning against his Maya congregants and the entire collected records of their past.

It all came out of a small find of human skulls and idols in a cave near Maní, a town in the center of the peninsula. There were forty of the sort of humble, everyday gods made of terracotta, wood, or animal parts that brought rains or good harvests or successful hunts. The friar in charge of the monastery, Fray Pedro de Ciudad Rodrigo, ordered forty locals arrested; they owned up, saying in mitigation that all the nearby villages had shrines like theirs. Ciudad Rodrigo made more arrests and began torturing the Indians, hanging them up by their wrists, attaching large stones to their feet, whipping them, and splashing them with hot wax. The torture, known as the *garrucha*, the hoist, was a makeshift equivalent to the better-known rack and worked on the same principle of gradual dislocation of joints, punctuated by snapping ligaments and cartilage, and the eventual destruction beyond repair of muscle fiber in legs and arms. Landa endorsed the procedure and, as confessions began to flow, took the investigation much further. By the time it ended three months later, some 4,500 Maya had been tortured; 158 had died; others had committed suicide; many were left crippled.

Landa's Franciscans were driven by disappointment at their flock's duplicity, and probably by fear. Their reactions had precedent in the conquest of Granada, during which the Franciscan Archbishop Cisneros publicly burned all the Arabic Qurans that he could collect. The first Spanish guide to Arabic translated the sacrament of "confession"—in the religious section—as *iqrār*, violent interrogation.[84] Any conspiracy theory evokes paranoia, and the universal flawed logic of torture follows. Desperation to stop pain makes people say what they believe their torturers want them to say; those "confessions" lead to more pointed questions that bring details, confirmation, and further denunciation of others. By the end, Landa—and only Landa—was extracting stories of crucifixion and human sacrifice in a rush to wrap things up before he was stopped. How much of any of the stories of exotic throwbacks was true is hard to discern.[85] It is a clear demonstration, though, of the latent violence of conversion, a heart of darkness with people like Landa in the role of Mr. Kurtz.

And yet the number of Kurtzes was quite low, and a system of checks and balances usually kept them within bounds. The lay Spanish, often enemies of the friars, could complain to the Church, the colonial government, or both. So could other churchmen, and in high-profile cases the Church generally responded. In 1563 Landa was driven out of Yucatán and back to Spain to defend himself, like any conquistador, against legal charges of an indiscriminate use of torture. (In Spanish law torture could only be applied once, for a maximum duration of an hour, and any testimony obtained if these rules were broken was invalid.)[86] Bishop Zumárraga was demoted after burning Don Carlos of Texcoco. Both men were allowed to return, even if in Landa's case it took a decade, but both were chastened, and did not repeat their violence.

More debilitating overall were the less committed or talented churchmen, the Keystone Kops of the spiritual conquest. Some struggled with both Nahuatl and Latin. "Latin in the Indians," one critic noted, "serves that they might understand in the saying of mass and the holy offices which of the priests are idiots, and that they might laugh at them or accord them less respect than is correct."[87] Letters to the emperor were harsher. Some friars were straightforwardly illiterate, they said; many priests were just in it for the cash.[88] A century after their first arrival, Franciscans on their way to Mexico were being described by a fellow traveler (albeit a Protestant traitor) as a crew of drunken gamblers, blasphemers, and silken-sleeved cynics, for whom "the love of money, of vainglory, of power and authority over the poor Indians, is their end and aim more than any love of God."[89]

At the same time as the more obvious opportunists began arriving, the revolutionary fervor of the first generation of missionaries tailed off. The Beast of the Apocalypse hadn't shown up, the Homeric marches and mass baptisms were all done, the disillusion of indigenous recalcitrance had taken root. A manual of "Counsels for Confessors" from 1600 is telling in its defeatism:

> Some of the habits of these natives gravely dishearten and arouse great scruples in their ministers' souls, and some have even retired from the Apostolic Ministry . . . Ministers are disheartened to see that some natives come to the Sacrament of Confession seemingly without suffering or repentance for their sins . . . [but] being often people of limited understanding they cannot attain that quality which contrition demands.[90]

Landa's rampage in Yucatán was exceptional for the period, his journey from ethnographer to witch-hunter mirrored by the exceptional journey of Fray Bernardo de Sahagún in the opposite direction. Everywhere else Zumárraga's demotion for excessive zeal was a lesson and turning point. Prelates might talk darkly of lapsing Indians and their syncretic rituals, but in practice they abandoned the more ambitious dreams of orthodoxy. Some Spaniards, after all, were themselves spectacularly heterodox: One Michoacán rancher, excommunicated for nonpayment of tithes, told the church bailiff, "I shit on the excommunication and he who informs me of it." Another rancher and scatological blasphemer was fond of the line "I offer little balls of shit for the saints."[91] The

Santo Oficio, the bureaucratic agency of the Inquisition, only arrived in 1571, and when it did it was underwhelming. The Jesuits, with all their energy and political clout, arrived in 1572, but they too were less doctrinally demanding than might have been expected.

After the first shock of monastic power there was in reality little religious repression. Priests in Oaxaca accused the caciques of two villages of a formidable degree of pagan backsliding: In the face of the drought and dearth of the mid-1540s they had gone back to sacrificing children and slaves. There were plentiful witnesses. Reverend Pedro de Olmos claimed to have actually seen a shrine in the Mixteca highlands where locals had surrounded a blood-covered stone idol with sixteen heads and put a child's freshly extracted heart in its mouth. Yet two years of trials ended with nothing more than a series of fines.[92] Across the whole of the 1550s inquisitors prosecuted Indians only once, and that was for cohabitation—a concern, naturally, but hardly the greatest of sins. A century and a half later the Bishop of Oaxaca offered a collective amnesty for paganism and collected over one hundred sacred texts of pre-Hispanic beliefs from thirty-seven thousand repentant—or more probably scared and relieved—Zapotec in the aftermath of a regional rebellion.[93] In Yucatán the cities had to be Christian, and Mérida became known for its baroque piety, but the old gods survived banishment to the countryside.[94] After the first wave of zealots died, churchmen worried more about undercover Jews, Moors, and European heretics, whom they garroted and burned, than about the quality of native orthodoxy. In doing so they were turning a collective blind eye.

So the first period of Spanish settlement ended in a curious mixture of spectacle and stasis. The early friars had tried to change most aspects of indigenous life and succeeded in building churches and monasteries, marshalling whole populations through the main sacraments, renaming people and places, putting on plays, taking over time with the new technology of the church bell, and policing the whole operation with the threat of hell. Yet for all the revolutions of culture and disease, much of the change was superficial. Indians certainly appreciated ecclesiastical buildings as music halls, schools, social security providers, and frontier fortresses. They saw them as community possessions, though, not necessarily the property of the newcomers, undeniably useful though their engineering skills might have been. The sacraments were of questionable meaning in many places, the Protestant critique of empty rote fair enough. The threat of hell seemed real enough; how could it not, amid the massive dying of the epidemics? But the god who administered the inferno was one more of many. Across much of New Spain Europeans and Indians lived in surprisingly separate mental worlds, a divide epitomized in the question of language: Next to no Spanish words, which would have expressed a new reality on a universal scale, crossed into indigenous lexicons. The hybrid culture of the future was still largely in the future, the changes of the sixteenth century its roots but not its fruition.

Yet to see this as a failure for the Spanish or a victory for the Indians, doggedly resisting colonial takeover, is to echo the critiques that came out of the bitter infighting of the Spanish or the just-so stories we like to tell ourselves. Both sides were acculturated, albeit to different degrees. There is some distance between learning Nahuatl and learning that your gods are dead. Compared to an earlier mission to a much smaller pagan land, England, the churchmen in New Spain were actually quite effective. There in the rain of the eastern Atlantic, far closer to Rome, their forebears needed ninety years just to convert kings and nobles. Everyday Anglo-Saxon folk remained unbelievers for centuries.[95] The depth and breadth of conversion in Mexico likewise depended on who you were and where you lived, and it was in much the same way uneven. In the first fifty years the more prominent indigenous urbanites may have been more the exception than the rule, well-schooled leaders in a land of uncertain converts. But they pointed the way to a coming and far more widespread cosmopolitanism, one exemplified in an exceptional feather painting from 1539. In the painting Christ appears to Pope Gregory, who had begun converting England a thousand years earlier, in the bread and wine of Mass, the miracle quieting a churchgoer's doubts over transubstantiation. The piece was commissioned in Mexico City by Fray Pedro de Gante and the indigenous governor Don Diego de Alvarado Huanitzin, Montezuma's nephew, as a gift to Pope Paul III. In short, a Flemish churchman and a Mexica royal paid a Nahua artist to use Central American feathers to imitate a European print of a Levantine holy man appearing to an Italian religious leader to confirm that a Georgian fermented grape juice was actually holy blood.[96] Further comment is perhaps superfluous.

Part Two

The Viceregal Years

1535–1821

Chapter Four

Distant Masters

The profoundly hybrid Spanish Empire endured some three centuries, stretching from the heady first years in the Americas to the great crash of the early 1800s. In Mexico the sixteenth century was a time of dramatic shifts: the alien arrivals of Europeans and West Africans; the mass dying; the ecological lurches of clear-cutting forests with iron axes and desertification by sheep; the ideological revolution of Christianity, with its carrot-and-stick approach to life and life after death. But after that unfinished conquest, surprisingly little changed in the basic structures of life until the last decades of imperial rule. Technology didn't develop much at all. Communications remained a matter of mules and sails. Work remained a mix of largely free urban labor, partially coerced fieldhands and slaves across the countryside, and a free peasantry that subsisted in those ancestral villages that survived. Politics remained divided between local indigenous authorities, partly elected Spanish town councils, and appointed royal bureaucrats in the higher courts and the executive. There was next to no army or police force. War was someone else's problem. The viceroy, "the king's image," ran a quite well-balanced executive, the office's power constrained but accepted. Both the independence and stability of the viceregal years were noteworthy.

For Spain, on the other hand, the seventeenth and eighteenth centuries were times of change, and the stories told about its sprawling and immensely diverse empire, both then and more recently, were of long decline punctuated by disaster. In the sixteenth century Spain had a head start in the geopolitics of modern European empire. By the end of that century it was almost gone. The Habsburg foothold in northern Europe, the small but economically potent enclave of the Netherlands, was increasingly expensive as its mercenary Army of Flanders fought the Protestant secessionists of the United Provinces, a war that lasted from 1567 to 1609 and soaked up a quarter of the Castilian budget.[1] The Dutch were rivals too, not just for their strategic position and business in Europe but also for their newfound oceanic reach, with interests stretching from the spice trade in Indonesia to sugar in Brazil and the Caribbean. While fighting the Dutch was the main drain on continental and global Spanish power, the wars were part of an ambitious series against the other major northern states, most either lost or fought to a draw. At sea, the Battle of Lepanto against the Ottoman Empire in 1571 was Spain's last significant victory. The last great Spanish offensive, the 1588 seaborne invasion of England by a huge fleet, was thwarted by an improvised English navy and atrocious weather; between the two they sunk a third of the Gran Armada's 122 ships. The Spanish navy never really recovered—in 1621 the royal aspiration was to reach 46 ships, about a third the size of the fleet of the glory years[2]—and its history over the next two centuries was one of repeated loss on a large scale: complete Dutch victories at Gibraltar in 1607 and the Downs in 1639, a one-sided catastrophe against the British at Cape Passaro in 1718, and the endgames of Cape Saint Vincent and Trafalgar at the turn of the nineteenth century. On each occasion the Spanish lost tens of ships and thousands of men.

On land the story was also one of a fighting retreat from dominance. The Thirty Years War, a Pan-European free-for-all, ended—after the Spanish had fought shifting combinations of Protestants and Catholics, Bohemians, Dutch, Danes, Swedes, and French—in the disastrous 1648 Treaty of Westphalia. For the Spanish, the treaty ended only some of the wars against their old and emerging competitors: They fought on against the French in Europe, suffered their first major territorial loss in the Americas—Jamaica, to the British in 1655—and another loss in Iberia itself when Portugal seceded in 1668. For Spain the greatest impact of the Treaty of Westphalia was not any redrawing of lines on maps: The treaty's codification of secular state sovereignty as the guiding principle of modern international relations was a profound conceptual blow to a theocratic, multiethnic empire. Above all, the peace deal inflicted significant economic and domestic political damage.

The Defeat of the Spanish Armada, 1588. Philip James de Loutherbourg (1796).

As Westphalia established other countries' sovereignty, it eviscerated that of Spain, cutting Crown revenues and forcing the Habsburgs to auction off key sectors of their own country's economy and bureaucracy just as the costs of geopolitics were rising.

In reality, Spain failed to live up anywhere close to its mercantilist promise to exclude foreigners from the profits of the Americas. Spaniards were frontmen for European merchant houses in Seville and Cádiz; numerous Europeans took Spanish nationality specifically to trade with the Indies; Europeans, Jews, Muslims, and the urban poor regularly slipped through the lines of Spain's rigorous emigration licensing, often shipping as soldiers or sailors and deserting once they made it to the Americas. (By one estimate as many as 50 percent of all seventeenth-century migrants to the Indies took this route.)[3]

Foreign banking houses directly controlled some of the new sectors of the economy: The German Fuggers ran the royal mercury mine, the German Welsers Venezuela. Spanish monopoly control of Atlantic production and exchange was always illusory.

After Westphalia, moreover, the Crown lost control of most of the strategic heights of the transatlantic economy, to the point of looking in places more colony than colonizer. The commercial clauses of the treaties set up foreign merchant enclaves with autonomous jurisdiction, rules, and authorities, and their representatives took over the powerful merchants' association, the *consulado*. The slave trade was opened to the Dutch in 1650 and the English in 1660. None of their merchants had to register imports to Spain; only a fifth of exports were declared to customs; detained smugglers were systematically released following euphemized bribes of gifts or loans. When French smugglers felt threatened in the 1670s, French diplomats threatened a naval attack on Cádiz. The entire system was a foreshadowing of informal imperialism, relying on an early form of gunboat diplomacy.[4]

Along with this hollowing out of economic control came a hollowing out of domestic political control as the Crown sold off positions of state. It was the obvious choice in the face of tax-dodging foreign merchants and Spanish aristocrats who straightforwardly refused to pay, leaving the burden on the Castilian poor. Consequently, government was progressively alienated: Municipal offices in 1606, then judgeships, then audiencia posts in 1687, and finally viceroyalties themselves were all put up for sale. As early as 1633 the Crown began selling off jobs in the Treasury, the ultimate level of tax farming. Investors who bought revenue-collecting positions looked aggressively to harvest returns, making them alternately bribable by the rich and extortion-prone with the poor. The sale of offices and tax farming were desperate, short-term fixes that were self-defeating in the long run, leaving little of a state in Spain. The upwardly mobile could buy titles, which in turn moved them into the realm of the tax exempt and reinforced a predatory aristocracy. Bureaucratic decline was exacerbated by failing leadership, exemplified by the handover in 1598 from the monastic workaholic Philip II to the playboy Philip III. The 1665 death of Philip IV brought the story to its terrible ending with Charles II, *el hechizado*, "the Bewitched," impotent, disabled, and long-lived, the last of the

Habsburgs. After thirty-five years of misrule and a famine he died childless in 1700, leaving Spain at risk of dismemberment and a new incarnation as a client state.

Instead there was a reconquista of sorts, an unforeseen recouping of lost ground under a new French dynasty, the Bourbons. Technocrat-kings, the Bourbons aimed to rule through enlightened absolutism; taking over in wartime as other European powers fought to install a more congenial alternative, Philip V found himself well positioned to make changes. He consequently ended the autonomies of Catalonia and Valencia and banned the entire Iberian aristocracy from the highest positions of government, replacing it with aspirational meritocracy. Habsburg institutions were scrapped en masse: In Spain the councils of state gave way to secretariats, in the Americas governors were replaced by military intendants, and tax farmers by salaried tax collectors protected by soldiers. The military itself was expanded, reformed, and dispatched to garrison the main cities and frontiers of the viceroyalties. A newly muscular, unitary, and ambitious government restored some control of the economy and its revenues, which more than trebled over the first forty years. Yet the Bourbons are traditionally remembered less than fondly, for the double standard of enduring corruption; the militarization and violence used to push through change; the tone-deaf anticlericalism that led them in 1767 to expel the Jesuits, those educators, bankers, and social security providers of viceregal Mexico; and for their final, ignominious defeat by Napoleon Bonaparte in 1807.

So for about 150 years, the *leyenda negra* goes, a fanatical Spanish superpower bet heavily on a unipolar world and lost. Its loss was not just geopolitical and fiscal but also moral, its imperial brutality laying the Americas and large stretches of Europe to waste. The eighteenth century was a comeuppance story of doomed efforts to claw back that bet. The Spanish had killed twenty million Indians, a seventeenth-century London pamphlet announced, and would live out the vengeful sentence of Deuteronomy 19:21: "life for life, eye for eye, tooth for tooth, hand for hand, foot for foot."[5] As one Englishman told Oliver Cromwell—who would recognize imperial brutality when he saw it, having practiced it himself in Ireland—"Though God be long-suffering, yet he is not ever suffering and ever bearing with a proud sinfull people;

but no people more sinfull than the Spaniards in America, both greate and small."[6]

That fanatical Protestants might have an axe to grind in telling such a story of moral and political collapse is obvious. More innocently, it is a story that relies on hindsight, mythologizes a sixteenth-century golden age whose perfection never existed, and overlooks the late Bourbons' success. At the turn of the nineteenth century Spain had recently won a critical victory over the British—the American War of Independence—contributing numerous troops and funds to their overthrow. Customs receipts had doubled, trade trebled; credit was good; silver production was at an all-time high, and the Rayas mine in Guanajuato was the largest in the world (even if the city was missing from most European maps). The winners of colonial rule were rich enough that one of them, the mining magnate Pedro Romero de Terreros, could give the king two 112-gun ships of the line as a present. The Bourbons enjoyed a certain level of political acceptance, aided by a new flexibility in dealing with Mexicans, ranging from the merchants they enriched to the poorest they vaccinated. At a time when hunger still drove much of politics, one scientist observed that Mexicans ate "infinitely more" meat than Parisians. The Bourbons even considered granting Mexico home rule: In 1783 the Count of Aranda proposed that New Spain become its own, separate Bourbon kingdom. In a different world, one not shattered by French revolutionaries and Napoleon Bonaparte, Spain's American empire might have survived and prospered.[7]

While the Spanish failed at great cost in European battles, they were in reality—smuggling aside, and that was a universal problem anyway—largely successful in policing the Americas. Other European powers that tried to stake their claim began relatively late and took pains to avoid the Spanish. The English (first stop Virginia, 1607), French (first stop Canada, 1608), and Dutch (first stop New York, 1624) were for decades marginal players, "upstart empires."[8] Their ships sniped at some of the main ports—Havana, Cartagena, Portobello—but without more intent than smash-and-grab. Their pirates were hardly advertisements for the greater efficiencies of private enterprise: The Atlantic silver galleons, floating equivalents of the Federal Reserve, were captured only three times across three centuries, the Manila Galleon twice. Spain was unable to prevent massive flows of contraband, but successful tax-dodging entrepreneurs were ubiquitous in both the Atlantic and the Pacific worlds in the early modern period; the Chinese empire's ban on international maritime trade similarly just made merchants into smugglers on a massive scale.[9] Moreover, too heavy a hand with smugglers was bad for political business. In France special law courts handed down draconian penalties for smuggling, the convicted providing about half of all the country's galley slaves; unsurprisingly, these were key complaints in the *cahiers de doléances*, the nationwide petitions of the distressed that foreshadowed and helped drive the French Revolution.[10]

Corruption, inefficiency, and weakness did indeed characterize much of the colonial state from the sixteenth to the nineteenth century. Government positions were bought and sold by ambitious men on both sides of the Atlantic, who then naturally enough strived to get returns on their investment—not a recipe for an icily neutral bureaucracy. Royal officials were not supposed to marry into the wealth and temptation of the societies they ruled—Philip II banned such compromising unions in 1575—but that was just one more piece of sexual regulation to be happily flouted. The demands of distant superiors (whether in Mexico City or Madrid) could safely be ignored; there was even a deferential formula for such passive resistance—*Obedezco pero no cumplo*, "I obey but I won't do it"—which was written into the Laws of the Indies.[11] Nepotism was likewise a norm, starting in Madrid, where royal secretaries were on several occasions succeeded by their sons, while in New Spain provincial worthies bequeathed their seats on town councils from generation to generation. As for financial mismanagement, the Crown defaulted on its huge debt six times in the first century of viceregal rule.

But none of these flaws in government was uniquely Spanish. The purchase of office was a European phenomenon, inevitably bringing uneven application of government with it. Nepotism was a European norm, the term itself something of an anachronism; one man's nepotism was another man's patronage or interest. And nepotism wasn't invariably inefficient, but at times something like on-the-job training—the sixth viceroy, Luis de Velasco, was the son of Luis de Velasco the second viceroy, both notably good at their job. Moreover, a generalized corruption was global: Britain's Royal Navy, the institution that destroyed Spanish sea power forever, was run from the Admiralty by a gang of unabashed crooks. The widow of a single high-ranking bureaucrat there received a bigger pension than the widows of thirteen senior officers killed in battle combined.[12]

At the very top, the financial management of the great expansionist, Philip II, was rational, in line with other states' practices and at the last gasp even prudent: He increased the empire's tax base and paid interest on sovereign debt through income and not further loans. When he defaulted it was not through insolvency but rather through temporary cash flow problems. During his reign Spain maintained a low enough debt-to-GDP ratio and large enough primary surpluses to have—with spectacular anachronism—qualified for Euro membership in 1999 and passed the IMF's sustainability test in 2002. Philip II was no dice-rolling idiot, and nor were his bankers; they knew the long-term fundamentals of the economy and its management were sound, and priced default into their loans.[13] At the other end of Spanish rule, the great late Bourbon technocrats like the second Count of Revillagigedo demonstrated an astute grasp of the three cultural beliefs central to any modern economy, namely that growth was desirable, possible, and achievable through their policy agenda.[14]

So when the wheels came off the empire fifty years after Philip II's death, it was not the inevitable consequence of longstanding mismanagement. The first century of Habsburg imperialism was more notable for its comparative successes: its bureaucratic expansion, the circumvention of an incipient conquistador aristocracy, and an extraordinarily productive alliance with the Church that the English failed to maintain and the French to use much at all. In the longer term, all European powers of the time were making similarly exaggerated claims to absolute sovereignty that were aspirational rather than real, and spending like sailors on shore leave to try and make them real. The French state, distinctly among the winners of the seventeenth and eighteenth centuries, remained riddled with holes and incapacities even after Louis XIV. Meanwhile contemporary Britain was not a particularly prudent nation of shopkeepers, running up a debt of nearly 200 percent of GDP in defeating Napoleon.[15]

Any assessment of Spanish rule should acknowledge the conventions of storytelling, with their strong propensity to plotlines of imperial decline and fall and death foretold. In the first great eponymous telling of this story, the historian Edward Gibbon's Roman Empire takes a good three hundred years to get on with its decline and fall. If modern empire is perforce global, then the Spanish remains the longest-lived of such enterprises. Spain's global empire endured far longer than any of its subsequent Western parallels, including the paradigmatic British Empire (which until the definitive takeover of India in 1757 remained upstart in many ways). As for comparison with the United States, a mere century into its own imperial history, that jury is out, for the moment at least.

Back in its sixteenth-century inception, the foreigners who aspired to rule New Spain were a mixture of optimists and pragmatists, idealists and cynics, often enough combined in the same person. They were universally jugglers of time, places, alliances, and responsibilities. They had little choice in the matter, whether they were a handful of Spaniards drawing up titles to an unbuilt frontier town or the handful of Europeans who, on scarce paper, ruled them from thousands of miles away across the Atlantic. The emperor to whom Cortés wrote his carefully crafted letters, the letters that sold his story of virtuous and individual triumph against massive odds, of wealth won and possibilities opened for Crown and Church, was in 1519 "by the grace of God, Holy Roman Emperor." He also held more than seventy other honorifics including King of Jerusalem, Lord of the Islands and Main Ocean Sea, and Lord of the Wendish March. In less formal terms, Charles V was a rather gormless-looking teenager from Belgium who didn't speak Spanish.

Teenagers in positions of high power were common enough in the early modern world, where kings and nobles died young like everyone else; the life expectancy for elites in southern Europe at the time was between fifty and fifty-five years.[16] Queen Isabella of Castile was eighteen when she eloped with the seventeen-year-old Ferdinand of Aragon

Emperor Charles V, Flemish School (1515).

(whom she had met only four days earlier). But it was not in the least part of those predecessors' plans that the next monarch should come from northern Europe, born in the rainy port of Ghent, raised and surrounded by courtiers from the Low Countries and the Duchy of Burgundy, a man who had never been to Spain until he succeeded to the Spanish throne.

Ferdinand and Isabella, like other teenage couples, had been poor enough to have to borrow money to pay for a wedding, but with that wedding they formed an alliance that was the political foundation of modern Spain. The idea of such a thing had been spreading before them, in geographical terms at least: The inhabitants of Iberia had described their peninsula as Hispania for centuries, and by the fifteenth century sailors spoke of coming home to Spain.[17] Yet linguistically and politically Iberia at the time was divided into five different kingdoms: Castile in the center, Aragon in the northeast and along the Mediterranean coast, Navarra in the mountains of the North, Portugal on the western Atlantic coast, and Muslim Granada in the South. Castile was both metaphorically and literally the heartland, the region's leading power in military, demographic, and economic terms despite its aridity and historical lack of access to the Mediterranean. Its success was founded on wool and warfare, its elites the leaders of the Reconquista, the centuries-long drive south against the Iberian Islamic kingdoms. Ascendant Castile was a hierarchical and pastoral country that would be neatly complemented by integration with declining Aragon, the more egalitarian kingdom that subsumed Catalonia and Valencia and bordered France. The Aragonese had the

Pyrenean and Mediterranean trade routes, merchants, and consequent diplomatic savoir faire that Castile lacked. The logic was consummated with Ferdinand and Isabella, who were not just dynastic jigsaw pieces but also intelligent, wily, and ambitious politicians: the *reyes católicos*, a power couple well matched in political and personal terms, who led the final defeat of the Muslim kingdom of Granada and the first steps of empire in the Western Hemisphere.

Yet with the accession of Charles V in 1516 the New World and its emerging Spanish metropole fell under the rule of a wholly different dynasty, the Habsburgs of Central Europe, whose rule endured for nearly two hundred years. Charles's family were Austrians who gradually acquired a patchwork of territories from 1279 onward, adopting the honorific title of Holy Roman Emperor in 1438. This did not add much substance to the rhetoric until the rule of his grandfather, Maximilian I. A strategic matchmaker, in 1477 Maximilian married Mary of Burgundy, who brought part of France and the Netherlands with her as a dowry, and in 1496 he married off their son Philip the Fair to Juana the Mad of Spain. Both nicknames are of debatable accuracy. Portraits of Philip give him a suspicious squint and the ubiquitous long Habsburg chin and drooping lip, while Juana's madness was politically convenient enough—she ended up confined to a convent for life—to reek of a dissident locked up in a dictator's asylum. Their marriage was the lesser of Maximilian's dynastic steps of the time—he simultaneously married off his daughter Margaret to the only male heir to the throne of Castile, John of Asturias—but it was the most fortunate one. An unusually intense pruning of Spain's royal line, culminating in the early death of Queen Isabella in 1504, left Juana's son Charles quite literally the last man standing.

He took over a Spain whose sudden expansion and coherence surprised contemporaries. "Who should have thought," wrote the priest Peter Martyr in 1489,

> that the Galician, the proud Asturian, and the rude inhabitant of the Pyrenees, would be mixing freely with Toledans, people of La Mancha, and Andalusians, living together in harmony and obedience, like members of one family, speaking the same language and subject to one common discipline?[18]

The Flemish Martyr was himself an outsider, but he went on to link his fate to those members of that one Spanish family. He represented the *reyes católicos* at the court of the Ottoman sultan and became the ultimate insider when Charles V made him a member of the Council of the Indies in 1518. In that strategic post he received reports, letters, and visits from many of the main travelers of the day, working all of it into the first history of the Americas, *De Orbe Novo.* Many of his informants brought "futile particulars" in "letters devoid of interest, written by correspondents bereft of intelligence." But others brought him enough intelligence to pen a contemporary history of Mexico and the Atlantic, which he revealingly called "our ocean." The Atlantic was "more prolific than the Albanian sow, to which tradition assigned thirty pigs at a litter; and more liberal than a generous prince." In 1525 there were, Martyr wrote, "as many fleets ploughing the ocean waves, and as many vessels coming and going from the New World, as there are merchants coming from Italy to fairs at Lyons, or from France and Germany to the fairs at Antwerp." This was wholly untrue—early colonial trade was nothing compared to European trade—but a fair reflection of his personal excitement. By the end of his life the newly cosmopolitan humanist had written about people across the Americas from South Carolina to Cape Horn.[19]

When Charles V came to the throne in 1516, the pithy motto *plus ultra*, "further beyond," was already on his coat of arms alongside the Pillars of Hercules, the two hills that flank the Strait of Gibraltar and symbolized the edge of the known world. The brag referred not just to the Americas but to a preexisting vision of dominating both hemispheres.[20] Yet the Habsburg Empire remained for centuries a geographical, institutional, and financial patchwork. Even before their arrival on the American mainland, the Spanish were driving ambitiously out of Iberia on all sides. For imperially minded adventurers, churchmen, and investors, the New World was only ever one of many options.

To the immediate east, ten years of war against the French ended with Aragon incorporating Naples in 1504, adding it to Sicily in what was known as the Kingdom of the Two Sicilies, and then pushing the French further back on the Catalan border. To the far west the Castilians by 1496 had stabilized the principal mid-Atlantic islands of Grand Canary, Palma, and Tenerife, the critical staging posts to the Caribbean. To the south they made their first ventures into North Africa at the small town of Melilla, following in 1509 with Oran; in 1510 Pedro Navarro, Count of Oliveto (and as the last name suggests, Navarrese), took the far more significant city of Algiers (temporarily) under Spanish control while six hundred miles to the east capturing the small town of Bougie in Libya. In 1511 Diego Velázquez conquered Cuba, the most important island in the Americas, nearly a quarter the size of Spain itself.[21]

In the Americas of the sixteenth century men like Navarro set out with the title of *adelantado*, forerunner, in a public-private partnership whose details would be arranged beforehand in a contract with the Crown, the *capitulación*. The contract typically surrendered much control of the territory conquered to the entrepreneurial type concerned, who became governor and enjoyed nonhereditary rights to assign political positions, treasure, and slaves. More permanent real estate in their realm was a provisional possession subject to eventual royal approval. In exchange the Crown took the *quinto real*, a 20 percent tax on profits, and kept the right to hire and fire leaders or reverse their distribution of wealth, while insisting on the most fundamental institutions of Castilian rule: at the bottom the *cabildo*, a town council, and at the top the viceroy, an executive doppelgänger of the absent king. Almost all sixteenth-century Spanish initiatives in the New World were undertaken by adelantados, from Argentina to Florida and from the Canary Islands to the Philippines. They reached as far as the Solomon Islands, specks of land in the South Pacific. (In 1568 Peruvian ships under Álvaro de Mendaña de Neira landed there while sailing toward Australia, at the time a hypothetical continent, which they never reached.)

The institutional outcomes of successful invasions varied greatly. Differences began at home in Iberia, where the kingdoms kept their own institutions and political cultures even as they became part of the larger enterprise of Spain. Castile was (appropriately enough) the most centralized, with a token *cortes*, the medieval consultative body representing the three estates of nobility, clergy, and towns; it met irregularly, its individual members were only allowed to attend by royal writ, and it lacked legislative power. The Castilian monarchy aspired to absolutism even as it faced down aristocrats and the everyday townspeople, who rebelled in the quixotic *comuneros* revolt of 1520. Aragon, by contrast, had much more representative institutions: The gentry of the *cortes* could veto royal legislation and taxes, and at least some of its members sat permanently in session to exercise vigilance over royal rule. A contractarian, rudely egalitarian political culture was summed up in the medieval oath of allegiance to the Crown, which promised in aggressively conditional language,

> We who are as good as you swear to you who are no better than we, to accept you as our king and sovereign lord, provided that you observe all our liberties and laws; but if not, not.[22]

Central authority spread slowly out of the Spanish heartland, its constituent kingdoms and provinces keeping their institutions and allegiances ambiguous to the point that Pedro Navarro, the hero of Spain's expeditions to North Africa, felt comfortable enough to defect and fight for the French a few years later. (When he was born, Navarre had still been the autonomous Basque kingdom of Naffaroako Erresuma, so this wasn't as perfidious as it might seem.)[23] In Portugal, part of Spain from 1581 until 1640, the *carta patente* of annexation specified that the king could not legislate on Portuguese affairs while outside the kingdom, whose soil he very rarely trod. The viceroy and the military and civilian leaders were all to be Portuguese, as were the king's advisors on Portuguese affairs. The *asiento*, the monopoly contract over slave trading to the Americas, went to the Portuguese; the voluminous colonial trade between Lisbon and Africa, Macao, Goa, and Brazil would stay in Portuguese hands; and those hands would pay Portuguese, not Castilian, taxes.[24] Portugal was an extreme example. Yet none of the Habsburg possessions, from Naples to the Americas, were belittled with the term "colony"; they were seen by their inhabitants with their diverse systems of rule as quasi-autonomous kingdoms.[25]

Royal forces and incomes were rarely used in forming the new kingdoms outside of Iberia, and the empire's institutional patchwork was extended by a financial patchwork. The victory over Granada was in terms of funding very much a Pan-European endeavor. The taking of Palma was a business venture for an Italian banking partnership. The tabs for Ferdinand's African expeditions were generally picked up by others, from the first conquest of Melilla, which was funded by the Duke of Medina Sidonia, to the weightier conquest of Oran, undertaken by twenty thousand soldiers paid by the Franciscan Archbishop of Toledo, Francisco Jiménez de Cisneros. As the contemporary historian Fernández de Oviedo put it, "Almost never do Their Majesties put their income and cash into these new discoveries, all is paper and fine words."[26] And beyond the deep purses of even the more crusading prelates like Cisneros, there were the bankers who decade after decade lent huge amounts to the Spanish Crown, rolled over existing debts, and tolerated periodic defaults, while in exchange enjoying high interest rates secured against the convincing collateral of the annual flow of silver from Mexico and Peru. It was not Spanish warlords but rather Dutch, Italian, and German bankers who were the ultimate backers of Spain's sixteenth-century power grab.

This meant that Charles V (1516–1555) and his son Philip II (1556–1598) could indulge in one of the most ambitious foreign policies in history on the cheap. For the Habsburgs the sixteenth century was a geopolitical telenovela, in which they alternately married into and fought against every other major European dynasty. The Habsburg women were marriage fodder, sent out with stiff upper lips against even those serial enemies the French: When Manuel of Portugal died, his widow Eleanor was promptly passed on to Francis I of France, himself en secondes noces. At the same time there was regular warfare between the Habsburgs and a shifting cast of enemies. Domestically the sixteenth century began in war, a major one against Granada having just concluded, a new one starting in Italy, a minor one taking place against Navarre in 1512, and another, more troubling, inside Castile itself in 1520–1521. This revolt began as a series of provincial risings in which disgruntled locals—*comuneros*, members of something like a county—ran royal officials and taxmen out of town and replaced them with elected councils. By September 1520 four cities, led by Toledo, had coalesced into a single rival government with an army and an agreed set of demands. The *comuneros* came from every urban class, from noble malcontents through a middle class of artisans, shopkeepers, and university graduates to commoners, and they were in many areas joined by peasants. Their goals were an end to seigneurial rights, a representative body, or *cortes*, with greater powers over taxation, greater rights for towns, and a king who served a kingdom rather than vice versa.

Charles met them with immediate repression followed by reform, spent the next seven years in Spain rather than in his other dominions, and finally learned the language. He replaced the outsiders in his entourage and administration with Spaniards and so tacitly fulfilled the demand of the rebels that he should live in the same place as his subjects and recruit them rather than "Flemings, Frenchmen, [or] natives of any other country." While he drew more and more on Castile as the treasure chest for his personal imperial policy, he did so in formal partnership with the *cortes*, an assembly of notables that was summoned far more often, giving legislation a collective sheen and helping co-opt provincial powerbrokers. Charles also began developing a bureaucracy open to the talents of clerics, gentry, and minor aristocrats, excluding the great nobility, whom he bought off with continued tax exemptions. It was not a profitable settlement, even if the king reliably got his way each time the *cortes* negotiated taxes, but it did provide decades of domestic stability and resources that made the Habsburgs creditworthy and secured them some of the down payment for empire.[27]

And every penny counted, because being a sixteenth-century superpower was a cripplingly expensive business. To the south the Spanish were caught between a persistent threat across the Mediterranean, where Muslim pirates and Ottoman forces—often one and the same thing—threatened the shipping lanes and the east coast. Even after the great Christian victory at Lepanto, where in 1571 an alliance with the Venetians destroyed the Ottoman navy, Spain feared attacks from the Mediterranean. It also feared subversion from its large surviving Muslim population, the Moriscos, who were particularly concentrated in the South and East, where they remained for decades a majority in Granada, and a third of the population in Valencia. Even after mass conversion, when they became New Christians, the Crown's Muslim subjects were subject to perennial political, economic, and cultural offensives perpetrated by petty officials, Christian arrivistes, and even parish priests. One village pleaded to have their priest moved as "all our children are born with eyes as blue as his."[28]

Moriscos' adherence to Christianity was understandably suspect. On Christmas Eve 1568, thirty thousand Moriscos revolted in Granada, leading to two years of bloody fighting—one of Cortés's sons was a casualty—and massive forced migration. It was, the Spanish commander wrote,

> the saddest sight in the world, for at the time they set out there was so much rain, wind and snow that mothers had to abandon their children by the wayside and wives their husbands . . . the saddest sight one can imagine is to see the depopulation of a kingdom.[29]

The uprising over, and with most New Christians staying on the sidelines, the royal administration still portrayed Muslims across Spain as fifth columnists, allies-in-waiting to North Africans, or even French Protestants. They were right, too: In 1570 the sultan ordered the governor of Algeria to send arms and troops to assist the Moriscos, who had petitioned him for support for an alleged 120 thousand rebels-in-waiting.[30] Between 1609 and 1614 the remaining three hundred thousand were deported to Africa. It was only then that the Spanish achieved a reasonable security on the sea lanes of the western Mediterranean.

The clash of Christians and Muslims was supposed to trump geopolitical rivalries among the northern powers. Yet any Christian cohesion was temporary and transactional. In 1520 Spain made an alliance with the Muslims of Tunis; seven years later Spanish and German troops attacked Rome; in 1540, peace made, a holy alliance between Spain, the papacy, and Venice fell apart when the merchant princes of *la Serenissima* serenely made a separate peace with the infidel Turk. In the late sixteenth century Queen Elizabeth flirted with the idea of a joint attack on the Americas with the Ottoman sultan, part of his seventeen years of letters to the woman he called Elzābet, queen of Anletār.[31] Both commerce and secular politics periodically trumped religious affinities to allow alliances across the Mediterranean and between Christian and Muslim worlds. For southern war with Islam was just one of several constants of sixteenth-century international relations in Europe. The first was, paradoxically enough, a general lack of any constancy in alliances. The second was the translation of Protestant ideology into Protestant factions and even government in England, the German states, and the Low Countries of Belgium and the Netherlands. The remaining included the growing reluctance of the people of the Low Countries to accept Habsburg rule; the reliable superiority of Spanish infantrymen, whose three-thousand-man tercios went undefeated for decades; the weakness, by contrast, of the Spanish navy; and, looming above it all, the century-long on-and-off war with France.

Such complexity demanded from the Habsburg rulers the sort of extraordinary juggling act of a modern US president—without, however, the attendant imperial bureaucracy and its extraordinary amount of data. Spain and its territories were run by prelates and minor aristocrats, small bodies whose members struggled to know what was going on and what to do about it in a frenetic world. In extremis, the collision of enduring personalist rule with the new scale of early modern politics was violent. In a mere five weeks in 1521, for example, France declared war (April 22); Charles V defeated the *comunero* rebellion (April 24); Charles concluded an imperial assembly in Germany, the Diet of Worms, by casting out Martin Luther, a declaration of war on Protestantism (May 25); and three days later he lost his lifelong consigliere William de Croy, Lord of Chièvres (May 28), allegedly to Protestant poison. At this time, Cortés began the siege of Tenochtitlán (May 13). Not that anyone in Spain knew—in the midst of all that was going on, a certain inattention to the Americas is unsurprising.

It helped that the Habsburg Empire was enjoying a free ride on the other side of the world, where international competition was minimal. The British of the sixteenth century were far from the maritime superpower of later centuries: In 1511, as the Spanish settled the Caribbean's last major island, Henry VIII's navy consisted of five ships. The Portuguese, a much more credible threat, were focused on Asia both by rational choice—they had been the first to travel the route and had all the economic advantages of early adopters—and because of the

Treaty of Tordesillas, the pope's division of the world into a Portuguese East and a Spanish West. The Dutch, future competitors in both hemispheres, were concentrating at this point on their long-running northern trade in textiles, herring, pitch, and timber. Some Muslims were optimists. "Let us hope to God," one Ottoman courtier wrote to the sultan, "that some time these valuable lands [the Americas] will be conquered by the family of Islam, and will be inhabited by Moslems."[32] These were pipe dreams: Islamic sea power, still critical in the Mediterranean, only rarely stretched into the Atlantic. (Though as late as 1631 two Algerian corsairs raided Baltimore, a village on Ireland's treacherous southwest coast, and there was more than one attack on the distant Canaries.)[33] The Spanish had pirates to fear on both sides of the ocean, and often lurking behind the pirates there were states. But even at its worst, early Atlantic piracy was a feeble proxy warfare.

A more rewarding start to Spain's empire in the Americas might have drawn more rivals, but the early rhetoric of effortless riches ran up against the realities of conquest within a couple of decades. The history of Iberian expansion became a cyclical one of action followed by delusion, disappointment, and passage on to the next frontier. Columbus was a serial liar in his letters, reporting gold that he never saw and making his entire fleet swear before a lawyer, under threat of dreadful punishment, that Cuba was not an island but rather an Asian peninsula. Against mounting evidence to the contrary, he seemed to believe it until he died; as Bartolomé de las Casas wryly observed, "When a man greatly desires something and fixes it firmly in his mind it is a wonder how all that he sees and hears, at every step, seems to confirm it." But by 1507 other navigators had already proven Columbus wrong, demonstrating that the Caribbean discoveries were islands, while Venezuela, Panama, and all points north formed a single land mass. In 1504 the Florentine sailor Amerigo Vespucci published the counterargument in his "Quattuor Americi navigaciones," and the German cartographer Martin Waldseemüller made the argument a map, inventing the new continent and calling it America in Vespucci's honor. There was no passage to the Indies on the other side of the Atlantic, no ready access to Chinese wealth. The main Spanish settlements were consolidated by the early 1510s: the big islands of Hispaniola (1493), Puerto Rico (1508), Jamaica (1509), and Cuba (1511), and the mainland foothold of Panama

(1510). Yet their profits proved ephemeral, and by 1520 an island pattern of limited loot, exhausted gold deposits, and indigenous apocalypse had made the extent of Columbus's lies quite clear.[34]

There were still some going concerns. For all its diminishing returns, Caribbean mining produced sixty tons of gold in the first half of the sixteenth century.[35] Hispaniola's other major export industry, hides, was worth three-quarters of a million pesos a year by the 1560s. Sugar was in its infancy but nevertheless mattered: The first canes brought by Columbus in 1493 multiplied enough to produce millions of pounds of sugar in the 1570s.[36] Enslaved divers brought copious pearls off the oyster beds of Venezuela. The first Spaniard there indicated his interest; four days later the local cacique brought him four pounds of pearls, some as large as olives, and by 1520 there were some hundred pearl farms.[37] Finally, there were humans. Demand was constant, as slaves were the only manual laborers and their numbers needed continual replenishment; few survived long. As a consequence, Cortés wrote, it was "custom in these isles that in the name of Your Majesties are settled by Spaniards to go for Indians to those isles that are not settled with Spanish in order to make use of them."[38] Those islands in turn depopulated, the Spanish shifted from island-hopping to transatlantic slave trading, the longer-distance trade still profitable through tight demand: The asiento, a monopoly contract for Spanish ships, helped keep competition down and prices up.

Mexico, though, had little of even these resources. Gold was scarce from the start; there was little tradition of working it, and outside the Oaxaca highlands there wasn't much to be mined anyway. For both gold and silver the smart money was on Peru, where the conquistadors of the early 1530s obtained huge amounts of both—in the division of spoils horsemen got 90 pounds of gold and 180 pounds of silver each—and where prospectors soon found the largest silver deposits in the world. Higher transport costs made hides and sugar in Mexico a more expensive business than in the islands. Cortés began cultivating cane in his tropical fiefdom but didn't see much profit in his lifetime, and his 1532 expedition to the Gulf of California revealed no viable pearl beds. Indian populations, even after the smallpox epidemics of the 1520s, proved more resilient than the islanders until the second-wave epidemic of the mid-century, but they were protected by a legal status different from those of the islanders. There was still money in slavery, and the odd windfall like Guzmán's conquest of the West, but criminalization of the indigenous slave trade left only the Chichimeca as legal targets—as warrior nomads they remained fair game—and they were harder (and a lot more dangerous) to catch. Mexico, in economic terms, was quickly found out as the sideshow of a sideshow.

So while European publics were captivated by the stories of Mexico—New Spain—the Spanish councils of state and their emperor were not. Four thousand books were printed about the Americas across the course of the sixteenth century.[39] There were by contrast no mentions of Mexico in Charles V's memoirs and precious few at the Council of Trent, the eighteen-year series of meetings to determine the Catholic Church's response to the Protestant Reformation. Attending prelates said nothing about the organization of the Church in the Americas nor about the theological and disciplinary challenges posed by its simple existence.[40] The main figures in the drama of early Spanish rule in Mexico struggled to be heard at home, however important their message: When Bishop Zumárraga dashed off a crucial fifty-five-page report to the emperor on postconquest coups and assassinations, he prefaced it with the plea "I beg that you might see fit to read all of this letter which is right and true."[41]

That was in 1529; that the plea was no literary or diplomatic device was made clear over twenty years later in a letter from the second viceroy, Luis de Velasco, to Charles V, which began,

> Sacred Catholic Caesarean Majesty:
>
> In every ship that has left New Spain I have written to your majesty, giving a long and detailed account of the state of things in the country and what has been done since my arrival, in fulfilment of your majesty's order and instruction, and I have had no reply from your majesty, nor even evidence that my letters have been summarized for you. It is two and a half years since I wrote the first of them.

As Velasco went on to surmise, the reasons for being wholly ignored were straightforward: finite time and low importance compared to "the great concerns and wars that have presented themselves."[42] It was a truism that the emperor had bigger fish to fry. "If, as the king of Portugal doth, [Charles V] would become a merchant, and provide shippes and their lading, and trade thither alone, and defend the trade of these Islands for himself," it might be very profitable, an Englishman in Seville let Henry VIII know. "But other greater business witholdeth him from this."[43] The first men to cross the Atlantic were like astronauts, sharing their courage to overcome the dread of the unknown and take the plunge into the infinite.[44] They changed the way humans saw the Earth, and they opened up vast opportunities for the future. But they were of about as much immediate use to their masters as astronauts; they provoked wonder but provided surprisingly little.

Chapter Five

Independence Before Independence

The piratical conquistadors, ironically enough, took more interest in a certain sort of state-building than did their distant masters. On the periphery they were first and foremost expeditionaries, their grand-sounding towns on the ground embryonic. But in the Valley of Mexico they were keenly interested in building the environments and ways of life of a major European city.

Doing so meant creating detailed codes to bring order out of chaos in everything from sex to the trade in turkeys. Rules were made initially by Cortés and subsequently by the *ayuntamiento*, the city council that began falteringly in 1524 to instill a more collective authority. Sweeping ambition came entangled with micromanagement from the outset. To populate this new world, Spanish men were to import their wives from Spain within eighteen months; bachelors were to marry within the same period.[1] (Regulating sex was also a concern of the emperor Charles V, who wrote to Cortés instructing him to punish any abuse of indigenous women with the utmost severity, as this was one of the main reasons for hatred of the Spanish in the other American territories.)[2] Trying to implement state-mandated monogamy in a violently promiscuous crusading culture was both utopian and authoritarian. Churchmen and their inquisitors were pruriently obsessed with the question for decades. But it was just one among many projects of social engineering and centralization of the first years.

In material terms, New Spain was intended to be a command economy from the start. A dire shortage of gold and silver coinage existed until the first mint opened in 1535, leaving barter rife, Indians buying things with their old currencies such as cacao beans, Spaniards "going around with pieces of gold, cutting off pieces in the shops to pay."[3] They nevertheless set everyday prices with careful detail. In the port of Veracruz wine was to sell at forty-eight grains of gold, the equivalent of half a one-peso coin, per *azumbre*, more or less a gallon. As Indian carriers lugged the precious stuff—the Spanish didn't indulge much in mushrooms, peyote, or the cactus alcohol pulque—up seven thousand feet to Mexico City, vendors were allowed to increase the price another forty-eight grains for every ten leagues. Chicken eggs taking the same arduous route went for the outrageous sum of thirty-six grains of gold each, part of the premium set on consuming rare European foods, far pricier than indigenous foods such as turkey, quail, deer, and maize.[4] Bread was the staple that distinguished Spanish elites from maize-eating plebs and was the only food sold by European rather than Indian vendors. It too was strictly controlled in consistency (it was to be well-cooked, dry to last longer) and supply; what the Nahua called the *Castilla tlaxcalli*, the "Castilian tortilla," was only available in the main square of the capital. The initial shortage of European crops was striking: All the first wheat in Mexico came, according to legend, from a single grain, a hitchhiker in a sack of rice.[5] The paucity of familiar food was to be remedied by fiat dictating that any Spaniard enjoying indigenous land and labor must cultivate European crops—wheat, barley, recognizable vegetables—in fenced-off fields, or face stiff fines.[6]

The first systematized body of regulations came in the *Ordenanzas de buen gobierno* of March 20, 1524, the "Ordinances for the Good Government of New Spain." Their rationale was straightforward, as Cortés explained in his fourth letter to Charles V:

> To seek all the good order that may be possible such that these lands be settled, and that the Spanish settlers and the natives of them might be preserved and maintained, and that our holy Faith might take root in all things.[7]

First of all, the Spanish were to be settlers and not raiders. Absentee landlords were banned: Men granted indigenous lands, labor, and tribute had to reside for a minimum of eight years in-country. They had to build houses and be ready to defend themselves and their neighbors, presenting appropriate weaponry when mustered for inspection. The minimum was a lance, sword, breastplate, and helmet; those with two thousand or more Indian tributaries had to have a horse, armor, three lances, six pikes, and four muskets. The Spanish were supposed to rule with that paltry force until they achieved lasting peace by turning Indians into Christians. That was, the Ordenanzas lectured them, really why they were there in the first place: "As Catholics and Christians our main preoccupation must be the service and worship of our Lord God, which is also the reason why the Holy Father granted the Emperor, our lord, dominion over these peoples." To that end four clauses of the Ordenanzas spelled out their evangelical obligations: to destroy idols and replace them with priests, chapels, and religious instruction for the elites. Money might be available to help the hard-up with costs; arms, passages on ships, and solid houses were all expensive. But the newly minted citizens had to comply with all provisions by the end of 1526.[8] With these provisions would come a leap toward the society the Spanish were supposed to be seeking. The revolution from above would create a peaceful, Christian, and yet also multicultural country, a mixture of the modern and the medieval in which their claim to greater seigneurial rights than back home in Spain would be accompanied by greater seigneurial duties. Anyone who didn't play by this book would forfeit their Indians, and with them any hope of joining a putative American aristocracy.

Above all, the conquistadors intended to restore the American Venice that had awed them the first time they crossed the valley rim. A rebuilt city on the lake was far more ambitious than a city upon a hill, because total war had erased central Tenochtitlán. The Spanish and their allies had destroyed the city's basic infrastructure, sabotaging the complex web of canals, dikes, and aqueducts that kept the city dry, watered, and fed. Merely restoring that life support system demanded massive engineering works. So Cortés considered abandoning the island to the stench of its thousands of Mexica corpses and rebuilding on the southern lake shore at Coyoacán, where he was headquartered. It was the practical thing to do; many argued as much. But with the megalomania that undergirds any decent urban planning, Cortés decided to rebuild Tenochtitlán as one of the world's great cities. It was to be Spanish in spatial terms, a grid centered on a huge square, the *plaza mayor*, where the cathedral and the house of government would stand, surrounded by the houses of the powerful. The rebuilt city was also to be Spanish in ethnic terms. Any emigrant accepted as a *vecino*, a townsman, would be allotted a plot measuring one *solar*, nearly twenty thousand square feet; two if he was a conquistador.[9] Their houses would form the city blocks of the new center, the *traza*, bounded to the north by a canal and on all other sides by an imaginary line. Indians would be forbidden to cross it—once, that is, they had built the hundred blocks the traza contained.

Reconstruction was planned by an amateur architect, the "geometrist" Alonso García Bravo, but it was achieved with the manpower of tens of thousands of the defeated Mexica. From the winter of 1521 onward, carpenters, masons, bricklayers, and workmen cleared the canals of bodies and rubble, restored the old avenues running to the four cardinal points, and carved out the new streets, their crowds packing them until a man could barely pass, their voices rising night and day. The island's marshy soil demanded copious men and materials just to sink foundations for the resurgent city's buildings, which sat on thousands of wooden columns. The Mexica dragged in timber and stones from around the lake, hundreds to a rope, and reused the beams and the huge slabs of volcanic rock of their own palaces and temples. Many died in the works, while the absence of crops from their untended floating gardens and lakeside fields increased the general level of hunger during those years; even workers went hungry if they didn't bring their own food. The construction of Mexico City was another of the plagues of conquest, Motolinía judged. But at least the workers didn't pay the taxes demanded from Indians outside the city, and for many there was a certain pride in what they did, even if their first constructions were fortified dockyards for the brigantines that had starved them during the siege and mansions for their enemies.[10]

These mansions were petty castles rising out of the destroyed center, with high walls, barred windows, embrasures for cannon, and turrets for sieges. There were at least nine of them, some with moats. Two on the main square belonged to Cortés, their foundations the imperial palaces of Montezuma and Axayácatl, and another two rose nearby for his captains Pedro Alvarado and Gonzalo Sandoval.[11] The private fortresses and the would-be apartheid of the traza were founded on Spanish fears that their abusiveness might combine with Mexica bellicosity to spark the sort of rebellion that happened elsewhere in the Indies. Cortés explained it pithily to the emperor:

> Causing them grievances that they were unable to suffer would be reason for them to rebel; and as they are already more dexterous with our things they might seek all sorts of weapons to counter ours in both defense and offense, for which they are greatly skilled; and as they are a people beyond number and we by comparison small change, they would in a very brief time finish us off.[12]

Yet the medieval fortifications proved unnecessary, because the much-feared Mexica rising never happened. The Spanish had planned to confine the defeated to Tlatelolco and the four indigenous neighborhoods on the periphery of Tenochtitlán: San Juan Moyotlan to the south, Santa María Cuepopan to the west, San Sebastián Atzacoalco to the east, and San Pablo Teopan to the southwest. But their apartheid failed, as indigenous domestics, tradespeople, watermen, and crowds of market sellers provided cover for a general freedom of movement. People who wanted to occupy Spanish space could; in the absence of interethnic violence, that was unimportant.

The other great failure of the Spanish, however, was important: They disdained the lake's ecosystem and the complex indigenous waterworks that managed it. Living at the heart of the Valley of Mexico meant securing freshwater for people and plants in the dry season and preventing flooding in the rainy season. This headache was exacerbated by the brackishness of the valley water. The Mexica had coped with the problem—because it could not be resolved, just managed—by creating three levels of water whose respective heights they could manipulate. They built five dikes separating the lake system into a freshwater reservoir to the city's west; two higher freshwater lakes in the south, in Xochimilco and Chalco; and to the east and north, lower and larger, the saline shallows of Lake Tetzcoco. Sluice gates were closed during the wet summer months to stop that salt water from backing up and contaminating the city's supplies; open the rest of the year, they allowed a steady flow of water downhill and eastward to maintain constant levels and to keep the city and irrigation canals clean. This demanded engineering on a pharaonic scale: The dike of Nezahualcóyotl separating east from west was sixteen feet wide and eight miles long. Building it had required tens of thousands of laborers to drive thousands of large tree trunks into the muddy lake floor, weave saplings in between them, and fill the resulting trench with stone. The conquistadors breached it and another key dike during the war, and then directed workers, stone, and timber elsewhere to the reconstruction of the city center. Even as they rebuilt it, the lake around them was draining eastward, drying up, and turning into polluted salt water, with a "stench so bad that it brought on plague."[13]

Putting aside sustainability and the noxious stench of sewage, dead animals, stagnant water, and the runoff from tanneries, though, the former Tenochtitlán was in a matter of decades restored as one of the world's great cities. The floating gardens called chinampas and the lakeside villages that fed the center recovered; to Motolinía there were "few cities in all of Europe that have such a setting and surrounding, with so many villages encircling it, and so well-founded; in fact I state and affirm that I doubt there is any place as good and as opulent."[14] By the 1550s the Spanish and their indigenous workforce had fleshed out the geometric promise of the center with paved avenues, restored canals, a town clock, townhouses, convents, monasteries, multitudinous shops, a viceregal palace, and a university, the Real y Pontificia Universidad de México. It was the first university in North America, predating Harvard by nearly a century and following close on the heels of Christ Church, Oxford's richest college. One of the first professors, Francisco Cervantes de Salazar, described the new city with an abundance of superlatives and exclamation marks. Ascending the Calle de Tacuba, one of the main streets, toward the plaza: "How the soul delights and the sight revels in the appearance of this street! How long and wide! How straight! How flat!" Arriving at the viceregal palace, he finds "not a palace, but another city." The plaza is beyond compare: "My God! How level and large! How happy! How adorned with high and proud buildings to all four winds! What symmetry! What beauty!" Classical and transatlantic comparisons are all favorable: More people walk the colonnades than did in ancient Rome, the town hall is as magnificent as any in Spain, the canals are once again Venetian. Even

The newborn Mexico City in 1557.
Giovanni Battista Ramusios, *Navigationi et Viaggi* (1557).

the clinic for venereal diseases is "a work of art."[15] Not every project prospered—Alonso de Herrera's brewery folded soon after the first beer left its gates in 1549—but to the poet Bernardo de Balbuena the finished city was the "center of perfection."[16] The urban planners of Madrid concurred: When building their own plaza mayor they took Mexico City's as their model.

But as the city rose, the conquistadors fell. A large part of it came down to mobility and high casualty rates: Gonzalo Sandoval, briefly governor, lived less than two years in his small fortress. Frontier warfare killed some of them, but poisoning was also rife and probably behind the deaths of Cortés's captain Ordaz, his secretary Juan "One Eye" Ribera (bacon), and the treasurer Aldarete (salad). Cortés himself may have murdered his wife Catalina that way; his family was still paying money to the in-laws a century later. (The use of the conditional is necessary in most historical accusations of poisoning.) Ill tongues whispered that he had similarly done away with the ex-governor of Jamaica, Francisco de Garay, and no fewer than three royal officials. Others were killed more visibly. Cristóbal de Olid was disemboweled by his own men, the crack cavalryman Pedro González Trujillo was hanged, and the blacksmith Hernando de Alonso was burned at the stake when found out a Jew. Most significant of all, Rodrigo de Paz, Cortés's cousin and representative in the city, was seized in 1525, waterboarded, burned, and finally hanged naked from the back of a donkey in the plaza mayor.[17] This was a coup, even if there wasn't much of an état to topple, and it proved the first of three turning points in the elimination of conquistador power. The second came in 1529, when the first royal government arrived, and the third in 1566, when its successor forestalled an alleged independence conspiracy and pushed the second generation of conquistadors from power.

Hernán Cortés had received the first postwar royal decrees in 1523, making him governor, captain-general, and chief justice of New Spain. His absolute power lasted only a few months before four crown officials arrived, and when Cortés left on the disastrous Honduras expedition two of them seized power and forced the audiencia to swear them in as the new rulers. The leader of the conquistadors, the royal entrepreneurs had been told, was dead; this seemed like their moment and they took it, denouncing him as a tyrant. The royal plotters were, of course, dead wrong, and lasted less than six months in power before a loyalist faction toppled them after learning that Cortés had survived. In June 1526 he returned to Mexico City in triumph, more of a proven state-builder than the royal officials who were sent to rein him in.

Yet contemporary history quickly repeated itself, wholly predictably, with the arrival two weeks later of a new set of officials who once again pushed Cortés from power, albeit by legal means this time. He was too much the overmighty subject for the Crown to leave in place, and was strongly suspected of defrauding his overlord by understating his profits from the wars. On July 2, 1526, Judge Luis Ponce de León arrived to take power and launch an audit, a *juicio de residencia*, of conquistador government. Dying in short order, the judge was succeeded by a Spanish colleague, Marcos de Aguilar, who likewise died quickly. (The first generation of royal officials, starting with the expedition's treasurer, had intriguingly short life expectancies.) Far from turning to Cortés, however, the third governor—yet another treasurer—exiled him and in 1527 installed the first royal government, a council of five men called the *Real Audiencia*. Cortés sailed to Spain, where he politicked successfully at court and with the pope. He came back to Mexico in 1530 with a ringing title, Marquis of the Valley of Oaxaca; a decidedly noble wife, Doña Juana de Zúñiga; a license to explore the Pacific; and a papal bull to legitimize his son by Malintzin. His was suddenly the third-richest family in the entire Spanish aristocracy. But he was also barred from Mexico City until a new government could arrive, and subsequently spent much of his time on the other side of the mountains in the warmth of his Cuernavaca estate, or hatching plans for unprofitable expeditions, sometimes accompanying them. When he returned to Spain in 1539 he was ordered to stay there until his audit, a decade in the making, was completed; it never was, and he died in a small town near Seville seven years later.[18]

Government by conquistador was not synonymous with government by Cortés or his long-time captains. The first Real Audiencia was run briefly by an arriviste conquistador, Nuño de Guzmán, who came late to the takeover of Mexico in 1527. He was a shockingly bad choice—incompetent, disputatious, in the end murderous—and was quickly dispatched: first to the west, where he killed and burned his way through peaceable towns, then to the north, where he wasted his own men, and then back to Spain in chains. In his place came the steady hands of the Bishop of Santo Domingo and four new *oidores*, councilors from outside Mexico. Adding more weight to royal government came the viceroys, who began their centuries of rule in 1535. For a while the conquistadors retained significant power, not just as wealthy individuals but also in institutional form as members of the ayuntamiento or cabildo, the council that ran Mexico City, the only body with the armed power and local knowledge to control the indigenous population. The ayuntamiento's territorial grasp actually extended rather than contracted in the first years of royal rule, the city jurisdiction defined as radiating some thirty miles from the center (except to the south, where it stopped at the boundaries of Cortés's estate). But it was a finite balance of power. The first generation of conquistador families maintained appreciable leverage vis-à-vis the Crown, and thanks to it their encomiendas; when the New Laws of 1542 decreed that those grants should not be heritable, vehement protests preserved them for a second generation.[19] That generation lost them in the 1560s, when an alleged conspiracy led by Cortés's three sons justified the Crown's ending the conquistadors' hereditary political positions, selling off their vacant seats on the cabildo, and appointing a Spanish bureaucrat to oversee the survivors.[20]

Their overthrow started with a series of arrests in 1566 of many of the city's bright young things, accused of plotting a coup against the audiencia that was to be followed by a declaration of independence and a Cortesian monarchy, backed by Franciscans and indigenous noblemen. Several Spaniards were tortured; two were hanged. Whether there was a conspiracy at all is questionable. The eldest Cortés, Malintzin's son Martín, was the city's chief constable, his unenviable job being to mediate between Spanish and Mexica. The younger Martín Cortés, son of a distinguished Spanish mother, was the Marquis of the Valley of Oaxaca. Unlike his brother, the marquis was a swaggering loudmouth who talked to other swaggering loudmouths about the conquistadors' hereditary rights and claims to *hidalguía*. It was a nervous time, worsened by the sudden death of a diplomatic viceroy, Luis de Velasco, in 1564. The Chichimeca were nowhere near defeat; they would be capable of raiding within fifty miles of Mexico City years down the line. The population of mestizos, indigenous, and Blacks in Mexico City had grown dramatically, the last particularly feared as potential urban cadres in a broader indigenous rebellion. The city-dwelling Mexica were outraged by new taxes, the first they had been asked to pay since the fall of Tenochtitlán. The Spanish were frightened that the emperor planned to dispossess them, ending the hereditary status of their encomiendas. The symbolism of the new viceregal palace, established in 1562 on Cortés's former mansion, itself standing on the ruins of Montezuma's palace, was unmissable.

So a certain paranoia among the royal bureaucrats was eminently understandable. The new viceroyalty of Peru had disintegrated after a conquistador rebellion in 1544; this opened the space for a resurgent Inca kingdom, which in turn backed Taki Unquy, a religious mass rebellion that broke out across the Andes in 1564 and was far from over in 1567. But a real estate deal, an angry protest march, and some entitled whinging do not a rebellion make. There is no hard evidence of a plot, and when tortured, Malintzin's son had nothing to say. The emperor would not have subsequently extended the conquistadors' encomiendas to a third generation if he believed them traitorous. The events of the late 1560s were nevertheless pivotal in the exclusion of creoles, Spaniards born in the Americas, from political power. They evolved something of a dual identity, Spanish and at the same time Mexican, a name they adopted early on.

Creoles were in many ways the obvious personnel to run the viceroyalty, but they were shut out from the top jobs, and across nearly three centuries only four were ever viceroy. They became, rather, second-class citizens and targets of undisguised racism: According to *peninsulares*, Spaniards born in Spain, the creoles—even if white and of the same bloodlines—were biologically inferior. American stars were different from European stars, and the creoles who labored under them would inevitably become degenerate like natives. (The British would later feel similarly about their own men in India.)[21] That degeneration, though an acquired characteristic, was hereditary through blood, semen, and breast milk. This Lamarckian idea was influential enough that even creoles espoused it. Mexico's first novelist, José Joaquín Fernández de

Lizardi, lamented in his 1816 classic *El periquillo sarniento* (*The Mangy Parrot*) that his mother had passed him around a series of wet nurses, because

> the first foods that nourish us lead us to acquire some of the properties of those who administer them . . . my first wet nurse was of an accursed nature, and so I came out ill-natured, and a lot worse given that it wasn't just the one who put me to her breasts, but rather one today, another the next, yet another the day after that, and all of them, or at least most of them, very bad; because the one who wasn't a drunkard was a glutton; the one who wasn't a glutton was syphilitic; the one that hadn't this evil had another . . . and these were just the diseases of the body, while it would be rare that those of the spirit were any lesser.[22]

This from a bitter critic of Spanish rule. Spain's nobles looked down on the conquistadors on grounds of class; they disapproved of their descendants, whether mestizo or white, on grounds of race.[23]

The exercise and reach of indigenous political power was in some ways more stable than that of the Spanish victors. There were profound differences between the peoples of the North, whose harsh environment ruled out cities, favored nomadism, and kept foreigners at bay; the Nahua and Mixtec of the central and southern highlands, numerous, who clustered in longstanding towns and cities; and farthest south the Maya, who spoke diverse tongues and were distributed from the cloud forest of Chiapas to the dry limestone plains of Yucatán. There was no single indigenous world: The Indian conquistadors of urban Tlaxcala had next to nothing in common with the Apache. For the majority of indigenous groups, however, there was the shared characteristic of surprisingly little change for the first century of Spanish rule.

Arguing for continuity in any facet of indigenous life is counterintuitive for peoples who were experiencing massive population collapse and a would-be cultural revolution. The personnel of the central valley's indigenous royal dynasties had shifted dramatically: excised in Tenochtitlán, transferred to a different family branch in Texcoco, handed over to a twelve-year-old godson of Cortés in Tlaxcala. In the cities the conquistadors replaced the tlatoani, the most important royal institution, with governorships. Outside the cities the more depopulated or far-flung indigenous villages were disappeared by the Spanish policy of congregación, which forcibly concentrated their inhabitants into larger units easier to oversee, tax, and convert. Spanish organizations replaced the institutions that were the building blocks of indigenous power. The Nahua *altepetl*, Maya *cah*, and Mixtec *ñuu*, all city-states in microcosm, with their own authorities, tutelary gods, histories, cultural identities, and markets, were subsumed into Spanish cabildos. In place of navigating the demands and aspirations of a single set of pre-Hispanic powerholders, the indigenous peoples now had to manage the often conflicting demand of two sets of masters in the persons of missionaries and secular Spaniards. Tlaxcala, as before the alien arrival, was the only exception, a kingdom that preserved its territorial, administrative, and fiscal autonomy while the aggressive new central power settled down next door.

Yet even among the losers forced to navigate these seemingly dramatic political shifts, the picture changes markedly once the focus on high government and the handful of histories of its vicissitudes is swapped for a look at humbler politics and more modest sources. The unglamorous paperwork of everyday life—notarial records, wills, land deeds, and town charters—tells a different story of indigenous continuity. Even where the Spanish presence was heaviest, most survivors got on with life much as they had before, using renamed institutions to preserve older social relationships. The *altepeme* might be redubbed a *pueblo de indios* but it generally preserved its boundaries and kin-based local government, a relative autonomy in internal affairs enshrined in Spanish law.[24] The most destructive Spanish policies were accommodated if necessary: Congregación might be enforced by Franciscans burning people's houses but it was also sometimes seen in hindsight as producing stronger homelands. Encomenderos, with all their potential for abuse and rapacity, were excluded from the villages, their Spanish and African overseers in the end dependent on indigenous leaders. Villagers rarely saw the new foreign overlords, whom they provided indirectly with tribute and labor through the old mechanisms of communal production and *coatequitl* or *tequio*, communal public service, all administered by their old lords. Those might be redubbed *gobernadores* instead of caciques or tlatoani, but they did the same job and often came from the same families.[25]

They were also among the few, outside the main cities, to become comfortable in Spanish. Until the mid-seventeenth century Indians adopted convenient words from Spanish but not much else, because they had very little reason to do so; their everyday lives did not depend on fluency and, with mass said in Latin (and often in their own languages), neither did their eternal lives. Revealingly enough, the Spanish largely gave up pushing their language as a universal standard as they moved out of the center, promoting Nahuatl as a lingua franca in the North and Maya in the South, where even the creole elites learned it out of necessity. A third of all books produced in the sixteenth century were written in indigenous languages. Some canonical works of European literature made it into Nahuatl, such as the playwright Lope de Vega's *Fuenteovejuna*—a morality tale condemning aristocratic rape, apt amid the sexual violence of some colonial relationships—which a Texcocan nobleman translated in the seventeenth century.[26] Hundreds of years later, rancher children across Mexico were still learning the basics of their area's indigenous languages.

Fundamental change in Indian government in the fertile, densely settled areas that produced decent tribute would have been costly and unnecessary, and in some cases the viceroyalty allowed local communities more rather than less autonomy. Local pride and corporate identity—a sort of village patriotism—survived in the center in the *xiuhpohualli*, alphabetic Nahuatl accounts of the indigenous past and near present. The names of the vast majority of altepeme were not lost but lengthened—it probably helped that Nahuatl, like German, is sympathetic to compound nouns—by tacking on a patron saint's name, often whoever happened to be having a feast day when the first missionaries arrived or the first church was built.[27] The division between religious and secular authority at the lay level was smoothed over by a revolving door between the two sets of officials. The net result, clear in the lack of the contact points of a shared language, was an indigenous rural world that changed comparatively little and slowly, keeping to itself, until the last decades of the seventeenth century.[28]

In the cities incentives and pressures to learn Spanish and join a new, hybrid society moved rather faster. Even in those very different contexts, though, there was a surprising degree of indigenous political continuity among the new institutions and amid the infighting of the Spanish. Tlaxcala, as a reward for its service, remained an untouched confederation of four altepeme with their own aristocracies. They still fought on occasion with the Nauha below, sending troops into Mexico City to help the Spanish put down riots.[29] The old families of the Valley of Mexico rebounded fast, promoted by the new viceroy and audiencia after the fall of that first, chaotic conquistador government. In Texcoco the line of Nezahualpilli, the patriarch who died just before the Spanish invasion, was restored to the throne. Don Hernando ruled for thirty years, an astute player who wrote regularly to the emperor and obtained recognition of Texcoco as a city with a coat of arms and a tlatoani, an indigenous monarchy until the end of the sixteenth century. While the title changed then to the Spanish *gobernador*, the institution and the family endured until the nineteenth century; meanwhile, the main nobles either served their old functions of running the city under new Spanish titles or else pulled the strings from behind the scenes.[30] The other regions with long-established cities, the South and Southeast, also continued under the administration of the old indigenous nobility. During the first decades after Spanish arrival they were indispensable to the point that even rebellion could be pardoned. In 1546 a coalition of eastern Maya in Yucatán tried to sweep the Spanish into the sea in the Great Revolt; though defeated, every single one of their caciques stayed in power.[31]

Finally, there was continuity in the least likely place of all, the ground zero of Tenochtitlán, where the Montezuma family returned to power and kept hold of it, with the odd interregnum, until the 1620s. *Gobernadores* to the Spanish, indigenous documents dubbed them tlatoani, emperors. They and other indigenous nobles ruled from a palace relocated to the southwest of the island, supported by the tribute and labor of the altepetl, as they had been before their defeat. They controlled the distribution and cultivation of the chinampas, the floating gardens vital to feeding the city. They ran the main business of the city, the huge market of the west side; the Spanish ran the small market of the plaza mayor, catering to their minority in their small area of the city. The Nahua nobility even named the market after one of their leaders, the *cihuacóatl*—a tlatoani's main deputy—Juan Velázques Tlactozin, Cuauhtémoc's nephew. The Spanish may have used the rhetoric of the tabula rasa to describe the resurgent city, and the downtown of the traza was indeed built from scratch on the classic Spanish grid system of a downtown of mansions, churches, and government buildings centered on a plaza. As a whole, however, Mexico City remained largely un-Hispanicized. This was perhaps not all that surprising: It was the urbanites of the indigenous nobility who actually understood the business of running a great city, not the provincial conquistadors.[32]

Across occupied Mexico indigenous political continuity declined around the middle of the seventeenth century and changed significantly once Habsburgs gave way to modernizing Bourbons. By then mestizos had been marrying into powerful indigenous families for generations, in the process adopting the standards and rules of those families and their communities. Local mistrust of interlopers gave them little choice. After 1650 Spanish language and culture spread wider roots: The Nahua chronicles of the *xiuhpohualli* moved toward the decadence of keeping accounts rather than memories, and caciques began to act more like hacendados, seeing common lands as alienable. The thin carapace of extractive Spanish rule, not concerned with much more than peace and reliable tribute, thickened with new involvement in the altepetl.[33] In the long run, though, everyone is dead, and this was in the center some six generations after the first Spanish arrived and declared Mexico subject to their far-off king.

The conquistadors, their creole descendants, and uneasy indigenous cohabitants were not the only rivals to European royal government. The Church collaborated with but also oversaw the local agents of the Crown. Churchmen enjoyed the spiritual power of possessing the keys to heaven and the pardon from hell. They also held earthier power as literate administrators, the shortage of which made them irritating but essential partners in government. The entire administration of the Indies from 1493 to 1524 ran through a single ministry, the Casa de

Contratación in Seville, which lay in the hands of a single cleric, Bishop Juan Rodríguez de Fonseca. The head of the first Franciscan mission to Mexico, Martín de Valencia, immediately claimed civil and criminal jurisdiction from the Mexico City ayuntamiento; the first competent head of the audiencia was Bishop Sebastián Ramírez de Fuenleal. When a civil viceroy became unavailable—by death or disgrace—his position was generally assumed by a prelate, a safe pair of hands, until a replacement arrived. They were sometimes more than just safe hands, and in the first century of Spanish rule prelates twice hastened their predecessor's fall, in 1584 by audit and in 1624 by coup.[34] The plotter of 1584, Archbishop Pedro Moya de Contreras, was briefly the most powerful man in the Americas: Viceroy, Archbishop, Captain-General, and Inquisitor-General of New Spain all rolled into one.[35]

The Church itself was no smooth-faced monolith. It was instead an umbrella term for several discrete agencies: the priesthood, organized territorially in parishes; and the four mendicant orders, Franciscans, Dominicans, Augustinians, and Jesuits. They were not in the least brotherly, and competition among them for souls, tithes, and buildings was complicated and hard-edged from the start. It stretched back to Europe: In Florence the Franciscans had destroyed the Dominican rabble-rouser Girolamo Savonarola in 1498. In the New World rivalries were exacerbated by opportunity and independence. The Franciscans had Mexico to themselves for only two years, and the Dominicans who joined them in 1526 immediately took the opposing side in the conquistadors' faction-fighting. Conflict was attenuated by a geographical division of labor: The Franciscans, the first arrivals and a majority across the colonial period, predominated in central Mexico, the northern frontier, and Yucatán; the Dominicans in the South and parts of the West; and the Jesuits, later arrivals, in the North. The Augustinians didn't count much territorially, providing only one in every forty friars, and ended up with only islands of rule across the center. (Perhaps because of that they solicited permission to convert China.)[36] The boundaries overlapped, though, and the orders quarreled vigorously in the cities where they rubbed up against one another. In Puebla, for example, Franciscans, Dominicans, and Augustinians all competed for souls and livings, which they amassed in quantities large enough to infuriate both bishop and priests.

To the Dominicans, the Franciscans were empire-building heretics. They built sumptuous monasteries and churches where there was no need and through naivety or dishonesty promulgated unsound doctrines.[37] Their industrial approach to conversion produced token Christians whose lack of basic knowledge threatened the Church. To the Franciscans, the Dominicans were armchair opportunists and arrivistes. The conflict between the two orders threatened positions and even freedom. When the Dominicans controlled the Inquisition they singled out Juan de Zumárraga, the Franciscan archbishop and leader of the first evangelization, as heretical: His *Doctrina Cristiana* did not promote the true faith but instead subverted it with its teachings on the blood of Christ. (God had collected some of it, Zumárraga wrote, in order to revive Jesus—a bit close to the bone among ex-enthusiasts for human sacrifice.)[38] Meanwhile the Franciscan Motolinía, the great protector of Indians, attacked that other great protector of Indians, the Dominican bishop Bartolomé de las Casas, as a windbag who didn't actually speak any indigenous languages. When Las Casas left his southern diocese of Chiapas to go to Spain (by traveling chair) in order to denounce the conquistadors' abuses of Indians, Motolinía, far from supporting a like-minded peer, accused Las Casas of sedition and apostasy for abandoning his diocese. The bishop should be confined, he argued, to a monastery cell for his lapses.[39]

This was the beginning of a struggle whose complexity increased when the Company of Jesus, the pope's shock troops in the fight against Protestantism, arrived in 1572. The Jesuits horrified members of the earlier monastic orders with their worldly realpolitik; one Dominican described them as a "cunning generation [that] studies purposely how to insinuate themselves with kings, princes, great men, rulers, and commanders."[40] The Jesuits did indeed enjoy a direct line to Philip II, whom they convinced with arguments regarding the shortage of priests in Mexico and the successes of their deployment elsewhere in his empire.[41] They obtained royal decrees to advance their own empire, staking claim to chapter houses and colleges in Veracruz, Guadalajara, Guatemala City, and Zacatecas, and winning substantial private donations: wheat haciendas, livestock herds, and mills. In the seventeenth century the Jesuits' herds of sheep ran into the hundreds of thousands; in the eighteenth century they operated the largest and most advanced sugar plantations, collectively the largest slaveowner in the Americas.[42] But they focused above all on education as their path for advancement.[43] By 1578 they had founded four colleges; one of their first requests was to take over the wealthy Franciscan college of San Juan de Letrán in the heart of Mexico City.[44]

Beyond Jesuit turf grabs, two other major divisions roiled churchmen in Mexico. The first lay between the squabbling friars and the parish priests. These later-arriving clergymen lived individually rather than communally, were bound by no monastic rule, and owed allegiance only to their church superiors. Conflict between these two very different species of churchmen grew across the second half of the century. In 1574 the *Ordenanza del Patronazgo* officially gave parish priests precedence over the friars. Priests never outnumbered friars, but their power grew steadily, and by the mid-seventeenth century they had the upper hand in terms of controlling bishoprics. The new power was etched on the landscape: In the countryside monasteries decayed while in the cities new churches and cathedrals rose.

At the root of the change lay money. Money that went to a priest in the form of the *diezmo*, the tithe equivalent to a 10 percent income tax, was money that no longer went to friars—if they collected it in the first place—and congregants who began attending a parish rather than a mission church for mass were lost constituents. So friars told their flocks that the new arrivals lacked the power to charge tithes or to understand their language or who they were—the latter charges quite often true—and told their superiors that priests were corrupt, entrepreneurial in the wrong sense, selling everything from candles to sacraments. The mutual loathing, institutional and personal, came out in lawsuits, lengthy processions through courts in Mexico City and Spain. In the countryside it came out in fisticuffs, iconoclasm, arson, imprisonment, grave robbery, and murder.

Early conflicts were particularly intense in Michoacán, where an empathetic and egomaniacal visionary, Bishop Vasco de Quiroga, fought Augustinians and Franciscans in his quest to establish an indigenous utopia. In the summer of 1560, while a court case over his authority dragged on in Spain, a group of Quiroga's men declared war on newly arrived Augustinians in the town of Tlazazalca. Fighting began in May, when the parish priest and cathedral choirmaster Don

Diego Pérez Gordillo y Negrón led armed men into the monastery church to destroy the baptismal font. A week later Gordillo came back and broke up an improvised baptism, allegedly killing the baby in the process. On June 13 he demanded that the Indians give him, not the friars, the decorations they had made for the Feast of Corpus Christi; when they refused he punched the indigenous mayor in the face and jailed his men. On June 23 Quiroga's thugs burned the monastery down, jailed witnesses, and then went back to court. A year later the priest completed his village jihad by digging up the bodies of dead friars from the former monastery, some still rotting, making onlookers retch from the smell. It was strong stuff, even by Michoacán standards, and it brought Gordillo back to Spain to answer charges; backed by Bishop Quiroga, he seems to have survived them.[45]

The final division between churchmen was ethnic, pitting mestizos against whites and peninsulares against creoles. It too could be violent.[46] Yet none of this would have surprised the lower-class population, who frequently saw clerics behaving badly. As New Spain aged, the priesthood attracted its fair share of shysters and wastrels, frequently the second sons of well-off families, and downright impostors.[47] The protagonist of *The Mangy Parrot* is told in no uncertain terms of the benefits of the job:

> Look: a clergyman is well regarded everywhere, everyone venerates and respects him even if he's a fool, and they cover up his flaws; no one dares to contradict them or accuse them of anything; they have a seat at the best balls, the best card tables, and even in the ladies' seats they aren't scorned; and last of all they never lack a dime, even if it comes from a Mass mumbled badly on the hoof. So don't be silly, study to be a priest.[48]

The corruption the author described was the least of it. The ecclesiastical higher-ups frequently investigated their parish priests for sexual abuse, assault, and rape, particularly of indigenous women. Friars were supposed to have prostitutes who specialized in their ilk, *putas fraileras*, which may explain why two of them helped a prominent Mexico City madam escape jail time.[49] Eighteenth-century inquisitors spent much time listening for pick-up lines in the shadowy mutterings of the confessional; three times as many priests were caught seducing "daughters of confession" in New Spain as in Spain.[50] Some devout parishioners accordingly hated their lecherous local clerics; one Maya group prayed, "God willing that smallpox be rubbed into their penis heads. Amen."[51]

For such churchmen it was good news that the Spanish Inquisition, once it came to Mexico, lost most of its teeth. In the nationalist mythology of independent Mexico, the Santo Oficio was an all-powerful institution of luridly depraved cynics, torturers, and sexual deviants; in reality it was a far more banal collection of bureaucrats, incapable of dealing with their inboxes.[52] Neither were there many inquisitors. Until 1700 only one tribunal covered all Spanish possessions north of Panama, three the entire Western Hemisphere. Together these guardians of orthodoxy managed less than three thousand trials.[53] In many places no inquisitors could be found at all; the Mexico City central office was run by two or three men.[54] Results were therefore understandably lacking. Between 1665 and 1703 the Mexican Inquisition burned all of sixteen heretics in the main square of Mexico City; far less than the Inquisition in Spain, less even than the good folk of Salem hanged in a single year, and orders of magnitude away from the witch-burnings of seventeenth-century Scotland.[55] After 1703 they never burned anyone ever again.[56]

Yet while the Church's assorted agencies were fractured and their representatives riven by human flaws, they shared a common ground beyond ideology. Churchmen everywhere were key political players in the early modern world: "Render unto Caesar the things which are Caesar's" did not apply to the sixteenth-century church, particularly not in Spain (although it was a safer place to be a political ecclesiastic than Tudor England, where Thomas Wolsey was accused of treason, Thomas More beheaded for it, and Thomas Cranmer burned for it). Clerics exercised soft power through education, business, and social services, their success most obvious when they prevented urban riot from escalating into rebellion. When in 1692 crowds of Indians set fire to the government buildings and market stalls of Mexico City, the treasurer of the cathedral went out at dusk with the Holy Sacrament and persuaded the rioters to go home peacefully.[57] Friars and priests also exercised hard power, above all on the frontiers, colonizers who drew on the violence of the nearest Spanish settlers and were sometimes quite violent themselves. They were essential to Spanish rule from the beginning to the end of the Habsburg Empire. And they were powerful enough for men like Vasco de Quiroga to dream of ruling alone, barring civilians and making New Spain a religious utopia.

On paper, however, the Church was unusually subject to the Crown in Mexico. The *reyes católicos* had negotiated a particularly uncatholic exception to universal papal authority for the entire New World, the *patronato real*. Under its terms any cleric wishing to go to the Americas needed royal permission; there was no papal legate and no direct contact between the pope and his representatives in the Indies. Papal bulls might be ignored.[58] A political church was no archaicism; wholly token prelates, like Talleyrand, were key players in the run-up to the French Revolution centuries later. But it was intended by the Crown quite consciously as one component of a much-enlarged and newly professional bureaucracy, packed—for the first time in history—with lawyers.

The majority of the more distinguished *letrados* came from a single elite institution, the Colegio Mayor de San Bartolomé at the University of Salamanca.[59] At the lowest level in the Indies, however, early lawyers were not the pick of the crop. The paleography of some seventeenth-century documents from provincial archives is telling, with the handwriting's stuttering, uneven lines, the ink blots, and the words that at times break in half and after a space resume their course with uncertain logic. But the institutional distribution of power was logical. Local residents could not profitably be shut out of politics, and so indigenous villages and Spanish towns were run by indigenous councils and creole ayuntamientos, both constituted through limited elections. They were overseen by outside appointees: *alcaldes*, mayors, for Spaniards, *corregidores*, correctors, for Indians. These were appointed by councils of royal officials based in the main cities, the audiencias, their members-at-large called *oídores*, hearers. The audiencias combined in a single body legislative, legal, and some executive powers and reported to the viceroy, the vice-king. Quasi-regal by force of distance from the metropole, the viceroy was nonetheless constrained by mulish underlings, turbulent priests, and the end-of-term audits conducted by metropolitan officials called *visitadores*, visitors. The terminology of hierarchy—visitors, correctors, hearers—encapsulates the principle of power in colonial Mexico: checks and balances or, in terms less Montesquieu and more Machiavelli, divide and rule.

The first viceroy, Antonio de Mendoza, arrived in 1535; the last, Juan Ruiz de Apodaca, departed at Independence in 1821. The first generation of royal officials had unenviable jobs, tasked with subordinating inherently insubordinate conquistadors and Indians, and they often died in mysterious circumstances. The early viceroys of New Spain, though, survived and prospered in two key areas where conquistadors failed. One was war: Mendoza opened a path to the north by dint of winning the Mixton Rebellion in 1542, ending a conflict that at one point had tens of thousands besieging the region's only city, Guadalajara. The other was long-range exploration: In 1557 Mendoza's successor, Luis de Velasco, put together the ships and men to send a flotilla across the Pacific. This was the first real flexing of the Crown's muscles, the viceroy appropriating as much as half a million pesos to follow Philip's instructions "to explore the Islands of the West, and colonize them, and put them in good order."[60] The people of New Spain were taught to welcome viceroys with baroque ritual: streets lined with ceremonial arches, progressions of townsmen in their finest, pacing slowly in intricately ordered hierarchy, Indians coached into decorous submission, Masses sung in the cathedrals of Puebla and Mexico City. The best viceroys were worth the obeisance because they faced serious and systemic obstacles to doing their job.

For a start, viceroys were almost always peninsulares, aristocratic outsiders appointed because of family connections, court politics, or royal whimsy, shipped across in pomp, and dropped into places of which they knew little. Their quality as they passed through gilded exile was predictably variable. Some triumphed as leaders and technocrats: Mendoza won the Mixton War and introduced the merino breed of sheep, Velasco's revolutionary Pacific expedition was a success, and the Count of Revillagigedo introduced a plethora of life-improving infrastructure ranging from highways to barroom toilets. Other viceroys fell short; all were mistrusted by both their subjects and their bosses.

Philip II, considering the corrupting effects of absolute power and distance, laid down revealingly strict rules. Viceroys were not to hand out tips, bonuses, or salary increases. They couldn't employ friends or relatives. They couldn't marry family members off to the locals. They couldn't accept loans or gifts of so much as a bottle of wine. They should "conduct themselves such that their life and manners might set a good example to those of the land." Life as a viceroy was supposed to be dull.[61]

The viceroys saw things rather differently. They longed for boring, their reports made clear; instead they had jobs from hell, besieged by people from uppity Indian litigants to grumpy local worthies and obstreperous bureaucrats. Churchmen were essential, they admitted, but many were fools or backstabbing knaves. They themselves, the king's alter egos, were penurious and staved off existential threats through hard work and political brilliance. The tropes were enduring, reflecting real frustration; they also reflected the fact that viceroys invested fortunes in winning appointment and had limited time to recoup the money. They knew perfectly well that they would be subjected to an audit by a Crown visitador at the end of their reigns and their profiteering questioned, and they tried to get their versions of events in first. The life of a viceroy was a tricky balancing act between the public-minded and the self-serving, but the two were not inherently opposed, and the best viceroys got things done even as they grafted. The far-off Crown had little option anyway but to rely on venal servants, flaws and all.

On the other side of the Atlantic the Spanish side of the equation was autocratically simpler. The Casa de Contratación on the Seville waterfront grew from a one-man customs house into a bureaucratic machine, with totalitarian ambitions to control everyone and everything that traveled the seaways. It in turn was subordinate to the lawyers and clerics of the *Real y Supremo Consejo de las Indias*, the Council of the Indies: executive, legislature, and supreme court rolled into one. All members were unelected; in the pursuit of the same divide-and-rule, all were also from the gentry or minor aristocracy. This was not just caution against overmighty subjects but also shrewdly meritocratic design; the sons of the great lords did not tend to go to university. They might, like Mendoza or Velasco, have training from birth for the sweeping executive tasks of a viceroy. But they were not generally trained in the niceties and tedium of paperwork, and across the sixteenth century the weight of paper required to administer a global empire grew heavy.

In Mexico bureaucracy began in the provinces, with the records of the mayor's or corregidor's administrative decisions and their verdicts in the pettiest of cases, such as the "suit for payment for some wooden beams brought by Nicolás Raya de Palos against José Gómez de Santiago."[62] The audiencias received their reports from below, their own cases and instructions from above, and wrote further reports and letters for the viceroy. The viceroys decided what to do about them and sent dispatches to the Council of the Indies, which digested them and sent on summaries and recommendations to the royal secretaries, who in turn prepared briefs for the king. Time added administrative layers; in the seventeenth century small specialist committees formed to help the council decide what did and didn't count and what should be done about it all. It was at this point in history that complaints about paperwork, a conversational staple of modern life, emerged. Whinging about pen-pushing became formulaic in a viceroy's letters, alongside the moans about useless subjects, insolent underlings, and the crises that these would doubtless cause despite the self-sacrificing zeal of the viceroy in question.[63] At the top of it all sat the king, who—supposedly at least—read everything, reflected, and then handed down decisions and himself wrote letters to his representatives across the empire. Philip II, who ruled Spain for nearly sixty years, did just that, reading, writing, and micromanaging the empire through its bureaucratic revolution. Fittingly enough, in his last year on the throne he began the division of the council into committees, the ancestors of modern ministries.[64]

Philip II was suited for the job by character: earnest, hardworking, and austere, all qualities reflected in the combined monastery and palace he built outside Madrid, El Escorial, a dour hilltop compound with all the seductive charm of a barracks. Madrid itself he turned into the permanent seat of government, the settled bureaucratic center that the empire lacked. He interjected himself into every aspect of a fast-changing and growing European state, from university curricula to priestly garb.[65] Yet there was more than personal inclination behind the long days and stream of instructions on the minutiae of empire. There was the strategic imperative of learning how to deal with vast territories and international warfare on an unprecedented geographical scale. And finally there was a cultural expectation of success, a habit of winning, that came through in places as disparate as national literature, Spanish infantry formations, and a refusal to learn other peoples' languages. Philip's reign was the peak of not just hard but also soft Spanish power, the *Siglo de Oro*, when playwrights, sonneteers, and the world's first novelist drew on classical, Arabic, and Italian influences to change their respective genres and reshape European culture. Spanish physicians moved across Europe, their mystique increased by Mexican herbaria, making Castilian, Catalan, and Portuguese scientific languages second only to Latin. Meanwhile Spain's representatives abroad remained strikingly, literally monoglot: the universal symptom and privilege of imperial accomplishment and arrogance.[66] They themselves knew it full well: "Language," the great grammarian Antonio de Nebrija wrote—back in 1492—"has always been the companion of empire."[67]

For all Philip's bureaucratic intent, however, he never managed to assemble a single coherent law code for New Spain. He oversaw the *Recopilación de las leyes de Castilla*, published in 1567, but its colonial parallel was only finalized in 1680, in the twilight of his dynasty. In 1700 the last of his line, the sickly Charles the Mad, died childless. The French successor dynasty, the Bourbons, brought a new zeal to broadening and enforcing the rational aims of an absolutist monarchy: heightened taxation, government monopolies, deferential churchmen, and the suppression of local creole oligarchies and their corrupt ways, all backed up by a peninsular military. Philip II would have approved of much of it in theory; in practice he was left waiting for a law code that never came.

The delay was eminently pardonable. It was indicative of the hands-off approach, at least de facto, of nearly two centuries of Habsburg monarchs in the Americas. It also stemmed from a contradictory de jure complexity, with metropolitan laws and viceregal decrees piling up across decades in an uneven heap of ambitious regulation. There were two distinct law codes for two distinct legal entities, the *república de indios*, which covered the hundred-plus indigenous peoples, and the *república de españoles*, which covered everyone else: Spaniards, Africans,

Asians, and all possible permutations. The coherence of those laws was not as important as the tension between an ideal of neat centralization and the reality of a messy, fluid, decentralized society.

In that society laws could be ignored. Ships were supposed to carry safe levels of freight; they sailed leaky and loaded to the gunwales, their masters blithely ignoring Philip II's assorted laws on the matter.[68] All aboard were supposed to carry state papers, registering their name, job, place of origin, age, and even physical description; the Casa de Contratación knew, for example, that Diego Fernández of Granada, who sailed in 1631, was thirty years old, "brown-skinned" (suspicious, given he came from a once-Muslim city), "with a large mole on the left wrist, lacking teeth in his upper jaw."[69] Nonetheless some ships sailed with twice as many voyagers as were registered, bringing in a considerable number of undocumented immigrants. In one mining town only half the whites had the necessary papers.[70] The Crown banned slavery more than once; the herds of branded men of the 1520s disappeared, but on the frontiers a profitable reality endured. Philip IV banned brothels; nothing came of it.[71] Blacks and mulattos were not supposed to carry guns; one of the master gunsmiths in Mexico City was a mulatto.[72] Indians were not allowed to hold more than small herds of sheep and pigs; some indigenous nobles possessed large herds of cattle.[73] When mixed with universal access to courts—this was a promiscuously litigious society, where indigenous plaintiffs generally won—the upshot was gridlock. Widespread tolerance for the state of affairs and grudging recognition of the law helped ensure that creoles did not become overmighty subjects, Indians did not revolt, and peninsulares went only slightly native. Most important for all involved, smugglers flouted on a massive scale the laws that specified what could or could not be traded across the ocean, and by 1680 French contraband alone constituted as much as 40 percent of all exports to Spanish America.[74] The viceroy might decree on pain of death that all silver go straight from the pithead to the Casa de la Fundición in Mexico City, the royal foundry, but huge amounts wandered elsewhere. By the late seventeenth century about half of all silver that crossed the Atlantic was smuggled.[75]

Yet throughout this period the bare essentials of colonial law and government worked. The encomiendas, the Crown's early grants of

Indian labor and lands to the conquistadors, were quickly recognized as exploitative and economically inefficient. In the gravest cases encomenderos alienated indigenous groups who had the wherewithal to do something about it, and revolt ensued: The Mixton War was basically a reaction to land grabs, according to one indigenous witness. Those rebels were only put down by a massive concentration of forces commanded by the viceroy himself.[76] Abolishing the institution would have been political madness, as officials on the ground well knew, and the encomenderos survived the first royal attack, the New Laws of 1542, because Viceroy Mendoza simply omitted to enforce them. The law limiting encomiendas to a single generation didn't stick either, and it was not state power but rather population collapse and indigenous litigation that drove the late-sixteenth-century transition to a less dictatorial and exploitative—and consequently more sustainable—form of great estate: the hacienda.

The haciendas' coexistence with Indian villages was conflictual over centuries, but functioning courts kept boundary disputes within bounds. Hacendados only rarely drove pueblos into rebellion or out of existence. Indigenous forced labor endured in many guises, such as labor drafts, debt peonage, and sharecropping, but these were not the same as the chattel slavery of the early years. Viceroys and their underlings often milked their posts for all they were worth, but at the end faced a visitador who, if dour enough, could forestall enjoyment of their profits. Habsburg monarchs got the fundamentals of what they wanted from New Spain. They kept the lid on a society thousands of miles away, so far away that when Philip IV died it took eight months for Mexicans to find out.[77] They did this without spending much money on a military, not a land-based military at least. They excluded their European rivals from the wealthiest and most accessible parts of the hemisphere. And under their rule Spain secured the extraction, conveyance, and taxation of unprecedented amounts of silver, making the Americas the center of a new global economy.

The ships that were the blood cells of that economy carried not just trade but also culture. By the early seventeenth century Pacific fleets had brought Mexico a Japanese embassy and a delight in things Asian. It is unlikely that they brought the *Tao Te Ching*, that classic of Chinese political thought, with them; the first Jesuit missionaries to China, arriving a generation earlier, ignored it in favor of Confucianism. It is pretty certain that no one in power in the Habsburg Empire ever read the *Tao*.[78] Had they done so, though, they might have recognized some of its less gnomic advice on governing an empire, such as the recommendation that "the best of all rulers is but a shadowy presence to his subjects." A quiet appreciation of the benefits of enlightened minimalism is not manifest in viceroys' letters, but it does come through in their actions, or rather their strategic inactions. That appreciation stretched up to the Habsburg emperors, embodied in *Obedezco pero no cumplo*, or in putting troublesome underlings in legal limbo rather than jail, or indeed in not calling Mexico a colony. New Spain was a viceroyalty, a semiautonomous kingdom, formally on a par with European territories such as Aragon, Valencia, and Italy. The Habsburgs' less malleable successors, the Bourbons, might have benefited from the same appreciation, summed up in the *Tao*'s ultimate plea for modesty in government:

> Whoever takes the empire and wishes to do anything to it I see will have no respite. The empire is a sacred vessel and nothing should be done to it. Whoever does anything to it will ruin it; whoever lays hold of it will lose it.[79]

Chapter Six

Traveling, Knowing, and Trading

It was very difficult to cross the ocean, and very difficult to know what was happening on the other side, but all it took was a small amount of traveling and trading to change drastically the lives of the world's people. Spain's occupation of the Americas was possibly the greatest case of unintended consequences in history; hoping to find a quicker route to the spices and textiles of Asia, their sailors bumped into the other half of the world. The subsequent comings and goings of a mere two ships a year between Manila and Acapulco and one fleet between Veracruz and Seville brought revolution to the global economy. They created it, in fact. Those voyages also made Mexico the world's first wholly multicultural place, the first-ever nexus for travelers, migrants, and traders from the Americas, Asia, Africa, and Europe. The prophet Isaiah had predicted that all the peoples of the world would meet in Jerusalem on the last day of history.[1] That meeting happened instead during the first days of modern history, and in Mexico City.

That this didn't happen earlier is unsurprising. The Arabs called the Atlantic the Sea of Darkness, and though they are supposed to have sailed nearly two thousand miles into it in 1420, that would still not bring them anywhere near the New World; from Andalusia to Havana is some four thousand nautical miles, and Veracruz another eight hundred miles west from there. That moreover is in a straight line, which no sailing master would have (or technologically could have) contemplated taking.[2] Their goal was to drive their square-rigged ships, machines deeply inefficient for going upwind, in front of as reliable a following wind as possible. This led Europeans in a great six-thousand-mile arc southward on the way to Mexico and northward on the way back, because the winds formed a giant clockwise system. The northern trade winds were the best conveyance westward across the Atlantic but could stop for weeks when they met mid-ocean with the countervailing southern trade winds, leaving ships stuck in a spreading circle of their own waste. The Spanish called this the equatorial "calm"; the English, mournfully, "the doldrums." Sailors finally arriving at Veracruz might meet with one of the frequent northerly gales that blew up without warning and kept ships trapped for days (or even weeks), sometimes low on food and water, within sight of a land they could not reach. The passage from Veracruz to Spain averaged ten weeks, but one seventeenth-century fleet took six months to navigate back through five major storms, suffering numerous sinkings, deaths, and a plague of rats en route.[3] At the beginning, in the 1530s, only about half the ships that set off on the Atlantic crossing actually made it, the rest either turning back or being lost at sea.[4]

On the other side of Mexico the crossing of the Pacific ended in Acapulco, a large bay surrounded by hills. It was a far more favored harbor than Veracruz but just as unfavored in terms of the tropical disease that greeted travelers and then bid them farewell; the local priest made a fortune from funerals, asking a thousand pesos to bury the well-off. Reaching the "first market of the Southern Sea," in reality a fishing village where the houses "were low and vile and made of wood, mud and straw," was the culmination of a ten-thousand-mile voyage.[5] It took as many as five months going west from Mexico to the Philippines and some four months coming back, the galleons called naos dodging the archipelago's pirates and cyclones before heading north to pick up the prevailing westerly winds across the Pacific.[6] They ran before them to California, where they could anchor and water. Even there they weren't home and dry: Over the years the English captured one galleon, a storm wrecked a second, and Pericú Indians attacked a third. The Spanish only established a port on the California coastline in 1730.[7] The final stage of the journey lay down the coast to Acapulco. The window for sailing from the Philippines to Mexico was narrow, opening in late April to take advantage of following monsoon winds and closing in June, when the likelihood of typhoons rose appreciably. Speeds varied greatly, but even on a long and fortune-favored run a galleon was unlikely to average more than five nautical miles an hour. Unfavored runs could be extraordinarily long and tempestuous: One nao weathered eighteen storms.[8] And consequently even in an age when all travel was slow, when it took two weeks to get a letter the five hundred miles from Venice to Paris, when news as vital as a revolution in Lisbon took a week to reach Madrid, sea travel was offputtingly slow and uncertain.[9]

So voyagers set off as prepared as possible, starting with a staggering amount of alcohol. On a typical passage each sailor's daily ration was a liter of fortified wine, insurance against the dangers of contaminated drinking water and misery. Keeping sailors half drunk and happy was international best practice; before discovering rum, the British shipped eight pints of (apparently quite nasty) beer per person per day. Spanish food staples were one and a half pounds of *bizcocho*, weevil-riddled sea biscuit, with small quantities of rice and broad beans and a varying daily protein: salt fish, salt pork, a pound of beef twice a week, and two ounces of cheese three times a week.[10] The sailors needed to work the ship were guaranteed three and a half thousand daily calories by their pursers; passengers, though, were at the mercy of their common sense, funds, and the sharks who sold preserved food in Seville and Cádiz.

Some private travelers fared better than their hosts. In the early seventeenth century, the English Dominican friar Thomas Gage was promised seductively lavish provisions:

> What dainties he had provided for us, what varieties of fish and flesh, how many sheep, how many gammons of bacon, how many fat hens, how many hogs, how many barrels of white biscuit, how many jars of wine of *Casalla*, and what store of rice, figs, olives, capers, raisins, lemons, sweet and sour oranges, pomegranates, comfits, preserves, conserves, and all sorts of Portugal sweetmeats.[11]

Most travelers fared much worse, even if those in the know told them not to skimp. María de Carranza, encouraging her brother to leave the poverty of Andalusia for the opportunity of Puebla, instructed him to

> be aware that anyone who brings children must come very well prepared: six hundredweight of hardtack will be enough, but better have over that than under, and make it yourself, since you know how. And buy four cured hams from Ronda, and four cheeses; twelve pounds of rice; chickpeas and beans, rather too much than too little; all the spices; vinegar and olive oil, four jugs of each; jerked beef and mutton, plenty of it and well dressed.[12]

No amount of material preparation, though, could save them from the constant thirst of being rationed to two pints of water a day under a tropical sun, or from short rations, disease, and even starvation if caught overlong in storms or calms. Even the well-provisioned wealthiest couldn't escape the constraints of space: There were far fewer cabins than passengers, and in 1570 a cabin seven by eight feet went for eighty ducats.[13] The question of how to shit with decorum must have been another daunting consideration, particularly for Spanish women in a culture of honor; in a seaborne world where generally only captains had their own loos, the rest of the passengers—presumably, because pudic history doesn't relate—were left with no choice but rudimentary heads, the communal seats for everyone else in the ship's bows. We do know that not everyone cared about privacy, though. One passenger's horrified letter laid out the problem in detail:

> Men, women, brats and old men, dirty and clean, all stewing together, crammed up one against the other; and thus next to you one burps, another vomits, another breaks wind, another voids his bowels; you are having lunch and cannot tell anyone that they are acting ill-bred, because the regulations of this [floating] city permit anything.[14]

It is wholly unsurprising, consequently, that other letters from Mexico should contain vigorous, almost standardized sales pitches explaining why their senders' relatives should, despite all this, chance the trip. Those daring or desperate enough could set off spiritually prepared: Reinforcing Christopher, the patron saint of travelers, was a more specialized Virgin of the Navigators, painted somber, suspicious even, in the chapel of the Casa de Contratación in Seville, sheltering the departing under her cloak.[15] They needed her, as they did her colleague on the other side at Veracruz, the Christ of the Good Journey ("very miraculous" according to Friar Francisco de Ajofrín, who was seasick for eighty days).[16] "For my sins I have sailed," wrote one chronically seasick passenger, and "when I heard the *Pater Noster* and the *Ave María* . . . I told my wife 'Señora, although I suspect we are in the devil's house, I have heard the word of God.' "[17] Yet whatever the consolations of faith, ocean travel was fundamentally horrible: nasty, brutish, and long. The Mediterranean could be loved as well as feared; a Provençal proverb ran, "*Lauso la mare e tente 'n terro*," "praise the sea and stay on land."[18] The Atlantic was unlovable.

Many never made it across. It was good counsel, one friar wrote, "that any man who takes to sea, whether it be in a galleon or a galley, make his confession and communion and deliver himself unto God like a good and faithful Christian; because the sea goer risks his life as one who enters a pitched battle."[19] At its worst even short-range seagoing was a death sentence: The life expectancy of a galley slave was four years.[20] A few of the long-distance dead died as a result of maritime natural causes: During the two and a half centuries of the Pacific crossing thirty-eight of the forty-two galleons lost were shipwrecked.[21] Losses of vessels of any size on the Atlantic run were relatively low, averaging roughly one in sixty over the course of the sixteenth century, even though a handful of crossings were catastrophic; one convoy's sinking in 1619 took more lives than the *Titanic*.[22] The Gulf of Mexico, moreover, was one of the more dangerous shipping zones in the Americas, and aging coasters broke up both there and along the Pacific Coast with some regularity. Yet while passengers, most of whom couldn't swim, had a horror of drowning that kept some up at night, it was a relatively improbable way to die; they were the nervous flyers of the early modern period.

Shipboard death from starvation or disease was a different matter, a distinct possibility realized at its cruelest in the shocking numbers of West Africans crammed by Europeans onto slave trading ships in the Old World who never got off again. Slave ships were small, generally less than one hundred feet, and packed to capacity with hundreds of slaves who were allowed at best limited time on deck each day. The cargo was assembled slowly, the ship moving down the tropical coast of Africa, the captain generally buying small lots from more than one dealer until he filled the hold; only then would he set off across the ocean. Between 1526 and 1700 some fifty thousand Africans died on Spanish ships sailing to Mexico and the empire's other Caribbean coasts, nearly a third of the people embarked on that forced migration.[23] Death was far less common among voluntary passengers, but it was still a universal reality: One ship setting out from the Philippines in 1629 lost one hundred of its crew and passengers, bringing many of their corpses into Acapulco for belated and malodorous burial.[24] Those who mustered the courage to sail might fall victim to any of the panoply of early modern microbes, and there was a certain realism in dealing with them as part of the package; only yellow fever and the plague brought a ship mandatory quarantine.

Added to universal diseases came a specific maritime plague, scurvy, which needed no microbe to spread throughout a ship. First came lethargy, lost teeth, and ulcers, then fever, hallucination, jaundice, bleeding, and finally coma and death. Scurvy's origins were dietary, stemming from a prolonged lack of fresh fruit and vegetables and a consequent severe vitamin C deficiency, though that would not be fully accepted for centuries. Belief in antiscorbutics such as lemon juice only became widespread in the mid-eighteenth century, and in the interim scurvy caused regular, at times extreme, mortality, killing most of the sailors who made circumnavigations with Ferdinand Magellan or that notorious pirate Sir Francis Drake (himself, however, killed by yellow fever).[25] Scurvy made even the less lethal voyages touch-and-go; the first nao staggered into Acapulco with only 10 percent of its crew able to work. Alongside water it was fresh vegetables that pushed Philip V to establish a port in California, in order that "the many deaths caused each year by scurvy may be avoided."[26] Passages lengthened by ambition or weather unavoidably brought disease and death.

Yet little could be done against the weather, bar choosing the least dangerous season to depart: spring for the Manila–Acapulco run, riding the monsoon winds, and summer for the run from Seville to Veracruz, slipping through the window between winter gales and autumn hurricanes. Six to eight months later the same fleet, now silver-loaded and far more valuable, set off on its return, following the same seasonal logic. Ships were built bigger and better and laws passed regulating build quality, seaworthiness, and maximum loads, even if those laws were promptly circumvented. The first caravels were under a hundred feet long and carried less than a hundred tons; the average ship size doubled to two hundred tons by 1600, and by 1700 the largest galleons were over a thousand tons.[27] Advances in meteorology, navigation, and engineering helped too; in 1571 the Council of the Indies created the position of cosmographer-chronicler, and in 1574 the first incumbent, Juan López de Velasco, produced a chart of the Atlantic that traced its coastlines with newfound accuracy.[28] In 1600 Veracruz, which took 40 percent of all trade to the Indies, was moved fifteen miles south from the unprotected mouth of the Antigua River to a better harbor in the lee of the island of San Juan de Ulúa, and the number of coastal wrecks fell notably. A similar move took place in 1670 in Spain, when the main port was relocated from Seville, fifty impractical miles up the silty Guadalquivir, to Cádiz, a large, sheltered bay to the south.[29]

But the cumulative impact of technological advance was not all that great. Ships remained vulnerable, their fundamental mechanical weakness—the limited ability to sail upwind—unchanged. A lee shore could sink a vessel of any size; the larger the ship, in fact, the less able it was to deal with adverse winds. In terms of sea time, the voyages of the seventeenth century were only slightly faster than those of the sixteenth.[30] Charts remained rudimentary, and the key measurement of longitude—how far east or west a ship lay—remained out of sight until the first reliable chronometer was invented in the mid-eighteenth century.[31] Technical advances in ocean travel were more questions of local tinkering than technological revolution. Local tinkering might catch on, the empirically demonstrated superiority of a new rig or hull shape becoming universal, the sum of all tweaking an innovation. The shipwrights of Hoorn took the Spanish galleon of the sixteenth century, made it longer and narrower, took out guns, put in higher masts, and ended up with the *fluyt*, the cargo workhorse of the seventeenth century. The new ships were cheaper and carried more freight than their predecessors, and were widely copied. But passage durations and numbers of sunk ships remained much the same.[32]

Human adversaries, on the other hand, could be dealt with, or at least managed. Pirates tried their luck in the eastern Atlantic from the start: The Frenchman Jean Fleury captured Cortés's second ship on its way home in 1522, taking among other loot Montezuma's feather-and-gold headdress.[33] Large-scale piracy was stimulated by silver shipments, the availability of safe harbors, and periodic international warfare, and consequently took off in the later sixteenth century and endured, with fluctuating intensity, until the turn of the eighteenth century. As in the Mediterranean, piracy in the Caribbean lay to some extent in the eye of the beholder, and many pirates, the British in particular, moved in and out of the formal service of their states. Some pirates were straightforward outlaws, above all the buccaneers of French Tortuga and British Jamaica, but even they could find routes to respectability: Henry Morgan, for example, sacked Panama in 1671 even though Britain was at peace with Spain and was promptly made lieutenant-governor of Jamaica in 1674. Many who prospered were knighted—Francis Drake, Walter Raleigh, Christopher Myngs, John Hawkins—and made admiral. Hawkins, checkered career behind him, ended up treasurer of the Navy.[34] They had their own ships, investors, and letters of marque, licenses from their governments that made them technically private warships and not criminals. It was the sort of promising public-private partnership pursued by Spanish Crown and conquistadors, but directed in this case against fellow Europeans rather than Indians, and rather less slaughterous.

For pirates did not generally sink ships; it was poor business. They looted them, at times even with a hammy courtesy, as when the buccaneer Diego el Mulato thanked the crew he had captured and robbed "for their good entertainment."[35] They looked for opportunities to knock off the great silver ships, but very rarely found them; Piet Heyn, the Dutch privateer who took eight million pesos from the 1628 fleet, was one of only three commanders ever to manage it. The pirates' main set-piece battles were amphibious attacks on key nodes of the mainland—the Spanish Main—such as Cartagena (1697), Panama (1671), Portobello (1668), Veracruz (1683), and island ports such as Havana (1555) and Santiago de Cuba (1603, 1662). Veracruz was generally safe, and the only Mexican port to suffer repeated attacks was Campeche, on the southeastern coast, which for all its relative insignificance was attacked twelve times between 1557 and 1708, in a revealing mixture of opportunist smash-and-grab and more thought-out, medium-term inroads into the indigo dyewood business.[36] (A nice, steady earner, indigo was a better blue dye than British woad and, like all the best commodities, imperishable, high value, and low volume.)[37] The pirates' earlier activities had the greatest consequences, however, because they helped push Spain into a permanent fleet system, consolidating by bureaucratic and naval force all sailings into two giant annual convoys, each carrying thousands of people and tens of thousands of tons of freight, with a huge impact on not just the material but also the political life of the empire.

The economic logic was clear. Silver went from a marginal to a central export from Mexico in the second half of the sixteenth century, and increased production was accompanied (counterintuitively) by increased price. With that incentive the volume of Spanish shipping boomed from a few hundred tons in the 1520s to tens of thousands from the 1560s onward; by the 1590s good years brought over fifty ships back from Veracruz. At the same time wars against the French in the 1550s and the English in the 1560s intensified the legal piracy of privateering, and in really bad years as much as a third of returning traffic was lost.[38] Privateers could be considerable warships, heavily manned for the cut and thrust of boarding, and even large individual ships could be outclassed. "In the month of February last," wailed one merchant's letter,

> Anchueta's ship, of more than 300 tons, left Sanlúcar for Nombre de Dios, with permission to sail alone. It cost us dear, because within four days after it left Sanlúcar the French took it; it was very richly loaded, with a cargo worth 60,000 ducats or more. The loss did great damage among the merchants here, and cost myself about 400 ducats.[39]

The obvious answer lay in the safety in numbers of the *flota*, the annual fleet that merchants suggested in 1522 and that Philip II mandated in 1561, using warships—paid by the merchants—to escort larger numbers of three-masted ships alongside smaller vessels such as brigs, schooners, and brigantines.[40] Consolidating all trade into a single sailing had other advantages: It emptied the ocean of ships for much of the year, which made the everyday business of piracy much harder, ameliorated a lasting shortage of skilled navigators, and made it easier for the bureaucrats of the Casa de Contratación to tax inbound and license outbound goods.

The flota worked well in terms of security, navigation, and mercantilism, and posed only one major problem: It restricted communications to two voyages every year. One set of letters and reports sailed with the silver fleet in the late summer or autumn and another in the late winter or spring with the *patache de aviso*, a small, fast dispatch vessel. Royal officials in Spain would get news from a year's worth of events in Mexico in the returning treasure ships in August or September; their responses reached royal officials or churchmen in Mexico only in the following spring, and they would not learn the effect, if any, of an instruction until at earliest the next winter, at which point they could issue further orders. This was in the best of cases; other transatlantic exchanges progressed far more slowly. In 1572, for example, Philip II issued a decree banning further monastic property-holding in Indian villages. In late September 1575 the archbishop of Mexico wrote a letter reporting that the decree was not being observed; receiving his letter in autumn 1576, Philip II issued another decree repeating his instructions, which arrived in Mexico in the summer of 1577. "It seems that you have not managed to observe [the decree] yet," he wrote again to the viceroy in 1579. That single cycle of government—the issuing of an important order, observation of its effect, and follow-up—took five years and achieved little or nothing.[41] The flow of goods was relatively efficient. The flow of knowledge was not.

And so the Europeans faced not just the tyranny of distance but also the narrow limits of the known.[42] It was not just useful knowledge of where things were or what people were doing that was slippery; the everyday exotica of the New World were likewise hard to grasp. For example, foreigners were not sure what to make of the iguana. It was clearly important to the locals; the Maya worshipped it as Itzam Na, one of their main gods.[43] Yet while the reptile was fascinating, it was also enduringly mysterious. The historian Gonzalo Fernández de Oviedo sent a specimen to Venice in the early sixteenth century, but unfamiliar with its diet, he provisioned it with a barrel of earth to eat en route, and unsurprisingly—despite the locavore logic—the beast died.[44] A century later the friar Thomas Gage, a good observer and writer, struggled to describe the species: The best he could come up with was "longer than a rabbit, and like unto a scorpion, with green or black scales."[45] (There was an upside to taxonomic bafflement, in that Yucatán's bishops decided it was acceptable to eat iguana during the Lenten fast.)[46] By the eighteenth century there was more certainty about what an iguana looked like, but not necessarily about its other properties, nor those of lizards in general. Dr. José Flores thought lizard flesh could cure cancer if eaten raw. Dr. José Vicente García de la Vega agreed but didn't see the need to administer lizard carpaccio when either lizard cream or a lizard pill could do the job. Two Mexico City doctors disagreed vehemently with both eminences, telling the cabildo that their own trials with these animals revealed poisonous salts. Another natural philosopher, Antonio de León y Gama, fought back, arguing that lizard did indeed have anticarcinogenic value, but only if the luckless specimen in question was both male and raw.[47] This was esoteric stuff, and of limited importance to most people in Madrid or Mexico City. However, three areas of useful knowledge were of vital importance to both rulers and ruled: geography, political intelligence, and the written word.

Geographical doubt and ignorance constituted the most worrying of these. Ocean voyagers crossed uncharted waters, prizing even the roughest ideas of land mass, coastlines, and distances; in 1527 an English merchant sent two spies aboard Spanish ships to get hold of their "navigation cardes," presumably the secret government master chart, the Padrón Real.[48] This was a rudimentary work in progress, which officials updated by quizzing returning sailors. They made some headway when in 1546 Charles V ordered the cartographer Alonso de Santa Cruz to piece together existing maps and charts with the writings of pilots and conquistadors to produce a global atlas. Santa Cruz was a sophisticate, the first to attempt charting magnetic variation, the difference between true and magnetic north that was for centuries the only way of estimating longitude. His atlas, the *Islario general de todas las islas del mundo*, was suitably ambitious.[49] It did not resolve navigational ignorance, though, and as late as 1674 one chart utterly deformed Yucatán, a vital landfall for ships from the Caribbean, while

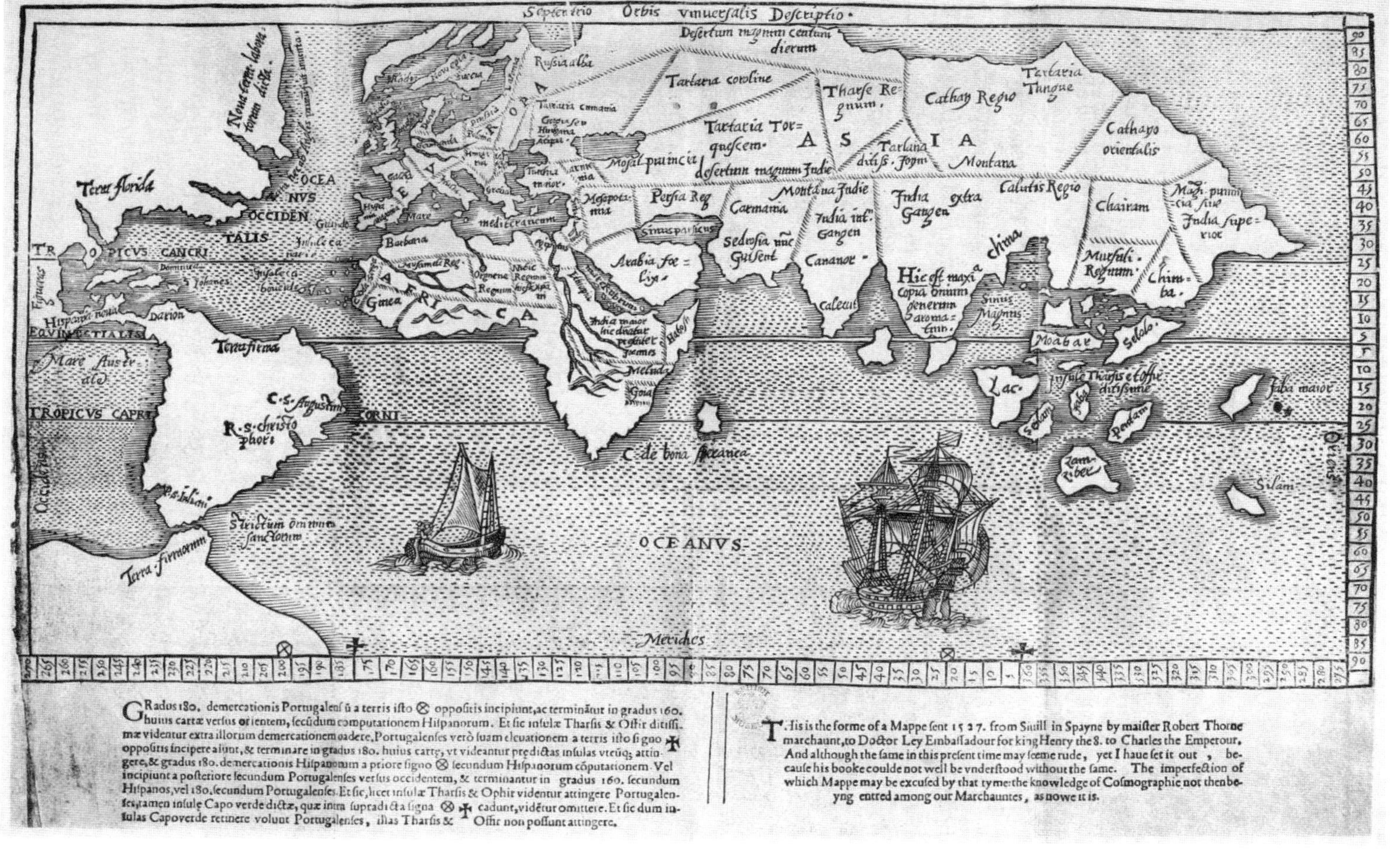

The most accurate chart of the Atlantic available in 1527, a Spanish state secret stolen by the English. Richard Hakluyt, *The Voyages* (1582).

showing California as an island.[50] A scientific chart of the coast from Acapulco to California did not emerge until 1802.[51]

Alonso de Santa Cruz's methods—standardized questionnaires for those in the know—were also applied in the Crown's first attempt to map terrestrial Mexico, the *Relaciones geográficas* of 1577. The king instructed officials on the ground to draw up *padrones de leguas*, scale maps of their areas of competence with distances marked out in the rational, standard units of leagues. They were to answer questions about land and sea, reporting whether the inhabitants of a place were watermen; how competent they were; what the prevailing winds were; how often there were storms; what the tidal variation was; whether the coast was rocky; whether there were reefs, ports, coves, or natural harbors; whether the bottom was clean or foul; and how many ships any shelter might accommodate. The exacting forms went far beyond this, with an encyclopedic set of forty-nine inquiries regarding the geography, culture, climate, history, and economic potential of each locality, concluding with a shotgun appeal for "all the other notable things in nature, and the effects of the soil, air, and sky that there might be anywhere and that might be worth knowing." Empiricism was to rule, the king told his men:

> For those questions for which you might have nothing to say, you will leave them without comment and pass to the next, until you have read all of them, and responded with what you might have to say; as already said, in all things with brevity and clarity, recognizing as certain that which is and indicating as doubtful that which is; such that the *relaciones* should be accurate.[52]

The result was in some places an unprecedented piece of research, the *relación* a rigorous coproduction of official and indigenous authors. The *Relación geográfica de Coatepec y su partido*, for example, takes over ten thousand words and three large maps to describe three villages in central Veracruz. Francisco Villacastín, its ghost author, was fluent in Nahuatl and sympathetic to his indigenous informants, who repaid him with detail; the elders consulted their "ancient paintings" before replying, and Villacastín cited them in his own replies to the questionnaire. The meticulousness after which Philip II hankered was there:

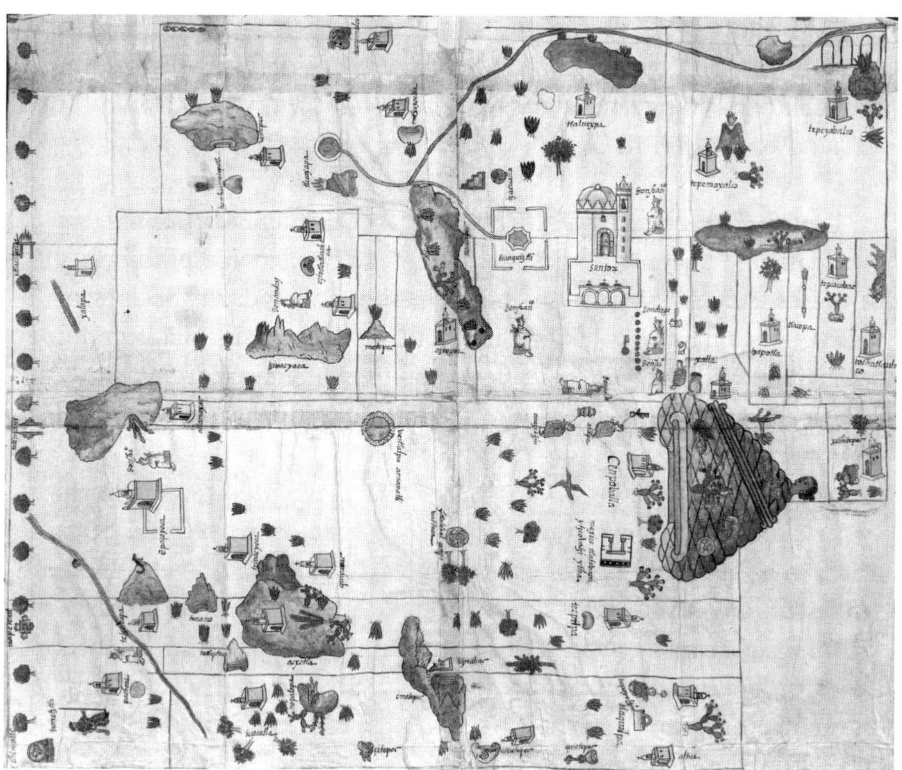

Relación geográfica de Coatepec, Veracruz (1577).

Among other impressive quantitative data the relación informed the king that it was "about" 168 years since the Mexica first appeared in the area, that the founder and first cacique had ruled for 36 years, and that life expectancy since the conquest had declined to a maximum of 50 years.[53]

In many other cases officials took up with cynical enthusiasm the preamble's invitation to leave difficult questions blank. Less than half the local officials answered the questionnaire at all. Given the state and speed of government, any sanction was improbable, and the bureaucracy was enough of a carousel that officials might well have moved on (or retired or died) by the time their lack of cooperation was noted. Professional rootlessness also meant that many of the ninety-eight who bothered to reply did so without much idea what they were talking about. That didn't bother one corregidor, who confessed his ignorance with blithe unconcern, revealing much about his relations with both Indians and superiors:

> The land is all mountains and ranges, so harsh and terrible that we are unable to apply a particular name to any of them because they are countless. Even so, in the past (and even today), the Indians have given names to all of them, but they sound dissonant in our Spanish language. Since we deal with these names so infrequently, using them here seems out of place because these names are not important.[54]

Even when officials wrote their own texts, they farmed out the visual mapping to indigenous subcontractors, who had very different understandings of space. The requested distances went unmarked on paintings that blended European with indigenous conventions, more like aides-mémoire than scaled representations of space.[55] Many indigenous cartographers oriented their maps with east rather than north at the top (and did much the same for the next hundred years).[56] Some didn't orient them at all, the cloths designed for readers to place on the floor and circumambulate.[57] The maps synonymous with state power didn't exist; both symbolism and reality are self-evident.

The upshot was a Mexico that remained unmapped in large swathes until well after Independence in 1821. At the beginning of the nineteenth century the north of Mexico was about as well surveyed as sub-Saharan Africa, the scientist Baron Alexander von Humboldt thought (and wrote, with the sort of supporting evidence that Philip II had long ago hoped for and rarely got). No one was quite sure where El Paso lay on the map despite its being the strategically critical "Pass of the North" where the Río Grande valley opened up a passage between uninviting mountain ranges. In the far South officials called the rainforest of Chiapas a "desert," where Spanish travelers were "discoverers."[58] The highlands north of Acapulco, the birthplace of maize, were a mystery. Most striking of all, the silver mines that had quickly become the raison d'être of Spanish occupation went either unregistered or unlocated by European cartographers. Most of their maps failed to note the city of

Guanajuato, with its seventy thousand inhabitants, and assorted famous mines; all of them ignored Real de Catorce, today a ghost town, then the home of forty thousand people and the source of twenty million francs of silver a year.[59] *"A la espada y el compás / Mas y mas y mas y mas"* (By the compass and the sword / More and more and more and more), ran one Spanish mercenary's doggerel, etched on the frontispiece of his book from the dying days of the sixteenth century.[60] The compass lagged a long way behind the sword.

Even established knowledge was hard to come by because of the dearth of books or any other written materials. Much of the known went uncodified, tacit even, passed on in person or by word of mouth, an essential but limited way of learning that relied on garrulous, generous, and mobile experts. The Spanish established the first printing press in the Western Hemisphere in 1539, produced over a hundred books and pamphlets across the rest of the century, and set up the first library in the Colegio de la Santa Cruz de Tlatelolco. As early as 1541 hawkers on the streets of Mexico City were selling a sensationalist report of the "dreadful earthquake" in Guatemala.[61] Yet stories like this were exceptional and confined to the big city. Most news traveled inside the Americas handwritten through the royal mail and the personal deliveries of travelers, traders, and muleteers.[62] Puebla opened a press in 1640, giving Mexico two of the entire hemisphere's four print shops, but thereafter regional expansion ended, and neither Veracruz not Guadalajara had a press until the 1790s. Outside the central valley printed matter was scarce and extremely valuable. The first Jesuits in Aguascalientes owned all of forty books.[63] When some Dominicans were shipwrecked they scoured the swampy Gulf shoreline for their books, nervously unstuck the pages of those they found, and washed off the mud page by page. (They succeeded in rescuing most of them, but the smell lingered.)[64] Demand was so high that one friar, urging his nephew to come to Mexico, advised him to invest his start-up capital in new Bibles from Ruperto Estephano of Salamanca.[65] Some classics never saw the light of day: No one printed Durán's and Sahagún's histories until the nineteenth century, long after the end of empire.[66] And—with an irony that the sarcastic Martin Luther would have relished—the Mexican Inquisition lacked copies of the *Index Librorum Prohibitorum*, their book that listed banned books.[67]

Despite this startling but inevitable ignorance, the global impacts of the new links were revolutionary. The extraction of unprecedented amounts of silver from Peru and Mexico doubled Europe's money supply in about a century. At one point it doubled that of France in a decade. The Spanish transmuted their silver into the world's first reserve currency, the peso, variously translated as *piastres fortes*, *stukken van achten*, *pièces de huit réaux*, or pieces of eight. It was a global standard accepted by everyone from sixteenth-century stockbrokers in Amsterdam to peasants in China, father of the modern reserve currency: The first US dollars were linked to the peso, which remained legal tender until 1857. At least a third of Mexican silver ended up in Asia, swapped by Europeans for everything they couldn't grow or make, from peppercorns to porcelain and silk.

Alongside American precious metals came plants of unprecedented efficiency in sustaining human life. Land planted with maize varieties from Mexico yielded far more calories than land planted with Old World carbohydrates such as wheat or rice. Together with South America's potatoes they underpinned a major expansion of the world's population, which grew by nearly a half between 1650 and 1750. By one estimate maize fueled a 20 percent rise in the population of nineteenth-century China; there and in India the growth was most pronounced, and these were the world's largest markets.[68]

Silver was by a long way the main precious metal in the Americas, but once long-assembled indigenous treasure had been seized or lost, it became scarce. For the first two decades of Spanish occupation the declining mines of Habsburg Europe, concentrated in Germany and the Balkans, produced four times as much silver as Mexico and Peru combined.[69] As exploration and failure debunked tales of golden cities, Spaniards listened to more credible indigenous rumors of silver deposits on the edges of the great northern desert. In August 1546 Juan de Tolosa, an undistinguished veteran, set off from Guadalajara to investigate. (His informant was a Nahua slave, another baffled by Spanish greed, who told him with a certain contempt, "If you're so worked up about these things, I'll take you where you'll stuff your hands and quench your thirst.")[70] In the highlands 350 miles north of

Mexico City Tolosa found that the rumors were true; numerous rich and shallow veins of silver ran through the dry hills around a deep and narrow valley. He named the place Zacatecas after the indigenous Zacatecos, who were the original population. It became first a mining camp, where within a few years the suddenly wealthy Spanish mine owners built five churches, and then a boomtown, incorporated in 1553, and by century's end one of the great American cities.[71] Tolosa's discovery was followed by another in 1550 at Guanajuato. Together with the lesser mines of Taxco and Pachuca they caused a silver rush. Only the Andean mines produced more, and between them the two complexes generated over three-quarters of the world's silver.[72]

At the outset, though, between scarce labor, indigenous guerrillas, and unsafe roads, the miners, often indebted, saw themselves as an endangered species. Their case was convincing enough to persuade the Crown in 1548 to halve the production tax, the 20 percent *quinto royal*, to the 10 percent *diezmo royal*. Spanish extraction was distinctly low-tech. Lacking explosives, workers carved out tunnels by pick and shovel and broke up ore with hammers before feeding it into wood-fired "Castilian" ovens (introduced, with cosmopolitan irony, by Germans). It took over a century just for the basic ore-grinding machinery of the *arrastres*—large drums in which heavy stones were pulled by mules—to become standard issue. Mining was a business whose yields progressively declined while running costs increased. Indian laborers had used their picks to dig out the silver closest to the surface and had cut down the nearest forests to provide fuel for the smelters. As ore became poorer, fuel became dearer; by the seventeenth century miners were buying firewood from thirty miles away.[73] They suffered, moreover, from the new cost of wages after the abolition of indigenous slavery in 1542, even if this took decades to translate into action.

A critical advance in metallurgy dealt with the biggest of these problems, drawing metal out of rock. In 1553 Bartolomé de Medina, an aging, comfortably established merchant from Seville, learned a revolutionary new chemical refining process from a mysterious German. Leaving behind his business and six children (and the mysterious German), he sailed to New Spain to experiment in the mines of Pachuca. The reaction worked, and Medina became the first to replace superheating ore with chemical extraction through the "patio process," in which laborers mixed pulverized ore with salt, water, copper sulphate, and mercury and spread the resulting paste on an open-air patio, where they trod it barefoot like grapes for wine. After about two months the mercury—"quicksilver"—drew the silver out of the rock to form an amalgam, which with a brief cooking split into the component metals.

The toxic mercury vapors ate away at the lungs of the Indians who trod it, killing them within a couple of years. Supply was tight, because there were only two mercury mines in the entire empire: Huancavélica in Peru, whose output went straight to the Andean mines, and Almadén in Spain. The royal mine there was subject to Crown taxes and the price-gouging Fuggers, German bankers who won the monopoly to sell its output in the Americas. Mercury smuggled from China was too impure to use. Neither did amalgamation benefit its promoter much. Bartolomé de Medina struck a deal with the viceroy to grant him a percentage of the silver his process produced; the deal was never honored, though, and when Medina set off for Spain to politick, his ship sank with all he had. He survived and returned to New Spain with his wife and children, where he died in old age, still without any great gain from having changed the world; because despite its shortcomings, mercury underpinned three centuries of massive silver production.

Getting hold of mercury was the only major bottleneck. Mines were not that labor-intensive—the Mexican workforce totaled about nine thousand people in 1590—and a new system in which salaried indigenous workers were supplemented by Black slaves did the job. Mines were capital-intensive, especially when stone-lined shafts replaced the larger open pits, but astute investors profited from simultaneously selling the pure silver that came out and the mules, food, wine, salt, mercury, and consumer goods that went in. After a rocky start, the supply of silver turned out to be high and comparatively reliable, as was demand, and mining became the world's most lucrative extractive industry.[74] More than that, Mexican silver changed the world economy in three ways: liquidity, long-distance trade, and the development of some components of capitalism. It connected economic cause and effect on a global scale.

Liquidity came in part from sheer volume. Constant long-term growth, during which only one downturn lasted much time (1640–1670), meant that by 1800 Mexican mines were producing 20 million pesos a year.[75] The actual coin was durable, of high and consistent value—a milled edge made post-1732 versions hard to shave or clip—and universally accepted, unlike rival long-range currencies such as Chinese paper, West African cowry shells, or American cacao nibs. It left the mints in Mexico City, Peru, and Seville and flowed around the world. Both coins and bars crossed the Pacific in limited amounts, albeit with important economic and cultural impacts, but most took the long way around to Asia, from Mexican miners to European traders and bankers to producers on the far side of the Indian Ocean and the South China Sea. The Habsburgs tried to control the flow of bullion by registering it on departure from the Americas and arrival in Spain, collecting tax and licensing only Spanish receivers. They inevitably failed, and by increasing margins as trade became more complex. After 1630 a majority of silver was siphoned off before the ships even reached Spain, disappeared en route from the mines to Mexico City and Veracruz or unloaded onto phantom vessels in the Azores, the Canaries, or the Bay of Cádiz. Most of what silver made it to Spain passed through unregistered and untaxed. Contraband silver could readily depart again, effectively never touching ground; an entire subset of smugglers, the aristocratic *metedores*, existed for the sole purpose of getting silver over the city walls of Cádiz and onto boats whose muffled oars rowed it out to waiting foreign ships.[76]

For the rest of the world, though, smuggling and a large informal sector were advantageous as they allowed faster and broader dissemination of colonial silver. The Crown's own money moved from its hands into those of its armies in northern Europe and its bankers in Genoa; merchants' money moved everywhere. It traveled around Europe in search of woolens, linens, hardware, and luxury goods. It returned to the Americas, temporarily transmuted into export goods, where it bought dyestuffs, hides, and tropical groceries like sugar and tobacco. Above all European silver went to Asia in exchange for high-value commodities like tea and spices and the manufactures that Europe, for a long time, could not make competitively, whether luxuries like silk or staples like cotton. Chinese and Indian producers dominated these markets until well into the eighteenth century, and as a result their populations, much larger than those of Europe, absorbed more silver than any other region.[77] It was a chronic imbalance of trade between East and West, founded on a basic verity: Europeans produced little else that Asians wanted.

Long-distance trade was a chancier proposition than selling grain in the local market, but profits were stratospheric. Even the most dynamic national economies before the Industrial Revolution had very slow annual growth, if any at all; between 1690 and 1830 the British economy grew an average of 1.08 percent per annum. Merchants who sent European goods on consignment to the Veracruz trade fair could expect anywhere from 40 to 75 percent profit.[78] Those who dared to buy Chinese goods and make the Pacific run marked them up 200 percent.[79] Wine, a risky commodity to ship given the threats of spoiling, leaky barrels, and thirsty sailors, was marked up 1,000 percent between Spain and Mexico.[80] Finally, silver trading went beyond agricultural commodities and manufactures. The ratio of silver's value to gold in China was six to one, while in India it was eight to one, and that difference meant currency arbitrage between the two largest Asian economies was lucrative to the extent of 30 percent earning per trade.[81]

So in economic terms Mexican silver changed what and how much was traded on a global scale, and to whose advantage. It made the world far more interconnected, to dramatic political effect. But Mexican silver did not revolutionize how things were made, whether in terms of materials, processes, finances, or ideology, whether through forward or backward linkages. It did not directly cause either industrialization or the rise of modern capitalism. The Industrial Revolution began in Britain two centuries after the silver boom. Scandinavian societies with next to no history of transatlantic trade or Atlantic World colonization—Denmark seized three out-of-the-way Caribbean islands, Sweden owned the stony ten square miles of Saint Barts—managed to industrialize nevertheless. The sixteenth-century need for pumps to clear water from deepening mine shafts or for vehicles that worked independently of wind or animal power did not lead to the technology of the steam engine. Burning enthusiasm for Chinese porcelain did not lead to European production until 1708, when a German in Meissen finally cracked the secret.[82] European empires failed to channel the American silver that entered their territories into favorable conditions for industrial takeoff, such as low taxes or state funding for technological development. Quite the opposite: They jacked up taxes and contracted the biggest loans possible to spend in their forever wars.

Spain suffered the most from this resource curse. The flood of silver from the 1550s to the 1650s constituted a perverse incentive to develop neither domestic industry nor banking. Longer-established foreign manufacturers already offered better value, and the inflation brought by silver increased their comparative advantage. The sheep oligarchs of Castile, organized since medieval times in a powerful business lobby called the *mesta*, were happy with their longstanding profits from the raw-wool trade. Foreign bankers were happy to extend the Crown substantial credit, obviating the need to develop a sophisticated tax system, a politically messy prospect anywhere. Spanish mercantilism, the policy of hoarding national wealth by excluding foreigners from transatlantic trade, failed. It wasn't just smuggling that doomed mercantilism: In the seventeenth century English, Dutch, and French merchant houses increasingly sent their progeny to Seville to be naturalized as Spanish, or employed Spanish frontmen, forerunners of modern shell companies. Dutch ships sailed under false Iberian flags.[83] For the greatest empire of the day, American silver led not toward but away from industrialization and a bourgeois society.

Some scholars identify a direct causal link between new colonial money and the ascent of capitalism. But capitalism is more than global commerce furthered by forward-thinking, financially agile, and creatively gifted individuals.[84] The sharper citizens of the mature Roman Empire managed that across their known world. Roman markets were intelligible and effective enough, and Roman law promoted private property, meaningful contracts, and business-friendly government. Capitalism is a vague concept, but it is certainly more than this: At its minimum it is a system founded on buying and selling human work to produce commodities with the help of machines, the profits of which then migrate from investment to investment in a restless search to maximize production and profit. In the process, old economic and cultural forms of life are destroyed—"creatively"—and revolutionary self-conscious social classes emerge, their members bound together by new, standardized ways of understanding, consuming, surviving, and thriving in a fast-changing world. Two classes are sine qua non: the proletariat of the wage laborers, whether in mines, industrial farms, or factories, and the bourgeoisie of their employers.[85]

Some components of capitalism did emerge in the sixteenth and seventeenth centuries. These included exploitative terms of international trade, as the Spanish inaugurated the forcible exchange of cheap American raw materials for expensive Old World finished goods; the rise of wage labor, human relationships distilled to their value in money, in what Karl Marx called the cash nexus; class differentiation, with entrepreneurial types rising through the ranks as they mastered the art of accumulating wealth and moving it around; and the rise of key institutions and financial instruments, such as insurance, bonds, and stocks, which smoothed their path. The whole, though, was no triumphant global capitalist system. It was instead a time when very different economic ways of life coexisted, with connections but considerable autonomy, in what Marxists call articulated modes of production: the slave, the feudal, the artisanal, and the capitalist.[86]

The newer parts, moreover, were not universally capitalist. The imperial diktats that supposedly bound Mexicans to send valuable resources to Spain on the cheap while compelling them in turn to buy marked-up European goods were systematically circumvented. The merchants of New Spain traded illegally with the rest of the Americas, while Dutch, British, and French merchants became transatlantic smugglers on a scale that subverted and eventually overthrew Spanish monopoly. The shaping of global trade by violence is historically part and parcel of capitalism, but it is not intrinsic to capitalism alone. It was also in this case part and parcel of mercantilism, the very different economic approach of cutting production, hiking up prices, and hoarding specie. This was both imperial and individual strategy: Merchants of all nationalities were free traders only when it suited them, and they aimed at monopolies either through royal decree or by amassing enough silver to buy all the imports at the annual trade fairs. The bigger merchants of Mexico City persuaded the Crown to curtail those fairs and compel Spaniards to ship unsold goods back to Europe, a law that drove prices down; Spanish merchants delayed the flota in order to drive up Mexican demand and prices. It was all rational choice, just operating under a noncapitalist logic.[87]

As for investment vehicles, Philip II successfully managed a complex and mutually profitable sovereign debt program with bonds that were both long-term, *juros*, and short-term, *asientos*. The bankers of Genoa worked together at key moments in negotiations with the Crown, ephemeral consortia. Simultaneously, stock trading took off in parallel with Atlantic commerce. When the first purpose-built stock exchange building opened in Amsterdam in 1631 it came complete with several hundred different stocks and crowds of shouting traders and clients. But sophisticated financial instruments predated contact with the Americas. A businessman in Genoa (where traders invented maritime insurance in the thirteenth century) was complaining about the dodginess of certain futures in 1428. The majority of joint stock companies operated inside Europe or to the East Indies, trading with people who made things using preindustrial workforces: artisans, peasants, or slaves.[88] And Philip's long-term bonds, the juros, discouraged Spanish entrepreneurialism and fostered rent-seeking. Juros' high interest rates, heritability, and fundamental solidity meant that investors could profitably and unthinkingly park their wealth in one place forever.[89]

Free wage labor spread slowly, involving only a small part of the world's population. Mexican mines ran on naborías, salaried and mobile Indian workers from the central highlands, but at their peak they never employed more than about fifteen thousand people. Sugar and woolen cloth were produced in quasi-factories, where large workforces with specialist tasks operated primitive machines to produce standardized goods. A sugar refinery as early as 1600 cost some 50,000 pesos to build and equip with presses for cane, boilers for syrup, buildings for purifying the molasses, and finally a smithy, a carpenter's shop, and a plethora of tools to keep the whole operation running.[90] The largest *obrajes*, early textile mills, had as many as thirty looms, one hundred spindles, and two hundred operatives, using technology that included hydraulically powered hammers. Raw wool went in, was spun into thread, and then woven into cloth. By 1600 more than one hundred of these vertically integrated businesses had been established in New Spain; Old Spain, by contrast, had almost none, and cloth was still produced by artisans with different stages taking place in different workshops. However, both sugar and textile sectors were manned by forced labor and not by any incipient proletariat, and their products stayed in Mexico.[91] The global sugar boom came later, out of Caribbean plantations, and didn't fund Europe's industrialization or shipping networks. The closest the early modern world came to a factory was a ship: a cutting-edge technological complex, manned by paid workers, characterized by a rigid division of labor, rigorous mechanical time, and the struggles of factory discipline, and susceptible to easy transfers of purpose and capital.[92]

Neither, until the age of revolutions of the later eighteenth century, is there much sign of any peninsular or creole bourgeoisie, a confident dominant class committed to transgenerational capital accumulation and mobility along with a distinct set of revolutionary ideas and values. Merchants aimed to form dynasties, but the larger ones generally wanted to move away from modern wheeling and dealing toward old-fashioned landed respectability. Successful Spanish families in Mexico might stop wanting to go home but they rarely stopped coveting the status and habits of a Spanish feudal aristocracy, hoping to alternate their time between townhouses and vast estates, practicing a longstanding lifestyle to which they hoped to become accustomed. (They often didn't: A sociologically cutting proverb ran, "Father a businessman, son a gentleman, grandson a beggarman.")[93] In economic terms, a few acted like capitalists, albeit capitalists with early retirement plans, but their businesses only looked futuristic in a context where most people made things with their hands on a small scale, grew much of their own food, bought little, and traveled little. Whether based in Mexico or on the peninsula, colonial merchants lacked key institutions of early northern European capitalism: corporations, joint stock companies, domestic banks, investment pools, and laws and judges that made sure that everyone paid up. Prevailing family ownership contained a time bomb in the form of Spanish inheritance law, which mandated an equal division of legacies among heirs—democratic in human terms, toxic in business terms. There was no wholesale shift underway from a feudal to a capitalist mode of production; there was coexistence and correlation, not causation. Capitalism didn't come out of sixteenth-century Mexico. Neither did it go back to Spain, where the resource curse of silver made people rich without having to make things.

What silver did in Mexico was to extend the Spanish presence into the unwelcoming North, developing complex towns and trading networks en route. As with the American West centuries later, the lure of minerals and livestock seduced both the foolhardy and the astute out of the more peaceful temperate zones to settle the drylands and frontier war zones. The discoveries of silver at Zacatecas were followed by others that pushed the frontier of Spanish rule: Guanajuato in 1550, Santa Bárbara in 1567, and Parral in 1623, the biggest European settlement north of the Tropic of Cancer.[94] Relatively few Spaniards clustered in those rowdy enclaves of wealth: At the beginning Zacatecas was home to about three hundred whites, not all of them Spanish. Smaller Real del Monte held only fifty-four Spanish men, half of them undocumented immigrants—they had omitted to apply for the Casa de Contratación's permit to cross the Atlantic—into the bargain. Don Fernando de Tapia, one of the founders of Querétaro, was Otomí.[95] Most laborers were Nahua, Tlaxcalan, or Otomí migrants from the altiplano, and even as the towns grew their populations remained predominantly indigenous.

The Spanish mines demanded numerous inputs: iron, timber, ropes, sacking, candles, oxen, and mules. Successful townsmen demanded luxuries: European clothes and paintings, Chinese silks, porcelain, and spices. Everyone needed food—unanimous carnivores—and drink, ranging from the cactus-based pulque—viscous, milky-colored and horrid, or at least an acquired taste—to cognac. The upshot was a series of backward linkages that developed the northern settlements into much more than shantytowns, and gave birth to new towns to supply them, like San Miguel (1555), Celaya (1571), Aguascalientes (1575), Saltillo (1577), and León (1585). Those new towns in turn demanded more food, which stimulated the rise of haciendas in their immediate vicinities. And there were dramatic forward linkages: Wealth from Zacatecas miners funded the colonization of Coahuila, Durango, and New Mexico.[96]

As in the American West, those getting rich were not so much miners as the merchants who supplied them. There were relatively few properly rich miners, but a lot of quite rich "middling people," the *gente intermedia*, merchants and shopkeepers who flocked to the boomtowns to set up businesses ranging from huts to hardware stores. Pedro Romero, esteemed the richest man in the world by 1771, started off as just another immigrant from Andalusia, a teenager working in his uncle's shop in Querétaro. With the profits he went into wholesale food and then silver, developing Pachuca's Veta Vizcaína as one of the world's largest mines. The rough garb to riches story continued as he transmuted financial capital into social capital. Romero married into an impoverished family of creole aristocrats and became a hidalgo; he lent money to the Crown and got a title, the Conde de Regla; he performed conspicuous works of public service and acquired titles for his sons. The Conde de Regla was also conspicuously pious, founding churches, convents, and colleges and funding scholarships for the poor. Like his American equivalents, he was also a transactional robber baron who forced indigenous laborers down his mines and pushed free workers so hard that they rebelled. He also owned pulquerías, the despised bars that separated the poor from their wages and sent them to lose their tools in the Monte de Piedad, the state pawn shop he funded. When the Count died, he was buried in Franciscan robes beneath the altar of one of his convents.[97]

Pedro Romero was exceptionally successful, but many like him moved quickly upward as the first settler families moved swiftly downward. One royal official, Gonzalo Gómez de Cervantes, had a foot in both camps, both miner and conquistador's son. His family, who claimed centuries of service fighting Muslims in Spain, may well have lost their lands in the 1560s when encomiendas were banned, and though Gómez did well in life, he left behind a bitter description of merchants replacing conquistadors:

> Those who but yesterday served in shops, taverns and other low jobs are today in possession of the best and most honorable positions in the country, whereas those the gentlemen and the descendants of those who conquered and settled it are poor, humiliated, disfavored and cast down.[98]

This was a bit rich; we don't know much about him, but we do know he prospered in the colonial administration, making it to the lofty heights of governor of Tlaxcala and possibly even the Real Audiencia.[99] There he would have rubbed shoulders with the new elite, the *almaceneros*, the import merchants of the capital, between ten and twenty wholesalers who distributed the world's goods across New Spain, making Mexico City the terminus of the Atlantic trade.

The almaceneros became extraordinarily wealthy. In the late sixteenth century they organized their own official body, the *consulado de México*, whose corporate clout bolstered autonomy in and control over the regional economies of the Americas. Even amid the downturn of the mid-seventeenth century the fortunes of the largest remained in the hundreds of thousands of pesos, at a time when the Crown's silver revenues averaged just over a million a year.[100] At the subsequent peak of silver production one small mining town was spending more than that annually on food and trade goods.[101] The almaceneros invested heavily in the trappings of merchant princes: townhouses, jewels, clothes, carriages, interior design, charitable endowments, aristocratic titles, elegant Black attendants "in brave and gallant liveries, heavy with gold and silver lace."[102] Paintings were shipped in by the crateload, mass-produced echoes of the *Siglo de Oro*, when Titian and El Greco painted in Spain for the metropolitan great and good. An estimated twenty-four thousand canvases were dispatched to the New World in the second half of the seventeenth century alone.[103] Like merchant elites everywhere they invested in the status markers of country estates, which spread across Mexico from the 1550s onward. Aristocrats in Spain, almost by definition, owned livestock; would-be aristocrats in New Spain imitated them. And landed ambition was not just a question of keeping up with the Joneses but also one of rational choice wealth management. Spanish inheritance law could with a single death destroy the fortunes of a merchant house by distributing it among legatees of variable abilities. A hacienda, on the other hand, could be converted into a trust through entailment and willed to a single descendant.

Haciendas were not money-making machines compared to trade, but they were essential to feed and clothe the growing towns and cities, and so they also drew in less prestigious provincial investors. There were two fundamental types of hacienda, meat- and plant-based, protein and carbohydrate, their specializations dictated by ecology, opportunity, and the local market. Sheep thrived in the temperate central highlands; cattle could survive most climates and colonized the North; in between the two zones, wheat, barley, and corn prospered across the fertile plains of the Bajío. Mountain ranges were unpropitious for haciendas, though they were used seasonally by huge migratory herds of sheep and goats, while the sparsely populated tropical lowlands were better suited to sugar and cotton plantations. Elsewhere, arable haciendas became the dominant type, cultivating European grain, fruits, and vegetables alongside the unfussy indigenous staples of maize, beans, and pulque, and they spread quickly from the well-watered central highlands westward into Michoacán and southward into Oaxaca. In most places there were some hybrids, their owners adapting to multiple ecologies or the mixed demands of a local market.

By the end of Spanish rule in 1821 there were some five thousand haciendas. The great livestock estates were territories unto themselves, complete with their own churches, *cascos*—fortified main houses—and small private armies. Shortly after Aguascalientes was founded, an impoverished laborer from Extremadura began farming cattle and sheep nearby; two generations later the family hacienda covered fourteen hundred square miles. The further north, the greater the potential for monopolization; one miner in Chihuahua bought rangelands that fed seventy thousand head of cattle. The very largest haciendas, also called *latifundios* or *estancias*, were the biggest private estates ever seen in the modern world, dwarfing even the great Australian cattle stations, Texan ranches, and Russian fiefdoms. A single family in Coahuila, the Marquises of Aguayo, ended up owning twenty-five thousand square miles, the equivalent of half of England.[104]

The typical hacienda was far smaller, and located not in the empty North but rather in concentric rings around Spanish towns. Farther south, towns grew sparser and haciendas as a result fewer, and as nearby as Oaxaca very few Spanish estates lay outside the valleys, while nearly a thousand Indian villages and their communal lands survived. The amount of arable land distributed officially by 1620 was actually quite small, not much more than two thousand square miles, though land grabs later legalized for one-off payments, the so-called *composiciones*, meant that much more than that was under Spanish cultivation. Once more the tyranny of distance determined key aspects of social organization; it was too expensive to transport most hacienda products any distance. By the time maize traveled sixty miles its price had gone up 50 percent. Prevailing mercantilist orthodoxy that privileged economic independence, monopoly, and boosting prices by cutting production didn't help. Neither did the Spanish ban on Mexican production of high-value, low-volume commodities that would have made long-distance hacienda trade more seductive, above all olive oil and alcohol. (Although there were regional exceptions, such as the Marquis of Aguayo's vineyards outside Saltillo, which sent wine from European varietals as far south as Mexico City.) Cow hides were the only items that haciendas could produce in real quantity for regional and international sales: The 1598 flota landed 150 thousand in Seville.[105]

As for plant products, the resilient cereals and maize could travel short distances cost-effectively, usually to places where other people's crops had failed. Vegetables and fruit couldn't survive the long journeys and bruising jolts of a mule train. The exceptions were high-value durable crops that couldn't be readily cultivated in Spain, above all sugar. The Spanish quickly spread the Southeast Asian grass from which this addictive product was derived, from Cortés's pioneering estates in Cuernavaca down to the subtropical coasts of Veracruz, Yucatán, and Oaxaca and across the temperate valleys of Puebla, Michoacán, New Galicia, and Colima. *Piloncillo*, the crude brown sugar they produced, was coveted wherever mule trains arrived. But sugar was fussy: It was a plantation crop requiring not just well-watered flatlands, themselves scarce assets, but also large amounts of start-up capital and forced labor, as opposed to the low quantities of all three necessary for livestock. Moreover, even as a low-volume, high-value commodity, sugar was still cursed by transport bottlenecks. The cost of transporting piloncillo from Veracruz to Mexico City tacked 50 percent onto the price, while competition with the Caribbean islands for international markets quickly overwhelmed exporters. Toward the end, sugar constituted only one percent of New Spain's agricultural production. Consequently, hacendados aspired to produce themselves everything they used, set out to dominate local markets rather than explore regional ones, and profited from times of hunger while suffering from times of plenty.[106]

This did not make them popular with either rulers or ruled. The parameters of acceptable business practice were set, as in most of the early modern world, by regulation and riot. Hacendados who hoarded maize and grain in hungry years to drive up prices were reined in by viceregal dictates establishing *pósitos*, public granaries, and punishing price gougers. Weighing the options of starvation or stone-throwing, the urban poor chose the latter often enough to discourage baronial rapacity. This does not mean that hacendados, hacienda workers, and their neighbors coexisted in forelock-tugging patriarchal warmth. At the outset of colonial rule extensive agriculture demanded a forced labor draft, the *repartimiento*, and throughout a resident workforce of peons who were often bound to their employers by debt, a legal relationship in extremis approaching chattel slavery. Sharecroppers, as everywhere, assumed all the risk and only some of the profit of crops that failed about once every decade.[107] But rooted belief in a moral economy—in which market relations coexisted with the moral imperative that no one, whatever their place in society, starve—allowed the hacienda to succeed as an institution at the same time as individual hacendados regularly failed. It was, perhaps, one more reflection of the ad hoc balance of power characteristic of so much of colonial Mexico. It was certainly a key determinant in what Mexican rural life looked like until the widespread arrival of capitalism three centuries later.

Until then, haciendas had little to do with the outside world. New Spain's second most valuable export after silver was not cattle hide but rather cochineal, a red dye produced by artisan farmers in the Oaxaca highlands. They collected tiny red beetles that lived on the nopal cactus, drowned, dried, and ground them to produce the world's most sought-after dyestuff. Once combined with Asian silks made by Chinese peasants it provided Europe's kings and archbishops with their robes (at huge labor cost; it took the harvesting and processing of seventy thousand insects to produce a pound of dye) in a microcosm of the new global economy.[108] Yet domestic agriculture was the cornerstone of Mexican economic activity: Even at the end of Spanish rule, when both silver and manufacturing production had risen steeply, a majority of Mexican wealth came from agricultural trades, and these were mainly local.[109] Hacendados had no monopoly there either, for all their aspirations; indigenous market farmers and self-sustaining peasants were critical in many regions. Meanwhile silver traveled directly from mine to royal mint to ship, and even with considerable leakage there were regular shortages of coinage in Mexico. The pre-Hispanic currency of cacao beans continued circulating for a long time after the silver boom, while the tlaco—a stamped strip of leather equivalent to one-sixteenth of a peso—was a staple of small change in the eighteenth century.[110] The greatest economic driver of change for everyday Mexicans was not silver but rather the new carbohydrates and, above all, proteins.

Abundant protein changed everyday life for everyone. Sheep and cows changed land use and ecologies, converting watered land in the center into pasture and arid nomadic territory in the North into vast Spanish estates. Mules revolutionized transport and together with oxen provided new sources of power. Horses changed warfare, first in favor of Spanish expansion, later in favor of indigenous resistance and even reconquest by fast-learning peoples like the Apache, who were subsequently followed onto horseback by the Comanche, Arapaho, Blackfoot, Cheyenne, and Lakota. When one sixteenth-century Indian was asked what the Castilians had ever done for him, he replied, eggs, horses, candles, and lamps. Far to the north, 150 years later, a Jesuit in New Mexico found that the O'odham people there "knew nothing of God, heaven, or hell but a great deal about cattle [and] horses." (They were doing better than their uncontacted neighbors in Baja California, who still ate copious rats and mice.) From early on even vagabonds ate the new animals: Bishop Zumárraga bemoaned the mestizo waifs, abandoned by their parents, who "wandered lost through the fields with neither law nor faith, eating raw meat." Old World livestock became all-pervasive: Fishermen who opened up a dead shark in Veracruz found a butcher's knife in its stomach.[111]

This was a marvel, though probably not for the knife's original owner, one of the many marvels the Spanish found in Mexico. It was a difficult place to get to, and remained that way for centuries, and it was a difficult place to know. The state didn't reliably reward people who came up with useful knowledge; the resource curse was also intellectual. Neither the inventor of the mercury extraction process, the pilot who led the first transpacific crossing, the friar who put together the definitive history of the fifteenth and sixteenth centuries, nor the bureaucrats who took the *Relaciones geográficas* seriously got much out of their hard work and creativity. Such lack of incentives is a major check on economic growth anywhere.[112] Yet despite the challenges of logistics and knowledge, the Spanish succeeded in extracting quantities of silver that revolutionized the global economy. Mexican silver drove economic and political change as it traveled by routes fair and foul across the world. Yet by a strange irony it didn't travel down far in Mexico itself, leaving indigenous worlds that changed remarkably slowly from their preconquest patterns of life.

Chapter Seven

Race, Idealism, and Realism

The idealism of racial hierarchy was central to New Spain. Like all Europeans, the Spanish hoped to construct colonial societies with the building blocks of race, inventing categories to order people on the basis of ancestry, companions, wealth, name, accent, language, vocabulary, geographical location, skin color, and lifestyle. All these characteristics combined to determine which race a person was ascribed in baptismal, marriage, and tax records, and with it, supposedly, what they could and couldn't do in life.[1] Races were also separated in death, the demise of whites recorded in different books from the rest. Yet when Spanish elites used race as a tool for domination, they brought to it a secondary idealism: that the concept enshrined rights as well as constraints. Priests and administrators treated the emperor's Mexican subjects differently according to their ascribed race, but those subjects were universally acknowledged to be fully human, enjoying certain universal rights. All had full access to the law, even if there were different codes and courts for different races. Hierarchical and humanist ideals were tightly intertwined; both, however, were subverted by realities. The same dictum applied to race as applied to most things in New Spain: *Del dicho al hecho hay mucho trecho*, between word and fact there's a big gap. When the ideals of racism and humanism met the realities of long distances and feeble government, they were only sometimes fulfilled. At other times those ideals were disdained, whether to the ends of unsanctioned oppression by rulers or undesirable freedom for ruled.

Interracial sex, the root of Mexico's hybrid society, threatened racial schema. It had done so in Spain before the conquest, where Christians, even prostitutes, were strictly forbidden from sleeping with Muslims or Jews, and by the 1400s prosecutions for interfaith fornication were everyday affairs.[2] In Mexico, however, the Spanish were given, or bought, or just seized indigenous women as concubines, starting with Malintzin. Wartime rape was extensive, and sexual violence deployed as a weapon or bonus. The authorities from the start aspired to regulate not just transactional and violent but all sex in order to stave off the threat of crossbreeding. They issued decrees demanding that the Spanish leave indigenous women be. In lieu of these, they required the settlers to bring in Spanish women; Cortés ordered his men to import their wives within a couple of years of the capture of Tenochtitlán, as did the emperor, while the Inquisition made the disciplining of Spanish bigamists its top priority. But all these measures failed, and as a result a large population of mestizos was quickly born. As Bishop Zumárraga reported to the future king Philip II in 1547,

> The married have been separated from their women for so many years that they are lost over there, and the men over here worse, almost all of them with *indias* littered with children, and there's nothing I can do about it, and seeing so much vice and sin makes me feel quite faint.[3]

This was not out of the settler norm: The first generation of North Americans in the West and of British in India also created substantial mixed-race populations. The difference lay in recognition, for all the qualms of Zumárraga and his peers. Eurasians, with some notable exceptions of nabob children, had little access to white status and its benefits; neither did those whom Americans later dubbed half-breeds, their numbers a lot greater than recognized, their claim on citizenship not much recognized at all.[4] In New Spain, by contrast, the children fathered by the first generation of Spaniards with indigenous princesses and noblewomen were incorporated into colonial society. Some of the more princely mestizos colonized Iberian society: Many of Montezuma's descendants with Spanish spouses moved to Spain to become members of the Order of Santiago, dukes, counts, viscounts, and marquises. Some sent European financial advisors back to Mexico to manage family affairs.[5] The last Habsburg viceroy was the Count of Montezuma, the last emperor's family back in power nearly two centuries after his death. Yet another Montezuma was the right-hand man of Guadalupe Victoria, the first president of independent Mexico.[6] Montezuma's descendants continued to receive state pensions based on their royal ancestry well into the twentieth century.[7]

It was not just the legitimate children of the powerful who held respectable places in the new order. Charles V and his empress demanded that the first viceroy, Antonio de Mendoza, do something about the numerous unrecognized mestizo children who they had heard roamed the city. He duly set up separate boarding schools for boys and girls with Spanish fathers. It was not just a holy but a pragmatic measure, "so necessary for our republic," Mendoza told his successor. Sex across racial boundaries might be feared and resisted, but a certain degree was also accepted as an inevitability to be dignified; in conservative Puebla, Mexico's second city, a third of the founders' families were based on marriages between Spaniards and Indians. In New England, by contrast, there is no record of a single interracial marriage before 1676. By the 1700s Mexican society was on the brink of baroque racial catalogues, with the general populace divided into sixteen meticulously (and wholly unrealistically) defined lineages and phenotypes, each one a distinct race with predetermined and distinct qualities. While slave traders used more than twenty shades of black to describe their goods, theorists coined strange names for the children of racially distinct sexual partners, such as *lobo* ("wolf," the grandchild of a Spaniard, Black, Asian, and Indian), *tente en el aire* ("suspended in air"), or *torna atrás* ("throwback"). Smart marriages, backstreet fumbles, and all the many possible sexual encounters in between created an ethnic diversity unmatched anywhere until the twentieth century.[8]

Apart from Mexico's unique position at the crossroads of the early modern world, four structural reasons created this multiracial society: a dearth of Spanish women, a slow-growing population of Spanish men, a collapsing indigenous population, and a substantial influx of African slaves intended to counteract that population collapse.

Spanish women did not come to the Americas in any numbers until, from the perspective of their social engineering superiors, it was too late. Even those who could expect the utmost luxury avoided the passage. Doña Ana de Castilla y Mendoza, the second viceroy's wife, left him on his own in Mexico City for years.[9] During the first thirty years of Spanish settlement on the mainland only one in twenty migrants was a woman; as late as the 1570s they were still less than a third of the newcomers, and their numbers fell steeply in the 1600s.[10] By contrast two-thirds of the passengers on the *Mayflower* were couples and their children.[11] Neither were there all that many Spanish men. An entire genre of letters from successful migrants to nephews back in Spain, pleading with them to come and partake of their uncles' successes, reveals an unsubtle desperation to attract more fellow countrymen. Many didn't; not all nephews had Pedro Romero's confidence. One cloth merchant in Puebla, writing in 1572 to his nephew, spelled it out particularly bitterly:

> I have been so unhappy that not one of you cowards, even having the support here that you have in me, should have had the courage to risk coming here to see me and help me enjoy my estate. I have written about it many times, as you well know . . . by God my only desire is to see people of mine in this land, in order to favor and aid them with my assets and have someone to look after me now in my old age when I need consolation more than ever.[12]

Whether his moral blackmail worked is unknown; what we do know is that less than 250,000 Spaniards moved to their entire American empire, from Patagonia to California, across the first century of its existence.[13]

This was the same order of magnitude as the slave trade, which in the early years of settlement brought in as many Blacks as whites. Cortés took three hundred Africans with him to Baja California; there were more with him on his disastrous Honduras expedition than there were Spaniards.[14] In 1550 the two populations were roughly the same size, each about 20,000 strong. While the slave trade was substantially illicit and so hard to quantify, Europeans may have brought as many as 150,000 West Africans to New Spain by 1640, shipping the registered into Veracruz and the unregistered into the muddy Gulf waters of Campeche or Pánuco. In some years smuggled humans outnumbered their legal counterparts by two or three to one. Their migration was a direct consequence of the mass dying of the indigenous peoples and the labor shortage it caused. It went back to before the Spanish arrival in Mexico, to the islands where indigenous populations collapsed completely, leading a 1516 commission of Hieronymite friars to recommend their replacement by African slaves with Old World resistance to disease. The recommendation was seconded by a young Bartolomé de las Casas. The emperor agreed and issued the first license, allowing the importation of four thousand slaves over eight years. Las Casas never forgave himself.[15]

For the overwhelming majority of the rest of society, though, the African slave trade seemed like a good idea that only improved over time, one justifiable once again by the sophistry of religious conversion. The many tribes of West Africa were considered a bunch of warring heathens (that the wars were often driven by slave raids was a dissident position); it was in their own interest to be relocated to New Spain and receive the salvation offered by its Church. Slavery was distinctly in the Crown's interest, as the Crown created and sold to merchants the import license called the asiento, a major and guaranteed source of revenue in a world of industrious tax evaders. It was in those merchants' interest, as they could either sell quotas from their license to slave traders at a markup or engage in the trade themselves. Whoever got the slaves across the Atlantic made a substantial profit; quite expensive even wholesale in Africa, slaves became extremely expensive retail in Mexico, fetching three to five times the price of an Indian, costing between 300 and 500 pesos apiece in the seventeenth century. Slavery was also in the buyers' interest, because the Africans and *afrodescendientes*, their descendants, supplied a workforce unavailable elsewhere. Black slaves cut sugarcane on the coasts, picked cotton, bolstered the muster of field hands on the mixed haciendas, acted as overseers and ranch hands on the livestock haciendas of the center, and unloaded the ships in Acapulco and Veracruz.[16]

The Mexican trade in African slaves fluctuated with demand and war. It started off quite slowly, increased rapidly in the last quarter of the sixteenth century, peaked during the seventeenth century, and then declined to a trickle across the eighteenth century. At its peak it was supplemented by an Asian slave trade, as the Manila galleons brought an estimated eight thousand servants from the Philippines and points further west (including Bishop Zumárraga's cook, probably the first from the Indian subcontinent to use the tomatoes and chiles subsequently central to Indian food).[17] The trade suffered a major interruption in the mid-seventeenth century when Spain lost wars against much of northern Europe and decided to cancel the asiento system and end slave imports. Economics and the fragility of imperial rule caused the government to reauthorize shipments, now largely in the hands of Spain's erstwhile enemies the Dutch, English, and French. But while slavery became increasingly lucrative in the emerging sugar economies of Brazil and the Caribbean islands, it was less and less important in Mexico; this was in large part because the labor shortage there was far less serious. Extensive interracial marriage, or fruitful interracial sex, had largely resolved the problem.

The only significant exceptions were higher-ranking Spanish women, who were confined to cities and within them to private houses or convents because of the constant danger their sex posed; in the contemporary culture of honor they could, with a single act of sexual transgression, bring down a family. Iberians recognized two forms of honor: *honra*, which was individual virtue, and *honor*, which was individual and family social status, accumulated painstakingly over generations by public acts of courage, wealth, community-building, and/or charity. Both forms could be lost with shocking speed through a lost virginity or an uncovered affair, and with them could go a family's access to not just social but also political and financial capital, because the dishonored did not attract patrons, business partners, or lenders. The contradiction between expectations of polygamy for successful men and monogamy for successful women was not confined to imperial Spain, but under such stringent conditions it was particularly bitter. And in the multicultural world of New Spain both illicit sex and its product could be catastrophic: Jewish, Muslim, or Black ancestors all polluted *limpieza de sangre*, blood purity, and could damn family members for generations.

This cutting logic applied across all ranks of Spanish society. The rich had more power to obey it: They enjoyed greater private space, favoring the defense of virtue; political contacts; and, when things went wrong, access to "private pregnancies" or even *probanzas de limpieza de sangre*, official certificates of blood purity. *Cacicas*, wealthy Indian noblewomen in Oaxaca or Tlaxcala who ruled their communities, were desirable marriage partners. Further down the class scale there was more opportunity for adultery, rape, or premarital sex because women were less attended, less likely to have servants, and more likely to have jobs, which took them out of the house to work, shop, and socialize. As they got poorer, and the population of impoverished Spanish women rose as time went by, so their chances of having mixed-race children grew. If they became pregnant while unmarried, they might be sent to a *casa de recogidas*, a house for fallen women, a priestly jail for the sexually unsound. Poorer and less successful men could be punished too: In 1667 the alcalde of Aguascalientes exiled Gerónimo de Medina for six years after the night watchman caught him "nude and lying in bed with this married woman" committing "an offence against God."[18] Serial wife-beaters were liable to be drafted. For the mighty whose families rather than womenfolk had fallen, there was the more decorous solution of the Convento de Jesús María, founded in 1582 specifically for the impoverished daughters and granddaughters of the conquistadors.[19]

Yet women in New Spain were more than unreliable reproducers, partners in or objects of pleasure, social and sexual control. Like women anywhere, across most of recorded history they were not much recorded, moving less seen than men through the archived past. They could not be politicians, priests, nor—until the dying days of the colony, when some took over the equivalent of social services—administrators. They could occupy a few of the heights of visible power in their own right as abbesses, indigenous cacicas, or wealthy widows. Spanish law allowed women to inherit before sons, leading to figures like Leonor de Alburquerque, nicknamed with eloquent simplicity *la rica hembra*, the rich female, who in legend could ride across Castile without leaving her own lands.[20] The precept crossed the Atlantic, and unless they remarried widows could run big businesses: One of the great sheep fortunes of seventeenth-century Querétaro was managed for decades by Doña Francisca de Espíndola.[21]

On a humbler, collective level, some social groups enjoyed clout because of their key economic and cultural functions. *Curanderas,* folk healers, were respected and feared. Market sellers were notoriously independent-minded; someone had to keep the supply chain moving, and they took advantage of that, and their clientele stood up for them. When the authorities in Toluca went to arrest the pulque vendor Margarita Bernal (for living in sin) she won over the crowd by telling the constable, among some really choice insults, that "the judge and his ministers were beggars and thieves to a man" and that she was a very respectable Indian lady and no fool and had the money to take them to court in the capital.[22] When food riots broke out more women like Bernal broke briefly into judicial records, because they quite often instigated or led them: Mothers and grandmothers did the family maths, and they worked out when the price of corn or grain no longer added up. In more decorous roles, the nuns of New Spain were far from cloistered religious automata. Convents were places of worship and discipline, but they were also refuges for numerous women who were either unmarriageable through genteel poverty or just not minded to marry, seeking greater independence or education.

At times individuals crop up in passing, tantalizing shadows: María de Estrada, a lethal conquistadora, Black slave-owning matriarchs, female cowboys, bandits, nuns with visions like Francisca de los Angeles. One bridged multiple categories: Catalina de Erauso, who in the early seventeenth century escaped her Dominican convent, exchanged her habit for a man's clothes, fought for the king on the Chilean frontier, murdered a man in Peru, got off in exchange for rejoining a convent, and ended up as a muleteer—a suitably difficult, hard-nosed, entrepreneurial job—in Mexico. She was rare because we know about her—she left behind something of an autobiography—and because she allegedly got a dispensation from the Pope to continue cross-dressing.[23] Some of this, the last flourish in particular, sounds too good to be true. A different sort of transgressor, however, generated copious records (including a biography and the outlines of an autobiography) that demarcate the boundaries of the permissible in gender relations: Sor Juana Inés de la Cruz, a seventeenth-century Hieronymite nun who turned her cell into a study and her convent's common room into a literary salon. By the end of her career she was recognized—by the leading male intellectual of her time—as "a phoenix in all the sciences, in the emulation of the subtlest of creations, immortal glory of New Spain."[24]

Her story is baroque not just in terms of the age. She was born to a Basque hacendado father and a creole mother, one of the many Mexicans born out of wedlock, in 1648, or perhaps 1651. According to her autobiography she snuck away to a girls' school when she was three years old—an eloquent anecdote—and learned to read and write. In 1664 she joined the entourage of Vicereine Leonor Carreto, Marquess of Mancera, and then took holy orders in 1669 in the Convent of Santa Paula. Sor Juana's independence was secured in part through such relationships with three Vicereines, above all the Countess de Paredes, ironically one more shadow despite her status. The aristocrat was beautiful, intelligent, and one might surmise bored to death with court life and a feeble husband, and she quickly struck up a close relationship with the famous nun. The Countess's patronage was more than protective and local: In 1689 she organized the publication of *Castalian Inundation* in Madrid, the first of three books that stayed in print in the metropole until 1725.[25]

Sor Juana produced enough work to choose from: plays, songs, sonnets, a theological essay, love poems, a eulogy to the synthesis of Spanish and indigenous culture and a lengthy defense of women's rights. She experimented with writing in Nahuatl. And she also wrote about sex:

> So I say, Inés, to one thing I aspire,
> That your love and my good wine will draw you hither,
> And to tumble you to bed I can conspire.[26]

This was not just explicit (and bawdier than anything else she wrote); it was sapphic enough to give a prurient future pause for thought. Her present was given pause for thought by her independence, manifested in among other works a terse condemnation of men's sexual hypocrisy:

There is no woman suits your taste,
Though circumspection be her virtue:
ungrateful, she who does not love you,
Yet she who does, you judge unchaste.
You men are such a foolish breed [. . .]
Who does the greater guilt incur
When a passion is misleading?
She who errs and heads his pleading,
Or he who pleads with her to err?[27]

Alongside her freedom she also managed throughout her career as Mexico's leading intellectual the pressure to behave, in the religious and gender terms of the day. One abbess admonished her that "study was a thing of the Inquisition" (this particular boss was, Sor Juana sniped, "very saintly" but soon transferred); the Jesuit Padre Antonio de Vieyra pushed her repeatedly to retire from public life and writing; her response to his criticism, *Response to Sor Filotea,* was Sor Juana's last major publication before she gave in, gave up writing, and retired to an anonymous convent life. She died soon afterward in an epidemic.[28]

Rather like the outraged pulque seller Margarita Bernal, or the cross-dressing muleteer, Sor Juana stood out in New Spain because she was a woman who left behind words in print, and defiant ones into the bargain. All three lived in a constant tension between the possible and the permissible; only one of them, the muleteer Catalina de Erauso, died having reconciled the two in her favor. (Bernal was arrested after market, when her crowd had ebbed away, and after days in jail apologized, pleading sunstroke and a glass of pulque, and married her lover.)[29] They illustrate the boundaries of the possible for the exceptional individual: impossible to ignore, but imperative to ponder just how much they reflect the stories of the mass of unrecorded lives. As with all unequal power relationships in Mexico, women's ability to shape their lives came down in part to realpolitik, both generally and case by case, a weighing up by the dominant of the cost of oppression against the cost of tolerance.

There were four main types of what euphemism called *mezclarse*, "mingling": indigenous women with Spanish men, Black women with Spanish men, indigenous women with Black men, and the many possible combinations of their descendants, generically grouped as *castas*. The people of New Spain enjoyed in practice, if not in theory, relatively liberated sex lives choreographed by clear codes of flirtation and seduction, and by the seventeenth century the results were towns and cities that housed substantial mestizo, mulatto, and casta populations.[30]

Contemporary and historic estimates of these populations' size are understandably all over the place. No viceroy attempted a general census until 1793, nearly three centuries after first contact, and while the Spanish were fond of counting, demographic data such as marriage petitions are few and far between until the eighteenth century. European observers probably overcounted. Two order-of-magnitude conclusions are abundantly clear, however: The Spanish remained a minority, and they were outnumbered in the seventeenth century not just by Indians and mestizos but also by the combined numbers of mulattos and Blacks. This was predictable in the frontier towns like Veracruz, Acapulco, and Guanajuato, where as late as 1755 some 70 percent of the population was mulatto. Yet it was also the story of Mexico City, where one early-seventeenth-century guesstimate had fifteen thousand Spaniards facing eighty thousand Indians and more than fifty thousand Blacks and mulattos; perhaps baffled by the multitude of other ancestral possibilities, the author omitted them, glossing over even mestizos. A more scientific estimate proposed a mere twenty-four thousand Indians, a newly made minority in what used to be their city, but still considerably more numerous than the Spaniards.[31]

In such circumstances sorting out who was ethnically who was a bureaucratic nightmare for priests, pen pushers, and everyday people. It was imperative, though, because African blood was considered a "stain" with powerful real-life consequences, and by 1650 New Spain was home to as many as 150,000 people of African descent. Racial classifications from slave sales were the simplest, based on the sole and casual qualifier of skin color: *negro*, *mulato, mulato prieto* (dusky), *mulato cocho* (sooty), *mulato blanco* (white), *mulato membrillo* (quince-colored), *mulato achinado* (Chinese-ish), *mulato morisco* (Moorish), and so on.[32] Such differences might matter greatly in terms of value, status, and job, of who was flogged in the cane fields and who rode behind carriages in Mexico City, but in terms of legal rights they didn't matter; a chattel slave was a chattel slave. Classifying the freeborn, on the other hand, was a different question.

To manage it the Spanish turned to paperwork. Books of genealogical merit are universal in one form or another: The royal genealogies that make swathes of the Old Testament or *The Anglo-Saxon Chronicle* so unreadable, the dictionary of privileged inbreeding that is *Burke's Peerage*, the more open *Who's Who*. In Mexico the books and dossiers that mattered were birth registers, marriage records, *informaciones de limpieza de sangre* (reports on blood purity), and *probanzas de limpieza de sangre* (certificates of blood purity). Priests defined and wrote down babies' race at birth, bureaucrats reaffirmed their decisions when those babies became adults and went for jobs or to court or back to the church to marry or baptize their own babies. As the Spanish occupation aged, so everyday people came to track their ancestors, in extremis for generations into the past, because it mattered greatly for their legal rights. Racial categories were fictions, whether the philosophical fictions of biological determinism or the biographical fictions people spun as they claimed the most advantageous identity. But viceregal Spain invented racial classification on supposedly scientific grounds, the first society to do so in history. From the sixteenth century on, Iberians spoke of *raza*, race, as the sum of inherited characteristics transmitted through blood, semen, and breast milk, and deployed it to determine where the Crown's subjects should live, what jobs they could hold, what law codes they had to follow, and even what clothes they could wear.[33]

The Spanish aspired from the start to a rigid spatial apartheid. The traza, that neatly delineated grid of downtown blocks open only to Spaniards, was exported from Mexico City to other cities, such as Oaxaca, in that case by the same ad hoc urban planner. Indians were legally excluded from living inside the traza, dispatched to surrounding barrios in the old cities and assigned separate villages outside the new towns. Frontier boomtowns like Querétaro started out perforce mixed up, all races jumbled together for safety in a small center; neither could the twelve founders of Aguascalientes, packed in adobe houses in what was basically a small fort, afford pickiness. As the vecinos consolidated their grasp and their towns spread out, they could engage in segregation, and when Aguascalientes was refounded in 1609 it came with a traza and a commuter *pueblo de indios*, San Marcos, a quarter of a mile west of the parish church.[34] But unlike apartheid, viceregal racial segregation was intended to run both ways and protect both groups. Just as the central grid systems that spread at the turn of the seventeenth century were supposed to be for Spaniards only, so the indigenous barrios and satellite communities were supposed to be reserved for Indians. There they would be protected from the iniquities of Spanish and mixed-race land grabs, violence, and disease, a measure the friars had called for from the outset, and which the Crown decreed in 1563. Encomenderos were not allowed to settle inside the boundaries of their encomiendas; anyone not an Indian was forbidden to live in an Indian town. The Spanish in the city centers, meanwhile, were to be secure from the perceived filth, economic competition, and potential violence of the Indians.

Employment was designed to follow the same lines, with the Spanish monopolizing the center of the economy. In the countryside, Indians were subject to coercive labor regimes that were legally defined and that evolved over the sixteenth century toward salaried work without ever wholly getting there. At the extreme was the mass slavery that had done so much to depopulate the Caribbean islands. During those early years of embryonic control in the altiplano and no-holds-barred raids in the North and West, slavery was legal and practiced on a massive scale. The rebuilding of the City of Mexico pulled in tens of thousands of *macehuales*, Nahua peasants, and *chichimeca*, northern nomads, in "herds as large as those of sheep," wrote Motolinía. There they were branded, first with the iron of Carlos V and subsequently with those of their private owners, scars building up across faces in a palimpsest of enslavement as they were bought and sold.[35] As early as May 1522 records show the Spanish paying taxes on eight thousand indigenous slaves in the Valley of Mexico alone. By the mid-century estimates ran from high tens of thousands into rhetorical millions.[36]

Neither Church nor Crown approved. In 1500, before the Spaniards even reached Mexico, the *reyes católicos* banned indigenous slavery in general. The monarchs were ignored (and swiftly opened up loopholes themselves), and when in 1511 the Dominican Antón de Montesinos castigated a church full of slaveowners, it was a revolutionary shock. He came before his congregation in Hispaniola, he said, to tell them that they were all in mortal sin and to ask them:

> With what right and with what justice do you hold in such cruel and terrible servitude these Indians? On whose authority have you waged such repellent wars on these people who were in their own lands, docile and peaceful, where so countless of them you have consumed, with deaths and travails never before seen? . . . Are these not men? Have they not rational souls? Are you not obliged to love them as you love yourselves? . . . Have no doubt that in your condition you will no more manage to obtain salvation than will the Moors or Turks.[37]

Montesinos—a "choleric and very effective man," according to one chronicler—was nearly lynched; he stood up the next Sunday and said it all over again. Or so his colleague Bartolomé de las Casas reported, decades later. By then Las Casas was the dissident ideologue of the Indies, a merchant's son who came out from Seville in the glory days of 1502, eighteen, arrogant, and with useful experience in conquered Granada. In 1510 he joined the Dominicans. Yet even he was not wholly convinced by Montesinos, and still accepted grants of Indian slaves to work his gold mines. Las Casas's Damascene moment came three years later, when he gave his own denunciation from the pulpit and sailed back to Spain with Montesinos to advocate at court for abolition. After four years of politicking he returned to the Americas in 1520 with the title "Universal Protector of the Indians." In an exceptionally long life—he died at eighty-one, a rare span for the time—he crossed the Atlantic another seven times to advocate for his flocks; became Bishop of Chiapas; wrote the first major attack on the Spanish occupation of the Americas, the *Short Account of the Destruction of the Indies* (1552); followed it up with the three-volume *History of the Indies* (unpublished for centuries); and argued for Indian rights in a set-piece debate at court. (In classic Habsburg fashion, no clear resolution was reached; seven years later the judges had yet to rule.)[38]

These were rhetorical and philosophical checks and balances; legal checks and balances on slavery also obtained. The branding iron that burned the seal of Charles V into an Indian's face and took his or her freedom was kept in a locked box with only two keys, one held by Bishop Zumárraga, at that point Protector of Indians.[39] The 1512 Laws of Burgos contained significant human rights provisions, including the prohibition of corporal punishment and child labor. The 1542 New Laws declared Mexican Indians "free vassals, so from here on, no Indian can be made into a slave under any circumstance including wars, rebellions, or when ransomed from other Indians."[40] After nearly fifty years of slavery in the Americas this was revolutionary legislation.

It was partially implemented. In 1549, for example, Las Casas was summoned along with another great defender of indigenous human rights, Vasco de Quiroga, to determine the race of a twenty-year-old servant, Catalina de Velasco. She claimed to be from New Spain, while her mistress claimed that she came from the Portuguese empire. If Mexican she would be free; if a Portuguese import she would be a slave. Phrenologists avant la lettre, the monks examined her skull and pronounced her indigenous and thus liberated. The same year two slaves called Pedro and Luisa sued their master, the psychopathic Nuño de Guzmán, for freedom and 200 pesos compensation and won. (Guzmán appealed and had the amount reduced.) That these cases came before the unresolved 1550 philosophical debate on indigenous freedom says a lot about Spanish society's indecision on the subject. But religious pressure on chattel slavery endured, and the Crown reiterated a partial ban in 1570. A century later, in 1679, they made the ban total.[41]

Slavery was not the only form of forced labor. Five of the ten plagues that Motolinía described as the consequences of conquest stemmed from the violent recruitment of indigenous workers. The Nahua were given no choice in whether to rebuild Tenochtitlán, wriggle through the narrow shafts of gold mines, serve in the labor drafts known as repartimientos, or pay tribute to and work for their supposedly Christianizing encomenderos. In the early years, Motolinía wrote, the *calpixque* who administered the new estates "were so complete in their mistreatment of Indians and in burdening them and sending them far from their lands and in giving them so many other tasks that many Indians died at their hands."[42] This was not missionizing hyperbole. The *Codex*

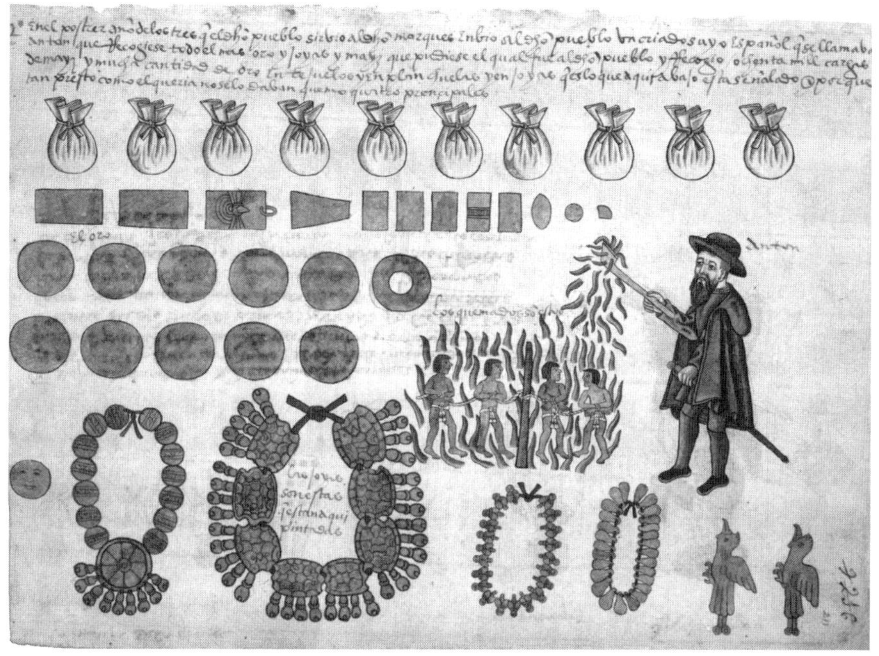

Cortés's overseer burns four indigenous noblemen to death, and is sued. Codex Tepetlaoztoc (1550s).

Tepetlaoztoc shows in graphic detail Anton, one of Cortés's overseers, burning four nobles in chains; they had been slow in coming through with their tribute payments.[43]

Yet all indigenous labor regimes were subject to opposition from their subjects, and the *Codex Tepetlaoztoc*, which combines hieroglyphs with Spanish text, was part of an elaborate lawsuit that villagers filed in the mid-1550s against multiple encomenderos. Two years later the viceroy named an indigenous justice to their estates with the explicit instruction to uphold Indians' rights. By then, a decade after the death of Cortés, it was open season on the conquistador's properties, and the audiencia ordered his mayordomo to pay large fines to assorted Indian plaintiffs.[44] As the sixteenth century aged, the number of Indians plummeted and the number of Africans rose, with a decline in the most coercive practices against Indians. The expanding haciendas replaced overt with covert violence. Indians, rather than being enslaved or drafted through the repartimiento, were increasingly compelled to work the land through debt peonage, which contractually bound them to an employer by cash advances. Some Indians took wage labor a step further by moving to mining districts and becoming free workers. They were not free in terms of choosing any asset or career; Indians were formally banned from owning livestock, the main rural path up the social ladder. Yet many indigenous men and women could make that most basic choice of all, the standard one of modern countrymen, to maintain traditional roles in the countryside or pioneer new lives in towns.

Those who did make the leap to the new Indian pueblos that supported Spanish towns, or the indigenous barrios of Mexico City, were supposed to bring with them those tight restrictions on which jobs they could and couldn't do. Indians were allowed to work as weavers (often compelled, the woolen mills being one of the main holdouts against emancipation), porters, market sellers, boatmen, potters, carpenters, masons, and manual laborers. They did the filthy job of manning the tanneries, where feces and urine were used to cure leather. They were initially banned from the lucrative skilled trades that proliferated fast in booming, free-spending Mexico City, where about half the Spaniards were artisans. Indians were not supposed to be bakers, wheelwrights, coopers, cobblers, glovemakers, glassblowers, bookbinders, tailors, barber-surgeons or, at the very top of those who added value, painters or silversmiths. Self-interest pushed the Spanish specialists in these trades to form guilds, the medieval European craft associations, and to exclude Indians and castas from membership. Within a couple of generations Spanish artisans had established over two hundred such guilds.[45] Their monitoring of who shod horses, hammered hoops onto barrels, worked silver into crosses or drinking cups, cut silks or painted for the rich, shaved the stubbly, and bled the sick was intended to be a legal check on the job prospects of non-whites.

Some regulations were about more than wealth and status. The Spanish had self-evident reasons for keeping their racial subordinates out of armories and gun shops, with their dangerous possibilities.[46] Race riots or would-be rebellions were an ever-present fear—the authorities thought they'd detected a Black conspiracy to seize the city in 1537—but one that rarely materialized. But the invocation of the colored horde in officials' reports was a genre standard, part of a paranoid (and profitable) line that they were keeping the ship of state afloat at huge personal cost and against overwhelming odds. "I am afraid," wrote the viceroy Velasco the Younger,

> that troubles very hard to remedy are going to come from one side or the other because the country is so full of blacks and mestizos, who greatly outnumber the Spaniards, and all of whom wish to purchase their liberty with the lives of their masters; this bad breed will join anyone who rebels.[47]

An audiencia decades later filled in more details of this nightmarish Spanish vision of gangs of Black slaves embedded in Spanish households inside the traza, plotting in their Black Catholic brotherhoods, armed to the teeth, "bellicose, bestial and ferocious."[48] The Nahua found the paranoia risible. When another supposed plot was identified, the historian Chimalpahin observed,

> We Mexica indigenous were not at all frightened by it but were just looking and listening, just marveling at how the Spaniards were being destroyed by their fear, and didn't appear as such great warriors [after all].[49]

The authoritarian's ideal solution, proposed over and over, was mass deportation. This was wholly undoable, but lesser answers to the intertwined concerns of safety and symbolism extended from bans on possessing really useful weapons—guns, horses, swords, owning any of which cost a Black slave one hundred lashes—to prohibiting the use of space. In 1598 the viceroy closed the Alameda, the park in Mexico City where people promenaded and rode to see and be seen, to prevent colored people and poor whites from meeting.[50] Blacks outside the city had to carry travel permits, part of a legal system of almost totalitarian ambition, shot through with a desire to see and control every single aspect of life. Legal distinctions between the rights of different phenotypes extended even to clothes and jewels; the Spanish, feeling that jewels and other finery might give their racial inferiors ideas above their station, barred Blacks and mulattos from wearing gold, pearls, and embroidered cloaks; Indians were forbidden to wear European dress.

Along with racialized rights came racialized punishments. Offenders got very different sentences depending on their racial category, much as in the modern American empire, but with the difference not implicit but rather explicitly laid down in law. A Spaniard who sold meat with rigged scales would be fined twenty pesos; his Black, mulatto, or mestizo competitor was liable to a hundred lashes.[51] Colored peoples' rights, though, were also written into law. Legislation of punitive violence against slaves was prefaced by strictures to slave masters to avoid unchristian cruelties like mutilation. The Spanish came to the Americas with laws regulating slaves' lives that stretched back to the Siete Partidas, an Iberian Magna Carta from the thirteenth century, and those laws gave slaves recourse to the same courts as Spaniards. They could sue to be either sold or freed, and that ability to sue owners theoretically protected their rights to own property, to marry and stay together as family, and eventually to be manumitted by self-purchase or by lawsuits they launched and won. The sheer numbers of the freed—over 40 percent of all slaves in Mexico City in the first century—substantiate the principle of the Siete Partidas, that slaves were Christians *in potentia*, their status no blemish on their human condition.[52] Viceregal Mexico was a slave society and remained so until Independence in 1821, but alongside the violence and the constraint there was also a society of rights.

No group, however, was as prone to take to the courts as the Indians. Amid the continuing conquest of the sixteenth century, Judge Alonso de Zorita wrote in amazement of their litigiousness, sounding like a tort reform enthusiast (with perhaps the same probusiness axe to grind). The damage and "enormous costs" of opportunistic lawsuits of "Indians against Indians within towns, of subjects against lords in all New Spain, of towns against towns, and dependencies against their head towns" had, he lamented,

> brought about great upheavals everywhere . . . false oaths, hates, enmities, the ruin of Indian towns and provinces, the many and grave misdeeds of those who incite and persuade the Indians in order to rob them, and finally the chaos that now exists among the Indians, which has become so bad that it seems impossible to end.

It was in his eyes a legal free-for-all, driven by lawyers, plebeians, crooks, and wastrels, a struggle for land, labor, status, and power that was destroying the fabric of native society.[53]

Inside what Zorita painted as lethal frivolity, though, lay much of the preservation of Indian rights and property. After indigenous slavery was banned in 1542, those Indians who sued their masters for freedom generally won, and as a consequence the market in indigenous slaves took a major knock.[54] Indigenous communities that filed suit against haciendas over boundaries, water, and commons prevailed often enough to preserve free villages across central and southern Mexico. Crooked officials and abusive landowners were always there, but the possibility of being sued provided some check on egregious abuses of power. The Nahua also had their crooks, and a group of forgers systematically produced and sold *títulos primordiales,* fake royal land grants.[55] The writ of *amparo*, a rough equivalent of habeas corpus, also protected those Indians savvy enough to get one against bureaucratic despotism or land grabs. When the Crown learned that Spanish defendants were getting lesser punishments when they lost to indigenous plaintiffs, the reaction was to order the audiencia to apply the reverse logic: Spaniards who committed offenses against Indians would receive stricter, not weaker, sentences.[56] Such royal paternalism was fair and necessary because Indians were "*niños con barbas*," children with beards.[57]

As ever, state fragility hampered smooth-running bureaucracy: Cases were costly to file; unsalaried functionaries were readily bought; and attempts to avoid the time and expense of a full trial, in which each side could call up to thirty witnesses, generally failed. Verdicts were systematically appealed in cases that dragged on for years. But as the legal system stuttered, the Spanish authorities did more than petulantly repeat the same lines. Viceroy Mendoza found a way around clogged and corrupt courts in the 1540s by reclassifying most cases as administrative rather than judicial; he then resolved them swiftly and cheaply in person, the interested parties present with interpreters on Monday and Thursday mornings. In the 1590s, looking for a more institutional solution, the Crown set up the Juzgado General de Indios, the General Indian Court. Indians wishing to sue Spaniards would still go to Spanish courts, but cases between Indians or with indigenous defendants went to the new court with its indigenous magistrates, free advocates and defense lawyers, and the simplified hearings and judgements reserved in traditional Castilian law for the weak or defenseless. The new system had flaws, but it was one of the main reasons that indigenous villages kept hold of their land, powers, and privileges, and the Juzgado General de Indios endured until Independence. Its strengths were clear to see once it was gone and a more typical North American dispossession began.[58]

As modern states were born, all the Christian ones endorsed earthly inequality as part of God's divine plan. Every creature had its place in a predetermined hierarchy, the Great Chain of Being, which ascended from the lowest creatures through the monarch to the divine. In Mexico the Spanish incorporated early scientific racism into this religious ordering system, extending its logic even beyond phenotype into the white elite. Spaniards born in the Americas were, some Europeans reasoned, lesser humans due to the baneful influence of climate and stars. Not at all, Mexican astrologers replied; it was not the patterns of their skies but their race that made other people, the brown and black ones, physically and mentally inferior.[59]

This racism did not preclude humanism; it could complement it, classifying indigenous people as the equivalent of the widows and orphans whom Spanish medieval law deemed *miserables* and for whom the king was supposed to take special care, systematically defending their rights against better-placed predators. The logic extended to encompass the rights of Blacks and mulattos, to sometimes unexpected lengths. In Aguascalientes in December 1669 Juan Francisco Ruiz, the town judge, heard that one of the town's notables, the widow Doña Catalina de Anguiano, was "greatly mistreating with lashes and blows" one of her slaves. Lacking evidence, the judge wrote in his report, he decided to see for himself. Visiting the widow's house, he inspected the girl, a seventeen-year-old mulatta, with a cold anger that comes through in his detailed cataloguing of her injuries. "Telling her to disrobe," he reported,

> I saw on her head many blows and contusions which it seemed had bled, seemingly given with a club or stone, and on her face marks and scabs seemingly from kicks and on her body a large quantity of

> scabs seemingly inflicted with some sort of leather whip and in the shackles the soles of the feet opened with a whip and flesh wounds four fingers long which seemed to be the abrasions of some sort of plaited rope.

He brought witnesses and took the girl from the house to convalesce and fined Doña Catalina 500 pesos and warned her not to leave town until definitive judgement had been issued. That could well have been banishment, an ostracism terrible to contemplate for a wealthy Spanish urbanite, about as close to social death as a member of the overclass might get.[60]

There is no record that the sentence in Aguascalientes was executed, and the outcome is unknowable. The last entry in the file says that a final binding decision can't be handed down because Ruiz doesn't have any of the special paper with the royal stamp, which comes from Spain, and he'll have to send to Zacatecas to obtain some. That might have been true; the next decision in the judicial archive comes a whole seven months later. Or it might be that the influence of Doña Catalina's class prevailed. And perhaps the only reason the case came to the judge in the first place was because of the girl's skin color; she was, the judge noted, "more or less white."[61]

This might also be an overly cynical reading of a semi-legible archive and the judge that lives on in it. His actions in an unresolved case in a dusty provincial town were not unique: Fifty years earlier fifteen hundred Blacks and mulattos demonstrated with a murdered slave's broken body in front of the viceroy's palace. Regulation and the threat of riot marked the boundaries of intolerable racial violence: The viceregal "Orders for the proper treatment of negros" offered rewards for whistleblowers.[62] The case of Doña Catalina and the tortured mulatta is a microcosm of the messiness of the history of race in Mexico, where the idealism of racial hierarchy and universal justice met with the realism of disorder. Unstable boundaries and an inability to police them allowed a greater Spanish oppression than society's rules contemplated, but also greater freedom and social mobility to the racial lower classes. Covert indigenous slavery endured in the North and the further reaches of the South past abolition and into the twentieth century. Simultaneously, all ethnic groups passed in numbers outside their racially allotted places in colonial society. Some individuals made history. Lope Martín, the expert navigator who piloted the lead ship on the first transpacific crossing, was a free mulatto from Portugal. He was disappeared from the narrative of the journey, and the record achievement was attributed to the Augustinian friar Andrés de Urdaneta.[63] Other individuals' gains were spectacularly visible: In the seventeenth century one head of the Franciscan Order, Tomás Manzo, was mestizo; one of the master gunsmiths, Agustín de Aguilar, was mulatto; and the most famous court painter of the eighteenth century, Miguel Cabrera, was Zapotec.[64]

Like his contemporaries, Cabrera painted the viceroyalty's leaders and religious tableaux, but he really stands out as a master of the niche genre of *pinturas de castas*, panels and canvas grids purporting to represent sixteen racial types of Mexicans. They showed parents of different ancestries and skin colors together with their offspring, their racial categories, and as many of their mœurs as the artists could symbolize in clothing, poses, places, and possessions. They were not mug shots in oils. The paintings were popular—over one hundred survive—as souvenirs for high-ranking retirees and as curiosities for the collectors' cabinets of European tastemakers, perhaps grouped with zoological curiosities like the armadillo.[65] Some artists crammed in a bit of botany for good luck, painting and labeling typical flora as backdrop to the human fauna. The pinturas de castas epitomize the racial curiosity of the Spanish and creole elites, in particular with detecting the contamination of African blood, but also the surrealism of operationalizing it. Seven racial categories were in meaningful use at the time, cropping up with regularity in written records: *español, indio, negro, mestizo, mulato, castizo* (three quarters Spanish, one quarter Indian), and *morisco* (the children of Spanish men and mulatto women).[66] Boundaries between even these were blurry in a world where priests carefully pondered the color, features, and crania of individual slaves to decide whether they were Indians from Mexico or Indians from India. Moreover, mere time made the emergence of twelve distinct hybrid types over the two hundred years or so since Europeans' arrival mathematically improbable. It was a nonsensical prospect; as a revolutionary priest summed it up, "beautiful gibberish."[67]

So the question of why pinturas de castas sold is curious, revealing, and controversial. The class of their consumers—they would have been expensive daubs—singled out their owners as wealthy and, in addition, inquisitive, well-traveled, learned in the exotic, rich in something more than assets. Some pinturas ended up in English country houses. The paintings simultaneously conferred an ethnographic distinction on the country itself, a complexity that lifted Mexico beyond the rest of the world. They conveyed that Mexico was different and special, as did portraits of the Virgin of Guadalupe, whose motto was *Non fecit taliter omni nationi,* "He has not dealt thus with any other nation." This was another stock-in-trade image, also painted by Miguel Cabrera; at least one of his colleagues, Luis de Mena, had the commercial savvy to combine the two genres—the Virgin and the pinturas—in a single hybrid work.[68] Such pictures had self-evident appeal to status-hungry creoles; they also suggested the sort of social order yearned for by any elite. Yet at least some of the paintings had satirical elements, the artists recognizing and mocking a degree of absurdity in their task even as they painted and fixed racial labels that didn't exist: One dubbed the eleventh generation of constant crossbreeding *no te entiendo*, "I don't understand you."[69] One interpretation is that the paintings were about domination through alienating colored people as other, different and inferior to whites. An alternative might be that the paintings were about domination through the quite different tack of folding colored people into an intimate if stern family, run by a paterfamilias both dictatorial and indulgent.

Both types of relationship existed, and alienation probably helped a widespread tolerance of indigenous slavery even after its official end in 1542. But these are murky waters in terms of both our interpretations and their ideals. Assorted other mechanisms of coerced labor complemented clear-cut chattel slavery: encomiendas, repartimientos, and debt peonage. These were all involuntary appropriations of indigenous muscle and craft backed up by violence. Sometimes they were indistinguishable from chattel slavery in practice. At other times the difference was clear. Indians on encomiendas were administered by their own caciques, did not work exclusively for the Spanish, and theoretically had the option of leaving. The encomiendas' replacement, Crown repartimientos of Indian workers to Spanish overlords, were limited-term corvée labor, a brute tax rather than a permanent loss of freedom. Corvée labor was a European commonplace of the time, slavery according to critical rhetoric rather than sociological exactitude. Finally, debt peonage could leave a peasant functionally enslaved through his mark on a poorly understood contract promising future labor for present cash for a marriage or festival. Yet this was not invariably a Faustian bargain. In other periods, the ability of peons to run up debts far beyond anything payable suggests that debt could be a measure of bargaining power and status rather than enslavement, an anachronistic peasant equivalent of running up mortgage or credit card debt.

The records of one eighteenth-century estate in Guanajuato, the Hacienda de Charco de Araujo, show just how far removed the social relations of debt could be from human bondage. The hacendado had no pressing need to ensure an adequate supply of workers, because there were many unemployed hands in the region. Wages, housing, and a patch of land were enough to keep people working. Nevertheless the accounts of the hacienda shop show the profits of the hacienda being redistributed in the form of loans for both subsistence—food, tools, medicine—and luxuries ranging from bulls for wedding feasts to smart *botas camperas*, the boots that were a major status symbol. The owner was tolerant with those slow to repay, and yet only a third of the workforce had long-term debts. These included not the lowest but the most valued employees: the administrator who ran up thirty-three pesos on soap alone, the cowboy whose boots were worth two weeks' salary, the stable boy whose family had been with the owners' family forever. Theirs was no euphemized slavery.[70]

Yet straightforward slavery, whether euphemized or outright, endured long past its decreed end. The 1542 New Laws and their restatements were taken in New Spain, several thousand miles from their framers, with equivocation and discretional enforcement. In Madrid or the Valley of Mexico courts enforced the ban; in the peripheries of New Spain they didn't. Slavery was politically useful as the only reliable profit motive for pushing on northward. Silver bonanzas were few and far between; merchant or hacendado fortunes needed long cultivation. Raids north of the forward lines to capture Indians, on the other hand, were risky but immediately profitable. Gapingly obvious legal loopholes even legitimated it. Criminals in severe cases such as homicide could be sentenced to penal servitude with private owners who could freely buy or sell them. Above all, captives in what theologians dubbed "just war," defined as one of defense against barbarian aggressors, remained fair game for unabashed enslavement. Christians interpreted "defense" in generous terms: According to Saint Augustine it was legal to wage war on enemies who obstructed free passage, even through their own lands. All of the prisoners from the Mixton War were (after consideration by the audiencia) classed liable for enslavement, and the Chichimeca Wars, melodramatically classed "wars of blood and fire," provided justification on the northern frontier up until the end of the sixteenth century.[71]

Even when legally questionable, the challenge of reconciling imperial ideals with economic and political realities, raison d'état by Viceroy Mendoza's admission, precluded a definitive, one-size-fits-all ban. In places beyond the war zones illegal slave raids and trading were still conducted with the winking tolerance of the law. One of the great slavers of the late sixteenth century, Luis de Carvajal y de la Cueva, made and sustained his fortune through decades of unlawful captures and sales of men, women, and children from small villages and peoples on the move across the North. His career peaked in the 1580s, when he was made the first governor and captain-general of Nuevo León, a territory of about thirty-five thousand square miles. In a dénouement eloquent of the ambivalent racial thinking of New Spain, Carvajal ended up in jail not for massive lawbreaking in dealing slaves but for bringing in a shipload of Jewish refugees from Portugal. He had been a crypto-Jew all along. He received a light sentence from the Inquisition but never left prison; discretional enforcement of slavery law allowed the authorities to keep hold of him for his professional rather than religious past. He was luckier than some of his passengers: The Inquisition garroted and burned his sister, nephew, and nieces.[72]

So the viceroyalty contained a multitude of opinions on the question of outright indigenous slavery. Banned for settled populations in 1542, its legitimacy for allegedly hostile nomads was considered by churchmen in 1546, 1569, and finally in the Third Provincial Council of 1585, where Mexico's bishops and monastic orders ended up fixated on the subject. Their main reading was the exterminationist report of Dr. Hernando de Robles, an ex–frontier functionary and expert on the Chichimeca. He argued that inside the war zones—which he admitted required careful delineation—all Indians were "enemies of the human race" and should be killed or enslaved. The audiencia of Mexico City was interested, with typical colonial fence-sitting, in what the churchmen thought of that. Secular Spaniards generally favored total war, the bishops broadly agreed, while the monastic orders were (with differing degrees of commitment) opposed. The Dominicans concluded that total war was only justified if it was utterly certain that the indigenous atrocities alleged in the Robles report were true; otherwise those who took the decision would go to hell. Without that certainty they themselves couldn't decide one way or another, but either way it was certain that the New World wasn't there solely for the good of the Old World. The Augustinians, less sophistic, concluded that they couldn't conclude. The Franciscans and Jesuits, who had the most experience on the ground and the most to win or lose, came up with the useful conclusions, recommending soldiers hold the existing frontiers and missionaries extend them.

Yet out of this strange brew, the Third Provincial Council somehow concluded with a formal opinion for Philip II that unequivocally condemned the war and slavery and blamed Spanish aggression as "tyrannical, impious, and to the injury and discredit of the gospel."[73] Nearly a century later the Crown issued new bans on indigenous slavery in Mexico (1672) and the Philippines (1679); the council's condemnation was a partial remedy at best. The Spaniards who invaded New Mexico in 1599, for example, sentenced prisoners they took to twenty years of personal servitude.[74] Yet the royal ban drove the volume of northern slaves down from the thousands to the hundreds and tens, and as the missions widened the Spanish sphere of influence, so slavers had to go further afield. Toward the end of his career Governor Carvajal was raiding as far north as the Río Grande. Profits declined as slaves became more expensive to catch; a major indigenous rebellion, the Pueblo Revolt, sealed off New Mexico from 1680 to the mid-1690s; in the same years the Spanish technological and comparative advantages ended, as the Apache, Ute, and Comanche adopted horses and guns and went into the slavery business themselves. Prohibition backed by theology reduced markets for the Spanish enslavement of Indians; economics and the practicalities of violence closed them.

On the other side of racial domination, humanism, pragmatism, and incompetence fostered a social mobility beyond the fictions of pinturas de castas or certificates of blood purity. As long as non-white subjects were not aspiring to administrative positions, which were racially ring-fenced—even creoles were out of the running for the highest offices—there were multiple paths across the boundaries of social order. Passing was in fact unnecessary when the ethnic regulations on jobs were ignored. In the countryside the rules against indigenous ownership of livestock were bent and broken with some regularity, the expansion of Spanish butcher shops into Indian towns and villages easing the way. Indians illegally entered long-distance trade and competed successfully with the other *tratantes*, peddlers, and middling traders, often cutting the Spanish out of business in cash transactions with Indians. But self-advancement was above all an urban phenomenon. Indians quickly colonized the guild jobs that were supposedly off-limits, skilled immigrants who provided cheap labor and were taken into workshops as apprentices and journeymen. Between the members of this artisanate and those in permitted jobs as market sellers, the more fortunate or astute Indians, mestizos, and castas formed an urban lower-middle class, not just in Mexico City but also in the new cities like Querétaro and Zacatecas, where Spaniards, mulattos, and Indians worked side by side in the workshops supplying the miners with tools, clothes, and carpentry.[75]

The middle class was also open to Blacks and mulattos. Wage labor—not always free, but providing at the minimum savings for manumission—spread in areas of high demand: The dockers of Veracruz and Acapulco were overwhelmingly Black and well paid. Skin color didn't get in the way of the leverage dockers anywhere enjoy, essential workers at the narrowest of bottlenecks. According to the English sailor Woodes Rogers, in late-seventeenth-century Acapulco Blacks disdained work that paid less than a piece of eight a day, a small fortune.[76] Mulattos were also important in the next stage of transportation, running the *recuas*, the mule trains that brought goods up from the coast and distributed them across the country; with so few navigable rivers, recuas of up to a thousand animals were often the only game in town. Success as a muleteer took literacy, local knowledge, violence, and management, a complex skill set that made its possessors rich.[77] In the cities, meanwhile, free Blacks and mulattos were key players in petty commerce and important intermediaries between Spanish wholesalers and indigenous consumers.[78] And less rule-abiding workshop masters trained their Black slaves in the same specialized tasks as indigenous apprentices, turning out jewelers, bookbinders, tailors, and smiths.

The very best passed far beyond any confines of race. A painter called Juan Correa was one of the most recognized in late-seventeenth-century Mexico, with more paintings than anyone else in the cathedral and an officer's position in the relevant guild. He was the son of a mulatto from Cádiz and a Black woman from Mexico.[79] Making it economically in the viceregal world allowed the non-Spanish to forget their social place, and travelers and officials were repeatedly

A Black woman beats a Spaniard in a *pintura de castas*. Andrés de Islas, *De español y negra, mulata* (1774).

shocked by their public displays of wealth and contempt. The city's Blacks and mulattos were characterized by "insolence," "a height of pride and vanity," "shamelessness," all racial code words equivalent to "uppity"; in less charged terms, self-confident, undeferential, and when possible giving as good as they got.[80] At least two pinturas de castas have a Black woman beating her Spanish lover with a hard-to-discern kitchen implement—possibly a meat hammer—an interesting twist in the broader tradition of pinning domestic violence on the non-white.[81] They ignored dress regulations, flaunting gold, pearls, and brocade when they could, and insulted whites on the street (because, one Italian traveler said hopefully, of the Europeans' greater sexual prowess).[82]

By the beginning of the seventeenth century poverty usually trumped race in popular politics: The primordial divide was between rich and poor rather than between Black, brown, and white. The ruled crossed color boundaries all the time, whether in sex or everyday socializing and living, and they had more in common with each other than with the rich; one group of bandits who worked the road to Cuernavaca consisted of a Spaniard, a mulatto, a mestizo, and an Indian, hanged side by side in Mexico City's plaza mayor in 1674.[83] Working together in piety rather than sin, a similar multiracial group joined forces in 1675 to fix the bridge over the Río Zahuatl in Tlaxcala.[84] Provincial *cofradías*, religious confraternities that organized much of such communal work and constituted the most important mass organizations of the period, were often multiracial. At the sharper end of politics, the most important riots were reported as racially segregated. The Mexico City conspiracies for mass rebellion, real or otherwise, of 1608, 1611, and 1612 were all attributed to Blacks and mulattos. The angry crowd of 1692 was reported by some as predominantly indigenous, driven by high food prices and triggered by moral outrage at the beating to death of an *india*, administered by a Black and a mulatto.[85] When the chips were down and huge crowds turned ugly, they were perceived as coming from a single race. Yet for a handful of scared Spaniards, parsing a large, violent crowd by phenotype and gossip was unlikely to give reliable conclusions. Few were that clear-cut; poorer mestizos were noted passing readily for indigenous rioters. To one of the sharper observers of 1692, the intellectual Carlos Sigüenza y Góngora, the rioters weren't any single race, but rather all races gathered together as "la plebe."[86]

Consequently, while a racial segregation of power worked in the assignment of political posts, in popular politics it was regularly traduced. At the same time as the genre of pinturas de castas was reaching its mid-eighteenth-century peak, someone wrote a vituperative satire entitled the *Ordenanzas del Baratillo*, supposedly detailed rules for a popular market run by castas. The otherwise unknown author, Pedro Anselmo Chreslos Jache, described a subversive "thieves' market" of secondhand tat, fenced goods, and pickpockets in the plaza mayor of Mexico City. His *Ordenanzas* were handwritten, never published; they were more interesting than what was generally printed, though, because they flipped racial categorization on its head, classifying the multitudinous world of the marketplace in terms of not how much degenerate blood people might have but rather how much Spanish. This was a society where multiracial decadents ruled. Outside the market, creole would-be elites were effeminate and ineffectual, hopelessly corrupted by, among other things, their womenfolk's reluctance to breastfeed. Creole children never stood a chance, in part because they imbibed racial inferiority from their Black and mixed-race wet nurses. Whether this was a peninsular attacking viceregal decadence or a creole attacking Spanish racism is open to question—both would permit a certain disgust at the plebs—but in this context irrelevant; like some of his artist contemporaries, Chreslos Jache was satirizing the racial basis of Mexican social order and its failure.[87]

In the end, the prospect of revolt kept racial hierarchies flexible and humanism in the minds of viceroys and archbishops. Some frontier wars brought different races together against the Spanish, the worst of the rulers' nightmares: Black slaves sought out Chichimeca allies during the northern wars and joined in the 1597 Guale rebellion in Florida.[88] More regularly Indians and Blacks opted out of social regulation by relocating to one of the "zones of refuge," the mountains, forests, drylands, or swamplands inhospitable enough to make the Spanish, learning from the conquistadors' experience, disinclined to venture into.[89] The communities they formed there—whether of *indios bravos, negros ladinos*, or renegade slaves, their permanent settlements called *palenques* or *quilombos*—could consequently thrive in autonomy along the swampier coasts of Guerrero and Veracruz. In the mountains of Guatemala and Nayarit independent indigenous kingdoms endured.[90]

Some sprung up closer to home; one near Puebla was allowed to survive by the Spanish on the condition that it accepted no more runaways, a distinctive but not unique arrangement, an exemplar of the sort of pragmatic deal found elsewhere in New Spain.[91] Unlike their Caribbean counterparts, however, maroon communities in New Spain tended not to endure in splendid isolation, presumably because intermarriage with indigenous people incorporated them into existing societies.

In the cities, on the other hand, the multiracial ruled first were coopted into and then themselves opted into Spanish-run society. And while the Spanish after the early seventeenth century were not particularly exercised by the prospects of rebellion—outside of the far North and the Southeast—in the cities the authorities remained paranoid about race riots and worse. Those illusions, mixed with the occasional real riot, kept them quite honest. The result, as in early modern Europe, was riot serving as a long-term bargaining tool rather than a prelude to revolution. Violent crowds often endorsed the system while lodging specific complaints against its bad representatives: In 1624 they shouted "*Viva el rey*" while they attacked the viceroy's palace, causing him to flee in disguise. In return they received light punishment and the backing of the archbishop and Jesuits.[92] *Viva el rey y muera el mal gobierno*, "Long live the king and death to the bad government," was a protest chant across the centuries, the popular equivalent of *Obedezco pero no cumplo*, a statement that the limits of the permissible had been passed.

The enforcement of racial barriers and order fluctuated. The early 1600s, for example, were a nervous time. In 1607 catastrophic flooding in Mexico City led the Spanish to divert the main river feeding the lakes through a system of canals, a dam, and a tunnel seven kilometers long. The dangerous work conscripted sixty thousand local Indians and reportedly killed many of them; it also killed part of their harvests, taking away both water and labor at a key point in the agricultural cycle.[93] Fear of a reaction may have underlain the next repressive step by the authorities. In the wake of the 1612 Black conspiracy the Spanish executed thirty-five, imposed a racially determined curfew, placed guards on all exit roads, and made leaving the city subject to magistrates' permission. Easter was canceled.[94] In 1692 the audiencia stopped the production and sale of pulque, insisted that Indians go barefoot and without cloaks, banned them once again from the city center, and forbade them from gathering in groups of more than five people.[95] The fortunes of mestizos ebbed and flowed dramatically, and in the eighteenth century they went from the early equivalence to Spaniards and a wide job market to strict discrimination and exclusion from the priesthood, their main route into the elites.

Some mestizos, like the Texcocan historian Fernando de Alva Ixtlilxóchitl, emphasized their indigenous ancestry for social advantage. A royal decree of 1697 made the advantage legally explicit: While mestizos at that stage might still enjoy the right to join the priesthood, the descendents of indigenous nobility "were to be accorded all the preeminences and honors, both ecclesiastic and secular, that are customarily conferred on the noble hidalgos of Castile."[96] Across the viceregal period the only unyielding legal bar to social mobility was Black ancestry, and by the end of empire the Spanish even had a legal procedure for getting around this, a Crown document called the *gracias al sacar*, which in exchange for a set fee formally changed a supplicant's ethnic classification, whitening Blacks and mulattos. It may be salient that almost none were solicited in Mexico, though, because Mexico stood out from other racialized societies in the permeability of its racial boundaries.[97] Indians could become officially white in four generations, but at times it was tactically more advantageous to pass as indigenous; unable to hold property in Indian villages, to marry elites there, or even to claim lands in the North, some Spaniards claimed to be indigenous themselves.[98] The gap between ideal and reality was yawning.

All attempts to police national and racial barriers failed to some extent. Permeability started on the other side of the Atlantic, where the Casa de Contratación's emigration permits were supposed to limit the flow of Europeans to the Spanish, and Castilians in particular. They didn't, and alongside Castilians came German miners, Portuguese, Basque, Venetian, and Genoese merchants, and many others. An altarpiece in San Cristóbal de las Casas, a remote town in highland Chiapas, is decorated with an engraving of Edward the Confessor, a very English saint.[99] Africans were likewise diverse: Alongside the animists there came three groups of Muslim immigrants alone, the Wolof, Mandinka, and Fula.[100] When these newcomers met with the 160 different ethnic groups of New Spain, the result was a population whose complexity only increased with time. It was a Great Babylon, complained Bishop Zumárraga; "the heart of the world," according to Mexicans who saw the first return passage across the Pacific in 1565, which confirmed New Spain as the bridge between the two great oceans; "the archive of the world," where all peoples' histories and treasures met.[101] They were all right in their way, because Mexico was not a caste but rather a hybrid society from the start, one in which Europeans, Indians, Africans, and Asians moved across spatial and legal boundaries to create the most complex human melting pot ever seen. It was one in which the divisions of ethnicity at times mattered greatly but so even more did those of class; where misery was widespread yet dramatic social mobility possible; where people of very different skin colors, ancestries, and cultures fraternized promiscuously, above all in the capital, Mexico City, in one seventeenth-century chronicler's eyes "the greatest city in the world."[102]

Part Three

Absolutism and Independence

c. 1750–c. 1877

Chapter Eight

Uncertain Rebels

In 1810, on the eve of a long and bloody war for independence, Mexicans were scared of the homeless. They had always been there in numbers, particularly in the cities. In a country where grim poverty was the greatest common denominator that was unsurprising. But the people variously despised as plebs, gypsies, lowlifes, impostors, beggars, lepers, vagrants, and vagabonds seemed increasingly numerous as the centuries changed. They were also increasingly grating, because the last decades of Spanish rule were years of wealth and progress. The world's first global vaccination program covered most of New Spain with startling success.[1] The homeless sat ill beside rapid economic growth, paved roads, clean underwear, rubbish collectors, firemen, a sewage system and a police force, not to mention cigarette factories and toilets for both sexes in the bars.[2] It was an uneasy juxtaposition that isn't beyond our own grasp.

Mexicans weren't alone in feeling that it was the best of times and the worst of times. On both sides of the Atlantic, city dwellers rich and poor, artisans, ambitious lawyers, radical philosophers, furious hacks, and future-seeking gentry were redefining how society and politics worked. The redefinition went as deep as language; in France the men and women of 1789 changed the meaning of the word "revolution" from the mechanical turn of a wheel to the human turnover of a world. In the florid speeches and angry put-downs of their assembly hall, French revolutionaries invented the primordial terms of modern politics, right and left, on the simple basis of where they chose to sit: conservatives on the right, radicals on the left. A decade earlier, British tax-dodgers along a coastal strip of North America had taken up the ancient idea of ditching a distant, exploitative, and incompetent monarch. (The medieval nobles of Aragon would have liked the slogan "no taxation without representation.") In England the industrious poor of factories, docks, and mines were meeting in church halls and taverns to swap stories of individual exploitation and invent a new group identity, the working class. In the Andes a wealthy mestizo cacique reinvented himself as Tupac Amaru II, the Inca emperor reborn, and in the early 1780s led tens of thousands of indigenous peasants in a cataclysmic effort to expel the Spanish. In Haiti the other great group of the racially defined oppressed, the cane-cutting slaves and free people of color, succeeded at huge cost in driving out their French masters a decade later. As revolutions like this changed the outside world, Mexicans were caught between enlightenment and incompetence, freedom and repression, and above all wealth and poverty.

Their society was dramatically split between a very rich minority and a poor majority. The eighteen wealthiest families in the Western Hemisphere, great miners and merchants, were all Mexican.[3] For them it was a time of mansions and fine art, the apogee of the Mexican school of painters, carriages of baroque decadence, a single haircut rumored to have cost an outrageous ounce of gold.[4] At the other end of the scale labor conditions were brutal for the thousands of desperate or imprisoned workers—some arrested for mere vagrancy—of the wool industry. Woolworkers were, an 1801 report recorded, enclosed semi-naked in unventilated rooms, light leaking in from a handful of fanlights, on their feet working the looms that threw off a thick dust, coated their lungs, and gave them tuberculosis.[5] Such primitive mills were on the way out, a different threat to lungs on the way in in the form of the huge cigarette factories that were spreading in the main cities. In the mines, another source of lung disease, owners were gouging salaries to help pay for deeper shafts and high-tech mills, calling in troops to put down strikers.[6] Across the towns and cities of New Spain real wages were dropping to the borders of survivability; malnourishment was making the poor notably shorter.[7]

In the countryside survival was yet more precarious. Disease and failed harvests, the natural disasters that devastated all preindustrial economies, were no one's fault, but they came with great frequency, roughly once a decade, and when they did people fled or starved. The year 1801, in which that horrified writer described the wool factories, was not a particularly vintage year for rural catastrophe. Outbreaks of disease were localized, although the yellow fever in Veracruz was bad enough that the government was urged to raze the coastal city and relocate it to the healthier foothills. Yet even an average year like 1801 brought home the fragility of all life across the Mexican rural world. In Coahuila and Yucatán the rains failed and the maize harvest was lost; in Oaxaca the rains were torrential and the maize harvest was lost. In some parts locusts ate the crops; in others livestock perished, drowned, or starved.[8] So did the least fortunate humans.

Yet if weather, microbes, and insects were beyond human control, economic models and political responses were not. The hacienda's profit-maximizing strategy—hoard grain in good times, mark it up in bad—wittingly aggravated the danger of food shortages. The harvest collapse of 1785–86, when early frost followed on the heels of failed rains, spread famine far and wide from Mexico City to the North; hacendados raised prices nearly 400 percent.[9] This was not just an urban problem. Villagers with their own fields and collective pastureland benefited from autonomy and a moral economy, the shared belief that in extremis helping neighbors to survive trumped profit-seeking, a categorical imperative to do unto others as you would have them do unto you. Overall, however, such peasants with social safety nets were losing ground to early agribusiness. The expansion of the commercial estates had turned more countrypeople into salaried workers, often migrant, reliant on buying rather than growing their food. At the same time population growth pushed salaries downward. There were more people than jobs.

Viceregal officials realized that a Malthusian stacking of odds was politically dangerous and tried to preempt mass hunger with export bans, price caps, and public food reserves. In the wealthy mining city of Guanajuato the top Spanish official, the intendant José Antonio Riaño, saw clearly how the region's commercial grain economy put farmworkers at a structural risk of recurring famine, and built a massive fortified depository to stockpile emergency rations, the Alhóndiga de Granaditas. Such forward planning was enlightened, essential, and not enough. Watching harvests fail in the autumn of 1809, Riaño wrote to the viceroy foreseeing the worst famine in living memory:

> Now mercury [for silver refining] is scarce, public and private funds exhausted, the population more numerous, business slowed down due to the lack of cash; and if maize goes to excessive prices, it will be impossible to employ thousands of families who have no other resources than their daily labour.

And yet, he ended, with that faith in rational government of his times, "I am not completely without hope."[10]

Riaño had reason for hope. In his lifetime he had seen a leap forward in Mexican science and watched similarly progressive peers applying its methods and results to rarified and everyday life. In the same years that thousands starved in the northern countryside, Creole thinkers were embroiled in scientific debates with critics on the other side of the Atlantic and launching a science of their own, American archaeology. In 1773 the priest Ramón Ordoñez led the first expedition to the great Maya city of Palenque, and in 1777 José Antonio Alzate explored the Temple of the Feathered Serpent in Xochicalco, Morelos.[11] The Crown passed from suspicion to endorsement: In 1786 Charles III ended the longstanding ban on the study of the indigenous past and in 1805 Charles IV instructed Guillermo Dupaix to draw up a catalogue of pre-Hispanic antiquities. In 1808 the viceroy set up an Antiquities Junta to regulate digs.[12]

It was one of a plethora of attempts to catalogue, chart, count, regulate, improve. The first Mexican census was held in 1790. In 1799 the Hydrographical Institute of Madrid printed charts of the Gulf Coast, while Alessandro Malaspina charted the Pacific coasts from Vancouver to Lima. These efforts were at once cosmopolitan and Mexican: The position of Los Cabos was fixed by three astronomers, one French, one Spanish, and one "a Mexican, and, what is more, the pupil of a very intelligent Indian in the village of Xaltocan."[13] The Bourbons managed the technocratic side of an Enlightenment self-consciously Mexican, one reflected from newspapers to ships: The first paper in the Americas was *La Gaceta de México*, while one of the ships sent to California was called *Mexicana*.

Above all, Intendant Riaño had seen what enlightened government could do to make people's lives better when it combined belief in science with attention to everyday sensibilities. In 1804 the Crown launched the Real Expedición Filantrópica de la Vacuna, a global campaign against smallpox. The campaign worked not just through empirical demonstration but also through a canny recruiting of local talent. Churchmen were intensively involved from the start, as bishops led processions to welcome the vaccine, had Te Deums sung in its honor and circulated pastoral letters urging priests to their greatest efforts. As the costs of professional vaccinators became prohibitive, administrators and churchmen took initiatives to get the job done by whatever tools came to hand. In some places, this meant anyone with experience of sharp objects, including barbers, curanderos, phlebotomists, and in one case hacienda workers with cactus spines. The Real Expedición's success was startling: As the campaign gathered steam officials were vaccinating more than one thousand people per month in Cholula, four thousand per month in Puebla, the vast majority of newborns in Chihuahua, almost all eligible children in parts of New Mexico.[14]

Yet for all they might keep children alive, vaccination campaigns didn't feed them when they grew up. Beyond the laboring poor were the many Mexicans with no wages at all, the ones who really worried rulers and the rich. Common across early modern Europe, the mobile destitute had always been particularly numerous in both Spain and New Spain, moving in search of food and shelter through the countryside and into the cities with their potential for casual work, begging, scavenging, and charity. In official eyes most were vagrants, because legally the term covered a multitude of sins. By one king's capacious definition, the criminal category spanned not just those who slept rough but also

> those who lack an occupation, benefice, estate, or income, living without knowing how to earn their income by licit and honest means. Those who have a patrimony or emolument, or are sons of a family, but lack any other occupation than gathering often at gambling houses, with individuals of bad reputation, or frequenting suspicious places. The beggar that is youthful, healthy, and strong, but has an injury that does not impede him from working.[15]

Even part-time laborers could be taken up as vagrants, and by the early nineteenth century they numbered in the tens of thousands in

Mexico City alone, where about 40 percent of the population were migrants to start with.[16]

Some rough-and-ready social security was in place: monasteries, confraternities, *hospicios de pobres*—poorhouses—and in bad times improvised shelters and food banks. A huge state-run pawnbroker, the Monte de Piedad, sat on the main square in Mexico City. The Conde de Regla, who founded it, also gave the authorities money to buy food for the hungry. The rich were becoming more considerate in death as well. In the 1710s only one-quarter of wills included a bequest for the poor; by the 1810s three-quarters of wills gave them some thought.[17]

And there was also repression. For centuries *alguaciles de vagabundos*, constables in charge of vagabonds, had the sole task of driving the homeless out of town, leaving behind a few locally born deserving poor with government licenses to beg.[18] During crises the bureaucrats intensified their efforts at social control: In 1809 the viceroy sent troops into Mexico City to confine the handicapped to poorhouses and press the rest—Spaniards, mestizos, mulattos, and Blacks alike—for military service in Veracruz, Havana, or the North.[19] The rest of the time some congregated even by the viceregal palace, eyeing up items they couldn't afford in the Baratillo street market.

Yet the vast majority of the indigent survived, at least into their thirties; how was something of a mystery. Some possessed nothing but a cloak, which served as clothing, bedding, and in the very last resort something to be sold or pawned. And so the assumption of the settled was that the poorest, sometimes called the *clase de mantas*, the cloaked class, kept afloat through lives of crime.[20] The ragged jobless were clearly getting by through age-old means—petty theft, pickpocketing, burglary, prostitution—their descent, or entrepreneurial ascent, into banditry a horse and dose of gumption away. The employed or wealthy also believed, with a culturally specific intensity, that the vagabonds who surrounded them were tricksters, impostors who practiced on the gullibility of all classes to pass themselves off as wealthy, holy, or medically trained. The first Mexican novel, *The Mangy Parrot*, was about just such an indigent swindler, who sermonizes (he does, after all, impersonate a priest at one point) that

> to be idle and useless is the worst fate that can befall a man; because the necessity of subsisting and the not knowing of how to go about it puts him, as it were, with a hand on the door of the most shameful vices, and that's why we see so many dope fiends, so many pimps for their own daughters and wives, and so many thieves; and for the same reason we have also seen and still see such crowded jails, forts, galleys and gallows.[21]

The narrator should have known, having ended up in jails and forts himself.

Tales of such *pícaros*, roguish tricksters, were an entire genre of fiction in the Hispanic world. But they are backed up by real lives with paper trails, the stories of men like José Lucas Aguayo. Born in Guanajuato to a fifteen-year-old father, Aguayo comes to life in the parish register for 1747, when he was baptized. His mother died young, his stepmother followed the cliché of disliking him intensely, his blood family ignored him, and so after a brief spell in a Jesuit school he took to the road, fourteen years old, and ended up in short order in jail. Released in 1767, he stole some clothes from a priest's house; chased down, he had to give them all up, and in addition surrender his own clothes. Aguayo at this point had the excellent (if unoriginal) idea of becoming a priest without any tedious training and was soon making a living by saying masses (half a peso a go) and offering useless absolutions. Keeping on the move, he raised his sights too far—passing as an Inquisitor, well-dressed, carrying a stolen, gold-capped staff of office—and ambition brought him low. He spent the rest of his life in and out of jails, both secular and Inquisition, sentenced to military service, exile, forced labor in Veracruz and Cuba, and public flogging, time and time again returning to the road and his imaginary priesthood and then back to jail. Aguayo was exceptional in his paper trail, and perhaps in his skills (although getting caught so often raises doubts; perhaps he was enthusiastic but second-rate).[22] But he was not at all special in being arrested over and over again; at the turn of the nineteenth century some 10 percent of all arrests were for drunkenness and vagrancy, a number that rose in harsh times to 30 percent.[23]

So there was a lot of raw material, qualitative and quantitative, behind Humboldt's conclusion, penned in the run-up to Independence: "Mexico is the country of inequality. Nowhere does there exist such a fearful difference in the distribution of fortune, civilization, cultivation of the soil and population." Less frequently cited is the great scientist's stress on Mexico's tranquility, "the long peace enjoyed by these countries since the commencement of the sixteenth century."[24] Mass misery might cause elite fear, but it did not cause the mass unrest that would justify it.

Instead of violence, the short-lived poor turned to social drugs. Peyote, mushrooms, and marijuana all occurred naturally, and one of the more outré bits of José Aguayo's prison record has him chewing weed while reading the liturgy and defacing icons. (The combination is, he's assured, an infallible spell for jailbreaking.)[25] But the more psychoactive drugs were the purview of shamans; it was banal cigarettes and alcohol that everyday people turned to. By the turn of the nineteenth century Mexico was a country of chain-smokers, the cigarette industry worth between three and four million pesos a year. Across the decade of the 1790s a single mining town spent a million pesos on cigarettes.[26] The tobacco industry, a state-run enterprise, was the second most lucrative in Mexico, surpassed only by silver, and the reason wasn't hard to see; smoking for the colonial underclass was one of the few reliable consolations in short, stress-filled, and uncertain lives. The result was what economists call inelastic demand, something central to basic survival: Every time the Mangy Parrot scrapes together a few coins, he spends them on cigarettes before anything else bar food.[27]

Alcohol was another prop. The *gente decente*, the respectable classes, got drunk on appropriately decent booze, brandy and wine, but it could only be imported from Spain and was correspondingly expensive. (Some indigenous villagers became wine connoisseurs in the early colony but reportedly went bankrupt.)[28] Everyone else drank pulque, the fermented juice of the maguey cactus. Once more the numbers were extraordinary: In Mexico City the average adult drank about two hundred gallons a year. Peasant production for local consumption went back to the Aztecs, but commercial production of pulque on dedicated haciendas took off in the second half of the eighteenth century, pioneered by Jesuits and developed by the great and good. The Conde de Regla brewed it on the Hacienda de Santa Lucía, where he cultivated maguey on an industrial scale, and sent it by mule train each morning into Mexico City, where he owned seven of the forty-five pulquerías, the large, disreputable, and ubiquitous taverns of the lower classes. Binge drinking was central to religious festivals everywhere, but it was the steady trickle of pulque from dawn to dusk that kept misery at bay. Builders started on their way into work, rubbing shoulders with the survivors of the previous night, before arriving at sites where they could drink some more. As the day wore on the trade became heavier, ending in out-and-out bacchanalia, lightly policed by bouncers. (One

The *pulquería*: to elites, a viceregal dive bar.
José Agustín Arrieta, *Tertulia de pulquería* (1851).

of the count's establishments, La Florida, featured heavily in arrests for indecent exposure and prostitution; the *corralones*, mixed-sex toilets, were notorious.) Lubricious stories of proletarian nightclubs may lie, but tax records—which undercount, missing the heavy illicit trade—do not, and by the turn of the century the tax on pulque was raising over 800,000 pesos a year. This was half as much as the total Indian tribute for New Spain, the flat head tax—the closest to an income tax the viceroyalty could collect—that formed a mainstay of government revenue.[29]

Thought differed as to the social impact of alcohol. Historically, lower-class boozing has been seen as destructive more or less everywhere, and Mexico was no exception. Officials occasionally (and surprisingly) dissented; a prosecutor's report from 1778 argued,

> The use of pulque in this crowded capital is of the greatest importance and has the most benign effects. If the Indians and other workers of the lowest sort who perform the most tiring and strenuous jobs were not to have its support, the prosecutor believes that it would be impossible they could stand them . . . in the midst of their most strenuous work it cools them down and feeds them and restores them that they might continue with greater vigour their exertions.[30]

The mainstream was more puritanical. Pulque was bad for public health. It made good workers go bad, pawning the tools of their trade for just one more bowl. It fostered gambling, lewdness, brawls, stabbings, and rape. It made a mockery of religion. Finally, it removed the inhibitions of crowds and made them riotous. In public, few of the elite thought pulque was the opium of the people; it was quite the opposite, their poison of choice, and it could transmute everyday misery into the political violence of the riot.

Riots were the constant preoccupation of administrators everywhere, from remote villages in the mountains of Oaxaca to the main square in Mexico City. The ruled very occasionally took to region-wide mass violence, mobilizing ragtag armies with overtly political talk, fighting for months and even years. Two were particularly vigorous, the Pueblo revolt of 1680 and the Yaqui revolt of 1740, but these were less rebellions than outright frontier wars, some thousand miles from the capital, lethal to pioneers but not to viceroys. For two centuries the only collective violence that threatened the entire system came in three great urban riots: 1624 and 1692 in the capital, and 1767 in Guadalajara. The riot of 1692 was the greatest in Mexico City; a bad harvest, cuts in public grain supply, higher taxes, corruption, a pulque ban, and other acts of misgovernment infuriated the poor, market sellers, and artisans. Once it was over the authorities emphasized the brevity of the violence—a single evening, June 8—and characterized it as a race riot, a spontaneous "tumult" of drunken Indians, a meaningless mass thuggery. It was in reality an outbreak of multiracial class warfare, uniting Indians, mestizos, and the poorer sort of Spaniards against the viceroy, as well as the inept Conde de Valde, the city's military command, and the main bureaucrats, all seen as his partners in crime. Their reports were written with the intention of depoliticizing the rioters; the rioters' words and acts, however, show quite clearly how coherently political the violence was.

It all started when a pregnant woman passed out and died in a hungry crowd outside the public grain exchange, where they had been denied subsidized maize. When no authority appeased the petitioners, they escalated into direct action, lynching members of the viceroy's bodyguard and burning half of the main square. The rioters shouted, "Long live the king and death to bad government," and chose wholly political targets. They spared the cathedral and the grain exchange while torching just about everything else: the viceroy's palace, the ayuntamiento, the gallows, the mint, a lieutenant's house, and, in a final touch of symbolism, the Cortés family mansion. What began as a protest within the bounds of the usual became something quite different. Some of the shouts were classic, puckish humor: One protester yelled, "Shoot! Shoot! . . . And if you have no musket ball, hurl tomatoes!" But the idea of shooting was no joke at all, and the riot became a congregation of the furious, who stood on the verge of a no-holds-barred rising; a crowd that threatened, quite consciously, viceregal power.[31] The crisis was so severe that the Dominicans allowed some of their friars to take off their habits and take up arms, joining the rest of the vecinos in what they feared might be a last-ditch stand against the hordes. In the aftermath the government established a curfew, forbade gatherings of more than four people, and arrested eighty rioters. They first tortured then hanged or beheaded twelve people, dismembered them, and put their heads up to rot on spikes.[32]

Yet the overwhelming majority of riots over the centuries weren't like this at all. The point of a riot, in Mexico as elsewhere, was to make a show of force—on both sides, rulers and ruled—while avoiding much actual violence. Riots were mutually understood as smoke signals communicating an urgent need for government attention to central questions of life: everyday people's food, religion, or health. They were acts of bargaining that followed the same choreography over hundreds of years. First, villagers would publicly protest an act by the powerful that they saw in grave and moral terms, such as a hacendado charging unaffordable prices for maize or making a land grab, or a governor imposing a smallpox quarantine that would bankrupt a town. The ruled would try to speak to the priest or mayor or would write letters of desperation to their higher-ups. Should authority prove silent or useless, someone would beat a drum, blow a trumpet, or ring the church bells. Men and women (women, universal domestic accountants and stealth executives, often led riots and provided many of the foot soldiers) would take up any weapon they could: rocks, kitchen knives, machetes, pitchforks, axes, clubs, hoes, the improvised tear gas of chili powder. Finally, the rioters would gather at the church and march on the town hall or jail, set fires, chant insults at the powerful, throw rocks, and run royal officials out of town. Sometimes they would beat or kill someone singled out as culpable. Pitchfork moment passed, the riot would burn itself out, often in a festive way. The authorities, meanwhile, might opt for masterly inactivity, or sending in the militia, or arresting supposed ringleaders. They would not engage in mass reprisals, the occasional whipping or hanging about as far as punishment went, and they would generally bargain their way to an acceptable solution to the original problem.[33]

Events like this were common enough: between 1680 and 1811 over 140 in central Mexico and Oaxaca alone.[34] But they worked to resolve some of the thorniest questions. In 1796, in an extreme example, smallpox broke out in Teotitlán del Valle, a small town of weavers in central

Oaxaca. Next door to the regional capital and closely integrated into its trade networks, Teotitlán was an ideal ground zero for an epidemic, and the Spanish reacted with drastic measures. They locked down the town, using militia roadblocks to stop anyone from leaving or entering; took sick children from their homes and forcibly confined them in a new infirmary, unable to see their parents; and denied church burial to the smallpox dead, burying them outside town in a new cemetery. The sum was a treble threat: to livelihoods, children, and souls.

The townspeople's reaction was a series of protests. When the lawyer they retained in Antequera, today's Oaxaca city, went unheard they escalated from protest to riot. A boy died in the infirmary and was refused church burial. A weaver, Francisco Ruiz, and a crowd of women with rocks led a march from the church to the hated infirmary, which they stormed to liberate the children. The rioters threatened a Spaniard with death and said, memorably, "that once they were together and the fire had been lit they should not stop until everything was burned." Two battalions of militia were sent in the next day, but no one received any meaningful punishment. Instead of confinement, the powers that be shifted to inoculation—by "persuasion" at that, not coercion—a return to church burial, and economic aid, buying the town's textile production at decent prices. The Teotitlán rioters won.[35] Yet they never threatened the fundamentals of Spanish power. Riots like theirs were the sharp end of local politics, confined to single communities, counterintuitive solutions to conflict. They propped up rather than subverted the viceregal system.

Until the 1760s, the only systemic, articulated central threat had been a farce. In 1642 an Irish immigrant called Don Guillén Lombardo de Guzmán planned to oust the Spanish king and install himself instead. A refugee from a far more oppressive monarchy, the English in Ireland, Lombardo had various of the qualities of a viceregal rogue. He was an impostor, who claimed to be the secret son of King Philip III and the (apparently stunning) Countess of Ross, exiled as a dynastic rival by his half-brother Philip IV. He abused drugs, and not alcohol but rather the more boundary-pushing hallucinogen peyote. He even believed in racial equality, to be established by force if necessary. So when Don Guillén persuaded a blind Indian to take peyote and prophesize, he was probably unsurprised to be told of his destiny to become king of an independent Mexico—with popular devotion and the devil's acquiescence into the bargain.

There were pragmatic reasons why the natives should want a revolution, Don Guillén confided to a neighbor: Creole political exclusion, indigenous labor abuse, Black and mulatto enslavement. His regime would offer political equality for all racial groups. The only problem was that none of those racial groups seemed to want it badly enough to put their lives on the line, some indigenous malcontents from Taxco aside, and even they never materialized. Neither did any other indigenous rebels, nor an insurgent creole militia, nor a spontaneous Black rising. As soon as Lombardo read his draft proclamation to neighbors he was arrested. He spent the next seventeen years in an Inquisition cell (and then hanged himself on his own execution pyre, cheating the law with a final flourish). His rebellion forms more than a picaresque footnote; it is suggestive that he didn't find any takers for it. Mexicans might want rid of a given viceroy, but a critical mass of all social groups accepted the idea of viceregal rule.[36]

So until the very end of Spanish power there was nothing more than the occasional provincial rebellion, founded more on specific tensions and messianic religion than on generalizable class or racial hostility. Outside the ever-dangerous North, only a few leaders managed to raise more than a few hundred followers, and those associations were short-lived. The limited potential of ideological risings was typified in the events of November 1761 in a village called Quisteil in Yucatán. Prominent villagers had gathered to plan their patron saint's festival, and as the meeting ran on—according to colonial reports, quite possibly libelous—Jacinto Canek, by some accounts a baker with some Franciscan education, suggested that they use some of the festival funds to continue drinking. When the local Spanish wine merchant refused to serve them, they killed him; the next day, perhaps rebuked during Mass, Canek threatened the parish priest, who fled crying insurrection. This was a self-fulfilling prophecy: Canek then called for rebellion, saying that "the day had come when all the Spanish were to die," sent emissaries out to the neighboring villages, adopted the cloak and crown of the church's virgin, and proclaimed himself Chichán Montezuma, "the Small Montezuma." He raised an army fifteen hundred strong, a substantial following anywhere in New Spain. He made a drink that would, he said, revive anyone who fell in his messianic war. Yet for all the sweep of the rhetoric and the magic and the impressive recruitment, the Canek rising remained local. His army's greatest achievement was the killing of a Spanish captain and his small company. In short order an unusually large Spanish force had mustered—the entire province's militia, give or take—defeated the rebels, executed Canek with exemplary gore, and razed his village, wiping it quite literally off the map.[37]

Such a draconian reaction was probably driven by the rarity of an ambitious and ideologically far-reaching rebellion, even one that never got near critical mass. There may have been appreciable numbers of the disenchanted in New Spain; they were unlikely to add up to enough to revolt.

Nevertheless, good immediate reasons for revolt existed in the 1780s, because at the outset of the Age of Revolutions the Spanish had imposed major political changes that dramatically increased Mexican grievances. Those changes, grouped under the heading of the Bourbon Reforms, provided the raw material for subsequent nationalists and historians to tell a just-so story in which independence was the inevitable result of a new imperial dictatorship.

The French Bourbon dynasty had taken over the Spanish monarchy in 1713, with a different, French view of government; absolutists and rationalizers, they brought with them the spirit of the age of Louis XIV and his grandson, the new king Philip V. Their revolution in government was clear in principle from the start. Under the Habsburgs the viceroys had been aristocrats; under the Bourbons they became military men, bloodline taking second place to ability. In later years some were not nobles at all. Under the Habsburgs the sale of government offices had grown steadily, until by 1687 the highest political posts in Mexico, seats on the Real Audiencia, went to the highest, usually creole, bidder. Under the Bourbons, many creole officials who had bought or inherited their positions lost their jobs. Between 1715 and 1727 Philip V's auditors got rid of more than half the judges and prosecutors on the Audiencia and suspended over 150 of their minions, including those key powerbrokers the notaries. And alongside the earthily bureaucratic business of good government came the pie-in-the-sky propaganda of a divinely appointed executive. The royal administration commissioned numerous portraits of the new monarch and strategically placed them across Mexico, decorating churches, government offices, universities, hospitals, numerous town squares, and the cathedral.[38] Pleb and plenipotentiary alike were meant to be impressed by a newly muscular state.

But paintings in town squares were perishable, and so were the practicalities of reform. Drastic change was desirable but not urgent. As ever, a far-off Crown faced enough problems in the rest of the world to relegate controversial changes in its American possessions to an ill-defined future, and across the reigns of the first two Bourbon kings the sale of offices continued. Outgoing government cronies were replaced by a new crop of creole buyers, more than a hundred under the first two Bourbon kings, and when the practice ended in 1750 a majority of the audiencia members were creole.[39] Underneath the new rhetoric there was substantial continuity across the change in dynasties, and a genuine revolution in government came only in the 1760s, when the ambitious Charles III took the throne.

The final push was fiscal, not philosophical; oceanic empire had become increasingly expensive as the French built up their land armies and the British their navy. A single ship of the line, three-masted vessels carrying seventy-plus cannon, cost around 100,000 pesos, and Spain launched fifty-four of them across the 1740s and 1750s.[40] It was no discretional expense, because ships of the line were the closest the day had to aircraft carriers, projecting massive force across imperial distance. With their new firepower came the imperative to build counterparts and beef up port defenses. The Seven Years War (1756–1763), which Spain and France lost to British sea power, brought home just how existential the business was; foreign naval squadrons temporarily occupied two of the keys of Spain's overseas world, Manila and Havana, and reaffirmed British ownership of the third, the Rock of Gibraltar, whose batteries and ships controlled passage between the Mediterranean and the Atlantic. The Treaty of Paris also ceded the British all lands east of the Mississippi. In practice that was pretty meaningless—Florida aside—given the lack of Spaniards north of the Texas borderlands, but in theory it set a terrible precedent. So the Crown for the first time needed a substantial military presence in the Americas as well as in Europe, and to fund it they turned to the peoples of the Americas. Tax-dodging colonials had long been free riders on Spanish greatness; now they had to pay their way.

The first army in Mexico was impressive: ten thousand regulars, including two regiments of light cavalry, and twenty-two thousand militiamen.[41] To pay for their military buildup the Spanish turned to new income taxes, sales taxes, export taxes, and a nationalization of the tobacco and salt industries, and pilfered the greatest asset holder in the Americas, the Church. The policy was exceptionally successful on balance sheets: Crown revenues went from six million pesos annually in 1763 to twenty million in 1782. Ten million of that went on hemispheric defense. Some gains were the wages of sin: Bourbon administrators taxed cigarettes, cockfights, playing cards, pulque, and prostitutes (the last in the progressive terms of a sliding, income-based rate). Bureaucratic avarice even hit sorbet, made with ice from the towering volcanoes, wrapped in cloth and grass, sold in the main cities to the sweet-toothed better classes.[42] Yet the impact of the new exactions went far beyond the frivolous. Policies that drove up the prices of pulque and tobacco were harsh in a society of hard-drinking chain-smokers and put numerous small producers out of business. Worse yet, the Bourbons targeted certain resources traditionally beyond the pale of government exaction, such as the tax-skimming of local collectors or the community banks of the cofradías, indigenous lay brotherhoods. Finally, taxes on food production meant higher retail food prices. Between all the new measures, Mexicans by the 1780s were paying 67 percent more tax per head than Spaniards. It was a squeeze that, compounded by population growth and failed harvests, had dramatic effects on living standards.[43]

Consequently, revenue needed for the military needed military collectors. Even a tax census could spark riots, now put down by the militiamen who perforce accompanied taxmen. Inefficient revenue collection formed one of the main practical reasons (backed by a philosophical rationale as to how modern absolutism should work) for a sweeping militarization of the entire political system. The Bourbons aspired to bring Mexico into line with Europe by replacing governors with military intendants, *alcaldes mayores* with subdelegates, and the viceroys' economic control with a centralized treasury system. An overwhelming majority of the new appointments were peninsulares, not creoles. Finally, the institutional casualties were not just creole bureaucrats. The new administrators established small forts called *presidios* along the entire northern frontier, from the Sea of Cortés to the Gulf of Mexico. As soldiers marched in, the old colonizers, the Jesuits, went out: a symbolic, spiritual, and subsistence loss to their flocks of indigenous peasants and nomads.[44]

This was part of a more generalized royal anticlericalism, a clawing back of power from the Church that culminated in 1767 with the greatest blunder in Spanish imperial history, the expulsion of all Jesuits from all Spanish territories. The savviest of the missionary orders, the Society of Jesus had been essential to settling the North, providing the advance guard of occupation along the risky frontiers of California, Arizona, New Mexico, and Texas. They provided social security to the poor; when in 1760 floods and smallpox brought mass death to Guanajuato, the Jesuits delivered food and sacraments, nursed the sick, and buried the dead. In 1762 they repeated the exercise when typhus broke out. They were also, more than any other order, the colony's educators and bankers; while salving Guanajuato's sons of toil, they were also building a college for the city's sons of wealth.[45]

Yet they fell victim to their own success. The Crown and its modernizers resented their allegiance to papal over royal authority, seeing them as wealthy, intriguing, and overmighty rivals for power. Their independence and critical thinking, even in an enlightened monarchy, didn't help. Shortly after the order's birth in 1540, a philosophically inclined Jesuit had written an apology for tyrannicide, making the argument for popular consent, not divine right, as the foundation of monarchy. In 1640 regional Jesuits had backed a rising in Portugal against the Crown. In 1758 another had published a satirical attack on the Franciscans, the Crown's oldest allies in the Americas.[46] In 1766 they were believed to be conspirators in a major riot in Madrid, by then (in Pope Clement's words) the target of "slanderous accusations" and "atrocious calumnies."[47] Adding to political paranoia, the idea of seizing Jesuit wealth was seductive in a time of fiscal paranoia. So in the summer of 1767 instructions arrived across Mexico for the new civilian bureaucrats to present themselves at Jesuit missions, churches, universities, hospitals, and businesses. There they were to tell the fathers to pack their essentials, leave their homes, and proceed peaceably to Veracruz, whence all 678 of them would be shipped off into impoverished Italian exile.

It didn't quite work out that way. Instead, simultaneous riots and peasant revolts broke out in strategic parts of the viceroyalty, including the mining capital Guanajuato; dozens of indigenous villages and towns in the forbidding Michoacán highlands; and around the city of San Luis Potosí, the strategic key to the mountains of the Huasteca. They added up to ideologically coherent popular rebellions; as one indigenous political flyer put it, the expulsion of the Jesuits was a "heresy" that would "destroy the kingdom," and good Catholics would themselves be heretics not to resist. They duly did, without much respect for rank. In San Luis de Paz the royal treasurer Felipe Cleere crept in the mission's back door to ask the Jesuits—almost certainly friends of his in a town with only five white families—to sneak out after evening mass to forestall riots. When his plan was rumbled, a mob chased him across the town's rooftops, coming within an ace of catching and killing him.[48]

Cleere escaped with his life, as did almost all Spaniards in the rebellious areas, leaving behind an eloquent account of the "incalculable conflict" in his letter to the viceroy, the Marqués de Croix. It was, among other things, a profoundly ethnic, even national, story. The luckless friars were probably Mexican, as were some three-quarters of all Jesuits in New Spain. The rioters were indigenous, some of them streaming down from the hills with what weapons they had to join the outraged townsmen.[49] Cleere, by contrast, came of Dutch family; he was writing to De Croix, a Belgian born in France. The troops who eventually turned up were Spanish. The man overseeing the purge, José de Gálvez, the visitador, was also Spanish, and worse yet *afrancesado*, frenchified; he had started his career as the French embassy's lawyer and advanced it by marrying a wealthy French woman.[50] Gálvez and his retinue didn't hide their anti-American biases. His long-time advisor, Antonio de Areche, dismissed New Spain as a wasteland peppered with a handful of primitive cities, condemned by its peoples' inferior character, made even worse by the promiscuous mixing of races.[51]

The counterinsurgency Gálvez launched was announced in terms of class, however, describing the rebellious as "the vagabonds and the lost who cluster around the mines . . . and the very poor plebe" of the indigenous towns. His decree, issued in San Luis de la Paz in July 1767, called the Spanish vecinos to arms and made it clear that his campaign would be brutal:

> I will order the troops accompanying me to treat all who continue their impertinent resistance to be treated with the utmost rigour of war; once such persons are arrested I will do justice with all the severity that is merited by the enormity of the crime.

Gálvez made good on his threat, executing eighty rebels, imprisoning hundreds, taking away community lands, and making public shows of bloody punishment, chopping off hands and crippling with hundreds of lashes.[52]

Community dispossession, mutilation, and death were all good enough reasons for everyday people to remember Gálvez, decades on, as a nasty piece of work. They were not the only reasons. Gálvez oversaw most of the Bourbon reforms, from 1765 to 1771 as visitador general, an effective dictator, and from 1777 to 1786 as Secretary of the Indies. He was held responsible for the most offensive of the tax policies, the Royal Tobacco and Salt Monopolies; for dispossessing churchmen, creoles, and Indians; for persecuting numerous smugglers; and in politics for bringing Spanish officers in and kicking Mexican administrators out. Moreover, while Gálvez hawked a new probity in imperial rule, he personally continued the old ways of nepotism and cronyism: Many of his retinue came from his hometown of Málaga, and his brother and nephew went on to become viceroys. It was part of a broader hypocrisy; the viceroy with whom he served got a nephew—yet one more nephew making good in the Indies—into the position of Comandante General de las Provincias Internas, the northern military commander. Even some of the most puritanical (and gifted) Bourbon administrators followed crooked paths to the top. The great viceroy Count Revillagigedo began his career in Mexico when his father—also viceroy—made him Captain of the Viceroy's Guard. He was nine.[53]

Elsewhere in the Americas the new ways of imperial power led to a wave of revolts, and in the case of the 1780 Tupac Amaru rebellion in the Andes, the near-total loss of the viceroyalty. There were undeniably more riots and petty risings in Mexico during the Gálvez administration, but 1767 aside, they were never particularly threatening. Many of the local political reforms he implemented were reversed in short order. At a colony-wide level there were no credible threats; only wartime xenophobia caused reports to be taken in earnest. Frenchmen, Indians, Englishmen, creoles, and proletarians were all denounced at one time or another as planning anticolonial rebellion; none of the alleged conspirators were much more viable (or organized) than the long-dead Irishman Don Guillén. In 1794 the capital's tiny Crown colony was supposed to be planning a Mexican Revolution; sixty arrests and a mass expulsion produced little proof. In 1799 two tax collectors led nine other men in talks to overthrow the Spanish and form an "American National Convention"; arrested, they turned out to have stockpiled all of nineteen machetes and five swords. (They were so unthreatening that they only got two and a half years in jail.) In 1800 a mad cacique in Durango tried to set up an indigenous monarchy; in 1801 another Indian, Mariano of Tepic, was supposed to be conspiring with the English. Across the Bajío the revolutionary potential of a hungry peasantry and a mining proletariat showed no signs of being realized.[54] The Jesuit revolts of 1767 were the closest Mexico came to wholesale rebellion against Spain, and they happened more than forty years before the War of Independence.

Other modernizing empires, long-term winners, were a lot less stable. Catherine the Great lost several major cities and thousands of men to rebel Cossacks and peasants in the 1773 Pugachev Rebellion. The British lost their American colonies to the equivalent of a creole gentry in 1783. The French Crown's own expulsion of Jesuits, tax gouging, bullying of smugglers, and racial oppression brought down the monarchy in 1791 and lost them Haiti, their most lucrative colony, in 1804. Later in the nineteenth century the new global superpower, the British, fought major wars with their indigenous neighbors in India—the Sikhs, the Afghans—and systematically bought off others in the princely states and on the North-West Frontier. They relied on a much larger military presence—more than ten times as many cavalry—and came within a whisker of losing the country anyway in 1857.

Nothing remotely like this happened in eighteenth-century Mexico; in New Spain the most important point was not what happened, but what did not.

In the end, what happened an ocean away counted most in a Spanish Empire. The French Revolution kept Spain in constant European war from 1793 onward. Spain fought on both sides: first alongside the British and Austrians against the French, and then from 1797 until 1808—interrupted by the brief 1802 Peace of Amiens—alongside the French against what was left of unconquered Europe. The wars ended the Spanish Atlantic trade. A tight British naval blockade bottled up most ships in Cádiz; those that slipped through at night or in fog were generally schooners and polacres, glorified yachts. In 1805 the same British warships that had cut off their merchant shipping destroyed Spain's navy at the Battle of Trafalgar. The world's largest warship, the *Santísima Trinidad*, ran away and sank; the symbolism was obvious. In 1807 no Mexican silver at all made it back to Spain.[55] The endgame came in 1808 when the French invaded their unreliable ally and installed Napoleon's brother Joseph as king. Mexico was left as the centerpiece of a global Spanish empire without a Spanish emperor.

This surreal situation gave Mexicans both political and economic problems. In politics there was a vacuum of power and legitimacy. Mexicans remained vocally loyal to their Bourbon kings, but in 1808 those kings became hypothetical; King Ferdinand VII was under house arrest in France. As the creole leader of the ayuntamiento put it,

> The crisis in which we currently find ourselves is a truly *extraordinary* Interregnum . . . for the legitimate authority of our sovereigns, separated from their thrones, in a foreign country, and with no liberty whatsoever, has been put in question.[56]

The creoles, feeling that if they didn't hang together they might well be hanged separately, had through all the isolation, extortion, and losses of wartime remained loyal to the viceroy, the king's alter ego. When in July 1808 they got the news from Spain they proposed an autonomous government of delegations from Mexican cities under Viceroy José de Iturrigaray; they would follow the example of the Spanish resistance, who argued that power under age-old Spanish political philosophy passed automatically to a junta of cities. These would fill the vacuum in the king's name until his restoration. However, the peninsulares who controlled the audiencia, the merchants' guilds, the Church, and the Inquisition decided that this was not in their own best interests. A viceroy heading up a series of popular, mildly representative governments was neither a loyal nor reliable viceroy. So on the night of September 15, 1808, they suborned the viceroy's bodyguard and the capital's only regiment, the aptly named Regimiento de Comercio, sent three hundred men to the palace, arrested the viceroy and the main creole leaders, and installed a Spanish general, Field Marshal Pedro Garibay, as the new viceroy. It was Mexico's first coup d'état, and it was launched by Europeans.[57]

This made 1808 a watershed. Across New Spain the coup destroyed the legitimacy of rule from Mexico City—illegitimacy heaped upon illegitimacy—and put the blame squarely on a single minority ethnic group, the Iberians. Creole loyalty was already counterintuitive in some ways because the second problem the Napoleonic Wars brought was economic, and it hit them particularly hard. Some economic strain was structural. Free trade, the new and universal liberal dogma, had opened up Mexican textiles to competition from cheap Catalan and later British imports. That drove down prices, and poverty trickled down from manufacturers to men herding sheep and women spinning at home. The great silver magnates were also modernizers, taking away the traditional mineworkers' share of their production, a percentage of what they dug up paid in silver ore, and driving down wages. The attack on workers' participation and pay wasn't purely philosophical or profit-maximizing; it was also driven by pressures on mine owners themselves, squeezed by shortages of mercury, that critical input, and by the costs of the ever-deeper shafts and tunnels needed to get at the remaining ore.

Other strains were harder to rationalize, and even in desperate times seemed more policy choices than imperatives. The principal one was the attack on Church business. The expulsion of the Jesuits may have shaken creole belief in the monarch and government of the time, but the ensuing liquidation of Jesuit land and businesses had also opened up opportunities. The next step in practical anticlericalism, by contrast, alienated creole as well as indigenous communities. Desperate to raise money for the war, Charles IV seized the assets of the Church's charities and endowments in New Spain, extending even to the cofradías that held villages' common lands. Most of those Church assets were the loans and mortgages that kept everyone from landowners to petty merchants afloat in a risky economy founded on cheap credit. When the Crown demanded their immediate repayment, large swathes of the propertied classes faced ruin. At the same time peasants faced not just a loss of their income for religious festivals but also a significant part of what had passed for social security. It was a break in nearly three centuries of successful collaboration, sometimes tense, always vital, between church and state.

Mexicans might have hoped for relief when a legitimate viceroy, appointed by a new Spanish government, arrived to take power in September 1810. However, three days after Francisco Javier Venegas arrived, before he could do anything to assuage discontents or crack down on conspiracies, a distinguished (but sidelined) parish priest launched a rebellion in the northern town of Dolores, tolling the church bells as though to start a classic riot and shouting, in myth at least, to the mainly Indian crowd that gathered below, "Death to the Spaniards! Long live the Virgin of Guadalupe!"

Chapter Nine

Freedom and Devastation

The priest who started it was Miguel Hidalgo y Costilla, a member of the provincial creole elite, son of a hacendado, trained at the seminary in Michoacán, where he was a prize-winning theologian. He went on to teach there for ten years and became friendly with the area's powerful, such as the bishop of Valladolid, Manuel Abad y Queipo, and the long-time intendant of Guanajuato, Juan Antonio Riaño, the Spanish official so worried about feeding the desperate. Hidalgo ended up in a small parish thirty-five miles outside Guanajuato, according to the risqué accounts of later conservatives, because his Catholicism was more theoretical than practical; he gave, they said, few masses but slept with quite a few parishioners. He was accused of gambling, failing to honor debts, reading bawdy French atheists, using the confessional to philosophically advocate fornication, and cracking jokes about Saint Teresa. At fifty-seven years old, the scurrilous version ran, he had turned from a formidable theologian into something of an aging roué.[1]

Hidalgo gave his opponents raw materials for their denunciations by using the rectory to host dances, musical soirées, and amateur theatricals, himself translating Molière's *Tartuffe*, a French satire on clerical corruption; that didn't make him a raving atheist, he said, but a moral despiser of hypocrisy and priestly malpractice. He was accused of harboring Voltaire and the encyclopedists of the European Enlightenment on his bookshelves, but there was no sign of their works in his catalogue, or, indeed, in the transcripts of the Inquisitors who questioned him when he fell into disgrace after 1810. Nor is there any sign of him being in disgrace before 1810. He was not evicted from his position in the College of San Nicolás for moral turpitude; he asked for a transfer to a parish because it would more than double his income, and like many other creoles the economic strains of war in Europe left him feeling the pinch.[2]

So he was far from one more picaresque churchman, or another of the parish priests mulling revolution in Mexico or France. Hidalgo embodied much of the poise, developmentalism, and critical thinking of the Mexican Enlightenment. He ridiculed other theologians for debating whether an angel could be in two places at once; when the Inquisition accused him of denying hell's existence, he refuted them with the line "They say that I deny hell, but then they say I said a Pope was in hell—how can it be both?"[3] He tried to set up new industries in Dolores, like a silk farm. The year before he rebelled, the *Diario de México* singled him out as an exemplar of "wise parish priests who use their moral advantage . . . to promote the industry of the Indians, instruct them in their duties, and inspire in them the finest ideas of civilization."[4]

In rebelling, Hidalgo was responding to the political and economic strains brought by war in Europe. He resented the Spanish coup in Mexico City and suspected that the illegitimate Spanish government there was about to hand the country over to the French heretics. He knew how hard wartime exactions had hit his parishioners in steep sales taxes, forced loans, and the hated Indian tribute. And Hidalgo knew firsthand about the effects of the Crown calling in church mortgages. It had put a lien on a family hacienda, driving him toward bankruptcy and pushing his younger brother Manuel into madness and death.[5] So his rebellion was not improvised. He had been in touch with conspirators in Michoacán the year before and begun talks with three other creole landowners, the militia captains Ignacio Allende, Juan Aldama, and Mariano Abasolo. He had joined them in the Academia Literaria de Querétaro, a dissident talking shop that gathered arms and recruited a Crown official, the corregidor Miguel Domínguez. In January 1810 Hidalgo went to Guanajuato and picked up a copy of the *Diccionario de Ciencias y Artes*, which had a handy article on how to make cannon, and a history that described the Catiline conspiracy to overthrow the Roman Republic. On the same trip he dined with the region's two most important men, the intendant Riaño and Bishop Abad y Queipo, and invited them to visit him and enjoy September's winemaking.[6] It seemed like a well-planned coup d'état.

But on September 13 things went awry when some of the Querétaro conspirators were arrested. The corregidor's wife, Josefa Ortiz de Domínguez, warned Aldama, who made it to Dolores at two in the morning on September 16. At eight Hidalgo tolled the church bells, the traditional call to muster, lynching, or riot, and gave a speech to the crowd that gathered in the plaza below. It was canonized as the *Grito de Dolores*; no one took his words down verbatim, but whatever his precise choice, they worked. They included a viva to the Virgin of Guadalupe and an offer of respectable pay: a peso a day for horsemen, half a peso for foot soldiers. It was Sunday, so there were copious peasants, Indians, fieldhands, ranchers, cowboys, and drifters in town for mass and market day. By the end of Hidalgo's speech he had six hundred listeners. The plan had been for a vanguard of civilian and militia officers to raise a disciplined multiracial army; to the conspirators there seemed no good reason why it shouldn't still work, even with an accelerated schedule.[7]

They recruited tens of thousands with startling speed. A majority were indigenous and mulatto workers and peasants, the ethnic makeup of the Bajío. These were improvised soldiers without much ideology beyond a generalized resentment of the wealthiest Spanish and a moral panic that these were selling out religion and country to the French. They were attached to the banners and insignia of the Virgin of Guadalupe, which they wore in their hats. Some fought because the depression of 1808–1810 had left them jobless and/or homeless, profoundly worried about hunger and the future. The last great food crisis in the Bajío in the 1780s had killed as many as three hundred thousand of their parents' generation. Others were taking the chance to settle local scores and sack the haciendas that price gouged in times of famine. Savvy muleteers, village empire-builders, and bandits saw opportunity. Many insurgents were single, but they were not just young adventurers: The average age was around thirty. They weren't ancient communities in arms either; most of the regions' Indians were Tlaxcalteca or Nahua migrant workers. Neither did they start out radical independentistas: The Grito de Dolores, relatively centrist, hadn't called for independence. On the contrary, it followed the old, widespread formula of combining a rebellious "death to bad government" with a heartfelt or bet-hedging "long live the king."

To contemporary conservatives the army was largely indigenous; to later nationalists, mestizo; to social historians, peasants. Arrest records show none of the above: Thirty percent were townsmen and miners, another 10 percent muleteers, traders, and shopkeepers (though peasants were probably better at avoiding arrest, skewing the sample). Junior officers included hacienda overseers. The great common denominator was region, the specific legacy of the Bajío's mining and commercial agriculture and the fragile, populous society they created. This helped make it—paradoxically—a very Mexican rebellion in the sense of ethnic diversity, the army a mixture of numerous mestizos and mulattos with an indigenous majority and a white minority. Creoles did not just lead but also fought in the ranks. Two entire militia regiments joined in, the Celaya infantrymen and the heavy cavalry of the Queen's Regiment of Provincial Dragoons.

For ten days it was more procession than war as the rebels mustered and headed for Guanajuato. They faced next to no opposition; the Spanish commander of the hastily constituted Army of the Center, Brigadier General Félix Calleja del Rey, needed weeks to muster and arm troops, his blacksmiths racing to make everything from machetes to cannon. Hidalgo sent two letters to Guanajuato's ruler, his old friend Intendant Riaño, asking him to surrender, but Riaño retreated with the town's Spaniards into the Alhóndiga, the public granary he had built to ward off starvation for the people now attacking his city. On September 28 the rebel militiamen stormed his redoubt and massacred most inside, leaving behind graphic memories: Riaño's corpse left out two days so that the mob could see whether he was a Jew with a tail, as rumored; the tax collector's daughter staggering into a neighbor's house, bloody, naked, newly orphaned.[8] The Alhóndiga, remembered an eighteen-year-old creole who survived the sack of Guanajuato,

> presented the most dreadful spectacle: the food that had been stored there was scattered all around; naked corpses were found half-buried in corn and money, all of it stained with blood . . . Hidalgo's Indians made the strangest figures of all, for on top of their own clothing they wore the clothes they had taken from the homes of the

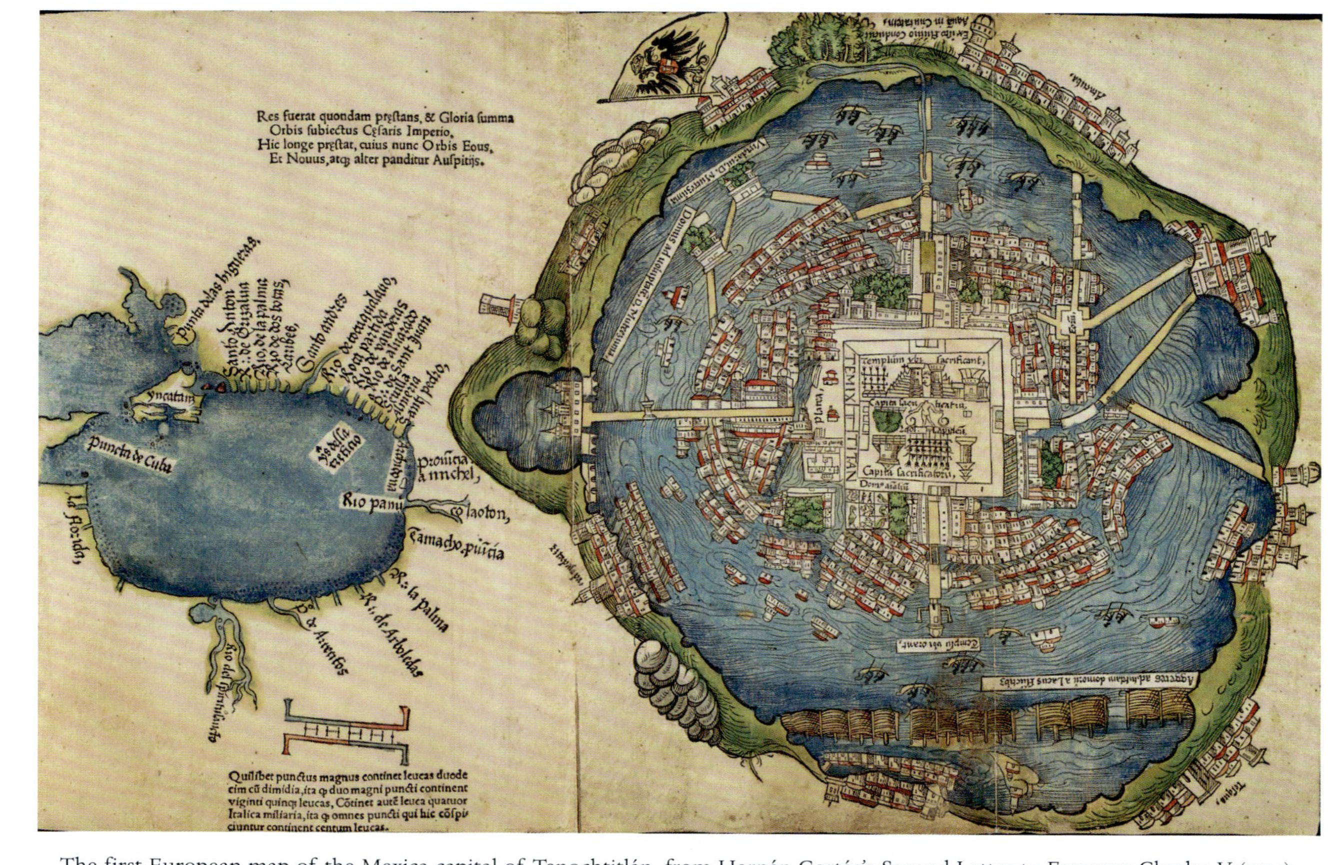

The first European map of the Mexica capital of Tenochtitlán, from Hernán Cortés's Second Letter to Emperor Charles V (1524).

The Spanish insist on meeting a reluctant Montezuma, as depicted in the bilingual chronicle (Nahuatl and Spanish) of the Florentine Codex Book XII (1576). The image is part-colored because the writers had to stop work and smuggle the book out of Mexico in a hurry, threatened with seizure by the Crown. The Codex ended up buried in the library of the Medici family, not to be disinterred until the late eighteenth century.

The horse offered the Spaniards their greatest military advantage. Early sixteenth-century chaffron, the warhorse's head armor.

Cortés hung Cuauhtémoc, "Falling Eagle," the last Mexica emperor, in 1524. Codex Vaticanus A (1565).

The Conquest of Mexico by Cortés (painted in c. 1650).

The apocalyptic visions that drove Franciscan missionaries.
Pieter Bruegel the Elder, *The Last Judgement* (1558).

Tapestry made of feathers commissioned by a missionary and an indigenous nobleman to send to the far-off pope. *The Mass of Saint Gregory* (1529).

The original Virgin of Guadalupe emblazoned on the peasant Juan Diego's cloak.
Attributed to Marcos Cipac de Aquino, mid-sixteenth century.

Philip II of Spain.

Dominican missionary Bartolomé de las Casas.

Sor Juana Inés de la Cruz, the woman who was the leading intellectual of her day, depicted by the leading artist of his day, the Zapotec Miguel Cabrera (c. 1750).

Anonymous artist, Pintura de castas, mid-eighteenth century, depicting the idealized and wholly unworkable sixteen different racial types of New Spain.

Napoleon's bloody takeover of Spain in 1808 left Mexico an empire without an imperial capital or emperor. Goya, *The Disasters of War.*

Miguel Hidalgo captures the granary in Guanajuato at the start of the Mexican War of Independence (1810–1821). This mannerly celebration by José Díaz del Castillo (1910) contradicts contemporary accounts of a disorganized massacre.

> Europeans, including the uniforms of magistrates, so the Indians adorned themselves with embroidered dress coats and gilded hats while barefoot and in the most complete state of inebriation.[9]

The eighteen-year-old was Lucas Alamán, son of a prosperous if declining local family (also friends of the prewar Hidalgo), who became the most prominent Mexican conservative of the nineteenth century: a politician, diplomat, businessman, and historian. Guanajuato left him convinced that the insurgents had launched both a race war—Indian hordes, mulatto cowboys—and a class war—miners tunneling into the Alhóndiga, a lumpenproletariat looting his city. Guanajuato was a bastion of the middle class that had been savaged because Hidalgo was "raising the proletarian classes against the propertied."[10] The looting and violence initially targeted the rich Spanish immigrants, whom rebels called *gachupines*, but rapidly expanded to encompass anyone else white or monied. It was a turning point: Creoles who might have rebelled shared Alamán's diagnosis and stayed on the sidelines. A new army of mulattos and Blacks mustering on the Pacific Coast sparked memories of Haiti's apocalyptic slave revolution. Hidalgo's army became browner and more military as it moved south, gathering Indians from the villages and deserters from the militias, and more numerous, reaching a proclaimed eighty thousand men when it climbed the capital's valley rim on October 30, 1810. Considered political revolt had turned to chaotic social revolution.

Alamán's diagnosis was wrong. While Hidalgo's army briefly occupied major cities, it remained amateurish and unambitious. Many rebels went home in the face of defeat or the aftermath of plunder; cowboys and Indians never stormed the heights of power. Hidalgo decreed the end of slavery but was otherwise reformist. There was no plan for a great redistribution of land or capital, a razing of conservative towns, or an end to monarchy. There were no new beliefs; everyday soldiers kept their popular religion, leaders their Catholic reformism. The execution of gachupines was a revolutionary terror, but it was ordered from the top, not demanded by a clamoring mob. At Valladolid and Guadalajara

Hidalgo tried to cover up the killings of some four hundred Spaniards.[11] The Indians who lynched a family of gachupín hacendados were creole-led.[12] Hidalgo's rising lasted only six months, and its redistribution was the pillage of an army living off the countryside and extorting townspeople rather than any thought-out revolutionary scheme. Generals and entrepreneurial types amassed wealth; classes did not.

The northern rebellion failed for structural and personal reasons. The rebel officers never much drilled their troops nor armed them: At the start one observer described them as "almost naked and armed with a few shotguns and lances"; bows, slings, machetes, and agricultural tools remained their mainstay. At one point royalists were confiscating kitchen knives.[13] The officer corps was bloated and incompetent, a core of professionals outnumbered by the promotions that Hidalgo scattered haphazardly, so many that he began inventing new ranks, such as Brigadier Brigadier. At its head Hidalgo assumed the tin-pot title of "His Most Serene Highness."[14] Critical decisions became erratic, taken against the advice of partners who actually knew something about war. Royalist troops, now concentrated and adequately armed, began to show the worth of even flawed professionalism. After Hidalgo beat the loyalists at the Battle of Monte de las Cruces on October 30, he had an open path into the Valley of Mexico, a possibly victorious end to the war; instead of pressing home his advantage he ordered an unnecessary retreat. In January 1811 a major defeat at Puente de Calderón in Jalisco was the definitive tipping point, winnowing the rebel army and leading Ignacio Allende to take over. Their reduced numbers marched north, where Hidalgo, Allende, and Aldama were captured on March 21 and executed. Their heads were hung in cages from the corners of the Alhóndiga.

The executions did not end the war, which dragged on until 1821. The great northern rebellion had been seconded by regional guerrilla forces, provincial lawyers and chieftains, and two disciples of Hidalgo who tried to unite them. His old secretary Ignacio Rayón set up a theoretical government in Michoacán; a former student, the priest José María Morelos, raised a real army in the South. Morelos had promising raw material in his mountain men, slaves, and mulattos, and he was better cut out to be a war leader than Hidalgo; not just a churchman, with all the legitimacy that brought, but also a mestizo muleteer with the local knowledge, contacts, and smarts of that job. He went about war in a systematic way, reading Frederick the Great and organizing a conventional military with clear hierarchies and logistics. He incorporated village recruits under their local leaders, the ranchers, priests, militia captains, and indigenous nobles who knew and could drill them. Racialized violence was punishable by death.[15]

As Hidalgo began retreating, Morelos began advancing, and in early 1812 he took and fortified Cuautla, a small city fifty-five miles south of the capital. He held it against the royalists for two months, grinding down the besiegers before retreating to continue war in the provinces, where he captured the strategic cities of Oaxaca, Orizaba, Xalapa, and Acapulco.[16] But the rebels didn't hang on to any of them for much more than a year, and a major defeat in Michoacán in December 1813 broke Morelos's army. The survivors turned to guerrilla warfare, ably enough to dominate large swathes of provincial Mexico. Spain didn't fund a big enough army to end the insurgency; on the contrary, it used the taxes it raised in New Spain to survive in Europe. In 1811, the thick of the rebellion, the entire year's revenue was sent home to pay for war against France.[17] Even after the Napoleonic War was over, Spain remained in ruinous condition, in Thomas Jefferson's judgement "a pigmy power" compared to Mexico.[18] The siege of Cuautla exemplified the pattern of the War of Independence. Rebels couldn't hold cities; royalists couldn't control the countryside.

Outside the warzones there were two political revolutions: on the rebel side, the constitution of an independent nation-state and complex indirect elections for its leadership; on the loyalist side, a liberal Spanish government proposing home rule inside a Bourbon empire, also with complex indirect elections for its leadership.

There had been a civilian government at Zitácuaro in Michoacán since 1811, aspiring to impose order on what a founder called the "so many libertine men" of the guerrilla bands. The Supreme Junta sent delegates and bureaucrats to rebel-held areas, raised taxes, issued identity papers, and minted coins. It was institutionally ambitious but constitutionally confused; sovereignty, Rayón explained, was founded on the people, was exercised by their congress in the Americas, and resided with the king in Spain.[19] In 1813 the Junta's divisions and incompetence provoked Morelos to convene an alternative constitutional convention in Chilpancingo, in modern Guerrero. He called it the Congress of Anáhuac, the Nahuatl name for the Mexica Empire, which Morelos said they would "re-establish, improving its government." After rhetorically summoning the spirits of the pre-Hispanic emperors, the constituents declared independence in November 1813. Mexico, the founding act said, had "recovered the exercise of her usurped sovereignty; and as such dependence on the Spanish Throne was dissolved and forever broken." In October 1814 the convention issued a replacement constitution for the country it was inventing, a color-blind democracy with three branches of government. What to call the new country was a good question: Some thought it should be Anáhuac, others called themselves *novohispanos*, *mexicanos*, and, like every other independence rebel in the Spanish Americas, *americanos*, Americans. Their first, short-lived choice was América Mexicana.[20]

They had Spanish rivals in revolutionizing government. On September 24, 1810, Spanish liberals, their country divided between French and British soldiers, had convoked a constitutional convention in Cádiz, one of the few places they controlled. (And that barely; at the outset they had to flee, attacked by twenty thousand French soldiers, to an island in the bay.) Their proposal—nothing to do with Hidalgo's rising, which they couldn't know existed—mixed Spain's medieval tradition of the Cortes and the commune with modern demands for elections, equality of representation, and tripartite government. Despite obvious logistical problems, *americanos* ran elections, recruited refugees, and came up with respectable delegations in both number and quality; New Spain sent twenty-one representatives, one of them Lucas Alamán, and provided six of the assembly's presidents. Five of the fifteen deputies on the constitutional committee considering the future of elections were from the Americas, and after lengthy debate they denied afrodescendientes suffrage but extended it to everyone else. Even the homeless could vote. It meant that future parliaments of a decentralized empire would be split more or less equally between colonial and metropolitan representatives; it enfranchised three million Mexican voters to determine who those representatives would be. Enfranchising as it did indigenous people, the poor, and the illiterate, the Constitution of Cádiz was one of the most inclusive constitutions of the nineteenth century.[21]

The central points of both rebel and loyalist constitutions were a strong legislature, a weak executive, and frequent indirect but meaningful elections. Neither worked. The Constitution of Cádiz led to exceptionally popular elections for the Cortes, the Mexican regional assemblies, and the city and municipal governments. They were fiestas, heralded by bells and fireworks, blessed by clerics; voting began with a mass and ended with a Te Deum. Nearly a million voters turned out.[22] Yet they only happened once, because in March 1814 a restored King Ferdinand closed the Cortes and abolished the constitution. In the war-torn rebel South of Mexico, meanwhile, it was difficult to hold elections, and the losers of the Junta boycotted them; half the initial delegates at Apatzingán were appointees. Those elections that did take place were managed from above, facilitated by the stricture that only priests and lawyers could be electors. Once the new state was constituted, its balance of power was inefficient: Morelos, as executive and *generalísimo*, had the de facto tools—control of the army, treasury, and caciques—to rule as military dictator. De jure, however, he was subject to congressmen who could inspect, question, debate, and overrule his decisions, even on campaign. They followed him around, looking over his shoulder; he took risks in trying to keep them safe from harrying royalist troops, and in doing so was captured, defrocked, and shot, just before Christmas 1815.

Morelos was the great charismatic of the insurgent movements, standing out among an Independence generation whom some dubbed mediocrities.[23] He managed for four years to hold together very different leaders, ranging from the Yucateco lawyer Andrés Quintana Roo to the Black muleteer Vicente Guerrero. Part of it was *don de gente*, the gift of getting along with people; when informed that a potbellied assassin was after him, he is supposed to have replied reassuringly, "There's no potbelly here but me, and since I've been ill, it has trimmed down."[24] He had a lasting media operation, keeping two portable presses running even as he lost the cities.[25] Morelos's government was a balance of personalism and institution-building, and when he died the fighting was taken over by lesser charismatics who stayed in their own fiefdoms. Some shared his democratic beliefs: Vicente Guerrero, talking to an Indian in the misty highlands above Chilpancingo, gave him a lecture on citizenship.

But they faced stiffer opposition and had lesser ambitions. While Morelos had got as far as sending scouts to the outskirts of Mexico City, his successors stayed away, aspirations to national power abandoned.[26] The king rewarded his commander in chief General Calleja by making him viceroy, and at the end of his term in 1816 he proclaimed the insurgency over. The new viceroy, Juan Ruiz de Apodaca, launched a hearts and minds campaign of pardons at the same time as a new offensive, and by 1817 the insurgents were at a nadir.

Yet while violence decreased, the mountains of the South proved (as they would over and over again) unconquerable. In his paper *El Pensador Mexicano* the opposition writer José Joaquín Fernández de Lizardi mocked the "Old Geezer" Calleja's overconfidence:

It's useless that he boast
Of enjoying a quiet night,
Because even if he kills a thousand Fleas
Another thousand will come.[27]

Jacqueries, conventional warfare, and counterinsurgency killed huge numbers. The three hundred Spaniards killed in Guanajuato paled alongside the two thousand Hidalgo lost outside Mexico City at Monte de las Cruces, minor in turn alongside the dead of an attritional counterinsurgency. Calleja dealt with the state's eternal problem of guerrilla warfare, the sea of popular support that sustains irregulars, with exemplary violence and collective punishment, a "new Cortés" to his enemies.[28] Villages adjudged to have aided insurgents were "tithed" in the random execution of one in ten. Disease and hunger killed far more: There were epidemics of typhus and yellow fever across New Spain between 1812 and 1814, their vectors of ticks and mosquitoes traveling long distances with the columns of soldiers. Typhus pathogens from the siege of Cuautla killed forty thousand in the Valley of Mexico alone, halving some villages, and then spread north to Zacatecas, west to Michoacán, and east to Puebla, where the authorities had to improvise four new cemeteries. Death, drought, and pillaging armies brought famine. Between 1810 and 1821 as many as six hundred thousand died; one in ten Mexicans.[29]

War-weariness, hopelessness, and economic devastation might have been enough to drive a peace deal. Generals and soldiers were certainly sick of it, senior commanders complaining in letters to the viceroy that their troops were demoralized, unwilling to fight. Uncertainty as to the loyalties of creoles weighed on their minds. They had proven unreliable in South America, deserting the Crown and creating new countries: By 1821 creoles had founded six republics, including Colombia, Chile, and Peru. The Spanish merchants had little faith in Mexican soldiers or their generals and paid for their own Spanish soldiers, but this gave mixed results, because the preference shown to peninsulares alienated creole officers. The coup de grâce came once more from Spain, where in 1820 liberals rebelled against King Ferdinand and restored New Spain to the uncertainties of distant parliamentary rule. In Mexico City creoles across the ideological spectrum began conspiring. There had for years been a secret network of rebel sympathizers, the Guadalupes, liberal intellectuals and professionals in Mexico City; priests and conservatives now began considering a different political end to the war than Spanish victory. But it was always going to be soldiers who decided the question; in the provinces they had taken over political power and much of the economy, and on February 24, 1821, in Iguala, a small city in northern Guerrero, Colonel Agustín de Iturbide declared for independence.

The creole progeny of a rich Basque hacendado, Iturbide had joined the provincial militia at age fourteen and done little until he was nearly thirty; when Hidalgo's rebels crossed into his homeland of Michoacán, however, he excelled at the bloody job of putting them down. He exemplified the entrepreneurial officers who combined able ruthlessness with business: jailing suspected insurgents' womenfolk, threatening their mass execution, declaring the countryside a free-fire zone, distributing recovered rebel loot to his soldiers rather than to civil authorities, trashing his own side's haciendas, and doing suspiciously well as a merchant on the side. A year after becoming Commandant General of the Army of the North in 1815, the complaints of the Guanajuato priesthood brought him down, and he spent 1816–1820 removed from the fray. In November 1820, however, a despairing Viceroy Apodaca gave him command of the Army of the South and sent him to crush the enduring rebellion of Vicente Guerrero.[30]

The viceroy's spies had failed him, because Iturbide—a talented networker—had already sounded out officers, churchmen, and the loyalist delegates to Cádiz about ending the war a different way.[31] His Plan de Iguala, quickly distributed across Mexico, was simple and hard to oppose: It proposed an independent Catholic state, ruled by a constitutional Mexican monarchy, inclusive of the entire breadth of viceregal society from casta rebels to wealthy Spaniards. Guerrero signed up to it within two weeks, becoming commander of the first division of Iturbide's army. Royalists followed suit, starting in March with the commander of the Veracruz garrison, General Antonio López de Santa Anna, and ending in July in conservative Puebla. Finally the Mexico City garrison forced the viceroy to resign. His replacement, the liberal Juan O'Donojú, sued for peace on arrival, and on August 24, 1821, signed the Treaty of Córdoba, which recognized Mexican autonomy.

It was independence by the backdoor; the treaty proposed a regency until a European prince be found, knowing that no one was likely to apply for the job. This sleight of hand conjured a consensual, almost wholly peaceful independence out of the viciousness of civil war. A firm but congenial separation from Spain was presented and received as a fait accompli when there was neither successor state nor government. Strategic vagueness, conciliation, and reassurance were the dominant tones, not Jacobin change: The Plan de Iguala "guaranteed" religion, independence, and union, to be won by the Ejército Trigarante, the Army of the Three Guarantees. It was Mexico's first *pronunciamiento*, a low-cost, Spanish brand of the coup d'état, a dangerous precedent. It was also one of history's great peace deals, a revolution wrapped as bland continuity that ended the first global empire. In its place came something that sounded like a centuries-long throwback: an *Imperio mexicano*, a Mexican Empire. It satisfied, for a few months, most concerned.[32]

Yet the next sixty years were more turbulent in Mexico than anywhere else in the Americas. Mexicans fought four major wars, one between themselves and three against foreign empires: Spain, France, and the United States. A country with historically next to no army fell prey to a predatory military, and paying off soldiers and foreign creditors soaked up most government money. An economy once at the center of the world collapsed, devastated by the destruction of mines, farms, and trade. The capital that might have restored them fled. For all the grim poverty of the colonial lower classes, Mexicans went into the Wars of Independence richer than the global average; they came out considerably poorer.[33] Between 1821 and 1855 the national executive changed hands forty-eight times, on average more than once a year. There were seven different constitutions. It was unsurprising that many tried to secede, opting out of being Mexican; the surprise was that all of them bar the Texans either failed or changed their mind. Across Latin America independence led to superstates, vast republics, and federations, some as big as the United States; by 1846 Mexico was the only one left standing.

Independence brought irreparable devastation that pushed Mexico into lasting poverty. But it also brought remarkable freedoms. The first constitution abolished slavery and the caste system, and, even as powerful racial divisions endured, Mexico elected the first Black and only indigenous presidents in North American history. Between 1820 and 1835 Mexicans enjoyed a wider suffrage than either the United States or Britain.[34] Impoverished Mexicans held real elections, their results unpredictable; polling days may have had their fair share of rough-and-tumble, their effectiveness waxing and waning according to circumstance, but some voters translated democratic aspirations into representation. Printers spread a culture of answering back, their numbers booming, their profit-maximizing ingenuity keeping presses rolling and controversy flowing.[35] Censorship fluctuated, but even generals were taken by Enlightenment thought. A new generation of young intellectuals argued the unsayable: In the literary salon of the Academia de Letrán one teenage provocateur proclaimed abruptly, "*No hay Díos*," "There's no God," decades before "God is dead" occurred to Nietzsche.[36]

The same brattish intellectual, Ignacio Ramírez, said that Veracruz was his favorite city in Mexico because it was the way out the door.[37] The jokey nihilism was in part another provocation—he was enjoying his show immensely—and in part a recognition of dramatic political instability. For the first thirty years after Independence, power was won by an unsettling combination of pronunciamientos and elections.

Liberal and republican reforms dramatically expanded the numbers of politically active Mexicans, and a vigorous press made mass politics an everyday pursuit. Some politicians made it from the colonial margins to the highest level. Guadalupe Victoria, the first president, was a moneyless orphan from Durango who rose in the world through a seminary and Morelos's army. Vicente Guerrero was an *afromestizo* from the indigenous highlands who learned politics running mule trains. But most executives were wealthy creoles or royalist officers. Between them they took Mexico through a regency, an empire, a triumvirate, two dictatorships, and three republics. For a generation two rival Masonic lodges were the main political organizations. Advocates for a restored European monarchy never vanished, and one finally materialized in the 1860s, when Mexico spent three strange years as an empire under a Habsburg princeling.

The sheer quantity of pronunciamientos and their generally low collateral damage made Mexicans blasé. Fanny Calderón de la Barca, a keen-witted observer of society high and low, picked it up quickly. At a slightly disreputable masked ball—the amount of cross-dressing stood out—she noted that "although a *pronunciamiento* [a fashionable term here for a revolution] was prognosticated, we found everything very quiet and orderly, and the ball very crowded and gay." The pronunciamiento was "a game of chess, in which kings, castles, knights, and bishops are making different moves, while the pawns are looking on or taking no part whatever."[38] Part of the problem was that pronunciamientos were easy. They required little creativity; the words, gestures, and sequencing of events were standardized. Neither was manpower a problem, because a couple of regiments in a strategic town were threat enough to change national events. Some were manned by a few dozen hopefuls. They weren't assuming much risk; survival rates among unsuccessful leaders were high, and the 1832 pronunciamientos, which killed some four thousand men over four pitched battles, were an aberration. The greatest exponent of them all, General Antonio López de Santa Anna, launched numerous pronunciamientos from 1822 to 1853, was exiled several times, cyclically loathed by politicians and plebe, and yet died in Mexico City of old age.

A pronunciamiento began with a disaffected or ambitious general or civilian convening plotters in the barracks or town hall before publicly pronouncing himself in rebellion due to the existential threat posed to the Mexican people, or a subset thereof, by the government. Secretaries took minutes, church bells rang out, fireworks exploded, bands played, people got drunk; the rituals and political electricity must have felt, ironically, like the contemporary elections. A manifesto was hastily printed and circulated as widely as possible, deals with opportunists and fence-sitters explored. If the *pronunciados* were numerous and timely enough, they stood a chance and might bargain their way into power, extending consideration to their defeated enemy. Pronunciamientos were often dubbed revolutions, but they were nothing of the sort. These were choreographed rituals, the rules understood by each side, the violence more threatened than realized; elite versions of a good riot.[39]

The Plan de Iguala set the pattern. At the end of the 1810s Agustín de Iturbide was an embittered and indebted outsider, living dissipated on a mortgaged hacienda. An appreciation of timing and others' disaffection led him into clandestine politicking followed by an unimpeachably vague consensus-building proclamation. Seven months and two hundred deaths later he was regent of an independent Mexico. Another seven months on he launched a second pronunciamiento and on May 19, 1822, became emperor, this time without any deaths at all. Six months after that, another disaffected ex-royalist, Santa Anna, launched a third pronunciamiento from his homeland of Veracruz. (A homeland was the best place to start a pronunciamiento, and Veracruz, with its port and mountains, was the best of homelands for the job.) It failed, but opened the way for a fourth, the Plan de Casa Mata. Santa Anna joined it, the pronunciados reached critical mass, and on March 19, 1823, Iturbide abdicated and was allowed to go into exile, another emerging norm. When he came back without warning, however, he was arrested and shot, leaving one politician wondering, in the privacy of his diary, "whether Iturbide had died like a Hero or a *pendejo* [dickhead]."[40]

Pronunciamientos were personalist; some were also ideological. Almost all politicians believed in two of Iturbide's three guarantees, religion and independence. Only union, conciliation with the Spanish, was traduced through two laws of expulsion. Even liberals, slurred as raving atheists, endorsed the Church's fundamental role in Mexico, and every constitution until 1857 stated explicitly that Mexico was a Catholic country.[41] Monarchists believed in autonomy, the sort of home rule that some Bourbons had mooted in the 1780s. In addition to that consensus few politicians publicly opposed voting. It was theories about who should vote that varied enormously, from universal to very limited suffrage. Opinion on what the vote should count for also varied greatly: Conservatives believed in a centralized republic with a powerful executive, while liberals believed in federalism with powerful regional legislatures. Conservatives and liberals belonged to different Masonic lodges, the Scottish Rite set up by the Spanish and the York Rite set up by the Americans, and they were different enough to constitute the party labels of the 1820s, conservative *escoceses* against liberal *yorkinos.* And in the midst of it all was General Santa Anna, backstabbing, trimming his sails to the prevailing wind, proclaiming adherence to one ideology or the other.

A Mexico without Santa Anna would still have seen its fair share of pronunciamientos, with their calls to and performances of honorable rebellion. As a bargaining mechanism it worked, and a wide range of people used it, from remote mountain villages to the national palace. However, Santa Anna was unusually talented at the pronunciamiento and pulled them off where others might have failed. In 1822 he rebelled for the reopening of Congress and a federation; in 1835 he rebelled for the closure of Congress and a strong central executive. He was very good at getting power and very bad at exercising it. More than once he became president and then retreated to his hacienda in Veracruz, Manga de Clavo, a fiefdom of some hundred square miles.[42] Absence sometimes insulated him from responsibility; blame for the turbulence of the day attached to his visible vice president. There was no panacea for disaster, though, and after his 1845 ouster—by pronunciamiento—he ended up in jail, swapping indignant letters with the new administration. In one reply the minister of war told him, "The entire nation would rise up at the mere idea of the possibility that Your Excellency might return to rule over its fate."[43] Eighteen months later Santa Anna was president again.

He ended up a national villain, his duplicity and hunger for power a way to understand the disillusion and disorder of the post-Independence years. The story and raw chronology of betrayal beg the question why anybody ever believed in him. But there were good reasons for Santa

Anna's success. He had the best stronghold in Mexico in his hacienda near Veracruz, with its customs duties, bankers, and strong military. He was brave, and until 1847 won enough battles to be a war hero. He lost disastrously in 1836 to the Texan secessionists, but he also in the eyes of the public saved independence twice, driving off a Spanish invasion force at Tampico in 1829 and scaring off a French expedition in 1838. The latter engagement was a half-hearted affair. The French were officially there to collect compensation for a compatriot whose Mexico City patisserie had been destroyed by boisterous Mexican soldiers; a brief naval blockade and some shelling was as far as it was likely to go. But the political effect of the *Guerra de pasteles*, the Pastry War, was outsize. As the French covered their shore party's retreat, Santa Anna, leading from the front, had his horse blown out from under him by grapeshot. He lost a leg, physically unfortunate—poor surgery made it painful for the rest of his life—but politically priceless. Hand-colored lithographs, newspapers, and pamphlets ensured that no one forgot his sacrifice for the newborn *patria*. In conversation he name-dropped the leg (which had received its own state funeral) with notorious frequency.[44]

Alongside his lasting rural constituency and military glory Santa Anna had the other two characteristics of a successful caudillo, intelligence and charm. Unlikely people like Guillermo Prieto, a liberal who saw Santa Anna up close at his dangerous worst, recognized it. The General was semiliterate, Prieto remembered, but

> he used to make sparkling conversation, animated by an extremely powerful imagination and a perception clear as daylight. When he was playful he would put on a *jarocho* [rustic Veracruz] accent that was funny; his large and penetrating black eyes were more persuasive than his words, and his quick and sweeping gestures made him seductive and irresistible.[45]

Other sharp-tongued observers and some painters agreed with Prieto on this physical magnetism.[46]

But there was more to Santa Anna's decades in and out of power than good eyes and a famous leg. There were few alternatives. Poverty and external threats made settled parliamentary regimes improbable.

Between 1830 and 1850 more than 80 percent of the paltry federal budget went to debt service and buying off overmighty soldiers.[47] Like other presidents, Santa Anna cast around for money, in one instance with the intelligent simplicity of basing property taxes on a house's number of windows (a widespread strategy of early state-builders). The best of measures failed, nevertheless, to ameliorate the structural problem. When the government ran out of money and suspended payments to either creditors or soldiers, conflict ensued. Soldiers toppled presidents, looking for backpay or profit; foreign powers launched wars looking for their interest, opportunistic profit, or land. One anticolonial war brought Santa Anna to power; another threw him out; the most catastrophic, against the United States in 1846, brought him back, then ruined him again; in 1865 he tried unsuccessfully to come back one more time to fight the French. In a vicious circle war was fueled by debt, which fueled poverty, which fueled yet more war.

So the Republic's first name, the United Mexican States, was a misnomer; four decades after Independence the conservative Francisco Pimentel lamented that Mexico was still not "a nation, properly speaking."[48] Mexico inherited New Spain's borders, that vast territory from Oregon to Texas to Central America, but it was politically divided into nineteen states, five territories, and a federal district. Their interests diverged widely, and one of their few common denominators was an enduring desire for autonomy. Bandits were endemic, ranging from gangs of silver-braided dandies like *los Plateados* of Morelos to rugged individualists like Heraclio Bernal, "the Lightning Bolt of Sinaloa." Like bandits everywhere they inspired a mixture of fear, romanticization, and good anecdotes: *La Carambada*, who dressed as a man to stalk the roads around Querétaro, was said to have flashed her breasts at her victims while shouting, "Look who has looted you!"[49] A count gravely told Fanny Calderón that he couldn't "understand why we complain of Mexican robbers, when the city of London is full of organized gangs of ruffians, whom the laws cannot reach; and when English highwaymen and housebreakers are the most celebrated in the world."[50] The difference, she might have retorted, lay in quantity, not quality; the royalists had pardoned some fifty thousand rebels in the 1810s, and many subsequently moved between army units, provincial militias, and robber gangs.[51] From the outset Mexico lacked one of the main attributes of a functioning state, a legitimate monopoly on violence.

Mexico also struggled with another basic test of sovereignty, preserving borders. Provincials seceded regularly, opting out of taxes whose results they failed to glimpse and the overreach of centralists they mistrusted. They could see the point of the borders and elected bodies of their own municipios and states, lent coherence by topographies, economies, race, and colonial administrative divisions; seeing the point of Mexico was more difficult. In 1822 only three states actually wanted a republic; in 1823 Oaxaca and Puebla voted out. They came back; the countries of modern Central America, nominally Mexican, went their own way permanently.[52] In 1835 Zacatecas seceded for three months, only brought back into the fold by Santa Anna's army; in 1836 Texans separated more permanently, Santa Anna failing dismally to bring them back at the Battle of San Jacinto (which lasted less than an hour, and which kicked off while the caudillo, his staff, and motley army were taking a siesta).[53] Texans and Yucatecos were reluctant from the outset, both Maya caciques and Mérida planters rooting for the monarchy, and after achieving their own independence Texans proposed a trans-Gulf naval alliance. Yucatán would give the Texan navy $8,000 per month, and in return Texan vessels would be stationed off the peninsula.[54] Yucatán agreed, and between 1841 and 1848 it was an autonomous state.[55]

The northern states, meanwhile, were war zones where small groups of Mexican settlers fought sophisticated indigenous rivals. In the Northwest, the Yaqui proclaimed themselves a nation and turned the symbols of Mexican independence against independent Mexico. Their "king and emperor" Juan Banderas said that he was the legitimate heir of Montezuma; his men followed banners embroidered with the Virgin of Guadalupe. The Yaqui didn't merely refuse to fight the neighboring Apache raiders; they egged them on.[56] Banderas's first peace treaty with Mexico secured his people ownership of the Yaqui River Valley and the lands of the Yori, the white men who had fled the war. In the Center-North the Comanche attacked ranches, haciendas, and even the occasional big town. They were helped by Mexican traders who acted as spies, local militias who fought only for themselves, border states incapable of mounting a joint defense, and a capital that prioritized other problems. It was a dirty war of everyday atrocity that revealed a fundamental lack of central power and unity.

Debility was founded on tax as well as politics. During the War of Independence the regional treasuries collected less revenue, as rebels occupied haciendas, devoured livestock, and ravaged mines. A French economist sneered that France's cobblers made more money than all the Americas' mines combined.[57] The provinces also remitted less of what they collected to Mexico City. When peace came Mexicans found it easy to continue evading tax, and the newborn states continued hanging on to as much as possible. The national governments of the 1820s surrendered. Iturbide tried to spend his way to popularity, cutting taxes and increasing spending to the benefit of bureaucrats, merchants, and military. The Plan de Casa Mata that toppled him promised states the majority of the revenues they collected; as a result, by early 1825 the Treasury had only 60,000 pesos cash in hand. An attempt to get off the fiscal brink through income and corporate taxes in 1827 proved unenforceable. In 1829 President Guerrero, struggling for survival, took desperate measures to raise revenue; his successors swung between such emergency expropriations and considered reform packages centering on income tax, which were also unenforceable.

Governments were not incompetents and often knew very well what they were doing, and what they couldn't do; they were horrified by deficits and the regressive nature of the value-added taxes called *alcabalas* charged at entrances to towns and markets. Yet they were damned if they charged taxes, which lost them popular and elite support, and damned if they didn't, running out of money to buy off a turbulent military. Their only great unforced error was to expel the Spanish in the two laws of 1827 and 1829, because the great merchants and landowners departed with their capital, most of them for good. Otherwise, failure was systemic and generally unavoidable; even the most successful of tax-gatherers, Santa Anna in his 1840s dictatorship, never came near balancing the budget.[58]

Neither was there much left to tax. In the 1820s the smaller, mainly domestic sectors of the economy began a patchy recovery: People bought textiles from Puebla and Guadalajara again, and some of the great haciendas began shipping grain and meat to the cities. British money went into the great mines, abandoned and flooded, promising Mexicans steam engines to drain them and shareholders the fabulous riches of New Spain. At their peak British companies had sunk more than 100 million pounds in Latin American mining.[59] White settlers came too, the human capital that elites hungered after, despite the myths of atavistic nativism generated by Hidalgo's rebellion. They were welcome, particularly those in the thinly populated North, like Moses Austin, who bought huge land concessions in Texas in the 1820s. Foreign businessmen were impressed by some of the politicians they met, such as Lucas Alamán, who as foreign minister negotiated loans in the 1820s and set up a state development bank in the early 1830s. The first Mexican bond issues sold well on the frenzied London stock market of the 1820s, keeping the Republic's first government afloat.

But creditors proved as predatory as generals. The great London banks like Barclays that sold Mexico's bonds took usurious commissions. The first two loans put Mexico 16 million pesos in debt; only six and a half million of that ever made it into the Treasury, in part because Barclays collapsed alongside the London Stock Exchange in 1826. British financiers' fraud and imprudence—a stock bubble founded on domestic cotton and Spanish American dreams—brought down the entire regional economy. Mexico tried to pay its obligations and even those of others, lending Colombia a month's interest payments, but in 1827, with domestic taxes paltry and import tariffs hard hit by the crash, the government ran out of money and defaulted. The Treasury committed the cardinal sin of taking out new loans to service old ones. Bent British financiers were replaced by outright loan sharks: One 1828 loan had an annual interest rate of 536 percent. Astute refinancing—new bonds with interest deferred for the first five years—briefly rescued the government, but it never managed to pay the interest because politics got in the way. The civil wars of 1832 diverted even more of the budget to the army and reduced revenues yet further. In 1833 ragtag pronunciados under Mariano Arista, a future president, looted the British-restored mines of Guanajuato; investment from Britain dried up. By 1837 Mexico was 50 million pesos in debt.[60]

So an intertwined, mutually reinforcing combination of poverty and political instability endured. It wasn't just the mines; the ruins of the great viceroyalty were ubiquitous, their descriptions a wistful trope for foreign visitors in the 1840s. The great highway that Revillagigedo had built was now a muddy, potholed track, an impressive single-arch bridge near Xalapa only emphasizing its decline. In Mérida one of the great Franciscan convents housed a handful of friars in crumbling cloisters, weeds growing through the paving and horses grazing in a garden gone to seed. Another of Revillagigedo's great roads ran north to Toluca, a major industrial and trading center, former capital of the province of Mexico; now the point of it was gone, because Toluca had become a ghost town where grass grew on the streets, town dwellers just walked away from their houses, and the very basics of city life had disappeared. All that was left were the ill-reputed poor.[61]

Yet devastation and freedom weren't mutually exclusive. Viceregal Mexico had shown notable mobility between racial categories: Stringent laws did not stop mestizo and mulatto individuals from colonizing the arts, professions, and large sectors of provincial economies. The settled indigenous peoples of the center had their own laws and governments; the Tlaxcalteca enjoyed their own governor and believed that they had won the Spanish conquest. In the South the Maya of Yucatán and Chiapas were left alone, their power forcing creole elites to learn their languages, revolt a constant fear. In the North the Apache, Comanche, O'odham, and Yaqui owned much of the mountains and drylands and were kept in check by trading and bribery. Mulatto militiamen moved up the social ladder, and some made it into local judgeships and ayuntamientos. In the cities afrodescendientes disdained the laws intended to keep them in humble subjection. One racial category was inflexible, however, and that was the exclusion of non-whites from all but the most local political and economic elites. In a terrible mistake, at the very top they even excluded creoles: The great merchants and viceroys were European.

Independence ended that practice for reasons both ideological and pragmatic. Rich creoles were the obvious heirs to the new country's strategic heights, but they fought from 1810 onward for the political rights of non-whites too; they needed them. Both globetrotting autonomists and mountain rebels overcame opposition to giving Indians the vote. The Spanish merchants had argued at Cádiz for exclusion of the Indian on the grounds that he was

> endowed with a laziness and languor . . . congenitally stupid, without either innovative talent or strength of thought . . . a drunkard by nature . . . sensual because of lascivious thoughts and bereft of chaste ideas about physical closeness, modesty or incest . . . as careless as he is insensitive to religious truths.[62]

They lost the argument. At the rebel constituent congress in Chilpancingo the mestizo Morelos insisted that indigenous peoples had "the right to vote, even though they might not seem competent."[63] When they did in Oaxaca they elected an ayuntamiento with four non-whites.[64]

In both Spain and Mexico indigenous enfranchisement passed; weakened Spanish radicals and Mexicans who argued that their polity was Aztec could hardly do otherwise. In rebel Mexico Black enfranchisement passed too, and in Morelos's army it was whites, not Blacks, who risked being subject to racial violence. In Spain reformist Mexicans advocated the Black vote too. Enfranchising the castas would give them many more deputies. At the Congress of Cádiz one described the castas as "the basis of our well-being and our happiness." Another, future justice minister Miguel Ramos Arizpe, told the assembled:

> I know descendants of Africans who are distinguished priests. I have seen countless such individuals employed in all fields. I have seen [casta] judges and just and zealous regidores of ayuntamientos . . . I have seen their families linked with distinguished Spaniards . . . do not sow the seeds of dissension and discord among these countless [casta] families.[65]

At Independence such egalitarians won, abolished racial classification, and passed a law affirming "the equality of civil rights to all free inhabitants of the empire, whatever their origin."[66]

It wasn't verbiage: In 1829 a Black president took office. Vicente Guerrero was installed by Santa Anna against the wishes of a thin

Vicente Guerrero.

majority of voters, only lasted eight months, and was murdered in 1831. His race fostered numerous attacks by his opponents, who included Simón Bolívar, using code words like a "lack of education," a "rural background," or "barbarism" versus "civilization." Yet the mere fact that he could be president, and that these attacks were dog whistles rather than avowed racial insults, was revealing. One writer who called him *el negro* took care to clarify (twice) that those were the words of others, and the year that Guerrero died a future indigenous president, the Zapotec Benito Juárez, won his first election. There was a meritocratic opening through which talent in war, law, or even poetry could bring outsiders by race or poverty into high politics. The deacon of Mexican letters in the second half of the nineteenth century, Ignacio Manuel Altamirano, was a Nahuatl-speaking Indian. Guillermo Prieto, a penniless teenager, burst in on the minister of justice, improvised a sonnet, and promptly got a government job, a place at the university, and a path toward the cabinet.[67]

This was not just because the minister, Andrés Quintana Roo, was himself a poet; even that self-fashioned man of action Santa Anna (whom one writer thought less philosophical than his warhorse) played the thinker. The general was keen on cockfights; he was also an opera buff and sponsor of the national theater.[68] More to the point, wordsmiths like Prieto who wrote sonnets, plays, and stories also wrote influential political journalism. The insurgents wrote freedom of the press into the Constitution of 1824, and by 1831 there were three major opposition papers in the capital, six in the provinces, and a steady stream of vituperative pamphlets.[69] Defamation cases abounded, but so did small, risk-taking print shops, whose owners called themselves "citizen printers," their profit-making idealism. It was probably both.[70]

Censorship materialized with press juries that settled complaints of subversion, immorality, or slander. After the 1820s, the decade of greatest liberties, both conservatives and liberals worked hard to control journalists and printers through emergency decrees and the replacement of juries with less tolerant judges. The governor of Mexico City banned the newspaper boys who shrilled out sensationalist headlines on street corners, seducing buyers and informing illiterates. Yet hardliners balked at prohibiting press freedom outright, and a critical tradition persisted, ironically upheld in censorship legislation; the preamble to an 1848 law preached that "to express thought through the press is one of the first rights of man."[71] Even the seemingly holier-than-thou men of Puebla's *La Abeja—The Bee*, whose first issue promised that its editors "would know how to extract honey and wax from the calyx of all flowers," avoiding "the unbearable nuisance that hateful party disputes leave in their wake"—confessed that they would cover politics, albeit without offending "the moderation, urbanity and decency" of their fellow *poblanos*.[72]

The struggle over press freedom reflected the struggle over elections, which, despite punctuation by coups, mattered. A national congress sat almost continuously from 1824 to 1857. Civilians and generals proved incapable of controlling it or its elections; campaigning was a long business, and deputies who triumphed usually represented a committed political faction rather than a readily distracted president. Indirect elections—parish voters voted for electors who then voted for state-level electors who then voted for deputies—meant that parties had to organize three times to get their man in, and this was easier done by locals who cared than by outsider fixers. Even a dictatorial Santa Anna proved unable to rig the 1842 elections and lost Congress.[73] He dissolved that congress, but when a year later his appointed governor rigged the Chihuahua state assembly elections, a broad coalition of locals got the elections nullified.[74] As with the press, Mexico's formal commitment to egalitarianism meant that while the competitiveness of elections might wax and wane greatly, holding them was a categorical imperative of power.

After the presidency, the further down the hierarchy of power the more the election counted. Presidents came and went with their retinues of old mates and new operators, but outside the capital and their homelands they were short-lived meddlers. The deep currents of provincial politics ran on beneath their terms, groups of men coming together on grounds of class, race, place, and belief to compete for places in town halls and state legislatures. Their labels varied from place to place: While in the 1820s national politics was divided between Scottish and York Rite Masons, city politics in Oaxaca was a bitter struggle between the patrician *aceites*, the oils, and the popular *vinagres*, the vinegars. (The name "vinegar," like *sans-culotte*, started out as a pejorative and was proudly adopted by the masses.)[75] By the 1830s they were calling themselves federalists, because across Mexico the main division between parties from the 1820s through the 1850s came down to whether their followers were federalists or centralists. Other ideological divisions were real but dramatized or simplified according to utility. The conservative bishop Clemente Munguía of Michoacán didn't reject Enlightenment political values wholesale but sought instead a synthesis of "revelation with the light of human reason."[76] Liberals like Prieto still believed in God, even if they didn't think much of his representatives on Earth; conservatives like Alamán believed some form of popular representation unavoidable, just not the mass politics he labeled demagoguery.[77] Even monarchists signed up to the basic beliefs of Independence, namely liberty, universal access to law, and predominance of a national will.[78] It was the function of the vote, who should have it, and how much it should count that divided them.

The baseline was the local democracy of one man one vote. Mexicans inherited a belief that the ruled should have a say in the choice of their rulers from both the Spanish commune and the indigenous *república de indios*. Both prized independence: The communes revolted against overly insensitive monarchs, while the repúblicas de indios were often pre-Hispanic polities renamed. The Constitution of Cádiz bowed to this legacy and liberal ideology, allowing towns and alliances of villages to form *municipios*, the equivalent of American counties, and to elect councils to run them; any polity of over one thousand people was eligible. When the law passed in 1812 it created 36 municipalities; by 1821 there were 630, concentrated in indigenous heartlands in the center and above all in Oaxaca, home to a third of them.[79] Their citizens chose their authorities by universal male suffrage, giving them power to determine the indirect election of state and federal politicians. But what really counted for municipal voters was the freedom to manage their religion, festivals, taxes, schools, public works, and above all land. The municipio helped them obtain and defend that freedom against a predatory outside world.

Elections were fraudulent and competitive. The romance of indigenous polities as soporific Athenian democracies doesn't stand up to the grit and complexity of village politics. Many Indians were royalists, particularly the Nahua of the altiplano. Their societies were pulled between aging patriarchs and younger men. Sometimes the polity was little more than the cacique and his family, who might be privatizing rather than preserving common lands. Which village would become the *cabecera*, the privileged municipal seat, and which would be *sujetos*, its subjects, was a burning question; it gave neighboring villages and municipios cause for generational feuds. In many areas Indians took over as regidores on the new councils but ceded mayoralties to mestizos or creoles. Yet they benefited from the new egalitarianism and their old experience in voting, greater than in most of the rest of colonial society, to expand their powers after 1821. They got to spend more of their own taxes; their votes, riots if necessary, enabled them to kick out nonindigenous superiors who let them down; in places like the Mixteca they were positively encouraged to buy up cheap the lands of departing Spaniards, which gave them greater community clout and cohesion.[80] Municipal governments were necessary for national politicians; they fed them intelligence, organized the nuts and bolts of their campaigns, and moved their pronunciamientos toward critical mass. Sometimes they launched miniature pronunciamientos of their own, as when in 1837 five Tlaxcalans pronounced against the abolition of their municipio, Zacatelco.[81]

Small Zacatelco was just one of the municipios abolished in the 1830s, as centralists countered their radical democratic possibilities with laws that narrowed the electorate and defined most municipios out of existence. The reaction had begun in the 1824 constitution, which allowed states discretion in deciding whether new municipios were viable; the Estado de México immediately raised the population bar from one thousand to four thousand, disqualifying most indigenous villages. But communities continued forming them across the country anyway; they were alluring rewards for national politicians to hand out, and mountain men like the peasants of the Huasteca rebelled for them. In 1835 a conservative government struck back, abolishing the Federal Republic, elected governors, state legislatures, and most municipalities by raising the bar to eight thousand inhabitants and applying it retroactively. At the same time, everymen, *don nadies*, were priced out of the vote. The new constitution of 1836 asked voters to prove that they earned 100 pesos annually before they got their ballots; in 1843 Santa Anna raised it to 200. When a new constituent congress was convened in 1846, the property bar for the vote was so high that in one state only seventeen people qualified.[82]

But there was always some distance between laws and realities, the *vía de derecho* and the *vía de hecho.* Disenfranchised peasants became idle workers, reluctant taxpayers, and ready rioters. Municipalities gone, self-rule endured by less official means; many indigenous villages just voted for their own unrecognized authorities and did what they said. In some places it had been that way since Independence; when estate workers in Nohcacab, Yucatán, still enjoyed the vote, they would line up on election day to deposit ballots for whomever they were instructed to vote for and then go home and secretly, democratically, elect parallel and more real governments. Getting rid of those authentic governments was difficult; it required a military force that the centralists didn't possess; moreover, these were the powers that actually got important things done. In arid Yucatán, the secretly elected Maya governments of Nohcacab had the essential task of equitably running wells that supported six thousand people from multiple villages. Municipios came and went, but the popular principle that underlay them endured: These were the units of Mexico that most Mexicans cared about most, their so-called *patrias chicas*, the little motherlands, and they cared to choose their own to run them. As Ignacio Ramírez put it, the municipio is the nation, and the *municipio libre*, the free county, was an ideal that shaped how Mexicans thought of and practiced politics for the next two centuries. It was a profoundly democratic principle that their New England contemporaries, busily voting and arguing over their own village affairs thousands of miles north, would have recognized quite well.[83]

Chapter Ten

Between Empires

In 1816 a small brig called the *Rurik* anchored off San Francisco and sent its crew ashore to provision and poke around. It was one of the first foreign ships to visit the harbor; it was Russian, sponsored by the imperial chancellor, and its interest was not wholly ethnographic. The crew were not the first Russians in the area; in 1811 others had settled thirty miles north at Bodega, where they stayed until 1839, harvesting otters as far south as San Diego, smuggling and buying wheat from the few local Mexican ranchers. They may have gone to services in the San Gabriel Mission, where some of the paintings have the outsize eyes and flat perspective of Byzantine art, perhaps the work of a homesick Russian painter. Bodega was a small, unprofitable colony, but the fort had a dozen cannon and was powerful enough to fight off any Spanish attack (the nearest soldiers hadn't been paid in seven years). Officially private, it enjoyed the Russian emperor's blessing as an extension of years of mild interest in New Spain's Pacific Coast. In 1799 Tsar Paul I had licensed occupation south of Canada, backed by the military; in 1805 Tsar Alexander's chamberlain told him that the entire California coast was open to Russian conquest.[1] President Andrew Jackson had his eyes on San Francisco too, envisioning it as a base for dominating the Pacific, and asked Mexico about buying it.[2]

Neither happened, but the existence of a long-lived Russian colony in California exemplified Mexico's vulnerability to foreign empires. Spain made a geopolitical comeback between the mid-1770s and the early 1800s, establishing presidios and rudimentary harbors in the North (in part for fear of Russians); dispatching ships to chart the Pacific and Gulf Coasts; and jostling up on Vancouver Island against Russians, Americans, and the British, with whom they nearly went to war in 1790 over "a few sheds erected on the coast, and a miserable bastion defended by swivel guns, and a few cabbages."[3] Humboldt might have mocked this overreach and the Nootka Sound Crisis it caused; no one mocked the real war in the East, where Spanish ships, soldiers, military supplies, and money were key in driving the British out of their American colonies. Yet the Napoleonic Wars threw the late Bourbon recovery into reverse, and between 1805 and 1867 Mexico was prey to numerous invasions of filibusters, indigenous raiders, and imperial expeditioners.

It began with the British, believed in 1805 to be dispatching ten thousand men under Sir Arthur Wellesley, the British general who later recaptured Spain from Napoleon; in 1806 he was reported to have actually set sail.[4] It wasn't true, but neither was it beyond the bounds of possibility. The British did attack the most profitable parts of the region, occupying Haiti, at the time the world's richest plantation society, between 1793 and 1798, and Buenos Aires in 1806. Both incursions had an immediate military rationale, but silver and trade wouldn't have hurt; Britain was running up a debt of approximately 200 percent of GDP in fighting France (far more overextended than Philip II had been during his bid for global dominance). Seizing vulnerable New Spain, the old center of the global economy, might have made good sense.

Yet military incursions went badly for the British. The Haitian expedition achieved little bar the deaths of thousands of their troops from yellow fever. The attack on Buenos Aires was beaten off by a local militia. Lord Cochrane, the privateer in command of the Chilean Navy, tried to annex Baja California for Chile and was driven off by a handful of *californianos*.[5] So instead the British chose informal empire, fostering trade monopolies with tame governments, their young consuls doing lucrative business on the side, the Royal Navy discouraging other European incursions, with fighting as an option only in extremis. As Foreign Secretary Lord Castlereagh put it in 1807, Britain's policy would be

> creating and supporting an amicable and local government, with which those commercial relations may freely subsist which it is alone our interest to aim at, and which the people of South America must equally desire.[6]

Free trade with Mexico made excellent sense. It allowed traders in military surplus, Lancashire cotton, and Sheffield steel to sell some of their vast surplus of aged muskets, cloth, and knives, and by 1828 the British had taken over most of the big trading houses in Mexico. It wasn't just the Industrial Revolution that favored British economic dominance. London was the financial center of the world, and a stock market bubble began there in 1822 that lasted until 1825. Nearly half of all new stocks were in Latin American companies; nearly three-quarters of bonds were in Latin American governments. Mexico's urgent need for capital gave the crooked financiers of Threadneedle Street an opportunity for usurious returns on bonds that they themselves, when crisis hit, failed to honor.[7]

Other powers took a more direct approach. The initial cordiality of Independence disappeared fast: Spain refused to ratify the peace treaty and the Spanish garrison stayed on the island of San Juan de Ulúa, its cannon commanding the entrance to Veracruz. This forced ships north to Tampico, whose appalling road to Mexico City made it a very long detour. Mexico only evicted the Spanish in 1825, taking an appreciable part of English debt to buy 7,500 old English guns from the Battle of Waterloo. Four years of Spanish blockade, the opposition of the Holy Alliance of Austria, Russia, and Prussia, and hereditary hatred of gachupines all nurtured fears of a reconquest, leading in 1829 to the expulsion of the remaining seven thousand Spaniards, even churchmen and those with Mexican families. Mexican fears were well-founded: In 1827 a revanchist conspiracy led by a Spanish priest came to light, and in July 1829 Spain sent thirty-five hundred soldiers to take back their old colony.[8]

The expedition failed dismally. It was intended as a new species of pronunciamiento: not so much a reconquest as a provincial show of force that would trigger a cascade of royalist risings and reinstall a viceroy. However, by 1829 that didn't count as saving the nation, the cut-and-paste justification for a pronunciamiento, and the only hint of support the Spanish got was a single pamphlet in central Mexico urging monarchist Indians to rebel. The logic was flawed, the execution too: General Isidro Barradas chose to disembark his troops on a waterless beach far south of Tampico and then quick march, slapping off mosquitoes, forty miles to take the port. He took the town without resistance and then, in classic pronunciado style, went nowhere fast.

Two Mexican forces moved in, one from Texas and a second from Veracruz, led by Santa Anna. The mosquitos began to win, as they always did, giving hundreds of Barradas's men yellow fever. He began preparing his retreat, building a stockade at the mouth of the Río Panuco. On September 7, 1829, Santa Anna attacked it, and without taking it forced the Spanish into unconditional surrender.[9]

Defeat at Tampico put Spain off military adventures in Mexico; only half of Barradas's men made it home. Inside Mexico it had two political effects. One was a call for land reform, the "just and egalitarian distribution of land," a resolution passed by the state of Mexico's legislators, stimulated by fear of royalist Indians.[10] This was revealing but of far lesser significance than the second effect, which was to give Santa Anna the enduring political capital of being the "Victor of Tampico." It had been an impressive victory, Santa Anna ringing out the church bells across his patria chica, raising without warning a small host, falling on the Spanish, and fighting through a storm to bring their colors down. A foreign pronunciado brought the prince of pronunciados to power.[11] This pattern, limping colonialism fueling dictatorial domestic politics, was nothing like unique to Mexico; it was a postcolonial story, told over and over again in different parts of the world for the next 150 years.

A few petty imperialists lasted longer than the transoceanic powers, but both sorts of incursions were the marginalia of empire. In Tabasco a Catalan filibuster named Francisco Sentmanat came from Cuba in 1839 with a small group of mercenaries and set up his own military fiefdom, which ruled some of Mexico's most obstreperous provincials for two years. It was a fellow Cuban who toppled him (and decapitated him, tried to preserve the head in oil to convince followers he was dead, and mistakenly deep-fried it when his cook overheated the oil). The governor of neighboring Chiapas a few years later was another Cuban, the strongman who succeeded Sentmanat a half-Italian Colombian who had fought for Napoleon, and the US consul who tried to deal with them all a Transylvanian count.[12] But Tabasco was a strange and watery place, nearly as much wetland as dryland, and not of huge significance to the embattled Mexico of the 1830s and 1840s. It was in the drier North that empire-builders posed the real threat.

American presidents and ideologues had imperial aspirations from the outset. Thomas Jefferson spoke of "an empire of liberty," Andrew Jackson wanted to push on from Florida to Cuba, Alexander Hamilton called the Republic "the embryo of a great empire."[13] They had two vanguards: the Anglo-American colonists of Texas, and the Comanche who threatened everything Mexican east of the Rockies and south from the Great Plains to the altiplano. Yet neither group were empire-builders themselves. Texan colonists started out as entrepreneurs seeking profitable autonomy, not a move from one unreliable federation to another. After their independence in 1836 the Texans offered the coastal states of southeastern Mexico the services of their warships, but as well-paid mercenaries; owning rich grasslands for cattle and irrigated valleys for cotton, the Austins and their ilk didn't aspire to conquer Tamaulipas, Tabasco, or the forbidding Maya interior.

As for the Comanche, by 1845 they had been the main power of the North American plains for a century, in one Franciscan's summary "a nation so bellicose and so indomitable that it rules all those of the interior country."[14] Like the Yaqui, they felt the self-confidence of a nation when Mexico became independent, sending representatives to Iturbide's coronation. In political terms their success was thanks to a militarized society, with superb irregular cavalry, in economic terms thanks to the sale of horses, cattle, and bison leather on a near-industrial scale. Shipping records show that between 1825 and 1830 Plains Indians sold 785,000 bison robes to New Orleans fur traders. (Robes were made exclusively from females, and the bison population had begun collapsing before white hunters made it much west of the Missouri River.)[15] The territorial sweep of the Comanchería was comparable to the old Habsburg holdings in Europe, and they had something of the Habsburg swagger of knowing that they were chosen above others, their name for themselves the Nʉmʉnʉʉ, "the people." The Comanche were politically dynamic, choosing wars and alliances with realpolitik care and flexibility. They formed multiethnic coalitions of convenience and absorbed large numbers of captives and slaves. Yet they were themselves a loose coalition of *rancherías*, independent kin-based bands of anything from a couple of dozen to a few hundred members, profoundly decentralized, with neither imperial metropolis nor aspirations to one, no direct or even proconsular rule over those they dominated, and no universalizing religion or ideology with which to incorporate the defeated. They were nomads and warrior-businessmen, not empire-builders.[16]

Their Mexican enemies weren't parsing indigenous political structures. The Spanish always struggled with their northern frontier, trying to hold a faltering line with convict-manned presidios, some of the more hardheaded missionaries, and the bribes of tribute and trade. The Comanche were early adopters of the first great technology that Europeans brought to the Americas, the horse, and at the beginning of the eighteenth century they moved south into the plains and used it to rise rapidly to preeminence. Long-distance hunting, horse-breeding, raiding, and trading gave them access to the second great technology, gunpowder; by the mid-eighteenth century they could outshoot Spanish infantry, as they did at the village of Wichita in 1759, where Comanche muskets behind breastworks proved unconquerable. Between 1750 and 1780 the Comanche population trebled to an estimated forty-five thousand, all of the males with mounts and military training. They forged useful in-between empire relationships with their European neighbors: Comanche horsemen took wealth from the Spanish Empire and used it to buy guns from the French Empire, which they then used to take more wealth from the Spanish. A later generation substituted Americans for French, in—from the indigenous perspective—a virtuous economic circle.[17]

Frontier wars had caused cyclical devastation ever since indigenous societies took to horseback at the turn of the seventeenth century. Alongside tribute, unpayable in hard times, only disease and wars elsewhere could check them. From the 1780s to the early 1830s smallpox, indigenous civil wars, and the United States expansion that fostered them gave Mexico on-and-off peace. That allowed Mexicans to expand their settlements and flocks, becoming in the process increasingly attractive targets; the need for large estates to support herds in the northern drylands meant that ranches and haciendas were widely dispersed and often on their own. As a consequence even small indigenous groups could inflict grievous damage in wars of burnt ranches and wiped-out villages, performative violence and vengeance, heads on stakes and tortured corpses. Comanche and Apache had little use for Mexicans, whom they despised but didn't aim to eliminate wholesale, because they were lucrative producing livestock. Mexicans on the other hand had no use at all for the northern barbarians, a different ontological class than the settled societies of the rest of Mexico, and often spoke of their mass extermination. The governor's palace in Santa Fe had two architectural curiosities, the German visitor Dr. Friedrich Adolph Wislizenus observed in the 1840s,

> windows of glass, and festoons of Indian ears. Glass is a great luxury in Santa Fe; common houses have shutters instead of windows, or quite small windows of selenite, (crystallized gypsum.) The festoons of Indian ears were made up of several strings of dried ears of Indians, killed by the hired parties that are occasionally sent out against hostile Indians, and who are paid a certain sum for each head. In Chihuahua, they make a great exhibition with the whole scalps of Indians which they happen to kill by proxy; the refined New Mexicans show but the ears.[18]

The government of Chihuahua offered one hundred pesos for the scalp of an Apache man and fifty for that of a woman; the other frontier states passed similar laws. It was good business, though open to abuse, not all scalps coming from Indians.[19]

Yet in the scheme of the frontier as a whole, the Apache were the lesser threat, even though the wars lasted into the 1880s.[20] The Comanche Wars were the main front, peaking after 1834, when the principal Plains Indians, the Texans, and the Americans reached a wide-ranging peace. The upshot was renewed indigenous attacks on Mexicans across the North, more extensive than anything seen before. Between 1840 and 1847 bands numbering more than a hundred warriors attacked Mexico at least thirty times. In December 1840 a force of four hundred rode as far south as San Luis Potosí, burning ranches and towns, killing the livestock they couldn't take with them, and gathering slaves; on the return north through Coahuila they eschewed the rich hacienda San Francisco de los Patos and instead attacked the state capital, Saltillo. In 1847 another band occupied part of the capital of Durango.[21] This was indigenous cavalry fighting on a regimental scale rather than in bands.

The warbands were more on the Mexican side; in 1839 the governor of Chihuahua paid through the nose for an Irish mercenary, James Kirker, and two hundred men to fight the summer campaign season.[22]

Mexico's inability to hold the frontier against these attacks helped materialize the greatest threat of all, war with the Americans. At Independence, Mexico was significantly more generous than the United States in granting settlers land, starting at nearly one thousand acres per family and seven-year tax exemptions. The stimulus worked. In 1821 Texas was home to about twenty-five hundred people; by 1836 it was forty thousand.[23] Three-quarters were Anglo.[24] The main colonist, Stephen Austin, negotiated exceptions to the national prohibition on slavery and proclaimed his loyalty to three successive regimes: the Spanish Empire, the Mexican Empire, and the Republic. He took Mexican citizenship and converted to Catholicism. In 1826 Austin fought for Mexico against a rebellion of his fellow Americans.[25] But in 1832 a colonist convention (to which *tejanos*, ethnic Mexicans, were not invited) petitioned Mexico City for statehood and continued tax exemptions: representation without taxation. Denied that, they rebelled, volunteers signing up to fight with the promise of twenty-five hundred acres each. In 1835 other northern states rose against the new centralist government and were defeated by Santa Anna; in 1836 he won a minor fort in Texas—the Alamo—before losing his army at San Jacinto and suing for peace. The Texans' independent republic stood, at very low cost. Their success inspired the Plains Indians; it also inspired the United States, and in 1846 it declared war on Mexico.[26]

The fighting lasted just under a year and a half, from April 1846 to September 1847, and ended with Mexico losing the territory that became the states of California, New Mexico, Nevada, Utah, most of Arizona and Colorado, and parts of Kansas, Oklahoma, and Wyoming. Lucas Alamán called it, in a line that stuck, half the national territory.[27] Most of the hundred thousand Mexican citizens living north of the new border sold up, were dispossessed by legal or violent means, or were sent to Indian reservations. Many of their successors were not, as mythology might have it, smallholders with an admirable work ethic, but rather crooked politicians and crony capitalists. In January 1848, eight days before the peace treaty was signed, gold was discovered northeast of San Francisco and the California Gold Rush began. The $40 million of gold taken out of the new mines in 1850 alone would have paid off nearly all Mexico's crippling national debt.[28] Instead the bonanza and its allure fueled the explosive growth of the United States.

The war had been some time coming. In September 1842 Commodore Thomas Jones landed with eight hundred men and took Monterrey from its twenty-nine Mexican soldiers. He had extrapolated from rumor that war had been declared and got it wrong; he said sorry and withdrew.[29] His mental workings, however, were sound, based on the three widely prevailing attitudes inside the United States of disdain, opportunity, and nationalism. The disdain was largely racial, taken up even by Stephen Austin, who switched from moderation to calling his adopted Mexican compatriots a "mongrel Spanish-Indian and Negro race." In extremis the rhetoric was genocidal: The governor of Mississippi, Henry Stuart Foote, mused that "extermination may yet become necessary for the repose of this continent."[30] The political opportunity was clear: Mexico was highly unstable, its provinces unreliable components of an unwieldy and bankrupt federation. It was incapable of defending its citizens against Indian depredation. Finally, a messianic nationalism was afoot in the US. The annexation of Texas was a given, the Democrat John O'Sullivan wrote in 1845. Mexico, "imbecile and distracted," should have surrendered it and California peacefully, and British Canada would be next, annexed from "the little island three thousand miles across the Atlantic." England and France might have "the avowed object of thwarting our policy and hampering our power, limiting our greatness," but it was—another line that stuck—the United States' "manifest destiny to overspread the continent allotted by Providence for the free development of our yearly multiplying millions." It was a Protestant update of the *requerimiento*, the Spanish declaration of God-given right to conquest, printed in New York rather than read out on a Gulf Coast beach.[31]

Peaceful recognition of that God-given right was unacceptable in Mexico. The annexation of Texas in March 1845 caused Mexico to break off diplomatic relations, and when President José Joaquín de Herrera seemed to consider a US offer to buy California and New Mexico for $25 million he was toppled by General Mariano Paredes y

Arrillaga. Paredes and the ubiquitous Alamán revived the old idea of a European monarchy in cahoots with the Spanish foreign minister, backed by conservative newspapers and pamphlets in Mexico City. Whatever the Monroe Doctrine, the logic ran, the US would pause before attacking a quasi-European state. But there was neither time nor inclination (on the part of the majority of Mexicans, or of any putative princeling) for a European king to act as a deus ex machina against the US, and on January 13, 1846, General Zachary Taylor and four thousand soldiers occupied disputed borderlands between the Río Nueces and the Río Grande. On April 25 the inevitable exchange of fire with Mexican troops happened, and on May 12 Congress passed a declaration of war.[32]

By then Taylor had already invaded and was marching south toward Nuevo León. A second army was hastily assembled to attack west toward California, a third to attack Veracruz by sea. A naval force landed at Mazatlán and marched up the Pacific Coast, and the same day that Mexico belatedly declared war, July 7, 1846, Commodore John Sloat declared California part of the United States. On August 18 General Stephen Kearny annexed New Mexico. The first major fighting came with the battle for Monterrey, Nuevo León, which lasted from September 20 to September 23 and ended in the very center of the city. While their artillery shelled the town, US troops burrowed from house to house, civilians fighting back, growing hungry, and being killed. The Mexicans made a fighting retreat to their last redoubt, the main square, and when the Americans got within a hundred yards and opened mortar fire, they negotiated a peace that allowed them to withdraw with their weapons. Many women and children went with them. By that stage, according to a Mexican journalist, there was only a block left untouched on each side of the plaza.[33] This was an unwanted defensive war, the self-pitying president James Polk said in his 1846 State of the Union address, forced upon the US after decades of extreme forbearance:

> The wrongs which we have suffered from Mexico almost ever since she became an independent power and the patient endurance with which we have borne them are without a parallel in the history of modern civilized nations.[34]

Much of the northern fighting was less conclusive than the victory at Monterrey. As Polk gave his State of the Union address Mexicans launched three risings against the occupiers in New Mexico and California, where they recaptured the coast from San Diego to Los Angeles. It took months to put them down. Guerrilla forces played havoc with smaller detachments and convoys. The decisive attack of the war however came at Veracruz, where General Winfield Scott arrived on March 7, 1847, with seventy ships and a large army. After landing and setting up batteries around the port, Scott shelled it for four days, hitting civilian targets such as churches, bakeries, and flyblown hospitals and setting fires throughout the city. When the consuls of Britain, France, Spain, and Prussia requested a ceasefire to evacuate themselves and Mexican civilians he refused, twice; when some tried to escape in small boats, the squadron fired on them and drove them back to the beach. A majority of the more than one thousand estimated casualties were civilians, many of them women and children. It was barbaric, the outside world said; militarily justifiable standard practice, Scott wrote in his memoirs; both barbaric and militarily justifiable, a charitable Mexican wrote, perhaps remembering the civilian slaughters of the Napoleonic Wars.[35] On March 26 the Veracruz garrison surrendered; Scott landed the rest of his troops and began moving uphill toward Mexico City.

Santa Anna, true to form of success in getting power and failure in using it, raised a numerically impressive army out of nowhere and then misused it with *élan* to lose the two key battles of the war, Buena Vista and Cerro Gordo. At Buena Vista he moved north without a supply train against General Taylor and on February 23 attacked at the pass of La Angostura, Taylor's choice of defensive position. The ill-trained and undersupplied Mexicans had to advance through ravines or directly up the road into artillery; despite that, two regiments of US cavalry broke and fled, leaving the Americans' eastern flank open. It was a promising position for the Mexicans, but in the rain of that evening, lacking water and food, Santa Anna decided to retreat and let Taylor come after him—which he might have done in the first place—and lost much of his disheartened army en route.

In early April he set off from Mexico City to block the American advance from Veracruz, this time fortifying a key pass at Cerro Gordo and waiting for the enemy to come to him. The ecology of the North had worked against him at Angostura, killing his troops in the desert; this time he planned to let the ecology of the eastern lowlands work for him, bottling the Americans in the tropical lowlands until the wet season's yellow fever could work its customary ravages. Santa Anna fortified only one of the two main hills, though, telling his engineers that not even a rabbit could climb the other. Without being a rabbit, as one acerbic wit put it, Scott nevertheless managed to ascend the hill with three heavy cannon.[36] Santa Anna also neglected to post scouts on his left flank, feeling that the scrub was too thick for the Americans to penetrate. Early on April 18 the Americans launched surprise attacks in both places, and having captured the hilltop drove the army below into chaotic retreat, capturing three thousand. On May 16, 1847, the Americans entered Puebla, the road to Mexico City open. Ten weeks later they left, some ten thousand troops, for three weeks of intensive fighting against Mexican regulars; National Guardsmen, many from the old rebel states of Michoacán and the South; guerrillas; and civilians of all classes. It nevertheless ended with the Americans capturing the capital.

The defeat could be laid at Santa Anna's door, and it was, vigorously, for his initial decision to concentrate his defenses in the east on the Puebla road rather than in the south, while Scott looped around to attack on two fronts. But Santa Anna was also once again responsible for the cross-class and multiregional coalition that made American victory so costly, an estimated twenty-seven hundred dead, for all their numerical superiority in individual engagements. He also made canny strategic decisions, such as flooding the Valley of Mexico and preparing fixed defenses to cover a withdrawal into Mexico City. He lost the first battle at Padierna in part thanks to his subordinate General Gabriel Valencia, who refused to obey orders and regroup in the secondary lines. Santa Anna nevertheless saved his army and negotiated a truce to consider peace terms and rebuild his forces. When fighting began again on September 6 his thought-out and disciplined defense made the next battle, Molino del Rey, an expensive win for the Americans. Finally, he foresaw that Scott's next attack would come from the west and prepared three regiments of cavalry to ambush them. But the cavalry did not follow orders and seize the opportunity, and Scott ended up with only one fortification between him and the city, Chapultepec

Castle. Despite a preparatory bombardment he took heavy casualties in capturing it. Afterward, however, Mexico City was inevitably lost, and the Mexican Army withdrew, hoping to fight another day. On September 15 the ayuntamiento surrendered, and the Americans took over the national palace.

It was not the end, because the handover came amid two days of bitter and largely spontaneous street fighting. As the Americans marched in on September 14, thousands of residents took whatever came to hand and attacked them. Accounts from both sides stress that this was a popular rising, not a riot. A contemporary letter described how civilians fought and soldiers reacted:

> Stones and bricks rained down from the rooftops, the ragged poor egged on those who drew near, in the alleys they provoked the soldiers who were breaking ranks to lure them in. Those [US Army] blacks, those drunkards who were shouting and throwing themselves like beasts on women and children killing them, dragging them away; it was horrible! It is believed that 15,000 men without arms, disorderly and frenzied, threw themselves against the invaders, who took over as though they were a horde of savages.[37]

It wasn't just men; women asked for medium-sized paving stones so they could throw them too. A friar from the Convent of la Merced rode the streets urging them on. While Scott's report minimized the violence for political reasons, the diaries and letters of American eyewitnesses numbered their dead in the hundreds. The American who raised the flag over the national palace was murdered, and generalized fighting only stopped when American artillery began knocking down buildings and shredding crowds with grapeshot. At its peak the rising stopped the Mexican Army's retreat north and drew them back toward the capital; Santa Anna even sent scouts into the city to assess the scale of resistance.

It wasn't enough to justify a reconquest, and so Santa Anna moved toward Puebla and a provincial government was set up in Querétaro to begin peace negotiations. The Americans had them over a barrel: As negotiations started they threatened Mexico's states with expropriations of four times the annual federal tax.[38] A rumor circulated that

Scott would kidnap the Virgin of Guadalupe's cloak for ransom.[39] The Mexican negotiators had little leverage: bankrupt, their army virtually gone, their ports and capital occupied, facing peasant revolts in the mountains of the Huasteca and outright wars against the Comanche in the North and the Maya in the Southeast. Ironically, the main worry of Nicholas Trist, the US negotiator, was that his government would use its power to seize all of Mexico. (Some elucubrations ran as far south as Patagonia.) Consequently he went rogue, ignored his recall to Washington, and pursued the less ambitious goals of August 1847, determined before Mexico's final defeat. In doing so Trist probably saved Mexico from losing sovereignty over Baja California and the Isthmus of Tehuantepec, the narrow strip of Oaxaca and Veracruz that offers a shortcut from Atlantic to Pacific. He nevertheless found the eventual terms of the peace treaty hard to take, as he explained to his wife:

> Could those Mexicans have seen into my heart at that moment, they would have known that my feeling of shame as an American was far stronger than theirs could be as Mexicans. For though it would not have done for me to say there, that was a thing for every right-minded American to be ashamed of, and I was ashamed of it, most cordially and intensely ashamed of it.[40]

Trist did penance: His sympathetic disobedience cost him his job, and he spent the next twenty years as a low-level railroad employee. The Treaty of Guadalupe Hidalgo was harder to take for Mexicans, who had little choice but to sign on February 2, 1848. The treaty extended their compatriots north of the new border possible US citizenship, guaranteed their property rights, promised to prevent indigenous attacks, and gave Mexico 15 million pesos to defray costs. In exchange the United States took everything above the Río Bravo and the thirty-second parallel north: 930,000 square miles.

Victory was neither easy nor cheap. In Congress a young Abraham Lincoln branded President Polk's ideas on the war "the half insane mumbling of a fever-dream"; this in January 1848, months after the supposed triumph of taking Mexico City.[41] By then about 13,000 American soldiers had died, out of a total of 108,000.[42] The inevitable tropical disease took most, but considerable casualties also came from the fighting, because for all the failures of their generals, the poor equipment, and the hunger, Mexican troops often fought well, whether regulars, National Guardsmen, or guerrillas.

The guerrillas, ubiquitous in the supposedly conquered territories of the North and along the major roads of the center, scared the Americans the most, raising the prospect of a lasting and unwinnable dirty war. Guerrillas were Mexico's best troops, the statesman Carlos María de Bustamante argued,

> the ones who had put up a genuine and tenacious resistance to the enemy, attacking and reducing their forces and curtailing their supply trains; . . . men learned in the countryside, robust, those who relate to their horses, face down bulls, and lasso in hand, packed close at the gallop, break the enemy ranks, those following them inflicting terrible destruction.[43]

As with guerrillas everywhere, they fed off the repression they drew down upon the villagers who supported them, or just those who happened to be in their areas of activity. At the beginning of his campaign in April 1847, General Scott issued a draconian order for mass reprisals against cities, towns, and neighborhoods whose authorities failed to hand over guerrillas. At the end, in December 1847, he was repeating himself.[44]

Scott believed himself a moral man, and in the center the promised repression didn't materialize with the vigor it had in the North. There Colonel Alexander Doniphan's Missouri Volunteers left a trail of burnt villages and hamlets on their march to Santa Fe, reprisals for the ambush of a wagon train by the guerrilla General Canales. It was morally justifiable, the expedition's Dr. Wislizenus felt, because

> the right of retaliation, as well as expediency, command, in my opinion, such measures against such unusual warfare; and when carried out with some circumspection, it will break up these guerrilla bands much sooner than too lenient a course.[45]

The erudite German had some unsettling habits—he decapitated a dead Indian shaman and boiled the flesh off his head to collect the skull—but he was voicing a regional commonplace.[46] His commander Colonel Doniphan ended up writing the first set of laws for New Mexico.

Volunteers like Doniphan's men also committed less systematic atrocities and were widely despised by Mexicans and Americans alike. There were three sorts of American soldiers in Mexico: the prewar regulars, mainly from the Northeast; the wartime recruits, among them many Irish immigrants; and the volunteers from the Southern and frontier states. The last weren't much good at soldiering. The Arkansas and Kentucky volunteer cavalry regiments broke and fled at Buena Vista; volunteer infantry refused to advance into heavy fire in Mexico City.[47] A detachment sent out near Saltillo neglected to post an overnight guard, their Major Borland saying, "They were out for a fight, and all he asked was to have the 'greasers' come and attack him, and he would show them what mettle Southern gentlemen were made of." When Mexican lancers showed up early the next morning he surrendered without a fight.[48] Yet while the volunteers' military impact was unreliable, their human rights abuses had a disproportionate effect, in the unintended sense of recruiting for Mexican forces. By early 1847 the guerrillas in the North were so successful in cutting American supply lines that Santa Anna sent precious regular cavalry north to join them.[49]

The volunteers came from slave societies marked by Manichaean racism and endemic vigilantism. United States law, unlike imperial Spanish law, did not define non-whites as fully human, did not offer them access to courts, and was not applied to defend them against racial violence. Volunteers applied similar standards to Mexicans, and were, in one's words, "wild reckless fellows" who elected their own officers. A stump speech in a Missouri bar gives an idea of how some got their commissions:

> Fellow citizens! I am Peter Goff, the Butcher of Middletown! I am! I am the man who shot that sneaking, white livered Yankee abolitionist son of a b---h Lovejoy! I did! I want to be your Captain, I do; and I will serve the yellow bellied Mexicans the same. I will! I have treated you to fifty dollars worth of whiskey, I have, and when elected Captain I will spend fifty more, I will![50]

Once in charge, officers like Goff couldn't impose discipline even had they wanted to. When Mexicans turned out to be less than yellow-bellied, and the good life volunteers had come for turned into boredom, disease, and ambush, they turned to theft, murder, and rape.[51] Regular US commanders were horrified: Scott said,

> Our militia and volunteers, if a tenth of what is said be true, have committed atrocities—horrors—in Mexico, sufficient to make Heaven weep, and every American of Christian morals blush for his country.[52]

Volunteers also motivated some of their own to fight for Mexico. Irish emigrants, fleeing British misrule, endemic hardship, and the Potato Famine of 1845, often found that they had swapped one set of racist sectarians for another. Some, looking at fellow Catholics despised and murdered, churches used for stables, padres leading guerrillas, followed the logic and swapped sides, egged on by Mexican pamphleteers. Religion was not the only logic at work; the Irishmen were part of a larger body of deserters with diverse motives: poverty, ill-treatment, or just the absence of choices for the international poor in the mid-nineteenth century. Only the Irish, though, used religion and nation to form their own unit in the Mexican Army, the Saint Patrick's Battalion, or *san patricios*, with a green regimental banner sewn by nuns in San Luis Potosí. Their commander, Major John Riley, wrote that he was fighting as an Irishman, under

> the glorious Emblem of native rights, that being the banner that should have floated over our native Soil many years ago, it was St. Patrick, the Harp of Erin, the Shamrock upon a green field.[53]

Ireland's sophisticated, precocious nationalism helped make the *san patricios* some of the most useful of Mexican troops; so did their skills as artillerymen, and their value as propaganda assets; so did forced recruitment by their own officers, and the strong probability of execution if captured. They weren't wrong. After two hundred *san patricios* fought a critical rearguard action at Churubusco, covering the main army's retreat into Mexico City, almost all the survivors were hanged en masse.[54]

Long-term American occupation would have led to quagmire, a prospect much on the minds of General Scott, the chief negotiator Trist, and even the narrow-minded expansionist Polk. It would have been a stalemate: The citizen-soldiers of the National Guard from the southern mountains would probably have fought on, and the guerrillas (and their cousins the bandits) would certainly have continued their successful hit-and-run attacks. Reconquest by a rebuilt Mexican Army, on the other hand, was off the cards due to the state poverty that dogged Mexico throughout the war. In 1847 massive popular support for a while compensated for some of the materiel that could not be bought, but there were limits to how many church bells could be melted down for cannon, musket balls forged out of whatever iron came to hand, gunpowder conjured out of thin provincial air.[55] The main reason that US forces won the war was that they were richer. The navy that Mexico lacked could land troops and guns at strategic points, economically throttle the country, and prevent arms imports. Mexicans fought with aging muskets that jammed repeatedly; the Americans by contrast had numerous and powerful cannon that were easier to transport on light, modern gun limbers. They had the engineers to move them across terrain that Mexicans considered impassable, like the hill at Cerro Gordo or the basalt and scrub to the south of Mexico City.

A unified Mexican state staging a comeback was also off the cards because of disunity among national elites. Santa Anna made some unforced errors, but he was forced into others by a hostile press, opposition factions, and disobedient generals. The choice to force march into ill-chosen ground at Buena Vista was driven by outrage in Mexico City at Santa Anna's perceived inactivity; his outflanking at the Battle of Padierna, which ensured the loss of the capital, by his political rival General Valencia's refusal to take the Army of the North where he was told.[56] A conservative coup toppled President José Joaquín de Herrera on January 4, 1846, days before the American invasion began; a federalist coup installed Santa Anna in September; in 1847 a third toppled his vice president, who was running the country, just as Santa Anna fought at Buena Vista and the Americans prepared to land at Veracruz. The war ended with the same president in charge as on its eve, Herrera. He was a *moderado*, a moderate liberal who accepted the lack of options beyond the Treaty of Guadalupe; against him he had both the *puros*, radical liberals who wanted to fight on, and the conservatives, led by Alamán, who formed a party and bemoaned the loss of "half the national territory."[57] Capitalino elites shared a basic agreement on the desirability of Mexico's existence and the imperative of fighting Americans to preserve it, and Alamán courteously took in his bitter rival Prieto when war reached the city.[58] There was little consensus on anything else.

Regional disunity also ruled out the possibility of a reconquista. The authorities in northern Mexico prioritized fighting Indians over fighting Americans, and when the Americans came to Tucson they were let pass without resistance, the local government saying they needed their men to fight the Apache.[59] The governor of New Mexico recruited two thousand men to fight Kearny's advance westward, but his officers fell out and the militia disintegrated.[60] When the federal government asked for troops from Zacatecas, Durango, and Chihuahua in August 1846, none came. One of the first US papers set up in occupied territory, *The Matamoros Reveille*, was playing to a receptive audience when it told readers that Mexico only cared for its heartlands, leaving the North "spurned as bastards."[61] Outside those heartlands, broadly the Valley of Mexico, Veracruz, Michoacán, Oaxaca, Guerrero, and the Bajío, the national territory was not that potent an idea. Peasants in the Huasteca region and Morelos seized the opportunity of the war to fight the central government and local landowners more vigorously than they fought the United States. The patria chica, the little motherland, counted everywhere; the *patria* without adjectives only in some places.

This was clearer than anywhere in the Southeast, where the state government seceded with the aid of US mercenaries and a bloody civil war left behind burnt towns, massacres, and a swathe of independent Maya territory in the east.[62] Yucatán had long been divided between the creole elite of the towns and coast and the Maya villagers of the interior. Spaniards were few enough that they were compelled to speak Maya; some of the poorer whites spoke only Maya, a linguistic world turned upside down.[63] It was a curious society whose parts nevertheless added up in the viceroyalty: Despite the thin, unwelcoming soil of the peninsula, indigenous farmers, smugglers, and export crops—sugar, rice, cotton, dyewood—sustained half a million people and two rich cities, Mérida and Campeche. It was one of the more dynamic regions of provincial Mexico, both for its economy and for its popular politics.

Independence broke the modus vivendi. Spaniards and mestizos moved into Maya regions to settle and accumulate land. A state law that allowed individuals to appropriate untitled (but often Maya-farmed) common lands upped pressure on subsistence peasants; it was compounded by new demands for taxes and conscription, particularly after the wars with Texas in 1836 and France in 1838. The Maya, some of them successful commercial ranchers, joined competing creole politicians, federalists, and centralists, but their promised redress never came. Ever-worldly priests continued to price gouge for sacraments, seize lands, meddle in local politics, and live in conspicuous sin. Maize harvests failed, the export sector withered, and the US invaded Mexico. In 1846 two petty revolts broke out in the south of the peninsula. By mid-1847 one disgruntled ex-soldier and *batab*—a Maya cacique—named Cecilio Chi had had enough; he conspired with another batab, Manuel Antonio Ay, and Jacinto Pat to topple the state government. When the local commandant found Ay out, he shot him and came after the other conspirators. On July 30 Chi attacked the town of Tepich, where his men killed every member of the twenty-five to thirty creole families (and their mulatto servants; only Maya residents survived) and detonated the *Guerra de castas*, the Caste War.

As with the Comanche conflicts, this was not a contest between poorly armed, improvising Indians and organized governments. The Maya rebels had British rifles smuggled in from Belize and military training, and they waged fluctuating but coordinated war for decades. Neither was it the straightforward race war that both sides advertised. Whether Yucatecos fought or not was also determined by region, personal loyalties, kin, and the murky dealings of political faction. The Caste War's class rationale was evident, but it was not a simple fight between rich and poor: Both Jacinto Pat and Cecilio Chi were estate owners who seized common lands and had both feet squarely in the capitalist economy. Ideologically the rebels were autonomists: federalists, secessionists, municipal libertarians, and seekers of an independent Maya state. They were also firmly anticlerical, killing one priest, proclaiming that they could kill them all, and founding their own syncretic religion in the cult of the Talking Cross. All this was rhetorically simplified into a war of savagery against civilization, mutual genocide avant la lettre. In reality, like the Yaqui Wars of the Northwest, it was a complex conflict between two embryonic nations.

The Caste Wars were not as significant as the northern wars for the development of Mexican history, because the foreign interventions they sparked were limited to British pot-stirring and mercenary opportunism. But in its length and devastation it was the greatest of the indigenous wars. At their peak in the mid-century there were as many as one hundred thousand Maya rebels who occupied the southeast of Yucatán and set up their own capital city, Chan Santa Cruz, which opened diplomatic relations with Britain and endured fifty years. This was a far more numerous force than the Continental Army that won independence for the United States. Full-scale warfare declined after 1853, but that didn't mean it was business as usual, because, as a government report noted, "Cities and towns, villages and haciendas, everything that was once in indigenous-occupied territory is now nothing but jumbled ruins, ashes, and unburied human remains."[64] Neither was there peace: Raids, massacres, and reprisals became standard features of the frontier between rebel Maya territory and the rest of the state, which outside the main cities became a place where curfews reigned and armed townsmen slept in barracks. By 1857 some two hundred thousand people, well over a third of the prewar population, had migrated, died in the cholera and smallpox epidemics of 1853, or fallen victim to scorched-earth strategies.[65] Fourteen years of war, wrote the government inspector, had shown that it was impossible to bring the Maya under control by force of arms.[66]

Above all, a reconquest was unthinkable because the lost North was not half Mexico's national territory; in 1848 there was no such thing as a Mexican national territory. Tens of thousands of Mexican citizens were living above the new border, but their political and emotional links with the independent state were feeble. California and New Mexico didn't elect any representatives to the 1812 Cortes of Cádiz; the first Mexican constitution didn't even mention California and Texas.[67] When congressmen were finally elected they tended to go to the capital and never come back. In reality, no one knew what was up there. Humboldt said that everywhere above Durango was as well charted as the African interior, and the state-of-the art map in 1807 backed him up, showing most of the lands Mexico went on to lose as blank space labeled "Unknown Quivira Tribes."[68] In 1845 Sullivan's jingoistic article that claimed California in the name of "manifest destiny" had it right when it dubbed the territory "a remote province in a slight equivocal kind of dependence on the metropolis."[69] Santa Anna himself had little idea what Mexico was losing in the Treaty of Guadalupe Hidalgo. In 1853 the great Mexican cartographer Antonio García Cubas visited him to show off a new map and got an unexpected reception:

> On observing on it the great sweep of territory that our neighbors so unfairly grabbed from us he uttered I don't know what words filled with bitterness, which didn't fail to shock me, as I realized that before the presentation of that map he hadn't the slightest idea of the importance of the lost territory.[70]

The line of forts and missions that constituted state muscle ran out at the Río Grande. There were only six tiny coastal settlements in all of Alta California. In 1835 Robert Dana, a Harvard student who had taken ship as a common sailor, visited them. The future center of San Francisco was a single "shanty of rough boards put up by a man named Richardson." San Diego contained forty huts, huddled below a presidio that boasted two cannon, one spiked, the other dismounted, and "twelve half-clothed and half-starved-looking fellows."[71] The seventeenth-century frontier of the Center-North and Northeast was no better secured. In 1840 the Ministry of War reported a combined total of 707 troops in all the presidios from Nuevo México to Tamaulipas. The twenty-two men defending Nuevo León had a total of twelve muskets and just five rounds apiece; they found it hard to defend their own forts, never mind the farmers, cattlemen, missionaries, and miners they were charged to protect. What sovereignty there was came from posses and state militias, and was local. In some years Mexicans in Chihuahua were desperately fighting Comanche at the same time as Mexicans in San Antonio de Béxar were busily trading with them.[72]

But if the lost North was not a national territory in the past, it was a hypothetical national territory for the future. The immediate effect of its foreclosure was the removal or marginalization of resident Mexicans, subject to rigged land deals, squatter invasions, legal bullying, beatings, lynching, and murder. In California poorer Mexicans were subject to an anti-vagrancy law whose text dubbed them "greasers" and provided for jail and forced labor. Mexican miners were excluded from the Gold Rush by a foreigner tax and the racist violence epitomized by the "Great Greaser Extermination Meeting" of 1850. As many as ten thousand Sonoran miners headed north in 1849; by the end of 1850 about ten thousand Mexicans had been driven away from the diggings.[73] Sedentary indigenous peoples like the O'odham never stood a chance of hanging on to common or mission lands, neither forms of title recognized by the US. Neither, however, did the private landowners, whose rights were protected by the Treaty of Guadalupe Hidalgo. Article 10 originally read, "All grants of land by the Mexican Government . . . shall be respected as valid, to the same extent that the same grants would be valid, if the said territories had remained within the limits of Mexico." But the Senate removed that article during ratification, leaving Mexicans to apply to the US Court of Private Claims to have their deeds confirmed, and there the burden of proof lay with them. Those Mexicans who stuck it out and presented acceptable claims received a combined total of two million acres. Their prewar titles covered thirty-eight million acres.[74]

In the longer term Mexico's loss of her colonial North was a decisive lost opportunity, a final chance to join the world's rich nations gone. In 1859 Robert Dana sailed back to California, no longer a student slumming it on a trade brig but instead a prominent Republican on a fortnightly steamship, the *Golden Gate*. San Francisco had changed, too. Richardson's single shack was now lost in a lamp-lit city of one hundred thousand people, wrote Dana,

> with its storehouses, towers, and steeples; its courthouses, theaters, and hospitals; its daily journals; its well-filled professions; its fortresses and lighthouses; its wharves and harbor, with their

> thousand-ton clipper ships, more in number than London or Liverpool sheltered that day; itself one of the capitals of the American Republic, and the sole emporium of a new world, the awakened Pacific . . . when I saw all these things, and reflected on what I once was and saw here, and what now surrounded me, I could scarcely keep my hold on reality at all, or the genuineness of anything, and seemed to myself like one who had moved in "worlds not realised."[75]

Had Dana been Mexican, he might have mused on a world not realized, where Californian gold fueled the explosive expansion of the United Mexican States instead of the United States of America. The silver of viceregal Mexico had supplied much of the world's money; gold now underpinned the world's main currencies, and an intact Mexican republic might have recovered its old position at the center of the global economy. The sophisticated development bank of which Alamán dreamed would have jumpstarted industries. A different scale of budget would have given Mexico the military to defend tariffs against the British and the borders against incompetent chancers like the Missouri Volunteers. The old viceregal dream of a canal connecting Atlantic and Pacific worlds might have run through a different isthmus, Tehuantepec; Mexican railroads might have brought cotton from the Bajío, Durango, Coahuila, Texas, Oklahoma, and Kansas to the mill towns of New England, grim sources of cheap labor; Mexican wheat and beef might have fed the cities of the East Coast. Mexican politicians might have deplored the weakness of the white race, sapped by inbreeding; Mexican journalists might have lamented the atavism of a neighbor disintegrating in civil war. Instead, as Dana steamed into San Francisco in 1859, Mexico was bankrupt and halfway through its own civil war.

Chapter Eleven

Independence

The war with the United States left Mexicans bitter, fearful, and in some cases more conscious of a collective identity. In 1847 the nationalist Carlos María de Bustamante wrote—just before he died, a seventy-three-year-old huddled at home in the capital with a rifle while the Americans marched outside—that while the enemy's cause was "theft, plunder and conquest," "the Mexicans' cause was the *patria*."[1] Guillermo Prieto called Mexico's volunteers "the family who fought to defend the great home that is called *Patria*."[2] There was everyman substance to the sonneteer's rhetoric: Some marched hundreds of miles to fight for their parasitical capital. Prieto himself joined up as an aide de camp. In 1848 the gringos left—a tribute in part to Mexicans fighting back—but their threat endured. In the 1850s seven different filibuster expeditions set off from US soil to seize Tamaulipas, Sonora, and Baja California.[3] The Democratic presidents Franklin Pierce and James Buchanan had the same idea. Traduced deals like the Horse Creek Treaty, an 1851 border agreement with the Plains Nations that the US immediately broke, showed a willingness to put that idea into action.

But war and its threat didn't stimulate political unity. Regular soldiers were unimpressed by civilian voluntarism: Minutes from a general staff meeting in May 1847 show their bafflement at the lack of resistance in swathes of the countryside and Puebla.[4] Conservatives and liberals in the Bajío rebelled against the government that signed the peace treaty. In 1852 a wave of pronunciamientos spread out of Guadalajara and brought Santa Anna back to power as a technocratic dictator. The dictatorial half began promisingly: He closed Congress, exiled dissidents, imported Swiss mercenaries, shut down the press, invited back the Jesuits, formed a secret police, instituted mandatory passports for internal travel, and titled himself His Most Serene Highness. The technocratic half didn't: He failed to produce the economic and administrative development his Conservative Party allies had demanded, and Lucas Alamán, formally foreign minister, in reality the government's brain, died shortly after taking office.

A broad opposition developed fast, and on March 1, 1854, an old caudillo from Guerrero, Juan Álvarez, rebelled for an elected constituent congress. His Plan de Ayutla was vague enough and the government unpopular enough to recruit moderates, hardline liberals, and peasants, and in August 1855 Santa Anna resigned and went into Caribbean exile on a steamer called *Iturbide.* The great survivor's last turn in office left three enduring legacies. He commissioned an excellent national anthem—from a Catalan, unfortunately—that mixed the operatic bombast he loved with the patriotically homicidal lyrics of any good anthem.[5] He sold La Mesilla, a strip of the North about the size of Oaxaca, to the United States for ten million pesos—an infamous concession in the eyes of history, but probably the best deal the country could get from a neighbor whose maximum demands included most of the border states.[6] Finally, Santa Anna oversaw the last stages of polarization between conservatives and liberals. The liberal government that succeeded him proved incapable of resolving Mexicans' stark political and philosophical disagreements, and in 1858 civil war broke out.

The liberals' takeover from Santa Anna was a generational and cultural shift. The soldiers who brought them to power were indigenous and afro-mestizo peasants from the southern coasts and mountains; fighting the conservatives, they were joined by northerners and mountain men from Puebla and Michoacán. Their generals looked like them in many ways. They were young provincials—nearly half of them came from the dangerous North, only one from Mexico City—who moved up the ranks from undistinguished backgrounds because they were good at war and had the ability to talk people into going to war, the egalitarian charisma called *don de gente*. In the absence of regular soldiers, the gift of signing up civilians was essential. But writing was a different matter, because only a quarter had more than rudimentary schooling and some were barely literate. The new generals weren't from the republic of letters.

The civilian liberals in stark contrast were well-educated urbanites. Most were born middle class and attended seminaries—those Catholic centers for cultivating Latin, science, theology, and anticlericalism—and lay universities. Two-thirds were lawyers, and almost all of them were wordsmiths of one sort or another, who published promiscuously in a newly sophisticated press, whether in short-lived propaganda sheets or the two institutions of liberal thought, *El Siglo XIX* and *El Monitor Republicano*. A quarter were poets, another quarter historians. One, Vicente Riva Palacio, was a master of all genres, knocking out plays and novels that combined sex and liberal nationalism at a furious rate (while also fighting as a general; he was as close to a polymath as the age allowed).[7] The writers, not the generals, were supposed to be the political elites of the future. As the intellectual Manuel Altamirano put it, they should "make *belles lettres* into a defensive weapon."[8] Yet the two most important fit neither mold. One, General Porfirio Díaz, excelled at university; the other, Benito Juárez, was undemonstrative to the point of dourness and only wrote when strictly necessary. They were provincials, self-made *oaxaqueños*, born politicians who started out poor and were certainly not white. Díaz's mother was Mixtec; both Juárez's parents were Zapotec. Between them they ran Mexico for more than fifty years.[9]

Their early trajectories ran parallel. Both attended seminary in Oaxaca, and both abandoned it in favor of the city's newborn, secular Institute of Arts and Sciences. Both were drawn by the Institute's offerings of law and egalitarianism. As Díaz remembered, "I was seduced by the open and straightforward manner of those important people, something I hadn't seen in the Seminary, where one couldn't even greet the professors."[10] Díaz joined up early, volunteering against the Americans in 1847 and leading a Zapotec National Guard company in 1855. Juárez went into civilian politics, starting off in his mid-twenties on the Oaxaca town council, impressing superiors with his grasp of the law—an achievement, given its strange hybrid of republican innovation and

Benito Juárez.

colonial leftovers[11]—and climbing the ladder of state government. In 1842 he was Oaxaca's secretary of government, on paper a follower of Santa Anna, and in 1847 he became governor. When Santa Anna returned as a dictator, Juárez went into exile; returning in 1855 he became minister of justice and then head of the Supreme Court. In 1858 he became president.

As governor Juárez was more technocrat than ideologue. A passage in a school notebook of his, though, is as revealing as any speech. Its pages pass with neatly penned, underlined titles for each century, almost all left blank until the thirteenth century, when "Magna Carta" appears, followed by a eulogy to its liberal values. For a young Juárez, 1215 was Year Zero.[12] Yet that didn't mean he and his fellow believers were wild-eyed democrats: When French workers rebelled in 1848, *El Siglo XIX* called them uneducated barbarians who were mere "*plebe, populacho*," plebs, dregs of society.[13] Neither were they—Ignacio Ramírez excepted—atheists. The liberals tried, like their Bourbon predecessors, to square the circle of state and church power. When they passed a new constitution in 1857, the president proclaimed it kneeling in front of the Bible and celebrated with a Te Deum.[14] The hardliner Prieto, accused of being a heathen, wrote indignantly about kneeling next to his mother after seeing a miracle and offering up "a fervent prayer that echoed in my spirit like a canticle of resurrection . . . and there are animals that might suppose me an unbeliever?"[15]

It was the power of the Church as an institution that the new generation opposed. In this they were direct heirs of the last viceroys. Churchmen and soldiers remained literally outside the law, thanks to the endurance of colonial *fueros*, states of exemption that made them liable only to ecclesiastical courts. Soldiers could steal livestock and priests could abuse their flocks, and civil authorities had no jurisdiction. Catholic liberals were likewise horrified by sacraments as earners, churchmen price gouging for the rituals that kept their congregants in a state of grace. Some parishioners didn't pay: One priest in Tabasco complained that all he'd received in tithes was a jar of preserved peaches.[16] Most Mexicans scrimped, saved, and indebted themselves to buy baptisms, marriages (six pesos for a mestizo or mulatto couple, four for an Indian), and burials, or else lived dangerously without them.[17] The dying who really crossed the Church might be refused extreme unction.[18] A liberal state was incompatible with such rival institutions, and the moral and financial damage their autonomy caused orderly citizens. But even radical liberals had no intent to make Mexicans atheists. Their legislation to reduce the Church's power on Earth was presented as the *leyes de Reforma*, the Reform Laws; but after three centuries of far-reaching ecclesiastical power, it was revolutionary.

The first step of the revolution was to exclude the clergy from voting for the constituent congress, which caused top-level resignations and split the provisional government. It was a first taste of the divisiveness of the Reform Laws. The first of these, the *Ley Juárez*, rationalized a justice system plagued by inconsistencies; it preserved special tribunals for the military and the Church but reduced their jurisdiction to criminal offenses. That made them subject to civil law for everything else, ending automatic impunity. The second, the *Ley Lerdo*, was a mandatory privatization of Church- and indigenous-held lands. The third, the *Ley Orgánica del Registro Civil,* ended the Church's monopoly over births and marriages, and the fourth completed the secularization of the life cycle by establishing government control of cemeteries. The fifth, the *Ley de Obvenciones Parroquiales*, established a poverty line and punishments for priests who charged the faithful beneath it.[19] The new constitution, inaugurated on February 5, 1857, incorporated and extended these reforms.

It was one of the most progressive constitutions in the world (although competition was at a low point, with slaveholders and *génocidaires* to the north, emperors and rattling republics to the south, and Europeans wary after the revolutions of 1848). The Constitution of 1857 centered on a lengthy and specific list of the rights of man, which occupied twenty-nine articles and included an imminent abolition of the death penalty, "to the glory of Mexico in the eyes of God and the world," a global first.[20] To guarantee those rights it established a federal republic with a single-chamber legislature and considerable autonomy for states and municipalities. The institutional logic was the avoidance of despotism. Presidents, legislators, and Supreme Court justices were elected by universal male suffrage. The president could veto legislation once and then had to accept any revised version that Congress might pass. It was a totemic piece of paper for the ages; more or less everyone hated it.

The Church rejected the Constitution of 1857 because it enshrined the secularization of politics and law. Constitutions since Independence had started off by declaring Mexico a Catholic nation; this one did not. Catholicism had a special place in the hearts of Mexicans, the final text conceded, but other religions were welcome and institutional privileges were finished. The Bishop of Michoacán summed up clerical rejection in a public letter, protesting Articles 3, 5, 6, 7, 9, 12, 13, 27, 36, 39, 72, 123, "and all others that directly or indirectly oppose religion and the Church."[21] The Archbishop of Mexico excommunicated officials who swore allegiance to it.[22] Conservatives called it government "in evil, by evil, and for evil."[23] More surprisingly, liberals disliked it too. While for puros it was too tepid, to moderados it was provocatively utopian, ignoring the reality that "the government had to govern women, the timid, the religious fanatics, as it were, because not everyone is a philosopher."[24] Both puros and moderados quickly realized that its institutional design made the president very weak and governing very difficult; as the minister of finance put it, "An office clerk has more power than the head of the executive."[25] So when the Bishop of Michoacán wrote of the "deep and general disgust with which [the constitution] has been received," he wasn't just talking about his flock.[26]

Liberals dealt with rejection with two tools: authoritarianism and nationalism. They were creating a modern state, and they shared much of the law-and-order rhetoric of conservatives when they spoke of how to do it. The difficulty of governing Mexico, the moderate liberal Manuel Siliceo wrote, was reconciling "progress with order and freedom with the law"; to Gabino Barreda the national priority was "liberty, order, and progress."[27] Liberals were prepared to cede quite a lot of liberty for order and progress. Concessions to overmighty prelates, on the other hand, were unthinkable. That institutional anticlericalism meant fighting was abundantly clear before the constitution even passed, as a series of counterrevolutionary risings began under the slogan of "religion and fueros." Numerous guerrillas took to the sierra; conventional rebel armies captured Puebla twice.

There was also an inbuilt resistance to liberals from many indigenous communities, whose common lands faced mandatory privatization. This was a threat to their moral economies; it was also a threat to saint's days, credit, and cultural autonomy, all funded by the cofradías' collective holdings. Dealing with these inevitable spiritual and secular conflicts required periodic suspension of the constitution, prolongation of presidential terms, election-rigging, abrogation of press freedoms, exiles, and murders. Order was to be enforced in the countryside by the *rurales*, crack paramilitary police who were allowed to wage summary judgement, the extrajudicial executions of the *ley fuga*, the law of flight, which empowered authorities to shoot "fleeing prisoners." The realpolitik was evident in its unfussy recruiting policies; Juárez's early rurales were quite often ex-bandits.[28]

As liberals turned to force, they tried to engineer consent through nationalism. They believed that substituting patria for patria chica was an uphill but vital struggle. "Let us lift," suggested Ignacio Ramírez in 1856, "the thin veil of the mixed race which is drawn across the country and we will find a hundred nations which today, vainly, we struggle to blend into one."[29] Their raw materials were race, anti-imperialism, and an improbable national reconciliation. Their tools were street names, monuments, civic ceremonies, village bands, literature, and schools. None of these were new. The recovery, re-evaluation, and promotion of the indigenous past went back before Independence. In public festivals Iturbide had dressed up indigenous women in Spanish garb and vice versa.[30] Santa Anna had promoted free public schooling.[31] From creole flattery of indigenous culture to the ideology of mestizaje, "the struggle to blend into one" was the obvious next step. A north-facing anti-imperialism was likewise obvious: Both conservatives and liberals had fought the United States. Finally, there was appreciable personal mobility between the two sides before 1858.

There was also a potential receptive audience—outside the war-torn peripheries of the North and Southeast. Mexicans after Independence were not natural individualists, wandering through a labyrinth of solitude; they were used to clubbing together toward shared goals. Between 1820 and 1850 they had formed hundreds of societies in the fields of education, development, arts and sciences, and social support. These were places where people acted like citizens, paying dues, electing officers, debating strategies, and assessing the results, with goals that stretched from fixing the price of pulque to burying comrades to building schools, as the Lancasterian Company did with lasting success in Mexico City. Some associations stretched across race and class: The Lancasterians rented their buildings cheap from the Nahua of San Juan Tenochtitlán in exchange for free schooling for barrio children.[32] Their rhetoric said that they were creating citizens in a "little republic."[33] Some groups had explicit nationalist messages: The *Juntas de Progreso*, which aimed to stimulate domestic industry through boycotting foreign goods, said that they were spreading a "nationalist spirit."[34]

The problem was spreading a specifically liberal message across that collectively inclined audience. A bankrupt country couldn't build schools, and an illiterate public couldn't read pamphlets, newspapers, and books. Those Mexicans who could devoured print: Riva Palacio's novels had print runs of six thousand copies, and even at the appreciable price of a real and a half they sold out fast in the provinces. *The Mysteries of the Inquisition*, a novel in which priestly torturers flog topless women while bishops host orgies, was such enticing business that its printer went to court for the right to publish. But the literate were a tiny minority, perhaps 1 percent, and a third of the population didn't speak Spanish.[35] Mexicans, particularly in the center, were keen on associative life. Citizenship also made sense to indigenous political cultures, if lands were left alone. Mixtecs and Zapotecs were happy to dub themselves citizens when the party line came from one of their own, such as Díaz, who discussed liberalism with the villagers of Ixtlán and persuaded them to sign up to the cause.[36] But the cultural reengineering that liberal nationalism demanded was inherently gradualist, and liberals in 1856 and 1857 didn't have time.

Instead it was a mixture of religion and pragmatism that determined the choice of sides. Priests hated Riva Palacio's political bodice rippers, "the most repugnant coquetry and lubriciousness," and at least one confiscated and burned copies.[37] This was literary criticism compared to the rhetoric of 1856 and 1857, which was homicidal: Religious pamphlets cited the "blasphemies vomited against the Vicar of Christ" to justify calls for "Death to the Puros!!" and "Death to the Enemies [of the Holy Religion of Jesus Christ]!!!" Liberals, who for a while had claimed Jesus as one of their own ("the healthy doctrine of the Savior of the World: *man is free: every man is equal to another: Jesus Christ taught liberty and equality*"), called for the deaths of his betrayers the pope, bishops, and priests. Manichaean policy accompanied Manichaean rhetoric: When the constitution was proclaimed, officials who didn't swear fealty were fired, while those who did were excommunicated. Community leaders and bureaucrats lost either their jobs or their souls; metaphorically damned if they didn't, literally damned if they did. Churches were the flashpoints of the first nationwide violence on the day the constitution was inaugurated, as liberals stormed in to ring the bells while priests and parishioners took up arms to keep them out.[38]

To conservatives and many liberals this was compelling evidence that the Reforma made Mexico ungovernable, even if subsequent negotiations between the government and the papacy gave peace an ephemeral chance. In November 1857 a reluctant Congress gave President Ignacio Comonfort the power to suspend constitutional rights, deploy twenty thousand militiamen, and exercise supreme authority over the ministries of finance and war. By then even this was perceived insufficient. Consequently, on December 17 General Félix Zuloaga launched a pronunciamiento with the Plan de Tacubaya, which called for the closure of Congress and a new constitution. The capital's garrison backed him, taking over the city and jailing key politicians, including Juárez. So did Juárez's compadre President Comonfort, ex–finance minister Manuel Payno, and the ex-governor of the Federal District, Juan José Baz. All of them, revealingly, were liberals, accepting a pragmatic coup d'état to forestall an ideological civil war. The conservative generals Luis Gonzaga Osollo and Miguel Miramón had been on the verge of mobilizing; moderados and puros decided to act first, and they were backed by the strategically critical state governments of Veracruz, Puebla, and Tlaxcala.[39]

The Plan de Tacubaya failed, and civil war did break out. Other liberal state governments didn't go along, Veracruz changed sides, and President Comonfort wavered. Fresh Mexico City pronunciados rebelled against him, dividing the capital's troops between Comonfort and General Zuloaga; ten days of street fighting ensued until conservative troops reinforced the rebels, consolidating a new regime with Zuloaga as president. Comonfort, however, had repented and released Juárez, who set up an alternative government in Guanajuato. It was, fittingly enough for the lawyer, the legal thing to do; the constitution specified that if a president was unavailable—Comonfort had headed for exile—then Juárez as the head of the Supreme Court was to succeed him. Yet it was radical in its improbability. Juárez's early cabinets consisted of himself and a couple of inexperienced others: His oaxaqueño schoolmate Manuel Ruíz and the puro intellectual Melchor Ocampo held most of the main posts. They were chased from town to town for three months, and Juárez only escaped being shot in Guadalajara because Prieto used his gift of gab to talk conservative soldiers into letting them go. Finally they made it by steamer to Veracruz, where on May 5 Juárez set up an enduring constitutionalist government.

Juárez got that far because he was the figurehead of not just an ideological but also a regional war. The conservatives only held the capital, Puebla, San Luis Potosí, Tabasco, Durango, and Tamaulipas. The liberals established an arc around them that stretched from the South through the center and Center-West up to the border. They were fighting the majority of the army, and in the first three months they lost almost all the major cities. However, commanders like Juan Zuazua in Nuevo León and Porfirio Díaz in Oaxaca had been organizing National Guards since 1855, and they proved talented soldiers. Over the summer the liberals began recapturing, albeit ephemerally, the main cities of the Bajío; the conservatives' initial advantage in men and funds waned; and their army was kept out of Veracruz by astute leadership and scorched-earth tactics. When Miramón marched on the critical port in March 1859 he found the fields and granaries burnt and a liberal force behind him attacking Mexico City. By then President Zuloaga had been overthrown by peace-seeking generals who proposed amnesty, a constituent congress, and a moderate liberal constitution. The proposal failed because Miramón, only twenty-five years old but "the genius of war" in conservative eyes, believed he could win on the battlefield; so he made himself president and fought for another two years.

It was more than just martial self-belief. The civil war began as a popular conflict, not a mere pronunciamiento, and the commitment of a lot of everyday Mexicans to settling it by arms was evident. The long history of villages hating both neighboring villages and predatory hacendados was exacerbated by the municipio libre, in which the prize of being head town caused bitter conflict, and by *desamortización*, the disentailment of property that promised legal land grabs. The result was the violence of vendetta, a neighbor-on-neighbor killing that made peace hard to imagine or make. There were reasons from the past and new reasons of revenge for atrocities, because the war wasn't just slaughterous, killing tens, maybe hundreds of thousands; it was also total, and performative, which meant killing, torturing, and burning out civilians. There were visible, major massacres, by liberals at Guadalajara in 1858 and by conservatives at Tacubaya in 1859, where General Leonardo Márquez executed prisoners and civilians, including doctors, foreigners, and children. And there were the invisible massacres that went into village memory.

Another reason that conservatives and liberals fought for three years was that their forces were relatively balanced. At the outset conservative regulars outnumbered liberal militiamen, but many were conscripts of dubious enthusiasm. While liberals used coercion too, calling up all men from sixteen to sixty, they offered more in institutional terms: National Guardsmen in the Sierra de Puebla could elect their own officers.[40] And both sides offered more than ideology and score-settling. Conservatives extended the spiritual benefits of Church backing and the security of collective land, which drew the support of many in the indigenous center. Liberals offered local autonomies and the opportunity to take over Church lands. In the first years, when the war was a dynamic stalemate, regions changing hands but national fighting deadlocked, many Mexicans changed sides according to the fortunes of war. Tlaxcalans who joined the National Guard while their state was liberal wrote to their bishop begging forgiveness.[41] Signing up or getting killed was not much of a choice when a new army came to town.

In addition, the more cohesive indigenous peoples might formally identify with one side or another but they fought for themselves, defending or winning autonomy and then staying put, doing little to aid either national government. Down much of the Sierra Madre Occidental powerful indigenous polities turned conservative. The Yaqui in Sonora fought the liberal state government; the Náayari and Wixáritari of Jalisco followed the mestizo cacique Manuel Lozada and secured Nayarit independence until the 1870s. These were pragmatists who could cancel out opposing national ideologies with an updated syncretism. Liberals everywhere fought under banners of the Virgin of Guadalupe; in Michoacán some Purépecha (who called the sun "our Father") conflated Christ and Saint Joseph into a single deity who worked miracles through the intercession of Benito Juárez.[42]

Finally, elite positions hardened as the war aged. At the outset there was considerable to-and-fro between sides. Not all priests started out conservative, despite their superiors; some secular Mexicans began as conservatives and ended up liberals; many moderados, on the other hand, went along with the coup. Most conservatives believed that some form of parliamentary government was necessary; God was sovereign, but, in one writer's words, the people "were the purest form of authority."[43] The first commander of the liberal army, Santos Degollado, called his troops the real soldiers of "the religion of The Crucified," their conservative opponents "hypocritical Pharisees who invoke the religion of Jesus Christ without really believing in it or observing its maxims of fraternity and peace."[44] Degollado entered peace talks with President Miramón twice, hoping for a British-brokered deal; the second time, in March 1860, Juárez fired him. (Degollado fought on as a foot soldier.) Such high-level peacemakers were stymied by Juárez's refusal to remake the Constitution of 1857 and Miramón's refusal to accept it. Many held their noses and settled into lasting allegiances despite disagreeing with the intransigents.

A clarification of international positions meant neither side got the money or military aid that might have tipped the scales. The United States and the European powers started off by recognizing the Zuloaga government. The US hoped to obtain more of the North and free passage across the Isthmus of Tehuantepec, its citizens' rights there to be protected if necessary by its army. President James Buchanan told the Senate that "it was beyond question that the destiny of our race is to extend itself across the entire continent of North America"; Senator Sam Houston suggested making Mexico a protectorate.[45] Meanwhile France, Britain, and Spain sent warships to Veracruz to ensure both sides paid interest on their debts and at the same time counter US expansionism. The conservatives thought that either Europeans or the United States might lend them decisive assistance, but in April 1858 the US broke diplomatic relations after they indignantly rejected an offer to buy Baja California and much of Sonora and Chihuahua. The Europeans never went beyond extending a single, usurious Spanish loan.

Far from deciding the war, foreign powers instead guaranteed stalemate. The liberals were far more accommodating to the US than the conservatives, who called the liberals traitors; Juárez's minister in Washington was prepared to accept the land sales in return for help. Although other constitutionalists ruled that out, Juárez agreed to a deal that gave the US the essence of the protectorate it sought. The McLane-Ocampo Treaty, finalized in December 1859, offered Mexico two million pesos in immediate cash in exchange for a permanent route across the Isthmus of Tehuantepec and the right to send US troops without prior permission to protect that route and Americans' private interests. In ceding sovereignty over critical territory, it made Mexico a predecessor of Panama. The treaty was rejected in May 1860 by northerners in the US Senate worried about the power the acquisitions would give the South, saving Juárez's historical image. In the intervening months, though, the desperate capitulation of the McLane-Ocampo Treaty brought decisive benefits, because it guaranteed the liberals' hold on Veracruz, their strategic base near the capital and source of customs revenue. Miramón had purchased two warships from Cuba to attack the port by land and sea, but when they sailed up in March 1860 Juárez informed the US that the ships were pirates and called for assistance. Three US ships promptly attacked and took them. This military support Juárez received from the US didn't win the war for him, but it may well have stopped him from losing it.

So instead of a decisive stroke settling the civil war of the Reforma, attrition prevailed, both sides building armies while they ran out of money. The conservatives went bankrupt faster; they relied on funding from the Church and the business community in Mexico City, and both became less accommodating as Miramón failed to take Veracruz. The liberals, likewise penurious, at least controlled the ports and growing swathes of the countryside, where they could sell off Church property and tax what businesses and trade endured. Both sides were running up debts they couldn't pay and turned to the risky business of seizing foreign assets. The conservatives lost more battles for finance and territory, and on Christmas Day 1860 the liberal General González Ortega captured Mexico City. But victory was a brief respite rather than a final settlement, because the Juárez government was unable to service its debts, and the Europeans seized on default as an excuse to invade and install a Habsburg emperor. Conservatives, many longtime monarchists, welcomed them.

Debt had plagued Mexico since the London stock market collapse of 1826. That disaster, largely the fruit of British financiers' incompetence and dishonesty, left Mexicans paying the bill for decades. The companies founded in the bubble had gone bankrupt, and Mexican bonds had become worthless overnight, leaving a country without significant tax income owing high interest payments on assets that had effectively ceased to exist. The $15 million the US paid Mexico under the 1848 peace treaty went straight to debt service. By the end of the civil war Mexico owed foreigners over 80 million pesos, and a single year's interest payment to the British alone was 2.5 million pesos. Shut out of sovereign credit, Mexican governments turned to extortionate private loans; the flailing conservatives took on an obligation for 15 million pesos from a Swiss financier, Jean-Baptiste Jecker, in return for $750,000 in immediate funds. When Juárez came to power he repudiated the Jecker loan, recognizing the validity of all other debts and Mexico's inability to service them. On July 17, 1861, he suspended all payments, with the assurance that it was a temporary measure.[46]

It wasn't just British debt; the Spanish and French had made lesser loans, and key members of the French government were involved in the swindle of the Jecker bonds. The French had considered military intervention to collect Mexican debt decades earlier.[47] On October 31, 1861, they formed a coalition with the British and Spanish, formalized in a Convention of London, under which the three powers' warships would seize the customs houses of Veracruz and Tampico and divert taxes on Atlantic trade directly to debt service. In the past it would have been a risky move, given the naval power of the United States and the Monroe Doctrine's prohibition of European adventures in the New World. But the US had been at war with itself since April 1861, and in July the government had lost the first pitched battle at Bull Run. The South was trying to establish good relations with the Juárez government; Coahuila and Nuevo León even raised the prospect of joining the Confederacy.[48] When Lincoln mooted assuming five years of Mexico's debt service in exchange for European nonintervention, Congress turned him down.[49] It was a propitious moment for muscular informal imperialism; some thought the mere arrival of the warships might restore debt payments.

Yet the Emperor of France, Napoleon III, was thinking more in terms of formal imperialism, a ground invasion of Mexico to install a European monarch. His wife, Eugenie, originally a Spanish countess, had been chatting to down-at-heel Mexican monarchists for years; in September 1861, reviewing minor European royals for a suitable candidate, she, Napoleon III, and a conservative Mexican diplomat called José Manuel Hidalgo y Esnaurrízar came up with an underemployed Habsburg. Archduke Maximilian was the younger brother of the current Austrian Emperor Franz Josef and was at a loose end. The plan got a chilly reception from British prime minister Lord Palmerston, a wily realist, and the Convention of London included a clause prohibiting the joint force from interference in Mexico's domestic politics. Seizing the customs houses if necessary was as far as the alliance would go. Napoleon III agreed and then inserted a get-out-of-jail-free card, a further clause that gave field commanders the discretion to respond to fast-moving events as they saw best fit. He then secretly ordered the French admiral to occupy Mexico City whatever happened.[50]

The fleet arrived in early 1862 with seven thousand troops (Napoleon III, a cheapskate, provided less than half of them), who occupied Veracruz without much fuss. When Juárez agreed to resume debt payments the British and Spanish withdrew; the French installed a puppet conservative émigré as president and advanced on Mexico City. For anyone who had studied past invasions—and the French had, drawing up a map of what the US had faced in 1847—it was clear that invaders had to leave the lowlands quickly, before tropical disease set in, and should expect stiff Mexican resistance.[51] The French found both out in short order. When General Élie Frédéric Forey arrived in the autumn he set out for healthy Orizaba too slowly, leaving behind 200 sick in Veracruz; out of his remaining 515 men less than half survived.[52] And Forey was a new commander in chief, bringing in fresh troops, because the first French regiments had been savaged by guerrillas and lost a set-piece battle at Puebla.

Puebla was the gateway to the central valley, and the Mexicans garrisoned it scientifically with twelve thousand men. Outside the city they turned two former monasteries into forts; inside the city they dug trenches and built parapets on rooftops. On May 5, 1862, the French, overconfident, launched an all-out frontal assault on the well-organized defenses and were massacred. In the capital Mexicans launched the first-ever Cinco de Mayo celebrations. The French only returned to Puebla a year later, after raising their own army to twenty-eight thousand men. This time they abandoned élan and inched forward behind siegeworks; it took them two months to capture the city, and only after agreeing to let the Mexican rank and file go free. Juárez's government left the capital for San Luis Potosí, and on June 10, 1863, the French finally marched into Mexico City.[53]

Nine months later Archduke Maximilian accepted the imperial crown, and on June 12, 1864, he arrived in the capital of his Mexican Empire redivivus. He was backed only by Napoleon III and King Leopold of Belgium, his father-in-law. Napoleon III was a self-made emperor, a naturalized Swiss citizen, a "parvenu" to Maximilian, "a princely lumpenproletariat" to Karl Marx. King Leopold was a recent invention too, a princeling who accepted the newly invented crown of Belgium after turning down Greece as a bit too risky. In the royal scheme of things, Maximilian had more legitimacy than either; his family had once ruled Mexico for nearly two hundred years. He nevertheless conditioned acceptance on a vote to confirm everyday Mexicans' agreement, and Napoleon III duly provided the numbers, claiming without any ballot papers that five and a half million Mexicans desired a Habsburg restoration. In reality there was a petition with six names. One gimcrack emperor installed another.[54]

There were well-placed skeptics to whom Maximilian might have listened. Napoleon III tried to bribe General Miguel Miramón into joining the first expedition; the ex-president refused because, he explained, there was no monarchist party in Mexico. After losing the Battle of Puebla the French commander reported to Paris that he had "never met a single supporter of monarchy."[55] The main monarchist émigré, José María Gutiérrez de Estrada, was clueless and utterly marginal in Mexican politics: He had been in exile for more than twenty years, after publishing a pamphlet—partly in English—calling for a foreign prince; he was from Yucatán, he married into a family of Spanish aristocrats, and his neck was saved by the French consul. He wasn't even charismatic; when someone asked Napoleon III what he thought of Gutiérrez de Estrada, the reply was "Nothing at all."[56]

Other monarchists were more useful. The French army was reinforced by the three most important conservative generals, Leonardo Márquez, Tomás Mejía, and, despite his misgivings, Miramón. They contributed four thousand experienced troops, including four hundred officers who, finding themselves without soldiers to command, joined up as rankers in a "legion of honour."[57] It wasn't an army of the white upper classes: Mejía was an Otomí cacique, and the conservative guerrillas were not the cream of Mexico City society. Not that the cream of society was useless; a competent and nationalist civilian elite backed the empire. Their logic preferred a progressive European monarch, weakly legitimate, keen on going native, above all Catholic, to domination by the racist Protestant republic to the north. The savvy Alamán had reached the same conclusions decades earlier. After observing the US in the intervening years, an appreciable number of moderate liberals agreed. Many took cabinet jobs, like Santiago Vidaurri, who abandoned Juárez to become one of Maximilian's main advisors; José Fernández

Ramírez, his first foreign minister; and General José López Uraga. His interior minister, José María Cortés y Esparza; his war minister, Juan de Dios Peza; and his minister of justice, Pedro Escudero y Echánove were likewise moderados. Even as the imperialists were enrolled in national legend as irredeemable villains, the historian Justo Sierra called the better of them "good republicans and reformists of honour and talent."[58] Napoleon III's rhetoric of "Latin America"—a phrase coined by a French journalist in 1856—was well chosen.[59]

The world of imperial collaborators, behind the façade of balls, arcane titles and baroque medals, was not one of lickspittle reactionaries, as liberal propaganda made out. The French had the last word during most of the regime because they supplied the soldiers who propped it up. But many policy makers, bureaucrats, and municipal politicos were Mexicans considering serious questions of how to make their fractured and battered country into a functional modern state. They subscribed to the Roman ideal of citizenship, equality under rational law, and came up with a modern judicial system that survived their defeat, accepted more or less wholesale by their bitter enemies. The majority of imperialists also subscribed to the Aristotelian ideal of representative bodies of citizens who ruled and were ruled, as long as citizens were defined by wealth as "useful men," assemblies of petty oligarchs (much like Aristotle's reality). Alongside dogmatic religious extremists were men who believed in the separation of church and state, freedom of belief, and development for indigenous Mexicans. Perhaps that was what the Church was good for, the pragmatic missionizing of viceregal times; even a bishop like Pedro Espinosa of Guadalajara could agree. There was more overlap between imperialists and *juaristas* than either would admit.[60]

Their emperor turned out to be one of the most liberal of them all. Postimperial history registered three versions of Maximilian: the villain, the romantic, and the idiot; he offered material for all of them. The war against guerrillas that his French allies ran was a war of terror against civilians. The leader of their counterinsurgent corps, Colonel Charles-Louis Dupin, warned the townsmen of Ozuluama, Veracruz, that their home "would be wiped from the map of the Empire" if they didn't obey him. They didn't, and two weeks later Dupin warned the residents of Pánuco, "If you do not comply exactly with what I have stipulated I will raze your village . . . I include a newspaper that you might know what happened in Ozuluama in the same circumstances."[61] In Michoacán imperial forces burned stubborn Zitácuaro three times.[62] Yet while Maximilian fired Dupin in July 1865, he then generalized the repression with the *decreto negro*, the Black Decree, which made anyone who gave guerrillas money, food, arms, shelter, or intelligence liable to summary court-martial and shooting.[63]

The dreamer version of Maximilian drew on his enchantment with places like Cuernavaca, his romanticizing against the odds of Mexico, and his relationship with the Empress Carlota, young, pretty, smart, and personable. (Although rumor held that a venereal brush with a Brazilian lover had left him sterile, or at least unwelcome, which may explain a bizarre attempt to kidnap and adopt an Iturbide grandchild.) The third personification of the emperor, the fool, draws on the chancers and opportunists of Maximilian's foreign entourage, his fateful combination of micromanagement and incompetence, his delight in pomp, and his distraction in hobbies. He undid the astute policy of appointing Mexican liberals to government with a kitchen cabinet of foreigners. All government correspondence had to pass through the Belgian Félix Eloin, an inexperienced engineer who didn't speak Spanish. While Maximilian personally disliked balls and dinners, he felt compelled to host them *comme il faut*; his plans for a national theater were so over-the-top that the director himself told him to rein them in as the money was needed elsewhere.[64] He invented impractical and detested uniforms—the Imperial Guard wore a scarlet blouse and huaraches—while he himself dressed as a charro, a Mexican cowboy.[65] The first *Diario del Imperio* consisted in large part of a list of new decorations and who could wear them, followed by a proud account of how the Ottoman sultan had received a Mexican envoy after two weeks waiting in a hotel.[66] (The ambassador was Leonardo Márquez, a famous Catholic extremist, which may have encouraged the sultan to take his time.) In December 1866 a German doctor observed in amazement:

> The Empire is nearing a lamentable ending; the French and the Austrians are getting ready to leave; the Emperor, who either doesn't understand or doesn't want to understand the state of the country, still doesn't think of retiring, and can be found in Puebla hunting butterflies and playing billiards.[67]

But while Maximilian was easily distracted and satirized, he was no idiot. Education had reportedly left him with a grasp of ten languages; inclination led him to progressive policies that might stabilize his unlikely empire. He and Carlota, very much a partner in the family business, arrived ready to out-Mexican the Mexicans. Before entering the capital he went to pray at the Basilica de Guadalupe. He immediately changed the celebration of independence from Iturbide's entry into Mexico City on September 27 to Hidalgo's Grito de Dolores on September 16, describing that divisive eccentric as the hero of an "indivisible nation" of mestizos. In 1865 he gave the Grito himself and unveiled a monument to Morelos. In 1866 he set up an Imperial Academy of Science and Literature to foster Mexican intellectuals of all political stripes. He printed decrees in both Spanish and Nahuatl. The Indians, he said, "were the best people in the country."[68] In that last he was more demonstrative than Juárez, who didn't go out of his way to advertise much *indigenismo*.

In terms of social policy Maximilian was likewise progressive. Alongside the list of decorations in that first government newspaper he reaffirmed the liberal privatizations of Church and indigenous lands.[69] At the same time he recognized that the law had brought substantial privations to some indigenous communities and founded the *junta protectora de clases menesterosas*, a consultative agency to receive complaints regarding land grabs; it didn't stop desamortización, but it did provide for stays of execution and give communities recourse against violent predators. To some it returned lands.[70] Maximilian's labor legislation aimed to end debt peonage and whipping, and instead of employing workers' children, hacendados and factory owners were supposed to provide them free schooling.[71] When Mexico City had an unusually heavy rainy season and ninety-six hours of straight rain drove water levels up six feet, he ordered emergency relief of one real a day to those flooded out.[72] Maximilian serially wanted to do the right thing by what he called his *nueva patria*. Yet from the start he was in most eyes doing the wrong thing, because he had incurred original sin in accepting the job at all.

Maximilian's progressive policies could have political impact only on territory he controlled, and that was confined, as it had been for earlier empires, to the central valleys, the main cities, and the corridors in between. In 1863 the French army had driven the liberal army and government into peregrinations around the North, and by the beginning of 1865 it had destroyed most of their regular regiments. Yet Maximilian's troops never achieved reliable control of the countryside in the face of tenacious guerrillas and National Guardsmen. In some areas, like Oaxaca, the government tacitly acknowledged its failure to win hearts and minds by allowing defeated liberals to name their new authorities.[73] Neither did the *juaristas* lack manpower; the organized militias of the mountains were the basis for a resurgent regular army.

And so when money and geopolitics turned against Maximilian, so did war. From the start he was cash poor and heavily indebted. After accepting the crown, he signed the Convention of Miramar with Napoleon III, under which he assumed responsibility for interest payments on Mexico's historic debt, an additional 270 million francs to cover retroactively the costs of intervention, and a future 1,000 francs per soldier per year. The French advanced his future government 40 million pesos but kept 37 percent for themselves as brokerage fees and half the rest toward costs already incurred. It was an accounting sleight of hand that meant most of the funds never left Paris, fictional bonds that left Maximilian with just over 4 million pesos in hand, mortgaged to the hilt before even sailing for Mexico, incurring debt to pay debt. Once in Mexico he needed 38 to 40 million pesos a year to make payments, when at best he could raise 9 million a year. It was impossible: In February 1866 he was forced to stop paying the conservatives' old war debts, and in July a skeptical France began taking 50 percent of customs revenues at Veracruz and Tampico. As one liberal put it, "The French government buried Maximilian when he signed the Treaty of Miramar."[74]

Americans and Prussians did the last of the digging. The US government made outraged noises about the intervention from the outset but was distracted by its own civil war. By 1866 that was over, and the victorious Union could do something about the European puppet state on its border. The government of President Andrew Johnson pressured the French to withdraw, and when Maximilian tried to recruit

Austrian troops to compensate, it threatened his elder brother, the emperor Franz Josef, with war. Juárez's minister in Washington, Matías Romero, convinced an American general to lead a US army to help expel the French, an idea that attracted the irascible commanding general Ulysses Grant. (The more politick State Department headed them off.)[75] Meanwhile in France a jaded public combined with the threat from another new empire, the Prussians, and in June 1866 Napoleon III agreed to withdraw. It was supposed to be a phased retreat, leaving Maximilian time to regroup, but in August fear of a rout made Napoleon III change his mind and withdraw his entire force all at once in early 1867. By the time the last French soldiers embarked in March, the *juaristas* had taken back almost all of Mexico.

At this point a chorus of voices were urging Maximilian to abdicate and leave. The Empress Carlota had already left to try to rally European support, been universally rejected, and suffered a nervous breakdown. Instead of following her, Maximilian took command of the remaining troops and headed north to Querétaro in full charro regalia. The plan was to meet there with his other forces, commanded by Miramón and Mejía, and push the *juarístas* back north. He ended up penned up in the city with ten thousand troops, facing forty thousand Mexicans armed with American guns under the competent Mariano Escobedo. Maximilian waited for conservative reinforcements from Mexico City that never arrived, and began running out of ammunition. His forces melted down the theater roof to cast bullets and the church bells to make shells. Escobedo cut the water, but supplies of champagne endured; supplies of meat failed, and the imperial chef began serving roast mule and cat pie. On May 15, after a two-month siege, Maximilian surrendered. On June 21 Porfirio Díaz took Mexico City and the war was over.[76]

The last edition of the *Diario del Imperio* unintentionally reflects the gaudy delusion, ambition, and pathos of the regime. Almost the entire first page is taken up once again by a list of decorations, headed by the Imperial Order of Guadalupe, a vulgarly large but impeccably Mexican medal that Maximilian invented. A short note reassures readers that there have been no military operations in Mexico City "up until now, which is nine in the morning." A bookshop advertises copies of the artilleryman's handbook. A compelling scientific disquisition, courtesy of the *Sociedad Mexicana de Geografía y Estadística*, expounds the health benefits of eating horseflesh. Less reassuring is an advertisement for cut-price do-it-yourself burials:

> Funeral Carriage. Quite a good one is available in the Hospice of the Poor: people who might need it for carrying cadavers can present themselves to the said establishment. There they will also find wax candles and all necessary for their ends.[77]

The same day as the paper came out, June 19, 1867, a firing squad executed the Emperor Maximilian on a hill outside Querétaro. He died after the formality of a trial with a quiet stylishness, accompanied by Generals Mejía and Miramón, shouting, *"Viva México, viva la Independencia,"* and leaving behind a note of encouragement to his executioner, President Juárez. In following through with the shooting, Juárez ignored pleas for clemency from Europe's monarchs and the US secretary of state. The night before the execution he explained himself to Princess Salm-Salm, née Agnes Le Clerq, a New Englander who came to Mexico with an Austrian princeling named Félix and a lapdog named Jimmy. She fell to her knees sobbing for the emperor's life; a damp-eyed president told her,

> Even if all the kings and all the queens were in your place I couldn't pardon his life. It's not me who takes it away from him; it's the people and the law that demand his death; were I not to follow the will of the people, then they themselves would take his life.[78]

Juárez knew quite well what he was doing in killing a European prince, something simply not done; it was a second declaration of Mexican Independence.[79]

The aftermath saw a purge of conservatives as a political group and some reconciliation with liberals on an individual, nonpolitical level. In 1870 Juárez declared a general amnesty for imperialists; Porfirio Díaz quietly paid for a small monument to Maximilian. The Church that had pushed Mexicans to the fatal last step in polarization was excised from politics. Its social power remained largely intact: There was a church-building campaign in the Center-West, *damas católicas* continued to be important models of pious discipline, and Díaz, after writing a secret letter renouncing the Laws of the Reforma, secured his first wife the last rites and his second a blessing.[80] All were subordinate, however, to a new liberal consensus that enshrined the disliked Constitution of 1857 as revealed truth and gave liberals ownership of a new Mexican nationalism. The war against the United States had inspired only a measure of national unity alongside dejection, self-doubt, and regional fratricide. The war against the French was an unambiguous victory, and the people who waged it remembered what they had achieved with ceremonies that stretched from Cinco de Mayo to village concerts by brass bands of veterans. To be patriotic was to be liberal.

Juárez enjoyed unparalleled power as the hero of two wars, personally honest, an indigenous man who led Mexico against both conservatives and foreigners, overcoming steep racial, domestic, and geopolitical odds en route. He founded schools and promoted press freedoms; he also centralized government, tried to neutralize Congress, and set up a system of *jefes políticos*, centrally appointed officials who ran multiple municipalities, downgraded the democracy of the municipio libre, and drew on rurales to impose their rule. He and his successor, Sebastián Lerdo de Tejada, governed with extraordinary powers, constitutional guarantees suspended, for nearly half their ten years in power, struggling against the serial revolts of disenchanted veterans.[81] His own election wins were clean; those of other elected officials murky. In the 1871 election his win over the other great winner of the French Intervention, the young general Porfirio Díaz, was tentative enough for Díaz to claim fraud and rebel.

Juárez was the first authoritarian liberal, and had he lived long enough might have reelected himself serially and reaped the ensuing discredit. Instead he died of a heart attack while in office in 1872. He left behind numerous social conflicts. Early in his first presidency there was a revolt in Chalco, just outside the capital, of workers who called themselves communists. The peasantry who fought for him remained the great losers of liberal reform, their land under unprecedented threat from predatory hacendados and land companies. They continued to pay a disproportionate amount of what taxes were paid, and on the peripheries continued to be subject to debt peonage. President Lerdo de Tejada wrote the law that permitted the new land monopolization. He made himself unpopular enough that a second Díaz rising, the Plan de Tuxtepec of 1876, toppled him with a manifesto that twinned a long list of Lerdo's supposed crimes with a single, gripping, democratic proposal: no reelection of presidents or governors. It worked, the last pronunciamiento, and installed a government with the charisma and competence (and favorable context) to settle the poisonous London Debt. In 1888 a new Mexican bond issue met enthusiastic takers; by the end of the century the bonds were some of the most sought-after in the world, a final recognition of Mexican sovereignty.[82]

The history of nineteenth-century Mexico could be written in terms of serial political failure, a people culturally fit only for token elections and rapacious generals. It frequently was written in like terms, particularly by foreign politicians and intellectuals. But it might more realistically be written as one of the longest independence struggles in history, and one that ended up successful against considerable odds. Mexico after 1867 developed economically with startling speed, in part because of rich resources and foreign investors, but also through political astuteness, hard work, and rugged individualism. Politically, generations of Mexicans struggled to make their votes count, to put flesh on enduring democratic ideals. Their struggles translated onto paper: The constitutions of 1810, 1824, 1857, and 1917 were among the most radically progressive of their times. In Mexico many believed firmly in citizenship, and when it was difficult to exercise it in politics, they found solace in civic associations that pursued everything from education to gardening tips. For all the enduring discrimination and marginalization of minorities, tantamount to genocide in the far North, nineteenth-century Mexico was far more racially fluid and messy, de facto and de jure, than both its European and North American counterparts. In Mexico everyone, whatever their skin color, was technically a citizen. This was not verbiage: Mexicans elected the first Black and only indigenous presidents in North American history.

Such a telling is not a rewrite of the classic story of liberal nationalism, one of sacrifice ending in the triumph of a single mestizo nation. There was never any such thing. Some indigenous peoples hung on to a separate culture and identity, as did some descendants of the creoles. Some people in the former New Spain, from Maya peasants to frenchified Mexico City elites, tried to opt out of or were embarrassed at being Mexican. Yet Mexico, despite its uniquely dangerous neighborhood—in a Porfirian cliché, "so far from God, so close to the United States"—ended up moving beyond imperial predation to become one of the most sovereign and modern of postcolonial countries. It didn't just happen.

Part Four

Hedonism and Revolution

1877–1940

Chapter Twelve

Trains, Opera, and Misery

It was, they did declare, *quite* as beautiful as Switzerland. And safe, too: The towns and highways of Mexico were as safe as those of any civilized country. And the people! Innately kind, unfailingly polite, as minutely ceremonious as the French, their main aim in life to be *simpático*. Rather dapper mounted policemen with jingling spurs, swords, and rifles had made highway robbery a thing of the past, almost. While there may still have been beggars and thieves in towns, the really degenerate ones were foreign. "As a rule," the enthusiastic guidebook went on, "the Mexican thief is not as malevolent as his foreign brother; if possible he prefers to rob without bodily injury to his victim."[1]

By the end of the nineteenth century Americans could easily see some of Mexico for themselves, for five cents if they went to a movie theater to see *Wash Day in Mexico*. But what that film's publicity called this "quaint and wonderful foreign country" wasn't too expensive to get to in person, because it lay "at the very gateway of our southern frontier."[2] Steamships ran from New York, New Orleans, and Galveston to Veracruz, from San Francisco to Acapulco, but it was the new trains that really counted for bringing foreigners into Mexico. By 1911 some twelve thousand miles of railway lines crossed the US border at nine different places, stretching improbably across deserts, highlands, and gorges all the way from California to Yucatán. Tourists, investors, and the creative types who lured them southward were coming in increasing numbers. It was easy and it was cheap; three or four dollars a day could see you right. The capital's Hotel Gillow offered both an elevator and rooms for one peso—fifty cents—a night. Mexico, after twenty years of order and progress, was shiny and new in some ways; quaint and exotic in others; modern and recognizable enough to get around, old and different enough to romanticize; "in some respects . . . highly civilized," in others "utterly barbaric"; in one publicity phrase, an "old new land."[3]

The exotica lay even in banalities, exotic just for lying on the other side of the border. *Wash Day in Mexico* lived up to its exciting name, consisting of twenty-five seconds of jerky, thirty-frames-per-second footage of women washing clothes in Durango.[4] Scenes like this might easily be found in the US. But other images were different, exciting, distinctively Mexican, sent to exhibitions abroad, printed in quantity for souvenirs. Carefully posed photographs of lower-class archetypes went down well: street sellers, fruit vendors, barefoot peasants, all doing appropriate things on mocked-up stage sets. National clichés went down well too: the *china poblana*, a pale mestiza in rather racy petticoats; the charro, a cowboy in tight trousers, a differently shaped hat, and glittery silver braid. The photographs were mass-market equivalents of colonial pinturas de castas, and like the pinturas de castas they were technically polished. ("Photographic art in Mexico is remarkably advanced," crowed one exhibition catalogue, and so it was.)[5] Bringing the black-and-whites home made tourists sophisticates. Couth visitors had books about Cortés and ruins and volcanoes to read, works like the stirring *History of the Conquest of Mexico* by the near-blind William Prescott, or the *Incidents of Travel in Yucatan* of John Lloyd Stephens, bushwhacking, ruin-hunting pioneer. Philip Terry, the author of the most popular guidebook, pieced together a lovingly detailed hotchpotch of train timetables, hotel prices, restaurants, travelers' tips, popular mores, and history, all punctuated by doggerel. Turn-of-the-century travelers had a lot of inspiration with which to plan and dream.

And it was all so remarkably undemanding, on the main routes at least. Food was recognizable: The unadventurous could eschew the local stuff and enjoy cosmopolitan suppers rustled up by European immigrants, posh ones at that. In Mexico City the great French chef Sylvain Daumont served *soupe à l'espagnole, boeuf à la valencienne, poisson à la princesse*, and *vol-au-vent à la truffe noire*. The best hotels were top-notch. Spanish, needless to say, was unnecessary. The better class of café used French or English, and there were two English-language newspapers, *Two Republics* and *The Mexican Herald*. Americans unsure of what to do could leaf through one or the other; if dusk was drawing in they might make out the adverts under an electric streetlamp, and if nothing appealed they might take a taxicab back to the hotel, confident that they would not be ripped off for any "time spent in repairing a machine by the wayside."[6]

Leaving the beaten path was a different matter. In 1901 the intrepid Mrs. Ethel Alec-Tweedie (author of *Through Finland in Carts*, *A Girl's Ride in Iceland*, and *A Winter Jaunt to Norway*) fustigated the uncleanliness of Mexico's more tropical hotels and advised her readers that "a rubber bath is a source of constant joy."[7] In a market town in the Chiapas jungle the default lodging for all comers, whether American, Swede, Pole, Spanish, Chinese, or Black, was underneath the arches of the plaza's colonnade. But such men were there for business of one hard-nosed sort or another.[8] Other jungles were for the frivolous, adventurous, or better-heeled. In Mérida one could stay in the pleasant-ish Hotel Moromuzo, whose American owner treated his compatriots to beds instead of hammocks. Moving east by (admittedly delay-prone) train his guests rode through a countryside of flowers and the odd pyramid, yellow butterflies boiling out of the bushes, pausing at interesting Indian towns "with curious Maya names," finding the station vendors' tamales unlovable but the cheesy tortillas rather good. Moving beyond the vendors' greasy reach, anyone with a letter of introduction—or possibly just the gift of gab—could mix with small-town politicians, doctors, priests, and the odd shaman.[9]

Really adventurous travelers could get off at the village of Muna as dusk fell, beg a bed for the night—there was no hotel—hire a nag and a guide, and ride the rest of the way to the Maya pyramids of Uxmal. There they could ponder the tricky choice of whether to scramble to the top or just contemplate the work of the noble savage at his dead finest. Graffiti on the walls of Uxmal had early visitors doing just that, at length. One F. Carillo dawdled with an unusually sententious vandalism, scratching into the stonework, "Poor travelers! Silent admiration alone remains to you before the eloquent antiquity of these ruins."[10] Admiring the eloquent antiquity of more remote ruins was even more of a slog: Chichén Itzá was a hard three-day trip from Mérida. Over the state line in Chiapas the going was the roughest of all: Getting to the palace complex at Palenque called for guides, tents, food, several days on steamships, and two more on horseback through the "almost suffocating heat" of the forest. And that was in the dry season. Travel in the rainy season was simplified by the fact that floods, ticks, and mosquitoes put indigenous guides off from even trying.[11]

The more touristed North and center of Mexico did a brisker trade in the indigenous past. By 1910 some of their great pre-Hispanic cities were partially excavated, linked to the outside world, and open for business. The greatest of them all, Teotihuacán, was only an hour and a half from Mexico City, the train stopping a mile from the colossal Pyramids of the Sun and Moon, an electric tramline planned to make things even easier. Near Oaxaca City sat Monte Albán, dull but accessible by bicycle, and Mitla; a railroad line was in the works there, too, but in the interim horse-drawn carriages did the job and an on-site caretaker would unlock an underground passage and explain the ruins. The government was building a more convenient temple to the indigenous past in the National Museum (another of the Emperor Maximilian's indigenista creations) to which Leopold Batres, the Inspector of Monuments, hauled in materials from across Mexico: He moved the sixteen-ton Coatlicue statue from Teotihuacán on a portable section of railway track, covering 250 meters a day.[12]

Mexico had a lot of the valuable commodity of difference, and the comparative advantages of proximity and antiquity. It wasn't just pyramids; three centuries' worth of colonial churches, monasteries, palaces, and plazas were gripping for Americans whose own colonial past hadn't left much in the way of architecture or the arts. The mainstream draws were much the same as a century later: cheap city life in exotic locales, ecotourism, adventure sports, sex, and romantic vistas. Only beach tourism remained to be invented: Until the second half of the twentieth century even Acapulco remained a village, and the population of swampy Cancún hovered around a hundred. All railway lines led to Mexico City, but en route they passed through geographical melodrama: Copper Canyon in Chihuahua, the gorges and forests on the climb from Veracruz, the great cavern of la Catedral on the Tampico line. Another train took mountaineers to the foot of Popocatépetl, the larger of the two active volcanos on the valley rim, where one early climber started his ascent in "an ordinary heavy business-suit" and green glass goggles. (Summit achieved, he tobogganed down on a rush mat.)[13] Hunters pursued the luckless mountain goat of the Northwest and the elusive puma of the South. Fishermen in Veracruz went after sharks, "long man-eaters," taking care not to join the numerous ranks of the boating dead. ("Fatalities among fishermen who come from the interior towns for an outing are numerous.") More passive sportsmen ogled cockfights and bullfights. Even the more culturally sensitive male travelers ogled the women, whom Terry found "charming" in Mexico City. In Yucatán life got steamier: "beautiful brunettes with rich complexions, fine black eyes and hair, superb teeth, and sweet, pensive expressions."[14]

Thus between 1876 and 1910 Mexico was redefined in foreign eyes. It exerted a cultured fascination over outsiders from Independence on, but it was a fascination reserved for a small number of the curious. In the 1880s political stability and trains on one side of the border met with disposable income, a middle class, a museumizing elite, and mass media on the other. The results spanned magazine articles, books, paintings, and photographs; a biodiversity of sightseers that included antiquarians, investors, prospectors, grifters, and bums, but above all tourists. The old gringo disdain for Mañana-Land endured—one book of the 1910s was called just that—but it was joined by a new enthusiasm for the fun and heritage of a different Mexico.[15] It was evident in tourism earnings, infrastructure, and hyperbole. An altered relationship was visible in the US, too, where architects in the 1890s created a pastiche of colonial Mexican building, the Mission Revival style, and deployed it (in the sincerest form of flattery) in new railway stations and schools across the Southwest. When wealthy Mexicans imported it to build their own restaurants and mansions the circle was complete.[16]

The shock of the new hit Mexicans above all. In the late nineteenth century two institutions marked any country as a place of sophisticates, fully paid-up members of the bourgeois world: train stations and opera houses. Mexicans had both. Even provincial cities had railway stations; far-off Mérida had four. As for opera, in North America only New Yorkers listened to as much. As early as 1876 the wealthier citizens of Mexico City were hearing everything from Offenbach to

Verdi. Capitalinos patronized a dedicated opera season, and some of the global stars of opera came to the Teatro Colón. Like most of their contemporaries Mexicans weren't into Wagner's marathons, feeling that four and a half hours of Teutonic pomposity wasn't as much fun as Germans thought. Yet the odd snatch of even that made it to their ears: In 1904 the Gran Café y Restaurante de Chapultepec put on a dinner concert that included an excerpt from *Tannhäuser*. The same year a developer laid the foundation stone of a dedicated opera house.[17]

In the provinces other buildings of modern life went up. In Oaxaca citizens complemented their stunning baroque architecture with a Parisian belle époque playhouse, the Teatro Macedonio; in Tlaxcala the Teatro Xicohtencatl acquired electric lighting.[18] It wasn't all fun: Key markers of progress included modern hospitals and factories. Even smokestacks were objects of pride to one writer, who enthused about how they dignified Monterrey, an industrial city that sprang out of next to nowhere.[19] Industry paid for a new swagger in government buildings. The burghers of Orizaba, home to a textile and coffee boom, got in touch with Gustave Eiffel (shortly after he'd finished a tower in Paris) and contracted him for an art nouveau town hall, importing steel plates from Belgium and dragging them three-quarters of a vertical mile from sea level. The ascent alone cost 10,000 pesos a ton.[20] Outside the elegant arches, trams completed a cosmopolitan vision.

For modern city life was about mobility as much as static magnificence. Orizaba was just one of the places transformed by electric streetcars; by 1910 any city worth its salt had a tramway. The Mexico City system notched up seventy million rides a year. Trams weren't wholly modern; the "indigenous and poor classes" were regularly killed or maimed, despised by their betters as too thick to judge their speed. A certain lack of savoir faire went on inside too, elites held, with second-class carriages stuffed with ill-smelling plebs.[21] While a reasonably hygienic first class was tolerable, the better sort of city dweller was an individualist. In 1895 a young businessman brought the first automobile to Mexico City, a French Delaunay-Belleville that could do ten miles an hour, and by 1910 some thousand motorists were enjoying newly smooth streets, colonial cobblestones going under to asphalt from the American oil fields in Veracruz.[22] And finally there was the recently invented bicycle—accessible, beloved, but also, like the tram, misunderstood

Cyclist in Mexico City (1899).

and threatening. It wasn't just that people walked under bicycles, which they did. It was also about illicit sex, which rubber tires clearly encouraged. Romantics could pedal away for quick trysts in the nearby countryside, perhaps on the longstanding lovers' lane that was the way to Xochimilco. The newfangled machines brought women out in bloomers and sports gear that some found ugly but others rather hot. They also seemed to encourage *marimachas*, unsettling new women who to fin de siècle eyes looked queer, or at least sapphic. And even among the straight, bicycles, it was feared, might—like trains—bring women to unhealthy solo orgasm.[23]

Thankfully other sorts of new fun were more decorous. There was a lasting passion for roller-skating—a pursuit of "respectability, morality, and healthiness," in one journalist's words—that took off in the 1880s. (Enthusiasm was such that skaters moved from custom-built rinks to the pavement, and the Mexico City chief of police ended up banning them.) Baseball came in with American sailors, railwaymen, and miners and quickly grew two leagues. Cornish miners brought soccer with them to Pachuca (as well as Cornish pasties, which crossbred with chilis and beans and went native) and in 1902 they too founded a league. Both had the huge advantage of being street sports, infrastructure an optional extra, and soccer ended up a significant part of Mexican identity. For the less active, another key part of Mexican identity began when in 1898 Salvador Toscano Barragán opened the Cinematógrafo Lumière—four years before California got its first movie theater—where ten centavos bought capitalinos a brief burst of flickery magic. There was even a YMCA; President Díaz himself laid the foundation stone.[24]

And for the monied who loved shopping, the pinnacle of evolution was the new department store, made possible by cutting-edge construction techniques, globalization, and disposable income. The Palacio de Hierro, opened in Mexico City in 1891, consisted of five stories of iron and steel, elevators, and goods from across the world. It would have graced New York, one columnist opined.[25] Like all department stores it was both functional and seductive, and the class of people who might raise eyebrows inside got vicarious pleasure outside through the display windows. These, moreover, could be admired day and night because the store acquired six thousand of the revolutionary light bulbs. By 1910 about a million of them lit up the capital. Electric bulbs weren't an unalloyed good: Women were unsettled by the cruel brightness that penetrated their foundation, some men censorious at better-lit bosoms. But they opened up a genuinely new world of a seeable and safer night.[26]

It wasn't just the big city; wealthier towns shared in the joys of the new capitalist Mexico. In southern Veracruz the townspeople of San Andrés Tuxtla got rich through hard work and global events: They planted copious tobacco on rich volcanic soil just as world demand grew and Cuban production collapsed, annihilated by that country's own War of Independence. Their town became a pleasant place where they might drink ice-cold Mexican beer—perhaps one of the nationalist brews, Indio or Victoria, perhaps the futuristic Dos Equis, the *XX* standing for the twentieth century, perhaps one of Veracruz's many own brands—before heading off to buy French cognac or English cashmere or European pianos or American Smith & Wessons. In Michoacán the people of San José de Gracia, traditional cattle ranchers, were less flashy; they would be using candles and kerosene for some time to come. But they were inside the new world too, as traveling salesmen began making the fifteen-mile trek from the nearest railway station with the staples of an easier life: Singer sewing machines for women, Aspirin for hangovers.[27]

Three interwoven ideologies were supposed to help Mexicans make sense of it all. The overarching one was liberalism, which was to replace unproductive Catholic reaction with utilitarian order and progress. The motto of the Escuela Nacional Preparatoria summed it up in those words: *AMOR, ORDEN Y PROGRESO*, love, order and progress. It was a trope across the contemporary world: The motto on the Brazilian national flag read *ORDEM E PROGRESSO*, the words stretching up toward the Southern stars, while the Germans enjoyed the motto *ORDNUNG MUSS SEIN*. Liberalism encompassed political stability, science, development, and industrialization: catching up. It demanded the second ideology of mestizaje, a pride in hybridity. This too was not unique: The idea was spreading outside Mexico in works like the Cuban José Martí's classic essay, "Nuestra América," "Our America." Mestizaje was intrinsically modern. And it necessitated a third ideology, *indigenismo*, the sine qua non claim that Mexico was exceptionally enriched and not degraded by its indigenous past. Mexicans had lived in sophisticated cities and empires centuries before the conquistadors arrived.

What Mexicans who didn't politick beyond the patria chica or write thought of each set of ideas depended on where they were in terms of geography, class, and ethnicity. Most northerners didn't think much of indigenismo; their history with indigenous peoples centered on brutal warfare with hard-riding Apache and Comanche warriors. The Nahua and Mixtecs of the central highlands or the Blacks of the southern coasts were unlikely consumers of mestizaje; the powerful families that traditionally fleeced them were generally white, stories of droit du seigneur commonplace. The entire coast of Guerrero was supposedly run by one American and three Spanish families, lording it with violence over impoverished peasants. Many guerrerense peasants were admixtures of indigenous, Black, and Spanish ancestry; that did not lead to a belief in the virtues of mestizaje. As for Yucatecos, they didn't think they were Mexican in the first place. Indigenismo had little appeal to many whites; some espoused a counter-ideology of *hispanismo*, an idolization of the Spanish past. A lot of people didn't think of ideologies at all; they had to be led toward them by earnestly nationalist rulers.

It was not that liberalism and mestizaje and indigenismo lacked the raw emotional content that moves people. In the countryside liberalism's core lay in the popular political freedoms that came with independence. Peasant and indigenous liberals cared deeply about local elections, traditional leaders, the independence of the patria chica, the broader independence of the countryside against outsiders, whether capitalinos, conservatives, or foreign soldiers. Patriotic liberalism happened when self-conscious citizens of the municipio libre met with collective suffering and a clear villain. Sometimes the villain was the village next door. At other times communities that disliked each other in peacetime formed alliances in wartime and made entire regions liberal strongholds. They had fought together for their immediate homelands and something called Mexico. Their national leaders who talked about it might still be friends of friends or compadres or second cousins twice removed. A combination of legends, bands, parades, and National Guardsmen, their officers elected, their arms still to hand, kept peasants inside a liberal, and hence automatically Mexican, fold.[28]

To get misty-eyed about mestizaje was harder. Yet the majority of Mexicans were by now mestizo, and so the reality of demographics and the threat of indigenous secession—away from the frontiers, not very likely—made celebrating the fact important.[29] In the 1870s Mexican leaders decided that after three anticolonial wars they had enough material for a viable liberal nationalism that would combine glorious victimhood, the classical indigenous past, and the progressive present. The tricky logic of race dictated that this new nationalism stress Mexico as the world's greatest melting pot, its people (as one history textbook said) "a single great family"; and so writers and politicians turned to inventing sentiment in favor of those whom their northern neighbors wrote off as mongrel half-breeds.[30]

The best creators were very successful. Several literary blockbusters of the time were written by that multitalented lawyer, soldier, and politician Riva Palacio, and they hammered the point home. One, the bodice-ripping *Martín Garatuza*, made the point as explicitly as could be: The last Aztec emperor, Cuauhtémoc ("Falling Eagle"), ends up in bed with the Spanish Isabel Carbajal. On their fertile last night together his postcoital musings turn, naturally enough, to state formation, and he tells her,

> The shadow of the eagle covered the dove, and a hope was born for my line and for my people; man of a new race, perhaps his descendants will break the chains of his brothers . . . if my name dies, my blood will make this earth fertile, because from my blood and your blood, Isabel, heroes could be born.[31]

The message was unmistakable to the readers who devoured it in weekly installments: Mexico was always meant to be a mestizo republic, born out of pre-Hispanic glory, Spanish seduction, and the sacrifice of centuries of war against empires.

To the same end Riva Palacio also produced serious popular history. In 1880 he lost his shot at the presidency but won as a consolation prize a government contract to immortalize Mexico's triumph over the French. He used the money instead to assemble an exhaustive five-volume history of Mexico since the fourteenth century. It was a Darwinian epic of linear human progress that led readers from the dark origins of the Aztecs through to Mexico's real declaration of independence under the liberals. The purpose of *México a través de los siglos* was spelled out clearly in the pitch, which promised the government

> the narration of the various evolutions of a society that through great difficulties consummates the evolutions which bring it to occupy a worthy place among the ranks of the most enlightened of peoples.[32]

The prose was poor but the message was clear. *México a través de los siglos* was scientific history as well as romantic epic. And it was, the work uniting the most important liberal experts on archaeology, colonial legislation, military history, and writers of literature. Contemporary ideas of what constituted a nation centered on a French work, Ernest Renan's *What Is a Nation?*, which rejected biology in favor of shared modern culture. Riva Palacio argued back, listing the colonial castas and arguing that they combined into an entirely new race. "All these castes were like streams born from foreign sources," he said, which lost "the memory of their origins" and became "a single current and a new race to form the Mexican nationality."

For mestizaje to work, indigenismo had to work too: Modern Mexicans' most numerous ancestors were indigenous. That they were worthy forebears was proven not just in cities, codices, and massive buildings, but in their very physiques, the hairlessness and the comparatively large skulls that craniometrists recorded. Big heads meant big brains, scientific consensus held.[33] The blood of a philosopher-king like Nezahualcóyotl coursing through your veins was as good as that of Socrates, an idea that creole elites had promoted under the Spanish.[34] Not only national figures like Riva Palacio proselytized for the Indian. In Tlaxcala the wily indigenous governor Próspero Cahuantzi commissioned a reproduction of his state's first history, the *Lienzo de Tlaxcala*. He too went for funds to the central government and had the advantage that he could give speeches in Nahuatl as well as Spanish, which he did deliberately even when facing uncomprehending audiences.[35]

Indigenismo was more than just the knowing cultural politics of the powerful, though; in some places it was genuinely popular. When Mrs. Alec-Tweedie rode through Morelos to Xochicalco (fondly remembering "a happy ride" in Iceland), she was met at the ruins by a delegation of villagers. Their young spokesman told her in Nahuatl (he spoke Spanish, he said, but that was "a foreign tongue"), "You have come from a land of great civilization to visit our wild country, but Señora, you must remember that five thousand years ago, when England was unknown, our ancestors raised these ruins."[36] He himself came from Tetlama, a tiny village nearby, whose people had already made clear that their collective pride was more than rhetorical. A few years earlier Leopold Batres, the Inspector of Monuments who dragged the earth goddess Coatlicue from Teotihuacán, came for Xochicalco's equivalent, a one-ton effigy of Tonantzin. Batres came, unwisely enough, without his customary armed escort of soldiers or rurales. A Tetlama elder gave him a stiff warning; the eighty villagers watched him haul their statue away and then heaved her back to their church, two and half miles away, to hide next to a codex. They seemed otherwise willing citizens of Mexico—when Mrs. Alec-Tweedie came they welcomed the governor enthusiastically—but it needed to be a Mexico that respected their own local indigenous past.[37]

For most people, both Nahuatl and racial science were incomprehensible. Parades and monuments were not, and so the government invested heavily in them. The new ideas of what it meant to be Mexican helped politicians conjure into being a whole new patriotic calendar, saint's days for the secular. They had a lot to celebrate beyond Independence Day or Cinco de Mayo; in one month alone the people of Guerrero were ordered to observe nine public holidays, including the birthdays of Morelos and Díaz.[38] Celebrants had aides-mémoire in the government gazette, but nationalist ceremonies were also popular: In one village a roof collapsed under the weight of gawkers at the Independence Day parade. And popularity was backed by state funding. In Mexico City massive crowds were nourished by free tram rides, the beginnings of a long tradition of shipping in audiences for political performances.

This was the final piece of a new nationalism: the foreign technology that underpinned its creation and dissemination. The British trams that brought in the masses from working-class suburbs were driven by electricity produced by German Siemens generators. American light bulbs fostered nighttime renditions of the Grito de Dolores. The national newspapers that coordinated it all were printed on high-speed rotary presses, capable of producing tens of thousands of copies per day. The government organized state funerals, more than a hundred of them between 1876 and 1911, for dead heroes who caught the train from distant states to be reburied in the capital.[39] The progress that nationalist stories aspired to explain also enabled rulers to explain them. And at the center of those stories were the great men of Mexican history, and key among those great men was the current president, General Porfirio Díaz, a man influential enough to give his name to the entire period: the Porfiriato.

Díaz presided for thirty-four years, from 1877 to 1911. Foreigners fawned over Díaz; in 1908 the US secretary of state gushed:

> No one lives to-day that I would rather see than President Diaz. If I were a poet I would write poetic eulogies. If I were a musician I would compose triumphal marches. If I were a Mexican I should feel the steadfast loyalty of a lifetime could not be too much in return for

> the blessings that he had brought to my country. As . . . an American who loves justice and liberty and hopes to see their reign among mankind progress and strengthen and become perpetual, I look to Porfirio Díaz, the President of Mexico, as one of the great men to be held up for the hero worship of mankind.[40]

By that stage many Mexicans would disagree. For decades, however, Díaz's career seemed ample justification for a long stay in power.

He was born in highland Oaxaca in 1830, to a Mixtec mother and a mestizo muleteer, that classic job for the upwardly mobile. But his father died when Díaz was three, leaving him to be raised first by his mother, then a seminary, and finally the liberal Institute of Arts and Sciences in Oaxaca City. In 1855 he won a provincial government position in the district of Ixtlán, back in his highlands, where he set up a National Guard militia of about fifty Mixtecs and two hundred Zapotecs, fought against the conservatives, and became the political boss of his state. The war against the French gave him his chance as a commander and he knew how to take it. Díaz played a key role in the Mexican victory at the Battle of Puebla and reveled in it. A letter to his sister spelled it out: "I have never had a more pleasurable day . . . I pray to God that I do not go crazy with excitement."[41] He fought successfully through the next five years and then, a national figure, spent the decade after the war's end maneuvering for the presidency. He lost three elections in a row, those of 1867, 1871, and 1876. The fourth, however, was his after he rebelled in Oaxaca, promising radical term limits for everyone from mayor to president under the slogan *no reelección*, no reelection. That said, he reelected himself seven times.

Other numbers of his time were likewise impressive: the miles of railway track laid and telegraph wire strung, the thousands of tons of minerals dug out or mahogany cut down, the teeming schoolchildren in far-off schools. Near the outset of his reign Mexico set up a dedicated ministry of statistics and exported its numbers in government reports, investor brochures, and international expositions—a game Díaz personally oversaw with excellent results: At the 1889 Paris Exposition Mexico nabbed the prime spot under the Eiffel Tower to show off, among other things, Bodo von Glümer's *Cuadro estadístico* and the pickled head of an Apache chief.[42] Many of the government's numbers were massaged or fictitious. As one satirist put it, "One of the most important tasks the dictator set himself was to cook up statistics for the benefit of the world at large . . . Not even Denmark could boast such statistics." The same satirist pointed out the difference between schools that taught and schoolhouses that didn't, indigenous children who spoke Spanish and those who sang the anthem uncomprehending to impress visitors, and telegraph wires that stayed on poles and those that ended up repurposed as decorations.[43] On paper the government tended to have a more balanced budget than in reality.[44]

Other statistics were less shaky. Railway lines were either there or not. Mines, oil refineries, factories, fields of waving sugarcane, and smart hotels were incontrovertible proof of a changed and booming economy. The American Smelting and Refining Company set up five foundries. By 1908, 65 mines were operational in Chihuahua, 208 in Sonora, the majority American-owned. The first steel mill in Latin America opened, its existence presumably verified for Wall Street in one of the lushly illustrated, handsomely bound shareholder reports that larger companies printed. Mexico was the destination of half of all American overseas investment. That industrial output had doubled seemed perfectly reasonable. The claim that the largest textile mill, Río Blanco, had six thousand looms could be easily verified. So could the governor of Veracruz's claim that his state produced forty-one different beers, provided the verifier had a decent liver.[45]

The claim that GDP per capita trebled over Díaz's thirty years might be open to questions of methodology, but bond yields were beyond argument. Mexico went into the 1880s with a substantial and unserviced foreign debt. It returned to the sovereign debt market in 1888 and by 1904 was getting credit at 4 percent. That most investment was international could be seen as a lack of domestic finance. It could also be seen as a vote of confidence, with US investors choosing Mexican national bonds on a par with their own municipal bonds, which suffered a catastrophic wipeout in 1873 and took years to make it down to 4 percent. Díaz was obsessed with bond yields and cut canny deals with the foreign banks that issued them; once creditworthy, he followed a strategy of divide and rule, never using the same syndicate of banks twice.[46]

This was part of a broader strategy to achieve as much diversity in trading partners as possible, minimizing any one country's leverage as far as was consonant with having the United States as a neighbor. The Americans would have the major mines of the North, Daniel Guggenheim sitting down with Díaz in person to negotiate huge concessions for lead, copper, gold, and silver mining and steel production.[47] The German Bleichröders would have the upper hand in finance, and the French would have a sizeable share of industry and commerce. A single Irish-American, Thomas Braniff, had such commanding positions in Veracruz textiles, Monterrey steel, and Mexico City paper that it was near impossible, they said on his death, to start up a business without his say-so.[48] The main firms in Gulf Coast oil, construction, and infrastructure were British, the obvious counterweight to the US. A single British businessman, Weetman Pearson, began by digging the thirty-mile drainage canal that was supposed to keep Mexico City dry; went on to build docks, tramways, water, sewage, and electricity systems; and founded El Águila Oil, dominant until the 1930s.[49]

These were the rich immigrants. Mexico's stability and possibilities also drew tired and huddled masses from the United States, Asia, and southern Europe. Blacks from the South came escaping Jim Crow, Mormons from Utah and Arizona escaping anti-polygamy laws, Italians the *Risorgimento*, Afrikaners the Boer Wars, Chinese the rubble of the Taiping Rebellion, Levantines sectarian conflict or Ottoman conscription drives. Under the terms of the 1886 Immigration and Naturalization Law any foreigner who had spent two years in the country, worked for the government, or just owned property was eligible to become Mexican. The government was enthusiastic to be seen as more advanced on the question of racial discrimination than the neighbors; when an American hotel owner in Mexico City tried to exclude three Blacks, the press protested bitterly, noting that "on this point we are much more civilized than them."[50] And so Mexicans extended a formal welcome that stretched as far as citizenship, even for the resented Spanish and the despised Chinese.

Some individuals prospered whatever their race, in a more inclusive version of the American Dream. Domingo Kuri, a Lebanese Muslim, came to Mexico in 1903 and in short order bought a large house in the port of Veracruz ("Vrkrosh" to his Maronite compatriots) and became an honorary consul, helping Ottoman immigrants find kin and work. William Henry Ellis, born a slave in Texas, crossed the border, started trading in cotton and cattle hides, and was reborn Don Guillermo Enrique Eliseo, a magnate with offices on Wall Street next door to J. P. Morgan. In Mexico he mingled in high society while launching a colonization scheme for Blacks at Tlahualilo, a hacienda in the new Mexican cotton country of the Laguna, the seasonal lake lands of Durango and Coahuila.[51]

Organized settler schemes had been common enough since Independence, and most had failed, brochure utopias in unworkable places. The colony of eight hundred former sharecroppers at Tlahualilo failed inside the first eight months of 1895, disease, poverty, gang labor reminiscent to them of old plantations, and sheer foreignness launching an exodus back north. In similar fashion the Afrikaners who fled the Boer War to Chihuahua left within two years. In Sinaloa, Albert Kimsey Owen set up a quasi-socialist cooperative to build a railroad from the Gulf of California to the Río Grande, but the coastal lands he chose lacked fresh water and his pioneers opted first for privatization and then for abandonment.[52] The Sociedad Dante Cusi e Hijos, on the other hand, founded the town of Nueva Italia in Michoacán and prospered, with three thousand Italian colonists bringing in water from two rivers to become leading producers of cotton, melon, and rice. And in the greatest example of successful colonization, immigrants from the poor town of Barcelonnette in the South of France founded the largest textile factories and department stores in Mexico: Both Río Blanco and the Palacio de Hierro were Barcelonnette businesses.[53]

Neither the farm nor the factory would have made it without railroads. Nueva Italia could only make a profit on its rice thanks to the government-subsidized Camino de Fierro Nacional Mexicano that ran to Uruapan (the hacienda's own railroad covered the remaining twenty-five miles). The government-subsidized Ferrocarril Mexicano took cotton cheaply to the inefficient Río Blanco mill and brought tariff-protected cloth back out. The same line brought Parisian fashion from the Veracruz docks to the Palacio de Hierro's windows. Long-distance trade in even the despised pulque was profitable when freight prices were low, 500 percent lower than in the time of mule and cart. Trains didn't integrate everything: Travelers taking the Ferrocarril Mexicano down to Veracruz found that time there remained eleven minutes ahead of Mexico City and adjusted their watches accordingly. But

Metlatonoc Gorge railway bridge (1906).

while tourists were important, trains counted most in terms of markets and culture. The train was an extraordinary force for economic development and with it, in Porfirian minds, the spread of civilization.[54]

In 1908 one train took an American called John Kenneth Turner to Córdoba in Veracruz, where he saw ten men with their hands tied behind their backs on the platform. The next day he took another train south to El Hule in Oaxaca, where the same ten men got out of a second-class carriage and were escorted by two rurales into the tropical forest. On the third day he caught up with them in a village, and on the fourth day he rode behind them as they walked into the picturesque Valle Nacional, admiring "the tropical green above broken now and then by a ridge of gigantic gray rocks, below a level meadow and a little farther on the curving, feminine lines of that lovely river, the Papaloapan."[55] There at the San Cristóbal tobacco plantation he shook hands with the ten men and left. Turner was an undercover reporter; the prisoners were, in his words, slaves; his investigation, paid for by the democratic opposition and published in the last year of Díaz's presidency, was damning.

Turner was a socialist and something of a gun for hire. He later wrote a hatchet job on a popular revolutionary, in part for $9,000 paid by that revolutionary's enemies.[56] The men Turner accompanied weren't going to be paid; they were trying to sell their city shoes, because they were penniless and knew they were unlikely to ever leave the plantations. We're being sent to our death, the man selling his shoes told him. They weren't even peasants, but instead a mixed bag from the jailhouse in Pachuca, the mining town three hundred miles to the north. There were two debtors, two drunks, a loudmouth, a would-be rapist, a quarrelsome boy, two army musicians who had gone AWOL, and a clerk of the rurales. They had, another rural said, been sold to the planter by Díaz's man in Pachuca for fifty pesos each. The only reason Turner got access to stories like this was his cover, a wealthy American investor with letters establishing political clout. Without them he would never have got near the place.[57]

Turner's reports of tropical slavery in the new Mexican South found corroboration in unlikely circles. In Chiapas the largest rubber plant in the world and dozens of coffee plantations had recently opened in the Soconusco region, a remote strip of mountains and Pacific coastline on the Guatemala border. Further inland were the lumber camps of the Lacandón Jungle, whose trees met global demand for commodities from railway sleepers to French-polished mahogany tables. No one wanted to work in the dangerous lumber camps; German coffee planters didn't want to pay decent wages when prices fell; indigenous peasants generally didn't want to leave their villages; so debt peonage was rife. A state survey in 1897 found 31,500 indentured indigenous workers, almost certainly an undercount. Mexican reporters serially denounced Chiapas as a "slave state," its entire economy resting on "commerce in human flesh." Some politicians agreed and denounced it as well: In 1896 Governor Emilio Rabasa held a conference exploring ways to end debt peonage and in

1907 Governor Ramón Rabasa—his younger brother—outlawed it. Both initiatives failed, thanks in part to disapproval from Mexico City. The state's economy was, after all, doing very well as things were. Coffee alone was worth $2.5 million in a good year.[58]

Valle Nacional wasn't the only place Turner found what was effectively chattel slavery. In Yucatán he visited the haciendas where they cultivated henequen, a succulent whose leaves could be turned into bailing twine for the fast-growing international market. Indigenous laborers slept in barracks, where they were woken up at 3:45 in the morning for the day's fieldwork weeding or cutting leaves. They might see a punishment before heading off: Turner saw one worker stretched out across the back of a large Chinese man and flogged with a wet henequen whip until "the glistening back lost its rigidity and fell to quivering like a jellyfish." He and the others went off to work then, each family earning twelve and a half centavos a day paid in corn, beans, clothes, and blankets at the *tienda de raya*, or twenty-five centavos in credit against their debt. The prices made twelve and a half centavos a bare subsistence wage; working off the debt was impossible.[59]

Not all the workers were tied through debt. Two groups of indigenous people labored on the henequen haciendas: local Maya and Yaquis from Sonora. The Yaquis had not signed contracts. Formally they were prisoners of war, taken in the long-running guerrilla war in the Sierra del Bacatete on the Arizona border. For much of the nineteenth century they had been more or less independent, but by 1908 very few warriors remained, a few hundred holdouts trapped in the mountains between soldiers armed with Mausers and a closed border. Most made peace and went to work on the new haciendas. Others were deported, first the leaders and nobility, then anyone found without the new registration papers. In 1907 the government ordered all Yaqui north of Hermosillo to be taken, women and children included, even if they had papers; in 1908, all Yaqui irrespective of where they were and what they did in life.

The reason for the deportation was not so much political as economic. The Yaqui and Mayo had owned the rich sedimentary lands of the Yaqui River Valley for centuries. Under Díaz the railway arrived and with it, agribusiness, and in 1894 the government granted 1.3 million acres of the valley to the Sonora and Sinaloa Irrigation Company, whose majority shareholder was the governor, Luis Torres. He transferred the title to a company based in Los Angeles, Richardson Construction. The federal Secretary of Development, Colonization and Industry, Olegario Molina, likewise had a large stake in Richardson Construction; Colonel Francisco Cruz, in charge of deportations (with whom Turner shared a stateroom on a steamer taking Yaqui south), got ten dollars a head from selling them in Yucatán. The rest went to the secretary of war. When an old-school hacendado outside the valley complained that his workforce was disappearing, he was told, "It has been resolved that there shall not remain a single Yaqui within these districts." The process was enforced by mass arrests and exemplary violence; given high death rates and forced miscegenation on the plantations, calling it ethnic cleansing is charitable.[60]

Turner saw quite deliberately the extremes of the human cost of development, guided to the worst of places by his job and the Mexican

Lynched Yaqui (c. 1900).

opposition. He would have heard stories of Maya deportation as far as Cuba and of slavery had he gone to Tabasco and followed the woodcutters recruited there up to the Chiapas lumber camps: many forms of indebtment followed by forced labor in grim, often fatal, places.[61] And if he'd gone into the Chihuahua mountains he would have heard the landmark atrocity story of the tiny village of Tomóchic.

In Tomóchic a couple of hundred typically independent mountain men, *serranos*, faced a carpetbagger mayor who made them work his lands and those of a top government official for free. The mayor's friends went unpunished when their livestock grazed the cornfields of the unconnected; he upped taxes and executed five men who protested on fictitious charges of banditry. When the village protested he called for the army, and when the soldiers arrived the villagers rebelled. Encouraged by the visions of a local teenager, Santa Teresa de Cabora, by their schismatic church, and quietly by out-of-favor elites, they fought off the army for nine months.[62] Their cause was helped not just by sharpshooting and local knowledge but also by military incompetence on the other side; one drunken federal commander led a cavalry charge against a cornfield, cutting down the stalks he'd mistaken for enemies. In the end Díaz demanded "exemplary punishment" and sent in 1,200 veterans of the Apache campaigns. In five days' fighting they fired nearly 60,000 rifle rounds, drove the mountain men into a last stand in the church and cemetery, and killed all 217 of them. The remaining 114 villagers were marched away, almost all women and girls; the only males left were 7 teenagers and 18 boys.[63] The village was burned to the ground, bodies smoldering, the remains howled over by the villagers' dogs and eaten by their pigs.[64]

In most of Mexico the means used to acquire lands and labor were less terrible. Two laws, the Ley Lerdo of 1857 and the ley de terrenos baldíos of 1883, mandated that communal lands be sold off, and untitled lands split between those who surveyed them and the state. Communal and untitled lands were two categories that encompassed large swathes of rural, and especially indigenous, Mexico. These were legalisms that could be fought, and peasants had centuries of experience disputing their lands with hacendados. In places like the hills of central Veracruz villagers made a mockery of attempts to survey municipal borders and appropriate communal lands. Some used tricks, like continually moving the stone boundary markers called *mojoneras*. Others used courts, land invasions, and the threat of violence. The art of the riot didn't vanish; surveyors found death threats pinned to their doors. Yet the deck was stacked against countryfolk and a majority lost. In 1895 one in five Mexicans owned land. By 1910 that was one in fifty; 80 percent of rural communities and half the entire rural population were on hacienda lands. A single hacienda in Morelos, Santa Clara, enveloped twelve villages and covered 10 percent of the entire state.[65]

Even without the extremes of slavery and ethnic cleansing, dispossession rested on violence, a growing state's backing for both legal and illegal land seizures. Unlike their colonial predecessors, modern judges generally ruled against peasants; dissidents were jailed or deported to the tropics, where disease could deal with them. Illegally, companies and landowners forced villages to surrender their lands with weapons ranging from thugs to water. Oilmen in Veracruz sent their lawyers into the Huasteca to pressure indigenous farmers to sell up, and when they failed sent killers after them, men who burned houses and murdered holdouts. Standard Oil only managed to buy Cerro Azul, soon the world's richest oil well, from the owner Eufrosina Flores after her husband met a violent end.[66] In Tequesquitengo, Morelos, indigenous villagers had successfully defended their communal lands since the early seventeenth century; the neighboring hacendado diverted his irrigation water into the village and drowned it. The only thing left behind was the church spire, looming ghostly from the lake bottom to just below the surface, pushing through it in drier years.[67]

The aftermath of dispossession was violent too, as foremen imposed discipline on unhappy workers. Sugar workers in Morelos remembered Cuban overseers with nail-studded leather clubs and a Spanish foreman who horsewhipped an unruly peon and shot him for fighting back. Murder without euphemism was still a risk, but there were euphemized death sentences in the form of arrest and conscription to serve in Yucatán, where many didn't make it through tropical disease. In Veracruz locals were conscripted to fight massive oil fires; across the country families were pushed from their homes to face the poverty and early death of life on the road.

One man's story exemplifies that existence. Gonzalo Gómez was one more peasant—if he hadn't later met an anthropologist he'd have remained nameless to posterity—born in highland Michoacán in 1898. Like Porfirio Díaz he had a mestizo father and an indigenous mother, and like Porfirio Díaz he lost his father when he was young. Gómez, though, didn't go on to a seminary and the army; he never went to school at all, going instead on the road with his family as a migrant farmworker. They made several trips a year to the tierra caliente, the hot lowlands where sugar grew, where they lived in shacks and earned thirty-seven cents a day. These were dangerous places, and as he entered adolescence fever killed his mother and two elder brothers. Gómez went to the revolution and became good at charming, drinking with, and killing people. He got the nickname "Bones." He was lucky in some ways: He became one of the big men of his village, lived longer than most, and died of natural causes. His village, though, remained divided and extremely violent; he found himself on a different side from his only surviving brother and spent the rest of his life warring with him and his neighbors. And Gómez's was a happy ending in his village, a place called Naranja that never recovered from the arrival of outside money.[68]

Naranja, a Purépecha settlement in northern Michoacán, was the synecdoche of the dark side of the Porfiriato. It was a small indigenous community, surrounded by mountains, centered on communal lands and a medium-sized lake, Lake Zacapú. Carbohydrates came from the land, the typical intercropping of maize, squash, beans, and chili. Protein came from the water, for the *naranjeños* gathered clams and snails from the lakeshore marshes and caught shrimp, turtles, and waterfowl. They collected limited cash, enough to buy salt, iron tools, needles, and the occasional brandy from the outside world, by selling the baskets and mats that they wove from reeds. Naranjeños had no intrinsic objections to the world of buying and selling, but their main goal in life, as for peasants across Mexico, was to guarantee that they and their neighbors grew enough food to feed their families between harvests.

In 1881 a surveyor arrived. Surveyors were well-connected military types and members of high society who set out, theodolite in hand, to make the ley de terrenos baldíos reality. The one who came to Naranja appreciated the quality of the marshy black soil, and in 1883 the Spanish brothers Iñigo and Remigio Noriega began a campaign to acquire it. The Noriegas were important businessmen with tobacco factories, a cotton mill, and wheat haciendas in the Valley of Mexico. In Naranja they suborned the mayor to lose the community's colonial deeds, the *papeles del pueblo* jealously guarded across village Mexico. Then they mapped the land, which gave them the one-third allotted by the ley de terrenos baldíos and allowed them to buy the rest cheaply from the government. Hacendados ended up with thirty thousand acres; villagers one thousand, an average of a third of an acre each. Finally, the brothers took charge of the water, drained the lake, rerouted the streams that fed it to irrigation canals, and made a fortune exporting maize.

The Noriegas called their hacienda Cantabria, after the region of Spain that was their homeland, and worked its fields with outsiders used to wage labor and unencumbered by local sentiment. Their state-backed sequencing of land seizure, lake drainage, and monocropping was a superb business model; they replicated it for their wheat haciendas in the Valley of Mexico, where railroads connected them to the city, even as officials criticized them as dangerous men who "submit[ted] everything to their own interests." The Noriegas' business model was politically less superb, though, combining the theft of indigenous lands with extreme inequality and proof that Mexicans were being sold out to foreigners. As one journalist put it,

> Never to even the most cretinous of Spanish monarchs . . . would it have occurred that a community could live [without lands]; and yet, it was necessary that a Spanish adventurer [Noriega] convince us that the pueblos of Mexico do not need more than the land where their shacks were located.[69]

In Michoacán the villagers of Naranja were left without jobs or the common lake lands that had fed them for centuries. The fish, duck, clams, and shrimp were gone; so were the reeds that they used to weave and sell. Some families fell back on foraging for squash and other foods up in the mountains. Some turned to a time-honored indigenous survival strategy, litigation. Many, like Gómez's family, took up the oldest indigenous survival strategy of all, migration. Some went as far as the United States, where a young man called Primo Tapia moved to Los Angeles and joined the anarchist Industrial Workers of the World. In the end, enough to count followed his example and became revolutionaries themselves.

Chapter Thirteen

Time, Oligarchy, and Caciquismo

There are three reasons that the fate of villagers in places like Naranja, Tomóchic, and Tequesquitengo didn't turn more Mexicans into revolutionaries. Not all villagers suffered as much as they did as early as they did, and revolution is a matter of, among other things, critical mass and timing. Some twenty years passed before the ravages of the new economic model made themselves felt across the entire country, and for oligarchs to become overmighty. Moreover, there was a stark divide between town and country, and the stories of city dwellers were different, some better than others, but none with the same brutal dismantling of collective lives. And Porfirio Díaz was, for those twenty years and more, very good at politics; and while there were ample structural reasons for rural fury, the Mexican Revolution broke out largely because of politics.

The liberal laws that privatized villagers' common lands or denied their titles' validity were not universally disastrous. Predators with theodolites did not constantly stalk village utopias, ready to use the fiction of *terrenos baldíos* to dispossess the innocent. Eleven out of thirty-one states never saw any surveyors at all. Where they did turn up, they didn't always win: In the northern Huasteca of San Luis Potosí only one indigenous community, Xilitla, lost lands to surveyors and the companies behind them. Other indigenous communities bought into the sales pitch that privatization would unleash economic growth, and for some, such as the vanilla growers of northern Veracruz, it did. In the Oaxaca sierra, Mixtecs seized the opportunity to turn communal lands into municipios, the common goal of Mexican peasants, and with them as political bases expand onto hacienda lands. Neither was every preexisting indigenous community utopian, self-regulating for the good of the many; sometimes individuals wanted out, and desamortización, forcible privatization, was one way of doing it.[1] And while in general large commercial farms took over from small farmers, in some regions ranchers grew and prospered. They were precisely the sort of rural entrepreneurs, up-by-the-bootstraps middle-class types, who were idealized across North America. That part of the American Dream was just as much a Mexican Dream.

The tobacco growers and cattlemen of southern Veracruz were people like this, their beliefs and hopes encoded in their business names. In San Andrés Tuxtla, for example, small businessmen named their grocery stores things like Hope or Nirvana, their cantina The Renaissance, their pharmacy La Moderna. Their customers got money from cigar factories with names like The Dream, Triumphant, Victor, Destiny, and Progress.[2] San Andrés had no less than nine, more than twice as many as Guadalajara, the country's second city.[3] Near there, other sorts of ranchers did well too, cattlemen in places like northeastern Michoacán or highland Jalisco. San José de Gracia showed just how well Porfirian development might work; it started out as empty fields in 1888 and by 1901 supported a barber, three butchers, eighteen small shops, and a cigar maker.

The village was founded when a family of patriarchs decided it should be. Guadalupe González Toscano had been a tenant on the isolated and declining Hacienda de Cojumatlán; a literate peasant, he saved up 750 pesos, married well, and bought the properties he farmed in the 1860s. He and his peers were cattle ranchers with sidelines in honey and maguey, the spiky leaves useful for booze and fencing, but they were in general a sober lot. In 1888 his three sons and a few neighbors decided that they needed a chapel. While they were at it, they agreed, they might as well do the thing properly and build a village. So on March 19 they yoked their oxen and ploughed out a grid plan for seven blocks, centered on a plaza and a church, and then built it. Within a few years they had a school and 150 houses, the better-off made of brick and tile with indoor patios; by the early twentieth century they had running water. Traveling salesmen came, a mail service began, and with it came newspapers, and with them inspiration and wonder in stories of electricity, cars, submarines, and even aeroplanes. It was in some ways typical of San José that one slightly offbeat type, Elías Martínez, built (and crashed) his own flying machine, a ranchero Wright brother.[4]

San José de Gracia was a distinctly middle-class boomtown, its backbone 140 cattlemen whose ranches averaged about four hundred acres each—not all that much land on a dry plateau, but enough to hire cowboys and fieldhands, pay them reasonably, and send cheese, pork, and leather on the train to Mexico City. There were middle-class success stories elsewhere in the countryside, particularly in the Center-West and the richer parts of the Huasteca, states like Hidalgo and San Luis Potosí, places like San José: strong communities with strong individual leaders, long used to private property, close enough to cities to send them goods but far enough away from them—the nearest railroad to San José was fifteen miles up a dirt road—to turn the covetous eyes of big business elsewhere. While ranches fell to the hacienda in places like Chihuahua, they grew impressively at a national level, with fifty thousand registered by 1910. The final factor was race. While members of many ethnic groups set up ranches—clusters of Chinese ranchers dotted the Mexicali Valley and around Torreón—mestizos predominated.

Above all, middle-class success stories took place in the cities. Consumption habits showed it—the shops, the newspaper ads, the leisure pursuits—but so did the drier numbers. The trebling of GDP was most visible there, as new, frenchified housing sprang up west and northwest of the Mexico City center in places like the Condesa or Roma neighborhoods. Professionals and businessmen multiplied to populate them: By 1900 526 doctors, 884 engineers, and 42 architects were registered in Mexico City.[5] At a more rarified level, these were years of a flourishing intellectual and artistic life, which culminated in the 1909 foundation of the Ateneo Mexicano, a society that brought together young poets, academics, writers, and painters. Many—the painter Diego Rivera, the writer Martín Luis Guzmán, the philosophers Antonio Caso and José Vasconcelos—went on to distinguished revolutionary careers. At this point, however, they were more theoretical critics, possibly in part because they were funded by the Departments of Education and Fine Arts.

Workers and the poor meanwhile were pushed northward and eastward toward housing tenements and shacks in the badlands and dust storms of Lake Texcoco. This was gentrification with teeth: To get the poor to their workers' colonies in Azcapotzalco the government drove an avenue over expropriated and razed houses and then taxed the displaced for digging up and relocating their ancestors' bones.[6] "The ugly barrios," wrote one journalist, "are retreating or disappearing." Yet workers in general didn't have it much different than the working class in industrializing countries anywhere: exploited to the hilt with the longest hours, the cheapest working conditions, and the tightest discipline that owners could get away with. Child labor remained commonplace. Textile workers lost hands in their machinery and died young from breathing dust and fibers; in extremis miners lost entire cohorts, as when a shaft in the Palaú mine collapsed and swallowed fifty-seven of them.[7] The most radical among them were subject to exemplary state and private violence. One of the principal horror stories of the Porfiriato was the 1907 massacre at the Cananea copper mine in Sonora, where miners struck against their American owner, William Greene. Twenty-three were shot down with dumdum bullets by company thugs and Arizona Rangers. The Mexican authorities kept quiet.[8]

The miners were subsequently remembered as revolutionaries in waiting; they weren't. Just across the border they had would-be leaders in the form of the Partido Liberal Mexicano (PLM), a misnamed group of anarchists. The leader, Ricardo Flores Magón, was a well-read ideologue, particularly keen on Kropotkin, and he drew strength from his brothers and from experience with the Chicago anarchist union the Industrial Workers of the World. Flores Magón—originally, like Díaz and Júarez, oaxaqueño—was dangerous enough to flee Mexico and live undercover in Los Angeles, to be hunted down by private detectives working for the Chihuahua government and their allies in the LAPD. Yet mineworker leaders weren't in touch with these émigré anarchists across the border, even if their incendiary newspaper *Regeneración* made it into the mining camp. They had nothing to do with the Flores Magón brothers in 1907 when they made their stand; a letter from the brothers to a follower in Cananea, just before the strike, didn't mention it. The miners' demands weren't radical. They were worried about a rumored contract change, resented racism—though they themselves were racist toward the Chinese—and felt overworked and underpaid. American miners earned twice as much as Mexican miners for doing the same job. As one folk song put it,

We're no anarchists,
Revolutionaries on the make,
We just want fewer hours,
And a fair shake.[9]

The other horror story of the Porfirian working class was the strike at the huge textile mill at Río Blanco. This was the peak of a major wave of strikes in central Mexico in 1906, a new militancy that fueled the first serious union, the Gran Círculo de Obreros Libres. The union was recognized by the government, and while its internal rhetoric was radical, its first public demands were moderate: better working conditions and 5 percent more pay. Díaz reacted with equal moderation, firing an abusive police chief, reaffirming a right to strike, and trying to broker a solution. He also threatened to send in soldiers if necessary. At Río Blanco, as in Cananea, workers refused a settlement. They had multiple grievances: pay cuts and new regulations that fined them for poor-quality products, charges to replace broken machinery, bans on newspaper reading, a mandate that they ask permission to host guests in company housing. As in Cananea, the owners were foreign, in this case the French directors of the Compañia Industrial de Orizaba, and intransigent. As in Cananea, the government feared the strike's spread, in this case more realistically: An earlier strike at Río Blanco had been followed by a wave of strikes elsewhere. When they came out again in December 1906, the millworkers inspired neighbors in Tlaxcala to follow them.

Millowners reacted with a national lockout. Díaz brokered another solution; even the government press had been sympathetic to the workers. But when a group of dissident workers blocked the return to work and torched the company store Díaz made good on the threat of soldiers. Workers in the town were shot in the back as they fled to the hills and executed in the burned remains of the company store. It was believed at the time that three hundred had died; that the number was actually much smaller didn't matter all that much.[10] The bloody conflicts at Río Blanco and Cananea became totemic; the first pro-democracy manifesto of the time mentioned them as reasons that the dictator had to go.

These were rare moments and came toward the end of the period. For most of the Porfiriato violence against workers was more quotidian than spectacular. They had some collective power too: Mutualist societies, worker organizations that charged petty fees and provided emergency assistance—for funerals, for medicine, for widows—also provided political bonds. At the outset of the regime a national congress of mutualist societies was important enough to attract the Cuban revolutionary José Martí, and across the period there were over 250 strikes. Women formed their own organizations early on, led by the cigarette workers. They needed all the clout they could get; they earned half as much as men, and sexual harassment was rife on the shop floor. A tight labor market limited owner dictatorship until the very end. Millworkers moved around a lot, in part because they could be fired at an instant's notice, but in part because they could shop around for the best deals.[11] And with the railroads came the option to migrate longer distances, to try their luck in far-off cities in Mexico and the US, and they took it.

With this labor organizing came a growing class consciousness and an urban radicalism expressed by working-class journalists, or journalists for the working classes, in newspapers like *La Guacamaya* and *El Diablo Rojo*, the Red Devil. They printed a curious combination of reporting, advice columns, moralizing stories, and political cartoons. They and their readers took the jeering label the richer used to condemn them, *pelados*, literally the naked ones, and—rather like the *sans-culottes* in revolutionary Paris—claimed it as a source of pride. Writers recast their readers as the true moderns, facing the dinosaurs of an immoral oligarchy, patriots against Jockey Club sell-outs. These papers weren't pamphlets; they were mass-produced and read by tens of thousands. Revealingly enough, the government had the power to shut them down through its monopoly on newsprint, but rarely did.[12]

It was also revealing that if the government wouldn't censor them, then factory owners would, as with the controversial ban on newspapers at Río Blanco. Factory regulations reflected the totalitarian dreams of big business. Yet they also reflected the everyday lives of factory workers, what bosses wanted them to do and what they actually did. Seen this way, work regulations paint a picture distinct from mechanical lives dictated by the factory whistle. Workers in the Santa Rosa textile mill weren't to disappear for days on end during the partying of saint's days. They were forbidden to have sex or practice bullfighting while at work. They were banned from carrying knives (murder rates on the shop floor were quite high).[13] Being a worker in industrializing Mexico was almost certainly preferable to being a worker in industrializing Britain. Certainly life expectancy was longer than the seventeen years prevailing in mid-nineteenth-century Manchester.[14] The litmus test of revolutionary fighting suggested as much; workers might read and feel radical, but they did not often stick their heads over the parapet and act radical.

It probably helped that city dwellers got the largest share of the public goods of the time. Turn-of-the-century administrators, technocrats, and urban planners were utilitarian and ambitious. In Tlaxcala, for example, the governor doubled spending on public education and raised the social services budget fivefold. The education minister Justo Sierra aimed for compulsory primary school attendance. Literacy rose, and with it the scope for cheap entertainment and the prospect at least of upward mobility. The most gripping novels sold out fast to people like the weaver Rafael Mendoza, whose three years of primary school left him devouring the masterly invention, wit, history lessons and schlock of writers like Riva Palacio or Manuel Payno.[15] In the capital the conservationist Miguel Ángel de Quevedo proposed numerous public parks and playgrounds, green spaces specifically designed for the lower classes; against some odds he carved a "workers park" out of ninety-six hectares in Balbuena.[16] People would no longer get lost, an engineer proposed, if the streets were rebaptized with numbers, as in New York, instead of magical names. Neither would young misses be embarrassed by addresses on Calle El Órgano, Organ Street, or worse yet Calle de las Arrecogidas, Foundling Street, with its perilously illegitimate implications.[17]

Above all, the city would provide real public toilets; the first such facility, a two-story iron structure, as big as the first tram station, went up in the main square. By 1908 there were eighteen of them—a return to the urban sophistication of the pre-Hispanic city—and a new sewage system, inaugurated by Díaz. Again like the Mexica, the government invested heavily in pharaonic water management, in this case finally achieving the centuries-old dream of the *desagüe*, an extraordinary system of canals and tunnels that led spring- and rainwater safely through the city, north across Lake Texcoco, and through a tunnel piercing the valley rim to drain downhill, gravity in theory cleaning the city. At the same time, the authorities realized that contaminated water from Chapultepec was more than a gustatory problem. The city's supply was killing people with dysentery, so they reengineered the system to provide drinking water from a new source, the southern lake of Xochimilco.

Not all of this worked. Compulsory education required more schools than the government could build and populate. Parks and playgrounds competed with property developers and decay. The thought of replacing "Calle de Plateros" or "Isabel la Católica" with numbers was loopy from the start, and capitalinos ignored the soulless optimists' idea. The sophisticated debate over whether to drain or do away with Lake Texcoco was resolved in favor of the drainers, ecologically on the wrong side of history. As conservationists had foreseen, the parched lakebed caused dust storms and subsidence, the outflow slowed as sediment built up in the Gran Canal, and the lakebed became a cesspool. The pipes for decent drinking water ran mainly to the rich. As the brilliant Quevedo put it, "We are very capable of forming model regulations yet very deficient or neglectful at carrying them out."[18]

Mexico City was always going to be an ecologist's nightmare—it had been one since the conquest—and one rich in environmental injustice. It was a source of great pride to most capitalinos, but it was also in their eyes filthy, smelly, disorderly, and medically dangerous. A physicians' committee concluded that only African cities had higher death rates. Yet at the same time tangible medical advances came to the capital and the provinces. There were more doctors and hospitals, a new political commitment; some companies set up hospitals for workers. And most city dwellers benefited from an eclectic combination of modern germ theory and belief in vaccination with antique ideas of miasmas, toxic vapors that arose from swamps or rotting lakes and did away with people, generally in the night.

Germ theory drove hygiene measures, ranging from fines for peeing in the streets to sewage removal, rubbish management, and street cleaning, trying to do away with mud, overflowing sewers, and dead animals. In the port of Veracruz citizens were ordered to clean, disinfect, and whitewash their houses in bad years. The new measures reduced dysentery, which killed some three thousand capitalinos a year; cholera, which came about once a generation and was devastating; and typhus, one of the two main highland killers, one particularly virulent outbreak believed to have killed eighty thousand capitalinos in 1892. Vaccination made inroads against smallpox, still endemic, still lethal enough to wipe out entire villages, the trope of "not enough survivors to bury the dead" still occasionally heard. Governors made inoculation mandatory, monitoring campaigns municipio by municipio. Miasma theory drove politicians on the Gulf Coast to drain swamps, the wrong reason for the right decision; with fewer mosquitos came fewer cases of yellow fever and malaria. At all the main ports, finally, health inspectors were supposed to keep away human carriers of yellow fever and bubonic plague.

It worked; the plague, pandemic in China, was confined to a minor outbreak in Mazatlán, and in 1908 the government of Veracruz reported no cases of yellow fever at all. (The government had spent a quarter of a million pesos on the problem.) Government medical policy was consequently popular, and when officials mounted a Popular Hygiene Exhibition in 1910 some hundred thousand capitalinos reportedly went to see it. (If true, that was more or less every adult in the city—one more dubious statistic, but indicative of at least quite a lot of enthusiasm.) Porfirio Díaz thought sanitation good sense and good politics: He personally inaugurated Mexico City's sewage and drainage systems, the latter twice, once when it was finished in 1905 and once for publicity in 1910, part of celebrating the centenary of Independence.[19]

That Díaz was ubiquitous cutting ribbons, laying foundation stones, and even burying a time capsule was unsurprising, for his regime was profoundly individualist and image-conscious. He was a larger-than-life dictator, charismatic, adroit at playing off underling factions against each other while controlling every element of the government machinery. It was Díaz who appointed and disappointed governors. He signed off on every congressman's election; one year he allotted over a quarter of the seats in Congress to fellow oaxaqueños.[20] He picked his own men to be *jefes políticos*, the three hundred political bosses who ran the provinces. Constitutionally the face-to-face institution of government was the elected mayor of each municipio; in reality it was the jefe político who ruled several municipios at a time, armed with broad powers to arrest, jail, and conscript to public works or to the army. They regulated teachers, doctors, priests, local taxes, spending, and municipal government. They handed out property titles and mining concessions to themselves and their cronies. In theory free traders, in reality they used their power to squash rivals. A jefe político in Veracruz, for example, opened a butcher's shop and told his neighbors how much he would appreciate their business. His competitor went out of business in a matter of weeks. The most egregious sold their prisoners to the plantations of the South. They were, naturally enough, frequently loathed: One article wrote them off as "parasites," "arbitrary despot[s]," "the coarsest men," "headstrong tyrant[s]." In the wildest parts of the country they were murdered with some regularity.[21]

This was unsurprising, because the institution of the jefe político ran against two of the elemental forces in Mexican political culture: the goal of representative local government, and the hatred of caciques who impeded it. These had come together in Díaz's rise; his slogan in trying to seize the presidency had been the pithy *no reelección*, which summarized the aim of democratic alternance in government at all levels. He traduced it completely: Elected in 1877, he ceded the presidency to his comrade in arms and puppet Manuel González in 1880, took it back in 1884, ended the ban on reelection in 1888, extended the presidential period to six years in 1904, and was on the point of making it eight when he was toppled.

Yet not until the last of his terms was there much opposition. There were two reasons for this national acquiescence, which Díaz's functionaries didn't enjoy. The first was generalized war-weariness; the second was dictatorial diplomacy, the smarts for even the streets he'd never see.

Díaz came to power only a decade after Mexico's real declaration of independence, the execution of the Emperor Maximilian in 1867. The intervening years, thanks in part to his own dogged pursuit of power, were times of uncertainty and economic stagnation. Authoritarian liberalism appealed across the political spectrum with its promise of development through benign dictatorship, lucrative free trade through unfree elections. Vicente Riva Palacio repeated Santa Anna's line that Mexico needed "a lot of administering and not much politicking." The conservative intellectual Francisco Bulnes held that it "was stupid beyond belief" to criticize Díaz "for not having pulled off the impossible: being a democratic president in a country of slaves."[22] The future revolutionary Antonio Díaz Soto y Gama concurred, ranting that this "country of Indians made brutes by alcohol" needed "enlightened despotism," because "the countryside was only ready for abjection."[23] Díaz put it more diplomatically. When he took power, he told a journalist, "The people were divided and unprepared for the exercise of the extreme principles of democratic government."[24]

Ditching the substance of democracy if not its outward forms went long uncontested. Particularly unlikeable candidates occasionally prompted riots, and Díaz's 1892 re-election caused a fuss in the capital that was only calmed with cavalry charges and quiet arrests.[25] But in Mexico City even the forms of democracy went under with the Municipal Law of 1903, which passed municipal government to an all-powerful triumvirate, composed of a governor, a Director of Public Works, and a Director of Public Health, all appointed by Díaz. The elected ayuntamiento kept only consultative, oversight, and veto powers.[26] Outside the capital elections continued, but they were smoothly won by fly-by-night clubs that gathered to cheer on the preselected, often single, candidate. (The intensity of the cheering was itself a useful barometer of local politics.) The occasional more combative affair called for haggling over results or more vigorous rigging. In Coahuila the jefe político of Matamoros discouraged unreliable voters by telling them that the polling booths had been removed, most unfortunately, to Ireland. In the same state, thirty years on, a presidential candidate got no votes at all in his hometown.[27]

Coahuila was an outlier in its recalcitrance, its elections bluntly rigged because of its people's cyclical challenges to the established order. It was at the same time an exemplar of a central component in the stabilization of the upper strata: the old provincial dynasties, rooted in the colony or nineteenth-century warlords, surrendering politics in exchange for business opportunities. Families such as the Maderos in Coahuila, the Maytorenas in Sonora, or the Neris in Guerrero generally accepted this, some more gracefully than others. The Maderos took part in an 1893 revolt that derailed the official candidate for governor and then retired into the serious business of building one of Mexico's great modern business empires. General Canuto Neri briefly rebelled before likewise retiring, leaving his dynasty to flourish for decades. He himself died within three years, in popular myth poisoned at a banquet by a sombrero; magical realism aside, such an assassination would have been quite out of regime character, because by the mid-1890s Díaz had convincingly dealt with the provincial pseudo-aristocracy by more peaceful means.[28]

In the old days Neri would have been gambling on his pronunciamiento's attracting enough disgruntled army officers to propel him to national power. Díaz's second political achievement was to make that impossible by neutering the military; his own was the last pronunciamiento. Every president since Independence had relied on the tolerance and goodwill of the generals, unreliable qualities, and many had been toppled by them. Even Juárez, with all the legitimacy of two wars won, was increasingly dependent on army backing in his twilight. Díaz himself had made two attempts to capture the presidency through rebellion. When he finally came to power, the army was fifty thousand strong and generals occupied eighteen out of thirty-one governorships. When he fell, the army was fifteen thousand strong. In 1880 the army took 45 percent of the entire national budget; by 1910 it was down to 20 percent. Neither did Díaz buy off soldiers with governorships. Of the seventy-one governors he appointed, the overwhelming majority—fifty-five—were professionals with degrees in engineering, medicine, or law.[29]

Díaz came to the job with the cachet and contacts of being one of Mexico's most successful generals. His deceptive first step was to increase the military budget, buying the soldiers new French equipment and founding a military academy. Legitimacy reinforced, he went on to weed out rivals and prune the officer corps, rewarding those left standing with padded payrolls, junkets to Europe, or, in the case of General Manuel Mondragón, the backing to create the world's first semiautomatic rifle (named, with a certain inevitability, the Fusil Porfirio Díaz). Generals were not allowed to put down roots in any one region where they might go native and become political threats. Instead they were almost invariably posted outside their home regions, and shuffled with a competent frequency unmatched before or after.[30]

The other institutional threat to Díaz's power was the Church, the sustenance of conservative opposition to and war against liberal governments since Independence. In the 1910 census 99 percent of Mexicans, conservative or no, identified as Catholics; Juárez and Díaz were themselves seminarians. As recently as the mid-1870s there had been a religious rising in the rural West, which, even if confined to Michoacán and parts of Guanajuato, recruited thousands, attracted appreciable middle-class support in the region's towns, and took three years to put down.[31] Díaz's solution was to leave the constitution's anticlerical provisions intact while looking the other way at legal and ceremonial transgressions such as religious schools, discreet convents, defiant bell-ringing and parades. He himself was married in the Cathedral by the conservative Archbishop Pelagio Antonio de Labastida y Dávalos. (Díaz's wife Carmen was notoriously devout.) A major religious revival in the Center-West was left alone, as were the powerful Catholic women's organizations, and as was Pope Leo XIII's 1891 encyclical *Rerum Novarum*, which enjoined respect for the working classes as a core Catholic value.[32]

This was more than just tolerance. Díaz managed a rapprochement with the papacy, allowing the return of an apostolic delegation (which arrived, provocatively, staffed exclusively by Italians). He worked well with modernizing prelates like Bishop Gillow of Oaxaca, whom he backed for the job and who in return collaborated in forestalling Catholic opposition and promoting economic development. Personal affinities aside, Díaz laid out a simple logic for all this: "Persecution of the Church, whether or not the clergy enter into the matter, means war . . . Without its religion, Mexico is irretrievably lost." In return, the bishops dubbed him "our only defense under God" and either left him alone or positively supported him. After all, the reform laws were dead, crowed one cleric.[33]

It was a combination that worked in the cities. Urban peace also benefited from a technocratic approach to law and order, exemplified in the Mexico City penitentiary of Lecumberri. This was star-shaped, corridors of cells radiating out from a vigilant center, a panopticon where large numbers of prisoners could be watched over by small numbers of guards. Outside its walls policemen were nicknamed *tecolotes*, owls.[34] The symbolism was self-evident: Díaz's was the most vigilant and scientific security state in Mexican history. On the ground reality was rather less impressive. One of the key functions of policing, keeping the poor and their crimes out of the center and out of sight, failed dismally. Underpaid cops took second jobs to get by. Yet increasing arrests and sentencing in the Porfiriato were more proof of efficiency than of soaring criminality. Arrests for sex crimes bear this out: Traditionally the least reported, they rose dramatically.[35]

But there was a lot more to Porfirian rule in the cities than aspirations to a technologically sophisticated control of space and violence. There was also some give-and-take, a tolerance for criticism of the regime that kept popular politics alive in places where elections no longer mattered. The government shut down the press jury, an institution that protected journalists from political prosecution, shut down print shops, and began jailing reporters serially. That old mainstay of liberal politics, *El Monitor Republicano*, went under; the officialist *El Imparcial* moved into its place. Yet Díaz's main way of controlling the press was through the payroll, and opposition endured in dailies such as *El Hijo del Ahuizote*, *El Diablito Rojo*, and *El Diario del Hogar*. They covered causes célèbres such as the Tomóchic massacre and the drowning of Tequesquitengo, and their cartoons—an ever-sophisticated genre in Mexico, both artistically and politically—took aim at even Díaz. And these papers were widely read. *La Guacamaya* had a daily print run of twenty-nine thousand and was sold in seven cities. It provided, its masthead said, "a newspaper of gossip and good humor, agile and a teller of truths, not puffed up or snobby, scourge of the bourgeoisie and defender of the Working Class." This was not abject docility.[36]

In the countryside likewise Díaz enjoyed a certain political legitimacy for much of his presidency. He earned it with industrious letter writing to governors and jefes políticos asking about local conditions and enjoining them to do right by their constituents—to respect, for example, indigenous property rights. His governors were more than technocrats or, later, oligarchs. Cahuantzi, the indigenous governor of Tlaxcala, was an autodidact who gave speeches in Nahuatl; he was the longest-lasting Porfirian governor. Manuel Alarcón, the long-term governor of Morelos, was a liberal hero from the war against the French with profound roots in the National Guard, good relations with the village powerful, and, rarest of things, acceptance as both jefe político and head of police. His was a legitimacy that survived even as his villages went under to the sugar plantations. These were the sort of regional patriarchs who implemented a national patriarchy, dictators who might be imagined benevolent. Díaz even intervened in some of the more vigorous local elections to preserve some liberal substance. At the lowest level of all, elections for *agentes municipales*, the administrators of the smallest villages, were widely competitive until the 1900s. The municipio libre was a distinctly endangered species, but it did not go entirely into extinction.[37]

The problem with this portrait of Díaz the master politician is that it is timeless, and time eventually caught up with him. If he had had the fortune to die at the turn of the century, a sprightly seventy-year-old, he would have gone down in history quite differently. But he didn't, and the result is a chronology of two different Porfiriatos: one of paternalist dictatorship, from the late 1870s to the early 1900s, and one of calcification and oligarchy. That second one ended in 1910, in one of the world's great social revolutions.

Oligarchy is common enough when rapid economic growth, technological innovation, and privatization coincide, and oligarchs came to the fore in many parts of the world in the late nineteenth century. The Spanish established a constitutional monarchy that rested on a pact between different factions of the oligarchy to take turns in power. In El Salvador fourteen families took over the overwhelming majority of land and the political system. In Peru the ruling party was the property of a narrow clique of wool merchants who diversified into mining, construction, and industry. Mexico was not as extreme a case, but by the early 1900s the main politicians had large business empires and had been in power for many years. They were bound together by peace as best business practice and by positivism, a belief in running society along scientific rather than ideological lines that was itself profoundly ideological. Positivists recognized three phases to human history: the religious, the metaphysical, and the scientific. They held that they could lead Mexico into the scientific phase, but Mexico would need more economic development before the plebe could be left in charge of it; in the interim, that was the task of the *científicos*, the closest Mexico had to a political party.

Their effective leader was José Yves Limantour, a rich, educated, first-generation Mexican of French parents who was secretary of finance from 1893 until 1910. His ability to win over foreigners was one of the reasons for the influx of investment, 4 percent bonds, and accession to the gold standard in 1905. As with other científicos, he applied acumen and contacts to simultaneous personal dealings in the railroad-driven export economy; his portfolio included 52,000 acres near the new port, oil refinery, and rail terminus of Coatzacoalcos, where his neighbors were William Randolph Hearst and the oil baron Weetman Pearson. He carved an estate through the middle of indigenous lands next to the new Ferrocarril de Tehuantepec, the line that crossed the Isthmus of Tehuantepec and formed a predecessor to the Panama Canal. Far to the north he owned 420,000 acres of the foothills of the Western Sierra Madre in Chihuahua, where the new North West Railway ran his lumber to the border at Juárez.[38] A colleague, the minister of development Olegario Molina, took over much of Yucatán's henequen industry, manning his estates with deported Yaquis (he had shares in the corporation taking over their land—two birds, one stone). He monopolized the supply of bailing twine to Cyrus McCormick, whose combine harvesters were the most important market for henequen fiber. At the other end of Mexico in Chihuahua Governor Luis Terrazas built a business empire of banks, cattle latifundia, timber concessions, and mines across the 1890s. In 1904 he handed it over to his half-American son-in-law, Enrique Creel, who was simultaneously governor and ambassador to Washington. Creel used the ley de terrenos baldíos to form a hacienda in San Carlos and then deployed rurales to defend it against the outraged dispossessed. Creel's power stretched over the border, where he had an enemy arrested, even though he himself had legal problems; in 1908 his partner organized a heist in their own bank to cover up the stock market losses he had made with depositors' money.[39]

Some científicos lived up to the promise of their prestigious educations, managing economic and social development to good effect for some Mexicans in some places. The most acceptable face of their group, Justo Sierra, was devoted to the cause of universal education. Neither were the científicos mere foreign pawns, as opponents painted them; they aspired to economic independence, and started policies like rail nationalization that would foster it. But collective corruption aside, the senior científicos were, like Díaz, living too long, well beyond the actuarial average. By 1910 they were no longer the bright youngish things of the 1870s, people like Carlos Pacheco, who fought his way up through civil war and French Intervention and became Minister of Development at forty-one. They were instead the bewhiskered monopolists of working-class cartoons; not progressives whose finesse was rebuilding Mexico, but a morally atavistic group of sellouts lording it over a moral, modern, and authentically Mexican people. The científicos were "doddering old fools," wrote an angry young northerner in his local newspaper, who had entrenched themselves in political and economic power and made the Republic ill with their "stagnant blood."[40]

There were two chances for a peaceful transition away from one-man rule and the sort of closed political system where men like Creel held multiple top political jobs while enriching themselves. Both centered on the vice presidency; Díaz was clearly going to die in office, so this was the job that would determine what came next. In 1903 General Bernardo Reyes, the progressive governor of Nuevo León, made his pitch. As Minister of War he had built up a thirty-thousand-man volunteer reserve, recapturing some of the enthusiasm of the old liberal national guards. He had launched a political campaign across the North. He would ensure stability—he wasn't shy in using guns against protesters—but he would also open up a sclerotic political system. But Díaz put down Reyes's movement and disbanded his associated guard. The indecisive general did nothing about it, and Díaz installed the already-unpopular Ramón Corral instead.

The other chance came in 1910. Díaz had been trailing a decision to retire since 1908, when he invited the prominent journalist James Creelman to Chapultepec Castle for an exclusive interview. The talk turned into a mixture of investor-friendly health report (the seventy-eight-year-old Díaz was described as running up the palace stairway two steps at a time), support for another North American caudillo (Theodore Roosevelt, then considering a third term in offiice), apologia for benign dictatorship, and promise of democracy. After delivering the Cincinnatus line common to caudillos since Simón Bolívar—long-time aspiration to leave office, wholly disinterested in power, dragged back reluctantly by popular acclaim—Díaz set off into surprising territory. "I have waited patiently," he told the egregiously sycophantic American,

> for the day when the people of the Mexican Republic would be prepared to choose and change their government at every election without danger of armed revolutions and without injury to the national credit or interference with national progress. I believe that day has come . . . No matter what my friends and supporters say, I retire when my present term of office ends, and I shall not serve again. I shall be eighty years old then . . . I welcome an opposition party in the Mexican Republic. If it appears I will regard it as a blessing, not an evil . . . This nation is ready for her ultimate life of freedom.[41]

Translated into Spanish, the Creelman interview horrified swathes of society, from the elites, who saw it as profoundly destabilizing, to the working-class press, who saw it as insulting to Mexicans and sucking up to Americans. A cartoon in *El Diablito Rojo* put it frankly in verse, addressing Díaz with the overfamiliar *tú*:

> What's wrong with you that you go saying
> What you'll do tomorrow or the next day
> To people who don't care about
> What goes on inside your home?
>
> What you should do
> Is live mistrustfully[42]

Díaz ended up taking the cartoonist's advice, though not in the anti-imperialist sense intended. When the 1910 presidential elections came around, he decided to rig them and stay in office. The usual supposed begging for him to remain, against his clear wishes, culminated with a unanimous call from Mexico's governors. The problem was that the opposition party Díaz said he would welcome had in fact materialized as the popular Partido Nacional Antirreeleccionista. So he had Vice President Corral begin criminal proceedings against the candidate, arrest his followers at their national convention, and finally, two weeks before election day, arrest the candidate himself, Francisco Madero. The predictable landslide followed; 98 percent voted for Díaz, a ridiculously unbelievable (and wholly unnecessary) majority. In a final confirmation that he'd lost his touch, Díaz released his opponent shortly after polling day. Madero skipped bail and fled to San Antonio, Texas, where he scheduled a revolution to break out across Mexico on November 20, 1910.

By this stage, accumulated grievances in the countryside had reached critical mass. In the mountains of the North, years of tax increases, caciquismo, and meddling in fiercely independent municipios had given very different people—cowboys, ex-miners, drifters, smallholders, petty cattlemen, merchants, and village middle classes—lasting grudges. A new generation of hacendados had blocked watering rights and seized common lands. In the South the old question of disputed common lands affected more people than ever before, as hacendados in places like Morelos took over free peasant villages. In the breadbasket of the Laguna the incipient proletariat of the wheat and cotton estates—some of whom had opted into the life, drawn by initially decent cash wages—now suffered the same low wages, high food prices, and price-gouging company stores as industrial workers. In the old frontier lands such as Tabasco and Chiapas, commercial opportunities and unwilling workers led to debt peonage and subsistence-level wages. Even some of the economic winners of the time, the new middle classes with their small mines, transport companies, and ranches, had run up against the ceiling of an inaccessible political system, with all the economic setbacks that entailed.

These losers of the Porfiriato formed the backbone of subsequent stories of revolution, and the stories were in the aggregate true.

Neither was the economic story of the Porfiriato the unparalleled state-led success that científicos claimed. Growth was a global product of the time, the second great globalization, rather than a specifically Mexican outcome of smart policymaking and diplomatic intelligence. The other two great economies of Latin America, Brazil and Argentina, make that abundantly clear. Both fostered a dramatic expansion of railroads that stimulated not just exports but also internal markets, just like in Mexico. Both channeled new economic growth into new cities, in part inevitable, in part joined-up urban planning. Buenos Aires, Rio de Janeiro, and São Paulo all experienced development comparable or superior to that of Mexico City. While Mexico City was building trams, Buenos Aires was building a subway. Brazil even had a provincial city that could be set alongside the Mexican capital: The burghers of Belém, rich from the rubber boom, built factories, breweries, a conservatory, an opera house, and six movie theaters.[43] Both countries' governments were obsessed with public relations, organizing the same sort of statistical assaults on foreigners. Mexico's economic development under Díaz was impressive, but it was not wholly exceptional.

Moreover, it came at a cost that went beyond the human. The most dynamic regions of the economy, the northern states, were verging on US property. By 1900 half of all overseas American investment was in Mexico, and it had purchased large swathes of the northern economy: copper, zinc, silver, and gold mines, huge cattle haciendas, and industries. By 1910 five US companies owned more than a million acres each in Chihuahua, and $100 million had gone into mining. In Sonora the Chicago-based Wheeler Company owned nearly one and a half million acres, and 90 percent of the mines were American. As for industrial finance, of twenty-five major financiers almost none were originally Mexican. The *científicos* who welcomed them were, it was believed, not very Mexican themselves, half foreign by kin or education. Mexico's lack of economic autonomy was demonstrated by the generous land and tax concessions given to these outsiders, and by the knock-on effects of US economic policies and downturns. When the US imposed tariffs on cattle and mineral ores in the 1890s, the Mexican economy slumped; when the US went into deep recession in 1907, Mexico followed.[44]

Given Mexico's position in 1877, however, a high level of foreign influence was inevitable. One of Díaz's major achievements was to manage it strategically, garnering investment from the broadest array of nations possible, an eye always on balancing the unavoidable power of the United States. The return to international credit markets, the image of order and progress that reassured private investors, the careful balancing act between different powers' places in the Mexican economy, and the export diversification that buffered price shocks were all political achievements. The idea that the científicos were foreign agents doesn't stand up to their biographies: Only Creel and Limantour had immediate foreign kin and education.[45] The revolutionary Francisco Madero's intimates were far more externally oriented: There were three US-educated people in a small group that met with a US journalist, one from Cornell, another a star of the Notre Dame football team.[46] The Porfirians were actually trying to reduce foreign ownership by the latter 1900s. The 1892 Mining Code had made it possible for foreigners to outright own mineral deposits; the proposed mining law of 1908 would have restricted new concessions to Mexican nationals. By then the railways had been nationalized.[47]

Neither were the human costs of the Porfirian economic model unique. Poverty and inequality attended the spread of commercial agriculture, industrialization, and globalization around the world. Italian immigrants flocked to the Americas from dirt-poor regions like Puglia, where to the old challenges of desiccation and socioeconomic polarization came the new challenges of aggrandizing landlords who ended even gleaning; that burnt wheat pasta (with turnip top sauce) is an Apulian specialty should be no surprise. In Central Texas the boom-and-bust economy of frontier farming led white settler families downward into child labor picking cotton.[48] All this was part of a universal logic for capitalist expansion, systematically laid out by Marx decades earlier. Commercial agriculture requires big estates; industrialization requires factories underpinned by cheap food and labor. In this process peasants and indigenous people are both obstacles, in their uncommercial landholdings, and prerequisites, in their labor, and policymakers turn to similar solutions everywhere. In Britain the General Enclosure Act of 1801 transferred the pastures, woods, and marshland that had provided grazing, lumber, and game from villagers to a new generation of British hacendados. In the US the Dawes Act of 1887 ended communal land tenure and divided Native American lands into vulnerable private allotments. These revolutions from above were all founded, as in Mexico, on the tenets of classic liberalism, an ideology that is not leftist at all, but rather freighted with regressive economic and social consequences. The ghost villages of Morelos, with their rubble houses dotting depopulated fields of sugar cane, had direct parallels in British counties like Northamptonshire, where all that remained, one contemporary observed, were

> the ruins of former dwelling-houses, barns, stables, etc. . . . An hundred house and families have in some open field villages dwindled to eight or ten . . . twenty or thirty farmers, and as many smaller tenants and proprietors . . . are hereby thrown out of their livings with their families.[49]

The capture of the peasantry, wherever it takes place, requires state-endorsed violence. So does the introduction of former peasants to the discipline of industrial labor. In Britain, Scottish sheep farming was predicated on the ethnic cleansing of the Highland Clearances, grain cultivation on the state power that sent the obstreperous to jail, the Royal Navy, or Australia. On the Brazilian, Argentine, and US frontiers cattle ranchers and the states behind them used extreme violence to do away with indigenous societies in the second half of the nineteenth century. In the 1870s barbed wire, Remington rifles, and machine guns drove the indigenous Mapuche south through Patagonia to free up the lands that made Argentina a global leader in beef and wheat, until the Depression one of the ten richest countries in the world. In global comparative terms the violence of Porfirian commercial agriculture and industrialization was nothing special.

The authoritarianism that rammed these changes through was nothing new in terms of Mexican history either. Benito Juárez acted on the Porfirian belief that political instability made full democracy unworkable, and that private land ownership was a universal good. Juárez himself harbored clear ambitions to long-term power: After fourteen years as executive, and with the war against the French won, he nevertheless had himself reelected again. A prospective minimum of twenty years in the presidency was only stopped by a heart attack. In policy terms, Juárez was a committed believer in privatization of Church and indigenous lands; in terms of state violence, it was he who founded the rurales in 1861, recruiting violent professionals without much discrimination to impose order on the countryside.

Neither were oligarchy and caciquismo uniquely Mexican evils. By the turn of the century caudillos were extinct across most of the Americas: in the US in 1837, with the death of Andrew Jackson; in Argentina in 1852, with the exile of Juan Manuel de Rosas. In this Díaz's Mexico was an outlier. But oligarchs were on the rise and caciques remained universal, whatever their name: ward bosses in the US, *coronéis* in Brazil, *gamonales* in Colombia. In Spain, the philosopher Joaquín Costa put the final loss of empire down to centuries of oligarchs and caciques with their "elections with electors," deadening personal interests, and systemic corruption. The disaster of 1898, when the US took away Cuba and the Philippines from a rusting Spanish navy and an underequipped army, demanded their excision from national life so that there could be a rebirth, a *regeneración*. Costa's solution was an "iron surgeon" along the lines of Porfirio Díaz, whom he specifically gave as a beneficial example, and a parliamentary regime as the point of arrival, not departure. It must have pleased Mexican elites.[50] His diagnosis, though, probably pleased Mexican dissidents; the Flores Magón newspaper was called *Regeneración*.

Three differences distinguished the arrival of liberalism and globalization in Mexico from their arrival elsewhere. There was the political question of timing. Díaz grew senescent in office: After meeting him Madero described him as "a child or an ignorant and distrustful rustic."[51] And as the aging dictator lost his way the costs of his overlong stay came to be identified very personally with him and his innermost circle, transmuting abstract concepts into easily grasped enemies. Even rustic caciques were cursed as científicos. Moreover, Mexico was geographically extremely hard to rule. The challenge to government went back centuries: Deserts, swamps, forest, and above all mountains favored independent-minded, democratic local societies, their loyalties summed up in the idea of the patria chica. Díaz's reduction of the army only exacerbated a standard problem. Ultimately, different people in very different places across Mexico shared the ability to do something collectively about genuinely existential threats. Long experience with courts, bullies, and wars had taught them how. And so in 1910, when courts and politics failed, rural Mexicans were well-placed to express their dissent with guns. Enough did so to start a political rebellion and end up with a revolution.

Chapter Fourteen

The Failures of Ideology

Francisco Madero was an unlikely revolutionary. He was the scion of one of the five richest families in Mexico, naturally linked to Porfirian luminaries such as Limantour, and heir to a colonial land empire and a range of businesses that outspanned most científicos: wheat, cotton, cattle, mining, foundries, coal, and banks. The Maderos were early adopters of rubber cultivation, an astute choice on the eve of its global boom. They educated their eldest boy abroad: five years in Paris and then on to Berkeley, where he briefly studied agronomy. He enjoyed a more luxurious upbringing than most científicos. Yet Madero was more than a trust fund child; he was the first to propose damming the Río Nazas, a project that eventually increased the region's agricultural production dramatically, and he made significant money in his own right.[1]

Madero was also an idealist, providing schools, doctors, housing, and community kitchens to his workers. It was an idealism that spilled over into the mockable in his belief in homeopathy and, above all, in the spiritualism that drove him. The garrulous dead, including Benito Juárez, began giving him inspiration and career guidance in the early 1900s, which he duly wrote down in a personal diary. Give up cigarettes, booze, and barroom pool was one piece of advice. Keep plowing through *México a través de los siglos*, the colossal nationalist history, was another. Take up politics, because "you are a knight . . . a member of the great spiritual family that governs the destinies of this planet, a soldier of liberty and progress." The otherworldly instructions grew more critical and precise with time, and by late 1908 Madero was being told that he would take on and defeat the aging dictator:

> Your triumph is assured in the first campaign. The General is making blunder after blunder and is powerfully influenced in making them by [us spirits], who don't want him to be an obstacle to the re-establishment of liberty in Mexico . . . Not even those who surround him feel the same personal loyalty of a few years ago, as with so much time in absolute power he has made himself each day more of a despot with those around him, who serve him through fear or self-interest, but not through love.[2]

Yet while Madero's automatic writings make him sound like a potty jihadi, spiritualism was common enough among Coahuila's dissidents, devotees ranging from liberal mayors to anarchists. It was in fact a global phenomenon: That prophet of reason Arthur Conan Doyle was another believer. And Madero's dead advisors were complemented by a worldly, strategically sharp approach. He took to politics abruptly in 1903 after the governor of Nuevo León shot seven opposition marchers dead. Madero began from the ground up, first in the municipio, then the state congress, then backing the opposition for governor, founding a serious newspaper (*El Demócrata*) and a satirical rag (*El Mosco*). Finally, in 1908, he self-published a call for national change, *La sucesión presidencial de 1910*, "The Presidential Succession of 1910." It was no call to arms; the book condemned one-man rule and election-rigging, but it eschewed social reform and recognized Díaz's many successes. It was pragmatically managerial; free elections for the vice presidency would suffice to keep Porfirian progress on track. He even sent the dictator a signed copy. "Luckily," Madero wrote in the appendix to the second edition, "the revolutionary spirit has disappeared among us."

He didn't mean it. In a 1906 letter he contemplated armed rebellion if elections failed; after meeting Díaz in 1910 he concluded that "it would be necessary to start a revolution to topple him"; in 1911 he said he had known all along that an armed uprising was the only way to win. But a bet on ballots was reasonable in 1908 and 1909. Díaz's political decay coincided with a major US economic downturn and bad harvests. In addition to the immediate challenges, a sizeable, long-gestating constituency yearned for political change: excluded professionals, aggrieved artisans, petty businessmen stymied by political impotence, countrymen on the losing end of land struggles, workers whose real wages had dropped sharply. When Madero began campaigning in June 1909, he found receptive audiences.

He was not the only opposition. His Partido Nacional Antirreeleccionista was competing with the Partido Democrático and the Partido Liberal Mexicano. The latter couldn't actually campaign; anarchists in exile, they had chosen bullets over ballots twice already, in 1906 and 1908. They had distinct revolutionary flair—disheveled romantic looks, flaming rhetoric, a scandal sheet, the legitimacy of being jailed—and they managed risings in Coahuila and Veracruz. Nationally, however, they were largely ignored. The Partido Democrático was a different matter, resting on a solid, middle-class constituency of tens of thousands, advocating the same goal as Madero: leaving Díaz alone but freely electing a vice president. That vice president would have been General Bernardo Reyes, though, and he had already shown himself indecisive in 1904. By August 1909 he still hadn't launched a campaign, and when he met resistance from the regime he folded, accepting the golden exile of a "military mission" to Europe. Meanwhile Madero launched the first modern political campaign in Mexican history, using trains to speed across the country from rally to rally, logistics arranged by telegraph, newspapers influencing voters, newsreels recording results. By the spring of 1910 he had covered twenty-two states, drawing crowds of thousands in the main cities. After his arrest and the absurdist election-rigging, he thought up a revolutionary manifesto while in jail in San Luis Potosí, an orderly revolution that would follow the rules of war and lead to an orderly electoral transition. Preexisting laws and foreign investments would be respected. The only remedy proffered for the structural miseries of Porfirian development was a promise to review the transactions of well-connected surveyors and land companies, restoring obviously stolen lands to their local owners.

Criticism was easy. Flores Magón sent around a circular a couple of days before the revolution was scheduled, laying it out. He would not be joining the Maderistas, he wrote,

> because what the liberals [i.e., anarchists] want in their programme is entirely different to that of the Partido Anti-reelectionista. The liberal party wants political and economic freedom by handing over the land to the people, the raising of salaries and lowering of hours

> of work and stopping the influence of the church in the government and the family. The anti-reelectionist party wants only political freedom, leaving the land to the capitalists, the workers as beasts of burden, and the clergy to continue to brutalise the people.[3]

There was something to the charge. It overlooked, however, the fact that again Madero was the one sticking his neck out. More importantly to most Mexicans, there was a potential for social revolution inherent in genuinely free elections and single term limits. The Maderista slogan *sufragio efectivo y no reelección* effectively meant "a free vote and no boss rule."[4] They were intertwined: One would ineluctably cause the other. The jefes políticos who translated central policies into local action, helping themselves liberally en route, stood no chance under the manifesto. As a British consul put it, they were "men who, to say the least, could never be elected." Once they were ousted, Mexicans would get on with their age-old dream of the municipio libre, local democracy. And from those grassroots a national democracy would follow, and from that national democracy, social reform.

So while Madero seemed an unlikely revolutionary caudillo—short, squeaky-voiced, eccentric, irredeemably posh, and promoting middle-class reformism—he was onto something for more Mexicans than might be expected. That much was evident in the devotion of a likelier revolutionary caudillo: a charismatic, hard-riding, bloodily gifted bandit called Pancho Villa.

Francisco Villa came from a family of mestizo sharecroppers who farmed a plot on one of the biggest estates in Durango. Like so many others—Juárez, Díaz, "Bones" González—he lost his father young and became the head of the family. As a teenager he shot a hacendado who was trying to rape his sister and then fled to the mountains, where he took shamelessly to a life of rural crime. After all, he recorded in his ghostwritten, questionably accurate memoirs, "men who pompously call themselves honest also kill and rob." His first robbery earned him 3,000 pesos, three times the annual salary of the miner he had briefly been, ten times that of the fieldhand he might have been. Like most successful bandits, he had a support network of scared, charmed, and purchased villagers, smallholders, shepherds, muleteers, and ranchers. Like some, he made sporadic attempts (according to himself) to go legitimate, and failed.[5]

Villa should have scorned Madero on grounds of class and education. He himself was an impoverished mestizo, well aware of what that meant in the social hierarchy. He could never be president, he told a journalist, because he wasn't educated enough; he could never be president, he told a fellow revolutionary, because he was dark-skinned.[6] He viscerally hated the Spanish, whom he said hadn't changed since the conquest: slavers, thieves, murderers, unwanted parasites. "We did not ask them to mingle their blood with ours," he complained.[7] He backed up rejection with massacres. Talking about Madero's upper-class political allies, he said that from the beginning he'd "loathed all the dandies to death."[8] However, on the subject of Madero himself Villa spoke quite differently, calling him "one rich man who fights for the people," "a little fellow" with "a great soul."[9]

Men like Villa, not dandies, made the liberal revolution work. The stereotypical Maderista conspirator, a well-meaning doctor or lawyer or carpenter, was not much fit for treason, stratagems, and spoils. They were moved by the sweet sounds of words, sometimes their own, but in practical terms they failed across the board, rounded up quickly by the Porfirian police (in itself, given their questionable efficiency, something of a condemnation). The first to be rumbled, a shoemaker named Aquiles Serdán, was the most successful of them; he managed to take Puebla's police chief with him before he died. Almost everywhere else cells leaked, pamphlets damaged their authors more than their targets, and workers and miners didn't rally to the cause. It was the sort of bourgeois amateurism that Lenin—listening to Wagner in Munich, mulling over a theory of professional revolutionary takeover—despised.[10] The regime did fall, and surprisingly fast, but not at all as planned.

Instead, a real and disorderly guerrilla war began on November 14, 1910, a week before the scheduled and orderly one, and not in the cities but rather the Sierra Madre of western Chihuahua. Toribio Ortega, a hatchet-faced local worthy in the village of Cuchillo Parado, learned that he was about to be arrested and headed for the mountains with sixty followers. Similar petty risings took place across Chihuahua over the next week, disparate collections of mountain men coming together under threat or opportunity and taking over their patrias chicas. The characters of the great novel of the revolution, Mariano Azuela's *The Underdogs*, form a reasonable sample: Some are outlaws (one a thief, another the unintentional poisoner of a girlfriend with Spanish fly), some are drifters, and their leader is a salt-of-the-earth rancher feuding with the local cacique. All are born guerrillas.[11] Their young real-life counterparts were too; bandits like Villa and entrepreneurs like Pascual Orozco, a muleteer whose small mining security company suffered from a lack of political clout. Such a combination of grievance, local knowledge, reputation, and networks of hard men was ideal, and Orozco quickly recruited a large following. Villa, with similar qualities—bar respectability—gathered three hundred men within a few days. By December the village risings had reached critical mass, and the rebels controlled much of the sierra and were spreading onto the plains.

Their explosive military success was due not just to their own talents but also to a feeble opposition. One of Díaz's great achievements, the shrinking of the army, came back to haunt the aging general; he had nothing like enough men to fight a guerrilla war. By 1910 all he had left were fifteen thousand soldiers, some nearly as geriatric as him, and seventy-year-old captains.[12] In reserve they had two thousand rurales, just enough to police railway lines and keep the lid on historically turbulent places like Guerrero. Tomóchic, in distant memory, must have seemed like a harbinger of doom. Subduing that small mountain village had taken what would, by 1910, have constituted nearly 10 percent of the entire army. Now Díaz faced, out of thin air, multiple simultaneous Tomóchic risings. The rebels were people like his old Zapotec soldiers, whom he once praised as "hunters, who have, because of that, a very good aim."[13] In the rebels he was fighting the sort of handy, dangerous everyman whom he had once, long ago, understood, recruited, and led himself.

Government impotence demonstrated, Mexicans outside the northern mountains began rebelling too. Field hands from the great estates of the Laguna, a lowland proletariat battered by economic crises, joined their highland neighbors. Further south, rebel bands mustered in Veracruz, Oaxaca, and Guerrero. In February 1911 revolts began in Morelos, quickly taken over by a savvy young countryman named Emiliano Zapata. By April, eighteen states were in revolt, and the people in arms—women were heavily involved from the start—were a lot more than dispossessed peasants and offended highlanders. Ranchers, indigenous peoples, and even some large landowners were going to war. Serranos, tough and independent-minded mountain people, had once fought as communities, rich alongside poor, against the Apache; as the revolution started, some picked up their parents' tradition.

As spring progressed small bands became armies that threatened the main cities. The bulk of the federal army was pinned up in Chihuahua City. In Campeche Manuel Castilla Brito, a hacendado's lawyer-son, set off toward the state capital with sixty escaped prisoners; by the time he got there he had eight hundred men following him—peons, fishermen, coffee pickers, political dissidents. Zacatecas, the center of the silver industry, came under siege. In the North, revolutionaries following Villa and Orozco were closing in on Ciudad Juárez, the main border crossing. On the Gulf Coast Gabriel Gavira, a carpenter turned general, was marching on the port of Veracruz, critical for taxes and weapons. In the lowlands of the Isthmus of Tehuantepec, hardly a revolutionary hotspot, there were reportedly eight thousand newborn Maderista soldiers. Even Mexico City had its natural defenses breached: Zapatistas captured Milpa Alta, a village on the valley rim.

So when in February 1911 Francisco Madero rode back across the border, much of the Northern Mexican countryside was under Maderista control. The question was whether it was under his. He was from the start enfiladed. On one hand there were the people who were good at war and who were doing the fighting. Not all harbored Villa's affection for the unlikely revolutionary; to some Madero was an irritant, increasingly ignored. In April Pascual Orozco fired his Maderista superior officer and in May he mutinied, attacked Ciudad Juárez against orders, and attempted to arrest Madero. To Emiliano Zapata, a thousand miles to the south, Madero was an abstraction, a man who sent some blank commissions and a notional commander who resigned within weeks.[14] Zapata's revolution was about his patria chica and his state. And on the other hand Madero had to deal with his own kind, starting with the upper-class mafiosi of his large family.

When he returned to Mexico five of his brothers joined him and began pressuring him to end the unwanted popular war, which some exiles described as "a family affair."[15] In mid-March his father, Don Evaristo, went to New York to meet with Limantour, the brain of the aging regime. In the same city the more steadfast Maderista Francisco Vázquez Gómez—although himself an insider as Díaz's personal doctor—pushed the family to keep fighting alongside the popular rebels. In April Díaz offered tepid concessions—a cabinet reshuffle, another promise of no reelection, the head of Ramón Corral. Madero was urged to cut a deal, not just by his family but also by the sort of urban intellectuals who were his natural allies. Luis Cabrera, an up-and-coming revolutionary journalist, summed it up in an open letter to Madero:

> The country finds itself almost wholly caught up in a conflagration more great and powerful than you yourself could have foreseen or hoped for; and understanding that this revolution threatens to become unstoppable, all we Mexicans have given ourselves up to the task of putting it out.[16]

Not all of them had. There were two parallel revolutions under way, one popular and the other political, and people in each realized the dangers of leaving the war half finished, the Porfiriato still breathing. Madero had appointed Senator Venustiano Carranza, one of the few big cattlemen to back him, his minister of war; Carranza was rich and slightly dull, but he clearly understood the dangers of what he called "sickly humanitarianism" and warned that "the revolution that cuts deals commits suicide."[17] Villa, with characteristic swagger, told Madero at a banquet that he was destroying the revolution, and that they should hang all the civilians in their frock coats before they themselves were hanged. ("You are a barbarian, Pancho, sit down," Madero replied cheerfully.)[18] But he recognized the danger himself, fretting, "It is preferable to continue the war and only cease hostilities when some arrangement has been reached."[19]

With Orozco on one side and his family on the other, though, he decided to end the war while he still had nominal control of the revolutionary army, and on May 21, 1911, he signed the Treaty of Ciudad Juárez. It was vague and generous. President Díaz would go into exile but would be replaced by his foreign minister, a Catholic lawyer named Francisco León de la Barra, until elections were held five months later. The president of the Supreme Court was Díaz's chief negotiator. The legislature would remain in place until 1912. The cabinet was concocted of Porfirians and Maderistas, nepotistic and conservative Maderistas at that; two of the five places went to Madero's brothers, who hadn't fought. While the Porfirian congress, judiciary, bureaucracy, and army were to continue business as usual, rebels were to hand over their weapons and go home. As for Article 3 of the Plan of San Luis Potosí, the promise of returning lands to the dispossessed, Madero declared it immediately unrealizable, to be determined through constitutional means at a later date.[20]

Díaz went into exile on the steamer *Ypiranga* headed for Paris, leaving behind a faux-naïf letter saying that he wasn't quite sure what he'd done to deserve it but was resigning anyway to prevent further bloodshed and falling bond prices. He is also supposed to have said, "Madero has unleashed a tiger. Let us see if he can control it." Carranza, out of a job, thought gloomily that the answer was obvious: Madero was presiding over "a dead revolution that will have to be fought all over again."[21]

Madero won in a landslide in October and then ruled for just over a year amid the rubble of central power. His progress southward after signing the Treaty of Ciudad Juárez was a triumphant procession; by one account nearly half the population of Mexico City turned out to greet him on June 7. So, unpropitiously, did one of the valley's frequent earthquakes. Madero was doomed from the start by the botched peace treaty and the politics that made it, one of fundamental division between those who fought the revolution and those who ruled afterward. Madero didn't take over as president until November, so he spent the first months in Mexico City with great responsibility and little power. In that time the pattern for the rest of his regime was set: in the cities, subversion by Porfirian survivors, armed with a newly free press; in an embittered countryside, wars with ex-allies.

The two were linked. Riots broke out across Mexico in the weeks after the treaty signing as local revolutionaries realized that neither Porfirian officials nor Porfirian property boundaries would move. The Terrazas would come home and their peons would still get paid fifty centavos a day in scrip for the company store. Contracts that caciques had taken from small businessmen like Orozco remained valid. Soldiers in places like Puebla were still ready to shoot protesters, as they did with machine guns in July, surpassing the death tolls of the great Porfirian massacres at Cananea and Río Blanco. Peasants in Morelos who took their lands back from planters were criminalized. Even in Coahuila, where Madero had the local knowledge to know better, federal soldiers were favored over local militiamen, hacendados over peasants, family and friends over the upwardly mobile.[22] Three weeks after Madero took office Emiliano Zapata summed up the widespread sense of betrayal:

> The so-called Chief of the Liberating Revolution of Mexico, Don Francisco I. Madero, did not bring to a happy end the revolution which he gloriously initiated with the help of God and the pueblo, since he left standing most of the governing powers and corrupt elements of oppression of the dictatorial government of Porfirio Díaz . . . [while] the immense majority of Mexican pueblos and citizens are owners of no more than the land they walk on, suffering the horrors of poverty.[23]

Zapata was in many ways the ideal rural Maderista. He was thirty, of impeccable liberal stock, his ancestors fighters against the Spanish, the conservatives, and the French. The family were rich smallholders and traders in the village of Anenecuilco. They were important in mediating between a peasant world stocked by countryfolk they understood and a broader world that they made comprehensible. His elder brother Eufemio was, like so many other revolutionaries, a muleteer, with the regional networks of merchants and remote villages that that implied. Emiliano had also dabbled as a muleteer and bred horses; he had been as far as Mexico City, where he briefly looked after the stables of a big planter, Díaz's son-in-law Ignacio de la Torre y Mier. He had taken a minor part in a failed gubernatorial campaign. When he went back to Anenecuilco in 1909, he was elected president of the village council.

Emiliano Zapata was more than a local worthy; he had the experience and legitimacy of a fugitive, arrested at seventeen for protesting against a neighboring hacienda's land grab. He was charismatic, an excellent horseman who despite showy, silver-trimmed riding clothes remained a straightforward man who enjoyed women, cockfights, and corridas. The combination made him a useful leader as Morelos's villages disappeared beneath the seas of sugarcane, and in the spring of 1910, with maize planting urgent, he organized the occupation of ancestral fields taken over by the neighboring hacienda. By late autumn he was adjudicating land disputes at the municipal level in Villa de Ayala, a village defense fund supporting a growing militia, the authorities intimidated into acquiescence. In late November the Zapatistas began conspiring to join Madero's revolution; in March 1911 they finally did. In May they took the major town of Cuautla and then, the war supposedly won, began the business of agrarian reform. Peasants with guns took over hacienda fields, and Zapata, chief of the revolutionary army in Morelos, backed them up.

A Maderista regime with a chance of working would have confirmed Zapata in power, allowed the people of Morelos to elect him governor, and granted him the autonomy to administer institutional land reform. But in the summer of 1911 Madero couldn't support Zapata, as this would have undermined reconciliation with the enduring Porfirians in government; he could only try and fail at mediation. President León de la Barra appointed first a planter and then a federal policeman to the governorship, sent in the counterinsurgency veteran General Victoriano Huerta, canceled the state elections, and declared martial law. Madero tried to negotiate by going to Morelos. He was not as well-meaningly myopic as all that, and knew that he was witnessing a microcosm of events across Mexico. On August 25 he wrote to León de la Barra with a list of complaints. Soldiers had jailed revolutionaries in Guadalajara, and Porfirian state legislatures had toppled revolutionary governors in Aguascalientes and Tlaxcala. Across Mexico interim governors were treating revolutionaries with contempt and violence as they took away their guns; of their triumphant forces only forty-eight hundred had been allowed to remain in arms; meanwhile León de la Barra's inactivity was allowing reyistas (supporters of Bernardo Reyes) to prepare counterrevolution. Madero ended with a threat and a demand: León de la Barra should remember the revolution's power and sack the hardline interior minister Alberto García Granados. Otherwise a civil war, for which he himself would prepare, was "almost certain."[24]

Yet in the end he backed the interim government. He had already supported the dismissal of Emilio Vázquez Gómez, the cabinet's main defender of the popular revolutionaries. In mid-August Huerta launched an offensive, burning ranches and executing more than sixty people. Yet as late as August 27, Zapata was still proclaiming loyalty. Only when the attorney general issued an arrest warrant did Zapata finally take to the mountains with his followers, growing in number and identifying themselves as rebel Zapatistas; the government called them "ridiculously pretentious bandits."[25]

Bandido and *abigeo*, cattle rustler, were terms long used to delegitimize rebels, branding them thieves—abigeos being the sort of thieves countryfolk particularly loathed—instead of political opponents. The Zapatista rebellion was the first of three such risings against the new regime, all branded banditry, all overtly political. In November the Zapatistas made the distinction clear with a manifesto, the Plan de Ayala, which called for peasants to get their lands back and for científicos and caciques to lose their own should they get in the way. Madero was to step down in favor of Pascual Orozco. In December they were followed in Oaxaca by the mayor of Juchitán—a troublesome city, fiercely autonomous—Che Gómez, who led five thousand men into renewed rebellion. Once again Madero tried to mediate and failed, the governor murdering Gómez—the classic ley fuga, "shot while running away"—as he prepared for talks with the president. In February disillusioned Maderistas briefly took Ciudad Juárez. And among multiple smaller outbursts—some manned by proper bandits, scofflaw opportunists—the most serious came in March 1912, when Orozco rebelled in Chihuahua.[26]

Orozco posed a major threat. He was not a stay-home rebel like Zapata; his northerners were dangerously mobile, capable of crossing long distances for a favorable fight, and they did, quickly taking every city in Chihuahua bar Parral, moving southward into the Laguna and westward into Sonora. Orozco was well-placed to take over the vital rail links to the US; he aspired to Mexico City because he had serious designs on national power, and numerous disaffected Maderistas were allies-in-waiting. In the South Zapata and the Isthmus rebels were allies in name at least. Finally, Orozco had Porfirian backers in the oligarchs of the Creel-Terrazas family, whose money helped buy him eight thousand salaried troops, and powerful sympathizers in the US, first among them William Randolph Hearst.

Yet Orozquismo turned out to have fatal weaknesses. The majority of his allies-in-waiting were doing just that, watching and waiting; his links to conservatives were not conducive to mass support. It was revealing that the people of his own patria chica did not rise with him. He could not get ammunition from the United States, which embargoed supplies to the rebels, and began running out of cartridges quickly. He had very good cavalry but little artillery. And he faced two gifted generals: Huerta the specialist in counterinsurgency, the old regime's fireman, and Villa the specialist in insurgency. Villa slowed the Orozquistas down enough at Parral to give the government time to save the key rail terminus that led to Mexico City, Torreón, and Huerta then drove them north in a methodical way. By the autumn of 1912 the revolt was over, and Orozco, wounded near the Texas border, had become one more Mexican exile in Los Angeles.[27]

It was then that Porfirio Díaz's nephew Félix launched the first of his coups d'état, with the timing that characterized a farcical but dangerous career. Félix Díaz was a clown prince; it took him eighteen years in the army to make captain. His uncle had shown admirable resistance to nepotism by giving him a series of lowly jobs—congressional deputy, consul to Chile—until those fatal last years when Díaz's political judgement failed. At that point he named the family mediocrity inspector-general of the capital's police and then brigadier-general. The sudden promotions gave Félix Díaz a top-echelon status to add to the surname. The combination might, he hoped, attract enough soldiers to topple Madero and restore his uncle. (He gave no specifics of his putative regime, but it "was natural that señor General Díaz should always be thinking about returning to his beloved country," he told a US reporter.) He launched his coup in the port of Veracruz on October 16, 1912; it was impressively incompetent. Díaz and his small force failed to seize the barracks, defend the railway lines, or even just cut the telegraph wires; they went nowhere for several days and then surrendered. "Poor Félix," commented his uncle in Paris.[28]

Yet the coup established three serious points. The manifesto followed most of the fuzzy, cut-and-paste lines of the old pronunciamiento genre—a rising "in the time of the Patria's greatest distress" to restore the honor of the nation and bring "peace and justice"—with one interesting variation: an attack on Madero's nepotism and profiteering. In power, the president had revealed "his true face, one of a being avid for wealth for himself and for his extremely numerous family," backed by an army infiltrated by "foreign adventurers and mere relatives."[29] Some Maderos indeed looked like they had fingers in the government till: Gustavo, who was being sued for fraud and defalcation when the revolution broke out, set up a company to bid for public work contracts. Others had deeply unsavory contacts: At the outset of the rebellion Ernesto had started peace negotiations with Iñigo Noriega, the Spaniard who had destroyed the village of Naranja.[30] Most demonstrably, many family members rode the presidential coattails: Ernesto the treasury secretary, Emilio the brigadier-general, Gustavo the head of the Secret Service and the *porra*, Madero's group of thugs-for-hire. The secretary of justice, Rafael Hernández, was a cousin; the secretary of defense, José González Salas, another. It was a reality that contrasted starkly with Félix Díaz's long exclusion from power and a criticism that stuck.

The coup was one more demonstration of Madero's weakness; not just because it occurred, but because it lacked real consequences for the plotters. Madero for once was happy to shoot an opponent, once duly court-martialed, but was balked by a Supreme Court stay of execution, and Díaz ended up in the Santiago Tlatelolco military prison instead. Above all, the coup made Madero more reliant than ever on the federal army, which he had been building up throughout 1912. Its share of the budget rose to 26 percent; its manpower to sixty thousand, four times the size of its Porfirian progenitor. Volunteers lacking, the government continued the loathed conscription; formally a lottery, in reality the same drumming up of the poor, the brown, the vagrant, the drunk, the dissident, and the jailed.[31] In charge of them, assiduously courted by Madero, were some hardline Porfirians, key among them Victoriano Huerta. As tends to happen with weak civilian regimes sustained by ambitious generals, the time came when they wondered why they needed Madero at all.

That time was early 1913. Madero's presidency was more than an uninterrupted slide downhill into military dictatorship. There were times of hope, such as the summer of 1912, when the government defeated Orozco and the Maderista Partido Constitucional Progresista won the congressional elections. His government had benefited from a more streetwise leadership, willing to follow his tougher brother Gustavo's advice to "govern with the law in one hand and a club in the other."[32] He signed a landmark treaty with the Yaqui that gave them autonomy and inalienable collective lands. The key cities were under control, major strikes like the Mexico City tram workers a thing of the past; the new Labor Department had proven popular. He managed to tax foreign oil companies and spend some of the results on social policy. When the government called for a territorial militia to defend the capital, five thousand volunteered.[33]

In sum, though, Madero oversaw a sweeping reversal of Porfirio Díaz's achievements. The economy was tottery. Credit was in doubt. The American ambassador was fiercely critical. The Church returned to politics with a vengeance; the main opposition party was Catholic. More important than the government's feeble electoral showing, though, was the enemy press, whose constant vituperation took the shine off Maderismo with impressive speed. Cartoons, that most Mexican form of political commentary, hammered home the message that Madero was not just dictatorial but also weak, eccentric, and incompetent. His former allies in the countryside were savages. The street theater called *teatro de carpa*, carnivalesque satire played on the cheap, reinforced the attack. The old regime had kept control of some strategic heights of the state, ranging from jefes políticos to the top ranks of the army. Committed Maderistas, on the other hand, were thin on the ground: One estimate is that at their peak only one in a thousand Mexicans fought against Díaz.[34]

Weighing up such a balance of forces, it is unsurprising that the generals in Mexico City should have decided to put together a more convincing coup. Their plotting began in autumn 1912; by winter rumors abounded. In the early morning of February 9, 1913, Díaz's old defense minister, Manuel Mondragón, freed Félix Díaz and Bernardo Reyes from prison. They marched with rebel troops to the National Palace, which cadets from the Military Academy were supposed to have seized. The teenagers hadn't, though, and loyalists opened fire on Reyes and killed him. After ten minutes of bloody fighting in the Zócalo (the nickname for Mexico City's plaza mayor, by then universal usage), the rebels retreated to the nearby city arsenal, the Ciudadela. Hundreds died, many of them civilians. Led by default by Félix Díaz, they took up positions with ample supplies of ammunition and began making war on downtown Mexico City.

The fighting lasted ten days, remembered as the *Decena Trágica*. On one side loyalist soldiers, rurales, and militiamen attacked the well-fortified Ciudadela; rebel machine gunners and artillerymen drove them back at point-blank range. Ill-aimed shells crisscrossed downtown, adding civilians to the dead. Food became scarce; looters proliferated; bodies piled up. In his diary the poet José Juan Tablada described where the dead ended up:

> The corpses of the combatants and the odd bystander are being brought down [to the monument to Juárez] from Balbuena, where they are stacked up, and doused with petrol to burn. The demi-circle at its base is, I'm told, an enormous heap of lifeless bodies. A strange offering.

When a general arrested Madero and ended it all, a relieved Tablada called him "a glorious soldier, an archetype of loyalty, a priest of honour."[35]

The general was the treasonous Victoriano Huerta, and so the hyperbole was particularly inapt. Huerta had been the first general to declare for Madero and consequently became his commander in chief. It was rapidly clear that neither side could win a military victory: Each had around two thousand troops. The rebels couldn't escape; the government couldn't storm their stronghold. The traditional belief is that Huerta and the plotters deliberately engineered a war of stalemate and terror, keeping loyalist troops out of the city, firing wide of the citadel walls and dispatching rurales down a narrow street straight onto machine guns. The reality is that the government never stood a chance of winning: They had half as many pieces of artillery as their opponents and only sixty mortar shells, while the rebels—they held the city arsenal, after all—had 13,000 shells and 120 machine guns. They certainly had a strategy of terror; they fired 11,000 of those shells into downtown Mexico City.[36]

Huerta had been invited to join the plot early on but had refused. When it became clear that the fighting was set to last, Huerta established links with the rebels but didn't get the reward he wanted, the presidency. So he let the insoluble military problem continue until the body count motivated those already disposed to get rid of Madero to do so. It worked: The American ambassador, Henry Lane Wilson, went rogue—the process had started a long way back with false reports to Washington of Maderista incompetence and bad faith—and rallied the diplomatic corps and Mexican Senate to request Madero's resignation, backed by a threat of US intervention. Only then, on December 18, did Huerta launch his coup, arresting the president and his consigliere brother Gustavo.[37]

They sent Gustavo to the Ciudadela, where he was lynched. Huerta and Díaz joined Wilson at the US Embassy, where the ambassador brokered an agreement, the Pact of the Embassy, making Huerta provisional president. The plotters staked a claim to legitimacy by pressuring Madero and his vice president, José María Pino Suárez, into signing a resignation letter. It promised the safety of Maderistas across the country and of Madero himself, guaranteed by the diplomatic corps. He and Pino Suárez were to be escorted from the National Palace to Veracruz and ushered into exile. Instead, the night before their departure two cars drove them to Lecumberri, the penitentiary that symbolized Porfirian order, where the lights went out and an officer of the rurales, Major Francisco Cárdenas, shot them and riddled the cars with bullets. It was a bloody mafioso ending to an unworkable regime, doomed by the gentlemen who botched its design.

Francisco Madero's government and its murderous dénouement convincingly demonstrated that liberalism didn't work anymore. In 1911 everyone claimed to be liberal, hearkening back to the men and ideas that had made Mexico genuinely independent in 1867. Díaz was a liberal; Madero was a liberal; Zapata was a liberal, appealing to "the immortal code of 1857," the "immortal Juárez." Even the anarchist Flores Magón brothers were in name at least liberals. By 1913 that consensus claim had vanished. Madero was the last important liberal in doctrine and in practice.

It was not just that Madero's ideals faltered when he was faced with the realities of holding power in a revolutionary, half-understood country, but also that he and his inner circle realized it and cut their cloth accordingly. They themselves turned away from their idealism in what one historian has called "a liberal apostasy," faith shaken and actions betraying a new appreciation of realpolitik. Elections were less than immaculate from the start. In 1911 Madero imposed an unpopular running mate—Pino Suárez, a Yucateco brought onto the ticket for balance—over the much more popular Francisco Vázquez Gómez, attracting suspiciously more votes in the countryside than in the cities. Subsequent gubernatorial contests were of variable probity, and in 1912 Madero sent governors in turn more direct messages to ensure the election of favored deputies. When *El Imparcial* wrote the elections off as wholly undemocratic, it was more of that opposition paper's propaganda; but neither were the "flagrant frauds and patent injustices" wholly imaginary.[38]

On the streets, meanwhile, the porra did the dirty work of beating up opposition candidates and their supporters and menacing the press. In Tabasco José Gurdiel Hernández, an opposition editor, was given the old extrajudicial death sentence of the ley fuga.[39] Eighteen journalists requested amparos, judicial protection against abuse of power.[40] In February 1912 Maderista deputies discussed outright suspending freedom of the press; later that year Madero asked Congress to allow the government to fine and arrest newsmen and force printed retractions. (Revealingly, the law failed to pass, and the Maderistas turned to either setting up their own papers or buying out the old ones, most significantly *El Imparcial*.) In the countryside constitutional *garantías*—a blanket term for due process and civil rights—were suspended in the conflict zones of Chihuahua and Morelos, where vicious counterinsurgency was the answer to rebellious ex-allies. In some ways Madero became reminiscent of Maximilian: well-meaning, hopelessly upper-crust, divorced from reality, his progressivism going against the nature of his times and allies.

Against a tired and self-contradictory liberalism, three ideologies stood out: the improvised rural socialism of the Zapatistas, a diverse Catholic conservatism, and a coherent but out-of-place anarchism.

The Zapatistas' dogmatic thinking was codified in the Plan de Ayala, put together in a hurry by Zapata and the schoolmaster Otilio Montaño, and the speeches of the urban intellectuals who later represented them on the national stage. Overt ideology, in the sense of a written systemic and totalizing belief set, was hard to discern. There are no consistent references to any universalizing political philosophy. God is there fighting alongside the pueblo; the Plan was typed up by Huautla's parish priest, and the Virgin of Guadalupe was embroidered on Zapatista battle standards.[41] On the other hand their slogan *Tierra y Libertad*, land and freedom, was taken from contemporary anarchists, and the Zapatistas' laws, letters, and actions once in power expressed a clear and constant ideology, a peasant socialism with complementary social, economic, and political predicates. It meant collective ownership of the means of production, in their case large estates; communal labor to work them; nationalization of those they didn't care for, namely sugar refineries; acceptance of a reasonable level of individual wealth, albeit in a free-market economy that was trumped by the moral economy, the categorical imperative to keep others from starving; all ruled by a popular democracy in a decentralized political system. (Which would be a formidable opponent: One American, looking at Morelos in 1919, wrote "You might as well fight the Swiss.") The central state wouldn't vanish, but it would shrink to the basics. Soldiers would choose their chiefs and could change units. They got land, and could go back to cultivate it when it was necessary and possible. This was more than a set of postulates: It was what Zapatistas did whenever they could.[42]

Likewise invoking the Virgin of Guadalupe was a reinvigorated political Catholicism. Churchmen and their congregations had been excised from public life in 1867, indelibly associated with the foreign empires of Spain and France. Civic Catholicism, on the other hand, had endured and rebounded in religious schools, orphanages, charities, cofradías—the Catholic lay brotherhoods that were officially extinct, unofficially enduring in assorted legal guises—and women's associations such as the *Damas de la Perpetua Vela*, who organized round-the-clock veneration of church altars. A crop of young bishops educated in Rome set up new parishes; Porfirian oligarchs like Olegario Molina helped fund their church-building and other projects. Regional bourgeoisies, like the tobacco growers of San Andrés Tuxtla, began building cathedrals. The Church's new recognition of the strains of capitalism, given the papal imprimatur in the bull *Rerum Novarum*, encouraged both churchmen and technocrats to incorporate labor into development through public works and mutual societies for factory workers and hacienda peons. Between 1900 and 1910 there were four Catholic Congresses to discuss social reform and the Church's role in furthering it. By the time Madero rebelled, all the elements of a return to political power were in existence bar a party. In May 1911, as his rebellion ended, a party formed, the Partido Católico Nacional, which became the main legal opposition.[43]

Like their colonial forebears, the political Catholics of the early twentieth century were not all of the same mind. Some were democrats who competed decorously in elections, even if those elections were sometimes rigged against them, as in Jalisco and Zacatecas in the summer of 1912.[44] Others were social Catholics who set up activist groups such as the Asociación Católica de la Juventud Mexicana, the Catholic Association of Mexican Youth, which drew in militant student types. And finally there were the hardliners in the press and episcopacy. Trinidad Sánchez Santos, the octogenarian editor of *El País*, wrote an opinion piece in the run-up to the coup calling on Madero to either resign or go out in a useless and sinful way by suicide.[45] The categories overlapped: Sánchez Santos had spent the Porfiriato as a prominent social Catholic, inveighing against the evils of the free market. Wherever they lay on this broad spectrum of beliefs and tactics, Catholics believed that they were better prepared to run Mexico than Maderistas or secular politicians in general and took appropriate actions. That meant at the least opposing Madero's rule, acquiescing to his fall, and accepting his dictatorial successor.

The third ideology was the anarchism of the PLM, powerful in exile, on stretches of the border, and, as elsewhere, in ports. Mexican anarchists combined the universal anarchic traditions of their peers in Barcelona and Buenos Aires with an established history of radical journalism, pamphleteering, and rebellion. The Flores Magón brothers had released a revolutionary manifesto in 1906, the Plan of Saint Louis Missouri, and persuaded small groups in Coahuila and Veracruz to rise under its auspices. In 1911 they briefly seized Tijuana and Mexicali. They were for the last decade of the Porfiriato the only revolutionary game in town, which earned them unmerited causal prominence afterward as *precursores de la revolución*, revolutionary trailblazers.

In reality, anarchism might have had an intrinsic appeal to autonomist revolutionaries across Mexico, but it never took. Villa was in the right place (by both geography and inclination) to take an interest in anarchism, but he didn't; instead he arrested members of the Partido Liberal Mexicano as part of the disarmament of 1911, and then fought them when they allied with the Orozquistas. Mexican anarchists were promiscuous in their choices of partners—one of the Flores Magón brothers, Jesús, even joined a counterrevolutionary cabinet—but not many wanted to dance with them.[46] When PLM members invaded Baja California, they were part of a motley band that included bandits and American filibusters, eyeing up the state for plunder and annexation. Fifty Italian anarchists who visited Tijuana wrote off the revolution there as fictitious. The real revolution lay in Zapatista Morelos, they wrote, but Zapata had little or nothing to do with them.[47] Anarchists were too distant and pretentious for the everyday; they were too frightening for the middle classes in search of an ideology. A young idealist in *The Death of Artemio Cruz*, one of the great revolutionary novels, puts it neatly:

> My entire life reading Kropotkin, Bakunin, old man Plekhanov . . . and at the moment of truth I have to join up with Carranza because he's the one who seems like a decent sort, the one who doesn't scare me. You see how limp-wristed? I'm scared of the plebs.[48]

The fictional medical student in Azuela's *The Underdogs* goes about things the other way around, tacking an ideological superstructure onto the straightforward serrano logic of the primitive rebels with whom he (accidentally, and to his horror) falls in. After the leader asks what they're fighting for, the student gives him a lecture:

> You still don't understand your true, high and most noble mission. You, a modest man without ambition, don't want to see the very important role that falls to you in this revolution. It's a lie that you are here because of Don Mónico, the cacique; you have risen against the caciquismo that assails the entire nation. We are elements of a great social movement . . . instruments of destiny to recover the sacred rights of el pueblo.

This comes as news to the rebel rancher, whose party line is "All I want is to be left in peace to go home."[49]

He was one of the majority driven not by ideology but by pragmatism. Aside from opportunism, revolutionary careerism, and the geography of conflict, there were convincing immediate and long-term reasons for joining the most convenient rebel group around. Regular meals alone counted, particularly in the years of great hunger like 1915, when the previous year's fighting had devastated the wheatfields and cattle ranges of the North and the cornfields of the South. So did exercising a choice of army while it still existed, going to the hills with Zapata, or with Saturnino Cedillo in San Luis Potosí, or with any of their lesser ilk across Mexico instead of waiting for conscription. So did protection in dangerous times. When John Reed asked one of the child soldiers he met why he was fighting, the eleven-year-old nodded toward his leader and answered, "The man who gets under a good tree gets good shade."[50]

In the longer term, the two traditional sets of enemies had to be dealt with, neighboring communities and the distant capital. Generations-old intercommunal grievances—land, personal feuds, municipal or parish dominance—often determined the choice of sides. In Jalisco, San José de Gracia leaned toward Villismo, so next door Mazamitla leaned the other way, denouncing the Villistas to all other factions as they passed through.[51] In northern Guerrero the villagers of Ixcateopan, liberals in the nineteenth century, became Zapatistas; those of neighboring Ixcapuzalco, conservatives in the wars of the Reforma, backed central government. It was a common pattern, exceptions like Morelos rare, even in the very center: The villages around Teotihuacán were also scenes of centuries-long disputes that carried over into political alliances and identities in the 1910s.[52]

Associated with this was the historic interloper, Mexico City. In much of provincial Mexico the question "What have the Romans ever done for us?" would have met with silence or ire. Revolutionary pragmatism might dictate conditional alliances with the national state, but it could also determine taciturn defiance or armed opposition. The northern risings in 1910 had, after all, strong roots in the meddling of a far-off city and government. The civil wars of the 1910s had different origins and courses in different regions of the country, expressions of the lasting improbability of ruling Mexico. There were of course common patterns, smaller groups whose raison d'être and way of doing things paralleled the greater movements of Villismo and Zapatismo, to which they often paid nominal fealty. The famous individuals of the revolution were synecdoches for obscure leaders and their followers. The greatest pattern of all, though, was the preeminence of pragmatism over ideology, local concerns over abstract systems, an approach of "whatever works" taken by both rulers and ruled. Ideological strands contributed to this: liberalism to enthusiasm for meaningful elections, anarchism for workers' definitions of a fair deal, Zapatismo for social justice through land tenure. Mistrust of formal ideology, however, ran deeper, and the failure of any single ideology to convince on a national scale was central to how politics worked not just for the next decade, but for the next century.

Chapter Fifteen

The Civil Wars of Revolution

The squalid back-alley killing of Madero set off a series of civil wars whose human cost surpassed anything capitalinos could have imagined. Between Huerta's coup and 1920, small farmers, peons, socialist workers, middle-class citizens in arms, entrepreneurial northerners, and a bloated federal army fought with an intensity that literally decimated the population, taking nearly one and a half million Mexicans. In relative terms Mexicans lost more people between 1910 and 1920 than Germans did in World War I.[1] They used many of the same tools: Mauser rifles that could kill from nearly half a mile away, machine guns that fired six hundred bullets a minute, barbed wire, mines, heavy artillery, armored vehicles, airplanes. Unlike the European conflict, however, this was a total war, one that moved across large swathes of the country killing civilians and soldiers alike. Atrocity stories became casual, recounted without fuss. It was the greatest mass dying in Latin America since the conquest.

There was a chronological rhythm to it, three different civil wars fought in sequence. The first was an all-out fight against Victoriano Huerta, whose actions in power pushed very different Mexicans into an improbable rebel coalition. This lasted from March 1913 until August 1914, Huerta only lasting slightly longer than Madero. The second war, from November 1914 to November 1915, was between the victors, who now had little in common. The third was a guerrilla war, extending from late 1915 until the summer of 1920, a bloody stalemate in which dozens of small bands fought a central government that secured the cities and not much else.

Survivors rhetorically simplified this decade of complex violence into "*La Revolución.*" Once underway it had a certain inevitability. Participants and observers alike talked about it in the language of natural disaster. (In this, metaphors were preceded by reality: In Mexico City one earthquake toppled the statue of the Angel of Independence, a second greeted Madero's triumphant arrival.) The revolution was a flood, a volcano, a hurricane; the man caught up in it a mere leaf in the storm, the great storm that swept Mexico.[2] It surpassed human understanding and trumped human morality; the nonsensical tautology "*La Revolución es la Revolución,*" the Revolution is the Revolution, it is what it bloody is, became the self-justification—in the words of the man who coined the phrase—of fighters who "killed, burnt, raped children, kidnapped, looted, stole and 'came into possession of' horses, automobiles, furniture, houses and even haciendas."[3]

That it should have started was less inevitable: Huerta took a series of decisions that pushed Mexicans to rebel again. A different set of decisions might have had a different outcome. A president installed by coup in a capital divorced from the rest of Mexico was not inevitably unpopular everywhere else; his predecessor had disappointed in social reform while presiding over several regional wars. A Mexico where Madero left for exile as agreed; where deals of the nineteenth-century sort were cut with warlords, their regional fiefs tolerated in return for tribute and fealty; where vague nostrums about social policy gained some flesh, promises—particularly in more recalcitrant regions—fulfilled with reconstruction funds for villages, rural education, clearly looted lands returned; and a paid army that fought only in the few remaining dissident regions, long-troublesome places like Guerrero: This was a Mexico that might have avoided rebellion and civil war.

Huerta was not the man to do this. He gestured toward political and social reform, drawing up an education plan and creating a Department of Agriculture. He appointed Genaro García, a leading advocate for the rights of indigenous peoples and women, to direct the Escuela Nacional Preparatoria, the prestigious gateway to the university. His presidency was hawked as an interregnum, with peace, amnesty, and land on offer for obedience and demobilization. But it was never going to happen. Huerta's personal qualities weighed against it; he was a power-hungry, politically dense alcoholic, a combination that favored what one writer called "the spurious regime of a dipsomaniac."[4] So did his philosophical qualities; Huerta shared the militarism of the Cold War's coup-driven generals like Augusto Pinochet in Chile, the ideological belief that soldiers made the most effective leaders and bureaucrats, and hence should run societies at every level. (Like Pinochet, Huerta had a thinking side: Both had taught at war colleges, and Huerta had excelled at mathematics.) So Huerta ordered all government employees—deputies, ministers, governors—to become soldiers, drilling alongside students, shop assistants, bankers, and office workers. This change was to be implemented by eminent Porfirians, starting with a restoration of General Mondragón as secretary of defense.[5]

The struggle that ensued was no-holds-barred. In the capital soldiers and policemen murdered top politicians. Abraham González, the governor of dangerous Chihuahua—a state with violent manpower, wealth, and a keen arms vendor to the immediate north—was shot en route to Mexico City "while running away," the ley fuga once again. Four policemen kidnapped and murdered Senator Belisario Domínguez of Chiapas; three senior congressmen met the same end. Death squads appeared, driving anonymous through Mexico City at night to disappear the inconvenient, another foreshadowing of the military dictatorships of the 1970s. In the countryside the war was the scorched earth of burned hamlets and villages and hungry towns. Senator Domínguez was killed because of a pamphlet he wrote saying that Congress should remove Huerta from office because he was prepared to "cover the entire land with corpses . . . rather than to abandon power." The deputies who insisted on investigating his death were arrested en masse, the legislature dissolved at gunpoint. This was in October, after nine months of the Huerta presidency, but the writing was on the wall from the beginning. At a US Embassy party on the night Madero was killed, Huerta, while pouring himself a drink, stuttered to a diplomat that his solution for Zapata was an eighteen-cent rope.[6]

Military violence reanimated the old Maderista coalition. It was not the instant revulsion that mythmakers down the line claimed. Some old rebels bought into the new regime. Others opted to watch and wait, a revival of the strategy of the pronunciamiento. Governor Maytorena of Sonora promised recognition of the regime and then said his state would be a "spectator" and departed for a leave of absence in Arizona. Even the soon-to-be leader of the coalition, Governor Venustiano Carranza of Coahuila, who had prophesied precisely such a dénouement, hesitated. As late as February 21, 1913, he was still negotiating with Huerta; he even sent a telegram acknowledging the general as "President of the Republic." Then, however, the news of the Madero assassination arrived alongside reports of federal troops heading up from the Laguna. At that point, on February 23, Carranza went out on the balcony of the governor's palace and gave the revolution's equivalent of the Grito de Dolores. He wasn't going to stick around to be murdered, he told those below, but instead he would go into the countryside and fight.[7]

Carranza has gone down in history as dull, vain, and pompous. A young member of his court, the writer Martín Luis Guzmán, went into well-penned, and hence unusually influential, detail. The Carranza with whom he spent the early days of the revolution was "somewhat bovine," with "something very reminiscent of Don Porfirio" about him. He had himself piped into dinner by a bugler every evening.[8] Despite questionable charisma and looks, he was obsessed with being photographed. In March, on the run, he issued the Plan de Guadalupe, a manifesto that declared his government to be Constitutionalist and himself to be First Chief and interim president-in-waiting. Yet whatever his character, there was a realpolitik to this formalism and publicity. Like other wartime leaders without much of a country—De Gaulle in London, striving to incarnate France itself—Carranza's narcissistic ceremony and self-promotion were important in those early days to keep the idea of an orderly, legitimate, civilian Mexico alive.

Carranza was also the first major leader to declare a rebellion, and he had the institutional equipment to fight one: Pessimistic from the start about the Madero peace settlement, he had kept a state militia intact and armed and could immediately muster a thousand troops. He was not the only politician to have converted mistrust into armed reserves. On the other side of the sierra the Sonorans had held on to their state militia too, cleverly adducing their need to defend against the Yaqui in uncertain times, and even added to the initial thirteen hundred men during the Orozco rebellion. Lower down the ranks municipal self-defense forces added to the military potential of the North: Men like Álvaro Obregón, an upwardly mobile local politician, had set up his own volunteer detachments a year earlier.[9] The Zapatistas, main force of the South, had been in arms throughout. But the far-off northerners were the key to fighting the military regime.

Alongside institutional recruitment ran the second track of grassroots rebellion. Small groups mushroomed. Pancho Villa, the most dramatic example, left his El Paso exile in late February 1913 and crossed into Mexico with eight men and nine horses. They were ill-equipped, though Villa—a teetotaler, counseling others to "drink, but don't get drunk"—had at least brought coffee beans. By the summer he had seven hundred men, to whom he added another five hundred when joined once again by Toribio Ortega. Suddenly rich—forced loans were the order of the day for all the early leaders—Villa turned from volunteers to a paid soldiery, and when in October he attacked his first major city, Torreón, he had five thousand men behind him.[10]

Yet while many of the same northern rough types turned out as had for Madero, a key difference in the coalition against Huerta arrived in a new group of first-time revolutionaries from Sonora. They had in the main abstained from the fighting in 1911, a solid choice given their isolation from the rest of Mexico and close links to the United States. Martín Luis Guzmán called Sonora a Mexican Far West: only recently settled in any depth, a territory taken with considerable fighting from Apache, Pima, and Yaqui, and for a long time severed by geography from the rest of the country, in this case not the Great Plains but the Sierra Madre. It was seven hundred miles from Mexico City, and there was still no direct railway line. Neither was there an equivalent to the US Cavalry, riding over the horizon to save settlers in their hour of need. The combination favored entrepreneurship, investment from an outside world, but also last-ditch community alliances. By 1913 it was an increasingly sophisticated and quite autonomous state. The war with the Huerta regime was, as one historian put it, a war between two distinct nations with parallel resources.[11]

Álvaro Obregón epitomized the Sonorans' potential, the military and political clout that the immediate past and fortress-like topography gave their upwardly mobile leaders. Obregón was a small rancher of pure Spanish descent, one of eighteen children, who dropped out of school at thirteen. Like Villa he left home as a teenager and had several jobs: carpenter, blacksmith, photographer, shoe salesman, and hairdresser. Unlike Villa he became a landowner, buying a farm and making a go of it specializing in chickpeas. He invented a mechanical harvester and shipped his harvests to Arizona. He went into local politics and succeeded; in 1911 he was elected mayor of Huatabampo.

As Obregón rose through the social and military ranks he maintained a strategically useful common touch. He could share (or make up) stories of a worker's past or a farmer's daily struggle; he also had the rancher child's familiarity with indigenous languages, fluent in Mayo, competent in Yaqui. He was also fluent in rancher talk, the mixture of slang, rough jokes, and country metaphors that gives speakers the innate legitimacy of people who know when to say *cabrón*. He recruited the future leader of his party in Congress with a dick joke.[12] More importantly, he recruited large numbers of Yaqui soldiers with, in lore at least, indigenous eloquence. (Their silent arrows were distinctly handy in bush fighting.) After Madero was murdered the governor of Sonora made Obregón head of the state militia, and by autumn 1913 he was commander in chief of the twenty thousand soldiers of the Division of the Northwest.[13]

To fight them, Huerta took the Federal Army that Madero had already inflated and used conscription to increase it to an alleged 250 thousand men. It was an army of the unmotivated and outclassed: ex-convicts, dope smokers, workers snatched by press gangs from night shifts, bootblacks, late-night drinkers, aficionados filing out of bullfights. Some weren't even men. In one photograph a child soldier stares out from a railway platform, his rifle taller than he is. He had a gun at least; on the other side many revolutionaries, among them more child soldiers, didn't. The US had from the outset banned arms sales to the rebels; in July they extended the ban to the Huerta government. In April 1914 the Marines occupied Veracruz—the surface reason the brief arrest of a few US sailors up the coast in Tampico, the underlying reason Woodrow Wilson's antipathy to the Mexican dictatorship—in what was intended, among other things, to end Huerta's arms purchases in the rest of the world. It didn't work; a German steamer just unloaded its shipment of arms further down the coast.[14] But the disparity in numbers and arms was insignificant next to the disparity in rank-and-file motivation and skills, and in general officers' talents for both regular and guerrilla warfare.

Child soldiers were common on all sides in the revolution.

So Huerta's army quickly abandoned the countryside and its big business to its fate. By the end of June 1914 the Constitutionalists had cleared Sonora, the border towns were falling, and the Villistas, by far the most active rebels, held Durango. In October Villa briefly occupied Torreón; in November he surprised the garrison at Ciudad Juárez and took it more permanently. In December he captured the capital of Chihuahua. Meanwhile Zapata's Army of the South pushed out of Morelos, creating a southern front that diverted thirty thousand men to defend Mexico City. The board set, Carranza ordered an offensive on three fronts from the North. Obregón was to move down the coast out of Sinaloa before curving inland toward Mexico City. Villa was to continue the more direct route south along the

Mexican Central Railroad; in the East General Pablo González to take his division toward Monterrey. González, another young northerner, was earning a reputation as pleasant, crooked, and incompetent; the acerbic Carranza described him as "the general who has commanded the most powerful forces of the revolution and has had the honour of never winning even the smallest of battles."[15] The serious campaigns would come in the West and Center.

The strategy worked surprisingly quickly. In February 1914 Wilson ended the arms embargo and the Constitutionalists went on a shopping spree. Villa incorporated his diverse bands into a modern army, the División del Norte, adding to the old tools of irregular cavalry the new ones of artillery and—confirming once again the complexity of his character—startlingly large numbers of hospital train wagons. Tactically he relied on terrifying mass cavalry charges, but for strategy he had the foremost military thinker of the Porfiriato, the enigmatic and humane Felipe Ángeles. In the first few days of April the División del Norte took Torreón and then wiped out ten thousand Federal troops at the Battle of San Pedro de las Colonias, ending Huerta's presence in the North. Pablo González captured Monterrey, and Zapata drove the Federal Army out of Morelos and took Chilpancingo, the capital of Guerrero. On June 23 a strong garrison made a last stand at Zacatecas and was carefully annihilated. Huerta's lickspittle cabinet called for his resignation. The game was up.

What happened next was what should have happened three years earlier: the prosecution of the war all the way to Mexico City, an unconditional surrender, and a wholesale changing of the guard. In May 1914 an international conference at Niagara Falls began, convoked by the major Latin American powers, its ostensible mission to settle the US occupation of Veracruz and thus avoid a Mexican-American war, its true purpose a negotiated stitch-up of the revolutionaries. It was supposed to be a replay of the Treaty of Ciudad Juárez; Carranza ignored it and pushed on toward the capital.[16] There the elite of Huertismo voted with their feet, or rather the carriages of the increasingly dangerous railroad, and headed for the coast while they still could. The clergy, powerful unelected politicians under Madero, led the charge: eight bishops, including Archbishop José de la Mora, who headed out in May. They were followed by more than one hundred generals and more or less the entire Huerta cabinet. Some of the wealthiest Porfirian families accompanied them into exile, as did intellectuals who had chosen poorly. José Juan Tablada, the thuggish poet who had welcomed the Huerta coup, kissed his favorite willow tree goodbye, literally, abandoned his garden, and headed for New York.[17] On July 15 Huerta went the same way; others chose Paris, as Latin American intellectuals and dictators traditionally have, where French governments handed some of them *Légions d'Honneur*.[18]

Huertistas gone, a government delegation met with Álvaro Obregón a day's ride north of the city and agreed to the Treaty of Teoloyucan, an unconditional surrender. Like so many of the revolution's key events, it was choreographed for media. Obregón was photographed signing the paper on the mudguard of an army truck and then filmed playing catch with corncobs, the message one of a brilliant general with a human, clownish touch. Yet he was already preparing to fall out with his allies. The treaty required the Federal Army to hold the southern front against Zapata until Obregón occupied the capital. It was clear, not just in retrospect but at the time, that the split between popular and northern armies was going to happen. Carranza had already ensured that Obregón would win the race to Mexico City, first by ordering Villa to divert from his push southward to take Saltillo and then by withholding coal for his trains. As Guzmán put it, witnessing the subsequent power-sharing negotiations, they came from "two irreconcilable worlds" with "two absolutely opposed categories of mind."

The two worlds met in a constituent convention at Aguascalientes in October 1914. On one hand was the superficially bluff, honest rancher Obregón, in reality a smoothly duplicitous power player; on the other was Villa, the "wild animal in its lair," "a jaguar whose back one stroked with trembling hand." He had already resigned once in protest at Carranza's orders. Zapata didn't come at all, sending some intellectuals with firebrand speeches and paltry experience, who turned up late. Carranza neither attended nor sent representatives. The only people with any power who showed up to negotiate, rather than put on a Villa-run show, were Felipe Ángeles and Obregón.[19] In November the

Convention of Aguascalientes ended with an interim president, Eulalio Gutiérrez Ortiz; an assembly; and a military run by Villa and Zapata. In December they occupied Mexico City with sixty thousand men.

This was the peak of the success of the popular revolutionaries, the collision of the two worlds in the streets of Mexico City, the Zapatista soldiers in the smart Porfirian Café Sanborns, the Villistas at Sylvain's Restaurant, their leaders sitting on the president's chair in the Palacio Nacional. The assembly and its puppet president were sidelined in short order. The real president had himself photographed on that throne, a chuckling, uniformed Pancho Villa. The suspicious glower of a showily dressed Emiliano Zapata at his side, foot propped arrogantly on knee, large sombrero in hand, is more revealing. Zapata felt out of place. Left in charge of the capital, he abandoned it to Carranza's army at the end of January 1915.

Villa, meanwhile, was literally out of place. After a brief stay in Mexico City he took the División del Norte northward to fight Carranza's

Confidence and discomfort: Villa and Zapata in the National Palace (1914).

Constitutionalists on multiple fronts. He ignored Ángeles's urging to concentrate forces and go immediately after the main Constitutionalist army and its government in Veracruz. Obregón, who had critically chosen to ally himself with Carranza, was left time to rebuild his army for a series of decisive battles. He even added to them; returning to Mexico City he recruited five thousand workers of the radical new union, the Casa del Obrero Mundial, to form "Red Battalions." And as World War I sent global prices of arms and ammunition sky-high, the Carrancistas controlled exports of other wartime necessities, oil and henequen, whose value rose in parallel. They could buy materiel from multiple suppliers and manufacture their own. The Villistas could do neither, and their homelands' export production of minerals, cotton, and cattle was devastated by two years of war. Printing worthless money as fast as possible, they ran low on dollars and consequently low on bullets.

As the balance of forces moved in Obregón's favor, he moved as many men as possible into the Bajío to draw Villa into attacking carefully prepared modern fortifications: trenches, often preexisting in the form of irrigation canals, dense fields of barbed wire, and numerous machine guns. In April 1915 Villa took the bait in two battles at the northern city of Celaya. Having disdained Ángeles's strategic advice he now disdained Ángeles's tactical advice, launching instead his customary cavalry charges. He hadn't attacked Obregón's supply lines; he'd written a personal letter to Zapata asking him to help out with that—"I have no doubt that, convinced of how important it is to wipe out Obregón, you will help me to defeat him and undertake the maneuvers I request"—but Zapata never answered and went campaigning eastward instead.[20] Finally, Villa hadn't concentrated his forces and hadn't formed any reserves.

Slapdash ferocity and embryonic blitzkrieg had worked before, relying on exceptional horsemen, charismatic leadership, and motivated infantry, driven on by Villa's innovations—cavalry deployed from trains, a massive if somewhat token railway cannon—and general aura of invincibility. Yet there was only so far blitzkrieg could go without the future's tanks, dive bombers, paratroopers, and three-ton trucks. Meanwhile Obregón had learned the relevant lessons of the previous autumn in Europe, where the Battle of Ypres had shown just how slaughterous entrenched modern weaponry was against cavalry. The

Villista approach was obsolete. As an aide recalled, their charges were like "devastating cyclones . . . but poor us when that cavalry charge was contained by the enemy! Wholly defeated inside five minutes."[21] The Bajío campaign stretched over three months and still followed the basic pattern of waves of Villista riders attacking entrenched infantrymen. One of Obregón's telegraph reports gives the heart of the matter: thirty-eight hours of "continuous and desperate assaults" along thirteen miles of front line, individual Villista brilliance undone by industrial weaponry and the tactical savvy to use it.[22]

Yet despite Villa's losses he had enough men to continue the campaign and, again ignoring Ángeles, deliberately drew Obregón into a major battle at León. This time, some lessons learned, the División del Norte dug themselves in, formed reserves, and persuaded Zapata to threaten Obregón's overstretched lines of communication. The two sides spent over a month in the cautious attrition of trench warfare until Obregón, running out of ammunition, began considering an assault. Before he could launch it, though, Villa lost his patience and attacked the Constitutionalist rear, throwing everything into a costly and eventually disastrous move. Obregón, his arm blown off, ceded command to his cousin Benjamín Hill. Hill followed an existing plan for a massed counterattack on the Villistas to his front, who broke and ran. They had one more battle in them, at Aguascalientes, but this was a minor rerun. The Battle of León of June 3, 1915, ended the División del Norte, and with it the civil war between conventional armies.

In its place came nearly five years of guerrilla warfare. At Celaya in 1915 Villa enjoyed an army of fifty thousand, a polished railway car, and a garde du corps in dressy uniforms: brand-name Stetsons, khaki drill, golden badges (hence *los Dorados*, the Golden Ones). The following year he was in a cave halfway up a cliff, where he and two others hid for a month from pursuing cavalry. It was, he told them sardonically, "his old headquarters from expeditions past"; back to banditry.[23]

His was the most dramatic rise and fall, but it was emblematic of the fate of popular revolutionaries across the country, "comrades in arms and ideals," in Zapata's words, "we the ignorant men who make war," in Villa's.[24] Zapata did the best in preserving his army: He didn't fight the lethal pitched battles of Villismo, and the invasion of Morelos in 1916 may have even increased his operational forces. In September that year the Constitutionalist General Pablo González ordered all of the free villagers of rural Morelos to "reconcentrate" in the cities, whence they could be deported to labor camps in Yucatán. The choice before many peasants between forced migration into hungry towns, conscription, or joining the Zapatistas was not much of a choice. As one put it, "If it was between their taking me to fight far away, God knows where, and staying here, it was better for me to fight here."[25] At Zapata's nadir in 1919 he still had thousands willing to fight for him, even if some were Zapatistas in name only: In northern Guerrero they raided the villages of supposed allies.[26] There were prosaic reasons to stay in rebel arms: avoiding conscription and obtaining food in famine times.

Elsewhere, in places where counterinsurgency was less implacable or peasant bonds weaker, smaller forces declined precipitously, returned to straightforward banditry, or just disappeared. This didn't mean the central government controlled that much of Mexico. Carrancista rule remained in many areas a hypothesis, a presence only when armored trains, twitchy patrols, or columns flying black flags with skulls set off nervously from northern cities. Self-defense militias stepped into the void, locals with guns, largely divorced from government, proliferating on ex-Villista turf—Villa was no longer trusted by many of his own people—and in areas with land conflicts. Places far from the main battle zones remained extremely dangerous. In Chiapas the rebels nicknamed *mapaches*, raccoons, had declined significantly by 1919. In only three months, though, armed men raided thirty-one towns and villages and robbed seventy-two trains.[27] Trains weren't safe anywhere: In February 1917, less than a month after the new constitution had passed, a train on the Mexico City–San Luis Potosí line ran over a mine that blew the first four wagons to pieces and was followed by a half-hour shoot-out. The story merited a quarter column on page four of *El Pueblo*, one of the main newspapers.[28] It was almost a banality, the stagecoach robbery of the nineteenth century updated with the mournfully whistling boilers of derailed locomotives and the bodies of the civilian dead.

Train destroyed by Zapatistas (c. 1915).

There was also an elastic quality to the guerrilla forces, which meant they could never be written off. There was more to the last civil war of the 1910s than raids, mountain ambushes, and dogged defense of homelands. Villa's followers seesawed between tens and thousands of men in arms, and his bigger comebacks posed serious threats to government outposts in the North. He took Parral four times between 1916 and 1919, mauled a series of Carrancista regiments in the summer of 1918, and briefly captured Ciudad Juárez in June 1919. Zapata's men descended from the mountains and retook all of Morelos in February 1917; they weren't driven back until the autumn. In the south of Veracruz the indomitable loser Félix Díaz made another comeback, funded by wealthy New York exiles: Invading from Galveston, Texas, he built up an appreciable army that was then cut down to one hundred men; he then rebounded to head, in name at least, a loose collective of serrano revolts in Veracruz, Oaxaca, and the Southeast. Finally, there were the newborn mafias with political labels, sophisticated criminal organizations selling protection to big business. In the most striking example, the oil companies of Veracruz paid Manuel Peláez, a nominal follower of Díaz, $25,000 a month to keep their oil fields and refineries safe.[29]

The national government headed by Carranza was in consequence more aspiration than reality. Inclined toward authoritarian centralism, Carranza was forced to put up with subordinates who ran their own fiefdoms, ripped off the Treasury with padded payrolls, and ran venal armies whose soldiers (with a certain shortsightedness) sold arms and ammunition on the sly to their enemies. General Jacinto Treviño sold his soldiers his own overpriced grain and drew salaries for troops who never existed; he was spectacularly found out when Villa attacked his garrison at Ciudad Chihuahua and found 6,000 instead of the 21,300 Treviño was claiming. By 1918 the autonomous generals had plundered Chihuahua's great estates so much that their owners no longer paid taxes.[30] Treviño continued his corrupt career for decades; neither did the flamboyant corruption of Pablo González in Morelos hurt his prospects. Carranza depended on them too much.

Carranza's government couldn't even control the frontier with a US that wanted him to win as the unlovable but only palatable option. On March 8, 1916, Villa crossed the Arizona border and attacked the town of Columbus. These first invaders since the British chose a strange target: Columbus was small and poor, with a few hundred dwellers and an appreciable garrison, the worst of both worlds. The Villista cavalry made a lot of noise in the early-morning dark, galloping through the streets, burning the hotel, and shooting randomly into the air or at houses. But they also attacked the army stables and not the barracks, leaving six hundred US soldiers in one piece, and failed to either take the bank or find a local merchant who had drawn Villa's ire. So the raid was a failure in immediate terms, American machine guns costing the Villistas far more casualties than the seventeen Americans they killed.

Exactly why Villa ordered the attack is unclear. Blind impulsivity might explain it: Villa had developed a bitter resentment toward Americans, once amicably disposed toward him, for their conspiratorial support of Carranza. He had lost a key battle in Sonora, he told his troops in an emotional speech, because the Americans had allowed Carrancista troops to cross their territory in trains to get there safely.

Moreover, everyday Americans were lynching Mexicans in the borderlands. Someone in El Paso had thrown a match at Mexicans soaked in kerosene for delousing and burned them to death. (The local American press wrote it off as an accident, caused by a Mexican heroin addict playing with matches.) The violent racism, Villa insisted, had become intolerable. A different version features the same impulsivity: A local merchant called Sam Ravel had taken money upfront for guns and never delivered them. A third scenario, a conspiratorial but rational choice, casts Villa as an instrument of German geopolitics, promised a reward if he could distract the Americans from entering the war in Europe. The German Foreign Office was indeed wistfully considering the difficulties of getting war materiel to Villa the same month as the Columbus Raid. A year later they tried to put the idea into action again, this time eccentrically promising to give back Arizona, Texas, and New Mexico to Carranza if he attacked the US. That one backfired spectacularly: The Zimmerman telegram communicating the offer was picked up by British intelligence and handed to the Americans, causing public outrage and helping the government to declare war on Germany.[31]

The fourth explanation is the most likely: that Villa, in one of his wilier moments, was provoking the US to attack Mexico. A limited intervention into northern Mexico would, by this logic, reveal Carranza's secret pact with the Americans, unifying the rest of Mexico—under Villa, hero for fighting them off—and toppling the government. Or it might drive Carranza into negotiating a favourable peace with Villa in a desperate search for national unity. Whatever the case, he was confident in his ability to evade US forces, damage Carranza, and bring a new generation of recruits to his nationalist cause; all bets he won, because the US reacted to the Columbus Raid hastily, immediately sending five thousand men under Brigadier General John J. Pershing into northern Mexico to destroy the dispersed bands who made up Villa's army. When Villa hid in the cave he was hiding from American, not Mexican, cavalry, and when he came out he recouped forces and arms supplies.

The American Punitive Expedition (its formal name) was an educational experience for Pershing, who went on in 1917 to command the American Expeditionary Force in Europe. He deployed unprecedented technology, above all trucks and planes, and it all proved barely adequate in the face of the challenge of supplying an army far from home with the very basics. The then-Lieutenant George S. Patton, one of his aides-de-camp, left behind in his diary a litany of the logistical and martial woes: the trucks that over and over broke or got bogged down, the roads on maps that didn't exist, the aeroplanes that got lost or blown off course, the absent bedding, the ever-present cold at night, the men, many "too small," with uncleaned rifles and overlong hair, at times even shoeless, falling out of columns to defecate by the roadside, the Mexicans who refused to talk to them. That a certain Colonel Beacome died of high blood pressure was, perhaps, to be expected.[32]

The American troops spent March 1916 to February 1917 in Villa's stomping grounds of Chihuahua and Durango. They grew with reinforcements to eleven thousand regulars and in early days penetrated as far as Parral, Villa's *patria chica*, over four hundred miles south of the border. Increasing tension with Carranza's government, however, led the US expedition to end long-range operations in the summer, and subsequently stay close to their main encampment at Colonia Dublán, Chihuahua, less than a hundred miles into Mexico. Boredom set in: Patton spent increasing amounts of his time hunting and practicing his swordsmanship, while the men played baseball, gambled, and made visits to a carefully controlled stockade of sex workers. (The low level of venereal disease was touted as one of the Expedition's achievements.) When Pershing withdrew after nearly a year he could claim victory, having driven Villa into hiding, but it was a threadbare claim. The US Department of War estimated that they would need two hundred thousand troops to occupy Mexico. Villa emerged unscathed, briefly restored to some popularity, building up several thousand regulars and reconquering most of Chihuahua.[33]

Villa had made the US look unlikable and incompetent. The US had passed the same favor on to Carranza, demonstrating his weakness, cynicism, and lack of political antennae. While complaining bitterly, he did nothing concrete about the invasion, choosing to avoid contact and allowing the Americans to bring in supplies by the railroad he controlled. At the same time a new US arms embargo left him without his own military supplies. The national militia he formed, echoing 1846 and 1861, was deliberately left standing around. Finally, he sent his own expedition into Chihuahua to hunt for Villa, tacitly cooperating with Pershing's force.[34]

It was all emblematic of the shadowboxing of Carrancismo in government. Everyone promised some sort of agrarian reform; even Félix Díaz had a plan. Carranza duly passed an Agrarian Law in 1915, but nothing came of it; instead of peasants his generals took over and restarted large haciendas, benefiting from the cheap labor of desperate former fighters and refugees. In other cases, Porfirians came out of exile and recovered their old estates. Even the Terrazas got their lands back.[35] In 1917 the Carrancista government passed a new constitution as a public relations exercise, drawing a line between their legitimate, sophisticated modern state and the guerrilla movements that the papers wrote off as hordes of troglodytes and barbarians. Elections held for the Constituent Congress returned the sort of revolutionary body found elsewhere, heavy on lawyers, light on popular leaders (sixty-two of the former, five unionists). Not many people voted, and the delegates debated a quick two months before producing 137 articles. Some were remarkably radical. Article 130 gave the government tight control over the Church's internal affairs, including the appointment of priests, and the ability to shutter churches altogether. Article 27 nationalized land, water, and mineral deposits, allowing the state to expropriate and redistribute according to its aims and the people's needs. The rural poor could petition the government for land grants to form collective farms called *ejidos*. Article 123 mandated an eight-hour working day, obligatory Sunday rest, a minimum wage, equal salaries for men and women, and paid maternity leave. The sum was the most progressive code in the world, far beyond anything Carranza wanted. (His pen broke as he signed it—perhaps pressing too hard in irritation, perhaps just an unhappy augury.) The constitution's potential was extraordinary, but its reality in 1917 was totemic, almost offhand—the sweeping social revolution of land reform passed in a single evening session—and its provisions went largely ignored. The reality of the Carrancista state was summed up not in legislation but in budget allocations: Between 1917 and 1919, 67 percent went to the army.[36]

So it was unsurprising that the sprawling frozen conflict should end in a coup d'état. By 1920 the civil wars—"Mexico's national sport," said an embittered Guzmán—were unwinnable.[37] The popularity of popular rebels had run its course; Villa maintained himself in part through a terrorism that left him more feared than loved. Mestizo communities in Chihuahua and Durango formed self-defense communities to fight his dispersed bands; indigenous villagers on the other side of the sierra, such as the O'odham of Nayarit, did the same.[38] Smaller bands and bandits had run up against their political and military limits as provincial leaders. The typically most violent age cohort, young men in their late teens and early twenties, had been utterly devastated. The highest of politics, the presidential succession, was in the hands of an unloved man without any delicate or common touch, who planned to rig the 1920 election in favor of Ignacio Bonillas, an exile without a military record or even, some said, much of a Mexican accent.

In the wings meanwhile there waited a consummate Machiavellian, disassociated from the worst of the regime by retirement to his ranch in 1917; a self-conscious Cincinnatus whose letterhead read, ÁLVARO OBREGÓN, FARMER.[39] In summer 1919 he began a presidential run, taking trains across Mexico from Nogales to Tapachula, cracking jokes, putting himself on the level of his listeners, and telling them that he had been dragged back from the land to politics by the disastrous state of the nation. Obregón had the advantage of being a wounded war hero, an arm blown off in battle; he also shrewdly retained his old persona of bluff clownishness, telling one journalist,

> They have probably told you that I am a bit of a thief. All of us are thieves, more or less, down here . . . The point is, however, I have only one hand, while the others have two. That's why people prefer me. I can't steal so much or so fast!

And at the same time he made more serious promises to Americans, capitalists, and peasants; he would preserve estates yet at the same time redistribute them. It was a populist's juggling act, and it worked to cobble together another broad and improbable revolutionary coalition. When Carranza sent federal troops to Sonora, dissolved the state government, and brought Obregón to Mexico City on charges of conspiracy, he was doing the farmer a final favor. The Sonorans launched a formal rebellion with the Plan of Agua Prieta, and Obregón, bringing the Zapatistas with him, became its caudillo. In

May 1920 Carranza fled the capital and was murdered in the night in a small highland village called Tlaxcalantongo. The interim president, the young Sonoran Adolfo de la Huerta, finalized a series of peace deals; Pancho Villa came in from the cold in return for a hacienda in his Durango patria chica and lands for his followers. On September 5, 1920, Obregón was smoothly elected president of a newly peaceful Mexico, its revolution past.[40]

It wasn't, though, for two reasons. Widespread and collective political violence continued. The period 1920–1929 saw numerous assassinations of leaders from mayors to presidents, mass murders, forced migrations, three military rebellions, and a fourth civil war, fought between a doctrinaire anticlerical government and Catholic counterrevolutionaries. Moreover, there was more than a decade's time lag between the civil wars fought in the name of a revolution and a genuine social revolution, the only one in the history of the mainland Americas.

Assassination had been a key tool in politics from the very beginning. Porfirian survivors killed petty popular leaders as soon as the Treaty of Juárez was signed, and under Huerta the killings became more visible, audacious, and counterproductive. In 1913 the murder of Abraham González, governor of Chihuahua, convinced northerners that the new dictator would come after them too; soon afterward the murder of Belisario Domínguez, senator from Chiapas, was the final straw for the civilian congressmen who had gone along with the new deal. Unintended consequences didn't put off plotters. In 1916 the Americans, frustrated by their failure to capture Villa, sent two Japanese agents to assassinate him. Their mysterious Asiatic poison was in fact a US Army prescription, supposed to kill Villa three days after he ingested it in his coffee, and it failed dismally. In 1917 Villa himself opted for the deus ex machina of killing Carranza, infiltrating two men into Mexico City to scout out the possibility of shooting the president when he went for his early morning ride in the woods. The actual hitmen, fifty of Villa's Dorados, couldn't make it into the city and the plan collapsed.[41]

Not all assassinations backfired. In April the Carrancista commander of the Fifth Regiment of Cavalry, Colonel Jesús Guajardo, set up a meeting with Zapata to discuss an alliance. Guajardo, whose five hundred men might tip the balance and allow the southerners to retake Morelos, was in reality feigning his desertion. He did it with great realism, mutinying and taking the town of Jonacatepec in Zapata's name. Habitual suspicions somewhat allayed, Zapata organized a meeting for April 10 at the Hacienda de Chinameca, part of his patria chica. They were supposed to turn up with thirty men apiece; Guajardo showed up with several hundred and a machine gun. When Zapata went into the hacienda, a guard of honor raised the rifles they had been presenting and shot him dead.

His murder seriously damaged a movement already in decline: It was followed by his chieftains' drawn-out politicking to succeed him, military inactivity, and negotiations with old enemies. Some Zapatistas surrendered to General Pablo González, despite his history of brutal counterinsurgency; some major Porfirian planters came back.[42] Without the fillip of the Sonoran rebellion, killing Zapata might well have made his followers ineffectual, hopeless participants in desultory, low-intensity warfare. The political culture of the civil wars was one in which personalism was still critical, in sociologists' terms a time when bureaucratic domination was uneven and charismatic domination central to any armed force. Consequently, the tactic of assassination carried high risks but also high rewards, and it was cheap. Just about every prominent politician of the period claimed to have suffered an assassination attempt. The American comedian Will Rogers joked about it, telling his audience one night, "I've just seen something incredibly rare: an ex-president of Mexico. Who is alive!"[43]

It wasn't much of a joke, the ex-president in his audience thought, but it was spot on: By the end of the 1920s assassins had done for all the main national leaders of the 1910s. Pancho Villa was gunned down in Parral on July 20, 1923, his body left slumping dramatically out of the front seat of his car. On July 17, 1928, a Catholic radical infiltrated a banquet in San Ángel in the guise of a pavement caricaturist and instead of drawing Álvaro Obregón shot him five times in the face. Key regional leaders came to similar ends. In Guerrero the Partido Obrero de Acapulco, an anarchist group, won most of the early elections along the coast north of Acapulco. Its leader, Juan Escudero, mayor of the city, was shot in 1922 by federal troops, ending up paralyzed; having learned to type with his feet and gone back to work, he was shot again, fatally, in 1923. Two weeks after that, Felipe Carrillo Puerto, the caudillo of the powerful Partido Socialista del Sureste, was taken by soldiers in the middle of the night to a cemetery in Mérida and shot dead.[44]

The coincidence of dates—Villa, Escudero, Carrillo Puerto, and assorted lesser figures all died in the second half of 1923 and the first days of 1924—was not casual. Obregón began his presidential term in 1920 with legitimacy and a comparatively democratic approach to the new politics. Political parties proliferated; congressional elections were relatively competitive; newspapers were allowed a free hand. But in 1923 Obregón changed his approach in the face of two pressing political problems. First, the United States continued to withhold diplomatic recognition from his government. Without that recognition Mexico could neither access vital international loans nor prevent arms from reaching future rebels. The US government, fully aware of its leverage, used it to negotiate the Bucareli accords, an exchange of recognition for reparations to US asset holders who alleged revolutionary damages and the protection of US oil companies from expropriation.

Obregón's second problem was the eternal one of the presidential succession. The revolutionaries had written Maderista no-reelection laws into the constitution. Yet while Obregón's term ended in 1924, his control of the government machinery gave him a decisive vote as to who should succeed him. There were two leading candidates, both Sonoran: the popular interim president of 1920, Adolfo de la Huerta, and Plutarco Elías Calles, the unpopular interior minister. Calles seemed the more promising puppet, and so, in myth at least, Obregón chose him with one more joke. He took the two candidates for a drive in Chapultepec Park, so the story goes, where he delivered a eulogy to de la Huerta's many talents. He then turned to Calles and listed his multiple failures in life, concluding that as he was more or less unemployable, he needed the presidency just to survive.[45]

Calles was in reality a gifted political strategist. He had a checkered pre-revolutionary career as barman, hotel manager, teacher, school inspector, and police chief—a past which, combined with a family broken by alcoholism, favored his combination of puritanism and bureaucratic levelheadedness. He didn't have much of a record as a fighting soldier, but he had shown what he could do as interim governor of

Sonora in 1915, where he preserved political stability, kept resources flowing to the army, and banned gambling, alcohol, and bullfighting. Success and alliance with Obregón brought him key national posts: Secretary for Development, then War, and finally the Interior. He furthered a reputation as a Machiavellian by implication in prominent assassinations, including those of Senator Field Jurado, an opponent of the negotiations with the US, and Pancho Villa, a possible rival for the presidency. At the same time he fostered important personal alliances with the Confederación Regional de Obreros Mexicanos, the main union; the peasants of the Partido Nacional Agrarista; and important regional bosses like Carrillo Puerto. By 1923 he had the mass backing for a presidential run.

His rival de la Huerta, on the other hand, had been a successful interim president and was supported by the Partido Cooperativista Nacional, which controlled the Chamber of Deputies, the Senate, and six governorships. He had led negotiations with the International Committee of Bankers in New York, agreeing to pay $1.5 billion dollars of questionable debt.[46] Nevertheless, with Obregón against him he could run as an underdog, a patriot opposing the Bucareli accords, a defender of democratic politics against fixers and murderers; he and the leader of the Cooperativistas, Jorge Prieto Laurens, claimed that *Callista* assassins were after them.[47] On November 30, 1923, a series of risings in the name of democracy began in Guerrero and spread across much of the country. Their figurehead was de la Huerta, their reality a mixture of provincial and Mexico City grievances; their threat lay in a surprising number of military allies. Two of Obregón's longtime personal friends were the first to rebel; he dispatched a third, General Fortunato Maycotte, to buy off rebels with 200,000 pesos only to see him join them.[48] In the end 102 generals and about half the army came out for de la Huerta, who fled the capital in a Ford, tires screeching as he shook off his government tail, and in Veracruz became the public face of the rebellion.[49]

The Delahuertista coalition fighting in his name was motley; even the Communist Party considered joining in.[50] It ended up a cobbling together of malcontents, crooks, political outs, dissident labor leaders, and provincial conservatives. The frustrated generals, concerned that Obregón's effective appointment of a successor foreclosed their own routes to power, disliking Calles, were the key movers. They used the language of democracy and socialism, now ubiquitous for the revolution's politicians, and not all were cynical. The British ambassador was an unlikely believer of sorts, serially insulting Mexico's elections as medieval or, on good days, seventeenth-century; even he admitted, though, that election results in the twenties would "probably be found to represent the majority of the effective opinion of those whose ideals have lent them the courage to partake in the dangerous pastime of politics."[51] *Sufragio efectivo y no reelección*, the Maderista slogan of "a real vote and no reelection," had enduring power and some reality. "A real vote" had been the goal of numerous Mexicans since Independence; in the 1920s, as in the 1820s, there were opportunities to get it. Most of Sonora's veteran Maderistas joined de la Huerta's rebellion.

So there were reasons beyond conservatism and elite infighting driving the Delahuertistas, and by January 1924 they controlled the cities of Veracruz, Xalapa, Guadalajara, Villahermosa, and Mérida: the main port, the oil, the agricultural heartland of the Bajío, the Isthmus of Tehuantepec, and Yucatán's lucrative henequen industry.[52] At the same time, however, rebel commanders were contacting Obregón asking for peace negotiations, because the rebellion was a mess from the start. On arriving in Veracruz de la Huerta had urged the commanding officer there to wait and sound out more allies; "El Mocho" González, "the Bible basher," told him not to be scared; the would-be revolutionary leader replied, *"Me sobran calzones"*—he had more than enough balls—but they were jumping the gun. De la Huerta was right: The lack of initial planning meant the Delahuertistas never fought as a coordinated force; "idiots," in one loyalist's crisp verdict. Against them they faced a patient Obregón, waiting in a well-defended Mexico City until arms and ammunition could arrive from the US, whose sympathetic government sold off World War I military surplus for cash in hand.[53]

The rebels, on the other hand, were getting none. Meanwhile the government was using Calles's work with popular organizations to good effect, arming their members and securing the backing of two major peasant leaders, Saturnino Cedillo in San Luis Potosí and Adalberto Tejeda in Veracruz. In February Obregón began his offensive proper, taking back Veracruz on the fifth and Guadalajara on the twelfth. In March de la Huerta sailed to New York, supposedly to raise funds, the writing on the wall. By the end of the month the majority of the Delahuertistas had surrendered; some holdouts in the marshlands of Tabasco were left to their own devices, Obregón relying on the appalling rainy season to do his work for him, and in July they too gave up. The boyish de la Huerta went off to an exile's life teaching singing in Los Angeles, his party was destroyed, and Calles became president, claiming an unbelievable 82 percent of the vote.[54]

In military terms the rebellion was a sideshow of the civil wars, remarkable for its ratio of theoretical combatants to comparatively low casualties, some seven thousand dead. Its consequences, on the other hand, were far-reaching. Most observers went on expecting more trouble from the army: In the course of a single month in 1929 Lloyds of London sold nearly half a million dollars' worth of "anti-revolutionary insurance" in Chihuahua.[55] After 1924 it could only be limited trouble, though, because Obregón seized the rebellion as an excuse to tame an unruly army. In 1919 it had taken up two-thirds of the overall budget; by 1926 that was only a quarter.[56] He had fifty-four generals shot for treason, purged many more, and curtailed the survivors' power with more numerous commands and consequently fewer troops per potential mutineer. Large contingents of active-duty soldiers were transferred into the reserves, notoriously reluctant warriors. Finally, the threat of an army so weakened that it couldn't deal with popular rebels was countered by keeping many of the rural militiamen who had fought the Delahuertistas in arms.

The cost was the risk that peasant and labor leaders might become overmighty subjects; the rest of the 1920s showed that it was a risk worth assuming. After 1924 Obregón came to the Porfirian conclusion that political parties were inherently threatening and gave up his promise of no reelection, changing the constitution to allow it through nonconsecutive terms and extending the presidential term from four to six years. His former chief of staff Francisco Serrano disagreed and ran against him, meeting with Obregón in 1927 to suggest "a campaign of gentlemen." Obregón told him that such a thing was impossible "given the fatal circumstances then prevailing in Mexico"; a third candidate, General Arnulfo Gómez, agreed, promising Obregón a place in the penal colony of Islas Marías or six feet of earth.[57] In the early autumn of 1927 Serrano, Gómez, and their followers began planning rebellion.

Serrano had led the army effectively against the Delahuertistas in 1924, but he was also a renowned playboy, who once lost so much in a night's gambling that the Treasury had been called in to clear his debt. Gómez had led the persecution of Delahuertistas in Mexico City and was generally unloved; he was sick into the bargain. These were ambitious, flawed individualists rather than ideological dreamers. Yet they used a rhetoric of democracy that resonated when Mexicans were vigorously competing in uncertain elections at all levels, and in the mouths of civilian allies might be taken at face value. But the popular appeal of democratic elections was outweighed by the fact that the rebellion was an open secret, snuffed out before even declared. Serrano and his main civilian collaborators were executed on October 3, 1927, on the road from Cuernavaca to Mexico City. Gómez was shot a month later. Elsewhere their few military sympathizers were shot or moved on, in the best of cases given the classic "military mission abroad"; the mass execution of all the officers of the 16th Battalion at Torreón encouraged the others to do nothing.

There was one more rebellion left in the revolutionary army, that of March 1929, when General José Gonzalo Escobar declared against the government in Hermosillo. Though Escobar took over a quarter of the army with him, the movement was from the start something of a farce. Everyone saw it coming, yet the US ambassador Dwight Morrow was sanguine enough to head off on holiday to the Bahamas. Escobar's rising started off promisingly enough with disgruntled garrison commanders taking much of the North and the key port of Veracruz, but within three days they had abandoned that traditional bastion of rebellion. The British ambassador portrayed the rebellion as a commercial enterprise: Northern generals, their cash flow hurt by an austerity budget, had weighed up their chances of restitution and took them.[58] The revolutionary ideologue Luis Cabrera dubbed it "the Railroad and Banking Rebellion . . . for all that it amounted to was the rebels taking money from the banks and withdrawing to the United States by the Central line and by the Southern Pacific line, destroying the railway communications as they went." It lasted about six weeks, cost two thousand lives, sent a fair number of dissidents into exile—a couple went into the film business—and politically never stood a chance.[59]

As a profit-making enterprise, though, the Escobaristas were onto something, alert to the many possibilities of the time. As the Escobar Rebellion came to its end, a ghost ship appeared in British waters, a steamer that had reputedly been traveling the seas for two years, seeking buyers for 5 million pounds worth of stolen Mexican government silver. It had docked in New York, but finding no buyers there had proceeded to the Channel Islands. A shady American intermediary had approached Johnson Matthey, Britain's largest bullion dealer, offering the silver at an 80 percent discount. The reason was simple: As there was no clear title, the buyers would have to melt and brand the silver themselves, effectively laundering money. Tempted, Johnson Matthey dithered, accepted, then sought advice from the Foreign Office—who told them not to tell the Mexican government, whatever they did—got cold feet, and pulled back. That several months' worth of the national production of silver should be floating around the world spoke eloquently of just how much revolutionary loot was up for grabs. The story never left the archives and never went into the history books. Where the silver ended up remains a mystery.[60]

Yet while there were strong political and economic reasons for the 1920s to be a decade of violence and unfinished business, the most serious conflict was over neither jobs nor riches but rather religion. The 1927 and 1929 fighting between soldiers and Sonorans mattered to relatively few Mexicans. But the same years saw a final civil war, fought over religion, that killed as many as one hundred thousand and drove far more into exile, leaving ghost towns behind them. Their church went with them, archbishops and priests and nuns deported or fled to the United States, holdouts celebrating nervous masses in clandestine basements.[61] It was a counterrevolution that mirrored the revolution of 1910: provincial, detonated by elites but manned by everyday people driven to arms by a politics that they could no longer stand.

The spark to this Mexican Vendée was President Calles's strange decision to put into practice the dormant anticlericalism of the Constitution of 1917. Several of the numerous hastily penned articles of that constitution had been profoundly anticlerical, enshrining liberal and even anarchist beliefs in the nefarious effects of the Catholic religion and its institutions. Article 3 had proscribed religious schools, giving government the right to eliminate those that already existed. Article 5 forbade the establishment of monasteries. Article 24 banned acts of public worship. The sweeping Article 130 was the coup de grâce: It banned Catholic political parties, newspapers, and foreign priests and gave the federal government jurisdiction over all religious services and church buildings, while state legislatures could determine how many priests they needed. The new revolutionary politicians were to issue the licenses churchmen needed to do their job; no license meant no priests, no communion, confession, absolution, marriage, baptism, or last rites; no Church, and no salvation.

This was a war on the fundamental beliefs and social organization of a majority of Mexicans. Sonoran governors in the Northwest and Southeast, including Calles, had essayed something similar in the 1910s and early '20s; earlier presidents had left the issue well alone. Calles—illegitimate, seminary-educated, admirer of Mussolini—began putting his campaign against the Church in February 1925, shortly after taking office. His first step was to facilitate the physical takeover of six Mexico City parishes, his union allies sending gunmen to back up a rogue priest called José Pérez, who set up a schismatic church, the Iglesia Católica Apostólica Mexicana (ICAM), and declared himself its patriarch. The French and Russian revolutionaries had done something similar, albeit with more success. Even in Catholic Mexico, though, the revolutionary church still ended up controlling some three hundred parishes, stretching from the diaspora to the central and southern highlands, tending to some two hundred thousand mainly indigenous souls. It gave a voice to villagers sick of priestly outsiders who price gouged for the sacraments while scorning the popular fiestas that linked Rome to a pre-Hispanic past, rites that bound local communities together in innocent heresy.[62]

It also gave a voice to the elite Catholic reformism that dated back to well before Independence, one that included many liberals, Mexicans who believed wholeheartedly in God but not in his representatives on Earth. The schismatics followed that enthusiasm for the primitive Church, preaching with indigenous interpreters against confession, a tool of blackmail and a get-out-of-jail-free card; the Latin mass as mystification; threats of hell; and the collection of tithes as dictatorial. They also followed liberals and revolutionaries in opposing Rome's authority with nationalist calendars and ceremonies. (Patriarch Pérez had form as a liberal revolutionary, having fought as a captain in Oaxaca's militia.) The schismatics celebrated Juárez's birthday and lifted the excommunication on Padre Hidalgo. There was a generous sprinkling of the failures and eccentrics who populate most heresies, and Pérez could seem a geriatric buffoon. But if the schismatic church was in ways risible, it was also credible, aligned with many Mexicans—including revolutionary anticlericals, men like labor leader Luis León, even Calles himself—who weren't atheists, Jacobins, or Bolsheviks, but rather Catholics disgusted with modern Catholicism.[63]

If Patriarch Pérez ended up recruiting many, though, he alienated more. Spitting, stone-throwing crowds attacked schismatic churches, kept back by lines of police and union gunmen. Middle-class militants formed the Liga Nacional Defensora de la Libertad Religiosa, the National Defense League for Religious Freedom, while the bishops tried to negotiate a détente with the government. But conflict escalated steadily over the next eighteen months. Some fuel came from provincial revolutionaries in places like modernizing Veracruz and socialist Tabasco who invaded churches, burned saints, smashed icons, razed gravestones, and drove priests out. The Southeast was in the vanguard: Even before Pérez detonated the conflict, the governor of Tabasco, Tomás Garrido Canabal, had got rid of all but one priest. The governor specified not just numbers but qualifications: Men of God had to be Mexican, over forty, and married.[64] Calles sometimes tried to defuse the situation and sometimes worsened it, as when he appointed a hardline *veracruzano* anticlerical, Adalberto Tejeda, to the powerful Secretaría de Gobernación, the Interior Ministry. The bishops and the Liga escalated their rhetoric. In April the pope was brought in to mediate and failed, and by the end of 1925 the Mexican hierarchy was petitioning Rome to come out against the revolution.

The surprise, perhaps, was that mass violence came so slowly. In February 1926 Calles ordered all governors to close Church schools and expel foreign priests; in June he passed the Calles Laws, which enforced among other measures the constitutional demand that priests register before exercising ministry. Aspirants had to be nominated by their putative flocks, who would control their church buildings. Local revolutionaries could mobilize their own flocks against that, or promote a schismatic. The clergy had to do all this inside a month. Thirty-seven priests in Mexico City had already been jailed for ministering without registering. In response the Liga called for a general strike of consumers, instructing devout Mexicans to avoid buying anything beyond the bare essentials of food, eschewing luxuries, lottery tickets, lay schools, and dances. Their aim was to bring the economy crashing down. The bishops' strike, *cessatio a divinis*, was much more serious: On July 31 they suspended all church services, leaving the government endangering the souls of the unbaptized, unconfessed, or unshriven. In the last days of the month, families crammed churches, the overflow catching trains to the bigger cities, where priests married, baptized, and confirmed at breakneck speed. On July 30 more than a hundred marriages took place in the Cathedral and Basilica of Guadalupe alone, and eventually policemen, soldiers, and firemen cleared the packed churches and confiscated the keys. In Mexico City churchgoers rioted from Tepito, the thieves' barrio, to the Roma, the colonia of the Porfirian bourgeoisie. In the countryside they took up arms and went to the sierra.[65]

The Liga didn't declare war until January 1927, being the Catholic equivalent of the Maderistas: heavy on young lawyers, urban, earnest, and ineffectual. The real war started much earlier, when the mountain men of the Center-West, equivalents of the Chihuahuans of 1910, came together in big enough bands to take on the substantial army units moving into their territory. In October they killed half a regiment in Durango; in December rebels in Jalisco wiped out the entire 59th Regiment. By the year's end they controlled large parts of those states and southern Zacatecas. With success and territorial bases came increased organization, the first bands coalescing, as the revolutionaries had in 1910, into more regular army units. The government tried to write them off in the classic cant as bandits and cattle rustlers. In Michoacán, Jalisco, Guanajuato, Zacatecas, and Aguascalientes this spin was difficult to sustain, though, because an initial twelve thousand rebels grew into a force of tens of thousands—estimates vary considerably—divided between a conventional and guerrilla army.[66]

They were called *Cristeros*, their slogan was *Viva Cristo rey*, Long live Christ the King, and their war was the Cristiada. The states where they were strongest were the most devout, places where the religious revival of the Porfiriato had had the greatest impact, and those the revolution had largely passed by. Rural priests were key leaders; in February 1927 the government ordered their blanket arrest in the warzones. It was right to see them as revolutionary cadres. The ranchers of San José de Gracia only went to war, despite the dread miracle of inerasable footprints showing the Holy Family leaving town in disgust, when Padre Federico told them to.[67] Padres José Reyes Vega and Aristeo Pedroza were two of the first five leaders in the region.[68] The bishops egged on their flocks: The pastoral letter of September 1926, sent out as the risings began, urged Catholics to "imitate the constancy of the early Christians . . . who died like good men, and their blood was the seed of new converts."[69]

Sympathetic outsiders stressed the sacrificial nature of the popular devotion that sustained them and made them such good listeners and useful troops. Years later Graham Greene (Anglo-Catholic, struggling with doubt) described a congregation in San Luis Potosí in straightforward terms of martyrdom:

> The peasants kneel in their blue dungarees and hold out their arms, minute after minute, in the attitude of crucifixion; an old woman struggles on her knees up the stone floor towards the altar, another lies full length with her forehead upon the stones . . . This is the atmosphere of the stigmata, and you realize suddenly that perhaps this is the population of heaven—these aged, painful and ignorant faces: they are human goodness.[70]

The first historian of the Cristiada echoed him, calling the Cristeros "an anonymous crowd of rural saints."[71]

By no means all were. Padre Vega, nicknamed "Pancho Villa in a cassock," slept around and shot prisoners. Even mannerly San José de Gracia contributed the odd criminal.[72] O'odham guerrillas who wiped out a federal column in the Durango sierra were unbaptized locals on the way back from a shamanic ritual.[73] There were three good reasons apart from religion to fight the government in the second half of the 1920s: caciquismo, land, and the winding paths of local history.

The Cristiada echoed the revolution in more than causes and strategy. The sociological types of those early movers of 1910—bandits, roughneck businessmen, local serrano elites—came out for the Cristiada too. Quite a few were Villista and Zapatista veterans. In Jalisco one of the handiest leaders was Victoriano Ramírez, *"el catorce,"* whose nickname came from the fourteen men whom he shot dead in a jailbreak. Like Villa, some saw el catorce as a sort of highland Robin Hood, others as a criminal pure and simple; the Cristeros themselves ended up believing the latter, arresting him and shooting him dead (during another jailbreak).[74] In northern Michoacán the powerful hacendado Ladislao Molina was a liberal cacique who wanted nothing to do with the Cristero leadership, but was, rather, determined to defend his family's hold on Pátzcuaro, a municipality founded on seized indigenous lands.

Molina rebelled because a meddling state was trying to nationalize his lands and redistribute them to the sort of people his father had violently dispossessed. It was a high-stakes case of the general phenomenon of jumped-up revolutionary bureaucrats and outsiders alienating provincials, especially conservatives, in an echo of the old jefes políticos. Molina, backed by gunmen and friendly with President Obregón, had fought the intruders and agrarian militants of Governor Francisco Mújica and won. As President Calles's dispute with the Church intensified, though, the government began giving out Molina's land to local peasants and arming them against the coming rebellion. Once it started, Molina joined in, reacting to the capricious nature of national politics and the threat it posed to his lands.[75]

Lower down the social ladder, ranchers, smallholders, tenant farmers, and sharecroppers shared some of Molina's secular rationale. They recognized that *agraristas*, the agrarian militiamen fighting against them, might be "just as Catholic as we were," one said, but they were after their lands, an existential question. When Cristeros caught agraristas they sometimes hanged them with a bag of earth around their neck and the sign AQUÍ ESTÁ SU TIERRA, Here's your land.[76] The agraristas mocked them back with similar didactic violence. One scornful corrido ran,

The *cristero* went off to fight
Shooting off his *pistola*
He knew it wasn't Christ
That brought him to the *bola*.

The priest and the sacristan,
The rich were all a-fainting,
At the mere thought that
Their lands might be taken.[77]

Land was important in driving Cristeros and agraristas to war in the first place; the government's thirty thousand militiamen, many invaders from different regions, were the cannon fodder that kept it going.

Beyond religion, caciquismo, and land, the eternal, divisive logic of local history held sway. People who had benefited from the development of the Porfiriato tended toward rebellion. People whose grandfathers had fought in liberal militias and done well out of the wars of the nineteenth century tended toward the government. Places without churches had few churchmen to miss. People whose grandfathers had been *religioneros*, guerrillas outraged by liberal anticlericalism, went the other way. Indigenous communities chose sides depending in part on geography, the possibility of making war that isolation and topography either opened or foreclosed, and the historical and contemporary impact of the nation-state on their autonomy. And for many concerned, whether inside the O'odham and Mexicanero communities of Nayarit or between the mestizos of San José de Gracia and its nearest rival, there was the unchristian legacy of intra- and intercommunal vendetta, the old injunction to hate thy neighbor.[78]

So the Cristiada was a civil war with many roots. Even Calles's decision to launch it, foolish for such an able Machiavellian, had earthly rationale in memories of the Catholic reaction to Madero, key to his fall. Moreover, the labor movement was his main base; the Confederación Nacional Católica de Trabajo, a Catholic union with eighty thousand members, threatened it. Calles wasn't alone, either, finding willing anticlerical allies in people like Obregón, who made priests sweep Mexico City back in the 1910s (and told the world that many of them had syphilis), or minister of war Joaquín Amaro, who called the clergy "the sole cause" of Mexico's problems since the sixteenth century.[79] The other side had a similar worldly defensiveness; Amaro's decision to impose *reconcentración*, the forced relocation of peasant communities, made many into Cristeros. So did the everyday atrocities of guerrilla war: the mass hangings, systematic torture, burnt villages, the twelve-year-old whose tongue was ripped out before he was shot.[80] And because of these many roots, the difficulty of ending irregular warfare, and the government's multiple distractions, the Cristero War—like the civil war of the late 1910s—was unwinnable.

Instead the fortunes of both sides fluctuated. The year 1927 went well for the Cristeros, whose numerous irregular cavalry (Amaro had modernized the army in 1925, and in doing so sharply reduced its own cavalry) gave them an edge; 1928, as the government mobilized more troops and militiamen, not so well; 1929 very well, as the Escobar Rebellion gave the government war on two fronts. While they diverted thirty-five thousand troops to the North, the Cristeros—led by an agnostic northern Freemason, General Enrique Gorostieta, another of the war's walking contradictions—launched a conventional offensive that captured most of the West. The government's counteroffensive drove Mexico toward bankruptcy: The military once again drained the budget, taking over 30 percent of the whole. The Depression, which hit commodity producers like Mexico early, had already cut tax revenues to the point where the government suspended interest payments to foreign bondholders, a step dreaded in a country where nineteenth-century defaults had destroyed the economy and invited foreign invasion.[81]

In high politics, meanwhile, Calles was widely believed responsible for the assassination of Obregón. On July 17, 1928, shortly before he was due to resume power, he was shot by a Catholic radical, José de León Toral, allegedly egged on by a nun, Madre Conchita. The conspiratorially minded thought that this was a cover story and that Calles, in cahoots with his union allies, had murdered his old partner. At the scene of the crime General Ricardo Topete, head of Obregón's party, picked up the murder weapon and handed it to Calles, asking whether he by chance recognized it. It was a *j'accuse* moment, followed up with substance; two days later Topete suggested to his brother, governor-elect of Sonora, Calles's homeland, that they launch a coup.[82] Even that incompetent bad penny Félix Díaz turned up again, his agents caught in California trying to smuggle in a thousand rifles, nine machine guns, and a packet of antiseptics.[83]

While soldiers considered coups, José Vasconcelos, a messianic young nationalist, launched a presidential campaign to restore a lost democracy. In 1929 Vasconcelos's vigorous campaigning mobilized large crowds across Mexico, crowds in which young people and women (he claimed Madero's mantle, and promised female suffrage) were prominent. In Mexico City some hundred thousand attended the Vasconcelista rally. Vasconcelos, rector of the university, was seen by some as too cultured to survive in gun-toting times, his followers too naïve and genteel. The US ambassador told him in person that he was unfit to be president because he was no good at shooting people. Calles couldn't be too sure about that, though; some in those genteel crowds turned up with guns and serenaded Vasconcelos with the war song *"Me importa madre,"* "I don't give a fuck." The philosopher publicly threatened violence should he be cheated out of the presidency, and was planning vaguely for rebellion. Worst of all, from January onward he was in contact with the Cristero leadership.[84]

There were consequently pressing reasons for the government to negotiate peace. On the Church side some also sought an end to the war: The hierarchy had realized they were enfiladed, losing ground to the schismatics while lacking effective control over the Cristeros and the rural priests who succored them. Only about one hundred of those remained, the rest reconcentrated in towns or exiled to the United States. The hierarchy was playing a double game: While some bishops cheered the rebels on, another, the Bishop of Chihuahua, threatened them with excommunication. The Vatican leaned his way; as the war gathered steam Pope Pius instructed the Mexican episcopacy to provide neither moral nor material assistance to the Cristeros and condemned lay organizations that did, such as the women's brigades. It was providential, opined one cardinal, that the Cristeros existed, and providential that they ceased to exist.

So the Church helped them cease to exist by negotiating peace over their heads. Brokered and approved by Washington, it exchanged demobilization for tolerance. The Cristeros would lay down their arms; the government would ease its religious crackdown and cease promoting the schismatic Mexican Church; the bishops would resume church services. It was a nebulous deal, revealingly dubbed the *arreglos*, the arrangements, rather than a treaty. The arreglos didn't work particularly well. The most anticlerical revolutionaries continued attacking churches and parishioners. Many Cristero irregulars never surrendered their guns. Many who did were murdered; only two of the leaders in Guanajuato and Zacatecas survived.[85] Enrique Gorostieta, the able national leader who might have restarted the war, was dead already: assassinated, like Zapata, by an infiltrator, a colonel who led federal cavalry to his quarters in the night. But the arreglos worked well enough to forestall a national war.

So did a second great political fix, the foundation of a single state party, the Partido Nacional Revolucionario, PNR. Calles had warded off a coup by ditching the labor boss Luis León and appointing a civilian interim president, the popular and competent Emilio Portes Gil, and scheduling new elections for 1929. He disclaimed any aim to succeed Obregón as a caudillo, telling Congress that it was time for "a truly institutional life, to manage to move on, once and for all, from the historical condition of a country of a single man to a nation of institutions and laws."[86] The radio passed on the message in bars, village shops, and streets across Mexico. Simultaneously he headed off any truly powerful candidacies for the 1929 presidential election by persuading leading generals not to run. In March nine hundred revolutionary leaders gathered in Querétaro to subsume several thousand local parties and their bosses into one. It was sleight of hand; in founding the PNR Calles neutered his main opponents and installed a puppet, Pascual Ortiz Rubio, as candidate. Ortiz Rubio had been a prominent enough civilian revolutionary until the early 1920s, when he went to Germany and then Brazil as ambassador. He never stood much of a chance, though he did at least survive an assassination attempt on inauguration day. Calles kept power even as he moved out of the presidency, following the constitutional ban on reelection while setting himself up as the so-called *Jefe Máximo*, the strongman peeping out from behind the scenes. But he did set up an enduring party mechanism and a rhetoric of civilian rule, fulfilling some of his political promises.

And so by hook or by crook, or in Mexican proverb *pan o palo*, bread or the club, the civil wars of the 1910s and 1920s ended in what was proclaimed to be the polar opposite of the Porfirian dictatorship. Under the PNR Mexico was formally an electoral democracy that precluded one-man rule and the overconcentration of the country's wealth in the hands of a few. Its founders were the pragmatic survivors of two decades of intrigue, idealism, nihilism, and violence, an impressive will to power fighting off war-weariness. But they were also heirs, like it or not, to a language of revolutionary nationalism, socialism, and radical redistribution. The people they ruled were often tired, accepting what they could get rather than what they had been told they should or would get. "The revolution never made it here" became a stock phrase in protests to the powers that be, letters sent to presidents by peasants who never got their land or kept suffering under petty dictators. But it was a line that implied that somebody else like them, somewhere else, had got something out of the promises of the revolution. That belief, and the freedom to write letters about it, meant that they were right, that some Mexicans did get some of the rewards of one of the world's few great revolutions, and that distinguished Mexicans from other Americans, Latin or otherwise, for the rest of the twentieth century.

Chapter Sixteen

The Only American Revolution

The Mexicans who fought the civil wars of the 1910s called them a revolution, the Revolution. The winners wrote themselves into history as men and women who had fundamentally changed who owned what and who ruled. They were in truth a new generation of politicians who had climbed over old barriers of poverty, education, and race. The disappearance of the loathed jefe político moved local power back toward local hands. The most important national politicians remained whites: the first three presidents, the first ministers of war, the interior, finance, and agriculture. Yet after 1920 a new ethnic, class, and ideological diversity obtained. General Joaquín Amaro, the man who brought the army to heel, was "el Indio" to his peers, "the Indian Who Sways Mexican Destiny" to a foreign pressman.[1] The leader of the main union, Luis Napoleón Morones, was an electrician from the ranks of the anarchist labor movement. Theirs was a genuine political revolution.

The 1920s did not, however, see a social revolution, a wholesale change in who owned factories, oil wells, and lands, a dramatic rupture in how Mexicans lived day to day. A blueprint was there in the sprawling Constitution of 1917, its 137 articles mandating expropriation of any and all natural resources, collective land ownership, the most progressive labor code in the world, strict control of the Church, and universal education to replace its obscurantist teachings. It was the first constitution in the world to mandate environmental conservation as a collective social good.[2] It was rightly seen as a totemic collection of ideals. It was also seen as impossible to make reality. The Sonoran rulers of the 1920s thought turning over agribusiness or oil to the people ill-advised, given the frailty of their post-conflict country; it was a moment for safe hands to manage capitalist reconstruction. So across the 1920s and early '30s the Terrazas family continued to own vast estates in the North, the plantocracy of Mérida held on to the henequén plantations, the Pimentels of Morelos kept their canefields and sugar mills, the Americans of Standard Oil and the British of Mexican Eagle retained their Mexican oil fields and refineries.[3]

Some elements of social revolution were there for those who looked in the right places. The freethinkers of the Calles government followed the letter of the constitution in closing down the Church and attacking the age-old power of the parish priest. The government trained and dispatched copious teachers, in their own metaphor missionaries, to replace religious with revolutionary evangelism in a dangerous countryside. Alongside them went teams of hastily trained rural health workers to treat endemic preventable disease. Where peasants fought hardest, in the patrias chicas of Zapata and his like, they wrested communal lands from hacendados. Doughty rural militiamen who held the line against military or religious rebels got some too. Hacendados threatened by peasants who answered back sometimes rediscovered their own manners. Unionized workers, particularly those who had fought in the red battalions of 1915, got some of their promised rewards: collective contracts, minimum wages, support for the sick or injured, pensions.

Foreigners who squinted also saw revolution and told the world. The visitors of the 1910s had been journalists, adventurers, and war tourists; they were joined in the 1920s by writers, artists, photographers, social scientists, filmmakers, and patrons of the arts. Many clustered in Mexico City, where they could experience radical chic without the inconveniences of Weimar Berlin or Soviet Moscow, foraging artistically in the provinces before returning to what was again one of the world's great cosmopolitan cities, in the throes of a Mexican Renaissance, its cultural power rivaled in the Americas only by New York. The two cities had a symbiotic relationship and creators moved between the two, American social scientists influencing Mexicans, Mexican artists changing the way Americans painted. Jackson Pollock studied with one of the great Mexican muralists, Davíd Alfaro Siquieros, and said that another, José Clemente Orozco, had produced "the greatest work of art in North America."[4] Outside Cuernavaca, eternal refuge of the well-off, interested capitalinos and other foreigners could see a toiling revolutionary peasantry. In fashion it really was a world turned upside down: While the half-German Frida Kahlo attended the capital's parties in tailored *huipiles*, indigenous blouses from Oaxaca, Huicholes in Jalisco attended indigenous boarding schools in shirt and tie.[5] Radical change for most Mexicans was in observers' minds, though, or on the walls of government buildings where a team led by Diego Rivera (the best-known painter of the revolution, who spent the war comfortably as a Cubist in Paris) painted the revolution as the triumph of centuries of racial and class struggle.[6] They worked fast and charged workers' wages. It was, President Obregón observed to Congress, a cheap way of redecorating.[7]

There were new backdrops beyond the Riveras of the National Palace. May Day 1923 was heralded in Mexico City by workers and peasants in the Zócalo singing the Internationale and waving banners with slogans such as "Bourgeoisie, shave your heads and get ready for the guillotine." The Sonorans didn't set off to create crowds like this one, but they invested heavily in the education that would soon foster them.[8] When Obregón appointed José Vasconcelos rector of the national university and head of the newly founded Education Ministry he allotted him a bigger budget than even that idealist had requested. Vasconcelos spent it on a wildly ambitious program to bring Mexican children everything from universal primary schooling to Homer (printed in government workshops in runs of twenty-five thousand) and free breakfasts. At bottom a conservative, Vasconcelos was functionally a radical in terms of understanding what education in 1920s Mexico should be—as accessible and rapidly deliverable as possible—and led what he called a crusade to do something about it. It was straightforward, he told the professors and students of the national university:

> I have reviewed, for example, the courses of this our University, and I have seen that here French Literature is taught even down to Racine's tragedies, and I would have been proud of that were it not that I have etched in my heart the drama of children abandoned in the barrios of all our cities, all our villages, children whom the State should feed and educate, recognizing in doing so the most elemental duty of a true civilization.[9]

Far from the national university, numerous rural teachers with rudimentary training, at times adolescent volunteers, "the Children's Literacy Army," set off to teach. There was a sense of vocation abroad, and not just in the rhetoric of missionary teachers: One small-town teacher, Evila Franco Nájera, who had improvised schools across the 1910s, now taught children by day and adults by night, staging plays like *Proletarian Redemption* in her spare time.[10]

The money didn't last, and many children read the same textbooks as their Porfirian forebears, with their values of material progress, order, and obedience. Rafael Aguirre Cinta's *Historia General de México* criticized Villa and Zapata as "obstructors of order."[11] Yet what provincial children were actually taught went beyond textbooks as radical ideas spread from Mexico City via the magazine *El Maestro*, traveling libraries, and parent-teacher meetings. Rural families became more literate—28 percent of Mexicans could read in 1921, 38 percent by 1934—and more formally ideological. And they had sway over what was taught, because they partially funded it, paying teachers and chipping in labor, building materials, and food.[12] In poverty-stricken Guerrero one builder traveled hundreds of miles to the new teacher training college at Ayotzinapa to donate his labor; his daughter had been one of the first graduates.[13] Such support flowed from communities across the state, who put up 276 schoolhouses in three years at a cost of over a million pesos. The Education Ministry, in the same period, found 20,500 pesos to contribute to the cause.[14] Yet while central funding fluctuated, education was the only revolutionary cause that fostered real consensus. Calles, conservative in many ways, appointed the Marxist Narciso Bassols to lead the secretariat and its turn toward "socialist education," and in one of his last speeches he said:

> The Revolution is not over . . . We have to enter a new phase, that I would call the period of psychological revolution: we must enter and conquer the minds of the children, the minds of the young, because they do and they must belong to the Revolution.[15]

But the litmus test of revolution was land: who owned it and who owned the labor that worked it. Most of the world until well into the twentieth century was a rural world, the majority of almost every country's people living in the countryside. The great social revolutions—the French, Haitian, Russian, and Chinese—took that land and labor from a few and handed it over to the many. The many didn't invariably benefit much from the transaction, the rulers of collective farms and centrally planned economies having the same potential for ruthless overlordship as the rulers of great private estates and free markets. Yet on paper, and sometimes in reality, social revolution meant peasant ownership in place of peonage or sharecropping, and with it greater guarantees of subsistence, and pride. And with peasant ownership came plans to reeducate, to turn new landholders into more productive, rational, healthy, and grateful elements of the new state, like it or not.

In Russia and China this happened quickly after the revolutionary seizure of power. The Bolsheviks took over on October 25, 1917, and announced Lenin's Decree on Land on October 26, abolishing private property and expropriating the land of the Church, gentry, aristocracy, and imperial family. The Chinese revolutionaries oversaw massive land reform between 1946 and 1948, before Mao had even proclaimed the People's Republic of China in October 1949.[16] In Mexico, by contrast, the revolutionary land reform of the 1930s lagged its announcement in 1917 by nearly two decades. When it did come it was accompanied by a dramatic increase in workers' rights and ownership; a cultural program designed to wholly reshape the everyday lives, health, and beliefs of peasants; and the unthinkable expropriation of Mexico's most lucrative industry, the foreign-owned oil companies. The reforms were flawed and often they just failed. The beneficiaries and their descendants complained vociferously of the gulf between promises and reality. The sum of the reforms of the 1930s nevertheless constitute one of the world's great social revolutions.

Pragmatic reasons separated Mexico's political and social revolutions. Mexico had a broader export portfolio than most Latin American countries, but it still relied heavily on primary products and US markets. In the first half of the 1920s the national economy was kept afloat by oil. Global demand had soared under the stimulus of World War I, when El Águila supplied Britain's Royal Navy and Standard Oil the US Navy. Across the 1910s the two companies succeeded in protecting their wells and even expanding, while Russia's own revolution ravaged its oil industry, decreasing supply. By 1920 Mexico was selling a quarter of the world's oil, and between 1920 and 1924 oil taxes brought in 309 million pesos.[17] But after 1923 the aging oil fields of the Gulf Coast began drying up; simultaneously new suppliers in the US, Persia, and Venezuela came online and demand fell, until in 1926 oil prices collapsed. They were followed in short order by those of minerals, the first signs of the coming Depression. Gross Domestic Product shrank, and with it government revenues, increasingly destined for the military anyway. At the same time job losses and deportation forced four hundred thousand unemployed workers back from the US.[18] In the worst year, 1932, Mexico's exports were down two-thirds while three times as many jobless wandered the towns and cities.[19]

The politicians who faced reconstruction and the early Depression were classical liberals, orthodox and unimaginative economists in terms of the decade to come. Their priorities were stabilizing the peso at two to the dollar, balancing the budget with higher taxes and lower spending, and servicing international debt. They were initially threatened by Washington, which refused diplomatic recognition and credit until Mexico agreed to pay US investors reparations for wartime damage and to leave foreign oil companies alone. Yet while the canny Obregón agreed to Washington's terms, he did not agree to changes in the constitution, allowing a window for future expropriations. Neither was the set of agreements known as the Bucareli accords a treaty, and thus only reparations payments had standing under international law. The sums finally agreed upon were on properties' declared tax value, well below market, payback for decades of privileged tax dodging. Finally, the Special Claims Commission lacked any effective enforcement mechanism, and by 1931 none of the reparations claims—more than three thousand of them, valued at $421 million—had been paid out. Mexican officials pleaded a lack of preparation to hold up subsequent negotiations and ended up, in 1934, agreeing to a one-off lump sum payment of $5.5 million. It was 2.65 percent of the agreed amount.[20]

Yet the US didn't need to blackmail the Mexican government into eschewing land expropriation and redistribution, because Obregón and Calles didn't believe in it themselves. "We have no agraristas here, thank God," Obregón said of Sonora in the early 1910s; agrarian reform "would nullify the effort for the country's economic reconstruction," agreed Calles.[21] The Sonorans believed in state intervention and founded appropriate institutions, such as the Banco de México, the Banco Nacional de Crédito Agrícola y Ganadero, and commissions for irrigation and roadbuilding. Yet these were all intended to support rather than supplant capitalist development, and capitalism, not socialism, was supposed to deal with the basics of popular land ownership, microcredit, and affordable technology from tractors to cornmills. Governors backed by agrarian radicals were allowed to win in states with significant commercial agriculture. In Coahuila, which produced nearly half of Mexico's cotton, the 1925 gubernatorial election went to an agrarista, General Manuel Pérez Treviño. Yet once in office he wasn't allowed to do much for his followers. In 1927 the federal government invested 38 million pesos in dams and irrigation canals for Coahuila's 130 haciendas; agraristas got ten of the collective farms called ejidos, all on marginal land.[22]

This successful opposition to agrarian militants was sustained from the top by Calles, who remained the power behind the presidential throne, apparent defeat converted into tactical retreat and enduring power. He founded the PNR with a ringing call to end the time of the caudillos, and promptly traduced it. He was more than an *éminence grise*, even if his persona was precisely a gray apparatchik; he was the Jefe Máximo, the Great Leader. Calles made and unmade three presidents: Emilio Portes Gil (1928–1930), Pascual Ortiz Rubio (1930–1932), and General Abelardo Rodríguez (1932–1934), a northern revolutionary businessman after Calles's own heart (with the exception of his gambling and bootlegging). Through all their terms in office he kept redistribution to a strategic minimum. In 1934 he picked a fourth president to continue the emerging tradition, a quiet young general from Michoacán named Lázaro Cárdenas.

Cárdenas was a modest man. He grew up in Jiquilpan, a small town in northwest Michoacán, with one foot in the middle class: His father had progressed from weaving to owning a small grocer's shop with a billiard table, and Cárdenas made it through three years of primary school. It was one where a single *maestro* taught three hundred pupils, but it was enough to teach him literacy and numeracy, and his first job was as a town council clerk. His other foot was in poverty: He was one of eight children, and his father died young. In the summer of 1913 the eighteen-year-old Cárdenas rode out to the nearest revolutionary group, proved that he could write, and was made captain. By 1915 he was in Sonora commanding the 22nd Regiment of Cavalry. He met Governor Calles there and remained a Callista for the next two decades, advocating for an extension of his patron's term in the crisis of 1928, leading the PNR, the Callistas in Congress, and the Secretariat of Defense. He called the Jefe Máximo *maestro* and *padre*; Calles called him *el chamaco*, the kid. At the same time Cárdenas established rare credentials as an agrarista, fostering peasant organizations and land grants when governing Michoacán. He was a competent and humane soldier, and an unusually broad range of politicians liked him.[23]

Cárdenas also enjoyed a solid reputation for stupidity. He was a listener, not an orator, and his appearance didn't help: The slightly Lombrosian impressions of more than one writer included a "pear-shaped head," a "forehead shaped sharply back," "thick lips," and a mouth that hung slightly open as others talked.[24] His nickname was *el burro*, the donkey, and "the mere mention of a donkey in a music-hall [would] raise a titter of laughter."[25] His journals are impeccably dull even by the low standards of political memoir, and one of the only glints of personality comes through when he says defensively that his three years of primary school gave him the equivalent of six years' learning. He seemed ideal material for a presidential puppet: loyal, likable, and thick.

Yet even observers who questioned his intelligence wondered if it were not a Machiavellian act, and if Cárdenas weren't playing a very long game. Being obviously clever in the 1920s was not always a clever move; feigning a measured stupidity was no bad idea at all. Skeptical foreigners were of two minds as to exactly what went on behind the blank expression: "Opinion is divided as to his intelligence," reported the British Embassy, "but he showed considerable skill in playing off political cliques against each other."[26] The sharpest Mexican observers on the other hand were in little doubt, describing Cárdenas as profoundly ambitious and fluently duplicitous. The ideologue Luis Cabrera held that all Cárdenas's politics were calculated to establish him as a

Great Man, making him the most ambitious leader of his generation. Another major politician, Gonzalo N. Santos—whose candid, well-penned memoirs of his murders and other peccadilloes smash genre rules—summed up the political acumen underlying that campaign:

> *Cardenistas* make Cárdenas out to be a Saint Francis of Assisi, but he was nothing like that at all; I haven't known any other politician who has known how to cover up his intentions and feelings as well as General Lázaro Cárdenas and it's me who says that, and I'm not exactly an amateur.

Santos should have known; during one election he machine-gunned the opposition-held polling station in which Cárdenas was intending to vote, hosed away the blood, and heard Cárdenas dryly observe how clean the street was.[27]

When Calles set him up for president in 1933 Cárdenas thanked him profusely and began planning his ouster. He flattered Calles with requests for advice, avowed his subordination, went yachting with him in Baja California, and quietly began recruiting his own peasant militias.[28] He upped the radicalism of the party's Six-Year Plan until the final draft held that the only limit to land reform was the complete fulfilment of the "agricultural necessities" of rural Mexicans.[29] He launched a national campaign that went into legend, taking planes, trains, cars, and horses to travel eighteen thousand miles, reaching beyond towns and cities to villages and hamlets that had never seen a politician before, at times traveling sixteen-hour days. Stories spread of a future president who sat down in village squares to ask everyday Mexicans what they needed, listening to answers such as a school, drinking water, fields, roads, a cornmill, some sort of medic, and taking notes to do something about it. Cárdenas had a life geared to understanding all this: His single mother had kept the family afloat working at home as a seamstress, he and his wife Amalia had lost a premature baby just before he departed on campaign, and he had observed obscene poverty in the armed revolution.

His travels gave him national and at the same time specific understandings of what might be done about that poverty, and built an unprecedented base of popular support.[30] At the same time, he was doing the usual round of sweaty political banquets—though he wasn't averse to dodging them from time to time in favor of tortillas with the unknown—and cutting deals with thuggish caciques and Porfirian survivors. Shoring up support in the provinces meant forging murky alliances with some of the same people his natural allies were fighting. In the municipio of Pisaflores in Hidalgo he befriended the Rubios, ranchers who had been mayors since the Porfiriato, grabbing land along the way, keeping it by murdering peasant leaders.[31] In Veracruz he allied himself with Manuel Parra, a mafia boss whose Black Hand gang waged war on agraristas across much of the state.[32] Yet the result of Cárdenas's tours was the broadest coalition since that of Obregón, put together with the same expediency, inclusiveness, and ruthlessness.

When he won the election his problem was how to govern with that coalition. Cárdenas himself voted left, for the socialist Adalberto Tejeda, but he was stuck with a cabinet of right-wingers. Calles appointed his own men to the most important positions, Gobernación and Guerra y Marina, the ministries that ran domestic politics and the army. His son Rodolfo was in charge of the Secretaría de Comunicaciones e Obras Públicas, giving him weighty patronage—generals had turned out to be remarkably good at construction, or at least at charging for construction—as well as a ready-made intelligence network. Calles could theoretically listen in on any telephone call or read any telegram in the country. His expectations were made clear on the eve of the inauguration; he invited the incoming president to his farm in Sinaloa and then kept Cárdenas waiting while he finished playing poker with two other generals (who were doing their damnedest to lose).[33]

After assuming office in December 1934, however, Cárdenas began encouraging workers to strike and agrarian authorities to redistribute land. In June 1935 Calles condemned his "marathon of radicalism"; Cárdenas, backed by the army, a new labor movement, and his motley regional powerbrokers, purged the cabinet and suggested that Calles leave the capital. It was the end of the Jefe Máximo; he came back months later to attempt a restoration and failed. On April 9, 1936, they arrested him while he was at home in pajamas reading *Mein Kampf*. This time Cárdenas exiled him properly, deporting him and a handful of key allies to the US with no chance of return.[34] He followed up by firing numerous governors, generals, congressmen, and party officials;

he even packed the Supreme Court, changing the constitution to make justices elected for six-year terms, not life, and replacing the old ones with his own men. (Franklin Roosevelt, who tried packing the US Supreme Court shortly afterward, may have been taking notes.) By the autumn of 1936 Cárdenas had as much power as he would ever have, and he used it to push and wheedle through radical policies in four areas: culture, labor, nationalism, and, at the heart of it all, land.

Cárdenas started with two big advantages. The former chancellor Alberto Pani, a veteran policymaker, had adopted counter-cyclical policies in the early 1930s: In the face of global economic collapse he boosted the money supply, allowed the peso to slide, and upped government spending. What was counterintuitive at the time worked, and Mexico spent its way out of the Depression early and fast. Between 1932 and 1934 the overall economy grew 19 percent; industry, 47 percent. By contrast the UK and the US followed orthodoxy, defending currencies, cutting spending, and increasing tax and interest rates; their result was further economic contraction and high unemployment. Meanwhile Mexico's cheapened peso increased exports of oil and silver and reduced imports. Taxing those exports, printing paper money, and tolerating a deficit helped fund government spending. Low interest rates and relatively resilient employment helped keep Mexicans spending for themselves. The result was a Keynesian success story (before Keynes had published *The General Theory of Employment, Interest and Money*): Loose monetary policy and deficit spending increased aggregate demand and caused high-quality economic growth.[35] Cárdenas was a relatively rich revolutionary.

Moreover, by 1934 rural Mexicans had formed myriad popular organizations, local face-to-face groups that pressed for the promises of revolution, Cardenistas before their time. Peasants across Mexico organized themselves into newly ambitious revolutionary groups. The Veracruz League proposed abolishing the political system and transferring all power to worker-peasant councils, elected in their workplaces, Soviets by another name. Militant workers and federal teachers egged them on. Peasants won local elections, clung to their arms in the village militias called *defensas sociales*, bombarded the government with demands for land, and fought big landowners. They were rooted in their patrias chicas, but they weren't perforce bumpkins: Many read Marx and Machiavelli, one had been an anarchist organizer in the Rockies, one traveled to the USSR, another visited the Rochester Clinic to treat his cancer. Some regional leaders were urbane, middle-class types: The Veracruzano Adalberto Tejeda was an engineer who played the cello and had a decent knowledge of Russian, French, and English literature. Yet less cultivated everyday leaders didn't need the recognition of outsiders for anything apart from their land petitions, which they sent from the countryside to the cluttered desks of the Departamento Agrario.[36]

In theory these reams of paper would spark a survey to determine the needs of or historical injustices perpetrated upon the signatories. Surveyors and agronomists would make recommendations on how much and what sort of land and from which hacienda the peasants deserved to form their ejido, collective farm. If they were acknowledged as centuries-long owners, dispossessed by modernizing oligarchs, they would get their land back in *restitución*, a return of stolen property; if not then it would be a *dotación*, a governmental gift. Whatever form the grant took, it was not freehold but usufruct, to be occupied and used in the long term but not owned. The entire ejido was administered by an elected council, the *comisariado ejidal*.

Until 1934 this arrangement had limited results for both formal and informal reasons. The bureaucratic process was slow, and the lands that were subject to expropriation were strictly limited in the first place. A series of laws and Supreme Court injunctions kept the numbers of eligible low. Only places with twenty families or more were allowed to apply; this excluded more than half of Mexico's rural communities, including those in the majority of the commercial haciendas, whose average resident workforce fell below this bar. If the workforce was large enough to qualify, hacendados could replace permanent workers with temporary, seasonal laborers, putting their lands out of reach. Threatened hacendados preserved their holdings by giving titles to multiple family members. Even where eligibility existed, the Department of Agriculture was notoriously conservative and slow-moving. In some places it was colonized by the people it was supposed to investigate: Oaxaca's agrarian commission was run by Porfirians and hacendados.

Landowners could fight adverse decisions for years, taking a series of cases against agrarian officials all the way up to the Supreme Court, where justices might award a stay of execution on even a presidential decree.[37]

Informally these constraints were overridden when the government desperately needed agrarian militiamen or rural warlords to fight rebels. Generally, though, informality worked against peasant claimants. Some large landowners had gone out of business, but their successors were a hardened lot who armed their retainers and the violent unemployed of the revolution to form *guardias blancas*, paramilitaries who killed peasant leaders with little repercussion. In Naranja, the disinherited village par excellence, federal soldiers murdered Primo Tapia, the hometown radical made good (a death distinctly foretold—the Abbot of Pátzcuaro put a bounty of $3,000 on his head).[38] The Sonoran presidents systematically obstructed land reform, and when it was unavoidable, they tried to avoid the legal process of an ejidal grant in favor of the murkier award of a *colonia militar*, a discretional collective grant to ex-soldiers. As a consequence, in 1930 there were nearly 2,000 haciendas of more than 62,000 acres left, and between them they covered more than half of Mexico's private lands.[39] The mainly indigenous peasantry of Chiapas, by contrast, had secured all of 447 acres, a medium-sized ranch.[40]

What land peasants got in the 1920s was most often poor quality. There were three categories: *tierra de riego*, irrigated land; *temporal*, seasonally cultivable arable land, watered by rainfall; and *monte*, everything else, pasture, scrubland, hill, and desert. Before Cárdenas, 86 percent of ejido land was monte, 2 percent irrigated.[41] In some areas, affected hacendados chose which lands they would give up. A few acres of monte was not enough to sustain an average family, even given the hardiness and productivity of the maize plant, and a few acres was all that peasants in central Mexico, the best located to buy and sell, got. The average seven acres in Estado de México or Tlaxcala was nowhere near enough to bring its owners into commercial agriculture, "so small as to be ridiculous" to one government official. Some ejidos didn't have enough drinking water for humans, never mind livestock. Few loans were available for start-up costs, and there were next to no plans to develop irrigation works for their fields.[42]

While campaigning, Cárdenas promised that his presidency would be different. In Yucatán he vowed to expropriate fifty thousand acres of the henequen estates for the Maya peasantry.[43] In Oaxaca he decided that one of his first acts would be to channel the waters of the Río Tehuantepec onto the fields of the fiercely independent Zapotecs of Juchitán.[44] Once freed from the dead hand of Calles, Cárdenas announced that he would consolidate rural communities to get over the twenty-family rule and expropriate haciendas to provide the land. He had four main agribusinesses in his sights: the cotton of the Laguna, expropriated in the last weeks of 1936; Yucatán's henequen, seized in late 1937; the sugar of Morelos and Puebla, consolidated into new businesses like the Emiliano Zapata refinery in Zacatepec; and the rice of the Cusi empire in Michoacán, seized in November 1938.

The reforms followed similar patterns. Government surveys established that land remained in the hands of a few large proprietors, to the historical detriment of their peasant workers and neighbors. Expropriation and redistribution didn't need justification by historic dispossession anymore, because the government had changed the law to give any countryman the right to enough land to live with dignity. Huge teams of engineers, lawyers, economists, professors, students, and soldiers descended to occupy the land and divide it among the new owners; the Laguna reform was put into action by three hundred specialists accompanied by five secretaries of state. The president intervened personally, and redistribution was rapid and spectacular. The new Banco Ejidal provided generous start-up loans: The new collective farmers of the Laguna were lent 30 million pesos for their first year.[45]

Ejidatarios did not find themselves in peasant utopias. Local Cardenistas were at times cut out of the process, while presidential clients survived and even profited; there were multiple foreseeable long-term flaws. In Yucatán Cárdenas redistributed 1.2 million acres of henequen land, turning in a question of weeks the old slave plantations Turner had visited into collective farms. Yet even that was not enough productive land to satisfy more than half the potential ejidatarios. The agrarian bureaucracy projected that new plantings would deal with the problem, but the agave plant takes seven years to mature to where it can be harvested. Politically, meanwhile, Cárdenas abandoned his natural constituency of urban workers and existing leftists in the interests of appeasing Yucatán's old political elites, and redirected declining federal funds toward other projects.[46] Ejidatarios were left in poverty under conservative politicians. Yucatán was the great failure of agrarian reform, but ejidos everywhere were vulnerable to similar problems: inadequate lands as communities grew, vanishing credit, unstable commodity prices, vicious infighting, and enduring bosses. Nevertheless they brought about social revolution.

First, there was the lasting psychological effect of a Mexican government simply favoring the rural poor over the rich. As one observer put it, "The sharpest change was intangible. Fear left the have-nots and was distributed to the haves."[47] Cárdenas's rhetoric was born out by the thirty-five days he spent in the Laguna, where thirty-eight thousand new ejidatarios in Durango and Coahuila got collective farms that covered more than a million acres. Redistribution's psychological effect was reinforced by a cultural campaign whose most tangible benefits were education and healthcare. The education budget in the Laguna went up by $350,000 in 1937.[48] Teachers and medics set out to remake rural society. (Cardenistas would have appreciated Bismarck's dictum that wars are won not by generals but by teachers and priests.) The most basic structures of livelihoods often ended up the same: Country people without much of a say in their own lives struggled to get by, the end users of their work outsiders, ranging from administrators to carefully masked foreign corporations and bankers. A few ejidos even proved ephemeral, the lands taken back when new capitalist opportunities knocked; in law, after all, they were grants to use land, not own it. Fourteen ejidos around Acapulco lost land when tourism took off.[49] In the here and now of the 1930s, though, expropriation and reform did away with swathes of the old landowners and predatory generals. Neither were foreigners exempt. For many it was a personal end of empire: One curious Englishman in Torreón "drove out to the Country Club, and drank cocktails with the disgruntled foreigners of the place, most of whom were busy liquidating their estates and seeing what could be salved from the wreckage."[50]

The raw numbers tell the story. Between 1935 and 1940 the government redistributed forty-six million acres, nearly half of all Mexico's cultivable land. Twenty-three percent of that was good arable land, either irrigated or seasonally watered. The new owners received generous government loans; the sugar ejido at Zacatepec had a budget twice as big as that of the Morelos state government. Eight hundred thousand lower-class Mexicans became landowners. It added up to the greatest agrarian reform in the Americas.

With the land came the aspiration, common in the 1930s, of engineering a new culture. The New Soviet Man was founded on Marxist theory and futuristic promise; the Mexican new man added eugenics and nationalism. Intellectuals, artists, and politicians since Independence had told a compelling story of greatness, past and future, that drew on pre-Hispanic societies' sophistication and power. Indigenous peoples had been corrupted by brutish colonial rule, which in a sympathetic anthropologist's words left them "vegetating in the lowest stages of evolution." They could be restored to greatness, though, if "friendly hearts" could "awaken" them, giving them the tools to escape their "anachronistic and inappropriate" cultures. Suitably retooled Indians would be raw material for a country that would lead the Americas, the US included, "a new *patria* made from iron and bronze intermingled."[51]

The bronze part of that excited foreigners greatly. Art collectors, anarchist refugees like the German novelist B. Traven, and American reporters like Carleton Beals saw a Rousseauian ideal in indigenous villages, which they contrasted with the degenerate materialism of the United States. Katherine Anne Porter, curator of the first international exhibition of folk art, wrote that the only important and living art in Mexico "grew in the soul of the Indian." Traven's novels set in Chiapas contrasted the Tzotziles' "gentle form of undoctrinaire socialism and co-operativism" with the corruption of an outside capitalist world.[52] Beals made other philosophical comparisons:

> We Americans are interested in new toys; the Indian peasant is interested in new beauties . . . We Americans shut out the roaring tide of life by externals, by living outside of our bodies and minds, by conquering nature instead of ourselves . . . But the Indian lives close to the spirals of nature itself. There is a healthy interpenetration of

himself and nature. The American lives for the future, he divides his life into time units . . . the Mexican peasant is time, in its Bergsonian fluid essence.[53]

Revolutionary governments encouraged such idealists to the extent of paying them to curate exhibitions, make films, and teach indigenous languages. Their Mexican intellectual employees and allies inherited the cult of the Indian, indigenismo, from the nineteenth century, but spent a lot more time and money promoting it than their predecessors did. They organized festivals of dance, theater, music, and handicrafts, like the *Guelaguetza* in Oaxaca. Some efforts were ham-fisted, like the beauty contest called la India Bonita, the Pretty Indian Girl.[54] Others were sophisticated, like the programs that integrated archaeological digs with anthropological studies and tailored development measures according to their findings. It was perhaps the most joined-up approach to indigenous culture in history.

The revolutionaries also inherited indigenismo's dark, inherent contradiction. At base it wasn't about handicrafts. It was and always had been about extolling the Indian past and mourning the present-day Indian's poverty, ignorance, and distance from mainstream Mexico. And both respect and condescending pity were founded on race, a race once triumphant but now unfit to survive a modern world, and because of that Indian culture should be history. Proponents of indigenismo were often social Darwinists, but they were not always cynics. Many were well-meaning, progressive humanists, and they showed a lot more respect and cultural pluralism than their counterparts elsewhere in the Americas. Yet while they and their foreign consumers anthropologized Indians, they also museumized them. The indigenous lag behind the rest of society demanded a top-down revolution of economic development and assimilation. Indigenismo was a form of modernism; critics called it ethnocide.[55]

Beals got the idea: The Indian was a soulful but ephemeral creature, and the best hope was that his spirit would endure in a biologically and culturally hybrid people, a "super race." Elements of Indianness should endure in weaving, basket-making, pottery, song, and dance, but they would be evolutionary artefacts, a sort of cultural appendix, present but not particularly functional. Indigenismo was a vital component of mestizaje, not its antithesis. The anthropologist Manuel Gamio, a central thinker in revolutionary nationalism, wrote that every Mexican had to identify in spirit with the peasant to be a real Mexican. However, he went on, real Mexicans shared a common language, aesthetics, morality, religion, and culture in general, and a successful patria was founded on that unity. Unpublished documents from the time make it clear that this unity was also believed to be biological, and that Gamio's eugenic beliefs and aims were commonplaces among the governing class.[56] Ex–Education Minister Vasconcelos, another key nationalist, adopted a more pluralist stance: All the great civilizations of antiquity were based on ethnic diversity. But Gamio and Vasconcelos ended up at the same conclusion. Latin America's destiny, wrote the latter with messianic swagger, was to be the cradle of a fifth, hybrid race, the *raza cósmica*, a cosmic race that would rule the world.[57] Indians were a bridge to be passed over en route.

Cárdenas shared this combination of romantic fetishization and racial engineering: It was necessary, he said famously, to "Mexicanize the *indio*." He also, like the anthropologists he employed, believed in fostering their political and cultural autonomy, and tried to square the circle of economic development, cultural assimilation, and at the same time cultural preservation. To deal with this objective he set up a federal agency, the Departamento Autónomo de Asuntos Indígenas, that would promote indigenous language learning and use and ask indigenous people what they thought they needed in annual regional congresses. Some, like the Yaqui, won a partial autonomy and the recognition of their rights to their homelands, substantiated by major expropriations of US-owned properties in the Yaqui River Valley. In 1938 a constitutional reform recognized the rights of indigenous societies to ancestral lands in general. Mexico City encouraged state governments to found their own indigenous departments as complements. In heavily indigenous regions, like the highlands of Michoacán, Chiapas, and Oaxaca, they were major forces for change. The main solution, however, remained the universal panacea of rural education. Unmanaged racial diversity aggravated and obscured common problems of class; there should be a "transition from caste to class."[58] Some policies would be tailored to indigenous populations, such as bilingual teachers or indigenous boarding schools. But most were for general consumption. In metropolitan eyes many rural Mexicans irrespective of race were at root the same: poor, unhygienic, illiterate, shamelessly misled religious fanatics, trapped by a colonial past from which they'd never recovered. Racialized nationalism was part of a broader remedy to national backwardness, namely education.

Cárdenas inherited a commitment to radical anticlerical schooling that was written into a 1934 revision of the constitution's Article 3, which read:

> Education will be socialist and in addition to excluding all religious doctrine will fight fanaticism and prejudice, to which end the school will organize its lessons and activities in such a way as to create in youth a rational and precise concept of the universe and social life.

It was an optimistic prescription. On taking office the Inspector-General of Education had delivered a depressing report on progress to date in education. State governments across Mexico didn't think much of the new socialist education and were refusing to implement it. One governor fired fifty teachers just for asking about it; teachers in Catholic states were going on strike. The Archbishop of Mexico sent out a pastoral letter telling parents who accepted socialist education that they couldn't receive the sacraments, and that the *maestros rurales* who promulgated it were heretics who would be excommunicated.[59] Many maestros rurales went unpaid. Some teachers were incompetent, and school buildings were in dreadful condition. In Chiapas they were like chicken coops.[60] In San José de Gracia one actually became a chicken coop.[61]

Cardenista solutions were budgets, boots on the ground, and political backing against conservative opponents. Federal funding for education went up 14 percent in the first three years of Cárdenas's presidency, and the number of teachers in the remote countryside soared, at least on paper. More than three and a half thousand new primary schools opened, pushing the education system into places where it had traditionally been anemic.[62] The government changed textbooks and ordered governors to circulate revolutionary comic books and Gildardo Magaña's two-volume history of Zapatismo.[63] Teachers joined the few Mexicans who were licensed to carry firearms, which they needed: In

1938 the Secretariat of Public Education ("SEP" in Spanish) reported that one teacher was being murdered every ten days. The Segunda Cristiada, a movement characterized by diffuse, petty, but numerous Catholic guerrilla risings, was in large part fueled by the heresies of the outsider educators. In the village of Hueyapan in Morelos, it didn't matter so much whether Maestro Eligio was actually having students strip in sex ed classes as that he was believed capable of it, and a man who had marched the children around the square shouting "*¡Viva el socialismo!*" would clearly stop at nothing. So even though he had been the popular village teacher for the previous fifteen years, even though the villagers themselves had made him teacher, he was fired and his school was closed. And Maestro Eligio was lucky, because elsewhere his ilk came to gruesome ends: raped, tortured, mutilated, lynched.[64]

Not all of the new education met such violent resistance. There was more to revolution by schoolroom than religion, politics, and land. Maestros and their technocratic allies in the cultural missions meant to reshape the basic rhythms of everyday life to everyone's benefit. Small technological imports had outsize effects. Community cornmills, rudimentary machines driven by coughing diesel motors, replaced the old *metates*, back-straining mortars and pestles made of volcanic stone. Peasant women who once rose before dawn to grind corn for the day's tortillas could now sleep an extra two hours. Communal sinks for washing clothes saved more of their backs. Communal sewing machines saved more of their time. Military engineers who installed the concrete slab of a basketball court gave children and adults new ways of socializing. Games were scheduled for Sundays, rivaling mass as entertainment and opportunity to gossip. Further entertainment and competition for church audiences were provided by fifty-four new nationalist ceremonies, commemorations of the secular great and good ranging from Hidalgo to James Watt, the Scottish inventor of the steam engine.[65]

With an enthusiastic maestro—and not all were, some fleeing the countryside for long metropolitan weekends—a community could find itself living a very different life in a matter of months. Teachers were supposed to put on at least one public event a week. But villagers accepted the bits of SEP programming that made sense to them and ignored or even sabotaged the rest. Eighteen-year-old teachers in unknown places would quickly find out which was which; a lot depended on how they got on with the village matriarchs. Some metropolitan transplants were unlikely to take root whoever was involved: Temperance drives and outdoor theaters, for example, rarely prospered. In the small village of Tetipac the keen maestro produced a morality play against alcohol and found, in his own words, that "the usual thing happened, the habitual drunks dragged the sober ones off for a drink to celebrate how good the play had been and the truth of what had been said."[66] Savvy teachers spent more of their time on new crop varieties, fertilizers, and farming methods, using their literacy to guide locals through the new bureaucracy.

Women got less attention in the revolutionary scheme of things, even though tens of thousands of them had played significant roles with the armies of the 1910s. *Soldaderas* were cooks, camp followers, lovers, wives and mothers, messengers, ammunition smugglers, spies and soldiers. Folk songs and photographs made them into rugged but submissive helpmeets in one archteype, subversively dangerous fighters in another. One woman became head of Carranza's Secret Service; Amelio Robles, one of Zapata's more dangerous colonels, was born Amelia Robles, and decades after the revolution had ended still inspired fear in government circles.[67] So when Pancho Villa killed ninety women prisoners in 1916 it was probably not just the deepening brutality of his war of reprisals, but also recognition of just how central women were in their military roles.[68]

And yet Cardenista programming for women was often about improving them in their old domestic roles: nutrition, hygiene, childcare. Policies for their cultural revolution, much like those for Indians, were folded into universal education programming. Government schools were coeducational, and by the early 1930s the ratio of girls to boys was almost equal in some states. The basic three years of primary schooling sufficed to teach literacy and numeracy; it also provided new models of equality, and of women leaders in the shape of teachers. Girls progressed through schooling to teacher training and finally positions of real power.[69] Yet as in other spheres, the Cárdenas government first egged on and then dropped women's popular organizations.

Revolutionary rhetoric of gender equality went back to the 1910s; governors like Salvador Alvarado in Yucatán convened a Feminist Congress in 1916 and did something about schooling, access to paid work, reproductive healthcare, and reducing domestic violence. There were nationalist women's organizations, such as the Hijas de Cuauhtémoc, and women joined the revolutionary bureaucracy and colonized the single party. Women also counted in communist and conservative parties, mobilizing the men's vote, and even the Catholic right included secretaries for women's action in their leadership councils. Women in village Michoacán wrote to the president about their "feminine mission" to work for "the collective benefit of our class brothers." In mill towns they fought strikebreakers and led riots against factory owners. They set up their own labor organizations in industries ranging from coffee to sex: In Veracruz prostitutes were at the center of a huge tenants' strike (which they won, securing rent control and public housing). Feminist activism even reached into the unacknowledged world of unpaid household labor, with the Marxist tenant newspaper urging proletarians not to replicate capitalists' class-based oppression with gender-based oppression.[70]

The disappointments were many. Feminists were subsumed into the Left as one more group of proletarians, transmuted into men for the working day; Cardenistas and communists remained deaf to questions of unpaid domestic and reproductive labor.[71] Social programs for women were among the most vulnerable, cultural programming the first revolutionary measure to be ditched in the face of opposition, corruption, or bureaucratic poverty. The anti-alcohol campaign was a prime example. As in the US, it was founded not just on abstract puritanism or a calculus of lost work hours, misspent salaries, and cantina fistfights. Sexual and gender-based violence was critical, even if propriety and honor meant that it was rarely acknowledged in the letters that women sent politicians. The government acknowledged the link in cartoons of grotesque men threatening terrified families with chairs, knives, and bottles. Drunken men meant beaten women. Cardenista promises mobilized women in thousands of local anti-alcohol campaigns and then abandoned them, sometimes in dangerous positions, without funding or government support. Drinking increased across the social revolution. Prosecutions for rape and domestic violence remained so low that they can only be seen as having been irrelevant to judges and attorneys. Moreover, the extent to which women reported rape is unclear; the assumption has to be that very many didn't, a more or less universal pattern. When they did, along the fiercely independent coast of Guerrero, the result was an improvised hearing outside the town hall and a fine for the rapist.[72]

Above all, Cárdenas promised suffrage and never delivered. The radical governor Tomás Garrido Canabal gave women in Tabasco the vote in local elections, but the rest of the PNR took a paternalistic line on female suffrage, one that mirrored the Porfirian line on men's suffrage: good in the future, unwise in the present because of their civic immaturity.[73] In 1935 the *Frente Unido Pro–Derechos de la Mujer* brought together fifty thousand Cardenistas, Catholics, communists, and feminists to push for lower utility prices, books for children, and the right to vote. The party promptly made several promises that "working women" would soon be voting in municipal elections.[74] Cárdenas made two major speeches and passed two bills calling for the reform of Article 34, which would have allowed women's suffrage; neither was put into action, and in 1940 Congress declared itself opposed. Women were finally allowed to vote in local elections in 1947, but not in presidential elections until 1958. Instead of being at the forefront of women's political rights, Mexico ended up just one more of the Latin American states that stalled on delivering votes for women until the 1950s.[75] As for the climb into national politics, there were no women in Congress until 1954.[76] No woman joined the cabinet until 1958, when the playwright and diplomat Amalia González Caballero became undersecretary of cultural affairs.

So the cultural revolution that was supposed to be the handmaiden of agrarian reform turned out distinctly partial. No great leap forward occurred in adult literacy. Indigenous boarding schools repeatedly failed and were shut down. Catholic strategies of resistance, from keeping children out of schools to lynching teachers, largely stymied socialist education, which was ditched in the early 1940s. Teachers gained power, but priests kept much of theirs. Cárdenas had to deal with the compromises that had brought him to power, but he also ran into the problem of many Mexicos: One size of reform did not fit all communities. And even local knowledge was insufficient when faced with competing agencies, villages, caciques, and peasant organizations. Cultural policy confronted pent-up demand for reform from thousands of grassroots organizations with well-meaning rhetoric. It left behind an expanded pool of people who bought into that rhetoric and those ephemeral social programs and gained experience in the dark arts of local politics. It also brought disillusionment. Communal cornmills broke down and were never replaced; in one village the *maestra* privatized it, while also rustling cattle and using school resources to set up a mescal distillery.[77] Anti-alcohol campaigns foundered, cooperatives were defrauded, and teachers turned out to be careerists and caciques as well as idealists and helpful pragmatists. The women's mobilization that had made them so important in revolutionary fighting and social reform won them jobs as teachers and administrators in political parties; community cornmills and sewing machines; places in schools and universities; it didn't win them the vote. In some places the only concrete result of revolutionary reform was a basketball court.

Industrial workers before Cárdenas had done better than country people; they were the lower-class winners of the revolutionary civil wars. The dominant union of the 1920s, the *Confederación Regional Obrera Mexicana* (CROM), secured its hundred thousand members higher wages, shorter hours, and some of the benefits promised in the constitution such as healthcare and pensions. It came at the price of subordination, corruption, and violence. Union leaders used gunmen to get to the top and stay there, with the closed-shop system giving them the power to hire, fire, and discipline workers. The CROM's leader, Luis Morones, was one of the most powerful men in the country, and he used his power to break strikes and protect government and big business. In the interests of empire-building and development policy, he waged war on the rival anarchists of the *Confederación General de Trabajadores* (CGT) and Mexico's forty thousand railwaymen. Rebellious and strategically vital, the Association of Railway Mechanics struck in 1926 and was defeated by scabs, soldiers, and mass layoffs. By contrast, *cromista* textile workers accepted Morones's instructions for "conciliation" with management and got their salaries increased by a third. The weavers of Río Blanco, symbols of labor resistance to Díaz, had a new swagger to them; unfirable, they could happily nip off for a beer mid-shift.[78]

Morones himself was spectacularly and unabashedly corrupt, throwing lavish parties and showing off luxury Packards, gaudy women, and diamond rings. Even this, though, may have helped bring the new expectations home into workers' lives. If Morones could make it up through the ranks, perhaps they could too. For the average man and woman, reduced work hours radically changed the rhythms of everyday life: The old Marxist aim of eight hours work, eight hours sleep, and eight hours leisure translated into workers playing baseball, putting on plays, forming bands, reading books. Paid weekends began, mill shifts ending at 1:00 p.m. on Saturday. The CROM even extended its benefits into the Mexico City penitentiary, where prisoners unionized under the slogan "Health and Social Revolution" and won matrimonial visits and a jazz band.[79]

The mixture of violent centralization with revolutionary expectations endured past the political demise of Morones in 1928 when, accused of organizing the murder of Obregón, his demise could well have been literal. Factory floor shootouts, army scabs, and barroom murders all continued. But so did a new quality of life as the state tried to balance the interests of bosses and workers to keep both in check. The CROM's immediate successor as the state's preferred union was the weaker but more radical *Confederación General de Obreros y Campesinos de México* (CGOCM), run by Vicente Lombardo Toledano, a Marxist university lecturer. It had to compete with the surviving CROMistas, the anarchists, railwaymen, and oilworkers, and lead its members through the pay cuts and layoffs of the Depression. As a result organized labor came to 1934 with a renewed sense of grievance and ambition. The PNR manifesto promised to increase support for workers but without much of the language of class struggle. They didn't need it. Cárdenas's electoral rivals were doomed from the start, and the Partido Comunista de México had no revolutionary potential at all: Crippled by prohibition, arrests, and fratricide, it was down to fourteen hundred members.[80] So all it took to produce major change was to open the tap on the growing radicalism of the mainstream workforce, which Cárdenas did through inaction and action. He systematically declined to suppress strikes; simultaneously he passed a labor law that threatened strikebound businesses with expropriation. The numbers of strikes boomed, from 13 in 1933 to 642 in 1935.[81]

Cárdenas, freed from the constraints of his rise to power, moved leftward and encouraged strikers. In Monterrey, the conservative industrialists' capital, he delivered a speech called the "Fourteen Points" that distilled to one point: Business had to cede workers very different living standards or else, for raison d'état. "The employer class should be very careful," he told them, "to ensure that their provocations do not become a political rallying point, because that will lead us into an armed struggle"; "Businessmen who are tired of social struggle can hand over their businesses to the workers or the Government."[82] While he insisted to the same audience that communists were an insignificant minority, he legalized the Communist Party, released its prisoners, and allowed it an impressive comeback. In short order, helped by the rise of European fascism, the party was a player again, recruiting from the students of Ayotzinapa to the metalworkers of Torreón, reaching a membership of seventeen thousand. With this encouragement and rivalry, Lombardo Toledano recreated the single-union hegemony of the twenties with his state-backed Confederación de Trabajadores Mexicanos (CTM), a grouping of more than three thousand unions that recruited 70 percent of the urban workforce. The founding charter defined its aim as the complete abolition of capitalism in Mexico.[83]

With initial successes came the increased ambition of sympathy strikes, evidence of more sophisticated, cross-class mobilization in a virtuous cycle. The expropriation of the cotton and wheat estates was preceded by general strikes that brought together workers and peasants, events uncomfortably close to mass rebellion.[84] In 1937 striking oil workers were quickly joined by Tampico's electricians. This was understandable; they were neighbors with skilled jobs in similar sectors in the same oil port. That the strike should be seconded in Guanajuato, Jalisco, Michoacán, and even Yucatán, none of whose workers had anything to do with oil, was less predictable. As a result real wages rose to the highest level ever.[85] Even domestic workers, overwhelmingly lower-class women, the worst-paid, least powerful sector, unionized and made big gains. In 1935 a maid's salary in Tampico was fifteen pesos a month; in 1940 it was twenty.[86]

The labor aristocracy of railwaymen and oil workers did best, consolidated into single unions with their hands on the strategic industries. In June 1937 the government nationalized the railway companies, a move that was not particularly good business (they had been making losses for their foreign owners for some time) but one that gave Mexicans the prime jobs. Cárdenas was pushed into it by the recently formed Sindicato de Trabajadores Ferrocarrileros de la República Mexicana. In 1938, in like fashion but with far greater impact, he was pushed into expropriating the oil industry.

Mexico's oil came to foreigners' attention in the 1860s, when a Boston ship captain found gas and oil bubbling up through the smelly ponds and wetlands of the Gulf Coast.[87] It was malarial jungle, owned in the main by the Totonac and Tének peoples, and outsiders didn't dawdle. At first Mexico's own minimal oil needs were met by refining US crude. As global demand boomed, though, the unusual forest ponds drew the attention of the first oil barons. The region's indigenous people had long fought off Mexican outsiders, but they were initially tolerant of foreign geologists, whom they led to the deposits for five pesos a trip, and to whom they sold these wastelands. Some oilmen, like the ubiquitous engineer Weetman Pearson, were already established. Others began from scratch; in 1903 the founder of Standard Oil, Edward Doheny, had to cadge 50,000 pesos from a hacendado to keep going. Big discoveries gave them the drive and funds to buy large stretches of land, though, and in 1907 production took off. Pearson acquired a thousand square miles and founded El Águila. Doheny bought a foothold for his Standard Oil, a multinational whose wells were appearing from Los Angeles to Lake Maracaibo.

The new companies needed large stretches of land fast; they turned when resisted to gang violence to get them, murdering holdouts, burning houses, and clear-cutting forest. They also needed large workforces and so paid wages and bought local food and services, which helped sustain peasant farms elsewhere. But working in the oil fields was dangerous, and the oil companies supplemented wages with yet more force. On July 4, 1908, the field at San Diego de la Mar blew up; the unstoppable fire lasted two months and burned off one million tons of crude. From then on, the companies pressed the indigenous Tének to work when fire struck, using good connections with Porfirian rural police to get locals to do the difficult, sometimes fatal job. By 1930 two-thirds of the resident Indians had left the region, their places filled by entrepreneurial highlanders and refugees from the civil wars.

Yet the revolution also turned the tables. Oil workers rapidly organized and took to striking. In 1914 three thousand men walked off the job at a single field, Potrero del Llano. The government initially backed them: In 1915 President Carranza stopped all work pending new legislation, and the Constitution of 1917 made the deposits national property. The oil companies could own the soil above them; they couldn't own the oil below, and were supposed to pay the state for concessions to pump it out. The presidents of the 1920s never put the slippery maneuver into practice, though, and despite new global competition and falling production the companies stayed and even expanded. Business was lucrative enough to assume the risk, even as they faced a radical new union, the Sindicato de Trabajadores Petroleros de la República Mexicana, the STPRM. After the huge 1934 strike at Poza Rica the British El Águila bought a further oil concession there, betting on their traditional exceptions to Mexican legislation, backed by their government's clout, to see them through.

The oil workers had been talking of nationalization even before Cárdenas took office.[88] They were encouraged by General Francisco Mújica, the young president's left-wing mentor—Mújica's family had looked out for Cárdenas when his father died—in secret meetings with union leaders.[89] It was a typical Cardenista meeting of minds. Multiple strikes culminated in November 1936 with the STPRM demanding a new collective contract, whose 240 clauses included a pay raise of $26 million, increased benefits, a forty-hour week, and the "Mexicanization" of the administration, replacing foreign with domestic specialists. In May 1937 the oil workers struck; the companies refused an Arbitration Board compromise, legally opening themselves to expropriation, and took the case to the Supreme Court. Much of the presidential cabinet and the CTM favored settlement, but the intransigence of both sides backed Cárdenas into a corner, and on March 18, 1938, he took to the radio to announce that Mexico was seizing the oil companies.[90]

From the Mexican side the expropriation was presented in terms of anti-imperialism. In his manicured diary Cárdenas recorded it as

> a step taken by the Government in defense of its sovereignty, taking back control of the oil wealth from which imperialist capital has been profiting in order to keep the country in an abject state . . . with

an act like this Mexico contributes alongside the other states of Hispanic America in shaking somewhat the economic dictatorship of imperialist capitalism.[91]

A more spontaneous oil worker shut a British official out of his refinery with the words "The ambition of the foreigner is at an end."[92]

The expropriation was also seen as anti-imperialist from the losing side, a moment foreshadowing later panicked flights from lost colonial wars. In the refinery town of Minatitlán the British chartered airplanes to evacuate the women and children; local soldiers were unlikely to protect them from the red mob, they were told. Looting began early as oil company officials were besieged by requests for packing crates and advice as to how to evacuate a grand piano. The tennis courts and golf course emptied. The hedonism of despair kept the club packed as "a brave effort was made by certain members to drink up the bar stocks before they fell into the hands of the invader. Champagne corks popped merrily." The remaining British finally fled en masse on a 6:00 a.m. train, the foreman waking up middle-class refugees with shouts of "Get up, you lazy bastard."[93]

Mexicans across much of the political spectrum, even the Church, enjoyed this. It came at a price, however: The US stopped buying artificially high-priced silver, oil production fell, and the peso slid. Inflation, already rising, accelerated. It was not the disaster widely predicted when twentysomething Mexicans took over. A British engineer instead emphasized continuity in production, as El Águila's fourteen wells continued pumping tens of thousands of barrels a day.[94] The expropriation did, however, up the pressure on an economy already under strain. There was a political cost too. The international backlash was weaker than most had expected, but then—as Cárdenas noted in his diary three days earlier—the Europeans had greater distractions in fascist expansionism. The Germans had invaded and annexed Austria the week before.[95] The front page of the government newspaper the day after expropriation juxtaposed the two: in bold caps: UNANIMOUS SOLIDARITY OF THE PUEBLO WITH THE PRESIDENT, in italics beneath: "*Mexico will not recognize the annexation of Austria.*"[96] The British cut diplomatic ties with Mexico; the US, which counted rather more, did little. Domestically the Right and the army were publicly supportive, and the only overt opposition came from the last agrarian strongman, Saturnino Cedillo, by then obsolete, terminally confused, in Graham Greene's description "bewildered."[97] His rising in the mountains of San Luis Potosí was easily crushed.

Elsewhere staged patriotic rituals were backed by real enthusiasm: women donating their wedding rings, children their piggy banks, peasants sacks of corn and chickens; wage earners buying bonds with uncertain futures. But the Right, while publicly supportive, also perceived the oil expropriation as more of the frightening left-wing radicalism that threatened Mexico, one more reason to cast Cárdenas as an American Stalin, to increase fear that another civil war was pending, akin to Spain's. The pressure pushed the government rightward in pursuit of Cárdenas's most basic goal: keeping disaffected generals, governors, landowners, and Catholics away from rebellion.[98]

Toward that end, revolutionary nationalism and internationalism had mixed effects. Like much Cardenista radicalism, it had underappreciated antecedents. Carranza had promulgated an anti-imperialist doctrine of nonintervention, pushed for the ideals of the Mexican Constitution to be written into the Treaty of Versailles, and declared the Monroe Doctrine dead. Obregón outmaneuvered the US in reforming the Pan-American Union, ousting Washington from permanent leadership in favor of an elected president and removing its right to exclude other countries. Calles sent arms and by some accounts men to Nicaragua to fight American Marines. The foreign minister invented the eponymous Estrada Doctrine, which prohibited countries from using diplomatic recognition, and with it access to international credit, to influence other countries' domestic politics. Revolutionary internationalism waned in the early thirties as Mexico broke off diplomatic relations with the Soviet Union; Cárdenas's Six-Year Plan revived it.[99]

The expropriation of foreign-owned land and oil was the most radical assertion of foreign policy independence, and made Mexico influential from Uruguay, where pro-democracy demonstrators carried placards with Cárdenas's face, to Cuba, where the future dictator Fulgencio Batista studied the agrarian reform. The Mexican government paid Latin American intellectuals to come and admire the work of socialist teachers and indigenistas. At the same time Cárdenas made Mexico a leader in the early struggle against fascism: When the Spanish Civil War started, he broke with craven Western neutrals to send arms and volunteers to the Spanish Republic and then, as Franco marched toward victory in 1939, accepted thirty thousand refugees and the entire government in exile. He also opposed, unlike most of the global Left, the Soviet Union's Winter War on Finland, and begrudgingly gave the main figure in internationalist communism, Leon Trotsky, asylum and police protection. By 1940 Mexico was being called "the lighthouse of America."[100]

On the Right, however, this brought more fear than pride. The Spanish Republicans were anathema, condemned by their murderous anticlericalism and the support of Stalinists and anarchists. Trotsky was second only to Lenin as an architect of international Bolshevism. Promoting the achievements of Mexico's social revolution to other Latin Americans reinforced conservatives' belief in a fanatical left-wing extremism at the heart of government. Russians would doubtless repay it with military assistance; Lombardo Toledano, vocally keen on the USSR, was rumored to be importing tanks.[101] An American journalist was told that Mexican Nazis had dispatched engineers to strategic points on the coast to land German arms.[102] Agraristas wrote letters to the government to report that right-wing landholders were smuggling in large quantities of weapons.[103] None of the rumors were true. But it was eloquent of how international events and foreign policy polarized Mexico that people believed them, and it was one more compelling reason for Cárdenas to retreat from radicalism after 1938. Faced with the phantasm of a Spanish Civil War in Mexico, he preferred to allow a conservative comeback. So when in 1940 he chose a successor, he overlooked Francisco Mújica, his leftist compadre, and handed over the presidency to a bland right-winger from Puebla, General Manuel Ávila Camacho.

Much of the tangible progress proved quickly undone. Ejidal grants and credits dried up. The new government wrote socialist education out of the constitution and halved the number of teacher training colleges.[104] Soldiers beat and shot strikers. A regime that freed political prisoners was followed by one that invented the Orwellian crime of *disolución social*, a law that enabled the government to jail dissidents for long periods on the vague grounds that they were socially divisive.

While Mexico grew significantly richer, its governments invested significantly less of their budgets on social spending.

Other Cardenista changes endured but went in unexpected directions. Ejidatarios who realized the dream of individual plots were impoverished by artificially low government-set prices for the food they sold. Ejidatarios who took collective ownership of supposedly lucrative henequen or sugar estates found themselves more like proletarians than planters, salaried labor on what were theoretically their own lands. The trickle-down economics of collective farming proved unreliable: Some ejidatarios went unpaid for months, and if they struck were put down by soldiers. Elsewhere, administrators dug themselves into dynastic power and took over the supposedly inalienable plots of their subjects. They weren't invariably opposed by the rural teachers, those intended counterweights to local boss rule, because often enough they were rural teachers themselves. Some ejidatarios began calling their ejidos haciendas.

Workers found out that their merger into a single state-backed union left them with less rather than more power. Fidel Velásquez, the national union boss whom Cárdenas installed in office, remained there for the next fifty years. His subordinates, the heads of the different trades, were replaced by stooges. Real wages dropped steadily, and in an economy partly run by the state were allowed to drop, even engineered to drop. And unionized workers were the lucky ones, because many of the new jobs in the fast-growing towns and cities were in the informal sector, powerless, lacking the state benefits that partly compensated for the lurch to the right.

Dividing the extraordinarily diverse population of Mexico into peasants, workers, and everyone else may seem schematic, but that is what the single-party reforms did. In 1938 Cárdenas turned the PNR into the Partido de la Revolución Mexicana, PRM, its huge membership organized into three branches; the third, the misnamed Sector Popular, brought together anyone who was not a unionized peasant or worker, and was the most powerful of the three. The party monopolized power for the next sixty years. Its leaders moved from side to side ideologically, but the basis remained the same, a single party monopolizing national power to run a profoundly unequal capitalist society.

This dramatic shift away from the years of rapid, comprehensive, and profound reform was seen by many as the end of the revolution,

Cardenismo as it was supposed to be: "A Socialist Hymn Book" with musical notation and lyrics, Oaxaca (c. 1936).

its Thermidor. The metaphor drew on the French Revolution, where in 1795 radical egalitarians, struggling to refound their world, lost power in the month called Thermidor to conservative juntas that ended reform. The metaphor worked in some political terms, as a declining Cárdenas and rising conservatives undermined popular militants; revolutionaries were indeed hijacked by authoritarian centralizers. In France, however, the end result was military dictatorship and the massive violence of Napoleonic expansion. In Mexico, by contrast, the single party managed an overall decrease in high levels of violence, even as it waged war on provincial insurgencies. It was run at a national level by civilians who rotated in and out of power through a never-broken series of punctual elections. Mexico, unlike every other country in Latin America, never went under to military dictatorship during the Cold War, and its civilian regimes spent less on the military than any other country in the hemisphere. And as in France, some revolutionary change could not be unmade. The new peasant ownership of land, for all its many and great flaws, endured. With it came an enduring shift in what the French call *mentalité*, a new way of conceiving the world, its possibilities, and the language that encoded it.

The revolutionary gains of the 1930s in Mexico were fragile, reversible, flawed. Yet they came at a far lesser cost than dramatic top-down change elsewhere. There were no gulags, concentration camps, man-made famines, or mass racial murders.[105] In the hemisphere only Bolivia came close to similar social change. There in the 1950s the Movimiento Nacional Revolucionario legislated large-scale land reform and universal suffrage, but for all their radical intentions the reformers achieved slow and incomplete redistribution. The living standard and political freedoms of the indigenous majority didn't improve all that much.[106] Nearly two centuries earlier, the proclaimed first revolutionaries in the Americas, those of the United States, left property relations and chattel slavery alone and accelerated the forced migration and elimination of indigenous peoples. The new gentry, merchants, and middle classes weren't much different from the old gentry, merchants, and middle classes. The only societies that experienced changes comparable to those of Mexico lay offshore in Haiti and Cuba. On the mainland, the Mexican Revolution was the only real American Revolution.

Part Five

People and Power

1940–2020

Chapter Seventeen

A Part-Time Dictatorship

Whether it was a dictatorship at all was debatable. In 1929 a single-party state emerged from the fervid intrigue, rebellion, and religious war of the 1920s, thousands of local parties and their political bosses forswearing personalist rule, with swaggering hypocrisy, to found the Partido Nacional Revolucionario. They changed the party's name and statutes in 1938 and again in 1946, at which point democratizing leaders settled on the final version of the Partido Revolucionario Institucional, the PRI. Of the major single parties of the twentieth century, only the Communist Party of the Soviet Union spent more consecutive years in power. Unlike the leadership of the Soviet Union, the PRI stayed in power through punctual elections, its civilian leaders circulating punctiliously in and out of office. Soldiers stayed in their barracks. And while in power, through all the cycles of half-hidden violence and betrayal, corruption and inequality, booms of hope and busts of disillusion, the PRI oversaw another incontrovertible success story, a structural shift that was the greatest social change of Mexico after the revolution: the most dramatic population growth and stabilization of any country in the world.[1]

Mexico passed through three periods as a single-party state. From the mid-forties to the mid-sixties it was a hybrid regime of dictatorship and democracy, in their own words a *dictablanda*. (A punning neologism that combines *dicta* from the noun *dictadura,* dictatorship, and *blanda* from changing the adjective from *dura*, hard, to *blanda*, soft.) From the later sixties until the mid-eighties the political system was less a soft than a straightforward dictatorship, the bottom line of survival an unambiguous state violence. In the countryside the army waged dirty wars, brutal counterinsurgencies in places like Guerrero, where lethal technology fought peasant stubbornness, a sort of Mexican Vietnam. In the cities the government sent out secret policemen to beat, arrest, and kill middle-class dissidents and urban guerrillas. The PRI's presidential candidates won by arrogant, cartoonish degrees of fraud, majorities of 88 percent, 85 percent, 93 percent.[2] Finally, the eighties and nineties were a long goodbye during which the PRI appeared bafflingly incompetent and the opposition, steadily more professional, won post after post. Economic mismanagement gave way to collapse and foreign aid conditioned on killing off the social programs central to PRI rule. Ivy League technocrats took over the party and began losing the big elections: the governorships and, in 1997, the mayoralty of Mexico City. In 2000 the PRI lost the greatest election of all, the presidential, and the single-party state came to its end.

None of these changes happened cleanly or overnight. School textbooks, political speeches, intellectuals, and social scientists once concurred that the party had quickly stabilized the country in 1940 through sophisticated institutional design, the adherence of a majority of Mexicans, and a rough-and-ready ideological consensus. Through the party, the national leadership—the *familia revolucionaria*—overcame fratricide. A critical mass of the people they ruled had been satisfied, or at least co-opted, by the social revolution of the 1930s. Diplomats reported approvingly that managerial politics were replacing ideology, sidelining both the "peasant socialism" of Zapata and Cárdenas and the homegrown fascism of the Catholic far Right, the Sinarquistas, who "preached direct action, the glory of martyrdom and the beauty of violence."[3] Aging, rough-cut revolutionary generals made way more or less gracefully for young democratic sophisticates, Brylcreemed lawyers with good teeth. And because of all that Mexicans from the mid-1940s to the late 1960s enjoyed not just considerable peace dividends but also exceptional economic growth, more than two decades' worth of booming wealth that they dubbed the Mexican Miracle.

This was a story that Mexico's leaders told themselves, their people, and inquisitive foreigners. Much of it was inaccurate. For starters, the party probably lost the 1940 presidential election, when it installed the conservative general Manuel Ávila Camacho over the more conservative general Juan Andreu Almazán. It wasn't much of a choice. Ávila

Camacho was blandly amiable and little else, "a steak with eyes" to his elder brother, "a slab of halibut" to the British ambassador.[4] His rival Almazán was an unlovable oligarch, duplicitous and corrupt. Officially Ávila Camacho won overwhelmingly; the embryonic spy services thought he probably lost, all the way from the Catholic highlands to the major cities. Ávila Camacho witnessed the lethal street fighting needed to rig the vote in Mexico City and tearfully agreed.[5] He moved into the presidential palace anyway, and his elder brother Maximino moved into the lucrative public works ministry, seizing the building with submachine guns and proclaiming himself minister. There he remained until he keeled over dead at a barbecue in 1945, officially a heart attack, in gossip a poisoning.

All the gaudy violence was emblematic of a basic political truth: There was no grand revolutionary settlement in the early 1940s and no righteously powerful central state overseeing it. The government employed more people than it had a decade earlier but was not ruled by meritocratic civilian administrators. The president's brother Maximino exemplified that: a general described as a "lord of knife and noose" thanks to his murderous political ways, a provincial warlord in Puebla who first got rich plundering in the Cristiada, and who was unstoppable enough to steal the best real estate in Acapulco—Caleta, the islet that separates the two beaches—from his own government.[6] But in 1942 German submarines helped out the more farsighted party men by torpedoing two Mexican oil tankers and forcing a reluctant government to war. While assorted cabinet members slept with the same elegantly debauched German spy—the interior minister paid her rent—and the president happily played wargames, they also enjoyed the excuse to put down unions, purge the Left, make peace with the bishops, consolidate the single party, and build a newly powerful Secretaría de Gobernación to run it all.[7] World War II was a godsend; as President Ávila Camacho put it, "In the face of the war to which Nazi-fascist aggression has driven us, internal controversies—no matter how respectable—must go silent."[8]

In the corridors of power they largely did, top Cardenistas accepting job losses and right-wing opposition its systemic exclusion. The Sinarquistas acted and talked like fascists; as a sharp diplomat put it, "They denounce as heretical democracy, liberalism, scientific progress, and modern education," but they were not, as Cárdenas told a US pressman, a "fifth column"; their once-close contacts with the Nazis had ended by 1940.[9] Instead of fighting the government they went in droves into exile in the US or to the mystic fringes of the Christian Democrat Partido Acción Nacional, PAN, or to a failed agricultural colony the government gave them in the unpromising dryness of Baja California. The baroque sociopath Maximino proved the last of his kind in national government, his presidential ambitions thwarted not by poisoners but by rioters of all classes at a bullfight; gaudy violence, this time by the ruled.[10] Yet if there was détente in Mexico City, bloody unresolved conflict rolled on where politics counted to most Mexicans, in intensely personal struggles for control of the provinces.

There, single-party rule, or even a single party, had yet to arrive convincingly. Governors and regional bosses ignored its central committee and the higher-ups it served and ran their own candidates for mayors and congressmen. Sometimes they rigged elections against their own party. At other times the PRI roundel was a fig leaf for conservative Catholics. Caciques new and old kicked PRI-supporting peasants off their lands, families of ejidatarios fleeing in forced migration. A bureaucrat sent to resolve conflicts in Naranja was run out of town at pistol point.[11] The less unfortunate merely lost their symbols and promised quality of life. In Nueva Italia the profits of one of the great irrigation systems of the Americas had funded, among other things, a public swimming pool; it became a dirty puddle. In places like the mill town of Santa Rosa workers got functioning swimming pools.[12] Yet this was not a tale of two swimming pools, the single party abandoning peasants while rewarding docile union backers, because the workers' pool came from a violent labor boss fighting to control them as real wages plunged. In 1944, despite all the cooption and coercion, more strikes occurred than in the last years of Cardenismo, and workers like the swimming weavers were at their forefront.[13]

So by 1945 there was a stark divide between capital stability and rural conflict, the Valley of Mexico once again the settled center of a tenuous federation of turbulent provinces and unruly frontiers. The leader of Congress called Mexican democracy a gangsters' farce; assorted governors just ignored the center's political directions. In January 1946 the army used rifles, bayonets, and a grenade to kill twenty-seven protesters during a demonstration against electoral fraud in León, Guanajuato.[14] The dead were mainly working-class; some were women and children. At its national convention soon afterward the party fell on its sword, shapeshifting from the Partido de la Revolución Mexicana to the Partido de la Revolución Institucional. The first line of the new old party's founding statement accepted "absolutely and without reservation the democratic system of government"; the revolution came in second. The PRI's presidential candidate for 1946, a young lawyer named Miguel Alemán, promised that he would campaign cleanly and accept the result, whatever it was.[15]

Alemán won the presidency more or less cleanly and went to the US to lecture Congress on the principles of democracy.[16] He was less of a democrat than he sounded. He had experienced firsthand the hollowness of revolutionary elections; in 1929 his father had followed one spurious democrat, General Escobar, into rebellion against another, General Calles, and been summarily executed. The son nevertheless rose rapidly through the ranks, from judge to senator to governor of his home state of Veracruz by 1936; in 1943 he became Secretario de Gobernación. His success was widely attributed to his savvy, the smartest of a new generation of lawyer-politicians, the children of 1910 who started off in the lecture halls of the national university rather than on the battlefield. Alemán had formed the equivalent of a student fraternity there, H1920, its members sworn to mutual back-scratching, and it was supposed to be this American approach to coalition-building that got him (and 20 percent of his law class) into office.[17] His up-by-the-lawyerly-bootstraps biography was only half-truth, though; alongside Alemán's merits came the patronage of a thuggish right-wing faction of the party, a suave talent for corruption, and the unattributed but helpful murder of rivals.[18] His personal driver was nicknamed *el asesino*, the killer.[19]

Yet when Alemán took over in December 1946, even Manuel Gómez Morín, the founder and leader of the PAN, was "very hopeful."[20] The new president was, the playwright Rodolfo Usigli adjudged, a "manufacturer and salesman of wholesale hope." Usigli's cynicism was founded on a moment emblematic of Mexico's democratic spring: Allowed to stage his satire on the revolution, *El gesticulador*, a sort of Mexican *Les mains sales*, he took a fist in the face on opening night and was shut down after two weeks.[21] Critical cabarets, a longstanding tradition, flourished briefly and then were shuttered.[22] While Mexico City was the cultural capital of Latin America, home of the most influential literary and academic journals, with an unrivaled concentration of universities and world-class intellectuals, its newspapers were barred from proper political reporting. Between 1948 and 1950 anonymous thugs attacked several national journalists with opposition magazines, something that wasn't supposed to happen under the PRI. Jorge Piño Sandoval, editor of *Presente*, fell from a second-floor balcony; Natalio Burstein, editor of *Impacto*, improbably blew his brains out in the back of a police car in Puebla; Fernando Sánchez Breton, editor of *La Semana Ilustrada*, suffered the lethal clarity of a professional hit.[23] The ambiguities of power were clear early on.

Those ambiguities were far more relevant in the countryside, the cradle of revolutionaries, than among capitalino theatergoers or magazine readers. Mexico's longstanding electoral culture found regional expression in the 1920s and '30s: In places ranging from cities like Acapulco to remote hamlets, local voters who cared enough got results often enough to make the game worth playing. This was, in the party's revealing code, "the electoral problem": how to balance caciquismo, the boss rule that was the bulwark of everyday control, against unruly crowds with memories of revolution and its promises; the cost of repression weighed against the cost of toleration. In their early years the PRI's leaders regularly judged the cost of toleration lower, and ceded voters new powers. They doubled the electorate by giving women the vote, finally making good on Cárdenas's promise. They cleaned up local elections to the point that the PAN won a handful of the several hundred municipalities they contested; in places like highland Oaxaca the cost of repression would have been high, the benefits far too low.

In most places the democratic spring never translated into true multiparty elections. Yet there was real competition, because the party replaced the bloc votes of rigged conventions with primaries. These offered political fixers and voters choices ranging from communists to Sinarquistas. They were not just for diehard party men of the PRI, the *priistas*; anyone could enter a party primary, and many winners were party men for the day, joining the PRI being akin to registering to vote elsewhere, a bureaucratic nicety rather than a profession of faith or loyalty. Primaries provided the sort of representation that contemporary voters enjoyed in the single-party states of the US or the safe parliamentary seats of the UK, in some cases more; few communists were running for office in Alabama or Surrey. Primaries mattered to everyday Mexicans, who fought for the right to hold them across the rest of the twentieth century.[24]

The struggle for primary elections was refought at least once a decade from the 1940s onward because the PRI's democratic spring was too democratic for party leaders, and they ended it as quickly as possible. When President Alemán teetered in 1948 he promised more to voters who felt unrepresented, those who wrote him plaintive letters asking questions like "Why vote, if the results are going to be the same whether we vote or not?" By the end of 1949, however, the president felt restored enough to abruptly ban primaries, and in 1950 the party reinstated the bloc vote. When Cárdenas called for renewed primaries, he was ignored. Across Latin America governments were shifting to the right and consolidating power as the Cold War began in earnest, and Mexico, for all its revolution, did likewise. At the same time as the PRI closed down internal competition, it banned the Communist Party from running in elections, despite its puniness; US diplomats, who one might expect would see a lot of reds under Mexican beds, estimated the party's membership at sixteen hundred in 1950, concentrated in Mexico City and a couple of states. Only seventy-six of them made it to their Thirteenth Congress, convened in a defunct brothel.[25]

The threat from the moderate left was greater. The party had coopted the unions, most of them grouped in the CTM, in two stages: In 1940 they replaced the intellectual Lombardo Toledano with the apparatchik Fidel Velásquez, and in the late 1940s they replaced independent leaders of individual unions with pro-government stooges. But in 1951 numerous old revolutionaries ditched the PRI to form the Federación de Partidos del Pueblo Mexicano, an improbable coalition of the excluded that attracted everyone from radical Zapatistas to conservative, money-grubbing generals. Their presidential candidate,

General Miguel Henríquez Guzmán, was close to Cárdenas, spending time with him and his son Cuauhtémoc; many believed that he enjoyed the ex-president's blessing. Henríquez Guzmán and his construction company had done well out of the PRI's economic policy, but he appealed to the growing numbers who had not. Moreover he was running against an uninspiring accountant, Adolfo Ruiz Cortines, whose main qualification for the presidency seemed to be dogged loyalty to Alemán.

So while the Henriquistas never achieved a national peasant following, they did well in several states and the capital—unquantifiably well, given that the PRI counted the votes—and protested their defeat on July 7 with a victory parade down the Alameda, the pretty colonial boulevard in Mexico City. Police and soldiers put them down with tear gas, cavalry charges, and some five hundred arrests.[26] Shooting went on for hours across the city center. Reports of the death toll varied greatly, corpses vanishing; ambulances picked up 130 wounded. Cárdenas kept quiet; key leaders in the provinces were jailed, threatened with life sentences for disolución social; Henríquez Guzmán flirted with rebellion through the autumn, summoning twenty-five thousand peasants to the capital for one meeting. In the end, though, he retired from politics with a state contract to build the highway and pipeline to Poza Rica, the country's main oil field. (Satirists put two and two together.) In 1954 the Secretaría de Gobernación broke up his party; there wasn't much fuss, and the center left remained inside the PRI for the next thirty years.[27] The lesson that presidential elections were the preserve of the state party, which would be violently intransigent if necessary, was quite clear. Years later a British diplomat asked Gómez Morín if he actually wanted a two-party system; the PAN leader confessed, "Good Heavens no, that would mean shooting and violence at every election!"[28]

However, Gómez Morín and his party followers insisted vigorously on the importance of local democracy. They were absolutely right: Mayors, often despised by their higher-ups, written off as irrelevant due to paltry tax bases, were still the politicians who counted the most for most Mexicans. They appointed policemen and judges, and handed out or denied permits for everything from trucks to cockfights; they controlled everyday state violence and access to the market economy.

By contrast, 1952 ended competitive politics in Mexico City for decades: The most cosmopolitan electorate in the country was ironically among the most disenfranchised, inhabiting a federal district that lacked municipios, its mayor a presidential appointee, the feisty local papers of some states replaced by the wire services, coded gossip, and rehashed press bulletins of stage-managed nationals. Capitalinos had little clue about events in the rest of Mexico, which were reported in telegraphic snippets by stringers, and little desire to know about them. They didn't pay too much attention even to national politics. In 1959 only 15 percent of urban Mexicans claimed to follow government news, and 40 percent of that sample came from Mexico City.[29]

Outside the cities, however, the disappearance of primaries had not wholly done away with representative politics. Provincial politicians who failed to realize this and resorted to visible violence lost their jobs. Even as the new status quo emerged, voters who really cared could still veto unsuitable candidates for mayor by rioting or storming town halls, effectively daring the authorities to shoot them. The PAN kept the pressure up by running hundreds of local candidates even as they stoically accepted national marginalization. In the North, the sierra, and the most Catholic places they occasionally won. In the run-up to provincial elections, the priistas at the Secretaría de Gobernación spied systematically on their own candidates, collecting gossip on their careers, reputations, and probity. Two of the boilerplate categories were "popular acceptance" and "criminal record."

That the reports mattered was clear from their results. During the 1950s Mexico's town halls were taken over by teachers, ranchers, petty businessmen, and successful peasants, notable more for their local acceptability than their party record. (Workers and women were excluded.) A large sample of mayors from the early 1960s revealed that half lacked any party record at all.[30] There were rogues, but rioters policed the margins, even in the cities: Big riots broke out in Zacatecas in 1958, Chihuahua and Baja California in 1959. Bloody-minded Catholic marchers got a conservative mayor elected in San Luis Potosí over the opposition of one of the most powerful and ruthless governors, Gonzalo N. Santos, a man who boasted of offering opponents the choice of *encierro, destierro o entierro*, jail, exile, or burial. President Ruiz Cortines was only part idealist when he summed up the division of power in Mexico as federal legislators and governors chosen by the presidency, local legislators chosen by the governors, and municipal governments chosen by the people.[31] Mexico was a single-party state where the single party lost elections.

Ruiz Cortines, who ruled Mexico from 1952 to 1958, exemplified the PRI at its competent peak, finalizing the *reglas no escritas*, the off-the-books but universally understood rules of politics. He made the party politically competent by institutionalizing the change of president as a wholesale change of the guard, breaking unexpectedly free of his powerful predecessor Alemán and leaving his own successor to his own devices. He made it economically competent by cutting the runaway corruption of the postwar boom, by fairly rigorous book-balancing, and by trading popularity for a timely and steep devaluation of the peso. Ruiz Cortines was not really cut out for popularity, anyway; he was a middle-aged accountant from the port of Veracruz, more apparatchik than flesh-presser. (He started his career with ten years in the Department of National Statistics.)[32] He lacked the smiling charm of Alemán, nicknamed "Mr. Colgate"; one cinema audience dubbed Ruiz Cortines "Dracula," and in a certain light he also resembled Boris Karloff.[33] Yet unlike other politicians described as vampires—a popular insult—he was glaringly honest, and largely delivered on his campaign promises of a sober administration that would guarantee political stability, economic development, and the basics of life to the poor.

In doing so he cemented a key aspect of priista Mexico, the avoidance of military dictatorship. The army was critical to civilian rule, as patrolling soldiers policed the countryside, guarded the main farms, and conducted unseen petty counterinsurgencies to forestall bigger ones. Soldiers were ubiquitous, with one garrison for every five municipios, and at times popular; one of their roles was development, and military engineers and medics laid water pipes, drained swamps, built roads, and handed out antimalarials. In times of dissidence they were less popular. Whenever the government faced a serious threat, it turned to soldiers: strike-breakers and union heavies in the mines, oil fields and railway yards; scabs in khaki when doctors struck; classroom monitors with guns when students rebelled. In the deep countryside some officers became petty dictators, either officially, as leaders of interim ayuntamientos when elections went wrong, or unofficially, as the best-armed men in town. A career in the army offered poor pay but enticing business opportunities, and generals logged forests, ran drugs, stole cattle, meddled in local businesses, and set up protection rackets. At times junior officers acted as contract killers, whether the contract was extended by the locally rich or an unhappy government.[34] In the 1940s soldiers were not just Mexico's enforcers of last resort; they were generally the first resort, the only competent source of state violence.

Yet while all bar one of the revolutionary presidents were generals, all bar none of the PRI's presidents were civilians. There was very nearly a coup at the outset in 1948, when outsize corruption, the excision of military men from government, and a collapsing economy pushed outcast officers into conspiracy. In July the peso lost more than half its value in two weeks; food prices soared while the value of savings crashed. Union members took to the streets, where government agents followed them. Government agents also followed the everyday Mexicans who went to cafés, markets, and cinemas, listened to the piping shouts of the newsboys as they spread bad news, read outraged flyers, listened to threatening corridos and cracked murderous jokes, complained to friends and strangers, and considered revolt.[35] What the agents heard was the unbound anger of a crowd that believed, as one miner put it,

> that the President of the Republic and the bunch of bandits who surround him were to blame [for the economic crisis], that they were sick of it and should exercise direct action against the Government, and that Chapultepec woods had lots of fine trees on which to go and hang every last one of them.[36]

It was the ideal time for a coup, and some unimportant officers got as far as a cut-and-paste manifesto to the nation, but it never happened.[37] Civilian rule was saved in part by Alemán's last-ditch stand that mixed emergency food supplies—"popular markets"—with cabinet firings and promises to generals of future submissiveness. He was supposed to be their puppet. Other generals, however, outweighed the malcontents and opportunists. The military ex-presidents Rodríguez, Cárdenas, and Ávila Camacho put aside their differences, set themselves up as an informal senate, and vetoed a coup. They persevered as a check on soldiers and presidents after the trouble passed; in 1952 they weighed in with Henríquez to help forestall rebellion; in 1955 they vetoed a military candidate for the presidency; in 1952 and 1958 they vetoed Alemán's reelection. As the others died off, Cárdenas endured, a sort of *jefe mínimo* who with proxies and quiet chats at his ranch reined in would-be strongmen and overmighty soldiers. Leading generals preserved a discrete influence in national politics—the first four leaders of the PRI were soldiers, the secretary of defense was believed capable of vetoing the president's choice of successor—but publicly they stayed unwaveringly loyal to the civilians. There was never wholesale demilitarization in the provinces, where generals kept much of their capacity to meddle and profit, but neither was there ever a coup. In one more paradox, soldiers kept soldiers out of politics.[38]

Moreover, with civilian presidents came civilian police forces: corrupt, of questionable competence, often just hitmen or soldiers with a change of uniform, but violent professionals nevertheless who could be deployed instead of the army, and who were subject to civilian law. Like the army they had the power to discourage peace spoilers, from career criminals to agrarian dissidents, with the simple choice of *pan o palo*, carrot or stick, *plata o plomo*, profits or bullets. There were political police too, the spies of the Dirección General de Investigaciones Políticas y Sociales (DGIPS) and the Dirección Federal de Seguridad (DFS), bureaucratic institutions that for all their initial weediness and military staffing were civilian-controlled.

The 1940s were also the last years of the great criminal warlords. The handful of *pistoleros* who still ran private armies came to sticky ends, ambushed by rivals or erstwhile allies in darkened streets on their way home from the bar or pool hall. A couple were murdered by the new political policemen of the DFS. In other cases the state just looked the other way, sometimes literally: While it was former employees who shot Crispín Aguilar, the main Veracruz gangster, it was the soldiery who confiscated his gun and patrolled the street shortly before the bullets flew.[39] Top-level political killings of the more kosher sort ended too. Unlike the postwar US, where every major progressive leader—MLK, JFK, RFK, Malcolm X, Harvey Milk—was assassinated, in Mexico from 1944 to 1994 there were not even confirmed attempts at assassination. The overall decline in homicide was remarkable and universal, from thirty-one per hundred thousand between 1941 and 1945 (a substantial undercount) to eighteen per hundred thousand between 1956 and 1960.[40] Part of it was down to a generational shift and a population boom: the men who had grown up with revolutionary violence and abundant firearms dying off by hook or by crook, the millions of newborns outnumbering the survivors. But the growing state was also ambitious with one of world's most rigorous gun control regimes, and comparatively adroit in managing violence, its men kept honest—in terms of murdering people, at least—by the crowd. Politicians who couldn't follow the new ways, who broke the reglas no escritas of no visible violence, were an endangered species.

Economic growth helped pacification. Part of Mexico's price for joining the allies in World War II had been forgiveness for 90 percent of the foreign debt, enabling substantial new credits for postwar development.[41] Tax breaks, cheap money, and a guaranteed supply of cheap labor and raw materials favored industry, protected from foreign competition by Mexico's refusal to enter the General Agreement on Tariffs and Trade (GATT), the cornerstone of the postwar economic order. Nacional Financiera SNC, the public development bank of the 1930s, trebled its loans between 1945 and 1953 and channeled them to a handful of key industries. It seemed like textbook import substitution industrialization, ISI, the dominant development theory of the time. But in reality foreign private investment, above all in electricity generation and manufacturing, rose steeply.[42] Companies like Westinghouse could buy decisive stakes in companies like the Corporación Industria Eléctrica de México SA while leaving 51 percent of shares in the hands of private Mexican investors; Mexican companies on paper, they then built factories that made American goods for Mexican buyers. Alemán personally courted CEOs in Acapulco. Individuals followed similar strategies with *prestanombres*, Mexican frontmen who lent their names to foreign businessmen like William Jenkins, a magnate in cotton, film, and finance. It was duplicitous but dramatic growth: GDP rose 63 percent between 1945 and 1953.[43]

Individuals who got a share of this could spend it on the new consumerism. These were the years of cheap wristwatches, Ray-Bans in provincial country clubs, mass ownership of Westinghouse fridges and General Electric radio sets, rebranded for the Mexican market as Azteca M-578s.[44] For five US cents Mexicans could see a subsidized film in one of Jenkins's hundreds of cinemas, getting there on subsidized public transport, smoking subsidized cigarettes while dissecting the subsidized film after (or indeed during) the showing. Even a family who lived in a single room in a tenement went most days to the matinées.[45] Politicians passed legislation to shove Mexican films down filmgoers' throats, theaters having to show a certain number each month, but with nearly a hundred a year to choose from that wasn't hard.[46] It was the *época de oro* of Mexican cinema, a golden age of art and soft power when only the US and India made more films, when the cinematographer Gabriel Figueroa taught John Ford how to shoot a brooding sky, when Mexicans began competing for Oscars despite the Academy's racism. The actresses Dolores del Río and María Félix were global stars. Alemán was a fan, in rumor enjoying a secret tunnel from his residence to Félix's mansion.[47] The university bookshop sold the Kinsey Report on credit.[48]

Alongside the consumption habits of a lubricious president came the goods of development. Politicians painted industrialization as a social good in its own right, the logical successor to social reform, "the constructive phase of the revolution."[49] The 1952 presidential report to Congress, the main political ritual of the year, told Mexicans—through compulsory radio coverage, amplified by speakers put up in the streets, rehashed in newsreels, brought home by new television sets—that "all the construction and the material improvements achieved have a profound human meaning."[50] Even priests agreed; in 1950 one threatened to excommunicate striking miners on the "Caravan of Hunger" march to the capital, even though they stopped off at the Basílica and paid their respects to the Virgin of Guadalupe.[51] Development was supposed to have trumped ideology: A government-leaning paper claimed that in Baja California the Sinarquistas of the Colonia María Auxiliadora worked hand in hand with the agraristas of the Colonia Benito Juárez.[52] At the end of his presidency in 1952 Alemán claimed to have spent 7.8 billion pesos on roads, railways, airports, docks, electricity cables, and irrigation canals.

Much of the money disappeared, but verifiable buildings and infrastructure endured. The 2.3 billion pesos of federal money for roads changed provincial life forever, bringing individual opportunity and hollowing out communities.[53] In indigenous Chiapas status used to come from age, politico-religious leadership positions called *cargos*, and corn harvests; now, in places like Zinacantán, a small Tzotzil town, status began to entail holding trucking permits or getting remittances from the US. Fewer people wanted cargos—expensive, grueling, and unpaid. Inequality grew; community cohesion declined.[54] In mestizo San José de Gracia outsiders and locals built a highway that brought in money, venereal disease, and dreams of the city. Young townspeople followed the highway out of town and never came back.[55] But for those who stayed behind life was revolutionized by doctors, hospitals, and everything from cantina latrines to military pesticide campaigns. By 1951 smallpox was eradicated; ten years later malaria deaths had dropped 75 percent. Infant mortality plunged as provincial maternity clinics, long demanded by grassroots feminists, materialized. In 1930 the national life expectancy was thirty-seven years; by 1960 it was fifty-nine.[56]

Neither was vanishing government money wholly wasted. While corruption was economically inefficient, it did buy political stability. Real, promised, or potential illicit rewards kept underemployed politicians inside the party and gave presidents leverage over those with jobs. If they followed the party line, they reaped rewards beyond their paltry salaries; if they didn't, they might be unmasked with a leak to the press. So the PRI deployed three sorts of corruption: systematic payoffs, one-off bribes, and graft. Even the puritanical President Ruiz Cortines generously topped up the wages of generals or congressmen.[57] Official salaries were low: One general's mistress was wiretapped complaining that he couldn't even stand her a soft drink, to which he suggested she should "come over anyway" (which she did).[58] Governors bought journalists and were themselves bought by the private sector, most notoriously by *narcos*: comparatively small operators before the 1960s, but already a force to be reckoned with in

Sinaloa.[59] The National Committee of Employers paid union bosses for controlling workers: In 1953 they fixed a dispute in the textile sector by giving Fidel Velázquez $100,000, Luis Morones and local CROM leader Eucario León $75,000 each.[60] Justice was negotiable for the well-heeled or prudent. Compromising documents were sold, disappeared, or misfiled.[61] Municipal books were cooked; prosecutors and judges turned improbably forgiving. One gang arrested for murder on the dangerous Guerrero coast walked, despite damning confessions and eyewitness testimony, by paying the district attorney the equivalent of seven months' wages.[62] There was a revealing vocabulary of corruption: the *carpetazo* of disappeared paperwork, the *embutes*, *igualas*, *sobres*, *rayas*, or *chayotes* of pressmen's payoffs.

Graft was the most important form of all. Mexico was a gatekeeper state: cash and tax poor, bureaucratically weedy, but empowered by regulating access to the country's massive natural and human resources. Governments' regulatory scope and power shot up under Alemán as trade controls and tariffs built a new series of gates to postwar wealth.[63] Businesspeople needed permits to operate, whether they were street vendors, market women, truckers, factory owners, or drug smugglers. Control of those gates stabilized the state, from the municipality up to the state oil company. Some of the most successful grafters received literal gates: Alemán's hated crony Jorge Pasquel got rich heading up the customs house in Veracruz, spending the profits on a baseball team, trips to Harrods, and an estate in Kenya.[64] Agents of the government import/export agency CEIMSA stole hundreds of millions of pesos from the peasants whose corn they bought.[65] It was loyalty purchased on credit, corruption without the need to put up cash. As the political veteran Aarón Sáenz put it, *"No me den, pero ponme donde hay."* ("Don't give it to me, just put me where it is.")[66]

This was common knowledge, grumbled about in the streets, markets, and cafés, occasionally breaking out in the soccer stadium or bullring in chants that had nothing to do with bulls or soccer. The disappointment, anger, and cynicism in people's voices were, however, a testament to the enduring appeal of revolutionary nationalism, the theory that Mexicans had earned social justice with the struggles of earlier decades. In 1959 four out of five city-dwelling Mexicans told pollsters, "No one is going to care much what happens to you, when you get right down to it," but at the same time they felt strongly that the revolution had brought democracy and modernization.[67] The education system was intended to make them believe it, even though it was far from infallible: Schools in Catholic areas ended up teaching Catholic lessons, some of the most activist teachers ended up teaching very little at all, and there weren't enough of them anyway. In the school year 1957–1958 more than 40 percent of school-age children weren't going to school.[68] But the PRI compensated with the new mass media, seamlessly transmitting its messages, and its messages alone, through radio, cinemas, and increasingly television. All were dominated by government stalwarts: By the 1950s William Jenkins controlled 80 percent of cinemas, and Emilio Azcárraga Milmo all of television, his Telesistema Mexicano the only game in town after 1955. "Radio and television have the social function of contributing to the strengthening of national integration," said the 1960 broadcasting law. And so they did, either cutting politically inconvenient people out of the news—the 1952 opposition campaign went uncovered—or branding them fanatics and criminals, as Azcárraga did the railroad strikers. The overlap was complete and unapologetic: The main news anchor, Jacobo Zabludovsky, was also a media consultant for the presidency. Azcárraga publicly described himself as "a soldier of the president."[69]

Yet there was enough substance to keep the show on the road until well into the 1960s. Alemán laid down some of the key patterns of Mexico's idiosyncratic authoritarianism: His government extended the tantalizing prospect of participatory politics in primaries, opposition wins, and a federal electoral commission, but engineered in practice a tighter grip on elections. A loyal opposition of the PAN on the Right and the Partido Popular on the Left provided cover for ending the brief democratic spring of the 1940s. Civilian centrism ruled: Alemán banned communists and the far Right but kept on good enough terms with them to be heralded "the best of sinarquistas" (by Sinarquistas themselves).[70] He reached a Faustian pact with the generals, excluding them from national politics in exchange for latitude in provincial politics and business. The pact was reinforced by muscle; before he even took office Alemán had created a *guardia presidencial* of four thousand elite soldiers garrisoned in Mexico City, commanded by his uncle.[71] Finally, both his own dictatorial ambitions and those of the army were checked by the informal senate, led by Cárdenas, which had emerged in the 1948 crisis. When Alemán wavered over whether to postpone elections for a successor, adducing the Korean War, they said no and it stuck.[72]

And so it was left to his successor, Adolfo Ruiz Cortines, to put the finishing touches to the one-party state. He started out as the outgoing president's personal pick, Cárdenas having established an unwritten rule that presidents got to choose their successor with what was called the *dedazo*, the tap on the back. But in his inaugural speech the accountant broke unexpectedly with the exuberant corruption of the previous regime. Alemán left office naming a lot of things after himself—roads, markets, towns, and even an oil tanker—and taking a lot with him too.[73] One estimate had the president and his inner circle syphoning off more than the entire external debt.[74]

Ruiz Cortines, by contrast, published a list of his own middle-class assets—a second home but a single car, an underwhelming savings account—and ordered the quarter of a million people who worked for the state to do likewise. Congratulatory gifts were returned to sender. It was an unprecedented austerity; while Lázaro Cárdenas enjoyed a (comparatively justified) reputation for probity, he also enjoyed a large ranch; the perks of running a large development agency, the Balsas River Commission; good jobs for relatives; and junkets such as a world tour that included $30,000 of government money for "expenses related to his travels." This was about as much as Ruiz Cortines's entire life savings; the accountant was straightforwardly honest, avoided cronies, and handed over office in 1958 without fuss or profit.[75] This conspicuous thrift helped recover some squandered legitimacy; as one cartoonist put it, "Why would we pick fights with politicians if they're going to come over all honest?"[76]

Crony capitalism reined in, it was easier to bring troublemakers into the system. Ex-communist teachers found congenial jobs as mayors, congressmen, and senators. A handful of young Cubans were arrested for training a revolutionary army, interrogated by the DFS, and released to pick up their guns and head off on a leaky motor yacht

Coup plotter, serial president, national villain, and national hero General Antonio López de Santa Anna.

Superior American firepower against Vera Cruz during the US-Mexican War, 1846–1848.

Édouard Manet, *The Execution of Emperor Maximilian* (1868–1869).

Benito Juárez by José Escudero y Espronceda (1872).

The new romance of the very old. Alice Dixon Le Plongeon with rifle and workers in Chichén Itzá excavation, 1873.

Porfirio Díaz as a young president.

The train, central to Mexico's economic development and dispossession.

General Victoriano Huerta and his cabinet.

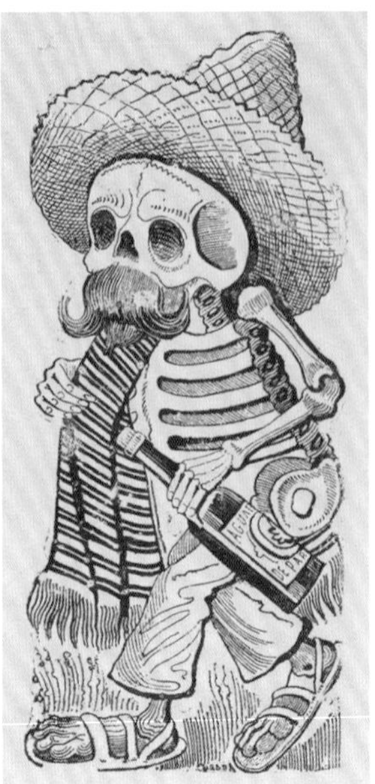

President Francisco Madero as a walking dead man. José Guadalupe Posada, *Calavera de Francisco Madero* (1912).

The media-savvy Pancho Villa as he liked to be seen, hard-riding and dangerous, during the Mexican Revolution.

Soldaderas were essential to the different revolutionary forces, not least as fighters. Hermanos Casasola.

So, often, were child soldiers.

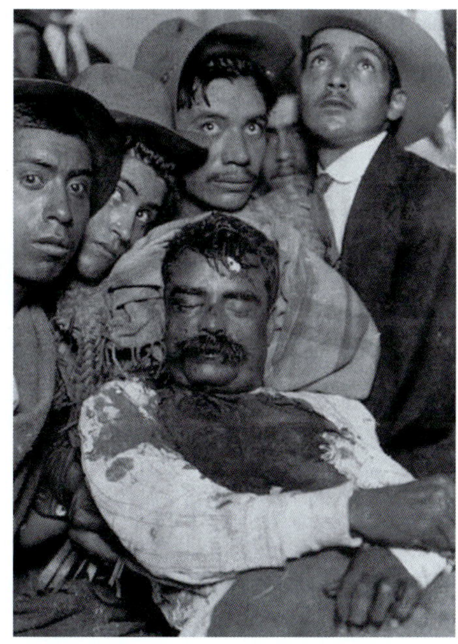

Emiliano Zapata, 1919. Hermanos Casasola.

Diego Rivera, *La maestra rural* (the rural teacher) (1932), symbol and reality of the social revolution in the countryside.

President Lázaro Cárdenas.

Miguel Alemán by Miguel Covarrubias.

Henri Cartier-Bresson, *Country Club, Aguascalientes, Mexico* (1963).

Tanks in downtown Mexico City, 1968.

The 1985 Mexico City earthquake, remembered in an *ex voto* by one grateful survivor: "I was going to cross Avenue Lázaro Cárdenas when I was at the lights I dropped my briefcase and on going back to pick it up this happened and the Virgin of Guadalupe saved me from death."
Alfredo Vilchis, sin título.

toward Cuba, where they seized power. Fidel Castro never forgot it. Disgruntled Mexican veterans were thrown the bone of a shell party, the Partido Auténtico de la Revolución Mexicana, with the congressional seats and payoffs that brought. The Cardenista labor boss Vicente Lombardo Toledano, periodically savaged in the press as a raving revolutionary, was encouraged to develop his Partido Popular, at the end of the day one more of the ruling class. The new tame union leaders, marshalled by the Machiavellian Fidel Velázquez, were periodically allowed to attack the government and reap their members pay raises and benefits. (Velázquez exemplified the PRI's stability; he ran the CTM, the giant government union, until 1997.) The great provincial caciques like Santos were tolerated but not promoted, and in 1958 he was compelled to accept a Catholic enemy, Salvador Nava, as mayor of his state capital. The PAN was ceded six seats in Congress. Higher social spending was built into even newly stingy budgets: The numbers of workers entitled to social security doubled.[77]

At the same time the main repressive strategies of the Alemán years continued. Workers who supported Henríquez Guzmán's presidential campaign in 1952 were fired en masse. The party leadership ruled out a return to primaries, mooted by Cárdenas and 170 allies in 1957.[78] The expansion of a civilian justice system didn't take the army out of the sharp end of controlling the countryside. Top generals had long wanted out of ad hoc policing, a dirty job they'd never been trained for, but Ruiz Cortines instead made their rural policing permanent, telling the defense minister that it was "in accord with national reality."[79] Working-class students at the Politécnico were arrested, their dormitories taken over by soldiers, their student organization taken over by government-backed stooges.[80] Soldiers shot at and arrested striking rail workers. Their main leader, Demetrio Vallejo, spent the next decade in jail. While many teachers joined the PRI's middle management, leaving *normales* (teacher training schools) like Ayotzinapa to become stalwarts of local rule, the dissidents of the Movimiento Revolucionario Magisterial struck and were likewise arrested, their leaders held in solitary confinement, their divergent paths the beginning of divergent politics inside the revolutionary profession par excellence. It was the balancing act that kept the PRI in power; Alemán began it, but Ruiz Cortines institutionalized it.

His final step was a peaceful transition to another civilian, Adolfo López Mateos. Well before maneuvering began, Cárdenas met Alemán—in Paris—and told him he wouldn't accept a soldier-president; subsequently Alemán was informed that he wouldn't make the grade either.[81] López Mateos, a labor lawyer, was vain and telegenic—screen presence, as John F. Kennedy was showing, now counted—with a penchant for oratory, travel, and transient love.[82] Precisely how many country people cared about him was open to question. They turned up in their tens of thousands to political meetings, but they went there as *acarreados* in hired buses and trucks, rent-a-crowds pulled by food and a few pesos and pushed by threats. Some peasants did care, though: López Mateos promised renewed land reform, did something about it early on, and purged some of the great provincial caciques. He was, like Alemán, like all Mexican presidents, a salesman of hope. City dwellers bought into it once more, reaffirming the ambiguities and downright surrealism of power in Mexico; six months into the López Mateos presidency a large sample told sociologists that they were very hopeful, and confident, and cynical, and alienated.[83]

The people who picked up the phone to give those sociologists answers, the minority with phones, generally did well out of the fifties and sixties. It was the golden age of global capitalism, when the dividends of peace, cheap food, industrialization, better transport, and free-spending states brought everyday people in the Global North unprecedented wealth. Mexico shared in it, helped along by oil and convenient neighbors, but also by a generation of talent. At the 1944 Bretton Woods Conference, Mexico chaired one of the three commissions and enjoyed major successes in shaping the foundations of the postwar order. A young Mexican economist called Victor Urquidi had the nerve to argue against John Maynard Keynes over development as a central goal for the new World Bank, telling him, "In the long run, Mr. Chairman—before we are all *too* dead, if I may say so—development must prevail." Urquidi won, and development went into the Articles of Agreement. The Mexicans also led in trying to water down overwhelming European and American control of the new institutions of finance and development. While a European appointee would run the International Monetary Fund in perpetuity, the director of Mexico's national development bank, Antonio Espinosa de los Monteros, negotiated veto power for a unified non-Western vote.[84] The Mexican government made itself a player in global economic rule at a key tipping point; they reaped benefits in credit and soft power for decades.

Domestically, the Mexican economy remained in steady hands across three administrations. The internationally respected Antonio Ortiz Mena served as a key advisor to Ruiz Cortines and as secretary of finance for the following two presidents, while Rodrigo Gómez was head of the central bank for the entire period. The set of policies that Ortiz Mena dubbed "stabilizing development" were effective in macroeconomic terms, and for middle-class urbanites in particular; their numbers and discretionary spending shot up. Labor was cheap and plentiful and industry profited from it to expand significantly. At the end of the sixties Mexicans became the first people in Latin America to have credit cards. In downtown Mexico City the first skyscraper, the Torre Latinoamerica, went up. Meanwhile those who watched it grow, and in this case their fellow Mexicans in the countryside, paid remarkably little in tax. ("If our government tried that tax business here, I believe it might even cause a revolution" was one capitalino's assessment.)[85] It was unsurprising that memory decades later was colored sepia. Some *chilangos*—the slang for people from Mexico City, an insult coming from the lips of people from the provinces, a term of jokey pride when used by capitalinos themselves—felt a sneaking shame at how good they had it under the politicians they scorned; Octavio Paz's divorce lawyer told a friend, "I vote for the PAN and cross my fingers that the PRI wins."[86]

It was clear even at the time that the economic growth branded "the Mexican Miracle" or "the constructive phase of the Revolution" worked for big buildings and big numbers but did not work for all Mexicans. Gaping inequality characterized the economy from the 1940s onward. When the World Bank began quantifying wealth distribution through a measure called the Gini coefficient, Mexico, for all its revolutionary past and rhetoric, was one of the most unequal places on Earth. The only places with comparable gulfs between rich and poor were Brazil and sub-Saharan Africa.[87] The deprivation was evident in the shantytowns in the red-dirt hills above Acapulco, the *colonias populares* that ringed Mexico City, and the dark tenements within sight of the restaurant on top of the Torre Latinoamericano. People down below inhabited different worlds. One of the few whose lives made it into recorded history grew up in the old thieves' barrio, Tepito, just twenty minutes' walk from the Zócalo, but didn't go there until he was eleven years old. His sister didn't make the trip until she was fourteen. Outside Tepito they felt like "fish out of water."[88]

And yet country people continued migrating into these new lives because they were the great losers of "stabilizing development." Ejidal grants and cheap money dried up after 1940. Meanwhile families grew bigger and cash inputs greater because the new crops of the Green Revolution, although more productive, demanded fertilizer, pesticide, and buying seed. So individual plots became uneconomic, and a class of wealthier ejidatarios, stealth ranchers, took over, buying rights to their perpetual grants from smaller fish, effectively buying their land. Those reluctant to go were sometimes pushed out by violence, because these stealth ranchers had become a class of new caciques.

On collectively farmed ejidos the problem was different; those who worked the cane fields of Morelos or Puebla or the wheat fields of the Laguna remained a semi-proletariat. They didn't choose what to grow, and they worked for cash wages on plantations; this was neither to their taste nor their advantage, because wages declined steadily from 1940 until the late 1960s. In terms of power, meanwhile, ejidal administrators like Cárdenas's brother-in-law parachuted in from Mexico City to run estates like Zacatepec in Morelos, a sugar mill that controlled nineteen thousand peasants on thirty-two ejidos. Neither tame outsider bureaucrats nor shop stewards did much to advocate for the ejidatarios who called the estate a hacienda, had their water supply cut off when they disobeyed, and might be kept in line by violence.[89] They too reacted by abandoning the countryside. They were displaced by economics and caciquismo; the unluckiest were displaced by the dams that made agribusiness and electrification possible on frontier lands like Chiapas, Guerrero, and southern Veracruz. Building Oaxaca's Papaloapan dam involved forcibly relocating twenty thousand Mazatec indigenous people. Despite the efforts of anthropologists—simultaneously government hegemonists and advocates for everyday people—the process was brutal and ineffective. The Mazatec villages were drowned in the name of modernization, their people dispersed randomly.[90] The parallel to Tequesquitengo, the Porfirian village flooded out of existence by a sugar planter, was clear enough.

Whether the entire regime was a Porfiriato redux was a reasonable question, and radical anthropologists like Arturo Warman and liberals like Daniel Cosío Villegas asked it.[91] Like Porfirian development, the PRI's development followed a global model: rapid industrialization with high costs for country people, a disappearing class. Forced migration to make way for dams was a global process. The Tennessee Valley Authority drove 125 thousand people from its catchment area, among a worldwide forty to eighty million watery refugees.[92] And unlike in many other countries, state profits in Mexico helped pay for a revolution in social services. Mexico spent far more money than its Asian equivalents on healthcare. In 1960 the government vaccinated fifty-six thousand children; in 1970 3.5 million. The number of people covered by the new Mexican Social Security Institute grew dramatically.[93] The livelihoods of many ejidatarios, particularly those who grew disappearing tropical crops like ixtle or henequen, or easily substituted oilseeds like coconut, were insecure; the basic numbers of survival—infant mortality, longevity, homes with running water—improved radically.

Workers had it better, at least those with unionized jobs. Their revolutionary unions were subsumed into a single conformist accessory to the single party, the CTM's leaders installed and maintained by violence, their primordial function worker control. The number of strikes testified to their success: In militant Veracruz, its port once anarchist, its rail and oil unions longtime fighters, the twenty-three strikes of 1949 shrank to three by 1952. Salaries fell accordingly. The cheap labor that industrialization demanded was obtained by depressing real wages across the economy from 1940 to 1967. This was thought-out, engineered policy. Yet to take wage trends as the whole story would be to mirror the airbrushed positive accounts of the Mexican Miracle, accepting big numbers as straightforward reflections of reality. Workers looked back at the 1950s as a time not just of repression but also of benefits: medical care, public housing, soft loans, and cheap nationalized electricity, free for Mexlight employees.[94]

The oil workers—alongside railwaymen Mexico's labor aristocracy, their work central to the economy—illustrated the contradictions. They had been the first to be taken over by the newborn PRI: In December 1946 and 1949 Alemán sent the army into the oil fields and refineries of Poza Rica and Minatitlán, on the first occasion arresting union leaders, on the second beating workers and breaking up dissident union meetings. Their new leaders were systematically corrupt, from the bosses of the Veracruz oil towns to the directors general in Mexico City: From 1946 to 1958 PEMEX, the state-owned petroleum company, was led by Antonio Bermúdez, one of Alemán's notoriously crooked inner circle.[95] Workers wrote to Mexico City complaining that while they lacked basic services, their managers lined their pockets and lived in opulence. In the 1940s some members still endured appalling living conditions in the boomtowns: lashed-together shacks, pariah dogs in dirt streets, raw sewage that killed children with endemic intestinal parasites.[96] By 1960 Poza Rica had the paving, drainage, hospital, and baseball team of civilization.

President López Mateos came to power in 1958 announcing himself part of the "extreme left" of the revolution. In domestic terms he partially substantiated this claim, engaging in major land reform in the Northwest to pacify militant agrarians. In international terms he guardedly welcomed the Cuban Revolution and famously defended the Cubans at the Organization of American States against the United States' attempt to banish them. The rhetoric on his many tours abroad—a nickname was *Das Paseos*, "you wander," which referred to both his traveling and his womanizing—was of the need for a third way, a progressive international left.

Backstage Mexico was less independent and more helpful to the US than public declarations asserted, and Americans like Secretary of State Dean Rusk liked it that way. When a promising third way through the Cold War materialized in the Non-Aligned Movement, López Mateos turned his back on it, sending observers to the founding conference in Belgrade but rejecting participation. Joining would have been of real geopolitical consequence, Spanish America's leading power allying itself with Asian and African states to reject the colonialism of Soviets and the West alike. But it would have upset Mexico's balancing act of a different and covert kind, in which politicians postured for Cuba while passing intelligence to the Americans. They even placed a CIA spy in their Havana embassy. Mexico also imposed informal economic sanctions on oil and food sales to the island. The productive double game was summed up in the detective novel *The Mongol Plot*, in which an aging *pistolero* outwits spooks from both Russia and America, or in the strange travels of the Soviet space satellite Lunik in Mexico City, the centerpiece of 1960's huge, extremely popular exhibition of Soviet achievements. The exhibition was enthusiastically backed by the López Mateos government, which hosted Soviet deputy premier Anastas Mikoyan; then, as the exhibition was dismounted, the Mexicans allowed the Americans to secretly disassemble the satellite and copy its inner workings.[97]

The balancing act allowed Mexico to maintain its relative autonomy after the revolution. Enough spies were running around Mexico City for it to be compared to wartime Casablanca; the Cubans maintained a big embassy and close relationships to Mexican intelligence, and the KGB legal residency was the largest in the Western Hemisphere. But in 1965 that meant only thirty-five agents, and it was only that big because it was a base for KGB operations across much of Latin America. As the Soviets and Cubans promoted guerrillas throughout the region, they made Mexico an exception, maintaining a policy of nonintervention that was important in a formally revolutionary country. Even people in Mérida, a most Catholic town, went weekly to the Cuban Consulate to watch its propaganda films.[98] The CIA officers were characteristically self-important—one station chief invited the president to his wedding, and wrote breathlessly of his "LITEMPO network" of leading politicians—and delusional. By the 1960s the CIA's top two men in Mexico City were failed writers.[99] The FBI was even worse: Its agents reported that a key government black ops team, the Olympia Brigade, were Trotskyite terrorists.[100] The Mexican institution that counted, the army, kept as much distance as possible from the US: Between 1950 and 1972 the US trained 61,000 soldiers from Latin America, but only 659 from Mexico.[101] When the US tried to impose itself—conditioning its supply of weapons and ammunition on the acceptance of US counterinsurgency training—the Mexican Army explicitly told them to get lost, and the Americans were forced to retreat.[102] The Mexican national security doctrine DN-1, logically enough in the light of history and location, established the US as the greatest potential threat.[103] Guatemala, Canada, and the Soviet Union were all unlikely invaders.

So Mexican tolerance of both sides in the Cold War made good sense, and may even have been a stabilizing force. In the corridors of power Mexican officials paid some lip service to the US, occasionally doing petty favors, sharing the burden of snooping on Eastern bloc embassies and once, in extremis, rounding up the usual suspects during a presidential visit. In exchange the CIA shared its dubious intelligence and counterbalanced the sharper, and hence more potentially troublesome, State Department. Foreign Service officers had a long history of skepticism toward communism in Mexico and the CIA's elucubrations in general: The Mérida Consul denied CIA reports of Soviet arms smuggling into Cozumel with the acerbic "The Consulate gives no repeat no credence to this report."[104] The KGB was unimportant inside Mexico and didn't seem to mind (though they did get Mexican agents to intervene when a bottle of "bourgeois Coca-Cola" snuck into a photo op for the world's first woman astronaut, Valentina Tereshkova).[105]

And bourgeois Coca-Cola counted for Mexicans, because for all the politicization of daily life, much was not about politics. A Catholic resurgence found concrete expression in provincial cathedrals, long in the making and now able to open in even the larger towns. In the mainstream of popular culture these were years of record players and *rocanrol* radio. Singers of a romanticized countryside, charros in tight trousers and big hats like Pedro Infante and Jorge Negrete, still did very well indeed; Pedro Infante's 1957 funeral attracted 150 thousand and ended up in a major riot as police clubbed mourners away from the grave, Beatlemania *a la mexicana*.[106] But their songs were losing ground: first to bowdlerized rip-offs of foreign hits, called *refritos*, rocanrol bands like Los Rebeldes Del Rock and Los Locos del Ritmo recording songs like *"Un Tonto Como Yo"* ("A Fool Like Me") and *"El Rock de la Cárcel"* ("Jailhouse Rock"); and then, once bans were revoked, to the original American and British groups. The Beatles caught up by issuing four albums in Mexico in 1964 alone.[107] One of Mexico's new film icons,

Cinco de chocolate, released December 1968.

Angélica María, spent the fifties as the demure girl next door; in the sixties she was suddenly a siren on psychedelic posters, unsubtle innuendos—"amiable bazookas"—surrounding or disappearing into one of the new "aggressive mini-skirts."[108] (Clothes which led to some classic mother–daughter exchanges: "Why are you going around with your arse hanging out? You don't know how to sit down into the bargain. I'd rather die than put on a skirt like that," and "One hundred and fifty pesos for that skirt! But it's not even a foot long!")[109] By the end of the sixties teenagers in Mexico City could listen to Jane Birkin having four minutes and twenty-eight seconds of sex with Serge Gainsbourg on the single *"Je t'aime . . . moi non plus."* Which they did, over and over again, thanks to Radio Capital and Radio Fiesta.[110]

It was the dawning of the age of the *churro*, the cheap film, and the *telenovela*, the cheap soap opera. It was also a time when Mexico City was the high cultural capital of the Hispanic world, rivaled only by Paris. Publishing houses, literary salons, magazines, and cultural centers abounded. Gabriel García Márquez wrote his first major novel, *In Evil Hour*, in Paris, but he published the first authorized edition in Mexico City, where he also wrote *One Hundred Years of Solitude.*[111] One of his major influences, the revolutionary novelist Juan Rulfo, lived there too, supported by a government job working on the Papaloapan dam commission. Rulfo was not the only great writer on the government payroll, the PRI realizing fully the benefits of soft power: The poets José Gorostiza and Octavio Paz both held high-ranking diplomatic jobs, folded into the establishment, Paz a friend of the telenovela magnate and regime propagandist Emilio Azcárraga.[112] (Paz had by then got over the visceral disillusionment he expressed in *The Labyrinth of Solitude*, a classic and misanthropic rumination on what it meant to be Mexican, described by one friend as a "go to hell" to Mexico.)[113] The CIA helped out in the world of soft power, in one of their only astute ideas for Latin America, covertly supporting non-Communist leftists and social democrats through the Mexican Association for Cultural Freedom.[114] The Mexican government was the player that counted, allowing erudite, metropolitan dissidents careers in a way unthinkable elsewhere.

Such a culture was possible because at national and visible levels Mexico was quite an open society. The Spanish director Luis Buñuel was allowed to make *The Exterminating Angel*, one of the great films of the sixties, to satirize the hypocrisy and violence of the upper classes and the state. When in 1962 the army murdered Rubén Jaramillo, the country's best-known peasant dissident, along with his wife and children, the New Left writer Carlos Fuentes was allowed to publish a furious condemnation linking the perpetrators directly to the president.[115] He was also able to publish two major Latin American novels, *The Death of Artemio Cruz* and *Where the Air Is Clear*, both bitingly critical of the post-revolutionary elites, with the Fondo de Cultura Económica, the government's own publishing house. When the government fired its director in 1965, he went immediately with five hundred other intellectuals to found an independent publisher, Siglo XXI, which ended up as prestigious as the Fondo.[116] The late forties' assaults on editors were seen as a shocking (if instructive) exception to the reglas no escritas, under which news critics were to be controlled by their supply of newsprint, the state agency PIPSA exercising a convenient monopoly, rather than by the crudities of beatings, street killings, or suspicious suicides. Outside of the newspapers and television, national politicians were allowed voluble criticism, whether live on the campaign trail or in interviews printed safely abroad. As Fuentes said in 1969, "To criticize Caesar isn't to criticize Rome. To criticize a government isn't to criticize a country."[117] By then, however, that idea was out of date.

Chapter Eighteen

Repression and Rejection

Over the course of the sixties the ambiguities of one-party rule decreased as the violence that underpinned it grew and became more visible. It was easier for city dwellers to decide whether the PRI ran a dictatorship when its leaders machine-gunned or disappeared students. The government's rhetoric had a newly dehumanizing, Orwellian ring to it. Young communist guerrillas were fascists, one president told the nation on prime time,

> the majority of them children who were slow learners; teenagers with generally greater degrees of maladaptation, with a precocious taste in their groups for the use of drugs, with a marked propensity for sexual promiscuity and a high degree of male and female homosexuality.[1]

Civilians kidnapped by the army were dubbed "packages" in military reports, sent in "for suitable inspection," from which a majority never returned. One counterinsurgent offensive was named "Operation Friendship."[2] The freedom of speech of the earlier sixties reined in, the capital's middle classes were left with gossip and misdirection. Even critical journalists like Julio Scherer followed the party line: Guerrillas were kidnappers and murderers.[3] The head of the army telegraphed the commander of the 35th Military Zone to "exterminate" left-wing guerrillas but "avoid displays of force might alarm civil population."[4] The army was on a "humanitarian mission" to bring medicine, clothes, and food to the poor, one press bulletin said.[5] But behind cover-ups the public knew that something big was going on in the countryside, and particularly in Guerrero, where Acapulco became a beach enclave in the middle of besieged villages scared of helicopters, car batteries, rape, and disappearance.

While unknown numbers of country people were disappeared, it was a very different population that made the new authoritarianism visible: Mexico City's students, especially from the two largest universities, the Instituto Politécnico Nacional ("the Poli") and the Universidad Nacional Autónoma de México ("the UNAM"). The capital's students were among the more privileged Mexicans of the time. Far from all were born into the middle classes, though it would have been difficult to find the sons and daughters of workers and peasants in the UNAM's law school or the Facultad de Filosofía y Letras. The more proletarian Poli, set up by Cárdenas, was flooded with immigrants from the suburbs and provinces. But whatever their background, students enjoyed something like colonial fueros, carve-outs from the rules of the rest of society. Hijacking public buses was a consequence-free student privilege, whether to get to protests or stadiums. The Poli, not the law, investigated fifteen students accused of sexually assaulting two prostitutes on a bus; their *compañeros* threatened the administration with consequences if they were not left alone.[6]

The authorities did use violence against political students: By the end of the 1960s soldiers had put down at least fifty-three provincial university protests. The student body of the University of Guadalajara was run by a party stooge backed by pistoleros. The government had sent the army in to take over the Poli in 1956.[7] Yet the capital's students, concentrated in the UNAM's sprawling campus in the city's south and in a Poli woven into the fabric of the downtown, were historically immune from the jailing, joblessness, and outright murder that other serial dissidents—independent workers, peasant militants—suffered. That changed in October 1968, when soldiers and policemen machine-gunned a peacefully protesting crowd of students in the center of Mexico City, in a square called Tlatelolco.

It was unthinkable. As one put it, "We expected bashed heads, mass arrests, we were ready for jail, well, more or less, but we didn't expect death."[8] It was 1968, and there were violent antecedents: In the spring the protest of a small group of student radicals in Paris had led to a brutal counterassault by riot police that set off seven weeks of marches and occupations of universities and factories and brought seven million workers out in a general strike. At its peak in May, President de Gaulle, not known for pusillanimity, dissolved the National Assembly and secretly left for Germany, fleeing revolution. Yet neither massacre nor revolution followed, and after settlement the crisis passed into French history under the bland name of *les évènements*, the happenings; it was, however, a startling, globally visible display of the power of the baby boomers.[9] In Mexico the spark was nonideological, a fight between street gangs from the Poli and the UNAM on July 22. As in Paris, though, heavy-handed state reaction followed: beatings by the *granaderos*, the riot police, and on July 29 a military assault on the Poli boarding school in the colonial Colegio de San Ildefonso. Shortly after midnight paratroopers blew the door in with a bazooka and beat the students inside before handing about one hundred over to the *granaderos*, who took them away in vans. A week later representatives from the UNAM, the Poli, the Colegio de México, the Agricultural College of Chapingo, and the Universidad Iberoamericana united with professors in a citywide strike.

The government was under time pressure to end it, because one of the fruits of Mexico's soft power was to host the Olympics in October 1968. But while President Gustavo Díaz Ordaz spoke of their willingness to negotiate, the downtown marches grew into the hundreds of thousands. *Niñas popis*, posh girls, came out alongside *porristas*, street fighters. "We don't want the Olympics," one chant ran, "we want revolution."[10] The strike leaders of the Consejo Nacional de Huelga (CNH) refused to negotiate unless the sessions were public and broadcast live—a nonstarter for a deeply unprepossessing president—and the army escalated, attacking a demonstration in the Zócalo. On September 18 soldiers took over the UNAM. Students formed "shock brigades" that pasted up posters and gave out flyers, burned vehicles, and fought the police with increasing sophistication. They began to make Molotov cocktails; their first dead appeared.

At the same time, however, the CNH was carefully signaling that it was not out to topple the government. The greatest march of all, some two hundred thousand people following the university rector Javier Barros Sierra down the Paseo de la Reforma to the Zócalo on September 13, was called the *marcha del silencio* because it was utterly silent, eschewing previous chants about Che Guevara. There was no demonstration against the presidential report on September 1, an annual state of the nation address of totemic importance, and the student leaders promised not to disturb the Olympics. On October 1, the army retreated from the UNAM, and the CNH convened a demonstration in the Plaza de las Tres Culturas in Tlatelolco, the old center of the indigenous city, now home to a church, the remains of a pyramid, a modernist public housing complex, and the Secretaría de Relaciones Exteriores.

On the morning of October 2· representatives of the president met with student leaders to discuss a settlement. At the same time the Secretario de la Defensa Nacional, General Marcelino García Barragán, met with the head of the Dirección Federal de Seguridad, Captain Fernando Gutiérrez Barrios, and the president's chief of staff, General Luis Gutiérrez Orepeza (who joined by phone), to plan a military operation against the afternoon's demonstration.[11] The main student leaders would be in Tlatelolco, its huge square easily sealed off, allowing a big enough force to detain students en masse and winnow out the would-be Ches. The DFS had been telling President Díaz Ordaz that the students had an "arsenal" of weapons and were preparing a revolution to coincide with the Olympics, due to start October 12. The governor of Mexico City, Alfonso Corona del Rosal, thought the students were riddled with KGB agents.[12] Incompetent Machiavellians, the spies found a credulous listener: Díaz Ordaz was the closest Mexico ever got to the typical cold warrior, an uncritical believer in reds under beds. Even the CIA thought him obsessed with "security issues."[13] He thus signed off on Operation Galeana, a deployment of several thousand troops to Tlatelolco. Once there they and political policemen would arrest the student leadership and scare their followers into ending the strike. It would be unanswerable raw power, involving Mexico's elite soldiers—paratroopers, *guardias presidenciales*, a newly minted special forces group called the Batallón Olímpica—and four mechanized squadrons of jeeps with heavy machine guns, armored personnel carriers, and light tanks.[14]

Unknown to anyone in this force, a parallel covert operation had been planned by the president's chief of staff, another fretful anticommunist. He stationed snipers from the guardias presidenciales on the rooftops of five buildings surrounding the plaza to act as agents provocateurs.[15] As the square filled—students, street vendors, women coming back from shops stopping to chat, neighborhood children playing, locals gawking—the strike leaders started speaking from a third-floor balcony of the Chihuahua Building, one of the main residential blocks. At the same time the army moved in and sealed off the exits to the square with bayonets fixed. At 6:10 two helicopters flew low over the square and fired two flares, and the president's snipers began shooting into the crowd and the soldiers below. The general commanding the paratroopers was hit. The soldiers, who had orders to fire back if fired upon, advanced at the double into the square, took up positions, and began shooting with rifles and machine guns at the rooftops and into the crowd. A Captain got on the radio to the Secretaría de la Defensa Nacional and told them "We're firing back with everything we've got."[16]

Dealing with the official target of the exercise, the student leaders, was easy enough. Members of the Batallón Olímpica, soldiers in civvies, a single white glove on their left hand identifying them to other security forces, were posted blocking entry to the Chihuahua Building. As the shooting began, they burst onto the balcony and arrested the orators. This turned out to be historically insignificant; what counted at Tlatelolco that afternoon was what went on in the square below. People ran in waves from side to side, trying to escape, but they were surrounded and just ran into other lines of soldiers. They dived to the ground and took cover behind pillars or among the pre-Hispanic ruins. A couple trying to run out of the square were bayoneted. A few students tried to shoot back, but the soldiers who were wounded were hit by their own men in the crossfire. At one point a tank opened fire. The Chihuahua Building began to burn. It was chaos: One Mexican reporter saw (and managed to get printed in *El Diario de la Tarde*):

> Women stitched at stomach height by the machine guns' bullets; children with their heads destroyed by the impact of high-powered shots, peaceful passersby riddled; street vendors and journalists fallen in the course of their everyday work; dead and wounded students, policemen and soldiers . . . Perhaps the most overwhelming sight was the numerous bloodied shoes strewn across the place, like mute witnesses to their owners' disappearance.[17]

One of the few snatched photographs from Tlatelolco, late afternoon, October 2, 1968. Anonymous.

After about an hour the most intense shooting died down, although bursts of gunfire continued through the rest of the evening. At some point it started to rain. Soldiers, policemen, and Secret Service agents went apartment to apartment in the housing block, kicking in doors, looking for people with student IDs, protest flyers, guns. There was some more shooting inside, blood in the stairwells and bullet holes in the elevator doors.[18] The security services shut civilian ambulances out of the square until 11:30, supposedly on the orders of the presidential Secret Service, while even wounded were lined up against walls, interrogated, put in vans, military ambulances, and troop trucks and driven away. About seven hundred went to the city's jails and the federal penitentiary; 363 went to the Campo Militar Número 1, the country's main army base in the west of the city. Some were tortured. Multiple destinations, the state's cover-up, and the victims' desire to emphasize losses meant that estimates of how many died at Tlatelolco varied widely, from the 26 reported in Mexican papers to the 44 cases documented in the archives to the *Guardian*'s 325. In the end a number of about 150 took root in Mexicans' collective memory.[19]

More than exact numbers of the dead, it was belief and memory that counted after Tlatelolco. In some ways, for all the unintended chaos of the shootings, the state did an efficient job. They achieved their goals of arresting the leaders and discouraging their followers, who went back to classes on December 4 after a peaceful Olympics. Firemen hosed away the blood the same night; builders, glaziers, and housepainters repaired the telltale damage in record time. The government held together; the only high-profile protest was that of Octavio Paz, who resigned his ambassadorship to India. The Church kept quiet; the devout Díaz Ordaz and the Archbishop of Mexico phoned the bishops to ensure their silence.[20] Future student mobilizations were forestalled by more mass arrests before the end of the year, and finally by another set of beatings and shootings on June 10, 1971, the Corpus Christi massacre, in which, according to the Secretaría de Gobernación, fifty students were killed. Again, no one knew the real number; the bodies were allegedly burned.[21] By then the Secretario de Gobernación, Luis Echeverría Álvarez, believed by many to be behind both massacres, had been elected president without fuss. There were no more major street protests in Mexico City until the mid-1980s.

Neither did the country outside of Mexico City seem all that bothered by Tlatelolco. The students failed to recruit workers or peasants to their cause, with the exception of dissident railwaymen who came to join them. In part this was because the CNH demands were very specifically for themselves and their city: the dissolution of the Mexico City riot police, the firing of the chief and second-in-command of the police, respect for university autonomy, compensation for families of their dead, and an investigation into the attacks on their peers. The only concrete generalizable demands were for the abolition of the crime of disolución social, totalitarian but unimportant to most Mexicans, and the freeing of political prisoners. In 1968 the students were not calling for free elections, although they were later associated with democracy, nor land reform, nor indigenous rights, nor an end to rural caciquismo, nor expanded social services, nor a clean-up of the unions, nor an end to the guerrilla wars in Guerrero. Politically they were not, in either the grassroots sense of the countryside or the totalizing sense of the Parisians, that radical.

Sociologically, moreover, they were isolated by class, place, and generation. Sporadic attempts at linking up with provincial activists in 1967 had failed. Poli students had tried several times, in alliance with northern militants, to free the Guerrerense peasant leader Genaro Vázquez from jail, falling short each time. When they tried to reach the coast to join protests against a massacre of coconut farmers, they were turned back by the DFS.[22] Rural teachers were key in the emerging guerrilla movements; Mexico City students were not. They said as much in interviews at the time. "The only real contact we had with the peasantry was in Topilejo, and Topilejo can't be considered a rural zone or 'countryside' because it's less than thirty kilometres from [Mexico City]"; "Workers don't know anything"; "Workers are way reactionary"; "They're heavy." In the municipality encompassing Naranja, the village that was the synecdoche of Porfirian oppression, one peasant said,

> The ejidatarios rejected the student mayhem and said that if the youths didn't want to study then the millions of pesos spent on their education that they were prepared to waste should be given to the workers of the countryside, because in the countryside it was money that was lacking to build public works.[23]

Yet peasant power was declining while baby boomer power grew, and the generation of '68 ended up in key positions in culture, the media, business, and politics. Senior figures of a future democratic opposition such as Heberto Castillo and Pablo Gómez were caught up in the student movement; so was the last president of the PRI, Ernesto Zedillo, arguing with granaderos outside the Poli and getting a clubbing.[24] For them Tlatelolco was the stuff not just of realpolitik but also of myth. There were a lot of reporters in that square on October 2, and they wrote some of the best journalism of their times, graphic and accurate beneath government-friendly headlines. Memoirs, poems, essays, and above all a single brilliant oral history, Elena Poniatowska's *La noche de Tlatelolco*, captured the images that photographers, harassed by soldiers, couldn't: the platinum-blonde anthropologist screaming about a massacre and combing the place for her missing son; the six-year-old shot while trying to wake up another six-year-old, already dead; the voice of Diana Hernández as she realized her brother was dying and called desperately for a stretcher; the shot woman slumping onto the horn of her car; Regina, one of the hostesses for the Olympic Games, dead in her striped uniform.

Even the place of the massacre was richly symbolic: the Plaza de las Tres Culturas, designed to represent national diversity and unity, Mexico's rich history summed up in the juxtaposition of a colonial church; Aztec ruins; and a new building complex whose high modernism housed elites, middle classes, workers, and the professionals of the Foreign Affairs Secretariat, the government's most impressive department. And so Tlatelolco changed the way the metropolis, its public voices, and its future powerbrokers saw the regime. It was worth it, said one activist, "if the Student Movement managed to lay bare the revolution, to show that it was an old, filthy and corrupt whore." Another told Poniatowska that "there was one Mexico before the Student Movement and another after 1968. Tlatelolco is the rupture between the two Mexicos." When Octavio Paz said an age in the history of Mexico had ended, he was repeating a trope.[25]

For the rest of Mexico the story was less clear-cut, because different turning points influenced different people on the road to a new authoritarianism. For party reformers it might have been their failure to reintroduce primaries. For Cardenistas it might have been the eclipse of Lázaro Cárdenas and the end of the informal senate; for many it was the ascent of Gustavo Díaz Ordaz, first Secretario de Gobernación and then president himself. His dramatic expansion of the state security services was a radical change in how power was exercised, an institutional and cultural inflection point with major impacts across Mexico. For street vendors in Puebla it was violent eviction from downtown by hundreds of policemen.[26] For peasants in Guerrero or Chihuahua it was guerrilla warfare, political and economic exclusion leading to minor rebellions leading to brutal counterinsurgencies.

The first few months of Díaz Ordaz's power seemed more of the same balancing act, Left and Right subsumed in a low-violence single-party regime. The president himself came from the Right but endorsed the introduction of the first proportional representation seats in Congress, opening the doors for some opposition congressmen. More significantly, he made Carlos Madrazo the first civilian head of the PRI. Madrazo stood out against the rising wave of apparatchiks as an old-school militant, starting off as a Cardenista youth leader in red Tabasco and making his career by winning elections. In the 1940s he had pressed the flesh, won a congressional seat, and become a prominent advocate for democratic reform; as a result he was set up on corruption charges and jailed. He got in line and made an unlikely comeback—at one stage he was reduced to working as a school inspector—in the fifties; by 1963 he was presidential material. Once again he got in line and was the first to endorse Díaz Ordaz, in return obtaining the somewhat token position of party president.

But then Madrazo departed dramatically from the official line. In his inaugural speech he accused the PRI of being out of touch with the regions and the poor, of forming a centralized electoral machine whose candidates "neither loved, nor felt, nor understood the Revolution." Its 8.6 million members weren't committed militants but herds of sheep, threatened and bribed into attending regular demonstrations of mass support that they didn't mean. The solution was democratic reform, a return to grassroots candidates, competitive provincial and union elections, and a revolutionary "mystique."[27] Achieving that goal would be institutionally simple: purging the party's corrupt state and municipal leadership and bringing back primaries.

Madrazo did so immediately in nine states: Baja California, Chihuahua, San Luis Potosí, Guanajuato, Michaoacán, Durango, Morelos, Estado de México, and Puebla. It was a patchwork of the dynamic North, the Cristero and agrarista heartlands, and the heavyweights of the center, all sites of discontent and disturbingly high abstention rates.[28] In June 1965 he extended the program south into Guerrero and Oaxaca; by July two-thirds of the party's municipal committees were directly elected. They began overseeing primaries for party candidates at the municipal level. Competition was genuine, turnouts shot up, and the PRI briefly returned to its initial self, the broadest of churches in which almost anyone could compete.[29] Yet democratic reform was a roll of the dice that Madrazo lost, overcome by the opposition of conservative governors and a more generalized fear that this was too much democracy, the sort of destabilizing popular mobilization that elites had sought to prevent since the revolution. They were unabashed, telling the papers that Madrazo's "wrong direction" had brought "vulgar squabbles" and "chaos." In November 1965 he was ousted, and party and electoral positions returned to central appointment rather than elections. The system endured until the 1990s. Madrazo didn't; on June 4, 1969, still pushing democratic reform, he died in a plane crash.[30] Given the modishness of suspicious car crashes and suicides, it was unsurprising that some believed he had been murdered.

Lázaro Cárdenas died a year later. His behind-the-scenes power had moderated both left and right since 1940, but by the late sixties he had lost much of his influence. His last hurrah had come with the Cuban Revolution: In 1956 he was behind the release of Fidel Castro, teaming up with the head of the DFS and going to see the president for one of his notorious little chats. (He had not, revealingly enough, done the same for the overtly communist Che Guevara.)[31] On April 18, 1961, when Cuban exiles invaded the island, he got on a plane to Cuba to fight them. But he was taken off again by the army, acting on the president's orders. The moment revealed the limits of his high-level power but also the endurance of his popular power; he immediately drew eighty thousand to the Zócalo to hear an impromptu speech defending Castro's Cuba against the US. Cárdenas continued for years to run an informal senate of ex-presidents, contacting them regularly in the cause of moderation. But increasingly they failed him: Ávila Camacho died, Alemán opposed him, Ruiz Cortines and Abelardo pleaded old age. The year 1961 was pivotal in Cárdenas's decline: Complaining to his diary about Mexico's "peaceful counter-revolution," in which profit-seeking had overcome social reform, he noted how his three attempts to ask the president for clemency for political prisoners—the railway union leaders Demetrio Vallejo and Valentín Campa, the painter David Siqueiros—had been rebuffed. The next day he accepted a role leading the Río Balsas dam commission, a megaproject that encompassed his home state and that he had asked to lead.[32]

For when difficult decisions had to be made Cárdenas reliably privileged stability over ideology; he would have agreed with Bismarck that "politics is the art of the possible, the attainable—the art of the next best."[33] When Cuba polarized the PRI it was he, not López Mateos, who suggested inviting the ex-presidents into a sort of government of national unity.[34] He helped defuse the leftist opposition movement of the early 1960s, the Movimiento de Liberación Nacional, which went into decline when his ambivalence became apparent; he tacitly backed the government in shunning the Non-Aligned Movement, the alliance of states rejecting both Soviet and US blocs in the Cold War; for all his antipathy to the cold warrior Díaz Ordaz, he stayed out of the 1964 election. He was a keen backer of an anti-imperialist Tricontinental Conference, but when it came to fruition in Havana in 1966 he quietly disappeared, pulling a prepared statement.[35] He initially denounced the student movement, and in the pages of his diary for 1968, as ever written cagily with one eye on history, he said nothing about its dénouement at Tlatelolco. At the end of October he wrote briefly of his sadness and belief that the massacre had damaged the democratic cause of the Revolution. A better future lay in the new generations, but "Mexico [could not] avoid contributing its blood to achieve progress." Meanwhile his own member of the new generation, his son and political heir Cuauhtémoc, spent most of the summer of 1968 in Europe. He too kept quiet about Tlatelolco, and left the country again in mid-October.[36]

One of Lázaro Cárdenas's signal achievements had been to reduce the state's reliance on its security services; in 1966 the government began reversing that. That year eighty-nine officers from the paratroopers and guardias presidenciales—a quarter of all those sent since 1950—went to the US for training.[37] The DFS went from a bureaucratic dwarf, commanding all of 120 agents in 1965, to an apogee of 3,000 in 1981, with 10,000 informants and field offices in every state. By the early nineties they had accumulated between sixty and eighty million fiches on more than three million people and institutions. The more hegemonic information gatherers of their sister service the DGIPS were sidelined, while the thugs of the DFS, nicknamed "gorillas," became central to state violence. They had useful new friends in the drug business and useful new enemies in guerrillas. Its directors moved into the highest levels of government: Fernando Gutiérrez Barrios ended up Secretario de Gobernación, running the country on a day-to-day basis, and his successor Javier García Paniagua took the portfolios of Reforma Agraria, in charge of relations with the peasantry, Reforma Trabajo, in charge of relations with the workers, and the party leadership. Both were seen as potential presidents.[38]

Mexico was not the United States, and that never happened. While Gutiérrez Barrios was something of a Mexican J. Edgar Hoover, accumulating dirt on generations of leaders, there was no equivalent of President George H. W. Bush, ex-director of the CIA, or of a military-industrial complex. Mexico was never a police state: The ratio of political policemen to civilians was nothing like that of East Germany or, closer to home, Brazil, where the Serviço Nacional de Informações colonized every branch of government, won veto power over all appointments, and provided two presidents. Neither were civilians incarcerated on anywhere near the scale of Uruguay, where one in six people went to jail at one stage or another during the military dictatorship.[39] However, under Díaz Ordaz Mexico's leadership began flirting with the idea of a security state. The rise of the intelligence services was both symptom and cause of rising authoritarianism. In 1965 a disillusioned American cultural ambassador called Mexico "that most subtly totalitarian of states"; under Díaz Ordaz the subtlety sharply declined.[40]

Mexico City was only ephemerally the strategic high ground for the new security state. Out of sight and out of public mind, the provinces were the center of the new repression, and in particular the cities of the North and the mountains of Chihuahua and Guerrero. There caciquismo and violent big business met with dashed revolutionary hopes and anticommunism; the result was a multiplicity of armed groups and state terror. Between 1965 and the early 1980s rural teachers, students, young peasants, and thwarted democrats fought it out against the army, the DFS, an array of police forces, and at least one death squad. It was a striking mismatch, tens of rebels against thousands of troops, the disparity in numbers and technology great enough to overcome the difficulty any state faces in a guerrilla war, which is not knowing who and where the enemy is. Solving that problem, as in any guerrilla war, implied extensive human rights abuse and war crimes, and the conflicts went down in history as the *Guerra sucia*, the Dirty War.

It started in the North on September 23, 1965, when thirteen young men calling themselves the *Grupo Popular Guerrillero* attacked a small town in Chihuahua called Ciudad Madera. It was a region where the government had given politically influential loggers more than one million hectares while locals struggled with poverty and were ignored, an epitome of the extreme inequality of rural Mexico. The attackers' intention was twofold. The attack would be propaganda of the deed, proselytizing through the publicity they would gain, using their success and the local radio station to spark a mass peasant rising. It would also provide them weapons from the garrison and money from the local bank. On both counts they failed dismally. Half the guerrillas didn't show up; those who made it brought two aged rifles, a shotgun, and a couple of .22s; they hadn't reckoned with a detachment of soldiers camped outside the barracks. Eight were killed, including the two leaders, rural teachers called Pablo Gómez and Arturo Gámiz. Only one peasant joined the attack, and the group never got near either radio station or bank. The army occupied the town, arresting, stripping, and holding overnight hundreds of locals; the governor then gave the municipio an ejido. The *pan o palo* worked. Sympathetic peasant risings never materialized, Cuba offered no support, and the largely student guerrillas, already a sparse force, split. By 1966 their group was almost extinct.[41]

The next year a more serious rising broke out in Guerrero. Lucio Cabañas, a rural teacher from the Costa Grande, the coast north of Acapulco, set up a village movement that started off calling for a conservative headmaster to be dismissed and ended up calling for the violent rich to be killed. In May 1967 he was attacked by state police while giving a speech in the town of Atoyac, long a center of bloody war between rich merchants and poor peasants; the crowd fought back, the police opened fire, and seven were killed. Cabañas escaped to the mountains and announced a revolutionary army called the *Partido de los Pobres*, the Party of the Poor. It was a hypothetical army, consisting of Cabañas and a friend with rifles, but villages, authorities, and agrarian militias allowed them free pass across the Sierra de Atoyac and recruitment slowly paid off. A greater massacre, of dozens of coconut growers in August 1967, helped. By the end of the decade Cabañas had about one hundred followers backed by a powerful network of local communities, and he began killing policemen, caciques, and, later, soldiers.[42]

Cabañas was not the only guerrilla in Guerrero. Another maestro rural, Genaro Vázquez, had been prominent in opposition circles since the late 1950s, when he was part of the teachers' strike in Mexico City. He had been part of the Movimiento de Liberación Nacional, the short-lived grouping of the revolutionary Left inside the system. Returning to Guerrero, he was watched by the DFS as he put together a coalition of independent peasant unions and an alliance with the dissident mayor of Acapulco. In 1962 he was involved in a gunfight with the police amid the repression of dissident voters, and fled the state to hide as a cotton picker in the Northwest. In 1966 he was arrested in Mexico City and sent to Guerrero's state penitentiary; in April 1968 he was freed by a commando unit of former civilian allies, and after several months' tortuous journey on foot he made it to the Sierra de Atoyac, where he set up his own guerrilla force, Asociación Cívica Nacional Revolucionaria, around a core of yet more teachers.[43] "Elections," he had concluded, "are a con."[44]

While teachers with some national experience led all the first groups, the most successful guerrilla forces were deep-rooted in local economic inequalities and politics. It was no coincidence that the centers of the new guerrilla wars were close to the old ones of Villismo and Zapatismo and the Cristiada; to the eyes of the everyday people who lived there, not much had changed, and many had memories of ancestors who had tried to do something about it. Cabañas was the third generation of agrarian rebels in his family. The network of local officials, coffee farmers, ejidatarios, and agrarian militiamen who made his rising sustainable had similar roots. The same place names cropped up in the sixties and seventies as had in the tens, twenties, and thirties. Atoyac had been a center of agrarian conflict since the 1910s, the same power structures of rich merchants, land monopolizers, bent policemen, and pistoleros at the heart of it. Kilómetro 30, one of the hamlets outside Acapulco devastated by army raids, had seen it all before; caciques there had murdered nine peasant radicals in a single year under Cárdenas.[45] El Ticuí, where Cabañas delivered his first call to kill the rich, was a factory town once owned by the main cotton-growing and merchant family on the coast, a pole for bloody land wars.[46] In the sierra of Chihuahua, conflicts over grazing land, water, and trees all echoed the distant past. Having failed in their attack on one sawmill's company town, Ciudad Madera, guerrillas in 1968 succeeded in blowing up a different sawmill: El Salto de Villegas in Tomóchic, the site of the most notorious massacre of the Porfiriato.[47]

Even in Guerrero it took a lot to push peasants into taking up arms. As Cabañas noted, a rebellion might be rooted in "poverty, the existence of revolutionary orientation, a bad ruling government, a direct mistreatment of the populace at the hands of government authorities," but the trigger would be "a massacre . . . that they will not silently endure."[48] The state economy rested on political violence: The success of hotel strips, logging companies, and buyers of coffee, coconut, cotton, and sesame would be impossible without cheap labor that accepted dispossession, inequality, and the rulers who administered it. Petty counterinsurgencies were standard, sustainable practice in the 1940s and 1950s: Flying columns of soldiers and state police used the dry season to pursue the undesirables they dubbed bandits and cattle rustlers—some political, others bandits and cattle rustlers—into badlands like the Oaxaca border. It took acts of misrule closer to the center to trigger the risings of the 1960s. The first was the massacre of twenty-one protesters in the state capital, Chilpancingo, in 1960. The governor responsible, General Raúl Caballero Aburto, was fired. But the national government adjudged the opposition movement that came out of the deaths, the Asociación Cívica Guerrerense, likewise beyond the pale, and its voters in the local elections of 1962 were violently disenfranchised. It was the beginning of a cycle of intensified repression that culminated in the 1967 massacres. Only after those could Cabañas recruit a petty army, because most peasant guerrillas didn't go to the hills; they were driven to them.

Across the Dirty War some forty armed groups arose in Mexico, spread across the major cities and the mountains.[49] They were so numerous not just because they were physically distant from each other but also because they disagreed vehemently over ideology, strategy, and who should lead. Yet whether they were students trained in North Korea or peasants fleeing the Guerrero coast, they shared three common points. All believed in offensive operations to kill members of the security forces and thuggish petty capitalists. Cabañas's army was called the Brigada Campesina de Ajusticiamiento, the Peasant Brigade for Executions. Over the summer of 1972 they killed thirty soldiers in ambushes. The days of armed rising as a tacitly understood form of bargaining, the shifting between election campaigns, riot, and rebellion, were gone. These were imagined as long and unwavering campaigns, apocalypse en route to utopia. One young woman wrote in a farewell letter to her family that she knew she wasn't setting off on an *aventura novelesca*, an adventure out of a novel; the army killed her a little over a year later.[50]

Long campaigns required funds, for which the new generation of guerrillas turned to the bourgeoisie. Over the course of the 1970s guerrillas kidnapped among others a US consul, a top businessman, one president's father-in-law, another president's sister, and a gubernatorial candidate. How much money there was in kidnapping is unclear because not all ransoms were disclosed, but the unintended consequences were drastic. The Monterrey businessman Eugenio Garza Sada died while members of the Liga Comunista 23 de Septiembre were trying to take him in 1973, which served as justification for an intensification of extrajudicial violence in the region's cities. The kidnapped Guadalajara consul lived but brought unwanted attention from the US; his ransom was the safe passage of thirty detained guerrillas to the archenemy in Cuba. In September 1974 the future governor of Guerrero, Rubén Figueroa, escaped after several months in captivity and launched a furious vendetta against his kidnappers and anyone else he considered a personal enemy, a large category. And the bungled 1976 attempt at taking Margarita López Portillo, favorite sister of the incoming president José López Portillo, convinced that weak self-proclaimed reformer to allow the secret police a continued and murderous free hand against the guerrillas of the North until they wiped them out.[51]

Ultimately all guerrilla groups were caught up in the force field of the Cuban Revolution of 1959. The improbability of a handful of men turning into an army in the mountains and toppling a US-backed dictatorship was the stuff of myth; Castro duly mythologized the war, minimizing the vital contribution of Cuba's urban guerrillas and a second rural front to create a compelling and historically inaccurate story, which Che Guevara and the French philosopher Régis Debray shaped into a new theory of revolution.[52] Peasants were not the people Marx described as a politically apathetic and atomized "sack of potatoes";[53] they were warriors in waiting, who could be sprung into action by a small vanguard to create a *foco revolucionario*, a nucleus of revolution. Both success and repression would multiply those nuclei until they fused and toppled a bourgeois regime. It was the vanguard theory of Lenin—another despiser of peasants—taken to the countryside. It was supposed to be generalizable. That Marxist revolution might be accelerated from the deep countryside did not, however, mean that the Cubans believed it was perforce rapid. Guerrillas had to be committed to violence over the long haul and be prepared for any sacrifice. They were not there to defend the country poor—in fact, state violence against rural noncombatants was no bad thing at all, pushing uncommitted locals off the fence—but to provide the spark to kindle revolution. The logic was win-win; guerrillas prepared for self-sacrifice would either survive and inspire or die and inspire. Either way, victory was doable in what would previously have been written off as impossible circumstances.

Yet Cuba had a lasting agreement with Mexico not to interfere, which it more or less honored. The only group with significant international contacts was the Movimiento de Acción Revolucionario, a group of fifty-three middle-class students who trained in North Korea, and their organization fell to pieces in short order on their return.[54] However, the government was convinced that all armed movements were expressions of the Cold War, existential threats controlled from abroad. And because of that perceived existential threat, the state's response went far beyond anything from the past.

The sheer numbers of soldiers and the strategy deployed were extraordinary. The governor of Chihuahua, an aging revolutionary veteran, wrote off the attack on Ciudad Madera as "absolutely nothing . . . a bunch of ill-advised madmen." Nevertheless the federal government sent in seven thousand troops from six states.[55] There were twenty-five regiments chasing bandits in Guerrero alone, claimed a sensationalist reporter.[56] Like the US in Vietnam, commanders measured success in body counts, with all the perverse incentives that implied. As one remembered, "We didn't have a problem with the dope growers; but we had to beat the guerrillas to fuck. I mean, terminally . . . the battalion commander used to say 'Don't bring me prisoners. How many dead were there?'" The soldiers' low morale and indiscipline made things worse for peasants, again like in Vietnam; undersupplied, troops pillaged for food, and the same officer, living in fear of being killed by his men, let them get on with it.[57]

Most brutality was top-down. Soldiers dispatched to locate guerrillas or their supporters would assemble the entire population of a village in the main square, raid the houses to ensure they had everyone, pick out people—the "packages" of army reports—using an informer or a blacklist, and take them away in trucks or helicopters. Family members of known guerrillas were targeted for arrest and imprisonment irrespective of whether they were involved, taken to clandestine jails or later Mexico City's main army base, Campo Militar Número 1, where Díaz Ordaz had built a jail for political prisoners in 1961.[58] The army made 1,421 documented arrests in Guerrero alone during the *Guerra sucia*; over 500 more were disappeared, the majority civilians. Historians found records of 207 "packages" for a single year, 1974, which saw the worst of the fighting. They managed to match names to 107 of them; 80 are on the list of the disappeared. Most packages went into custody and never came back.[59]

Between 1974 and 1980 the army began disappearing people by throwing them out of airplanes over the Pacific. Prisoners were transferred to Military Air Base number seven, just behind one of Acapulco's prettier beaches, walked stumbling outside in the middle of the night, shot in the back of the neck, and loaded onto small propeller planes. These would fly fifty miles out, descend to a few hundred feet above sea level, and open the hatch; military policemen would bundle blood-stained canvas sacks out of the plane, commenting sometimes on the package's weight. The pilots heard things they'd rather not have: on one occasion the sounds of prisoners who weren't yet dead. The planes' logs, found by military prosecutors decades later, showed 54 flights that disposed of an estimated 350 people.[60] The technology was much the same as the notorious death flights of the Argentine military dictatorship, which used navy helicopters to drop dissidents dead or alive into the Río de la Plata. The numbers weren't from a wholly different world, either: While Mexico has yet to complete the same exhaustive accounting for the dead as Argentina, where over a thousand people disappeared from the city of Córdoba alone, the regime clearly killed thousands, not hundreds.[61]

The army and other federal forces were not the only operators in an institutionally chaotic counterinsurgency. Governors, their policemen, and their pistoleros were key in a war that was partly personal. In Guerrero Rubén Figueroa, the scion of a revolutionary dynasty, had a prior history of political violence; running for Congress in 1940 he had machine-gunned voters at a polling booth and killed five, including a child.[62] After escaping from his kidnapping in 1974 he recruited thirty ex-policemen and soldiers into his own death squad, the Grupo Sangre, and went after Cabañas, his family, and other enemies. They were, the DFS reported,

> in charge of taking revenge for insults against the Governor, or people who had had problems with the army, drug traffickers (to make a deal); the majority of those detained are disappeared . . . they only report their activities to the Governor and on occasion to the Military Zone Commander in Acapulco. The dissatisfied citizenry is afraid of lodging complaints to avoid reprisals and because no authority will listen to them anyway.[63]

The army killed Cabañas in December 1974; Figueroa kept after his family, sending various members to Campo Militar Número 1 and raping the dead guerrilla's teenage wife, Isabel Ayala. She ended up pregnant; the child died aged four months; in 2011, nearly forty years later, she and her sister were murdered by persons unknown on their way out of church in Xaltianguis, a small town outside Acapulco.[64]

In the cities and the North, personalist and extrajudicial campaigns took a different course. Peasants never joined organizations like the Liga Comunista 23 de Septiembre (LC23S, or just "la Liga") in significant numbers, and most of the fighting stayed in the cities, where urban guerrillas distributed propaganda and attacked policemen and people who symbolized the bourgeois regime. They came from an idiosyncratic mixture of middle-class radicals, farm-boy graduates of rural teacher training schools, and fairly innocent barrio gangs like *los Vikingos* of Guadalajara.[65] In their new political organizations the upwardly mobile Vikings learned ideology, the maestros rurales learned city life, and the middle classes learned violence. The fight against them was led by the DFS, which faced the same problem as the army in the South, that of distinguishing combatants from noncombatants when they looked the same. Their solution was much the same: wide-ranging arrests, disappearances, and murder. Torture and the anonymity of the city made infiltration of the far Left much easier than in the countryside, and most revolutionary groups harbored informants from early on. Cell structures helped some guerrillas prolong their careers, fleeing from safe house to safe house, slipping out to strike and then moving on, but the overall structure of the war was against them. Their best end was retirement, and not many made it.

As in the South, the prominent botched kidnappings of the mid-1970s intensified an already bloody counterinsurgency. The state set up another specialist, no-holds-barred force, the Brigada Blanca, and by 1981 the desultory fighting was over, the hundreds of disappearances eliminating the committed and discouraging their possible replacements. The guerrillas achieved publicity through propaganda of the deed for more than a decade and had shown some of the professional ruthlessness called for by Che Guevara, killing not just minor state figures but also their own suspected moles. Those who fought them, however, had the resources and greater tolerance for extreme violence. The commander of the Brigada Blanca, DFS director Miguel Nazar Haro, was personally notorious for torture, remembered by victims who went through the entire gamut. Women experienced systematic sexual violence in addition to the universals like waterboarding and electric shocks to the genitals, their torturers taken aback by the upending of gender scripts. "At first we went easy on the chicks," Nazar Haro remembered, "but when we realized they were bigger bastards than the men our consideration ran out."[66] In the end most, whether men or women, broke; the guerrillas, by contrast, never managed to infiltrate the DFS.

Both urban and rural guerrillas might have had more chance of enduring had they been open to alliances. Instead ideology, parochialism, and personalism got in the way. In the South Genaro Vázquez met with his experienced predecessor in Morelos, Rubén Jaramillo, when he was first contemplating war, and subsequently with Lucio Cabañas; he came to an agreement with neither. When he ended up in the same mountains as Cabañas in 1969 he moved away from him into his own homeland of the Costa Chica. Vázquez found it hard to keep even his own small Asociación Cívica Nacional Revolucionaria together, expelling the three guerrillas who had broken him out of jail. A brief trip outside Guerrero by Cabañas led him to conclude that his peers wouldn't accept his terms, which were to supply arms while respecting his independence.[67]

The bookish street fighters of the cities and the North were yet more fissiparous. The full range of debates internal to Marxism was on display, the questions of how and when to topple the bourgeoisie a source of vigorous, movement-splitting disagreement. Even those with training in North Korea, which might be expected to instill disciplined unity, argued over who should lead them and what they should actually be doing, whether they were behaving like professional revolutionaries or dilettantes infected by subjectivism, romanticism, and adventurism.[68] It was rather like Mensheviks versus Bolsheviks before 1917, but with Lenin, Mao, Kim Il Sung, and Che Guevara added to the mix. Disagreements continued even through the potentially bonding experience of jail: Prisoners found it impossible to agree on whether watching soccer on TV was selling out to the bourgeoisie or uniting with the proletariat. The only exception was the LCS23, which managed to absorb and recruit several hundred militants, and even send a diplomatic mission to the South in 1967. A dynamic of smaller local groups uniting to wage wider war had prevailed in the Mexican Revolution, when the pragmatic possibilities afforded by alliance and agglomeration trumped personalism and localism. In the 1960s and 1970s the addition of ideology led to fragmentation.

But the revolutionaries of 1910 had also faced a very different state, characterized by a weak military without technological superiority, a dictatorship that offered little hope or ambiguity, a cross-class disenchantment, and a useful ideological simplicity. In those circumstances rapid recruitment and coalition-building came easy. The revolutionaries of the 1970s, on the other hand, faced helicopters and wiretaps with little in hand. When they sprang Genaro Vázquez from jail, the escape car wouldn't start.[69] Their groups never reached critical mass; they peaked at less than two thousand men and women. The deaths of the main leaders devastated their organizations. In 1974 the army killed Cabañas and the DFS disappeared Ignacio Salas Obregón, founder of the Liga. Their groups never wholly recovered; the mass killings of 1974–1975 and 1977 did away with possible successors and, in the case of the peasantry, their most committed civilian supporters. Critically, the guerrilla groups were incapable of drawing much support from the working or middle classes. The government line, with its talk of North Koreans, bomb makers, and wild-eyed kidnappers, worked to preempt broad middle-class sympathy. Mexico's guerrillas had nothing like the popular support of another contemporary group of urban guerrillas, the Irish Republican Army, likewise born out of an army massacre and much more prone to bombs and assassinations. The dissident cartoonist Abel Quezada summed up the rationale for rejecting violence as a political path in Mexico:

> Look: Of all the countries in Latin America, only four still have civilian governments: one of those is ours. The rest are dictatorships, colonies or chaos.
>
> The path to dictatorships of the right or left was always injustice followed by terrorism and crime.
>
> We Mexicans must defend what we have: we will never allow murderers to take away our liberty.[70]

In the end, for all Mexico's revolutionary past and rhetoric, despite the mass student protests and massacres, the new revolutionaries were out of step with too much of Mexican society to stand a chance.

Chapter Nineteen

The Long Goodbye

The main stories of the seventies and eighties were not the presence so much as the absence of guerrillas and their Latin American corollary, military rule. The latter stemmed in part from the PRI's enduring pact with the generals, who swapped national subordination for regional autonomy and its profits. Soldiers and spies were fundamental to the regime's endurance; with them there was little chance of a violent challenge to the PRI succeeding. That ruled out, endurance in a newly hardline one-party state was made bearable by the hope and dread of baby boomers, the economics of populism, the promise of meaningful elections, and the rigging of key ones. Together they kept the PRI in power, through crisis after crisis, in a long goodbye that lasted until 2000.

The social makeup of Mexico at the start of the 1970s was very different from that of the revolutionary years. The urban middle class had grown dramatically to nearly a third of the population and had profited from two decades of economic growth. In the 1940s the government sent spies to markets, cafés, and cinemas to eavesdrop; in the 1970s they frequented dry cleaners, banks, and petrol stations.[1] In the cities and their shantytowns a huge nonunionized lower class emerged of street vendors, casual laborers, servants, rubbish pickers, guttersnipes, and the underemployed; in 1974 40 percent of capitalinos had no steady job.[2] Unionized workers mirrored some of the gains of their US counterparts in housing, cars even, as Volkswagen began producing the Beetle—*el vocho*—in a factory outside Puebla. The country people who nourished them all were in demographic and economic free fall. The numbers who were wageworkers, a rural semi-proletariat, had more than doubled. Mexico had undergone one of the most notable population expansions in world history: In 1940 there were twenty million Mexicans, in 1970 forty-eight million.[3]

Despite increasing inequality and social strains it was a more conservative Mexico; repression, cooption, resignation, and social services had seen to that. Rural migrants in shantytowns might live longer than their parents, but they lived in squalid conditions, while the winners of the postwar economic boom drove past them in imported cars. Successive governments created far more school places, but there were even more children; one in ten Mexicans finished primary school at the start of the decade, one in twenty at its end.[4] Social mobility was in decline as new dynasties settled into politics, business, and bureaucracy. President Echeverría, anointed in 1970, was a visible example: Son-in-law of a major regional cacique, he went straight from the UNAM law school to a top party job to top bureaucrat in the Education Ministry to the cabinet. Sturdy upward ladders, like rural teacher training colleges, were removed under Díaz Ordaz, who shut down half the *escuelas normales* and made the remaining half more selective in admissions.[5] Relative deprivation—the powerful feeling of injustice when some get rich far more quickly than others—was a very real political problem in the cities. So was absolute deprivation, particularly in the countryside: In 1975 90 percent of rural Mexicans said they ate less than the government-defined nutritional minimum.[6]

The government's reaction across the 1970s was to talk and spend its way out of its dilemmas. Echeverría wanted to be Lázaro Cárdenas redivivus; he said so himself. In 1970 he launched a similarly exhaustive campaign, asking about the needs of everyday Mexicans in village after village, and made sometimes confusing promises to meet them. He was hammier than Cárdenas: In the village of Ixcateopan, Guerrero, he stood by the bones of Cuauhtémoc, the last Mexica emperor—notorious fakes—and spoke of how he—Cuauhtémoc, that was—had "assumed the responsibility of public power, when public power, far from being attractive, represented a challenge." He—Echeverría, that was—would, like Cuauhtémoc, be "the most valiant defender of the preservation of our principles, our postulates of social justice, our sovereignty, our cultural and historical heritage and our democratic institutions." As for "the youth of our century," who despised the incoming president for his role in the student massacres, they should learn from Cuauhtémoc "to manifest [their] rebellions based on reason, because [Cuauhtémoc] was in his time the archetype of restless youth, incapable of backing down in the face of cowardice and fatalism."[7]

Echeverría as Cuauhtémoc seemed a hard sell, especially when restless youth was trying to topple the government from the nearby hills. But while it foreshadowed the tangled weirdness of Echeverría's presidential utterances, and while Echeverría went on to intensify repression, he also tried to flesh out the rhetoric of a return to social justice and nationalism. Once in power, he expropriated a quarter of a million hectares from the logging company Bosques de Chihuahua, the target of the first northern guerrillas, to form Mexico's largest ejido.[8] In 1972 he launched Plan Guerrero, which funded new roads, schools, drinking water, electricity, loans, and rural health clinics in the state at the center of the Southern guerrilla war.[9] There was both symbolism and counterinsurgent rationale in these decisions. But they were also part of a far broader program of classic Latin American populism, a combination of revolutionary style with reformist policy and cross-class coalition building.

It was populism in the face of endemic skepticism. As Octavio Paz put it in 1973, "The Mexican people, after more than two centuries of experiments and failures, no longer believes in anything bar the Virgin of Guadalupe and the National Lottery."[10] Echeverría spent like someone who had won it. Mexican politicians had historically been sober in their budgeting, scarred, perhaps, by the fatal legacy of nineteenth-century debt. Even Cárdenas was a fiscally prudent revolutionary. Echeverría, by contrast, set off a decade-long spree that took the federal budget from 1.1 billion to 1.2 trillion pesos.[11] The largesse was for the battered countryside, the numerous new urban poor, and a far larger public sector; it was to be a whole new economic model he dubbed *desarrollo compartido*, shared development, which was to be funded by Keynesian growth and progressive taxation. There was ample room for tax increases, because Mexicans paid less than anyone else in the Americas, contributing less as a percentage of GDP than even the citizens of weak states like the Dominican Republic, Paraguay, or Guatemala. Mexicans reliably rioted against politicians who tried to change that, and governors who persisted had retreated or fallen. At a federal level big business wielded a similar veto; tax-dodging was part of the revolutionary pact undergirding the state. And so Echeverría's tax reform never passed, and in 1972 he turned instead to borrowing and printing money. His handpicked successor, José López Portillo, followed suit.[12]

Cheap money allowed these leaders to find something for everyone. Between 1970 and 1980 the agencies for health and welfare won budget increases of 1,000 percent, covering three times as many people through more than twice as many hospitals, free health clinics, doctors, paramedics, and nurse practitioners. Both urban and rural poor had access to subsidized tortillas, canned food, clothing, and shoes through government shops and food trucks that offered "popular subsistence." Sponsored markets cut out middlemen to offer cheap farm-to-shantytown fruit and vegetables. Unlike Brazil's *favelados*, Mexico's squatters in colonias populares and *colonias proletarias* got new levels of attention from bureaucrats and touring politicians. It became an informal rule that migrants who occupied land around cities and started building would get legal tenure, by hook or by crook, and down the line electricity, drinking water, and sewers. A new public housing agency, INFONAVIT, began building one million homes for the poor. In the country, people got thirteen million hectares of land for ejidos, new credits, infrastructure, and comprehensive development projects in poor, particularly indigenous, zones like the Sierra Tarahumara. The projects were accompanied by ad hoc ethnically defined political structures, *consejos supremos*, billed as empowering indigenous autonomists; in reality they became part of the PRI's peasant sector, one more mechanism for cooptation. At the end of Echeverría's term he redistributed one hundred thousand hectares of the Yaqui Valley, the synecdoche of violent dispossession of indigenous people.[13]

Without the social spending of the 1970s swathes of the countryside would have become apocalyptic. But the greatest beneficiaries were not the dirt-poor but the labor aristocracy. Railwaymen, oil workers, and bureaucrats got their own dedicated social service agencies, a major transfer of wealth from the general population. Public sector jobs boomed for underemployed graduates; six hundred thousand state employees in 1970 turned into 2.2 million in 1980.[14] Gains in education funding went to universities over primary schools.[15] Echeverría's term was a giveaway to students, who kept on hating him anyway; when he visited the UNAM in 1975 they chanted "go fuck yourself" and hurled stones (one hit him on the head, a tribute to either baseball or street fighting).[16] Bustled away, bleeding and cursing, he might have thought it a good thing to have spent so much on his security apparatus, because the regime police were some of the greatest winners of his budgets.[17]

At the start of the decade, however, Echeverría promised an *apertura democrática*. At breakfast with the editors of the main newspapers he claimed to be committed to "self-criticism."[18] That included press freedom and the incorporation of leftist or opposition thinkers into his government. Echeverría got rid of the totalitarian law of disolución social, amnestied the student prisoners from 1968, and allowed them to climb through the ranks: One took over the Fondo de Cultura Económica, the ultimate cultural sinecure, and later became his economic advisor. Carlos Fuentes came in from the cold with the ambassadorship to Paris. The president welcomed leftist intellectuals fleeing military dictatorships from across Latin America. He made Pablo González Casanova, the political scientist whose book *La democracia en México* had eviscerated the regime, rector of the UNAM. Daniel Cosío Villegas, the great liberal critic and historian, the first major intellectual to put the boot into the PRI in 1947, was awarded the national prize for literature. He accepted it because, he said, Mexico was beginning to breathe a climate of intellectual freedom.[19]

But Echeverría's greatest contribution to intellectual freedom was unintended. His muddled bons mots fueled savage jokes about his intelligence: In one much-quoted gaffe he described Mexico's relationship with the United States as one that "neither benefits nor harms us, but quite the opposite."[20] In March 1973 Cosío Villegas published a piece in the broadsheet *Excélsior*—once dull and officialist, now enlivened by some of the sharpest journalists—that called the president "monomaniacal and genuinely mentally disturbed."[21] The editor who published him was Julio Scherer, whom the DFS had long watched but who also enjoyed a productive if complex relationship with power. His headlines had to be pro-government; inner material, editorials, and cartoons in particular could be more critical. Scherer now became more overtly challenging, and in July 1976 the government sent pistoleros to depose him and his inner circle. He promptly set up *Proceso*, a weekly that revolutionized Mexico's investigative journalism. When the government cut off Scherer's newsprint, other papers sent him some of theirs. In the honeymoon of the next presidency José López Portillo allowed other journalists to set up *Unomásuno*, a left-leaning tabloid whose most popular columnist, Miguel Ángel Granados Chapa, was nationally syndicated, reaching even officialist papers. Censorship endured, but it often backfired by turning into a headline in its own right. The government even gave money to *Unomásuno*. One authoritarian created a critical press in Mexico City; another propped it up.[22]

Similar unforeseen results attended Echeverría's other political initiatives: electoral competition and international leadership. He appointed a historian, Jesús Reyes Heroles, to lead the PRI, and they passed an electoral reform allowing more parties into congressional and municipal elections. But Reyes Heroles, facing voluble conservatives and unsettled party leaders, opted for candidates chosen in smoke-filled rooms. The new electoral law's small print nullified its reformism.[23] The opposition chose not to even contest the 1976 presidential election; presented with an unopposed candidate, however, 20 percent of Mexico City still voted against José López Portillo with write-in or spoiled ballots. Many Mexicans didn't bother voting at all. The PRI was almost compelled to pass electoral reform if elections were to keep any legitimacy, and so the 1977 *Ley Federal de Organizaciones Políticas y Procesos Electorales*, designed by Reyes Heroles, made 25 percent of congressional seats proportional representation and gave the Supreme Court oversight of electoral fraud. Proportional representation was introduced at the most competitive level of all, the municipio.[24] It was a lot more democracy than either president wanted.

The gap between desire and performance was starkest on the world stage. Echeverría was an ambitious globetrotter: He traveled to China, Moscow, Brussels, and Washington and proclaimed a new "Third Worldism," but then failed to join the organization closest to incarnating it, the Non-Aligned Movement. Instead Mexico maintained "observer" status in the most promising radical institution for the Global South, signed up for the same compromise with the Soviet Bloc, and maintained a solid backstage relationship with the US. Posturing at the UN's General Assembly meeting—misrepresented as a distinction, in reality a fairly empty ritual—he spoke of Mexico's numerous contributions to international relations.[25] Some of the ways he tried to contribute were personalist and risible. He allegedly sought the pope's blessing for contraception and asked Mother Teresa to support his candidacy for the Nobel Peace Prize. The next secretary-general of the UN was, in line with the organization's policy of rotating between regions, going to be from Latin America; Echeverría said that he was ready.[26]

Yet his government's main initiative was not risible. Mexico had decades of history of advocacy in international relations: radically egalitarian in the interwar period, developmentalist after the war. Mexico, for example, did more than any other country to advance the seminal doctrine of Argentina's Luis María Drago regarding debt in international law, establishing debt as a two-way street: Creditors who profited had duties as well as rights, and their rights did not include violent coercion.[27] In 1971 Mexico began promoting a UN Charter of Economic Rights and Duties of States that extended the fundamental concept. Structural adjustment, internationally imposed changes to how countries spent their money, should also be a two-way street; as the Mexican drafters put it,

> Developed countries have the duty to adopt and apply specific programs of conversion and structural adjustment in their economies with the goal of bringing about a rapid transformation in the world economic order that does justice to the developing countries.[28]

The Global North should lend to and buy from the Global South without political discrimination or protectionism; the countries of the Global South should have the autonomy to regulate foreign investment, nationalize resources, and form trade associations. The charter passed the General Assembly in December 1974. Six countries, including the US and the UK, voted against it; as a General Assembly rather than Security Council resolution it was unenforceable anyway. It was, however, a coherent set of principles for a more egalitarian international order, a product of Echeverría's insistence, and for a while it was called the Echeverría Doctrine.[29]

Rather than accumulating global clout for Mexico, however, Echeverría lost it, because in August 1976 the combination of his borrowing—he quadrupled the national debt—and a global recession crashed the Mexican economy. Individuals and households had taken to ambitious borrowing too, egged on by credit card companies and the Fondo Nacional para el Consumo de los Trabajadores, a government credit agency that offered low-interest loans to minimum-wage workers.[30] Tariffs intended to stimulate Mexican manufacturing had been undercut by massive smuggling of the better foreign products, a black market known as *fayuca*. Mexicans continued not paying tax. Businessmen reacted with political organization and capital flight. As a consequence Echeverría was forced into a 58 percent devaluation of the peso, and an administration that sought economic sovereignty for the Third World was forced to cut state spending in return for an emergency $600 million from the IMF.[31] The anti-colonialist president had increased the power of colonialists, with the exception of those other reckless populists in the British Labour Party, who increased spending on healthcare 20 percent between 1974 and 1976 and needed their own, far bigger IMF bailout to survive.[32]

By then Echeverría had chosen as his successor an equally clueless economics advisor, his former law partner José López Portillo. It was a continuity choice in important ways. López Portillo was happy with extralegal repression as long as his "boys" in the DFS or his generals kept him out of the loop. They continued the death flights out of Acapulco across the first half of his term, and student disappearances rose. The perpetrators were personally and collectively rewarded. In 1980 López Portillo promoted the DFS director who oversaw the disappearances, Javier García Paniagua, to his cabinet. He doubled Gobernación's budget.[33] Like Echeverría he supported revolutionary guerrillas abroad—the Sandinistas in Nicaragua, the FMLN in El Salvador—and eliminated them at home. And as with Echeverría, far from all the spending went into state resources.

The plundering was quite witting: López Portillo made key appointments despite extensive files on their recipients' corruption. The chief of Mexico City's police, Arturo Durazo, was not just a counterinsurgency specialist but also his playground friend, he told the US ambassador, and so he would promote him despite his cocaine smuggling and extortion, which had earned him an arrest warrant in Miami. Durazo became the epitome of the administration's corruption, using racketeering profits, state funds, and dragooned policemen to build two magnificently vulgar mansions, one on the outskirts of Mexico City and the other, with an ugly irony, on ejidal land in a Guerrero beach town. By the end of his time in office he was believed to have made off with $1 billion.[34] López Portillo himself indulged on an unprecedented scale. Seven family members joined the administration; as the state pumped money into the new resorts of Cancún, Puerto Vallarta, and Ixtapa, his mistress became minister of tourism.[35] He built himself a mansion on a huge stretch of expropriated public land outside Mexico City. López Portillo left office in 1982 with between $1 and $3 billion; the estimated total of his inner circle's peculation was tantamount to the interest on the national debt for 1983, 1984, and the first five months of 1985.[36]

That comparison rankled in particular because López Portillo's great legacy was debt. He inherited a broken economy kept afloat by an IMF loan, but within months discoveries of oil in the Southeast and the Gulf made Mexico the world's fourth-largest producer and the loan unnecessary. It was an extraordinary windfall: Proven reserves went up more than 1,000 percent and commercial banks resumed lending. By 1979 interest on the national debt cost 175 billion pesos a year, but oil production was scheduled to reach fifty thousand barrels a day. Economic policymaking was divided among the incompetent in the presidential palace; a group of inexperienced Keynesians in the new Secretariat of Programming and Budget, among them the incompetent's son; and the more experienced monetarists of the Secretaría de Hacienda, the Ministry of Finance and Public Credit. In immediate policy terms the monetarists' only success was a hard-to-dodge, wholly regressive value-added tax of 15 percent. Otherwise they lost: Public spending remained high, inflation was ignored, and private spending on imported consumer goods went up sixfold. Borrowing against future oil revenues would not necessarily have been bad policy had the investments been productive, export diversity encouraged, and oil prices stable. But the borrowed money was spent poorly through multitudinous overlapping agencies, social spending went to alleviate declining real wages, white elephants emerged in herds, and Mexico became dependent on a single export. When López Portillo came to office in 1976 oil constituted 15 percent of exports; by 1981 it was 73 percent.[37]

At that point oil prices collapsed.

What happened next became an economist's morality tale. López Portillo refused to accept the decreased market price of oil, fired the director of PEMEX, and told his replacement to up the price of Mexican oil. In a reality of globalized commodity prices there were no takers, and Mexico began short-term borrowing at high rates to service its debt and prop up the peso. Wealthier Mexicans bought the ensuing artificially cheap dollars and sent them abroad into solid assets like American real estate. When the US Federal Reserve raised interest rates Mexico was unable to make its debt payments, and in February 1982 the peso collapsed from twenty-two to seventy to the dollar. By July Mexico had the largest external debt in the world. In August, as foreign exchange reserves ran low, the government froze private dollar bank accounts and converted them into pesos at below-market rates, wiping out middle-class savings. In September López Portillo nationalized the banking system. In November, having failed to raise enough money or stop capital flight, he agreed to an IMF program of structural adjustment. The IMF would reschedule debt payments and provide cheap money to help Mexico meet them; Mexico in exchange would fire state employees, privatize state enterprises, and cut social services. On December 1, 1982, López Portillo left office, a pathetic cartoon villain with a nice house and a new mistress in his future, a Montenegrin star of sex comedies; the story was an exemplar for the Reagan era of how deficit spending was morally wrong. It was a morality tale for the Left too: The Colossus of the North had imposed an extremist economic philosophy called neoliberalism on the Global South, which came at a crushingly high, ultimately counterproductive human cost.

Both versions were simplifications. Mexican politicians were under substantial pressure from Washington and the private sector, but they also had choices, and some wittingly chose a path of maximum austerity. Despite his free spending, López Portillo had been promoting monetarists since 1979; he named their leader, Miguel de la Madrid, his successor.[38] De la Madrid was yet another UNAM law student, the fourth the PRI had made president, but unlike his predecessors he held a foreign postgraduate degree, a master's in public administration from Harvard. The head of the transition team was a Harvard-trained economist, Carlos Salinas de Gortari, part of an Ivy League invasion of the cabinet.[39] De la Madrid had opposed the eccentric bank nationalization and campaigned on a platform of expertise and honesty; early in his term he pleased the crowd by jailing the director of PEMEX for embezzlement. De la Madrid's response to Mexico's financial meltdown was ideological, although he kept that quiet; he agreed with the IMF prescription for extreme austerity and even went beyond its strictures. This was not a rational choice.[40]

As for López Portillo's own irrational choice to splurge irredeemably, it was neither his alone nor wholly outside the bounds of international standards. For years the US had been encouraging Latin American countries to take cheap loans from the newly rich oil countries, brokering and making commission on the deals. Neither government institutions nor private banks did due diligence.[41] Meanwhile the Mexican government had long been under pressure to confront dramatic inequality. Echeverría was vulnerable to his unions: Strike petitions across his term soared, and when he tried to marginalize the national labor boss Fidel Velásquez, he was forced instead into an across-the-board salary raise. A rewritten labor law called for annual salary revisions, writing pay conflicts into the calendar. Land occupations, for both farms and shantytowns, grew dramatically.[42] State-led industrialization drove both; as a poetic federal planner said, "We create factories but also human deserts and slums."[43] A broad consensus backed the policy of spending both the oil bonanza and future wealth, agreeing with López Portillo that the main challenge was "administering abundance."[44] There was a risk of squandering, the president admitted; but as he told oil workers,

> In these times, in the last third of the twentieth century, it would be very grave if a country with oil could not resolve its social and economic problems. Such a country . . . would not deserve a dignified place in history.[45]

In January 1979, a month after that speech, the IMF's executive director for Mexico endorsed López Portillo's economic policy.[46]

Neither was oil money wholly dissipated in corruption, idle bureaucrats, white elephants, and middle-class giveaways. There were tangible gains in the fundamentals of development: the thousand new electrical plants that came online in the first half of López Portillo's six-year term, the newly watered fields of small farmers as well as agribusiness. By 1982 nearly twice as many houses enjoyed the holy trinity of piped water, sewage systems, and electricity as a decade earlier. Eleven million more Mexicans got social security coverage. There were ten thousand more doctors; thirty thousand more nurses, midwives, and paramedics; twice as many medical centers. Vaccinations went up over 250 percent. Half as many babies died from dysentery and pneumonia, the great childhood killers of the slums. Improvised shantytowns were turning into neighborhoods.[47]

After 1982 there were no such positive stories to tell, because living standards went into reverse for 90 percent of Mexicans. Language reflected it: In Mexico it was *la crisis*, which gave birth to "the lost decade." De la Madrid's main pledge to the IMF was to halve the deficit within a year through retrenchment, austerity, and liberalization.[48] Mexico sold off state businesses, closed parastatal industries, cut subsidies for the poor, and fired state employees, from middle managers to nurses. Even education, supposedly untouchable under both revolutionary and neoliberal philosophies, suffered budget cuts of nearly 30 percent.[49] Inefficient industries—in whose terms? some wondered; they did after all employ people—sheltering behind tariff barriers would be exposed to the harsh but fair light of the global free market. American companies with operations in Mexico could import American-made parts duty free for cheap assembly and re-export, creating over a thousand borderland sweatshops called maquiladoras. As they grew they negotiated better deals, including the ability to set up elsewhere in Mexico and to sell 20 percent of their production inside the country, displacing local manufactures.[50] Some displacements were literal; in Puebla armed police evicted two thousand market sellers from their downtown building "La Victoria," a belle époque landmark, to make way for a shopping center dominated by a Walmart subsidiary.[51]

By 1984 the minimum wage was less than half of what it had been in 1976; a quarter of rural families existed on less than $200 a year.[52] Unemployment rose sharply. For people across Mexico, particularly single young women from the provinces, late-night shifts in maquiladoras became positively aspirational. The urban middle classes were hard hit as state employees lost their jobs, small businesses went under, and savings were devalued as the purchasing power of the peso shrank.[53] The lower classes had it worse. A brief stabilization was undone in 1985 by another drop in the price of oil, and the peso slid through two orders of magnitude. By the end of 1987 it was at two thousand to the dollar, and annual inflation was well over 100 percent. Real wages had halved since 1982; the price of tortillas had risen 400 percent.[54] There were fortunes to be made, as in any crisis; one joke compared it to a mid-level bureaucrat, kind to those at the top, harsh to those at the bottom.[55] Another joke ran that de la Madrid's campaign slogan *renovación moral* had actually been *renovación del morral*, not renewing morality but restocking the backpack. It wasn't very funny, even at the time. Despite all of this, on September 18, 1985, the IMF froze Mexico's credit line; the institution's enhanced surveillance had concluded that Mexico was not in compliance with its promises.[56]

The next day, September 19, 1985, an earthquake hit the center of Mexico City. It started at 7:18 in the morning, lasted two minutes, and measured 8.1 on the Richter scale; the soil of the old lake floor was soft and unstable; the combination leveled entire blocks, knocking down over four hundred buildings. Between ten thousand and forty thousand died; at least thirty thousand were injured; hundreds of thousands were left homeless. The earthquake swept away an entire old world, ranging from the luxurious Hotel Regis with its Rivera mural, its bar once haunted by stars, politicians, and pistoleros, to the sixty blocks of old inner-city tenements around the Zócalo to the high modernist apartment buildings in Tlatelolco, like the Nuevo León, whose base crumbled and left fifteen floors lying on their side, surrounded by furniture, toys, and the bodies of people who jumped out their windows

Downtown Mexico City, September 19, 1985.

as the tower came down. The three main public hospitals, Televisa's studios, the telephone exchange, and assorted ministries were all gone. Houses from the genteel Roma to the mean streets of Tepito turned into heaps of brick. A fine gray dust cloud spread. Burst water pipes caused floods; burst gas pipes, fires. There was no electricity, water, television, or phone. The next evening a second earthquake brought down twenty more buildings and shifted the rubble heaps, killing more of the people who had been buried alive.[57]

The first reactions were shock, disbelief, and a horror that would last: Octavio Paz on a corner of Reforma, staring blankly at the devastation; the evening papers with their one-word headlines, taking up half the front page, like TRAGEDY or ¡OH, DIOS![58] There was an instant emergency response from civilians, who organized themselves into teams to dig for survivors, get the wounded treatment, and get food and shelter to the displaced. Groups of everyone from *chavos banda*, street punks, to housewives to the tenor Plácido Domíngo cleared rubble by hand; volunteers nicknamed *topos*, moles, tunneled into the collapsed buildings to bring out survivors. The metro down, students pedaled bikes in from the south of the city to help. It was the stuff of myth.

By contrast the authorities were first absent and later wholly incompetent. There was no disaster plan in place because the IMF austerity program had eliminated the Prevention of Disasters Office and officials failed to improvise. The housing director for the devastated Tlatelolco housing complex, home to 40 percent of the citizens caught up in the quake, told the first residents who came to him in the morning—no emergency services had arrived, so they'd headed for his office—that he couldn't make time to see them; perhaps later in the week. It was the first of a series of surreally cloddish official responses. The president, absent from any of the scenes, told the press the same day, "We are ready to return to normal life," and said they didn't need outside aid. Three days later, as volunteers were still looking for survivors in the wreckage near Televisa, a TV show host told viewers, "Everything is the same, minus a few buildings." The army had a good reputation for disaster relief, but when the soldiers turned up they tried to cordon off the destruction and bulldoze the ruins of tenements and hospitals while they still contained survivors. Some looted the Nuevo León apartment building, one of the main symbols of the disaster. Within a day the earthquake had become unmissably visible and profoundly political.[59]

A second storyline ran alongside the incompetence and disdain, one of corruption made flesh and blood. The nature of the ruins substantiated old rumors of government connivance with fraudulent constructors, slum landlords, and sweatshop owners. Public buildings showed a greater propensity to collapse, their structural pillars turning out to be filled with sand. The earthquake revealed two hundred illegal textile factories in the area, buildings unfit for the machinery they contained; the floors collapsed down through the buildings and killed sixteen hundred working women. Six hundred more were trapped for over a week; only twenty-five made it out. The sweatshop tragedy was also a story of collusion between venal bureaucrats and sociopathic businessmen. Owners dug out safes, documents, and machinery before workers. In early October the Garment Industry Association, backed by the city government, recommended (at a banquet) firing the remaining forty thousand workers without severance pay. The hubris of thinking this wouldn't leak, from a dinner for a thousand guests, or indeed of holding the banquet at all, was eloquent; as it was, a *Jornada* reporter had snuck in. When the party newspaper *El Nacional* belatedly joined in the coverage, it stressed how many of the sweatshop owners were of Jewish and Lebanese descent, not really Mexicans at all.[60]

The third story of the earthquake was the reaction of chilangos to the disaster, a story both real and politically crafted. The volunteers who dug out the living and the dead, opposed by the authorities, persisted and formed their own parallel authority, the Coordinadora Única de Damnificados, CUD. It was a political coalition that stretched from student radicals to unemployed middle classes to parish priests in the city's north. The intellectual Carlos Monsiváis codified it early on as a cross-class "civil society" seizing power from a failed state. So it was; the CUD was also heavily salted with experienced left-wing activists, cadres who shaped the story of a unique democratic takeover; as one said later, "The narrative that we began to invent was that 1985 was the outburst of citizen participation, the breaking of all the mechanisms of control."[61] The CUD used mass marches, media appearances, and negotiation to push city and federal governments into a relief and reconstruction project in which the tenement dwellers were, for once, the great winners. The first offer was to relocate them seventy miles north of the city; the CUD drove the government instead into expropriating thousands of buildings and empty lots to build public housing. About 70 percent of the original residents stayed in updated versions of their old neighborhoods. The more middle-class residents of Tlatelolco had a more ambiguous, neoliberal ending. They too got to stay; their homes were rebuilt, but they were turned into condos.[62]

The earthquake brought mass politics back to the city. Capitalinos had long voted for opposition congressional candidates, but that was as far as it went.[63] More than half the major cities in Latin America saw massive popular protests against the austerity programs of the lost decade; Mexico City did not.[64] A majority had been politically quiescent since the early years of the PRI, and even the 1968 massacre didn't shift that more than briefly. They had been violently dissuaded on Corpus Christi and at Tlatelolco, and before that by the election massacres of 1940 and 1952. Moreover, citizens in Mexico City lacked the institutional outlets for meaningful local politics that existed in the provinces: In place of a mayor, the president appointed a *regente*, a regent, and instead of elected municipal governments the regent in turn appointed delegates. And at the same time, chilangos were seduced by a city that, for all the strains of vertiginous growth, benefited disproportionately from the PRI's rule. Life in México Distrito Federal—DF, the *Defectuoso*, the *Detritus Federal*—was subsidized by a massive transfer of wealth from the countryside. Monsiváis, a chilango to his bones, summed up the 1960s as "the property of the middle class."[65] For the capital's chattering classes it was a charmed life, one with more possibilities, for even the poorest, of sociability and social mobility than anywhere else. The old colonial jibe *"Afuera de México todo es Cuautitlán,"* "Outside Mexico City it's all Cuautitlán"—metonym for a dump—still applied. Tlacotalpan was *precioso*, Cuernavaca *hermoso*, Acapulco *chido*, but you wouldn't want to live in any of them.[66]

That political separation ended after the earthquake, when the capital experienced the sort of mass mobilization that periodically shifted provincial power. In 1987 the CUD gave way to the permanent pressure group called the Asamblea de Barrios, leaders-in-waiting for an opposition party. The earthquake activists formed alliances with other nongovernmental organizations like the Fondo Regional de Mujeres.[67] When the PAN in Chihuahua launched a major protest over rigged gubernatorial elections, one of the leaders of the earthquake protests, the capital's left-wing luminary Heberto Castillo, traveled there to offer support and propose a national campaign for democracy.[68] In 1988 Castillo put the capstone on a broad left-wing coalition, the Frente Democrático Nacional, bringing his Partido Mexicano Socialista together with three others and a powerful leftist faction of the PRI, the Corriente Democrático; that in turn brought along disillusioned union leaders and experienced wheeler-dealers like Porfirio Muñoz Ledo, a former party president, cabinet member, and UN ambassador. The new party even got the blessing of Genaro Vázquez's ex-guerrillas. As a presidential candidate for 1988 they chose the most totemic figure of the revolutionary party, President Lázaro Cárdenas's son, Cuauhtémoc.[69]

The Frente Democrático Nacional wasn't very democratic. Rather than run primaries it anointed Cárdenas, proposed by the Partido Auténtico de la Revolución Mexicana, a small, notoriously corrupt party of opportunists.[70] Had it been a popularity contest, Heberto Castillo might well have won. He was everything Cuauhtémoc was not: former political prisoner, internationally renowned engineer, hardline opposition journalist, fierce critic of oil dependency, earthquake activist who oversaw the engineering of reconstruction. He had even set up a socialist taqueria.[71] Moreover, Cárdenas wouldn't have left the PRI in the first place without that party's continued rightward shift, which culminated in de la Madrid preferring the economist Carlos Salinas as his successor in 1988.

Yet while not democratic, the Frente Democrático Nacional was genuinely national, and it drew on the democratic culture that went back to the colony and centered on the municipio libre. The PRI always recognized the power of local democracy and never wholly monopolized local government. Between 1962 and 1978 they allowed the conservative opposition to win some of the biggest municipios in Mexico, including the state capitals of Sonora and Yucatán. After 1977 left-wing parties were allowed to compete again, and in the next ten years they and the PAN took over half the main towns and cities.[72] These were victories earned by electoral savvy, conviction, and violence, the generations-old bargaining by riot still a default tool. In the 1982 municipal elections a political scientist found that thirty-five out of a sample of fifty protests ended up with the opposition slate forcibly seizing the town hall. In 1988, leftists who won twelve municipios in Yucatán broke through police cordons to take up their offices.[73] By bringing together the newly politicized Mexico City crowd with older provincial election fighters Cárdenas could run a competitive countrywide campaign for the presidency.

An impressively dull speaker, he nevertheless turned out huge crowds in old Cardenista strongholds like Michoacán and the Laguna, on new turf like Baja California, and in Mexico City, where nearly a quarter of the electorate lived. By contrast the governing party machine was breaking down. In the early 1960s 25 percent of Mexicans had joined the PRI; by 1990 less than 10 percent could be bothered.[74] In 1986 the party was reduced to threadbare fraud to keep the governorship of

Chihuahua, and in the 1988 congressional elections its share of the national vote dropped to 50 percent.[75] Priistas became quite willing to change parties according to which way the wind blew.[76] Their candidate, Carlos Salinas, was a politically questionable choice: a Harvard-trained budget slasher and another fortunate son. His father had profited as secretary of industry and commerce, and Salinas, like Cárdenas, had grown up wealthy. Old-school party men, *dinosaurios*, disliked him on personal and policy grounds.

Salinas proved better at politicking than expected. In the Secretariat of Programming and Budget he formed a tight group of the like-minded and made a gifted negotiator, Manuel Camacho Solís, his consigliere. He and Camacho stood out from their peers in dealing with the earthquake survivors: Camacho signed a pact with them, recruited Heberto Castillo, and got nearly fifty thousand houses built within a year.[77] Salinas knew how to play the press: He dined journalists and ended up recruiting one respected for independence as his press secretary.[78] He was also an unexpectedly committed touring politician, putting his face to popular government spending. But he was running against three structural problems. His generation was committed to an economic model the majority of Mexicans detested. His timing coincided with the lost decade that toppled governments across Latin America. And he also faced a technological challenge: A public and press that could easily record and share data formed an empowered electorate, and by the time Salinas ran for office, critical papers pooled stories and used computers to send them across Mexico.[79]

But the PRI had a more sophisticated computer, which it used to rig the election. The Secretario de Gobernación, the dinosaurio Manuel Bartlett, installed a mainframe in the basement of the ministry to deliver same-night election results. After news leaked, he agreed to share the results in real time with opposition representatives, who could watch monitors in a different building with its own dedicated election computer. In reality those monitors were linked to the Gobernación mainframe. As results came in to that mainframe a program divided them between two folders. One held results from PRI-favoring districts; those would be visible in real time to the opposition. The other folder, kept off grid, held results from districts where the PRI was losing. These were to be released only when the party had the numbers to declare victory.

By election evening on July 6 this looked like foresight, because the polls were unexpectedly strong for Cárdenas. Televisa's coverage overwhelmingly backed the PRI; unknown gunmen killed Cárdenas's aide in charge of election monitoring. Traditional on-the-ground election rigging was widely reported—the repeat voters, the heavies, the stuffed ballot boxes, the disappearing polling booths—but its efficacy seemed questionable, and governors were telling Bartlett that it would be close. At that stage a PAN election official hacked the off-grid results and found that the opposition was winning the cities. An official physically tried to pull the plug in the monitoring room and was stopped by a scuffle. Screens went blank. The government announced that computerized vote counting had failed: "*Se cayó el sistema*," "the system had crashed." The opposition candidates pushed their way into Gobernación and their representatives into the basement with the real mainframe, whose operators admitted that it was working. Bartlett hurriedly gave the election commission printouts from eleven hundred precincts, which showed Cárdenas winning. Two hours later he gave them results from four thousand PRI-leaning districts and lied that they were the complete set to date. Salinas refused twice to declare victory; President de la Madrid, who had army detachments in the basement of the palace, ordered the party president to do it for him.[80]

Long afterward de la Madrid and others owned up to what vox populi knew on that night, that the PRI had committed a sweeping, sophisticated, and yet incompetent fraud.[81] Salinas may have won anyway. In the end he supposedly got 50.5 percent of the votes as opposed to Cárdenas's 33 percent, and he was awarded all but three states and Mexico City. This was clearly untrue, but surveys suggested that the rural vote held up better than expected and that Cárdenas was less successful in mobilizing long-term abstainers than he'd hoped he would be.[82] It was impossible to tell because no one ever saw the actual ballots. When PAN legislators tried to get at them in the basement of Congress for a partial recount, they were kept out by soldiers. Salinas secretly offered Cárdenas a full analysis in the run-up to inauguration day; Cárdenas declined.[83] The electoral commission was given a brief period to inspect 162 thousand vote tallies; those they managed to digest proved full of the clumsy trails of analogue fraud. Some vote tallies surpassed the entire district's population; others had zeros added to the PRI's score. In the end, the PAN and the PRI came to an agreement and the lot was burned.[84]

By then it was irrelevant. The losing parties agreed to push for the election to be nullified, but three days later Cárdenas changed his mind and called for his victory to be realized. This divided him from the PAN, and they decided to recognize Salinas's win. In exchange they negotiated an electoral reform that would hand over election running from the government to nonpartisan bodies. Rather less idealistically, they sought the assurance that they would be allowed to win the upcoming gubernatorial elections in Jalisco, Guanajuato, San Luis Potosí, and Zacatecas.[85] In the short term, it was the continuation of Mexican pragmatism meeting Mexican authoritarianism; in the long term, it was the beginning of the end.

The PAN had no problem with cutting taxes, privatizing state companies, reducing social spending, or opening up Mexico to foreign trade and investment. They were neoliberals themselves, without the intellectual clout of the new PRI: Ivy League PhDs against ranchers, businessmen, and devout Catholics. Who should implement these changes was what the PAN disputed. Electoral reform passed in 1989, but the electoral commission was still controlled by a government majority. *Panistas* didn't get the governorships they had discussed, although they were allowed Baja California and Chihuahua. Salinas knew that the PRI had lost the North years ago; his priority was holding on to the rest of the country and the capital and choking the Left. When Cárdenas formed his own party, the *Partido de la Revolución Democrática* (PRD), provincial priistas were allowed to kill 265 of its militants in five years, an average of one per week.[86] Proclaimed decentralization was, in the words of the PRI's leader, a decentralization of problems, the president passing the buck of spending cuts on to the governors. In political terms Salinas was actually recentralizing by hiring and firing locally rooted politicians according to expediency: Over six years he fired seventeen governors, and for five of those years he was remarkably successful.[87]

Salinas started off in his predecessors' footsteps, combining proclamations of democracy with attacks on corruption. In January 1989 he had the notoriously crooked PEMEX union boss Joaquín "La Quina" Hernández Galicia arrested, charged with murder, and jailed for thirty-five years. It was a productive scandal: He used it to fire 120 thousand oil workers and cut the PEMEX budget.[88] He bought lower-class support with a new development program called Solidaridad, which bypassed the old agencies to distribute $18 billion to Mexico's poorest. Rather like his arrest of La Quina, it looked like an assault on corruption, slimmed down the state, and increased his personal popularity. Solidaridad was billed as revolutionary in its grassroots deals for local communities, funding their priority projects in return for contributions in labor; in many places this was old wine in new bottles, the mandatory work details, called *faenas*, often constituting forced labor, rebranded as dynamic empowerment for the 1990s. Solidaridad did however result in a burst of the nuts-and-bolts development—new schools, drainage, electricity—that went missing during the peak years of austerity, and Salinas was careful to be filmed standing next to its results.

The final piece in his popularity lay in economic recovery. Salinas was counterintuitively lucky in his disastrous inheritance: The earthquake pushed the outside world to ease the terms of Mexico's debt repayments, and a steep devaluation in 1987 made Mexican products and assets cheap. Salinas privatized state companies including the national bank, Banamex; the national airline, Mexicana; and the national telephone company, Telmex. Foreign investors were encouraged, and the state got a cash windfall. More popular in US government and financial circles than any Mexican president since Porfirio Díaz, Salinas managed, like Díaz, to negotiate greatly improved debt terms. A nascent stock market boomed. Much growth was low quality: The cheap sell-off of Telmex, for example, helped make its buyer, Carlos Slim, the richest man in the world, but it neither ended the monopoly nor cut Mexicans' phone bills. It actually made them some of the highest in the world.[89] Mexican bankers continued to lend to their wealthy friends rather than everyday Mexicans.[90]

For a while the middle class did well. It was obvious on the roads, where Beetles proliferated; production at the Volkswagen Puebla plant went up 500 percent.[91] By the end of 1993 the number of Mexicans with cars had risen from 5.8 to 8.1 million (they were cheaper because the autoworkers' collective contract had been terminated).[92] Their drivers might read *Reforma*, a new centrist broadsheet comfortable criticizing the PRI, or watch TV Azteca, a new and marginally less sycophantic channel. If they preferred to read the leftist *La Jornada*, they had the cartoons of El Fisgón to tell them that Salinas's modernization was smoke and mirrors. In the long term, one of his fat capitalist caricatures said, trickle-down economics worked:

> I generate a lot of jobs:
> I have 12 drivers, 9 secretaries, 15 housekeepers,
> 7 cooks, 2 pilots,
> 15 stockbrokers.

But if those pilots were chilangos, they could also speed to Acapulco on a spectacular toll highway with revolutionary ease. As one of El Fisgón's oleaginous technocrats put it, "Before Salinas everything was Cuautitlán."[93]

It was a revolution in the Thatcherite sense of macroeconomic recovery combined with dramatic social disruption, rising inequality, and immiseration. El Fisgón sketched the costs to Mexicans in cartoons with text, statistics, and footnotes. The numbers of the poor had risen by four million, according to even Solidaridad; 73 percent of the population was in poverty according to the United Nations. While the government claimed that unemployment was under 3 percent, an independent consultancy put it at 10 percent.[94] Privatization meant selling off the government paper monopoly PIPSA in 1993, and with it went the mainstay of censorship, withholding newsprint. Yet increasingly critical media didn't translate into opposition gains, and the PRI even recovered in the 1991 midterm elections. At his peak Salinas had enough power to take previously unthinkable steps, like declaring the revolution's agrarian reform over. It had accomplished its purpose, he said in 1992—while touring the country on *Emiliano Zapata*, the presidential jet—and ejidos should now be privatized to increase production. And in a move against the most fundamental Mexican strategic doctrine—mistrust your neighbors, a popular, political, and formal military principle—Salinas negotiated the North American Free Trade

Agreement, a treaty that united Canada, the US, and Mexico in a single trading zone with few barriers to trade and investment. NAFTA was the final step in opening up the Mexican economy; "modernization," the slippery concept that obsessed Salinas, had arrived.

An economic shock and a few years made it clear that NAFTA brought most Mexicans something between disappointment and devastation. GDP per capita didn't grow faster. Export manufacturing output rose but inflation-adjusted wages did not, and nearly half of the growth was in the maquiladoras, the tax-free, foreign-owned factory sweatshops where low-paid workers pieced together foreign-made components.[95] Trade and investment were not liberalized in key areas: Foreigners couldn't put much-needed money into PEMEX, Mexican truckers couldn't operate in the US, American avocado production was protected by tariff. Competition in maize cultivation, critical to rural Mexico, was ironically unfair. After 1994 small growers had to compete with the rugged individualists of Iowa, whose substantial subsidies and protection enabled them to undercut the Mexican product par excellence. Consumers saw shrink-wrapped, shucked American corn appear on the supermarket shelves; they bought mole in Walmart with American Express cards. For US and Mexican elites it was confirmation that an old and inferior Mexico was in retreat, even if that idea needed some selling to a US public. When Salinas was invited to dinner at the Bush White House, the chef came up with a dessert called "Mexican Fantasy," which featured a sugar Mexican in a sombrero asleep against the wall of an adobe hut; Barbara Bush found out just in time to junk it.[96] The libertarian Ross Perot had no such qualms. When he was told that NAFTA might be as important to the US as the purchase of Alaska or Louisiana, he retorted that they hadn't been full of Mexicans.[97]

Alongside generic idleness, another key US racial stereotype of Mexicans was their cultural predisposition to violence. Mexicans found this rich coming from a country founded on not just the Declaration of Independence but also the deliberate elimination of indigenous peoples and a civil war, fought over the tardy abolition of slavery—forty years later than in Mexico, later than everywhere in Spanish America bar

Cuba—that killed six hundred thousand. Mexicans did on the other hand have a long history of revolting against injustice, and on January 1, 1994, the day that NAFTA went into effect, some of them expressed it in a rebellion in the southern highlands of Chiapas. Several thousand indigenous men and women in black balaclavas took over major towns, including the old capital of San Cristóbal de las Casas, released indigenous prisoners, burned land records, and fought with police and army for several days before retreating into the Lacandón Rainforest. They called themselves the *Ejército Zapatista de Liberación Nacional*, the EZLN; the *Washington Post* came up with its own analysis in the headline INDIANS RAMPAGE IN SOUTHEAST MEXICO.[98]

The EZLN was actually rather sophisticated, as its next steps and later intelligence reports revealed. They were militarily unimpressive, limited to hunting rifles, grenades, and the odd Kalashnikov, but they had the old guerrilla advantage of home ground, and the forested mountains of Chiapas might have been shaped for hit-and-run war. The Zapatistas were certainly not rampaging, and although they spoke like utopians they were not fantasists; they were never going to set out for Mexico City, and neither did they stand much chance of becoming a *foco*, inspiring enough like-minded into the sierra to topple the government. They combined instead something like the old pronunciamiento, the performative manifesto of rebellion, with the collective bargaining by riot of outraged communities that went back to the sixteenth century. Their strategy was to storm provincial town halls, show their potential and willingness to fight, make stretches of their countryside dangerous for the army, and get a series of utopian declarations out to a fascinated world. It was in the short term successful, because on January 12 the government declared a unilateral ceasefire and began talking with the Zapatistas.

The late-twentieth-century Zapatistas said they wanted land, equality, democracy, and an end to selling out to foreigners, a blend of autonomy and egalitarianism that echoed their forbears. And they went beyond their forbears, adding indigenous rights, women's rights, environmental justice, and a downplayed Marxism. It was all put across by a northerner who had won the prize for best dissertation at the UNAM's Facultad de Filosofía y Letras, Rafael Guillén Vicente, a pipe-smoking, balaclava-wearing charismatic with the nom de guerre Subcomandante

Marcos.[99] The mysterious Marcos—he started off anonymous, and it took a long time for the state to work out who he actually was—was the media presence and apparent leader of the revolution, but he titled himself Subcomandante because he obeyed, he said, the indigenous councils of the Tzotzil, Tzeltal, Tojolabal, and Chole peoples and, behind them, the people plain and simple.

The Zapatista rising was a triumph of revolutionary style over military substance. (The bandolier that Marcos wore to the first peace talks held bullets of a much bigger caliber than his gun.)[100] In talking to the Mexican and international press, which he did a lot, he used pathos and humor and swore like a trooper, projecting the image of a man on horseback who was more self-deprecating ironist than caudillo. He was a bit of a clown, he said, who made his points through a performance of bluff, candor, jokes, and children's stories about a beetle who steals his tobacco and chats with him about the future of the revolution against neoliberalism. (The bookish beetle reassures the Subcomandante that the revolution will triumph; he's just not sure quite when, because "many things have to be taken into account: the objective conditions, the ripeness of the subjective conditions, the correlation of forces, the crisis of imperialism, the crisis of socialism, etc. etc.")[101] For the domestic and international left, Marcos was a sort of Che without that Argentine's earnest machismo or contempt for locals.

The objective conditions were in the Zapatistas' favor. Chiapas was one of the poorest states in Mexico, famous for a series of revolutionary potboilers, B. Traven's "Jungle Novels," the indigenous slavery they depicted, and the coffee and mahogany those slaves extracted for a tiny elite and a global market. White and mestizo cattle ranchers had struggled with the Maya over land since the revolution. In the few places where indigenous peoples had the upper hand, like San Juan Chamula, the PRI egged their leaders on to revolutionary caciquismo.[102] Giant dams on the Usumacinta and Grijalva Rivers powered much of Mexico, but building them displaced indigenous communities and offered few jobs—not even electricity, in many places—in return. Chiapas was at the bottom of the entire country by key development statistics such as literacy rates, but at the top of the country in the size of its indigenous population, largely still organized in the free villages of the past.[103] As for the subjective conditions, the beliefs that push people to rebel, Chiapanecos had their own autonomy-seeking histories and revolutionary nationalism. They also had a network of radical priests and lay preachers who brought to the highlands liberation theology, with its potent ideal of a socially just, grassroots church, and a handful of ex-guerrillas who had headed there for shelter in the 1980s.

The Zapatistas didn't win, beyond autonomy for a handful of rebel municipios and an increase in development funding for the entire state. About two hundred of them died; the army launched a surprise offensive in February 1995 but was pulled back by public opinion and appalled priistas, including the Secretario de Gobernación. Soldiers and paramilitaries moved into the state long term; a massacre by paramilitaries of forty-five Tzotzil civilians at a prayer meeting in Acteal in 1997 caused international outrage but went unsolved. The EZLN wasn't joined by similar indigenous movements elsewhere in Mexico, although they nodded respectfully to a small Maoist group that appeared in Guerrero in 1996, the *Ejército Popular Revolucionario*. As the frozen conflict aged, Marcos's jokes grew thinner, the self-deprecation laid on a bit too thick, the personality cultish. A controversial novella was a straw in the way the wind was blowing; it imagined the Subcomandante signing a publicity contract with United Colors of Benetton.[104]

But the Zapatistas were no joke and neither did they lose, because the PRI collapsed six years later and they played a roundabout part in its fall. The party had been caught in a long goodbye from the early 1980s onward, its balancing act incompatible with neoliberal economic policies, local-level democratization, and a soaring population. The end was hastened, however, by the three interlinked crises of 1994. The Zapatistas' rebellion, immense visibility, and adroit media campaigning was the first, and it helped push the PRI a step further toward meaningful electoral reform. It helped detonate the second, a wave of unprecedented political murders. And its threat to Mexico's international reputation led Salinas into the third, an overspending that aimed to reassure voters and investors and helped crash the economy instead.

The first victim was Cardinal Juan Jesús Posadas Ocampo, archbishop of Guadalajara, who was shot dead in the parking lot of the Guadalajara airport in May 1993 while he waited to greet the Papal Nuncio, the Vatican ambassador to Mexico. The next was the PRI's presidential candidate Luis Donaldo Colosio, shot on campaign in Tijuana in March 1994. The third was the secretary-general of the PRI, José Francisco Ruiz Masseiu, shot in September 1994 in central Mexico City after a party meeting. The three murders broke the greatest unwritten rule of the PRI, thou shalt not kill top politicians. No one had ever killed a bishop, not even during the Catholic civil war of the 1920s. Neither had anyone murdered a president since 1928. The law never solved any of the killings to popular satisfaction; while incompetent narco hitmen, an unbalanced lone gunman, and a rogue congressman were duly provided, it was generally believed that all three murders were ordered at the highest levels of the PRI, and that belief in political terms was what counted.[105]

The murder of Cardinal Posada might have been an honest-to-God mistake by narcos, most of whom were quite religious—devotees of the Virgin of Guadalupe, it went without saying, but also of the patron saint of drug dealers, San Jésus Malverde, a mythical Sinaloan bandit who lived on across the North in shrines and plastic figurines. The police version was that Arellano Félix cartel gunmen had gone to the airport to ambush Joaquín "El Chapo" Guzmán of the Sinaloa Cartel, who, like the churchman, was supposed to be dressed in black and traveling in a white Grand Marquis. The murder was a case of mistaken identity. Vox populi held that the authorities killed Cardinal Posada because he was a popular and active opponent of the PRI who breached the longstanding rule that churchmen stay out of politics. Guadalajara had been a center of the Cristiada; it was also the center of the contemporary drug trade, the base of Miguel Ángel Félix Gallardo's Federación, an umbrella organization labeled the first cartel. Posadas had called for the governor to resign over his mismanagement of the city, particularly after two huge natural gas explosions. The next step might have been to denounce government ties to narcos.

There was promising raw material for the theory: an unusually heavy police and army presence in the parking lot that afternoon, bystanders locked accidentally on purpose into the bathrooms shortly before the shooting began. All of this could also have preceded a narco hit. But in July 1994 it leaked that the Arellano Félix brothers had met in secret with the Papal Nuncio, Girolamo Prigione, not looking for absolution but rather to deny vigorously that they had done it. There was enough confusion to bring that version beyond the bounds of conspiracy theory and into the realm of the possible; if that weren't bad enough for the PRI, the killing also brought home the power of a new generation of narcos. Few had known who El Chapo was before the Cardinal's murder. The government was damned if they'd killed him and damned if they hadn't.[106]

The next murder, ten months later, was even more damaging. Luis Donaldo Colosio was supposed to reinvent the PRI, one more of the presidential candidates who drove the party's boom-and-bust cycle of hope. Salinas had chosen him as a puppet, one more of his breaks in the reglas no escritas, and in November 1993 Colosio seemed ideal for the role: young, mildly charismatic, popular thanks to his leadership of the social program Solidaridad. As a candidate he was out of his depth, but he was a good listener who talked to a wide range of people and was widely liked. As the left-wing journalist José Woldenberg remembered, Colosio was

> the polar opposite of the overbearing, know-it-all and in the end insensitive politician. On the contrary his humility, ability to listen and to pose questions without deviousness really caught your attention. Despite his rapid political career the fumes hadn't gone to his head.[107]

Colosio was also from Sonora, by now politically peripheral, lacked the networks and top jobs of most of his predecessors and competitors, and for that reason was in hock to Salinas. In the aftermath of the Zapatista rising he faced unprecedented competition from the president's other protegé, Manuel Camacho Solís. Camacho was a better candidate: smarter, more experienced, and popular as a reformer who got things done. He had been highly successful in turning around the government response to the 1985 earthquake, and in 1994 he was again drawing a favorable public eye as the government's peace negotiator in Chiapas.

So both a public motive—shock at the Zapatista rising—and a private motive—political self-defense—led Colosio to depart abruptly from the script. On March 6, 1994, he stood in front of the Monumento de la Revolución and told the Mexico City crowd:

> I see a Mexico of indigenous communities who can't wait anymore for the demands of justice, dignity and progress . . . I see a Mexico of peasants who still don't have the answers they deserve . . . I see a Mexico of workers who don't find the jobs or the salaries they demand . . . I see a Mexico that is hungry and thirsty for justice. A Mexico of wounded people, people wounded by the deformations the law inflicts on those it should be serving. Of women and men ravaged by the abuse of the authorities or the arrogance of government offices . . . Change with purpose and with responsibility cannot wait.[108]

Just over two weeks later he was dead.

As with the Cardinal's killing, copious raw material existed to support public belief in a government assassination. A motive was clear: The talk of justice threatened some leaders of a party whose skeletons—massive defalcation and close links to narcos—were emerging from the closet. As for opportunity and method, Colosio had been on a chaotic campaign walkabout in a poor barrio of Tijuana, Lomas Taurinas; security was provided by three different escort groups, but the closest ones were from Salinas's elite guardia presidencial, and they somehow failed to stop an amateur gunman from putting a bullet clear through Colosio's head at point-blank range; the guardia presidencial then hijacked the critical first hours of the investigation and botched it. Credible reports emerged that the gunman, Mario Aburto Martínez, was tortured into claiming fictional sole responsibility. The head of Tijuana's police force, run by the PAN, launched his own investigation and was promptly murdered, one of ten lawyers and security personnel linked to the case who died in violent circumstances. Six years of investigations under different attorneys general moved through a bewildering pile of conspiracies—second gunmen, state police, vigilante retired federal police, presidents, dinosaurios, narcos—to end up back where they started, with Colosio the victim of a mentally ill lone gunman. Very few believed that; the labeling of Colosio as a Mexican JFK had a double meaning of tragedy and conspiracy.[109]

The assassination had major elite and public political impacts. The search for a replacement candidate revealed the PRI's major divisions and Salinas's tendency to go his own way. Right-wing governors and dinosaurios favored either the ex-director of the DFS Fernando Gutiérrez Barrios or Fernando Ortiz Arana, president of the PRI. Technocrats favored an economist such as Pedro Carlos Aspe, who had led both the Treasury and the Secretariat of Programming and Budget, or Emilio Lozoya. But both were ineligible, as constitutionally any candidate had to be six months out of office prior to the elections. Salinas instead imposed over considerable opposition yet another economist, Ernesto Zedillo. Zedillo's qualifications were expertise, a reputation for honesty, and a biography that made him the first candidate since Adolfo Ruiz Cortines in 1952 to come from outside the charmed circle of privilege: His father was a mechanic, and he had worked his way up through the Poli to Yale. Alongside intellectual affinity with the dominant economic model—his PhD was on the evils of Mexican debt—Zedillo's other qualification was his potential as another puppet. At forty-two he was very young. His immediate prior jobs had been as secretary of education, where his attempt to write some glaring nationalist untruths out of school textbooks caused a scandal, and as coordinator of the Colosio campaign. His biggest job, heading the Secretariat of Programming and Budget in the first Salinas years, hadn't left him many friends. He had no party base and wasn't much of a public speaker; the secretary of defense was rumored to have warned Salinas that "the army would not look kindly on the candidacy of someone who has characterized himself by his discourtesy with military personnel."[110] Zedillo was not beginning from a position of strength.

But while the choice of Zedillo turned out to carry major unintended consequences for Carlos Salinas, the greatest impact of the Colosio killing was public and systemic. It did away with the PRI's last reasonable qualification for office, the decades-long, partly substantiated image as a safe pair of hands, a one-party state whose civilian leaders, for all their flaws, knew how to manage the peaceful transition of power. After 1994 that was no longer the case, and in September there was more confirmation when two unknown hitmen killed the secretary-general of the PRI, José Francisco Ruiz Massieu. His brother, assistant attorney general Mario Ruiz Massieu, was put in charge of the investigation; he resigned within weeks, saying that high-ranking party members were obstructing his work.

By then Zedillo had won the August presidential elections running under the unintentionally mafiaesque slogan of *Por el bienestar de su familia*, "For your family's well-being." Turnout was the highest in years and Cuauhtémoc Cárdenas, the PRI's failed nemesis, came in a distant third. The Instituto Nacional Electoral, a new semi-independent body, found the elections fair in terms of voting and vote counting.[111] It had been less fair in terms of the financial and media resources available to the PRI, as Zedillo recognized, and the Banco de México had helped out by buying pesos to keep the dollar exchange rate artificially high. Voters able to buy foreign goods cheaply would appreciate that NAFTA had paid off and vote for its authors. But when investors compared this exchange rate to economic fundamentals and political violence, they began pulling out. Soon after Zedillo's inauguration the peso slid; an attempt to stabilize the devaluation at 15 percent failed, and it fell another 30 percent. When the Banco de México raised interest rates to draw back foreign investors, it caused everyday Mexicans and their businesses to default, bringing down several banks. Keeping the entire financial system from collapse necessitated a $65 billion bailout, much of which went to Mexico's private bankers. It was the last bill of the Salinas years: a deep recession and another transfer of public money to private allies.[112]

Some $50 billion came from Washington, and again it was conditioned on an austerity package of spending cuts, tax increases, and inflation-controlling interest rates. In 1995 1.2 million people lost their jobs, swelling the numbers heading north to the United States or eking out a living at the Mexico City traffic lights. Some took up their squeegees and washed windshields whether drivers liked it or not. Others breathed fire or juggled. Street kids formed and collapsed ambitious human pyramids and collected tips in the space of a single red light. Sunburned Mennonites in overalls sold their cheese. And alongside the street vendors' chewing gum a new keyring appeared, a big-eared Salinas cast in blue plastic as the Sorcerer's Apprentice, the Disney naïf whose clueless experiment brings the whole house crashing down.

Mexicans pinned the new crisis on the ex-president for more than hubristic foolery and failed magic. The 1995 collapse was also popularly understood, as previous devaluation crises had been, as a consequence of presidential corruption. Salinas had weathered corruption scandals while in office, most notably surrounding the privatization of state businesses, but the real threat came from his elder brother Raúl, an indiscrete bon vivant labeled the *hermano incómodo*, the inconvenient brother. He had made his way through Salinas's six-year term moving millions in and out of American and Swiss accounts, investing en route in some of Mexico's top businesses. This was nothing revolutionary: Presidents Alemán and López Portillo had done the same, and in far greater amounts. The difference was that Raúl Salinas's corruption involved rumors of narcos and killers, and in February 1995 the attorney general arrested him on charges of ordering the Ruiz Massieu hit.[113]

It turned into the greatest political scandal in Mexican history: a telenovela of money-laundering socialites, spiritualists, sex, drugs, and even rock and roll. The story unfolded across the press for years in all its sleazy glory. Ruiz Massieu had been more than head of the PRI; he had also been Salinas's ex-brother-in-law. Shortly after Raúl Salinas was arrested, Ruiz Massieu's brother Mario, the first head of the murder investigation, fled to the US and was arrested at Newark Airport for money laundering. Ex-President Salinas went on a brief hunger strike and then into exile in Dublin. (It was noted that Ireland had an appalling climate but no extradition treaty.) Raúl Salinas was accused not just of ordering the assassination, but also of disappearing his partner in crime, congressman Manuel Muñoz Rocha. On October 9, 1996, he seemingly reappeared as a mutilated skeleton on Salinas's ranch *El Encanto*, "The Spell." The police were guided there by a medium called La Paca, who said that she had felt "a bad vibe" emanating from the shallow grave.

La Paca was friends with María Bernal, Salinas's embittered Spanish mistress, whom he had dumped in favor of Paulina Castañon, a society figure on the rebound from dictatorial president Díaz Ordaz's son Alfredo, a music producer with a drug habit who had dumped her for the Mexican pop idol Thalia. La Paca was quickly unmasked as a fraud who had taken a bribe from the case's special prosecutor to disinter her father-in-law and reinter him on the ranch. In November Paulina Castañon (granddaughter of one of Mexico's more disreputable generals, the coup-plotting grafter Antonio Ríos Zertuche) fled to Switzerland, where she was arrested trying to withdraw $84 million from a numbered account. The special prosecutor himself fled, accused of witness tampering, only to be arrested in Madrid. A Swiss prosecutor identified the Salinas millions as the profits of money laundering for the cartels, "facilitated"—in the words of the US Government Accounting Office—by Citibank. It was breathless, compelling, hard to summarize; in January 1999 a Mexican judge somehow managed it and sent Raúl Salinas to jail for fifty years.[114]

The saga was more than titillating; it was a microcosm of the PRI in free fall, and it was rich material for Zedillo to use in breaking with both Salinas and the dinosaurios. In 1996 he reduced their power by mandating primaries, that decades-long goal of party reformers, for all candidates. He founded an independent Instituto Nacional Electoral to organize and monitor elections, well-funded, citizen-staffed, presided over by an admirably measured journalist, José Woldenberg. Certifying and if necessary investigating results was taken away from Congress and handed over to the Tribunal Electoral, a branch of the judiciary wholly separate from the executive.[115] Mexico City was taken out of the hands of the federal government, the presidentially appointed *regente* replaced by an elected mayor. In 1997 clean voting gave the job to Cuauhtémoc Cárdenas. (In the crowd that greeted him on election night in the Zócalo a parrot chanted, "One, two, three, *chinga su madre el PRI*," a call for the PRI to commit maternal incest that expressed considerably more emotion than the candidate himself.)[116] More than half the country's municipios went to the opposition. The PRI lost Congress; the PRD was allowed to win its first governorships in Zacatecas, Tlaxcala, and Baja California Sur. In 2000 they even formed alliances with the PAN to win Nayarit and Chiapas.[117] By then the only thing left to go was the presidency itself.

The race for president was gripping and nasty. A populist priista, Roberto Madrazo, lost the primaries to the Secretario de Gobernación Francisco Labastida, a feeble safe pair of hands. The PRD's primaries were so flawed that the party annulled them; they ended up choosing Cárdenas and in the bitter process lost his rival Muñoz Ledo, who ended up endorsing the PAN. The PAN in turn chose a foul-mouthed young Turk, Vicente Fox Quesada: a Coca-Cola executive who campaigned in cowboy boots, gave the PRI candidate a homophobic nickname, called the electoral tribunal swine, and cracked *ranchero* jokes. As a young congressman he walked out halfway through the president's state of the union address, telling reporters that he had better things to do, and besides, it was the only way he could get on TV.[118] He said "fuck" a lot. In the first presidential debate he told his priista opponent, "They might be able to stop me from swearing, but they'll never stop you from stealing."[119] Which was partly true: Labastida had been governor of Sinaloa, with all the narco baggage that suggested, and Fox could stop swearing when occasion demanded, a chameleon who could change rhetorical gear and talk like a gringo businessman. He combined impossible promises with earnest and uncomfortable policy proposals, like raising taxes. As a governor he had worked successfully with people ranging from a feminist to a conservative priista; he was an arch-pragmatist. The sum was a compelling candidate who appealed to unlikely constituencies, including some leftist intellectuals.[120] His own party was never keen on him, and his opponents disliked him viscerally, but President Zedillo stayed out of the entire democratic mess, and when polls closed on July 2, 2000, Fox seemed to be winning.

President Zedillo had been denigrated as a politically weak technocrat from the start, easy bait for the likes of Manuel Bartlett. He passed over serious abuses by the dinosaur governors of the South in Guerrero, Tabasco, and Chiapas. His predecessors had lost much of the labor vote, and the customary rent-a-crowd had shockingly begun filing out of his campaign launch before it was over, fans abandoning a flailing soccer team before the final whistle. The PRI's image was devastated by the devaluation and recession, and so were government budgets. His treasury continued picking up the bills for the crony privatization of the Salinas years.[121] Yet more worrying, for the first time since the 1940s the military had become unreliable. They allegedly came close to vetoing Zedillo's candidacy, the secretary of defense telling Salinas grimly that the armed forces wouldn't look kindly on his pick.[122] The day before the transfer of power Salinas said that Subcomandante Marcos was a force for moderation who should be taken seriously; on his subsequent flight home four fighter jets appeared out of nowhere, unordered, and engaged in close maneuvers around the presidential plane.[123] Across Zedillo's presidency generals used their counternarcotics role to expand their traditional power in the countryside; the extent of the President's control over them was never clear.

Yet despite these disadvantages Zedillo oversaw two major changes. He was a greatly underestimated social reformer, who moved money away from the PRI's traditional clients and toward the genuinely neediest. Development funding under Salinas had remained a tool of cooption, politically targeting battleground communities. Zedillo replaced this practice with two programs, PROGRESA for the cities and PROCAMPO for the countryside, which focused on ameliorating extreme poverty irrespective of the recipients' politics. Education funding was redistributed from universities to primary schools, less visible but life-changing for more Mexicans. The same approach characterized healthcare, where his administration increased the budget 11 percent and extended means-tested insurance outside the formal sector. The vaccination rate trebled; infant mortality dropped sharply. The program was knit together by direct cash transfers to 80 percent of the rural poor in exchange for school attendance and regular health checkups.[124] It foreshadowed Brazil's famous, globally influential Bolsa Familiar policy, Zedillo's perhaps less credited due to context: One was implemented by a charismatic trade unionist, Luiz Inácio Lula da Silva, the other by the technocratic leader of a collapsing one-party state.

Zedillo also managed the final steps of democratization. Salinas passed electoral reform out of necessity; Zedillo was a democrat by conviction. In three speeches the week after taking power he acknowledged that the recent electoral laws were insufficient and that Mexico needed "definitive electoral reform." He spelled out precisely what that meant:

> Party financing, caps on campaign spending, access to media, the autonomy, the full autonomy of the electoral bodies . . . our common aim has to be that the 1997 elections be unimpeachable and that we all emerge satisfied with their implementation, regardless of the results.

He met with the leaders of the PRD to tell them that unlike Salinas, who favored a centrist two-party system, he was convinced that Mexico needed a strong left-wing party to complement the PRI and PAN. In July 1996 the legislature unanimously passed constitutional reforms that met most of his declared aims.[125]

Zedillo was also critical for what he didn't do and what didn't happen on his watch. He couldn't maintain the consensus on reform all the way to cap campaign funding, and the PRI pushed through far higher (and for the richest and incumbent party, more beneficial) amounts. He didn't end state violence: The Acteal massacre was never cleared up, the army attack on the EZLN went against society's consensus for peace, and Governor Figueroa of Guerrero felt that he could get away with killing seventeen peasant protesters near Atoyac. However, the most egregious events came in the first months of the Zedillo presidency, as he struggled for policy autonomy. In the 1970s Figueroa's father got away with plentiful extrajudicial killings and disappearances; in 1996, by contrast, the Atoyac massacre pushed the governor out. Most of the Zedillo presidency was remarkable for what never happened. As the system disintegrated, there was no military coup, nor the army takeover of security and public sectors that lay ahead in the 2000s and 2010s. Zedillo left gubernatorial elections alone, believing central meddling undemocratic. At the end no last-ditch stand of violence, bribery, or election-rigging kept the PRI in power in 2000; unlike in that year's US election, no rioting lawyers blocked a vote count, and no partisan Supreme Court decided the result.

Instead Zedillo stayed out of the race even as the PRI's early lead vanished. The legacy of the Right's generations of grassroots opposition, of leftist activists sticking their necks out in the face of state violence and providing a critical intelligentsia, was realized. On election night early counts left the TV commentators of the old state television visibly shocked as they came out in the PAN's favor. The president told Fox, whom he cordially detested, that he believed he had won early on. He pressured Labastida to concede before any last-minute PRI fiddling, and as the official candidate resisted, Zedillo recorded a televised statement recognizing Fox's win. He ordered it broadcast as Labastida began his own speech, the one-party state's last president conceding the election from a desk beneath a portrait of Benito Juárez, the totemic president who consolidated Mexican independence and was also Mexico's first great liberal authoritarian. The symbolism was possibly more ambiguous than President Zedillo intended.

Chapter Twenty

Sex, Death, and Leaving Home

At the twentieth century's end about as many Mexicans lived in the United States as had lived in all of Mexico a hundred years earlier.[1] In 1900 Mexico was home to 13.6 million people, three-quarters of them in the countryside. By 2000, 100 million Mexicans existed there, three-quarters of them living in towns and cities.[2] That growth came despite the fighting, famine, and disease of the 1910s, which killed an estimated 1.4 million people.[3] In the following eighty years Mexico went from a set of small, rural societies with high birth and death rates to a big, urban society with low birth and death rates. When government and society began to see explosive population growth as a problem they ended it with speed and without totalitarianism.[4] Not even China went through such a dramatic revolution in its demography, adding so many people so quickly and then stabilizing so fast.[5] It was the greatest single change in modern Mexican history.

The population had grown very slowly for centuries. It is difficult to know just how slowly, because many Mexicans wanted none of being counted, rightly thinking that little good could come of it. (States, after all, count people so they can tax them.) The first census in 1795 was seen even at the time as an undercount; an 1808 estimate came up with 6.5 million Mexicans. Mexicans were having a lot more sex than their French or English contemporaries, according to Humboldt's scientifically prying eye; it was only natural "where there is a robust race of men incited by nature to marriage at a very early age." But the main reason for population growth in this period was a rebound from the disastrous 1780s, when smallpox, pestilential fevers, and hunger killed an estimated three hundred thousand people.[6] It was one of the deadliest decades in Mexican history; it was also a generational microcosm of the two eternal checks on the population, hunger and disease.

Nutrition was a constant challenge. Mexico has few rivers and fertile plains; most of the territory is mountain and dryland. Maize was exceptionally well adapted to terrain like this, a triumph of indigenous bioengineering, but even maize harvests sometimes failed. Some areas produced wheat on an industrial scale, but wheat was feebler than corn and failed with too much or too little rain. The topography that hindered agriculture also blocked long-distance food transport, so even when there was abundant grain in most places, the hungry found it difficult to get. There was only so much concerned churchmen or sympathetic administrators could do. And the powerful often didn't help: Transport taxes, the *alcabala*, were a major drag on food commerce (and continued to be until at least the 1950s, well beyond their official abolition). Meanwhile hacendados harvested fortunes by hoarding their own grain and buying up all they could in neighboring markets.[7]

Where the supply of water was more reliable, in the tropical lowlands, so was the prevalence of disease, the second great demographic check. Malaria and yellow fever made prolonged sojourns on the Gulf Coast or the Yucatán Peninsula lethal for outsiders. One nineteenth-century writer, a fairly sober Austrian botanist, claimed that two-thirds of European immigrants who stayed in the port of Veracruz were dead inside a year.[8] Casualty statistics from the French Intervention—or from the British in Haiti in the 1790s or the Spanish in Cuba—back up his somber estimate. The reporter John Kenneth Turner, writing in 1910, went further: Slavery in the tropical valleys of Oaxaca or conscription to Yucatán were, he proclaimed, death sentences.[9] The highlands were healthier but still home to the two most ubiquitous killers, malaria and tuberculosis, and vulnerable to the regional epidemics that until the 1940s came every generation or so.

Finally there were the great pandemics. They were global: In 1833 the cholera bacillus sped along the arteries of imperial trade, moving from Bengal to England and thence worldwide; in 1903 plague-bearing rats crossed the Pacific in ships from rebellion-torn China; in 1918 the Spanish flu, a new and deadly variant of the influenza virus, took the train south from the United States. But their local impact in Mexico was particularly brutal. Within a month of cholera's arrival in San Andrés Tuxtla, Veracruz, some two hundred were dying a day. About 40 percent of the entire town died, a far greater death rate than that of packed, filthy London when cholera struck that city.[10] Even in times of bacterial or viral peace, life expectancy was low by twentieth-century standards, as reflected in the biographies of the famous: Benito Juárez, Porfirio Díaz, and Lázaro Cárdenas all grew up fatherless.

Times of war brought worse. The revolution of the 1910s literally decimated Mexico, killing one in ten Mexicans, 1.4 million people. Hundreds of thousands more were "lost," in demographers' language, babies that would have been born in peacetime never materializing because potential parents were dead or diseased. War, famine, and epidemic took young men in particular, and while particularly prevalent in the main combat zones of the Center-North and Morelos, they afflicted most of Mexico. When a US consul in Yucatán reported, "Peace is raging down here, as usual," he was reporting an anomaly, the peninsula once again a different country.[11] In a third of Mexico's states, more than half the males alive in 1910 had disappeared by 1930. Neither was death picky about sex: In 1914 female life expectancy at birth was seventeen.[12]

The revolution caused few deaths from actual battles, particularly compared to the slaughter of the World War that was going on at the same time across the Atlantic. Mass executions made for ugly sights and stories: the three hundred hanged Villistas on the trees lining the streets of Ciudad Juárez, or the three hundred men whom a single Villista shot in groups of ten in a corral, telling them that anyone who made it over the fence would live. One did.[13] New technology eased the burden of mass killing; the dynamite-loaded locomotives called *máquinas locas*, mad machines, caused numerous casualties among soldiers waiting on station platforms or traveling on troop trains. Every element of war on the Western Front was there, bar tanks. Yet the lack of set-piece battles and trench warfare, the meat grinder of the European conflict, combined with comparatively small armies to keep military casualties low in Mexico. In 1916 more British soldiers died on the first day of the Battle of the Somme—nineteen thousand—than did Villistas during three months of battle in summer 1915.[14]

Instead the real killers of the revolution were disease and famine. In the worst years food supplies broke down and towns and cities, free from fighting, began to starve. In some places the Spanish were blamed, believed to be once more profiting from hunger. Some undoubtedly were, gachupines being prominent among food wholesalers; but farmers devastated by revolutionary expropriations or scared off from sowing would not have produced enough anyway. The train network, broken by armies seizing rolling stock and destroying rail lines, faltered in getting what food there was to market. In Mexico City the government introduced rationing cards, the literate scanned the papers for news of food shipments, lines sprang out of nowhere at food dispensaries, and some in the poorer barrios scratched for weeds to eat. Maize prices went up more than tenfold between the harvests of 1914 and 1915, twentyfold according to some estimates; the pinch-faced, skeletal needy collapsed in the streets and died.[15] In each of the years 1915, 1916, and 1918 roughly one in twenty inhabitants of Mexico City died. The survivors never forgot; as one put it, "Those who didn't live that year in Mexico City will hardly understand some things."[16]

The mortality was greater in provincial cities: In 1916 typhus killed a third of the population of Guanajuato.[17] Villagers could grow food but were defenseless against the pillaging hordes who took it—unless they formed militias, as Chihuahuans did to fight off Villista bands—and had little chance of buying it. When the 1917 corn harvest failed in the Nahua village of Acxotla del Monte, Tlaxcala, famine halved the population.[18] Disease and hunger spread outside the main warzones, affecting soldiers as well as the civilians whose animals they stole and whose grain stores they sacked. In good times eating well was a perk of joining up; in bad times revolutionaries suffered like everyone else. The Zapatistas who invaded northern Guerrero "arrived almost naked, thin from the lack of food. They opened the stomach of one of them who had died in Mexicapán and found nothing more than a few pieces of cactus."[19] As fighting tailed off in late 1918 the Spanish flu began. In Morelos whole villages filled with corpses, the survivors fleeing south; Coahuila's mines closed, the tight-packed, airless shafts lethally congenial to the virus; in the city of Zacatecas they stacked bodies like logs.[20] The revolution proved one of the most lethal wars in modern history. Mexico lost about as many people as did Germany in the First

World War, and far more relative to population.[21] It was the greatest population collapse of anywhere in the postconquest Americas.[22]

The mass dying of the revolution was the first demographic peculiarity of Mexico; the explosive growth that followed was the second. Mortality plummeted after 1920, while fertility remained high and constant. The result was the classic S-shaped population curve of a typical demographic transition. But the scale and speed were utterly exceptional. Between 1920 and 2000, Mexico's population rose 702 percent. The population of China, by contrast, only grew 246 percent.[23]

The population didn't just grow; it moved in huge waves across Mexico and northward into the former Mexican territories of California, Arizona, New Mexico, and Texas. Violence, hardship, and opportunity had already made numerous Mexicans into internal migrants at the turn of the twentieth century. Country people, newly landless or fighting to hang on to small family farms, traveled to earn wages in the new factories and industrial-sized fields. Some went permanently: The population of booming fin de siècle Coahuila trebled.[24] Many more moved seasonally. Poor, often indigenous smallholders and peons came from the mountains to the oil fields of the Gulf, from Michoacán to the tomato fields of Jalisco or Colima or the sugar plantations of the tierra caliente, from the highlands of Chiapas to the coffee farms of Soconusco, and from all over the Republic to the textile mills of Veracruz or Puebla.[25]

Migration shot up as the armed revolution laid waste to the states of Morelos, San Luis Potosí, Durango, and Chihuahua in particular, where set-piece battles gave way to guerrilla warfare. It pushed people toward new regions: The population of the state of Veracruz rose across the 1910s. Above all, people abandoned the dangerous, hungry countryside for the cities. Refugees swelled the populations of Guadalajara by 20 percent, Durango by 23 percent. They catalyzed a boom in the Valley of Mexico, where—in the face of food shortages, typhoid and even smallpox, which continued to kill thousands for decades—the Distrito Federal's population rose by nearly a third, eloquent of the greater horrors outside.[26] It seemed even more to the burghers watching the influx of pelados, peasants turning into capitalinos; one US journalist in the 1920s was told that the population had trebled.[27] It was the beginning of an extraordinary concentration of humanity in the capital.

Over the rest of the century three other trends emerged: Mexicans moved north, moved downhill into the tropical lowlands, and moved across racial boundaries as increased intermarriage changed the country's ethnic composition.

In the North many unskilled jobs arose in the newly irrigated fields of Baja California, Sonora, Sinaloa, and Tamaulipas that produced food for the United States. The Green Revolution, a global shift to higher-yield seed types along with extensive use of fertilizers and pesticides, came to Mexico first. US economic and demographic growth provided the motor for export sales; Sinaloan tomatoes began their lucrative travels to New York City in the depths of winter. New jobs were available in northern industry, and not just in Monterrey's existing factories and breweries—though the latter had done very well out of Prohibition; by the mid-1920s brands like Dos Equis were contributing more than a quarter of all Mexico's taxes on manufacturing.[28] In the late twentieth century a new species of factory sprang up, the maquiladora, assembly lines where shantytown workers from across Mexico took foreign-made components and pieced them together before returning them, sped on their way by tax breaks, back across the border.

The second move, downhill into the sweaty tropical lowlands, was another product of the postwar global boom. In the late 1940s Acapulco, long seen as a disease-ridden hellhole, was transformed into a glamorous tourist destination, its Hotel Los Flamingos a home away from home for Frank Sinatra, its charms broadcast by Elvis in the film *Fun in Acapulco.* The foreign tourists drew huge numbers of workers, who clustered in the colonias populares of the hills to service tourists on beaches. In the first two months of 1958 alone, five thousand squatters moved onto a single property, the Barranca de la Laja, forming an overnight slum of street vendors, shoeshine boys, waiters, chambermaids, and kitchen staff.[29] On the other side of the country the small town of Loma Bonita, Oaxaca, boasted four pineapple canning plants by 1952.[30] Such development was only possible because of a mid-century road-building boom, which connected remote places to international markets—Acapulco had no outside road until 1929—and by the retreat of tropical disease, in the case of malaria beaten back by an actual military campaign that drained swamps, distributed quinine, and sprayed DDT.[31]

A striking if hard-to-quantify shift also occurred in Mexico's ethnic makeup. An ascribed quality rather than an attribute, racial identity was eminently malleable, subject to the interests and biases of observer, respondent, and society at large. After 1921 the only national source for race statistics, the census, asked loaded questions regarding "cultural characteristics" instead of outright definitions. In 1940 and 1950 census takers asked Mexicans whether they wore shoes or sandals or just went barefoot; whether they ate wheat bread ("in the European way") or not; whether they slept in a bed or on the floor; and most salient, whether they spoke an indigenous language, and if so, whether they were monolingual. When choices in fashion and diet were taken off census forms after 1970, only language was left as a much-criticized but irreplaceable indicator of race.[32] Ethnic self-identification, allowing people to determine their own racial ascription, was only introduced in the twenty-first century. As for the third major root of the modern Mexican population, the African, it was glossed over completely until 2020.

Yet for all the uncertainty and conceptual caveats, the broadest of brushstrokes are clear: The history of race for the twentieth century was one of continuing indigenous decline, caused by higher mortality rates in indigenous communities and by intermarriage. In 1810 an estimated 60 percent of the population was indigenous, 3.3 million people, distributed in four and a half thousand *pueblos de indios*. Individual villages didn't disappear in the nineteenth century, the numbers staying constant since the seventeenth century; individuals and languages did, on a dramatic scale. By 1900 only 1.8 million Indians, 13 percent of the population, spoke an indigenous language.[33] The white population had been reduced by crossbreeding and outmigration from an estimated 23 percent to 10 percent. So mestizos were the new majority, forming an estimated 59 percent. The numbers, it will be noted, don't add up; but however inaccurate the estimates were in details, the shift was too large to miss, and it continued until a rebound of indigenous populations began at the turn of the twenty-first century.[34] Indigenous Mexicans, concentrated in the South, died younger and in greater numbers than their compatriots. The reasons were clear enough; as the Zapatistas said in 1994, *chiapanecos* had historically got "nothing, absolutely nothing, not even a roof over our heads, no land, no healthcare, no food nor education."[35]

These were big processes. Yet they were secondary compared to the greatest migration of the century, which was the exodus from the countryside toward the cities and the United States. The urban growth of the 1910s was never reversed; it continued and accelerated between 1940 and 1960, when for the first time more Mexicans lived in towns than in rural areas. In 1995 nearly fifteen times as many towns and cities existed as in 1900. Some, like Mexicali and Ciudad Juárez, were new cities, created by new industries out of nowhere. Others were newly important: The population of Monterrey, the industrial giant of the North, grew 4,000 percent across the century.[36] The government engineered tourist meccas—Puerto Vallarta, Ixtapa, Acapulco, and Cancún—using subsidies, infrastructure, publicity, and corruption. But urbanization was above all centered on Mexico City. In 1900 there were 344,000 chilangos; by 2000 the Distrito Federal alone housed 8.6 million, and its boundaries had blurred into the Estado de México, forming a conurbation of more than 20 million.[37]

The quality of urban life changed profoundly after 1940, as the nation industrialized and the towns and cities boomed. In the second half of the century urban Mexicans overwhelmingly worked for wages (both formal and informal) in shops, restaurants, factories, bureaucracies, markets, or on the streets. They bought food instead of growing it; they followed mechanical time—half the tenement dwellers in one study had wristwatches—instead of the sun or the church bell; they commuted to workplaces on buses or subway cars; when they got sick they sought out doctors more than healers. They bought consumer goods: The majority of tenement dwellers owned radios and over a fifth had television sets.[38] By the end of the century, the urban rich and the urban poor, even across the enormous wealth gap that separated them and across the apartheid that gap created, had more in common with each other than with their rural ancestors.

The social revolution of city life was founded partly on opportunity, both real and imagined. Mexicans were readier to move in search of better lives than before, and towns and cities seduced them with work and play. City life offered salaries, cheap consumer goods, better healthcare and schools. On a less noble note, it offered the seedy glamor of 1940s or 1990s nightlife—the dancers for hire in the cheaper dancehalls, *lugares de mala muerte*, the ask-no-questions motels on the Calzada de Tlalpan, the amphetamine-fueled abandonment of the Pervert Lounge—or the kitsch beauty of wrestling, the street theater called *teatro de carpa*, the subsidized movies, the sweltering seats on the sunny side of the bullring (*sol general*). The city sucked in all classes and groups. Tax breaks, infrastructure development, government subsidies, and artificially low food prices all served to concentrate industries there: By 1970 half the country's industrial workers lived in the central valley, and buses brought more commuting in from the Tlaxcala highlands.[39] They and the soaring numbers of administrators they dealt with created demand in other sectors, like construction, bringing in yet more migrants. Urban pioneers helped kin to follow in their footsteps. Migration to the capital was consistently led by women, often working as domestic servants—classic agents of modernization for the countryside—who brought families in their wake.[40]

The city remained a chimera for many. Even the government admitted it, adopting the slogan "Let's have fewer illusions" for a 1974 campaign to persuade people not to migrate to the overcrowded cities.[41] Government officials reported consistently low unemployment statistics, but they were just lying, and an enduringly large informal sector belied the promise of leaving poverty behind. Country people might move to the city dreaming of well-paid jobs; they stood a good chance of ending up the cannon fodder of urbanization, eking out marginal and unstable lives as street hawkers, pickpockets, or prostitutes. There were caciques in barrios just as in hamlets, and just like their country counterparts they used violence to control and tax the basics of existence for the luckless. In 1990s Mexico City, *Doña Loba*, "Madame Wolf," ran one poor municipio with an iron hand that grasped everything from the water supply to rubbish picking; she lived off, among other things, charging the poor to sift landfills, collecting recyclables ranging from empty cans to the stained cotton of diapers and sanitary napkins.[42] Life could be nasty and brutish in the tenements of poor neighborhoods like Doctores, or in the shantytowns that encircled Mexico City outside the great ring road of the Periférico.[43]

Yet it wasn't all that short. Life expectancy rose steeply during the peak period of urbanization, climbing from thirty-seven to fifty-nine years between 1930 and 1960, and the benefits of better access to clinics and hospitals in the cities canceled out the stresses of unsanitary overcrowding. Death rates were much the same for peasants and proletarians. Educational opportunities were far greater for the proletarians: In one tenement in Tepito, the centuries-old thieves' barrio, the average child spent nearly five years in school in the mid-1950s, and the children always had comic books to practice their reading. By contrast, in rural Veracruz, the origin of one tenement family's patriarch, only 2 percent of children made it into the fourth year; and Veracruz was a leader in provincial education.[44] Access to the benefits of healthcare, education, and public works required some initiative, a reality lampooned in the 1949 film *Puerta, joven* (*The Doorman*), in which the comic actor Cantinflas serenades a doctor to get an operation for crippled stunner Silvia Pinal, pays the fees by winning a horse race, and saves the barrio school by out-blustering a bureaucrat.[45] But migration and early urban life tended to self-select for those with initiative.

As for unionized labor, while real wages declined steadily from the 1940s onward, the state bought acquiescence not just with violence but also with cheap credit for housing, privileged access to the doctors of the Instituto Mexicano del Seguro Social (IMSS), and better educational opportunities.[46] Bureaucrats, railwaymen, and refinery workers enjoyed their own hospital systems; the children of textile workers in Ciudad Mendoza, Veracruz, attended a union secondary school that offered workshops, a theater seating two thousand people, and a twenty-five-meter swimming pool.[47] Until the lost decade of the eighties, even the people of the shantytowns were upwardly mobile, as local party bosses delivered stuttering gentrification in the form of water, electricity, and sewers to the *colonias populares*. Politicians had little choice. The sprawling urban populations became the strategic high ground of the postrevolutionary state, and they were willing to collectively protest collective mistreatment. Besides, endemic dysentery—in the 1940s less than one in four Mexicans had access to piped water—was uneconomic.[48]

Yet Mexicans were not just drawn to the cities; they were driven from the countryside. Population growth outran supplies of land and credit; governments gutted agrarian reform after 1940, adducing congenital low productivity.[49] Farmers' role was to send export crops to the North and cheap food to the cities, enabling workers to eat on the low wages that made industrialization possible. The government supported agribusiness through massive irrigation projects, such as the Balsas or Papaloapan dam systems, and through credit. They undermined ejidatarios and smallholders with price controls on maize and beans.[50] Capped maize prices were static across the 1940s; they dropped by a third between 1957 and 1973.[51] Things got even worse in the 1990s, when NAFTA allowed subsidized corn farmers in the Midwest to outcompete unsubsidized Mexican farmers, pulling down prices yet further. Mexican peasants were damned by both their own and the US government, by both state intervention and free trade. Industrialization and then globalization presupposed a massive and systematic transfer of resources from country to city. People followed, pushed out by poverty and unemployment, at times by hunger. In really bad years villagers took in their corn half ripe, while local authorities struggled to enforce colonial-style bans on corn leaving their districts.[52] Mexican cities, on the other hand, weren't as lethal as the early modern towns of Europe, slaughterhouses for an excess rural population, or England's dark satanic mills.[53]

President Echeverría's generous land grants in the 1970s were last efforts to correct some of the stark imbalances between countryside and city; they did not work particularly well, though, and were followed by the official end of the land reform program in 1991 and the inauguration of NAFTA in 1994. It is difficult to overstate the impacts of these imbalances. Peasant household income was statistically, judged one anthropologist, "not merely insufficient but ridiculous."[54] The Gini coefficient, which quantifies the equity with which national wealth is distributed, ran at an average of 0.56 between 1950 and 1968; in all Latin America only Brazil had less equitable wealth distribution. The only global region with anything like the same inequality was sub-Saharan Africa.[55] This extreme inequity in the distribution of national wealth was largely rooted in the poverty of Mexico's remaining rural population, subject since 1940 to a history of managed and foreseen decline.

Many Mexicans went north to the border and then kept on going for both political and economic reasons. The poverty of the 1900s combined with the opportunities of American economic growth—railroads, mines, agribusiness—to begin this great migration; the civil wars of the revolutionary years intensified it massively, the two phenomena driving about a million Mexicans across the border, huddled masses in strange new worlds.[56] The poet Rafael Buelna, Villista general by the age of twenty-four, ended up running a Mexican restaurant in El Paso. (It failed; the ex-Villistas he brought with him were better guerrillas than waiters.)[57] During the Cristero War, roughly twenty-five hundred monks, nuns, priests, and seminarians ran or were run out of the country. More than forty parishes in and around Los Angeles took in Mexican priests.[58] Elite Mexicans, like other rich Latin Americans, had long had a foothold in New York. Mass migration by the poor was something altogether new, and it lent the US the manpower to build modern cities and irrigated empires in the dry universe of the American Southwest.

Most migrants stayed within 150 miles of the border or the Pacific and worked on America's new latifundios. They picked cotton in the Río Grande valley, ran cattle in the rangelands from the Texas panhandle to the coast, and harvested grain in Arizona's Salt River Valley. At the beginning of the Great Depression an estimated quarter of Arizona was first- or second-generation Mexican. In booming California they grew vegetables in the Imperial Valley, picked almonds, grapes, and tomatoes in the San Joaquín Valley, and harvested lemons and oranges in the south. City-goers congregated in Los Angeles, San Antonio, El Paso, and Chicago. By 1930, sixty thousand Mexicans had turned El Paso from a village into a city of a hundred thousand; in San Antonio, longer established, eighty-two thousand Mexicans made up one-third of the entire population; Mexicans in Los Angeles, the largest of them all, trebled to ninety-seven thousand. The only major destination outside of the borderlands, Chicago, drew twenty thousand migrants, starting its journey to becoming one of the biggest Mexican cities in the world. The US Government census takers of 1930 registered 641 thousand Mexican migrants and a total first- and second-generation population of 1.4 million. And the men knocking on doors on April 1 only counted the people they found at home that day; it was, perhaps appropriately for April Fools' Day, a major undercount.[59]

Going was not a choice made lightly. Brown people were legally supposed to get a better deal than Blacks south of the Mason-Dixon Line, having attained full citizenship and exclusion from Jim Crow laws in the 1848 Treaty of Guadalupe Hidalgo. They were supposed to be free to ride in any railroad car they wanted, share restaurants, and vote freely if citizens, but as ever money whitened while its absence dragged people down the racial ladder. In South Texas, towns like Cotulla were segregated by the Missouri-Pacific Railroad tracks, and Mexicans on the wrong side of the tracks lived in termite-infested hovels on dusty streets, their lives defined by many of the problems they had tried to leave behind: grueling heat, landlessness, poverty, and pistoleros. Their children's teachers told them they could learn their way out, and then themselves left to move up the ladder. In Cotulla a young Lyndon Baines Johnson inspired as a teacher for nine months before going on to teacher training college and thence politics (a path any ambitious Mexican would have recognized).[60] New migrants heard the horror stories of powerlessness: the delousing with kerosene, the beatings, the labor recruiters who, like their counterparts in the old Mexican South, used wage advances to seduce the hungry into forced labor camps in Texas and the Arkansas Delta. Rather than encouraging its people to leave, revolutionary governments preached caution:

> Our Government does not forbid you from leaving national territory in search of better salaries, but it does try to prevent you from being perniciously exploited by labour contractors; brutally extorted by inhumane businesses; jailed in foreign prisons; fined by harsh authorities; and above all that, unable to obtain the protection of our Nation, be driven out poor and sick, as is currently the case for thousands of Mexican workers.[61]

With the coming of the Great Depression the migration reversed, and 423 thousand first- and second-generation Mexicans returned to real or imaginary homes. Some went voluntarily, helped on their way by Mexican consuls, subsidized railway tickets, and charitable relief. Others were rounded up and forcibly deported by local authorities in the US. Los Angeles County became notorious for indiscriminately detaining people who looked Mexican, including legal residents and US citizens, and shipping them over the border. In the early 1930s their places were taken by domestic refugees, "Okies," the people of the Great Plains driven west in their hundreds of thousands by sudden desertification. The Dust Bowl created a homegrown cheap migrant labor force for agribusiness; Mexicans became superfluous. Leaving the US, they were relocated by the Mexican government, in an attempt at state support, to often ill-considered areas: Some twenty returnees from industrial Detroit ended up in a doomed agricultural colony on the conflict-ridden coast of Guerrero. Yet the mid-1930s were also the years of promised land, agrarista rhetoric substantiated with massive redistribution. Part of that was a utopian plan to bring Mexican migrants home to farm their own plots, settlers with new skills learned in the North, walking nationalist testaments to the new society.[62] The landmark moment, the 1937 expropriation of large parts of the Laguna, made land available to everymen in a region that large numbers of their families had left.

During World War II, however, living conditions in the Mexican countryside worsened while in the US men went to war, leaving arms manufacturers, food producers, and railways understaffed.[63] To resolve the labor shortage the US began recruiting workers in Mexico under the Bracero Program, a state-run system that granted annual Alien Laborers' Permits to Mexicans to work as fieldhands and railwaymen. They and Rosie the Riveters made America's war economy work. The Bracero Program was highly successful, lasted from 1942 to 1964, and brought 4.6 million Mexicans north. En route it gave many families the skills and incentives for the next half century's intensive migration, both documented and undocumented.

Being a bracero was tough from the start. Migrants who turned up to the recruitment centers in the main cities and later along the frontier often slept in parks and streets while they endured long waits for contracts and demands for bribes.[64] Some were swindled, swapping bribes for permits they never got. Those workers who got jobs went by train to the border, where they were made to strip, examined, and sprayed with DDT for lice before being transported by ranchers to the work camps, where sixty-hour weeks were the norm and pay was suspended when rain stopped work. Such conditions made the program politically unpopular, a "National Shame" to one newspaper. Yet it was oversubscribed, particularly in the Center-North and Center-West. Nearly half of all braceros came from five states—Aguascalientes, Guanajuato, Jalisco, Michoacán, and Zacatecas—refugees from religious civil war and landlessness.[65] When the program ended in 1964, wages in that "emigrant heartland" were still beneath the national average.[66] The logic was clear: Many had little to leave behind.

So bracero permits were coveted resources that the federal government allotted on a quota basis to state governments, who passed the buck on to the municipalities, where local governments were supposed to distribute them by lottery to the landless. Village mayors often subverted the system, selling the permits or keeping them back for relatives and cronies. As one man put it in a protest letter, using some classic political insults of the time, his town council was a pack of "thieving vampires" and "scamming mafiosos" who had distributed permits not to farmworkers but instead to an assortment of the undeserving, including a pastry chef, a shoeshine boy, and a dredge operator. The individual deprivation that was supposed to be a factor in eligibility for permits was ignored and local priistas were enriched. Catholic opposition organizations joined in the crony handouts, sometimes through clout with sympathetic locals, at other times in tacit agreement to dispatch their dissidents north.[67]

Many would-be migrants without papers left anyway. Between 1945 and 1946 the Immigration and Naturalization Service intercepted 155,000 of them, nearly twice the number of registered braceros. In times of labor shortages or political conflict, the US positively encouraged the migrants they called "illegals"; in January 1954 the government announced that any Mexican who managed to cross the border would get a bracero contract, before making a volte-face in June and launching a deportation campaign, "Operation Wetback," to get rid of them.[68] The undocumented could face even worse conditions than the documented, and Mexican government circulars told village politicians to warn their constituents of the "grave consequences" and "serious dangers" of work that could approximate bonded labor.[69] Yet drastic

Competition for *bracero* permits was fierce.

warnings did little to stop the flow north. Some were driven by ambition. The first workers from Santa Ana del Valle, a Zapotec community in the foothills of the Sierra Madre, left in the 1950s and returned rich to set up businesses and climb the political ladder.[70] Others were driven by desperation, staggering into northern recruitment centers, "souls in anguish . . . all dirty, in rags, and starving . . . so weak that the strong Mexicali sun made them walk like drunkards."[71]

Most US employment, however exploitative, was preferable to life in a collapsing rural community, and the collective contract with the US government held protective clauses regarding wages and working conditions.[72] The Mexican government tried with some success to hold the Americans to their word, blacklisting abusive counties and entire states; Texas was more than once forbidden from receiving laborers.[73]

Yet the braceros whom one ne'er-do-well chilango met in the tomato fields of Southern California concurred that the United States was "*a toda madre*," "awesome."[74] The conservative Catholics of San José de Gracia found that the wages, bars, brothels, and health insurance made up for discrimination, hard work, and risk, and in some years as much as 20 percent of the male working population took crash courses in English and headed north.[75] So the number of migrants rose steadily, and leapt upward in the 1980s. By the end of that "lost decade" a majority of households in Santa Ana had at least one migrant; according to those who stayed behind, half the municipio of Ixcateopan, Guerrero, was in the United States.[76] Villagers tended to head together for the same places: *santaneros* to Santa Monica, *ixcateopenses* to Chicago, *poblanos* to the Bronx, and *zapotecos* to Los Angeles in big enough numbers to found a league for their idiosyncratic brand of basketball.[77] Where they went changed dramatically at the turn of the twenty-first century. Mexicans had traditionally headed to California, Texas, and the large cities of the Northeast, but in the 1990s they broadened their range and increasingly moved to the South. North Carolina's Latino population grew nearly 400 percent; Georgia's 1,000 percent.[78] By 2000 conservative estimates put the sum of permanent and seasonal Mexican migrants in the US at nearly twelve million.

Migration was lucrative for Mexico. Remittances became the second largest source of foreign exchange after oil, and once invested back home they multiplied: By the end of the century each migrant dollar produced another three in Gross Domestic Product.[79] Most braceros, moreover, did return home, and states like Jalisco, which received a disproportionate number of permits, saw a corresponding jump in development.[80] Yet the numbers braving the human traffickers ("coyotes"), the desert, and the looking-over-your-shoulder life as an undocumented worker were also an expression of the strains of the demographic boom.

Revolutionaries had debated from the outset the pros and cons of population growth. "Unlimited procreation should be avoided," admonished anarchist union leaders, and some of the more conservative revolutionaries like Vasconcelos agreed. The technocratic Calles did something about it, setting up three family planning clinics and distributing leaflets calling for abstinence and contraception. More revolutionaries were fiercely pronatalist, though, printing textbooks that equated large populations with national success, banning over-the-counter contraception, and offering prizes for fecundity.[81] Some went to totalitarian extremes: In 1938 the governor of Tamaulipas began taxing celibacy with payroll deductions for men over twenty-five who were single, divorced, or childless widowers.[82] By the 1970s the average mother gave birth to seven children, the population was rising at circa 3.5 percent a year—one of the highest rates in the world—and the economy had slowed from the gallop of the postwar years. Faced with this combination, the state abruptly changed policy. In 1974 President Echeverría passed the General Law on Population, establishing fertility targets, along with free family planning and contraceptives to achieve them. The government founded a National Population Council (Consejo Nacional de Población, CONAPO) attached to the powerhouse of the Secretaría de Gobernación. In 1975 Mexico City hosted the first major international women's conference; in 1977 and 1985 the capital hosted international meetings to discuss world population growth.[83]

Unlike most of the policies of the 1970s and early 1980s, Mexico's population planning was highly successful. Family planning services were offered to all Mexicans in the urban and rural health clinics that proliferated in the period. Government posters, television ads, and radio spots equated contraception with both social mobility and patriotism. Soap operas were pressed into service to help with those awkward conversations: In 1977 Televisa came up with *Acompañame* (*Come with Me*), in which the vampish Silvia Derbez pushed family planning five days a week at 9:00 p.m. The message was explicit, the publicity department promoting the series as "a great telenovela with profound social content, where education and family planning are the main topics."[84] By the 1970s, one Mexican historian noted, "Just like the French, certain methods of birth control, once used only in the brothel, [were] now also in the conjugal bedroom."[85] (Presumably he didn't mean the lambskin condom of an earlier century.)[86] There was a certain justice to this: A Mexican chemist, Luis Ernesto Miramontes, first synthesized the hormone on which the Pill was based.[87] Women took to contraception even in rural, socially conservative Catholic towns like San José de Gracia, where the Pill became commonplace.[88] And this was the third particular feature of Mexican demography in the twentieth century. Once technocrats, intellectuals, and governments started seeing population growth as a problem, they countered it faster and more effectively than in comparable countries.[89] This was recognized by the United Nations, which awarded Mexico a "population prize" in 1986.[90]

So Mexico's demographic history over the twentieth century was unique for the apocalyptic losses of the revolution, the unparalleled population boom that ensued, and the speedy and consensual fertility decline that ended it. The population growth might be explained by three structural rather than human arguments. In ecological terms Mexico had been underpopulated since the conquest: By the most optimistic estimates, central Mexico alone had been capable of supporting some twenty-five million people before the conquest.[91] The decimation of the revolution only increased this gulf between carrying capacity and reality, the large numbers of humans that Mexican soil could theoretically support and the small actual population. Given basic stability and modern economic development, rapid growth was inevitable.

Moreover, such growth was not exclusive to Mexico: It was structurally determined by global advances in medicine. Between 1879 and 1900 European scientists identified the microorganisms that caused some of the world's main diseases at a rate of one a year. Effective vaccinations followed for anthrax, rabies, diphtheria, typhoid, tetanus, and eventually tuberculosis. By the 1940s pharmaceutical companies had begun mass-producing sulfa drugs, a class of potent antibacterial medicines, and the first antibiotics. At the same time the great everyday killer malaria was curbed by mass production of quinine. Alongside it came a new and therapeutically significant understanding of the plasmodium parasite's life cycle. Village medics began identifying it as a cause of death, changing their recordkeeping to replace *calenturas*, sweats, or *fiebres*, fevers, with *paludismo*, malaria.[92] By 1960 infectious disease deaths were roughly half what they had been in 1931. That year malaria killed thirty-six thousand people; in 1970 it took only thirty-three lives across the entirety of Mexico, about as many as it might have killed in a single year in a single town a generation earlier.[93]

Finally, Mexico was distinguished from the rest of Latin America by its neighbor, the United States. Geography gave Mexico a comparative advantage in terms of investment, trade, and remittances, enabling Mexicans to marry younger and helping with the economics of supporting the ensuing population boom.[94] Migration offered some a way to avoid the worst extremes of hunger or want. Proximity offered privileges in terms of large-scale technical assistance and funding, even if the ends—diplomacy, public relations, the safety of occupying troops, the protection of the borderlands and South from contagion, and access to experimental human subjects—were in part self-serving. Americans, newcomers to the game of tropical imperialism, had been horrified by the scale of casualties from disease among their troops in Cuba in 1898 and Veracruz in 1914. So between 1921 and 1923 the Rockefeller Foundation spent $100,000 a year on a campaign in Veracruz that eliminated yellow fever; the malaria campaign was both funded and partly operated by the US.[95] Between 1947 and 1954 half of all US development funding for Latin America as a whole went to a campaign against foot-and-mouth disease in Mexican cattle.[96]

Yet human choices more than big structures made Mexican demography unique. The population boom was down to more than benefiting from global medical advances: Mexicans had begun living much longer before everyday lifesavers like antibiotics became commonplace. Instead, the infrastructure of nutrition and hygiene, democratic healthcare, revolutionary empowerment of women, and a compromise with the Church made Mexico different from everywhere else in the mainland Americas.

As in Europe and America, much of Mexico's mortality decline was the result of public health measures: governments pushing better hygiene, sanitation, and nutrition and laying down pipes for drinking water and sewage.[97] These were the obsessions of all stripes of revolutionary, from Calles to the village leaders who pestered their superiors for everything from water pipes to cantina latrines.[98] When cities built sewage systems, deaths from dysentery and typhoid halved.[99] When tax revenues were insufficient, governments used soldiers, chain gangs, or peasants forced into faenas, collective public works, a corvée tax that survived into the 1990s in the Solidaridad program. While the voluntary participation of the poor in all of these initiatives was often involuntary, they got the public works central to improving health on the cheap.

Federal governments also spent heavily and astutely on humble medical personnel: crash-course paramedics, medical interns, barefoot midwives.[100] Mexican leaders consistently decided, unlike their US counterparts, to invest uncommonly large portions of their budget in unglamorous but democratically effective healthcare for the poor. President Obregón set up a public health ministry in 1922 and incorporated healthcare into the educational missions that set off into the deep countryside. The Cárdenas administration pushed further these programs of *medicina social*, "socialized medicine." The agrarian reform that gave Mexicans better diets than before also delivered far better medical services. *Ejidatarios* went to permanent health units in their central offices for preventative and palliative care. This institutional infrastructure was key to the rapid implementation of malaria prevention and birth control. It was generously funded: Spending on health rose sharply, from 3.7 percent to 6.0 percent of the federal budget; mortality rates began to decline steeply; life expectancy soared.[101] In the US, by contrast, public spending on health declined as a percentage of GDP across the 1930s.[102]

Mortality decline was above all caused by plunging infant mortality. Comparative studies stress just how much such advances come from women's education and empowerment, how strong the correlation is between increased female literacy and declining infant mortality. Mexican women's access to those key first three years of primary school increased dramatically after Cárdenas. Eighteen percent of women born in the late 1920s completed elementary school; that figure rose to 73 percent for those born in the first half of the 1960s.[103] And Mexicans' improved reproductive health was not just the gift of a socialist or cosmopolitan elite: Grassroots feminist organizations across the country campaigned hard for maternity clinics in the 1930s.[104]

At the core of explosive population growth, in sum, lay a combination of phenomena common to several Latin American countries, but of peculiar intensity in Mexico: vigorous public health campaigns, persistent and astute popular mobilization for social development, rapidly rising women's autonomy, and generous state investment in education and healthcare. The same fusion of popular demand and comparatively competent state services was also behind Mexico's exceptionally rapid fertility decline. Everyday Mexicans had taken note of the strains of population growth before their governments had, and increased their use of birth control even when it was difficult to access: A 1965 survey from Mexico City's Hospital Inglés found that nine out of ten women accepted contraception.[105] Once contraceptives were freely available their use soared, from 30 percent of women in 1976 to 66.5 percent in 1995, a rate close to that of the United States.[106] The Total Fertility Rate (the average number of children a woman has in her life) plummeted: In 1970 it was 6.7, in 1981 4.3, and in 1996 2.7.[107] Women opted overwhelmingly for voluntary birth control, whether their husbands liked it or not.

This was in part because the Catholic Church, in stark contrast to elsewhere in Latin America, did not oppose intensive promotion of contraception. President Echeverría even claimed to have the sympathy of Pope Paul VI.[108] Parish priests, who contributed to revolutionary healthcare by promoting hygiene and preventive medicine from the pulpit, by and large kept their noses out of the whole question.[109] The national government corresponded by neither legalizing abortion nor reintroducing sex education. This quiet, pragmatic compromise was a legacy of Mexico's hard-won modus vivendi between church and state, whereby the Church kept social power and autonomy in exchange for public discretion and an avoidance of political involvement.[110] And so a drastic change in Mexicans' reproductive choices took place with little coercion or resistance. Some individual doctors pressured women to accept intrauterine devices or sterilization immediately after giving birth. Government publicity campaigns, on the other hand, stressed that women's reproductive choices were their own business. In India, by contrast, Indira Gandhi's Emergency government engaged in forced vasectomies; in China the "one child family" policy meant compulsory abortions and as many as twenty million forced sterilizations.[111] Both population explosion and fertility decline were strongly shaped by both Mexico's rulers and ruled, and owed heavily to revolutionary medical and land reform.

Mexico would have experienced a demographic transition under any conditions; that much was inevitable in the modern world. There were structural reasons for it to be an intense population boom. An important one was proximity to the US: a liability in the nineteenth century, an advantage at times in the twentieth. But the main reasons for Mexico's peculiarly large population growth and subsequent peculiarly rapid control of fertility lay in the choices of politicians and everyday people, and in their freedom to choose. Across Latin America countries that were significantly poorer than the Asian Tigers matched their public health records because of strong state commitment to goals like cutting infant mortality.[112] Mexico was unusually free-spending and smart in pumping resources into education, public health, and medicine, particularly under the leftist governments of the 1930s, 1950s, and 1970s. It was surpassed only by Cuba's revolutionary healthcare system, which followed the same precepts. The result was a population that multiplied sevenfold in eight decades. The structural impacts of that explosion were all-pervasive, ranging from the creation of one of the world's biggest cities to politicians' enthusiasm for neoliberalism in the 1980s. Fertility decline likewise showed the political impacts of social revolution at their most effective. Governments deftly forestalled Catholic opposition; broad provision of contraception was met with broad uptake, due to education and women's empowerment; the coercion of other countries' campaigns was largely absent. Shaping how and when people have sex and die is difficult anywhere. In Mexico, the revolution and its ghost produced a peculiarly successful demographic transition.

Chapter Twenty-One

Rupture

July 2, 2000, should have been the end of this history. The last words would have belonged to an unlikely trio: Ernesto Zedillo, the last president of the one-party state, promptly conceding defeat to forestall any attempts to fiddle the results; Vicente Fox, beaming out over a crowd at the Ángel de la Independencia at 2:00 a.m., saying, "Today we celebrate . . . tomorrow we work"; and Subcomandante Marcos, pointing out that he and Fox were diametrically opposed but had bad jokes in common.[1] On July 3, interviewees told journalists that they were waking up to a different and probably better world. Not everyone saw it that way, some bemoaning the fact that it had been a conservative Coca-Cola macho and not a leftist who had toppled the PRI. Barrio dwellers in Mexico City were soon telling an anthropologist that their lives hadn't changed much at all.[2] The singer Natalia Lafourcade wrote a song calling the new First Lady a racist worm.[3] When the new president proposed putting clocks forward for Daylight Saving Time the mayor of Mexico City refused, opening up the enchanting prospect of different time zones in the same city, of gaining an hour by crossing a street.[4] Most agreed, though, that democracy was like that, that the election had been a democratic one, and that Mexico was better off without the PRI.

Two decades on, the story looked different. Mexico had been at war for nearly fifteen years, a War on Drugs that looked more like a civil war. It was a war on three fronts: The army fought cartels, cartels fought cartels, and cartels fought civilians. Large numbers of combatants inflicted heavy losses on each other and civilians in battles for territorial, social, and even ideological control.[5] It was early to write drug history, and the standard thirty-year lag in opening even banal document collections made all administrative documents unavailable for the 1980s onward. Governments since 2000 had opened, closed, moved, redacted, reclassified, and re-released intelligence records, and aside from the sabotage that may well have happened en route, their chronological coverage ended in 1985 anyway. The US Drug Enforcement Administration (DEA) claimed that much of its archive had been lost when it moved out of its old headquarters above The Golden Eagle, a topless bar.[6] The Mexican Army denied that the most bureaucratically routine materials, such as state-by-state administrative reports, even existed.

What could be known by the early 2020s came from leaks and some very good investigative journalists and researchers. It was hard-won knowledge, because the attrition rate among journalists was high. Between 2006 and 2020 more than one hundred were murdered, making Mexico one of the most dangerous places in the world for reporters. It became something of a cliché to describe Mexico as second only to Iraq in terms of risk to journalists; by 2020 that wasn't true anymore, because Iraq was safer.[7] The effect on press freedom was chilling, but despite that, stories came out on who was killing whom, and why, and which politicians, soldiers, and policemen were complicit, bought, or threatened off. Sometimes these stories brought the guilty down. In 2019 the secretary of public security in the administration that started the war, Genaro García Luna, was arrested in Dallas for taking millions of dollars of bribes from the Sinaloa Cartel; *Proceso* magazine had run some one hundred articles on his links with the narcos since 2005.[8] More often journalists ran up against the limits of the knowable, in a shadowy world of conspiracy, gossip, and fear where most stories were believable and few provable.

The case of Javier Valdez Cárdenas epitomizes the difficulties of knowing. Valdez was a prize-winning Sinaloan investigative journalist who was taken out of his car and executed in Culiacán in May 2017. He had covered the Sinaloa Cartel extensively in the weekly he cofounded, *Ríodoce*, and the assumption was that they had killed him; an article he had published had peeved one of El Chapo's sons. No one claimed the killing, though, and different explanations began doing the rounds, centering on the idea that Valdez had been the victim of a political, not a criminal, assassination. That wouldn't be anything new: By some estimates about half of all journalist murders were ordered by politicians, not narcos. Valdez himself had been writing about it. He said that he was more afraid of politicians than drug gangs, and his last column was about a corrupt congressman murdering a journalist. And a third, yet more conspiratorial theory circulated: He had been killed not because of any article he had written or was ever going to write but just to embarrass the governor. Valdez was famous enough for his murder to cause a scandal and distract the incumbent from investigating his predecessors for corruption. Whether the twisted explanation was true or not is of less analytical importance than the fact that it might well have been, and there was no way of knowing for sure.[9]

Some things, though, were evident. Between 2006 and 2020 the War on Drugs killed more than two hundred thousand Mexicans.[10] About one hundred thousand more disappeared or were disappeared.[11] Another two hundred thousand became refugees, according to the UN—many more according to asylum claims.[12]

Meanwhile, the consumption of cocaine in the United States, the main reason for the War on Drugs in Mexico, increased year by year after 2011 as it got purer and cheaper. So did the use of methamphetamine and heroin.[13] Undisclosed additions of fentanyl made them all more dangerous. Between 2010 and 2020 the number of Americans using illegal drugs went up 50 percent.[14] Overdose deaths from cocaine and heroin more than quadrupled.[15]

The business of getting recreational drugs to American consumers took provincial Mexico back to the mass dying, child soldiers, and everyday atrocities of the revolution. Some narcos enjoyed brutality for its own sake, psychopathic successors to men like the Villista Rodolfo Fierro or the pistolero Crispín Aguilar. In Tamaulipas, members of the Zetas cartel took 193 people off buses near San Fernando and killed them at a ranch called La Joya; before they killed them, they raped the women and made the men play gladiator, fighting each other to the death with machetes, clubs, and hammers.[16] Street kids and kidnapped children, if taken young enough, could be desensitized to others' suffering. El

Ponchis, a prepubescent hitman who tortured and decapitated prisoners and posted the videos on YouTube, started age eleven.[17] By 2011 an estimated thirty-five thousand minors were working for drugs gangs.[18] Revenge was another motive for atrocity, a spiral of retribution and escalation that characterizes civil war. And beyond pathology was the strategic logic of staging gruesome death, standard issue in conflicts from Colombia to Afghanistan: The greater fear that performative murder causes makes it more effective than simple killing to deter rivals and control civilians.[19] In Mexico a new tool, social media, increased the terrorist leverage of attested painful death.

As in the civil wars of the Mexican Revolution, the majority of the dead in the War on Drugs have been civilians, collateral damage in the fighting among cartels and between narcos and the security services. It hasn't been all about drugs, though: Alongside political violence, which the War on Drugs has enabled and helped cover up, paramilitary criminals in the 2010s broadened their portfolios, expanding into robbery, kidnapping, extortion, human trafficking, forced sex work, and illegal logging and mining. Migrants were easy pickings, the Central American ones vulnerable to arrest as soon as they crossed into Mexico or were deported from the US, and narcos price gouged them, taxed them for the right to cross their territories, or forced them to act as drug mules or sex workers. Migrants were readily disappeared; one early Zeta mass grave near the Texas border contained seventy-three bodies. By the mid-2010s many smaller gangs were earning more from this kind of rent-seeking than from drug production or smuggling.[20]

For Mexicans, consequently, civil-criminal relations were a catch-22. When cartels fought for turf, noncombatants suffered the violence of armed conflict. When one side achieved victory and a rough peace, on the other hand, its constituent local gangs forcibly recruited civilians, stole with impunity—it was safer and cheaper than long-distance shipping of drugs, and provided a steadier income stream—and charged for the *derecho de piso*, an informal license to operate. If drug taxes went unpaid—a local furniture maker having a bad month, a trucker's vehicle needing expensive repairs, a car mechanic getting injured, a child needing an operation—then threats, beatings, kidnappings, and killings followed. Small businessmen became the most frequently targeted group in provincial society.[21] A majority paid. That, however, opened them up to reprisals when rival gangs went to war. When the Cártel de Jalisco Nueva Generación (CJNG) went after its competitors in Ciudad Hidalgo, Michoacán, it publicly announced:

> Anyone found making payments to and backing the filthy *Correas* or *Familia Michoacana* will suffer consequences and very grave ones . . . first and only warning. Anyone who ignores it will have a response from us in the next few days.[22]

The leaders of CJNG were part of a new, post-Zetas generation less concerned with the diplomatic side of earlier drug organizations. The once-upon-a-time, sedulously cultivated Robin Hood image—the grim-looking Pablo Acosta distributed photos of himself hugging a young girl whose eye operation he paid for—was hard to sustain in times of war and shadow-state terror.[23]

The petite bourgeoisie, migrants, peasants, and the urban poor weren't the only ones vulnerable. The fight for control of the avocado export industry killed numerous ranchers, laborers, members of cooperatives, and community self-defense force members. This too was rational choice: Between 2016 and 2020 the business took in more than $2.5 billion a year. As early as 2009 the Knights Templar, an eccentric Michoacán cartel, raised an estimated quarter of a billion pesos in extortion payments from avocado growers; this was equivalent to over a third of the Michoacán state government's tax revenues.[24] It was also another case of drugs detonating a broader social conflict, based on preexisting tensions. Avocado cultivation had boomed in the 1990s, as ejidos were privatized and NAFTA opened a whole new market. Avocados replaced traditional small-scale crops such as maize, coffee, marijuana, and poppy. Ranches and large estates grew at the expense of small farmers, who went from being landowners to laborers. Poverty and inequality also grew.[25] When drug gangs arrived, local communities formed *autodefensas*, community vigilante groups that were legatees of the agrarian militias of the revolutionary period. They were partially effective in repelling narcos; they also themselves became implicated in intercommunal violence, like some of their ancestors, and they were also unsafe. As with the *defensas sociales*, their leaders were often killed.

Even students seemed fair game to those with short memories. In 2014 narcos, local police, and soldiers disappeared forty-three trainee teachers from the Escuela Rural Normal de Ayotzinapa, the revolutionary college in Guerrero that had turned thousands of impoverished country people into maestros rurales (among them the guerrilla leaders Lucio Cabañas and Genaro Vázquez). The students had gone to the city of Iguala and hijacked three buses to get to a Mexico City commemoration of the 1968 Tlatelolco massacre. The dominant drug gang in Iguala, Guerreros Unidos, mistook their trip for an offensive by a rival gang, Los Rojos. (They may also have had a heroin shipment aboard one of the buses.) Consequently, when the local police arrested the students and handed them over to the Guerreros Unidos, its leader told his men to err on the side of caution and "kill them all, [because] Iguala is mine." Six survivors of the initial murders were handed over to the colonel of the 27th Infantry Battalion, who after a couple of days killed them too. The narcos dismembered and burned their victims and disposed of them in various places—a river, a well, a mine—only to dig them up and rebury them elsewhere when the case became a scandal. Some remains were supposed to have ended up on the 27th Infantry Battalion's base; like the overwhelming majority, they were never found. The attorney-general at the time, Jesús Murillo Karam, came up with a version of events, based on tortured witnesses, that left the army out altogether. Eight years later he was arrested for his part in the affair.[26]

In extremis, cartels took over entire cities. In October 2019 the army arrested Ovidio Guzmán, one of El Chapo's sons, in Culiacán; gunmen immediately moved in, made blockades of burning cars, and drove out the security services with machine guns and Barrett sniper rifles. Twenty-nine people died in the *Culiacanazo*, "Black Thursday," before the government released Guzmán and the narcos pulled back. When, years later, the government dared a repeat operation, they came with Blackhawk helicopter gunships.[27] And Sinaloa, securely controlled by the oldest and largest cartel, was one of the safer states for everyday people. The Sinaloans shared a duopoly of violence with the government security services, an arrangement that at its most functional made them a parallel state. They didn't just tax; they took over entire businesses. But they also provided some social regulation, including policing against street criminals and kidnappers. In some areas (with some irony) they provided protection against corrupt taxmen and health inspectors.[28] They also had better public relations, astutely using false flag operations, plausible deniability, and propaganda to cast themselves as the most socially concerned of narcos. In 2010 one of the two founders, Ismael "El Mayo" Zambada, gave Mexico's main news magazine a chatty, candid interview; in 2016 the other founder, El Chapo, gave one to *Rolling Stone*.[29]

The most dangerous regions were those without a single dominant cartel. There had always been competition for *plazas*, politically sanctioned trade routes, but in the twentieth century the competition was moderated by territorial demarcations that were accepted and policed by politicians and the cartels themselves. The most lucrative zone, the border, was divided among coalitions that answered to the Sinaloa and Tijuana Cartels in the Northwest, the Juárez Cartel in the center, and the Gulf Cartel in the Northeast. The pattern was similar to crime organization territories elsewhere: As with the Five Families of the Mafia in New York, stability was better business than violence, and so periodic wars were the exception rather than the rule. Politicians were bought off, communities too with some redistribution of drug wealth to the poor, providing social services where the state had faltered or just been disinterested. That too was good business. Drug violence was ever present and increased toward the end of the century as profitability rose. Yet it was of a wholly different scale and quality than what came next, a forever war between cartels and the state.

The old organizations split, and with the exception of Sinaloa declined or went under to new combinations of gangs. In 1997 the Gulf Cartel set up a paramilitary wing, the Zetas, whose first soldiers were all former Mexican Special Forces. In 2010 they rebelled and seized plazas for themselves. While the Gulf Cartel was busy on multiple fronts, the Sinaloans moved east against the Juárez Cartel and south against old allies on the Pacific Coast, the Beltrán Leyva brothers. Soldiers, fighting all of them, were ineffective or bought off. In Michoacán, a center of violence and rapid turnover between cartels, the army started using helicopters to resupply their bases. Narcos controlled transit with systematic roadblocks and IEDs, improvised explosive devices. Some IEDs went airborne, commercial drones carrying payloads of

C-4 explosives and ball bearings. In Tamaulipas, just one Zeta convoy of several that attacked the city of San Fernando in 2010 numbered forty-nine vehicles: improvised armored personnel carriers, pickups mounting machine guns, and an adapted school bus.[30] The logic of fission applied to them too, however, and by the end of the 2010s the Zetas had lost much of Mexico to CJNG.

Some of the soldiers that narcos fought became predatory empire builders themselves, another return to revolutionary days. Major government infrastructure projects such as the new terminal at Mexico City's airport or the tourist train in the Southeast were handed over to the Secretaría de la Defensa Nacional, to the personal benefit of personnel from the ground up.[31] Generals were convincingly linked to specific cartels and occasionally prosecuted: In 2012 the former undersecretary of defense Tomás Ángeles Dauahare was arrested, as was the former secretary of defense, the head of the armed forces General Salvador Cienfuegos, in 2020.[32] It was the Americans who arrested Cienfuegos, and it was a major diplomatic gaffe that Mexico forced them to reverse by threatening a complete withdrawal of security cooperation. He was released and left alone, like most of his colleagues.[33] Impunity was furthered by the army's takeover of civilian policing: In 2019 the Federal Police was replaced by a paramilitary Guardia Nacional, part of the Secretaría de la Defensa Nacional, its men and women—80 percent of them ex-military—subject to martial rather than civilian law. The national spy agency, the Centro Nacional de Inteligencia, was supposed to be civilian, but in 2018 it was taken over by a general, Audomaro Martínez Zapata, who appointed army officers to run key departments. The exception was the main coordinating unit, the Centro Nacional de Fusión de Inteligencia, which was run by Luis Rubén Sandoval Medina, a civilian. His father was General Luis Cresencio Sandoval, the head of the army.[34]

Drugs, not elections or economic reforms, were thus the main determinants of the new democratic Mexico. This was ironic, because drug consumption had never been a public health problem inside Mexico. When the War on Drugs started in 2006 Mexico was in the bottom 20 percent of cocaine-using countries. Nearly one in six Americans had tried cocaine at one stage or another. One in forty Mexicans had done likewise. One in a thousand had an opiate problem. Combined illicit drug usage in Mexico was about a third the global average.[35]

This was not a supply-side problem. Coca bushes are fussy, preferring terraced hillsides at medium altitudes in damp, semitropical climes, and Mexico, unlike the Eastern Andes, doesn't have many of those. Neither was there any tradition of indigenous coca leaf use. Yet neither obstacle mattered, because from the 1980s onward enough processed cocaine was traveling from South America to the United States to meet any potential Mexican demand. There were several native psychedelics—psilocybin mushrooms and ololiuqui seeds in the central highlands, peyote cactus further north—which had long and rich indigenous histories, but they were niche products. The only cultivars to really take off across the twentieth century, providing between them enough domestic narcotics to satisfy the most demanding of societies, were poppies and cannabis.

Poppies were recent imports, linked to Asian immigration in the late nineteenth century and the hard work of German chemists at Bayer, who in 1895 invented heroin. Marijuana, another Asian drug, had a longer history; it migrated with the Spanish to Mexico in the sixteenth century. It was essential technology, its fibers the basis for the hemp ropes and sails that all ships needed, and the Crown ordered the colonists to cultivate it. Once the start-up problems of a lack of seed were overcome it wasn't difficult: Cannabis was happy in all sorts of soils, climates, and altitudes. It enjoyed being near humans, with their sunny cleared fields and fertilized soils, but it was also an adventurous traveler, sending seeds and pollen long distances on the wind to grow on stonier ground. Its place in polite society, however, was uncertain. Even as the Crown sought rope, its officials and churchmen chastised the Nahua for eating a psychoactive herb called *pipiltzintzintlis*, which turned out to be a product of the same cannabis plant. After Independence marijuana became associated with jailhouses, soldiers, and violent psychoses; during the Revolution General Huerta was insulted for being not just an alcoholic but also a stoner.[36]

In this stigmatization of marijuana, modernizing Mexico was ahead of the rest of the world. The main Western powers of the nineteenth century were blithely unconcerned about the trade in drugs: The British went to war in China (twice) to protect their right to sell opiates to the Chinese, while US consumers could in the early 1900s buy heroin by mail order from Sears Roebuck.[37] But this attitude shifted around the turn of the century. The widespread use of morphine on the battlefields of the Civil War and Cuba created a generation of addicted veterans; at the same time, growing US puritanism opposed any and all social drugs; finally new sources of migration, especially Mexican and Chinese, led to the rhetoric of drug use as "a racial problem." Mexicans were dangerous degenerates because of their use of marijuana, the Chinese because they used opium, Blacks because they used cocaine. Whites who used these drugs might take their race down the same paths.[38]

Consequently, in 1909 the US government began criminalizing various narcotics until it arrived at the Volstead Act of 1919, the legislation that introduced the Eighteenth Constitutional Amendment, banning alcohol. By the early 1920s all social drugs were illegal in the US. Demand, on the other hand, remained strong, and so supplies started to flow north across the Mexican border. Prohibition fueled the explosive growth of beer production in Mexico, which ended the 1920s as the country's second most profitable manufacturing industry.[39] The ban on other drugs opened up an entirely new cross-border trade in marijuana, brought transoceanic opium shipments into Ensenada and Tampico, and drove entrepreneurial farmers in the mountains of Sinaloa, Durango, and Chihuahua to start growing their own poppies.

Mexican political and cultural reactions to this new business, one more in a long line of shady border businesses, were complex. Puritanical northern revolutionaries wholeheartedly shared their US counterparts' ideological enthusiasm for proscription. Prohibition came to both countries' states in the mid-1910s—1914 in West Virginia, 1915 in Sonora and Yucatán. In Mexico City there was even an attempt to outlaw pulque.[40] Revolutionary politicians bemoaned the damage that alcohol and drugs inflicted on society; Carranza banned opium imports in 1915 because they "seriously damage[d] society."[41] Some shared the Lamarckian racial thinking of their northern neighbors, the idea that acquired characteristics—in this case the debilitating, morally corrupting effects of drug taking—were heritable. Mexico's

1920 law banning marijuana was called "Dispositions on the Cultivation and Commerce of Substances That Degenerate the Race."[42] In 1923 Obregón sent the embryonic air force to the US border to interdict drug exports and declared a fifty-mile dry zone on the Mexican side. Soon afterward the government banned the import and export of all nonmedical narcotics, and in 1926 it banned the domestic cultivation of poppy and trade in opium.[43]

But business imperatives trumped the aspirations of a weakened state. While border politicians used the new income from drugs to enrich themselves, they also used informal taxes on narcos for reconstruction and development. In the 1910s the governor of Baja California, Esteban Cantú, charged Mexicali's main Chinese opium syndicate $10,000 per month for protection and spent the money on public goods: new roads, drinking water, drains, rubbish collection, and a postal service. He made education compulsory until the age of fourteen and built the schools to make law reality. Enrique Fernández, the first major narco in Ciudad Juárez, spent money on rural schools, playing Santa Claus for the children of the poor and paying for their parents' funerals. The man who ousted and murdered him, Governor Rodrigo Quevedo, promised "to transform the state of Chihuahua with gambling, whores, and addiction." The pioneering Cantú was notoriously honest, keeping himself afloat after the glory days with a series of humdrum bureaucratic jobs. Quevedo and his ilk were not. All, however, used drug money to pay for roads, hospitals, and schools that would have otherwise gone unbuilt. It was a mixture of criminal entrepreneurship, high-quality development, and populist redistribution that set a pattern for drug dealers across much of the century.[44]

This was not the only lasting pattern from the early days. The first narcos pioneered most of the global routes out of or through Mexico and into the US. In the Northwest muleteers brought opium down from the mountains of Durango, Sonora, and Sinaloa to the ports of Mazatlán and Ensenada, where it added to the Hong family's transpacific shipments. More came from Europe via the Panama Canal.[45] Some drugs took fishing boats up the coast to California; others went by land, first through Mexicali, later Tijuana; others traveled over Ensenada by plane at night.[46] Smugglers used the same technologies on the Gulf Coast: Drugs came in by steamers from South America,

Europe, and Asia and went out by plane or ship. In the early 1930s the American oil tanker *Dungannon* made ten trips in a year from Tampico to ports in Texas, Virginia, Delaware, and Rhode Island, taking drugs each time.[47] In the center, drugs clustered at the rail hub of Torreón, where lines from Durango, Tampico, and Mexico City converged, and then went north to Juárez. When the Pan-American Highway was finished in the mid-1940s it followed the same route.[48]

Drugs came to be cultivated across much of Mexico as the business developed, but the main opiate production zone—the "Golden Triangle" of Sinaloa, Durango, and Chihuahua—also dated back to the thirties. It covered ten municipios in the Western Sierra Madre, mountainsides punctuated by forests and deep valleys, watered by rain-bearing clouds from the Pacific, a place difficult to cross but close to ships, railways, and roads going east into central Mexico and north to the US. Retail drug busts in the markets of Mexico City or the nightclubs and pharmacies of Juárez were straightforward. Production was a different matter: To burn the poppy fields of the Golden Triangle, soldiers had to struggle against terrain and the early warning systems of the locals. If they reached them, they often found the harvest already reaped, the trip a waste of time. The poppy, like any good weed, sprang up again next season.

Yet by the standards of the future, or contemporary production zones like Turkey, Mexican growers were small-scale. World War II increased demand and cut off Asian and European producers, leading to a minor boom: In 1944 Mexican soldiers and US customs officers destroyed a six-hundred-acre poppy field with a sophisticated irrigation system in Durango. (The raid foreshadowed the future in more than one way; the growers were tipped off and brought in their harvests before the soldiers arrived.)[49] Opiate industrialization was ephemeral, however, foreshadowing the ease with which drug routes could shift, because when global smuggling hubs like Marseilles, Hong Kong, and Naples came online after the war, Mexico's international importance dropped precipitously. Old World white heroin was of far greater quality than Mexico's black tar heroin. In 1948 customs agents on the California border seized only six pounds of opium; by 1952 the Customs Bureau there was more worried about an illicit trade in sick parrots.[50]

A few of the leading families of the future emerged. In the small town of Badiraguato, the center of opiate production and export out of the highland poppy farms, the fathers and uncles of a couple of the great cartel founders were getting into the business. Their day came decades later, though. The best-known traffickers of the time were big fish in small ponds. The heroin dealer Ignacia "La Nacha" Jasso founded a family business that lasted into the 1970s but never left Juárez, and continued to live modestly even when she was a rich and distinguished local citizen, president of the committee for free school breakfasts and a board member of the Escuela Benito Juárez. Lola la Chata, another famous female narco of the mid-century, foreshadowed later cartel leaders: She had a diverse portfolio, spanning hash and heroin; was a public figure, well linked to the police (her husband was a former policeman, and cops formed a substantial contingent at her funeral); and was capable of conducting business in some comfort from within federal penitentiaries. Brought to trial, she pointed to the philanthropic work she'd done in the community. Yet when she was arrested she had a mere $9,000 in cash in her house, a pittance by subsequent standards. For all the patterns laid down in the first half of the century, the drug business was in those years a cottage industry.[51]

Mexican governments were nevertheless concerned about the health impact of drugs, and from the 1930s onward they adopted three coherent policy approaches: accommodation, harm reduction, and eradication.

Accommodation was the first and most venerable. Regional governments like those of Sinaloa and Chihuahua worked smoothly with growers and traffickers to maximize profits and minimize risks. The main politicians and policemen were narcos themselves; Governors Rodrigo Quevedo (Chihuahua, 1932–1936) and Rodolfo Loaiza (Sinaloa, 1940–1944) led the way. The Sinaloans unofficially prohibited the in-state retail of the heroin they made; the trade was only socially acceptable when it was wholesale and export. The World War II opiate boom took the Sinaloa state government overnight from debt to surplus, and alongside their conspicuous consumption its members also built numerous rural schools. Politicians from a single-party state could control the drug business, licensing production and trade routes to gangs that generated profits and stability.

Harm reduction was founded on a philosophical acceptance of the inevitability of some drug use in any society. By the late thirties the government was making serious and sustained attempts to treat drug retail and consumption as a medical rather than criminal problem. They differentiated between different drugs and adopted different approaches. Marijuana, for all its panic-inducing history, was recognized as a sideshow, in the view of one astute policymaker less damaging than tobacco. Cocaine was a rare beast, sold in luxury brothels in Mexico City.[52] Opiates were a different matter. Mexicans injecting in Mexico City markets or Ciudad Juárez shooting galleries were harming themselves and society, yet they too were understood as unstoppable. Up-and-coming doctors persuaded politicians to respond accordingly, founding a rehab clinic and leaving drug policing to the Ministry of Health. In 1939 the Cardenista government took the logical next step of setting up cheap morphine clinics, managing harm to addicts and reducing profits for retailers. In 1940 they argued for this generally effective approach on a global level at the League of Nations and were vehemently shut down by the US representatives, who told them that users were "criminals first and addicts afterwards."[53]

In 1947 much the same US drug delegation went to the UN Commission on Narcotic Drugs and bullied Mexico away from medicalized policy and toward eradication and interdiction, and in 1948 Mexico deployed the army for the first time in a national campaign.[54] Sending soldiers and federal policemen into the deep countryside to find and destroy marijuana and opium fields became a permanent program, taking up four to six months a year, and not just in the Golden Triangle; by the end of the 1950s they were burning fields in several states, from Baja California to Yucatán. The Secretaría de la Defensa Nacional claimed that they were reaping remarkable results, hundreds of fields burned in campaigns covering thousands of miles. Deployment records gave them the lie: Up until 1954 they never committed more than half a battalion to the job, less than 1 percent of the army.[55] While soldiers took the field for four to six months of the dry season, the best growing areas were giving three harvests a year, including one in the rainy season. The quality of eradication was questionable too. Burnt fields were often harvested beforehand, major plantations bypassed. But the new militarized approach was a restatement of what the US thought

Mexico's role in the international drug trade should be. Americans' recreational drug taking was Mexicans' responsibility, and they were duty bound to use their budgets, police, courts, and soldiers to live up to it.

The Mexicans were never going to succeed because they shared a two-thousand-mile land border with the US, long the world's biggest market. In 1895 Americans consumed nearly four times as many opiates per capita as the Germans, inventors of heroin.[56] In 1911 the US Opium Commissioner Hamilton Wright told the press that Americans were "the greatest drug fiends in the world, not excluding the Chinese." But until the 1970s that wasn't Mexico's problem, because after World War II old global supply routes reopened and Mexico went back to being a bit player. In 1955 the total value of all narcotics seized coming across the US-Mexico border was less than half a million dollars.[57] The opiates that preoccupied the US came overwhelmingly from the poppy fields of Western allies like Turkey or client states like Iran and Indochina, processed either in-country or in the heroin factories of another Western ally in Marseilles. At the beginning of the 1970s estimates of Mexican heroin production were one ton a year, between 1 and 2 percent of world production. It wasn't enough to get Mexico anywhere near the list of countries of concern to the UN in 1970.[58]

Four things changed that: the taste of American baby boomers for marijuana; the conservative reaction to the counterculture they created; the bite of global prohibition on traditional opiate trade routes; and the revolutionary effects of a new mass market drug, cocaine.

Marijuana caused moral panics in both the US and Mexico from the nineteenth century on, and Mexicans led the way in divorcing the actual effects of the drug from hysterical perceptions. Yet even hard-line American drug warriors considered marijuana more an artisanal than industrial problem. Harry Anslinger, the alarmist (and xenophobic, red-baiting) bully behind the US counternarcotics bureaucracy, saw it that way. In 1937 he wrote an article for *American Magazine* called "Marijuana: Assassin of Youth," which repeated the old Mexican tropes of reefer madness—the drug "as dangerous as a coiled rattlesnake," driving heedless youth to sex crimes, suicide, and murder—but surprisingly didn't blame Mexicans or organized crime. Hash, he wrote, was "a weed that grows wild throughout the country," which consequently had not been taken over by "gangster syndicates" because there was already more than enough to go around.[59] Customs officers bore him out: In 1961 only three hundred kilos of marijuana were seized crossing the border from Mexico.

By 1970 that had risen to eighty-one tons.[60] The counterculture took marijuana mainstream, its use trebling between 1962 and 1967;[61] demographics and wealth meant that there were a lot of young middle-class Americans with the spare time to read *On the Road*, published in 1957, or to follow the ramblings—literal and musical—of the Grateful Dead, formed in San Francisco in 1965. Like Kerouac they could drive into Mexico—"a pornographic hasheesh daydream in heaven"—to buy a product far better than anything domestic. They were ambitious, entrepreneurial: One Kerouac crackpot suggests taking "a road that goes down Mexico and all the way to Panama?—and maybe all the way to the bottom of South America where the Indians are seven feet tall and eat cocaine on the mountainside?"[62] More considered travelers stuck to high-quality, standardized product like Acapulco Gold, smoking, smuggling, and dragging up supply. Customs couldn't keep up: By the end of the sixties technological developments at the California border hadn't run beyond a single German shepherd, and the dog turned out to be something of a prima donna, requiring, President Nixon was told, "considerable time, manpower and effort to sustain" while putting in a four-hour working day.[63]

Even when Customs got more manpower to search more incoming people and vehicles, their pressure and the trade's profitability led to professionalization on the other side, syndicates with Cessnas replacing amateurs with backpacks or hollow surfboards. Nixon accelerated the process in September 1969 by declaring drugs public enemy number one, with his aide John Ehrlichman—shortly afterward a felon himself—in charge of an "Action Task Force." They singled out marijuana as the greatest threat, closed the border, and crashed the regional economy with Operation Intercept, which required Customs to search every single vehicle coming in from Mexico. Like other border policy initiatives, Operation Intercept was both publicity stunt and blackmail stratagem; like other drug policies, it was rich in faulty assumptions, perverse incentives, and unintended consequences, and in twenty days it was over.

The faulty assumptions were that marijuana was replacing opiates as the main source of human damage in American society and that aggressive interdiction would lead to long-term changes in aggregate drug consumption. The perverse incentive was that increased enforcement led to dramatic growth in the scale, sophistication, and political links of drug trading organizations. These were the years when Mexican policemen, protected by governors, emerged as major dealers: In Sinaloa Miguel Ángel Félix Gallardo, founder of Guadalajara's Federation; in Durango Jaime Herrera Nevárez, founder of the Herrera heroin empire; in Tamaulipas Juan Nepomuceno Guerra, founder of the Gulf Cartel.[64] The unintended consequences of US drug policy were to lay the foundations for the dynastic powerhouses of the future and drive them toward heroin.

The push was exacerbated by another prohibitionist initiative, the US-led United Nations Single Convention on Drugs of 1961. This multilateral treaty bound UN member states to stop producing and trading drugs, with narrow exceptions for medical use and for Coca-Cola, whose use of coca leaves as flavouring was protected in perpetuity under Article 27. (The corporation got a better deal than indigenous Andeans, whose ancient right to chew coca leaves was to be phased out over twenty-five years.)[65] The result, combined with the US breaking the French Connection supply chain in 1972, was a sudden dearth of heroin in North America. Growers in Mexico moved into the gap in the market. Peasants began growing more poppy in more places, spreading out of the Golden Triangle into states further down the Sierra Madre, like Michoacán and Guerrero. By 1976 Mexico provided an estimated 90 percent of the heroin consumed in the United States.[66]

This provoked a second prohibitionist surge, a joint US-Mexican campaign against heroin producers called Operation Condor. It featured pronounced differences from traditional eradication efforts, starting with funding: In 1975 Mexico spent $35 million on the campaign, 10 percent of the entire military budget, and the US increased its contribution from $1.3 to $15.6 million. This funded a year-round commitment of 5,000 troops and 350 federal agents to the cause, assisted by

30 DEA advisors; as in Vietnam the term "advisor" was a loose one, concealing a high degree of operational authority. As in Vietnam the war relied heavily on remote forward bases and helicopters, and air power was not just about transporting troops but also about spraying herbicides. The two most used were the carcinogenic paraquat and 2,4-D, a key component of the Agent Orange used in Vietnam, where it left behind permanently destroyed land, unusable water supplies, and 150 thousand birth defects.[67] Ingesting small amounts of paraquat caused lung damage; large amounts caused organ failure and death. This was known on both sides of the border: Herbicides had long been controversial in Mexico, while the US had banned Agent Orange in 1971 and worried that as much as a quarter of the marijuana imported in 1976 contained paraquat. In statistical terms of fields destroyed, estimated drug flow, and that most reliable number, street price and purity, Operation Condor was successful. At its start Mexico supplied close to the entire US heroin market; by its end, perhaps as little as a third.[68]

It was a diplomatic success too, far from unalloyed US imperialism, because President Echeverría's government was an enthusiastic, proactive host that profited from US resources. Condor helped him go after two important groups of political rivals: governors and guerrillas. Gubernatorial autonomy was a permanent concern to Mexico City, and Sinaloa was an extreme example, wealthy not just through opium but also tomatoes and other cash crops, and virtually independent. In the 1960s its government had been a leader in thwarting the PRI's democratization initiative. In the early 1970s the Policia Judicial de Sinaloa outnumbered the entire federal police force by more than fifteen to one.[69]

As for guerrillas, while Guerrero was tangential to national poppy cultivation, it was the center of the Dirty War and took priority over the Golden Triangle at the start of the campaign. "Mexico's war against the poppy," contemporary analysts concluded, "may be more accurately termed a war against the peasant and the real or imagined guerrillas of the sierras."[70] It was not a hearts-and-minds campaign: Soldiers, spies, and police agents all used mass killings, widespread torture, and systematic rape as weapons. Everyday objects like water buckets, car batteries, soft drinks, cigarettes, and chiles became terrifying in the hands of men who used waterboarding, applied electric shocks or burns to genitals, and sent explosive jets of fizzing liquid up noses and through sinuses. When questioned, the government justified its brutality with the claim that communist guerrillas were swapping narcotics for guns.[71] Operation Condor was also a personal success for the national elites of the time because it allowed them to displace less powerful or gifted regional drug leaders and move into their places.

Yet the success in terms of policing and diplomacy was ephemeral, in part because heroin production rebounded completely once the campaign ended in 1979, but mainly because in the 1980s heroin took second place to cocaine. Cocaine was a new arrival to the mass market, until the 1950s produced and traded on a small scale by amateur types: There were no significant export networks linking Andean production sites to the rest of the world, and cocaine production was concentrated in a single valley in the Eastern Andes. Until the 1980s about half of all the cocaine in the world started off there, in Peru's Huallaga valley, moving out of crude peasant laboratories down the Amazon or the River Plate toward the ocean, and beyond it to Florida and New York.[72] A global boom changed all that, with astute Colombian businessmen taking over first shipping and then cultivation, and as shipments escalated into the hundreds of tons, the US began shutting down the Caribbean routes and the cocaine began to flow through Mexico. By 1988 it was worth about as much as heroin to the Mexican narcos, and this in mere commissions paid by the Colombians for shipping services.[73] Once again established networks proved their worth; in 1990 the Gulf Cartel moved forty tons into the US in a single shipment.[74] And as Colombian cartels began to crumble under the pressure of another US-backed prohibition campaign, the Mexicans took over their vertically integrated business, no longer just porters but wholesalers and retailers in their own right.

The new narcos were products of old ties. All bar the Gulf leaders came from Sinaloan families. A couple were metropolitan types from the state capital, Culiacán: Miguel Ángel Félix Gallardo, "The Godfather," who spent time in business college, married money, and became the greatest of them all; Ramón Arellano Félix, keen on leather jeans, fur coats, and discos, founder with his brothers of the Tijuana Cartel. Rather more came from a single highland town, Badiraguato, among them Rafael Caro Quintero, a third-generation cannabis man; the Beltrán Leyva brothers, who controlled key shipping routes; and Joaqúin "El Chapo" Guzmán—"Shorty"—a hillbilly who set up the Sinaloa Cartel. Amado Carrillo Fuentes, who ran the Juárez Cartel, was an anomaly in that he hailed from Guamuchil, eighty miles up the road. His uncle and mentor, however, was Ernesto "Don Neto" Fonseca, another Badiraguato luminary.

Promiscuous intermarriage and *compadrazgo*, the tight bond of godparenting, strengthened their hometown and business ties; shared opportunities and threats brought them together. In the late 1970s, on the run from Operation Condor, they relocated to Guadalajara and formed a loose common front they called the Federation. It was more trade association than corporation, members working together to minimize conflict, divide responsibilities, and exploit synergies. Yet for all its efficiency the Federation was brought down in 1989, four years after key members tortured and murdered a DEA agent, Kiki Camarena. Camarena had helped destroy Caro Quintero's Rancho Búfalo, an industrial-scale marijuana plantation; the narcos' bloody revenge set up their own destruction. The US got the narcos' main state enablers—the agents of the Dirección Federal de Seguridad—fired or jailed and their institution abolished. Fonseca and Caro Quintero were arrested. Congress passed the Anti–Drug Abuse Act of 1986, which licensed a greatly expanded DEA to kidnap foreign narcos abroad, an early form of extraordinary rendition. Economic assistance, including IMF credit, was conditioned on annual certification by Congress that Mexico was doing all it could to end the drug trade.

This was uneuphemized imperialism, the kidnappings a breach of sovereignty that broke international law. It outraged Mexicans, but it also shaped Mexican government policy. More troops were deployed and more arrests made. Between 1987 and 1988, 60 percent of all prosecutions were drug-related, in a country whose citizens didn't really do drugs themselves. A further 18 percent of cases were for the possession of illegal firearms, most of which were from the US—as Mexico had some of the world's stricter gun laws—and in the hands of narcos. By

1990, forty-six thousand people were in jail for drug offenses; not all that many by the standards of America's carceral state, but an unprecedented number by Mexican standards. The Procuradoría General de la República adopted under pressure the Americans' kingpin strategy, founded on the premise that arresting or killing top narcos would bring their organizations tumbling down.[75] Major figures duly went to penitentiaries: the chief of the Mexico City Police, Arturo Durazo; the army's drug czar, General Jesús Gutiérrez Rebollo ("a guy of absolute unquestioned integrity," according to his US counterpart); El Chapo Guzmán; even Miguel Ángel Félix Gallardo.[76]

Yet even while big names were arrested and the Mexican justice system became choked with drug cases, drug shipments and violence grew. By the mid-1990s Mexico was supplying 30 percent of the US market's heroin, 80 percent of its marijuana, and 70 percent of its cocaine. Amado Carrillo Fuentes, *El Señor de los Cielos*, the Lord of the Skies, was using decommissioned Boeing 727s to fly industrial shipments direct from Colombia to the Texas border. And alongside the glamorous technologies—the airliners, the mile-long air-conditioned tunnels, the mini-submarines—ran the unstoppable conduits of licit free trade. Part of the reward for Mexico's cooperation on drugs had been the North American Free Trade Agreement, which allowed easy cross-border passage for thousands of trucks every day. They couldn't all be searched; as much as half of all cocaine coming into the United States just drove straight through Nuevo Laredo in shipping containers.[77] The profits of smuggling rose from billions to tens of billions.

As profits rose, so did killing. Old agreements between politicians and narcos expired when the former lost elections or the latter lost leaders. Opposition governors in the border states lacked the clout of their single-party predecessors, able to make everything right with the federal government or bring down its power on the locals. In place of a single partner in law enforcement, the spies of the defunct DFS, narcos could recruit from multiple competing police forces and military units. Democracy and its competing parties gave the narcos new opportunities and threats, and they began encroaching on each other's production and shipping zones. By the mid-1990s politicians no longer invigilated the smuggling routes or told drug dealers the limits of the possible; the old relationship flipped, and it was the narcos who now ran smuggling routes and told politicians what they could or couldn't do.

Once clearly demarcated territories now came up for grabs. Local gang wars broke out in Tijuana first, where in the early 1990s the Sinaloa Cartel attacked the Arellano Félix brothers, owners of the main northwestern route into the US. In 1997 the Lord of the Skies either died on or disappeared from an operating table where he was having extensive plastic surgery. It was a classic instance of drug history's unknowability: Appearing to die mid-surgery, temporarily unrecognizable, would have been in keeping with Carrillo Fuentes's ingenuity. His three surgeons were found dismembered in oil drums by the side of the Acapulco highway. Yet there is no evidence of a plot, and the surgeons might have died as revenge rather than silencing.[78] Anecdotes didn't really matter; what counted when narcos left the scene was the aftermath, in this case a three-way fight for control of the central route to the US that set Carrillo Fuentes's heirs in Juárez against both Sinaloa and Tijuana cartels. Finally, in 2005 the Gulf Cartel went to war on Sinaloa, generalizing the fighting across the entire border.

The struggle had a dystopian impact on an entire society. Graves began appearing in the desert, and in a foreshadowing of times to come the greatest number of victims were civilians. At least seven hundred young women disappeared from Ciudad Juárez's maquiladoras, some reappearing raped and strangled. A new noun gained currency, *feminicidio*, femicide, the massive and systematic killing of women because they're women. The Juárez femicides would have been far less probable under the old one-party state that refereed the most violent players, powerful enough to threaten narcos out of the murders if they were the perpetrators, or employ them to end the killings if they were not. Had the guilty been a single, politically well-connected serial killer he probably would have been stopped in the end by his own contacts. Yet the classic reglas no escritas, the rules of the game, were finished and in the North a war of all against all prevailed.

It had not been a war of all against all throughout Mexico in the past because in the 1990s the PRI still controlled most of the country and tacitly favored the Sinaloa Cartel, foreclosing all-out national conflict. President Zedillo kept the army on the sidelines as much as possible; making episodic arrests and tolerating the DEA kept the Americans quiet. Personally honest, Zedillo faced structural problems beyond repair: the rent-seeking of generals, bureaucrats, lawyers, and policemen, and the intimidatory power of the drug organizations. President Fox found himself in much the same situation; as with Zedillo, his top drug policeman, Genaro García Luna, turned out to be working with top drug businessmen.[79] In the second month of Fox's presidency, El Chapo escaped from the supposedly high-security Puente Grande penitentiary, hidden in a laundry cart according to some, ushered out the front door according to others.[80] Fox had promised on campaign to resolve the drug war; his approach in office was a tepid continuation of the status quo, altered only by a new policy of mass extradition of narcos to the United States. Murder rates, flatlined since 2000, didn't fall; neither did the flow of drugs. He was widely criticized as incompetent. By the standards of what came next, though, Fox's drug policy looked like masterly inactivity.

His successor, another panista, did things differently. Felipe Calderón had likewise campaigned with promises to resolve drug violence, and on December 11, 2006—ten days after he took over the presidency—he donned an unflattering flak jacket and helicoptered into Michoacán, where he told Mexicans that he had ordered sixty-five hundred troops into that state and Guerrero as part of an all-out war on all cartels. It was life-and-death, he told them:

> We are doing it for the good of Mexicans to come, we are doing it for the good of our families and for new generations of Mexicans who have the right to a safer and better country, we are doing it for the good of Mexico.[81]

He was widely understood as doing it for the good of himself. Calderón officially won the presidency by a quarter of a million votes, half a percent of the votes cast, and election day was questionable enough to put his victory in doubt. The losing candidate, the leftist Andrés Manuel López Obrador, declared a parallel government; hundreds of thousands of his followers occupied downtown Mexico City. Declaring a new War on Drugs was Calderón's bid for khaki legitimacy. There was no raison d'état to justify the wholesale militarization of the Mexican countryside, and a relative increase in domestic drug use had still left the country itself with one of the lower rates of consumption in the world. Calderón started a civil war that left more Mexicans dead or displaced than the Cristiada, the war against France, the war against the United States, and the last colonial smallpox epidemic: a devout conservative's morally bankrupt, reckless choice of an unwinnable war.[82]

There was enough moral bankruptcy to go around. The Americans of the DEA had long known that the kingpin strategy was ineffectual, yet they continued to promote it vigorously. By 2006 most of the major dealers of the eighties and nineties were jailed or dead: Miguel Ángel Félix Gallardo, Rafael Caro Quintero, Don Neto Fonseca, and Juan Matta-Ballesteros (Guadalajara); Javier Arellano Félix (Tijuana); Amado Carrillo Fuentes (Juárez); Joaquín "El Chapo" Guzmán (Sinaloa); Juan Nepomuceno, Juan García Abrego, and Osiel Cárdenas Guillén (Gulf); and Arturo Guzmán Decena (Zetas). Ensuing disruptions in the drug supply chain had all proven ephemeral, and the medium-term flow of drugs rebounded or increased. After the triumphalist, misspelled press bulletins—more than one bungled the kingpins' names—had been digested, the only discernible effect was the growth of the DEA's budget.[83] In 1973 it was $75 million; in 2020, $2.5 billion. The DEA wasn't very good at drug control, but it was exceptionally good at empire-building.[84]

The kingpin strategy was founded on three theoretical assumptions. The first was that the drug trade was structurally quite static and for that reason could be ended by a combination of eradication, interdiction, and security campaigns against cartels. The second was that these organizations were analogous to licit corporations, with pyramidal power structures overseeing vertically integrated operations. The third was that at the apex of those massive illicit corporations sat boards of directors, CEOs and CFOs, "kingpins," and when elite security forces removed them the entire edifice would come tumbling down. Everyday soldiers and policemen could then mop up the rest. Given enough governmental funding and ruthlessness a violent war on drugs was winnable.[85]

None of these assumptions stood up. The drug business wasn't at all static or cumbersome; it was late capitalism at its dynamic, nimble, globalized best. Drug markets were very efficient in maintaining equilibrium, the point at which supply and demand match. Demand for specific products might rise and fall according to fashion, technology, or availability, but aggregate demand was relatively inelastic: Just as many colonial Mexicans put buying cigarettes and pulque above most other needs, so many modern Americans valued marijuana, cocaine, and opiates above other consumables. Should their drugs of choice grow more expensive, they would keep buying as long as they could or shift to cheaper alternatives. When campaigns against marijuana in Mexico and Colombia drove up prices, it encouraged the take-off of cocaine, equally unfrightening to middle-class users. (As an early dealer put it, coke was "almost in the same category as marijuana, only a hell of a lot better . . . It became an accepted product, just like marijuana.")[86] The price of cocaine, kept artificially high by hype and government efforts to stop its trade, helped turn the poor onto the cheaper crack in the 1980s and 1990s and crystal meth in the 2000s. In the 2010s the forever war on heroin opened the door for the synthetic opioid fentanyl, which by the end of the decade had almost entirely replaced heroin in New England.[87] In drug study argot it was called the balloon effect: Squeeze producers, shippers, or consumers in one place and they will shift their production, shipping, and consumption to another.

On the supply side, meanwhile, state success in eradicating crops, interdicting product, and busting gangs was just evolutionary pressure: It didn't get rid of drug trading organizations; it just selected those better adapted to any given moment. When coca cultivation fell in Colombia in 2008, Bolivians and Peruvians increased their own production to compensate.[88] When the atrocities and territorial successes of the Zetas made them public enemy number one (for both the military and the other cartels), they were replaced across much of Mexico by the (just as terrorist) Cártel de Jalisco Nueva Generación. Capitalism was once defined as "a perennial gale of creative destruction," and that definition fits the illicit drug industry well: The destruction of one zone of production or cartel inevitably created others.[89]

The second assumption, that cartels were centralized corporations, was also wrong. The very word "cartel" is misleading and rejected by some analysts in favor of labels such as DTO, drug trafficking organization. Most use it because of its ubiquity: It is, ironically, confusing not to talk in terms of cartels, even though the term obscures more than it reveals. The first modern narcos, Félix Gallardo and his associates, didn't call themselves the Guadalajara Cartel; they called themselves *la Federación*, the Federation, and the rest of Mexico called them that too. That reflected the structural reality of the grouping, a loose, decentralized franchise operation. Regional and mid-level associates worked with a high degree of independence: They were licensed to sell a standardized product sourced from specific suppliers and routes and to open new branches in return for minimizing violence and paying the top narcos a percentage. That aside, they were left to their own devices.[90] Even many of the big shippers, the heart of the business model, were independent subcontractors rather than integrated employees.[91] This was not a cartel in any technically accurate sense.

The idea of the Mexican drug cartel was popularized in the 1980s by outsiders: a journalist with close connections to the DEA, Elaine Shannon and an American political scientist.[92] It seduced reporters, DEA agents, and their employers with its compelling simplicity, which magicked a complex story of cops and robbers into a final struggle between Good and Evil. Narcos were Bond villains, and Bond villains were good for selling media coverage to consumers, expensive policy proposals to politicians, and politicians to voters. For a long time narcos were keen too; leading a cartel sounded flashy and overstated their individual sophistication and significance, which helped with self-esteem, social capital, and intimidation. In their glory moments some may have believed it.

In the end, however, the idea was profoundly flawed as a basis for history or policy. The DEA publicly presented cartel maps that looked like maps of nation-states, large colored blocs representing a few great powers. A leaked insiders' map from 1986 showed a rather different reality of sixty-two different local gangs.[93] Some journalists knew and said as much; security analysts captured the divorce between language and reality in reports filled with stories of cartels splitting on a more or less annual basis, cartel factions, cartel splinters. The "franchises" of the Beltrán Leyva Cartel had at one stage ties to Juárez, CJNG, and the Zetas, mutual enemies all. With that level of

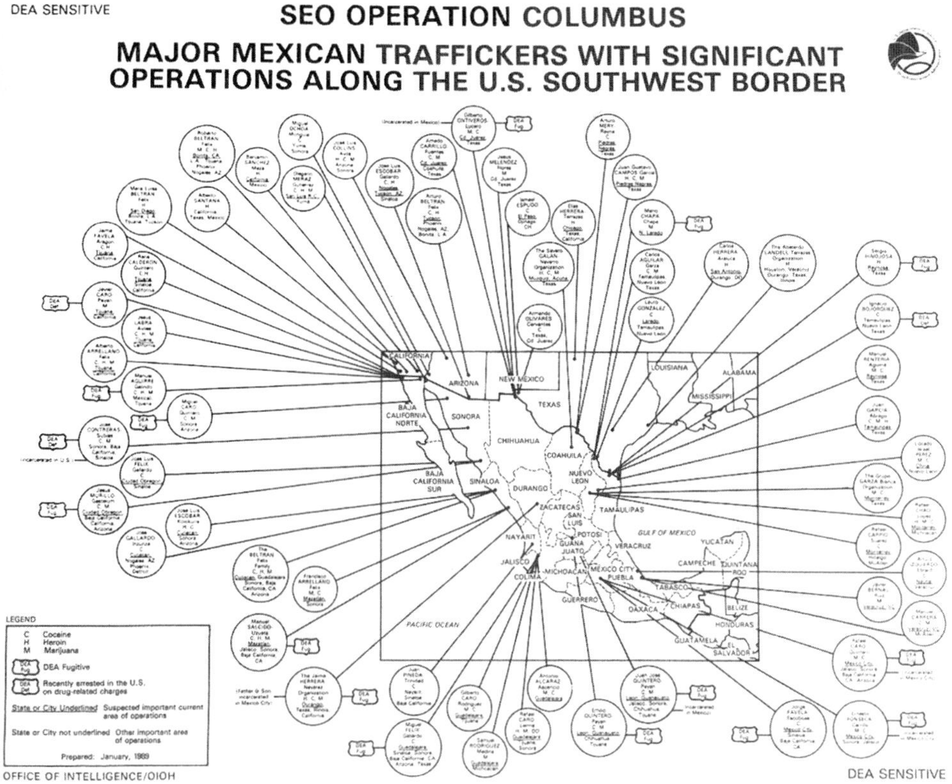

Little sign of cartels: leaked DEA map of drug trading organizations (c. 1986).

fissility, an obvious question was how much stability there had ever been. Even narcos criticized the concept. When the DEA reported a growing "influence" of the cartels in the US, a Sinaloa Cartel interviewee rebutted the entire idea as "bullshit," adding, "We wholesale to [US-based dealers], and what they do to that merchandise is their problem. We don't give a fuck. They can lose it, sell it, snort it, whatever, as long as they pay up."[94]

In light of this franchise or cell model, the third assumption, that removing top leaders will seriously reduce drug trafficking and violence, has long been untenable. A leak from the Customs and Border Protection in 2011 said as much, concluding,

> The removal of key personnel does not have a discernible impact on drug flows as determined by seizure rates. [Drug trafficking organization] operations appear to have built in redundancy and personnel that perform specific duties to limit the damage incurred by the removal of any one person. By sheer volume alone, drug operations would require more than one individual to coordinate and control the process.[95]

El Mayo Zambada said much the same a year earlier, telling a journalist, "They shoot me and euphoria breaks out. But after a few days we start to see that nothing has changed."[96] The arrest of his partner, El Chapo, bore the point out. He was on the run for years, moving constantly, working through multiple cutouts and burner phones, but his arrest had no impact on the flow of cocaine, which increased. Neither, with El Mayo and other leaders around, did it end Sinaloa's preeminence. Hunting the main narcos had broken up Colombia's cartels, the DEA was fond of pointing out. What it omitted to say was that successor gangs and Mexicans kept the trade going; the only difference was that in Colombia damage to cartels reduced damage to civilians. In Mexico the effect was the opposite; the increase in cell structure, local gang numbers, and autonomy all boosted violence.

The United States' drugs enforcement officers and foreign policy makers might, up to a certain point, plead ignorance; in 1975 the DEA said that its knowledge of Mexican narcotic production was "so lacking in detail and documentation as to handicap any detailed analysis."[97] Yet bad faith was more significant than bad intelligence. Insiders gave different stories: One DEA brief told its privileged readers that the Juárez Cartel—at its late-nineties peak—was not actually a cartel, functioning "more as a loose federation of trafficking organizations than a regimented, organized mafia group."[98] That few news stories about corruption on the American side of the war have emerged is in part a function of not wanting to know. The narco links of State Senator Joseph Montoya of New Mexico, for example, never made the national papers even after his 1990 conviction for extortion, racketeering, and money-laundering; he had twice stopped police from searching large drug transports, one of them a plane on which he was traveling.[99] Persistent rumors had numerous Federal Bureau of Narcotics agents on the take before that agency's 1968 abolition; retired DEA agents cast off-the-record doubts on former colleagues. One of the few DEA agents to be arrested died after a week in prison; a researcher was told that "all documentation" relating to the agent had "been destroyed."[100] Collectively, civil asset forfeiture laws meant that between 2007 and 2016 the DEA got to keep an average of $400 million a year in cash it seized from alleged drug business, the majority without due process, to the Department of Justice's concern.[101]

The most significant corruption was along those lines, institutional and not individual, and it rested on serial and knowing misrepresentation to superiors and the public. Busts were hawked in terms of street and not wholesale prices, a sleight of hand that made seizures seem far more damaging to drug organizations than they really were, and those organizations far wealthier than they really were. It was a long tradition: In one year during the heroin boom the DEA estimated that the Herrera gang had exported 746 pounds of pure heroin, but they reported it as 8.14 tons, which was what it would have weighed once cut for retail.[102] Directors lied with a firm belief in the gullibility of their audience. In 2010 former DEA director Richard Bonner wrote that the 1970s heroin trade was of "small quantities" to argue that the government faced a new level of threat with cocaine but could win if it spent enough on his kingpin strategy. In 1975 his predecessor had argued for funding and similarly aggressive intervention on the opposite grounds that massive amounts of heroin were coming up from Mexico.[103] Whatever the data, the conclusions were the same: The drug enforcement empire needed more. It was not an empire in anyone's interest except its own, and with a bitter irony it helped create and sustain a Mexican empire, once more at the center of the world, of a very different caste.

Epilogue

The history of any country is full of caveats and unknowns; Mexico's caveats and unknowns are unusually full of history. There is eloquence in the fact that we don't even know what Cortés looked like; we don't know how many Mexican politicians and American law enforcement agents were on the take from narcos; our not-too-distant ancestors couldn't find El Paso on the map. The dead are elusive too: Estimates vary hugely as to how many people lost their lives in the epidemics of the sixteenth century, or the 1910 revolution, or the 1985 earthquake. Archives, raw materials of history, are also weapons, and as such have been burned by the unruly or disappeared by the rulers. The chorus of voices that all histories miss is particularly faint for numerous periods, peoples, and regions of the many Mexicos.

Even with so much silence, diversity, and contradiction, some things can be asserted. Contemporary Mexico is subject to not one but three empires: one of domestic criminal bosses, one of American drug warriors and their tame politicians, and one of American drug consumers who regale dinner party companions with happy memories of child soldiers selling them whatever they wanted on Pacific beaches. Mexican history could be told as a single story of a series of empires, from Mexica to Americans, and sometimes that was indeed the dominant key. Rather more often, though, Mexican history is characterized by many and distinct stories of lives lived in the face of empire, of people succeeding in being left alone despite great disparities of power. Spain rarely succeeded in imposing more than the most tenuous control over New Spain, which it never had the temerity to call a colony. The United States had to live with a proper revolution on its doorstep and like it, or at least put up with it.

Mexican history could be written as a tragedy of race: the slavery of West Africans, the forced migrations and ethnocides of the North, the complex wars of the Southeast simplified into caste wars of brown against white, the systematic impoverishment of the Maya peoples in modern Chiapas, the eugenic hunger for white migration that continued well into the twentieth century.[1] None of that would be wrong. Another story of race in Mexico can be written looking across the Atlantic or to the north, where one Supreme Court ruling determined that indigenous people were "an inferior race" with "diminutive rights" (*Johnson v. M'Intosh*, 1823). A second ruling determined that Blacks were not liable for United States citizenship and had no recourse to federal justice (*Dred Scott v. Sandford*, 1857). The readers of such a story might wonder at the Canadian Indian Act that forbade indigenous communities from hiring lawyers to sue the government, or at George Washington's dentures, made from a mixture of ivory and his slaves' teeth.[2]

Such a history of Mexico would register the difference of a country where Blacks were acknowledged to be fully human, their abuse punished, their lynching unknown, and where Indians were full citizens, whose protective courts worked, who often kept language and lands, several hundreds of villages staying in the same place with the same political borders from the fifteenth century to the present;[3] indigenous peoples who were celebrated while intact rather than safely dispossessed, their names turned to brands of cars, sports teams, and helicopters. It would be a story in which social and sexual mobility across supposedly strict racial boundaries was a given from the start; in which there was sometimes status to be had in claiming Indian ancestry; in which mestizos of all castes climbed high in the arts and professions; a story of a racially fractured society that elected the first Black and the only indigenous president in North America.

Another supposed constant of Mexican history and culture is intense violence, whether during Independence, the revolution, or the War on Drugs. Yet Mexican violence is comparatively unremarkable when set alongside the long homicidal sweep of American or European history.

While Mexicans were fighting a cruel War of Independence, Napoleon was continuing a centuries-old tradition of European fratricide; while hundreds of thousands of Mexicans were dying in places like Chihuahua and Morelos, cannon fodder for the revolution, millions of Europeans were dying in places like Flanders and Verdun, cannon fodder for World War I. There is no Mexican equivalent to the political violence of the postwar United States, where the five main progressive leaders of the time—the Kennedy brothers, Martin Luther King, Malcolm X, and Harvey Milk—were all assassinated.

Neither is there a death penalty on the books in Mexico; the last judicial execution of a civilian took place in 1937.[4] There are no school shootings in Mexico, whose gun control regime since the revolution has been among the world's most restrictive. The Sackler family knowingly killed more Americans with prescription opioids than the Sinaloa Cartel did with heroin.[5] Mexican culture celebrates death with baroque flair; societies that enjoy zombies, death metal, and soap operas about serial killers shouldn't find that particularly foreign or distinctive. Mexico City's carnivalesque Day of the Dead parade isn't actually Mexican in origin; it was the invention of English film director Danny Boyle, painting a backdrop for the stylized violence of a Bond film.[6]

Violence is often seen as central to Mexico's politics, which are widely viewed through the lens of extreme skepticism. Mexicans and foreigners alike see corruption, rigged elections, violent bosses, dynasticism, dictatorship, and political turbulence as historical norms. Yet seeing these phenomena as peculiarly Mexican requires a blinkered view, and not just of the world at large but also of the countries that pride themselves on being the democracies par excellence. The British have always enjoyed an unelected head of state, until recently an unelected senate in the form of the House of Lords, and until well into the nineteenth century a Parliament in which 20 percent of the members were appointed rather than elected, delegates for the private owners of so-called rotten boroughs. Between 1979 and 2020 five out of Britain's seven prime ministers came from the same university, Oxford. The US lost its last caudillo when Andrew Jackson died in 1845, but it continued to produce numerous caciques, ranging from Governor Huey Long in Louisiana to the Daley family of Chicago, and never wholly abandoned election-rigging, whether practiced by Franklin D.

Roosevelt's Democratic Party, George W. Bush's rioting lawyers, or gerrymandering electoral commissions.

Mexico was a one-party state for much of the twentieth century, true competition confined to the single party's primaries; the same applies to many states across America, similar political monocultures. Until the 1960s the states of the American South voted almost universally for Democrats. The British don't even have primaries; parties choose candidates. Mexican presidents were traditionally seen as political untouchables, idolized by a brainwashed people and a sycophantic press; but only one country has a Presidents' Day. A quantitative analysis of two major Mexican newspapers between 1951 and 1980 revealed a far higher percentage of politically critical articles than on Americans' front pages in the immediate aftermath of Watergate.[7] Mexico has no political dynasties the likes of the Roosevelts, Clintons, and Bushes; Porfirio Díaz kept his nephew Félix, the only other family member with political ambitions, an army captain for eighteen years. Conservative verities about Mexican politics, whether coming from Díaz or Donald Trump, are rather one-sided.

Some progressive verities are questionable too. It is hard to reconcile the stereotype of the macho with a long line of distinguished women writers, religious leaders, and drug dealers, or with the fact that Mexicans adopted the Pill faster than most other societies, or with the life of Sor Juana Inés de la Cruz, a seventeenth-century nun acknowledged in her time as one of Mexico's leading thinkers, or that of Colonel Amelio Robles, a famous transgender revolutionary.[8] Mexican working-class newspapers of the nineteenth century pushed progressive gender norms; a writer of the time penned an essay deploring the oppression of women in Western society.[9] Mexican voters of the twenty-first century elected North America's first female president. The atrocious level of femicide in modern Mexico is part of the rupture of the present with the past, not its continuation. Mexican history is intrinsically a story of patriarchy sustained by violence. So is that of just about everywhere else on Earth.

So Mexico's story can be told as one of victimhood, sacrifice, and triumph against the odds, an exemplar of what one Ukrainian historian called lachrymose history.[10] It can be, as a Mexican historian wrote, a sort of moral kitsch.[11] Skulls, murals, narcos, the paintings of Diego Rivera and Frida Kahlo, and the existential navel-gazing of intellectuals like Samuel Ramos and Octavio Paz all favored both, creating an iconography of Mexico that writes off the cosmopolitan and the universal in favor of the exotic, the singular, and the peripheral. Mexico has been anthropologized and culturally critiqued to death. Some of it is romantic, flattering; some of it patronizing; much of it damaging and historically wrong. Thinking about Mexican history demands thinking about empire, race, violence, political fragility, and gender; but Mexico's is also a history that mocks those categories as default ways of thinking about countries, and particularly countries outside the United States and Europe.

Another way of thinking might be to consider the everyday universality of much of the past of the *Estados Unidos Mexicanos*, the United Mexican States, and only then, against that backdrop, the uniqueness of the peoples who made the first truly global society.

Acknowledgments

> *[The traveling scholar] will discover how many truly kind-hearted people there are with whom he had never before had, nor ever again will have, any further communication, who yet are ready to offer him the most disinterested assistance.*
>
> Charles Darwin, *On the Origin of Species*

I owe what I know about Mexico to a multitude of archivists, librarians, everyday Mexicans, colleagues, and friends, so many that naming them all would take another—though slightly slimmer—book. I hope those I don't specifically name will forgive me and accept my profound gratitude for all they have helped, taught, and encouraged me over the years.

First thanks are due to my peerless agent Alison Mackeen, quite superb in conceptualizing and communicating what this book hoped to be to my publishers. It would not exist without her. Second thanks go to those publishers, George Gibson at Grove Atlantic and Simon Winder at Penguin UK, for their enduring encouragement, patience, and meticulousness. From their teams, a special thank you to the outstanding copyeditor Alicia Burns, whose painstaking work saved me blushes in more than just grammar. Logistical and scholarly support from Oscar Altamirano, my special advisor in Mexico City, was as ever key.

Without archivists there is no history, and I appreciate enormously their erudite and enthusiastic support, starting during my earliest work in Mexico at the Archivo General de la Nación, marshaled by the redoubtable Roberto Beristáin, and continuing with that of Olivia Domínguez Pérez at the Archivo Histórico del Estado de Veracruz. In more recent times I have profited greatly from the Jesuit archive in Rome, where Mauro Brunello saved me days of work, and the state archive in Aguascalientes, whose director Mtra. Aurora Figueroa Ruíz likewise helped cram a lot of fruitful research into a little time. A heartfelt thanks to that first generation of archivists in the intelligence archives of the AGN, whom I'll leave anonymous, whose above-and-beyond and even subversive help gave me a different understanding of Mexico.

Without librarians there are no historians, and I have had the fortune to profit from some of the best. I'm indebted to librarians from the Bodleian and the Latin American Centre in Oxford, University of North Carolina in Wilmington, Northwestern University, the University of Chicago, the Newberry Library, Columbia's Butler Library, and critically that of the Colegio de México. The New York Public Library has been fundamental, lending me for years a vital calm workspace in the Vartan Gregorian Center for Research in the Humanities and speedy access to their extraordinary holdings.

As for colleagues, it is hard to know where to start, and invidious whom to single out. A host of historians ranging from Alan Knight in Oxford to my graduate students at Northwestern have taught me about Mexico. So I'll confine myself to those who have read part of the manuscript or heard about it at tedious length. The usual caveat, that they own their many ideas and saves and I own the misses, is more than a formality. The most sincere thanks to Randi Epstein, my first general reader and companion in Martinis; Paul Ramírez, whose enlightened suggestions are still being developed; Margaret Chowning, whose generosity goes beyond searching comments; that erudite magpie and stand-up comedian Ben Smith; the ever-welcoming, calmly clever Pablo Piccato; and Mauricio Tenorio-Trillo, who didn't just review but also played a part in the basic idea of the book by suggesting I write something without footnotes. (It didn't quite work out that way, but I hope to have preserved some of the idea, as well as a punch line he suggested.) As for the ever-uplifting Carla Zurita Grigsby, words are, for once, inadequate.

One specialist, Erika Pani, and one scholar from another field, Alison Richards, read the entire manuscript. They combined enthusiasm with the most straightforward and candid commentary, in Alison's case a line edit and question about coverage that put me to shame, in Erika's a list of misses and a big idea. I am extraordinarily grateful for the time they took from unusually busy professional and intellectual lives to think about my own.

I have been very fortunate with a number of research assistants over the last decade. But particular recognition is due to the drive of three at the beginning of interesting careers: Alan Fernando Medina Díaz, Lucia Barnum, and Luke Bannerman. The initiative and care for their work they displayed was impressive. Even if the biographies didn't go in, they counted; the bigger stories, reliable minutiae, and illustrations did survive the cut and make this a better book.

Finally, my thanks to my mother, father, and in particular Sarah and Josh for the support and sympathy over the years. They have chased me down by phone to recall me to normal life when I am down the rabbit hole. Above all, my work would have been very different without my son Alastair, the beloved tough guy who makes me think daily about the challenges, triumphs, and unknowability of other people's lives. And it would have been impossible, unthinkable even, without Snježana, who deserves another book; not, before she recoils in horror, of history, but rather of gratitude and love for the myriad ways she makes things possible.

A Timeline of Mexican History

1492 First contact between Europeans and indigenous peoples in the Caribbean.

1511 First contact between Europeans and indigenous peoples in Mexico, when Jerónimo de Aguilar and Gonzalo Guerrero are shipwrecked off the Yucatán Peninsula.

1516 Sixteen-year old Charles I of the Habsburg dynasty, born in the Netherlands, doesn't speak Spanish, becomes King of Spain.

1517 First Spanish expedition from Cuba to Mexico sets out under Francisco Hernández de Córdoba, loses half its members to Maya attacks.

1518 Second Spanish expedition from Cuba to Mexico sails under Juan de Grijalva, proceeds up Gulf Coast to northern Veracruz, learns of the Mexica Empire.

1519 Hernán Cortés sets sail from Cuba, founds first Spanish town in Mexico at Veracruz; forms military alliance with Tlaxcalans; is invited into Tenochtitlán.

Smallpox reaches Cuba.

1521 Smallpox epidemic breaks out in Valley of Mexico.

Indigenous and Spanish armies capture Tenochtitlán.

Charles I made Holy Roman Emperor, declares Martin Luther an enemy of the state, goes to war with France, defeats domestic *comuneros* rebellion.

1522–1540 Reconstruction of Tenochtitlán.

Cortés's captains lead expeditions across Mexico.

1524 Twelve Franciscans arrive at Veracruz, led by their superior Martín de Valencia.

1527 Conquistador rule replaced by Crown rule with the first Real Audiencia.

1528 Franciscan Juan de Zumárraga appointed first archbishop of Mexico.

Laws of the Indies passed.

1529 Cortés made Marques de la Valle de Oaxaca, overlord of c. 23,000 Nahua.

1531 Juan Diego in legend has vision of Virgin of Guadalupe.

1535 First Viceroy of New Spain, Antonio de Mendoza (1535–1550), arrives.

First Royal Mint opens in Mexico City.

1536–1537 Franciscans found Colegio de Santa Cruz de Tlatelolco for indigenous nobility.

1537–1540 Re-establishment of indigenous royalty in Tenochtitlán, Texcoco.

1540–1542 Mixtón War.

1542 New Laws prohibit indigenous slavery.

1545 First *cocoliztli* epidemic.

1546 Discovery of silver mines at Zacatecas.

1550 Viceroy Mendoza leaves, replaced by Viceroy Luis de Velasco I (1550–1564).

1550 Start of Chichimeca Wars, continue until 1590.

1553 University of Mexico opens.

1556 Philip II (1556–1598) becomes King of Spain and the Indies.

1562 Bishop Diego de Landa burns nearly all Maya codices in existence as part of campaign against alleged human sacrifice.

1565 First Manila Galleon.

1567 Alleged conspiracy of Cortés's sons and other conquistador scions against Spanish rule.

1572 Arrival of first Jesuits.

1575 Second *cocoliztli* epidemic.

Lifetime of encomiendas extended to the conquistadors' grandchildren.

1576 Bernardino de Sahagun's *Florentine Codex*, thirty years of ethnohistorical work, is banned.

1585 Third Provincial Council of Mexican bishops condemns slave trading and Chichimeca Wars.

1588 Sinking of Spanish Armada, failure to invade Britain; beginning of Spanish military decline.

1592 Foundation of Juzgado General de Indios.

1607 First attempt to drain the Valley of Mexico.

1609 Final deportation of 300,000 Muslims from Spain to North Africa begins.

1612 Alleged Black conspiracy in Mexico City.

1624 Riot in Mexico City topples Viceroy.

1648 Treaty of Westphalia.

1649 Virgin of Guadalupe cult spread across Mexico by Luís Lasso de la Vega Nahuatl-language account of apparition.

1648–1695 Sor Juana Inés de la Cruz, theologian, essayist, poet, and proto-feminist.

1672 Ban on indigenous slavery in Mexico.

1680 Pueblo Revolt in New Mexico.

1692 Food riot in Mexico City, attack on Viceregal Palace.

1695–1768 Miguel Cabrera, Zapotec court painter and master of *pinturas de casta*.

1700–1713 War of the Spanish Succession installs Philip V, ending the Habsburg dynasty and replacing it with the Bourbon dynasty.

1754 Pope makes Virgin of Guadalupe Patroness of New Spain.

1765–1771 New Spain run by authoritarian Minister of the Indies José de Gálvez.

1767 Expulsion of Jesuits.

1778 Free trade between Mexico, other American colonies, and Europe.

1785 Harvest failure in Bajío leads to famine, hundreds of thousands dead.

1789–1794 Second Count of Revillagigedo viceroy oversees major social reform and infrastructure development.

1797–1808 Spain sides with France in the Napoleonic Wars; British naval blockade ends Spanish trade with the Americas.

1808 French invade Spain, imprison Ferdinand VII, make Napoleon's brother king.

1810–1811 16 September revolt of Miguel Hidalgo, ends with capture and execution after defeat at Puente de Calderón near Guadalajara.

1812 Cortes of Cadíz draws up liberal constitution for Spanish Empire.

1811–1815 Insurgency led by José María Morelos.

1814 Insurgent constitution drawn up at Apatzingán.

1815–1821 Vicente Guerrero becomes principal of several rebel leaders.

1816 José Fernández de Lizardi publishes *The Mangy Parrot*.

1821 Agustín de Iturbide defects from royalists and joins with Guerrero in Plan de Iguala, leading to Mexican Independence and First Mexican Empire.

1826 Collapse of London Stock Market saddles Mexico for sixty years with "London Debt."

1829 Vicente Guerrero becomes first Black president in North America.

Guerrero abolishes slavery, as earlier abolition decrees of Hidalgo and Morelos were ineffective.

1830s–1840s Comanche Wars.

1836 Texas secedes.

1846 United States invades Mexico.

1848 United States takes California, New Mexico, Nevada, Utah, most of Arizona and Colorado, parts of Kansas, Oklahoma, and Wyoming in Treaty of Guadalupe.

1857 Liberals' passage of Constitution of 1857 sparks civil war with conservatives.

1858 President Benito Juárez becomes only indigenous president in North American history.

1861 Liberals win war.

1862 French, British and Spanish force arrives in Veracruz to enforce debt collection.

1862–1867 French Intervention: seize Mexico City and install Habsburg Maximilian as Emperor of Mexico.

1867 Júarez's forces capture Maximilian and execute him.

1872 Júarez dies in office.

1876 General Porfirio Díaz rebels under Plan de Tuxtepec and obtains presidency under slogan of "No re-election."

1884–1911 Díaz dictatorship from office of presidency.

1910–1911 Francisco Madero rebels against Díaz, becomes President.

1913 *Décena trágica*: Madero toppled and murdered by General Victoriano Huerta in Mexico City.

1914 August: Revolutionary armies of Venustiano Carranza end Huerta regime.

November: Revolutionaries split between popular armies of Emiliano Zapata and Pancho Villa and northern army of Álvaro Obregón, war begins.

1915 Obregón defeats Villa at Battle of León, winning conventional war.

1915–1920 Guerrilla warfare.

1917 Revolutionary Constitution passed.

1920–1934 Rule by Sonora presidents Álvaro Obregón (1920–1924), Plutarco Elías Calles (1924–1928).

Rule behind puppet presidents by Calles, dubbed the *jefe máximo* (1928–1935).

1926–1929 The Cristiada, civil war between anticlerical government and Catholics.

1934–1940 Revolutionary land redistribution and labor reform under President Lázaro Cárdenas.

March 28, 1938: Mexico nationalizes oil, evicts US and British oil companies.

1936 Beginning of Golden Age of Mexican cinema (1936–c. 1956).

1942–1945 Mexico joins allies in World War II.

Bracero program (1942–1964) of Mexican guest workers launched to fill wartime labor shortage in US.

1946 Foundation of Partido Revolucionario Institucional (PRI), rules Mexico in competitive authoritarian regime until 2000.

1946–1952 President Miguel Alemán oversees postwar economic boom (1945–1973).

1948–1963 Stabilization of PRI's regime.

1940s–1970s Mexico literary capital of Spanish-speaking world (Octavio Paz, Juan Rulfo, José Gorostieta, Carlos Fuentes, home to Gabriel García Márquez as he writes *One Hundred Years of Solitude*).

1960 For first time census counts more urban than rural Mexicans.

1965–1982 *Guerra sucia*, Dirty War, of counterinsurgency against small guerrilla groups.

1967 Mexico brokers Treaty of Tlatelolco, prohibiting nuclear arms in Latin America and the Caribbean.

1968 October 2 massacre of student protesters and civilians at Tlatelolco.

October 12 opening of Mexico City Olympic Games.

1976 Near-collapse of Mexican economy, propped up by $600 million from the International Monetary Fund (IMF), conditioned on cuts in state spending.

1978 Emergence of first large-scale drug trading organization, *La Federación* ("Guadalajara Cartel"), co-ordinated by Miguel Ángel Félix Gallardo.

1982 Near-collapse of Mexican economy, propped up by IMF loans, conditioned on massive reduction in state spending.

1982–1990s "Lost decade" of stalled growth, crippling debt burden, and extreme austerity.

1987–1988 Left-wing group splits from PRI, runs Cuauhtémoc Cárdenas as candidate for president; Carlos Salinas (PRI, 1988-1994) declared winner.

1990s Mexican cocaine boom.

1993–1994 Assassinations of Cardinal Juan Jesús Posadas Ocampo, PRI presidential candidate Luis Donaldo Colosio, PRI secretary-general José Francisco Ruiz Masseiu.

1994 January 1: North American Free Trade Agreement (NAFTA) comes into force.

January 1: rebellion of Ejército Zapatista de Liberación Nacional breaks out in Chiapas.

Ernesto Zedillo (PRI, 1994–2000) wins presidential election.

1997 Opposition win Congress, multiple governorships, mayoralty of Mexico City.

2000 July 2: PRI loses presidency to Vicente Fox (Partido Acción Nacional, 2000–2006).

2005 Foreign oil companies allowed for first time since 1938 into offshore oilfields.

2006 Felipe Calderón (Partido Acción Nacional, 2006–2012) wins presidency and declares War on Drugs, deploying army against narcos across the country.

2006–2020 War on Drugs kills over 200,000 Mexicans, makes over 100,000 refugees, creates 100,000 more disappeared.

2010–2020 Number of Americans using illicit drugs goes up 50 percent.

2024 Mexico elects North America's first woman president, Claudia Sheinbaum.

Glossary

afrodescendiente Mexican with African ancestry
agrarista agrarian militant
altepetl pre-Hispanic central Mexican city-state in microcosm
Audiencia/Real Audiencia de México Royal council for New Spain, based in Mexico City
ayuntamiento city or town council
Cabildo colonial city or town council, Mexico City in particular
cacique political boss
capitalino inhabitant of the capital, Mexico City
Cardenista follower of President Lázaro Cárdenas
casta colonial racial classification for people combining Spanish, indigenous, and African ancestry
charro Mexican equivalent of gaucho or cowboy
chilango slang, possibly pejorative, for inhabitant of Mexico City
científicos "scientific" developmentalist elites of the late nineteenth / early twentieth centuries
cofradía lay religious community
compadre godfather to one's son; a close friend
Cristero Catholic counterrevolutionary
desamortización forced privatization and division of communal lands
dictablanda hybrid regime of dictatorship and democracy
dinosaurio late-twentieth-century member of the PRI old guard
encomienda sixteenth-century grant of land and indigenous labor
encomendero possessor of an encomienda
ejido community of collective farmers
ejidatario member of an ejido
gachupín pejorative term for Spanish settler in Mexico
hacienda large estate or plantation
hacendado owner of a hacienda
jefe político late-nineteenth- or early-twentieth-century political boss
ley fuga the practice of shooting prisoners who were allegedly fleeing, i.e., extrajudicial execution

maestro rural rural teacher

mestizaje the sexual and cultural blending of indigenous and European peoples; nationalist ideology promoting that end

mestizo Mexican of mixed indigenous and European descent

moderado moderate nineteenth-century liberal

municipio municipality, county

municipio libre democratic and autonomous municipality

PAN Partido Acción Nacional, conservative party with close ties to the Catholic Church (1939–present)

panista member of the PAN

patria the homeland

patria chica "little homeland," a Mexican's local place of origin

peninsulares Spaniards living in Mexico, born in Spain

peón peon, a generic term for lower-class agricultural laborers, seventeenth to twentieth century

peso Mexican unit of currency since sixteenth century; originating in colonial silver coin weighing 3.4 grams

pinturas de castas colonial paintings describing sixteen supposed racial types

PNR Partido Nacional Revolucionario, state party ruling Mexico from 1929 to 1938

PRD Partido de la Revolución Democrática, left-wing party (1989–present)

prdista member of the PRD

PRI Partido Revolucionario Institucional, state party ruling Mexico from 1946 to 2000

priista member of the PRI

PRM Partido de la Revolución Mexicana, state party ruling Mexico from 1938 to 1946

pronunciamiento high-level, often performative and bloodless rebellion

pronunciados those engaged in a pronunciamiento

pueblo village, or "the people"; (nationalist) the masses, Mexicans

pulque milky, viscous cactus alcohol, strength equivalent to beer

pulquería drinking establishment, often rowdy, specializing in pulque

puros radical nineteenth-century liberals

repartimiento indigenous forced-labor draft, viceregal period

rurales paramilitary mounted police force (1861–1914)

serrano n., mountain dweller; adj., from the mountains

Sinarquista member of far-right Catholic organization the Union Nacional Sinarquista

tlatoani Nahuatl, literally "he who speaks"; Mexica emperor

terrenos baldíos supposedly empty land for settlement; undeeded land for development

vecinos lit., neighbors; official Spanish residents of a colonial town

Villista follower of revolutionary Pancho Villa

visitador political auditor of viceroy

Zapatistas followers of revolutionary Emiliano Zapata

Select Bibliography

Principal Archives

Archivo General de Indias, Seville
Archivo General de la Nación, Mexico City
Archivo Histórico del Distrito Federal, Mexico City
Archivo Histórico del Estado de Aguascalientes, Aguascalientes
Archivo Histórico del Estado de Guerrero, Chilpancingo
Archivo Histórico del Estado de Veracruz, Xalapa
Archivo Histórico de la Secretaría de la Defensa Nacional, Mexico City
Archivo Histórico de la Secretaría de Educación Pública, Mexico City
Archivo Histórico de la Secretaría de Hacienda, Mexico City
Archivo Municipal de Ixcateopan, Guerrero
Archivo Porfirio Díaz, Universidad Iberoamericana
Archivum Romanum Societatis Iesu, Rome
Fundación Miguel Alemán, Mexico City
Hemeroteca Nacional de México, Mexico City
Instituto Nacional de Antropología e Historia, Acervo Sonoro, Mexico City
General Archives of the Ordo Fratrum Minorum, Rome
The National Archives, London
The National Archives and Records Administration, College Park, Maryland
The Newberry Library Ayer Collection, Chicago
University of Chicago Library Special Collections, Chicago

Printed Sources

Aboites Aguilar, Luis. *Chihuahua. Historia breve*. Colegio de México, 2016.

Aboites, Luis, and Luis Jáuregui. *Penuria sin fin: historia de los impuestos en México siglos VVIII–XX*. Instituto Mora, 2005.

Acevedo Rodrigo, Ariadna, and Paula López Caballero, eds. *Ciudadanos inesperados: Espacios de formación de la ciudadanía ayer y hoy*. Colegio de México, 2012.

Acuña, René. *Relaciones geográficas del siglo XVI: México tomo primero*. Universidad Autónoma de México, 1985.

Agostoni, Claudia. *Monuments of Progress Modernization and Public Health in Mexico City, 1876–1910*. University of Calgary Press, 2003.

Aguayo, Sergio. *La Charola: una historia de los servicios de inteligencia en México*. Raya en el agua, 2001.

de Aguilar, Francisco. *Relación breve de la conquista de la Nueva España*. Edited by Jorge Gurría Lacroix. Universidad Autónoma de México, 1977.

Aguilar, Rubén, and Jorge G. Castañeda. *El narco: la guerra fallida*. México DF: punto de lectura, 2009.

Aguilar Camín, Hector. *La frontera nomada: Sonora y la Revolución Mexicana*. Fondo de Cultura Económica, 2017.

Aguilar Camín, Hector. "Nociones Presidenciales de la Cultura Nacional de Alvaro Obregón a Gustavo Díaz Ordaz, 1920–1968." In *En torno a la cultura nacional*, by José Emilio Pacheco. Secretaría de Educación Pública, 1976.

Aguirre Beltrán, Gonzalo. *Regiones de Refugio: El Desarrollo e la Comunidad y el Proceso Dominical en Mestizo América*. Instituto Indigenista Interamericano, 1967.

Aguirre Benavides, Adrián. *Errores de Madero*. México, 1980.

Ahmed, Azam. *Fear is Just a Word: A Missing Daughter, a Violent Cartel, and a Mother's Quest for Vengeance*. Random House, 2023.

de Ajofrín, Francisco. *Diario de viaje que hicimos a México Fray Francisco de Ajofrín y Fray Fermín de Olite, Capuchinos, con una introducción por Génaro Estrada*. Antiguo Librería Robredo, de José Porrúa e Hijos, 1936.

Alamán, Lucas. *Semblanzas e ideario*. Edited by Arturo Arnáiz y Freg. Universidad Autónoma de México, 2010.

Alanís Enciso, Fernando Saúl. *They Should Stay There: The Story of Mexican Migration and Repatriation During the Great Depression*. University of North Carolina Press, 2017.

Alba, Francisco, and Joseph E. Potter. "Population and Development in Mexico since 1940: An Interpretation." *Population and Development Review* 12, No. 1. 1986.

Alberro, J. Solange. *El águila y la cruz. Orígenes religiosos de la conciencia criolla. México, siglos XVI–XVII*. Colegio de México, 1999.

Alegre, Robert F. *Railroad Radicals in Cold War Mexico: Gender, Class, and Memory*. University of Nebraska Press, 2014.

Alemán Velasco, Miguel. *Miguel Alemán contesta . . .* Austin, 1975.

Altman, Ida. *The War for Mexico's West: Indians and Spaniards in New Galicia, 1524–1550*. University of New Mexico Press, 2010.

Allier Montaño, Eugenia. "Memorias imbricadas: terremotos en México, 1985 y 2017." *Revista Mexicana de Sociología* 80, núm. especial. (Septiembre, 2018).

Alvarado Tezozómoc, Fernando. *Crónica Mexicáyotl*. Universidad Nacional Autónoma de México, 1975.

de Alva Xitlilxochitl, Fernando. *Obras históricas*. Edited by Alfredo Chavero. Oficina tip. del Secretaría de Fomento, 1891.

Almond, Gabriel A., and Sidney Verba. *The Civic Culture: Political Attitude and Democracy in Five Nations*. SAGE Publications, 1989.

Anderson, Jon Lee. *Che Guevara: A Revolutionary Life*. Bantam Press, 1997.

Ann Sumner, Jaclyn. *Indigenous Autocracy: Power, Race, and Resources in Porfirian Tlaxcala, Mexico*. Stanford University Press, 2023.

Anderson, Rodney D. *Outcasts in Their Own Land: Mexican Industrial Workers, 1906–1911*. Cornell University Press, 1976.

Ankerson, Dudley. *Agrarian Warlord: Saturnino Cedillo and the Mexican Revolution in San Luis Potosí*. Northern Illinois University Press, 1984.

Anna, Timothy E. *Forging Mexico, 1821–1835*. University of Nebraska Press, 1998.

Aizpuru, Pilar Gonzalbo, and Lira González, ed. *México, 1808–1821*. Fondo de Cultura Económica, 2014.

Austin Nesvig, Martin. *Ideology and Inquisition: The World of the Censors in Early Mexico*. Yale University Press, 2009.

Aviña, Alexander. *Spectres of Revolution: Peasant Guerrillas in the Mexican Cold War Countryside*. University of Oxford Press, 2014.

Azuela, Mariano. *Los de abajo*. Fondo de Cultura Económica, 1994.

de Balbuena, Bernardo. *Grandeza mexicana*. Universidad Nacional Autónoma, 1941.

Bartolomeus Heller, Karl. *Alone in Mexico: The Astonishing Travels of Karl Heller, 1845–1848*. Translated by Terry Rugeley. University of Alabama Press, 2007.

Batra, Armando, ed. *Crónicas del sur: Utopías campesinas en Guerrero*. Ediciones Era, 2000.

Beals, Carleton. *Mexican Maze*. J. B. Lipincott Company, 1931.

Beezley, William H. *Judas at the Jockey Club and Other Episodes of Porfirian Mexico*. University of Nebraska Press, 2004.

Benjamin, Thomas. *A Rich Land, a Poor People: Politics and Society in Modern Chiapas*. University of New Mexico Press, 1989.

Benjamin, Thomas, and William McNellie, *Other Mexicos: Essays on Regional Mexican History, 1876–1911*. University of New Mexico Press, 1984.

Benton, Bradley. *The Lords of Tetzcoco: The Transformation of Indigenous Rule in Postconquest Central Mexico*. Cambridge University Press, 2017.

Bermejo Mora, Edgardo. *Marcos Fashion: O de cómo sobrevivir al derrumbe de las ideologías sin perder el estilo*. Editorial Oceano, 1996.

Bernal, Ignacio. *Arqueología ilustrada y mexicanista en el siglo XVIII*. Centro de Estudios de Historia de México, 1975.

Bernal, Rafael. *El Complot Mongol*. Grupo Planeta, 2013.

Berlin, H., and R. Barlow, eds. *Anales de Tlatelolco*. Porrua, 1948.

Bethell, Leslie, ed. *Cambridge History of Latin America*. Cambridge University Press, 1985.

Blasco Ibañez, Vicente. *El militarismo mejicano: estudios publicados en los principales diarios de los Estados Unidos*. Madrid, 1920.

Blázquez Domínguez, Carmen. *Estado de Veracruz: informes de sus gobernadores, 1826–1986*. 20 vols. Universidad Veracruzana, 1986.

Bleichmar, Daniela. *Visual Voyages: Images of Latin American Nature from Columbus to Darwin*. Yale University Press, 2017.

Bonfil Batalla, Guillermo. *Obras escogidas*. Instituto Nacional de Antropología e Historia, 1995.

Bonfil Batalla, Guillermo. *México profundo: una civilización negada*. Grijalbo, 1987.

Borah, Woodrow. *Justice by Insurance: The Great Indian Court of Colonial Mexico and the Legal Aides of the Half-Real*. University of California Press, 1983.

Bortz, Jeffrey. *Los salaries industriales en la Ciudad de México, 1939–1975*. Fondo de Cultura Económica, 1988.

Brading, David. *Peasant and Caudillo in the Mexican Revolution*. Cambridge University Press, 1980.

Brading, David. *The First America: The Spanish Monarchy, Creole Patriots and the Liberal State, 1492–1867*. Cambridge University Press, 1991.

Brading, David. *The Origins of Mexican Nationalism*. Cambridge University Press, 1985.

Brading, David. *Miners and Merchants in Bourbon Mexico, 1763–1810*. Cambridge University Press, 1971.

Braudel, Fernand. *Civilization and Capitalism 15th–18th Century*, vol. 1, *The Structures of Everyday Life*. Translated by Siân Reynold. Fontana, 1981.

Braudel, Fernand. *The Mediterranean and the Mediterranean World in the Age of Philip II*. Collins, 1973.

Braudel, Fernand. *Civilization and Capitalism 15th–18th Century*, vol. 2, *The Wheels of Commerce I*. Translated by Siân Reynold. Fontana Press, 1981.

Brennan, James P. *Argentina's Missing Bones: Revisiting the History of the Dirty War*. University of California Press, 2018.

Brenner, Anita. *The Wind that Swept Mexico: The History of the Mexican Revolution 1910–1942*. Harper & Brothers, 1943.

Buchenau, Jürgen. *The Last Caudillo: Alvaro Obregón and the Mexican Revolution*. Wiley Blackwell, 2011.

Buffington, Robert. *A Sentimental Education for the Working Man: The Mexico City Penny Press, 1900–1910*. Duke University Press, 2015.

Bulmer-Thomas, Victor, et al. *The Cambridge Economic History of Latin America*. Cambridge University Press, 2008.

de Bustamante, Carlos María. *El nuevo Bernal: Memorias de la Guerra México-Estados Unidos*. Fondo de Cultura Económica, 1997.

Butler, Matthew. *Mexico's Spiritual Reconquest: Indigenous Catholics and Father Pérez's Revolutionary Church*. University of New Mexico Press, 2023.

Butler, Matthew. *Popular Piety and Political Identity in Mexico's Cristero Rebellion*. Oxford University Press, 2004.

Cabildo de la ciudad de México. *Actas de Cabildo de la ciudad de México*. Imprenta de Aguilar e Hijos, 1898.

Cabrera, Luis. "La Revolución es la Revolución" in *El Pensamiento de Luis Cabrera: selección y prólogo de Eduardo Luquín*. Biblioteca del Instituto Nacional de Estudios Históricos de la Revolución Mexicana, 1960.

Cancian, Frank. *The Decline of Community in Zinacantán: Economy, Public Life, and Social Stratification, 1960–1987*. Stanford University Press, 1992.

Calderón de la Barca, Fanny. *Life in Mexico*. Oakland: University of California Press, 1982.

Campos, Isaac. *Home Grown: Marijuana and the Origins of Mexico's War on Drugs*. University of North Carolina Press, 2012.

Cañizares-Esguerra, Jorge. *How to Write the History of the New World: Histories, Epistemologies, and Identities in the Eighteenth-Century Atlantic World*. Stanford University Press, 2001.

Calvo, Thomas. "Soberano, plebe y cadalso bajo una misma luz en Nueva España." In *Historia de la vida cotidiana en México*, edited by Pilar Gonzalbo Aizpuru. Fondo de Cultura Económica, 2014.

Carballo, David M. *Collision of Worlds: A Deep History of the Fall of Aztec Mexico and the Forging of New Spain*. Oxford University Press, 2020.

Cárdenas, Enrique. *La hacienda pública y la política económica 1929–1958*. Colegio de México, 1994.

Cárdenas, Lázaro. *Obras I – Apuntes 1913/1940*. UNAM, 1972.

Cárdenas, Lázaro. *Obras I – Apuntes 1957/1966 tomo III*. UNAM Nueva Biblioteca Mexicana, 1973.

Cárdenas García, Nicolás, y Enrique Guerra Manzo, coord. *Integrados y marginados en el México posrevolucionario: Los juegos del poder local y sus nexos con la política nacional*. Universidad Autónoma Metropolitana, 2009.

Carey, Elaine. *Women Drug Traffickers: Mules, Bosses, and Organized Crime*. University of New Mexico Press, 2014.

Carillo Dewar, Ivonne. *Industria Petrolera y Desarrollo Capitalista en el Norte de Veracruz, 1900–1990*. Universidad Veracruzana, 1993.

Carr, Barry. *La izquierda mexicana a través del siglo XX*. Ediciones Era, 1996.

Carrera, Magali M. *Traveling from New Spain to Mexico: Mapping Practices of Nineteenth-century Mexico*. Duke University Press, 2011.

Casans, an eye witness. *The Tears of the Indians: Being An Historical and true Acount of the Cruel Massacres and Slaughters of above Twenty Millions of innocent People*. Nath Brook, 1656.

Cabrera, Luis. *La revolución es la revolución: antología*. Comisión Nacional Editorial del C.E.N., Partido Revolucionario Institucional, 1985.

Castañeda Batres, Oscar, Horacio Labastida, and Ernesto Lemoine. *Documentos para la historia del México independiente*. Porrúa, 2010.

Castañeda Batres, Oscar. "Revolución Mexicana y Constitución de 1917." In *Documentos para la historia del México independiente*, edited by Ernesto Lemoines et al. Porrúa, 2010.

Castellanos, Laura. *México armado 1943–1981*. Biblioteca Era, 2007.

Ceballos Garibay, Héctor. *Francisco J. Múgica: Crónica política de un rebelde*. Ediciones Coyoacán, 2002.

Ceballos Ramírez, Manuel. "La enciclica Rerum Novarum y los trabajadores catolicos en la Ciudad de Mexico (1891–1913)." *Historia Mexicana* 33, no. 1 (Jul.–Sep. 1983).

Cedillo, Juan Alberto. *Los Nazis en México*. De Bolsillo, 2017.

Celia Toro, María. *Mexico's "War" on Drugs: Causes and Consequences*. Boulder, 1995.

Cervantes de Salazar, Francisco. *México en 1554*. Universidad Nacional Autónoma, 2001.

Chaunu, Pierre. *Séville et L'Amérique aux XVIe et XVIIe siècle*. In collaboration with Huguette Chaunu. Flammarion, 1977.

Chamberlain, Samuel E. *Recollections of a Rogue*. Museum Press Limited, 1957.

Chevalier, François. *Land and Society in Colonial Mexico: The Great Hacienda*. University of California Press, 1966.

Chowning, Margaret. *Catholic Women and Mexican Politics, 1750–1940*. Princeton University Press, 2023.

Clendinnen, Inga. *Ambivalent Conquests: Maya and Spaniard in Yucatán, 1517–1570*. Cambridge University Press, 1987.

Cohen, Deborah. *Family Secrets: Shame and Privacy in Modern Britain*. Oxford University Press, 2017.

Cole, Felipe. "When Debt Made Sovereignty, 1820–1933." PhD diss. Northwestern University, 2023.

Un compañero de Hernán Cortés. *El conquistador anónimo: Relación de algunas cosas de la Nueva España y de la gran ciudad de Temestitan Mexico*. Editorial América, 1941.

Contreras Martínez, José Eduardo. "La confrontación tlaxcalteca ante la Conquista." *Dimensión antropológica* 61 (2014).

Contreras Valdez, Mario. *Nayarit: historia breve*. Colegio de México, 2016.

Córdova, Arnaldo. *La política de masas del cardenismo*. Serie Popular Era, 1974.

Cornelius, Wayne A. *Politics and the Urban Poor in Mexico City*. Stanford University Press, 1975.

Corona del Rosa, Alfonso. *Mis memorias políticas*. Grijalbo, 1995.

Cortés, Hernán. *Cartas de relación de la conquista de Méjico*. Espasa-Calpe, 1940.

Cortés Basurto, María Angeles. "Cimientos del impero de la familia Guggenheim en México, 1890–1905." In *Negocios, empresarios y entornos políticos, 1827–1958*. Colegio de México, 2015.

Costa, Joaquín. *Oligarquía y caciquismo como la forma actual de gobernar en España: Urgencia y modo de cambiarla*. Madrid: Imprenta de los hijos de M.G. Hernández, 1902.

Cosío Villegas, Daniel. *El Porfiriato: la vida política interior*. Hermes, 1972.

Cosío Villegas, Daniel, et al. *Historia general de México*. Colegio de México, 1977.

Cosío Villegas, Daniel. *Memorias*. J. Moritz, 1976.

Craib, Raymond B. *Cartographic Mexico: A History of State Fixations and Fugitive Landscapes*. Duke University Press, 2004.

Crosby, Alfred W. *The Columbian Exchange: Biological and Cultural Consequences of 1492*. Connecticut, 1972.

Dana, Richard Henry. *Two Years Before the Mast*. Penguin, 1948.

Deininger, Klaus, and Lyn Squire. "A New Data Set Measuring Income Inequality." *The World Bank Economic Review* 10, no. 3 Oxford University Press, 1996.

DeLay, Brian. *War of a Thousand Deserts: Indian Raids and the U.S.-Mexican War*. Yale University Press, 2008.

van Deusen, Nancy E. *Global Indios: The Indigenous Struggle for Justice in Sixteenth-Century Spain*. Duke University Press, 2015.

Díaz, Lilia. "El liberalismo militante." In *Historia general de México*, by Daniel Cosío Villegas et al. El Colegio de México, 1976.

Díaz, Porfirio. *Memorias de Porfirio Díaz con un prólogo de Moisés González Navvro*. Vol. 1. Conaculta, 1994.

Díaz Díaz, Fernando. *Caudillos y caciques: Antonio López de Santa Anna y Juan Álvarez*. Colegio de México, 1972.

Díaz del Castillo, Bernal. *Historia verdadera de la Conquista de México*. Madrid, 1982.

Díaz y de Ovando, Clementina. *Vicente Riva Palacio y la identidad nacional*. UNAM, 1985.

Douglas Cope, R. *The Limits of Racial Domination: Plebeian Society in Colonial Mexico City, 1660–1720*. University of Wisconsin Press, 1994.

Drelichman, Mauricio, and Hans-Joachim Voth. *Lending to the Borrower from Hell: Debt, Taxes, and Default in the Age of Philip II*. Princeton University Press, 2014.

Ducey, Michael T. *A Nation of Villages: Riot and Rebellion in the Mexican Huasteca, 1750–1850*. University of Arizona Press, 2004.

Dulles, John W. F. *Yesterday in Mexico: A Chronicle of the Revolution, 1919–1936*. University of Texas Press, 1961.

Durán, Diego. *Historia de las Indias*. Kessinger, 2010.

Dwyer, John J. *The Agrarian Dispute: The Expropriation of American-Owned Rural Land in Revolutionary Mexico*. Duke University Press, 2008.

Earle, Rebecca. *The Return of the Native: Indians and Myth-making in Spanish America, 1810–1930*. Duke University Press, 2007.

Eckstein, Susan. *The Poverty of Revolution: The State and the Urban Poor in Mexico*. Princeton University Press, 1988.

Elliott, John H. *The Old World and the New: 1492–1650*. Cambridge University Press, 2000.

Elliott, John H. *Imperial Spain 1469–1716*. Penguin Books, 1963.

Elliott, John H. *Empires of the Atlantic World: Britain and Spain in America, 1492–1830*. Yale University Press, 2006.

Escobar Ohmstede, Antonio, et al. *Agua y tierra en México, siglos XIX y XX*. Colegio de Michacán/Colegio de San Luis, 2008.

Esposito, Matthew. *Funerals, Festivals, and Cultural Politics in Porfirian Mexico*. University of New Mexico Press, 2010.

Falcón, Romana. *El agrarismo en Veracruz: la etapa radical (1928–1935)*. Colegio de México, 1977.

Fallaw, Ben. *Cárdenas Compromised: The Failure of Reform in Postrevolutionary Yucatán*. Duke University Press, 2001.

Fane, Diane, ed. *Converging Cultures: Art & Identity in Spanish America*. Brooklyn Museum and Harry N. Abrams, Inc., 1996.
Farriss, Nancy. *Maya Society*. Princeton University Press, 1984.
Félix, María. *Todas mis guerras*. México DF, 1993.
Fernández, Claudia, and Andrew Paxman. *El Tigre: Emilio Azcárraga y su imperio Televisa*. Grijalbo, 2000.
Fernández-Armesto, Felipe. *Our America: A Hispanic History of the United States*. W. W. Norton & Company, 2014.
Fernández del Castillo, Francisco. *Libros y libreros en el siglo XVI*. Fondo de Cultura Económica, 2017.
Fernández de Lizardi, José Joaquín. *El Periquillo Sarniento*. Alexandro Valdés, 1816.
Fiscalía Especial para Movimientos Sociales y Políticos del Pasado (FEMOSPP). *Informe Histórico a la Sociedad Mexicana*. Comisión Nacional de los Derechos Humanos, 2006.
El Fisgón and Helguera. *El sexenio me da risa*. Grijalbo, 1994.
Flandrau, Charles M. *¡Viva México!* Eland Books, 1985.
Flores Pérez, Carlos Antonio. *El Estado en crisis: crimen organizado y política. Desafíos para la consolidación democrática*. CIESAS, 2009.
Florescano, Enrique. *Etnia, estado, nación*. Aguilar, 1997.
Florescano, Enrique, and Pablo González Casanova, eds. *La clase obrera en la historia de México Vol. 1: de la colonia al imperio*. Siglo XXI, 1996.
Florescano, Enrique. *Memoria Mexicana*. Fondo de Cultura Económica, 2014.
Forment, Carlos A. *Democracy in Latin America, 1760–1900: Volume I, Civic Selfhood and Public Life in Mexico and Peru*. University of Chicago Press, 2003.
Fowler, Will, ed. *Forceful Negotiations: The Origins of the* Pronunciamiento *in Nineteenth-Century Mexico*. University of Nebraska Press, 2010.
Fowler, Will. *The Grammar of Civil War: A Mexican Case Study, 1857–1861*. University of Nebraska Press, 2022.
Fowler-Salamini, Heather. *Working Women, Entrepreneurs, and the Mexican Revolution: The Coffee Culture of Córdoba, Veracruz*. University of Nebraska Press, 2013.
Freije, Vanessa. *Citizens of Scandal: Journalism, Secrecy and the Politics of Reckoning*. Duke University Press, 2020.
Frías, Herbierto. *Tomochic*. Fundación Carlos Slim, 1905.
Friedlander, Judith. *Being Indian in Hueyapan: A Study of Forced Identity in Modern Mexico*. St. Martin's Press, 1975.
Friedrich, Paul. *Agrarian Revolt in a Mexican Village*. University of Chicago Press, 1970.
Friedrich, Paul. *The Princes of Naranja: An Essay in Anthrohistorical Method*. University of Texas Press, 1986.
Fuentes, Carlos. *La Muerte de Artemio Cruz*. Fondo de Cultura Económica, 1962.
Fuentes, Carlos. "Un día en la tierra de Zapata." *La Cultura en México. Suplemento de Siempre!*, July 11, 1962.
Gamboa Ojeda, Leticia, ed. *Los Barcelonettes en México, miradas regionales*. Benemérita Universidad Autónoma de Puebla, 2008.
Gamio, Manuel. *Arqueología e indigenismo*. Secretaría de Educación Pública, 1972.
Gamio, Manuel. *Forjando Patria (Pro-Nacionalismo)*. Porrua Hermanos, 1916.
García, Alberto. *Abandoning Their Beloved Land: The Politics of Bracero Migration in Mexico*. University of California Press, 2023.
García, Inocente. *Hechos históricos de California, as told to Thomas Savage, 1878*. University of California Press, 1974.

García Acosta, Virginia, Juan Manuel Pérez Zevallo, and América Molinar del Villar. *Desastres agrícolas en México. Catálogo histórico*. Fondo de Cultura Económica, 2014.

García Martínez, Bernardo. *El Desarrollo regional y la organización del espacio, siglos XVI al XX*. Universidad Autónoma de México, 2004.

García Díaz, Bernardo. *Un pueblo fabril del Porfiriato: Santa Rosa, Veracruz*. Fondo de Cultura Económica, 1981.

García Martínez, Bernardo, and Gustavo Martínez Mendoza. *Señorios, pueblos y municipios*. Colegio de México, 2012.

García Quintana, Josefina. *Cuauhtémoc en el siglo XIX*. México DF, 1977.

Garner, Paul. *Porfirio Díaz*. Longman, 2001.

Gauss, Susan. *Made in Mexico: Regions, Nation, and the State in the Rise of Mexican Industrialism, 1920s–1940s*. Pennsylvania State Press, 2010.

Gibson, Carrie. *El Norte: The Epic and Forgotten Story of Hispanic North America*. Grove Atlantic, 2019.

Gill, Mario. "Los Escudero, de Acapulco." *Historia Mexicana* 3, no. 4 (Oct.–Dec. 1953).

Glantz, Susana. *El ejido colectivo de Nueva Italia*. Instituto Nacional de Antropología e Historia, 1974.

Gonzalbo Aizpuru, Pilar, ed. *Historia de la vida cotidiana en México*. 3 vols. Fondo de Cultura Económica, 2014.

Gonzalbo Aizpuru, Pilar, and Andrés Lira González, eds. *México, 1808–1821: Las ideas y los hombres*. Colegio de México, 2014.

González Casanova, Pablo. *Las elecciones en México: evolución y perspectiva*. Siglo XXI, 1985.

González, Alberto. *Doña Loba: una historia de cacicazgo y poder*. Penguin Random House, 2013.

González Sierra, José. *Monopolio del Humo (elementos para la historia del tabaco en México y algunos conflictos de tabaqueros veracruzanos: 1915–1930)*. Universidad Veracruzana, 1987.

González y González, Luis. *El indio en la era liberal*. Colegio de México, 1996.

González y González, Luis. "El liberalismo triunfante." In *Historia general de México*, by Daniel Cosío Villegas et al. Colegio de México, 1994.

González y González, Luis. *Pueblo en vilo: una microhistoria de San José de Gracia*. Colegio de México, 1995.

González Navarro, Moisés. *Cristeros y agraristas en Jalisco*. Vol. 2. Colegio de México, 2001.

González Navarro, Moisés. *El Porfiriato: La vida social*. Fondo de Cultura Económica, 1957.

González Navarro, Moisés. *Memorias de Porfirio Díaz*. Vol. I. CONACULTA, 1994.

González Navarro, Moisés. *Población y Sociedad en México (1900–1970)*, 2 vols. México DF, 1974.

Gómez-Galvarriato, Aurora. *Industry and Revolution: Social and Economic Change in the Orizaba Valley, Mexico*. Harvard University Press, 2013.

Gómez Serrano, Jesús, and Francisco Javier Delgado Aguilar. *Historia breve de Aguascalientes*. Colegio de México, 2012.

Gootenberg, Paul. *Andean Cocaine: The Making of a Global Drug*. University of North Carolina Press, 2008.

Gootenberg, Paul. "Secret Ingredients: The Politics of Coca in US-Peruvian relations, 1915–1965." *Journal of Latin American Studies* 36, no. 2 (May 2004).

Greene, Graham. *The Lawless Roads*. Penguin, 1982. Originally published in 1939.

Greenleaf, Richard E. *La Inquisición en Nueva España Siglo XVI*. Fondo de Cultura Económica, 2015.

Gruening, Ernest. *Mexico and Its Heritage*. D. Appleton-Century, 1936.

Guardino, Peter F. *Peasants, Politics, and the Formation of Mexico's National State: Guerrero, 1800–1857*. Stanford University Press, 1996.

Guardino, Peter. *The Time of Liberty: Popular Political Culture in Oaxaca, 1750–1850*. Duke University Press, 2005.

Guardino, Peter. *The Dead March: A History of the Mexican-American War*. Harvard University Press, 2017.

Guillén, Clemente. *Explorer of the South: Diaries of the Overland Expeditions to Bahía Magdalena and La Paz, 1719, 1720–21*, translated and edited by W. Michael Mathes. Dawson's Bookshop, 1979.

Guillermoprieto, Alma. "The Riddle of Raúl." *The New Yorker*, 2 June 1997.

Gutiérrez, Ramón A. *When Jesus Came, the Corn Mothers Went Away: Marriage, Sexuality, and Power in New Mexico, 1500–1846*. University of Stanford Press, 1991.

Gutmann, Mathew C. *The Romance of Democracy: Compliant Defiance in Contemporary Mexico*. University of California Press, 2002.

Guzmán Urióstegui, Jesús. *Evila Franco Nájera, a pesar del olvido*. México DF, 1995.

Gruzinski, Serge. *El águila y el dragón: desmesura europea y mundialización en el siglo XVI*. Fondo de Cultura Económica, 2018.

Gruzinski, Serge. *What Time Is It There? America and Islam at the Dawn of Modern Times*. MA Polity Press, 2010.

Gurría Lacroix, Jorge. *Hernán Cortés y Diego Rivera*. Instituto de Investigaciones Historicas, 1971.

Gustave Desmond, Lawrence. *Yucatán Through Her Eyes: Alice Dixon Le Plongeon, Writer & Expeditionary Photographer*. University of New Mexico Press, 2009.

Guzmán, Eulalia. *Una visión crítica de la historia de la conquista de México-Tenochtitlán*. Universidad Nacional Autónoma de México, 1989.

Haber, Steven. *Industry and Underdevelopment: The Industrialization of Mexico, 1890–1940*. Stanford University Press, 1989.

Hahn, Steven. *A Nation Without Borders: The United States and Its World in an Age of Civil Wars, 1830–1910*. Viking, 2016.

Hammond, Norman. *The Maya*. Folio Society, 2000.

Hernandez Chavez, Alicia. *Morelos: historia breve*. Fondo de Cultura Económica, 2002.

Hernández Garcia, Erasmo. "Redes políticas y sociales. Consolidación y permanencia del régimen posrevolucionario in Veracruz, 1920–1970." PhD diss., Universidad Veracruzana, 2010.

Hernandez Llamas, Héctor, ed. *La atención médica rural en México: 1930–1980*. Instituto Mexicano del Seguro Social, 1984.

Hernández Rodríguez, Rogelio. *El oficio político: La élite gobernante en México, (1946–2020)*. Colegio de México, 2021.

Hernández Rodríguez, Rogelio. *Historia mínima del Partido Revolucionario Institucional*. Colegio de México, 2016.

Hernández Rodríguez, Rogelio. *La formación del político mexicano: el caso de Carlos A. Madrazo*. Colegio de México, 1991.

Herrera Calderón, Fernando, and Adela Cedillo, eds. *Challenging Authoritarianism in Mexico: Revolutionary Struggles and the Dirty War, 1964–1982*. Routledge, 2012.

Herrera Pérez, Octavia. *Tamaulipas: Historia breve*. Colegio de México, 2010.

Hirales Morán, Gustavo A. *México, ajustando cuentas con la historia (justicia transicional fallida)*. Comisión Nacional de los Derechos Humanos, 2017.

Hu-Dehart, Evelyn. *Yaqui Resistance and Survival: The Struggle for Land and Autonomy, 1821–1910*. University of Wisconsin Press, 1984.

de la Huerta, Adolfo. *Memorias de Don Adolfo de la Huerta según su propio dictado*. Instituto Nacional de Estudios Históricos de las Revoluciones de México, 2020.

von Humboldt, Alexander. *Political Essay on the Kingdom of New Spain*. Translated by John Black. 3 vols. Longman, 1814.

Iber, Patrick. *Neither Peace nor Freedom: The Cultural Cold War in Latin America*. Harvard University Press, 2015.

Informe de la Presidencia de la Comisión para la Verdad y Acceso a la Justicia del Caso Ayotzinapa. August 2022.

Iturriaga de la Fuente, José. *Anecdotario de viajeros extranjeros en México. Siglos XVI–XX*, 5 vols. Fondo de Cultura Económica, 1993.

Jacoby, Karl. *The Strange Career of William Ellis: The Texas Slave Who Became a Mexican Millionaire*. W. W. Norton & Company, 2017.

Jackson Albarrán, Elena. *Seen and Heard in Mexico*. University of Nebraska, 2015.

Jaurrieta, José María. *Seis años con el general Francisco Villa*. Fondo de Cultura Económica, 2023.

Jones, Halbert. *The War Has Brought Peace to Mexico: World War II and the Consolidation of the Post-Revolutionary State*. University of New Mexico Press, 2014.

Joseph, Gilbert M., and Timothy Henderson. *The Mexico Reader: History, Culture, and Politics*. Duke University Press, 2002.

Joseph, Gilbert M., and Daniel Nugent. *Everyday Forms of State Formation*. Duke University Press, 1994.

Joseph,Gilbert M., Anne Rubenstein, and Eric Zolov, eds. *Fragments of a Golden Age: The Politics of Culture in Mexico Since 1940*. Duke University Press, 2001.

Justo Sierra, Carlos, Fausta Gantus Inurreta, and Laura Villanueva. *Breve historia de Campeche*. Fondo de Cultura Económica, 2011.

Kamen, Henry. *Empire: How Spain Became a World Power, 1492–1763*. HarperCollins, 2003.

Katz, Friedrich. *The Life and Times of Pancho Villa*. University of Stanford Press, 1998.

Katz, Friedrich. *The Secret War in Mexico: Europe, the United States, and the Mexican Revolution*. University of Chicago Press, 1981.

Katzew, Ilona, ed. *Painted in Mexico, 1700–1790: Pinxit Mexici*. Prestel, 2017.

Kelker, Nancy L., and Karen O. Bruhns. *Faking Ancient Mesoamerica*. Left Coast Press, 2010.

Keller, Renata. *Mexico's Cold War: Cuba, the United States, and the Legacy of the Mexican Revolution*. Cambridge University Press, 2015.

Kiddle, Amelia. *Mexico's Relations with Latin America during the Cárdenas Era*. University of New Mexico Press, 2016.

Kloppe-Santamaría, Gema. *In the Vortex of Violence: Lynching, Extralegal Justice, and the State in Post-Revolutionary Mexico*. University of California Press, 2020.

Knight, Alan. "Cardenismo: Juggernaut or Jalopy?" *Journal of Latin American Studies* 26, no. 1 (Feb. 1994).

Knight, Alan. *Mexico: Volume 1, From the Beginning to the Spanish Conquest*. Cambridge University Press, 2002.

Knight, Alan. *Mexico: Volume 2, The Colonial Era*. Cambridge University Press, 2002.

Knight, Alan. *The Mexican Revolution, Volume 1, Porfirians, Liberals and Peasants*. University of Nebraska Press, 1990.

Knight, Alan. *The Mexican Revolution, Volume 2, Counter-revolution and Reconstruction*. University of Nebraska Press, 1990.

Krauze, Enrique. *Francisco I. Madero: Místico de la libertad*. Fondo de Cultura Económica, 1987.

Krauze, Enrique. *La Presidencia Imperial: ascenso y caida del sistema político mexicano (1940–1996)*. Tusquets Editores, 1997.

Krauze, Enrique. *Mexico, Biography of Power: A History of Modern Mexico, 1810–1996*. HarperCollins, 1997.

Labastida Martín del Campo, Julio, and Martín Armando López Leyva, "México: una transición prolongada (1988–1996/7)." *Revista Mexicana de Sociología* 66, no. 4 (October–December 2004).

de Landa, Friar Diego. *Yucatán Before and After the Conquest*. San Fernando, 1991.

Lafaye, Jacques. *Quetzalcóatl y Guadalupe: La formación de la conciencia nacional en México*. Fondo de Cultura Económica, 1995.

Lear, John. *Workers, Neighbors and Citizens: the Revolution in Mexico City*. University of Nebraska Press, 2001.

León-Portilla, Miguel. Informe referente al Colegio de Santa Cruz de Tlatelolco (1570), in *Códice franciscano*, ed., *Historia Documental de México*, vol I.

León-Portilla, Miguel. *Los franciscanos vistos por el hombre náhuatl: Testimonios indígenas del siglo XVI*. Universidad Nacional Autónoma de México, 1985.

León-Portilla, Miguel. *Visión de los vencidos: relaciones indígenas de la conquista*. Universidad Nacional Autónoma de México, 1992.

Lepore, Jill. *These Truths: A History of the United States*. Norton & Company, 2018.

Lewis, Stephen E. *The Ambivalent Revolution: Forging State and Nation in Chiapas, 1910–1945*. University of New Mexico Press, 2005.

Lewis, Oscar. *The Children of Sánchez: Autobiography of a Mexican Family*. Vintage Books, 1963.

Lieuwen, Edwin. *Mexican Militarism: The Political Rise and Fall of the Revolutionary Army, 1910–1940*. University of New Mexico Press, 1968.

Lira González, Andrés. *Comunidades indígenas frente a la Ciudad de México: Tenochtitlán y Tlatelolco, sus pueblos y barrios, 1812–1919*. Colegio de México, 1995.

Livi-Bacci, Massimo. *A Concise History of World Population*. Oxford University Press, 2007.

Lockhart, James. *The Nahuas After the Conquest: A Social and Cultural History of the Indians of Central Mexico, Sixteenth Through Eighteenth Centuries*. University of Stanford Press, 1992.

Lockhart, James, and Enrique Otte. *Letters and People of the Spanish Indies, Sixteenth Century*. Cambridge University Press, 1976.

Lomnitz, Claudio. *Death and the Idea of Mexico*. Zone Books, 2005.

León-Portilla, Miguel, ed. *Historia Documental de México*. 2 vols. Universidad Nacional Autónoma de México, 1964.

López de Gómara, Francisco. *Historia general de las Indias*. Memoria, 2014.

López, Rick A. *Crafting Mexico: Intellectuals, Artisans, and the State after the Revolution*. Duke University Press, 2010.

Loret de Mola, Rafael. *Manos sucias: crónicas verdaderas del poder*. Tiempo de México, 1996.

Luis Guzmán, Martín. *El Aguila y la Serpiente*. Ed Anahuac, 1949.

Lynch, John. *Spain 1516–1598: From Nation State to World Empire*. Blackwell Publishers Limited, 1991.

Madero, Francisco I. "Los diarios espiritistas de Francisco I. Madero." *Letras libres*, 28 February 1999.

María Jaurrieta, José. *Seis años con el general Francisco Villa*. Fondo de Cultura Económica, 2023.

Martínez, José Luis. *Hernán Cortés*. Fondo de Cultura Económica, 1990.

Martínez, José Luis. *Documentos Cortesianos*. Fondo de Cultura Económica, 1991.

Martínez, José Luis. *Pasajeros de Indias: Viajes trasatlánticos en el siglo XVI*. Fondo de Cultura Económica, 1999.

de Mauleón, Hector. *La ciudad que nos inventa: Crónicas de seis siglos*. Cal y Arena, 2015.

Macauley, Melissa. *Distant Shores: Colonial encounters on China's Maritime Frontier*. Princeton University Press, 2021.

MacEwan, Colin, and Alejandro López Luján, eds. *Moctezuma: Aztec Ruler*. British Museum Press, 2009.

Magaloni Kerpel, Diana. *Albores de la Conquista*. Artes de México, 2016.

Mann, Charles G. *1491: New Revelations of the Americas Before Columbus*. Vintage Books, 2011.

Manthorne, Katherine, ed. *California Mexicana: Missions to Murals, 1820–1930*. Laguna Art Museum, 2017.

Marett, R. H. K. *An Eye-Witness of Mexico*. Oxford University Press, 1939.

Marichal, Carlos. "The Spanish-America Silver Peso: Export Commodity and Global Money of the Ancien Regime, 1550–1800." In *From Silver to Cocaine: Latin American Commodity Chains and the Building of the World Economy, 1500–2000*, by Steven Topik, Carlos Marichal, and Zephyr Frank. Duke University Press, 2006.

Marichal, Carlos. *A Century of Debt Crises in Latin America: From Independence to the Great Depression, 1820–1930*. Princeton University Press, 1998.

Marnham, Patrick. *Dreaming With his Eyes Open: A Life of Diego Rivera*. Alfred Knopf, 1998.

Martínez, María Antonia. *El despegue constructivo de la Revolución. Sociedad y política en el alemanismo*. México: CIESAS, Porrúa, 2004.

Martínez Assad, Carlos. *El henriquismo, una piedra en el camino*, Colección Memoria y olvido. Martín Casillas Editores, 1982.

Martínez Assad, Carlos. *El laboratorio de la Revolución. El Tabasco garridista*. Siglo Veintiuno, 2004.

Martínez Assad, Carlos, ed. *Estadistas, caciques y caudillos*. UNAM, 1988.

Martínez Baracs, Andrea. *Un gobierno de indios: Tlaxcala, 1519–1750*. Fondo de Cultura Económica, 2014.

Martínez Baracs, Rodrigo. *Convivencia y utopia: El gobierno indio y español de la "ciudad de Mechuacan", 1521–1580*. Fondo de Cultura Económica, 2005.

Martínez, María Elena. *Genealogical Fictions: Limpieza de Sangre, Religion, and Gender in Colonial Mexico*. Stanford University Press, 2008.

Martyr, Peter. *De Orbe Novo*. Vol. II. Knickerbocker Press, 1912.

Marx, Karl. *Capital Volume I*. Penguin, 1990.

Marx, Karl. *The Eighteenth Brumaire of Louis Napoleon*. Marx/Engels Internet Archive, 1995 [1852].

Matthew, Laura E. *Memories of Conquest: Becoming Mexican in Colonial Guatemala*. University of North Carolina Press, 2012.

McCaa, Robert. "Missing Millions: The Demographic Costs of the Mexican Revolution." *Mexican Studies/Estudios Mexicanos* 19, no. 2 (Summer, 2003).

McNamara, Patrick J. *Sons of the Sierra: Juárez, Díaz, & the People of Ixtlán, Oaxaca, 1855–1920*. University of North Carolina Press, 2007.

Medel y Alvarado, León. *Historia de San Andrés Tuxtla (1525–1975)*. 3 vols. Xalapa, 1993–1994.

Medin, Tzvi. *El minimato presidencial: historia politica del Maximato*. Colegio de México, 1982.

Melville, Elinor G. K. *A Plague of Sheep*. Cambridge University Press, 1997.

Mendiola García, Sandra C. *Street Democracy: Vendors, Violence and Public Space in Late Twentieth-Century Mexico*. University of Nebraska Press, 2017.

Meyer, Jean. "Mexico: Revolution and Reconstruction in the 1920s." In Leslie Bethell, ed., *Mexico Since Independence*. Cambridge University Press, 1991.

Meyer, Jean. *La Cristiada*. 3 vols. Siglo Vientiuno, 1970.

Meyer, Jean. *The Cristero Rebellion: The Mexican People Between Church and State, 1926–1929*. Cambridge Latin American Studies, 1976.

Middlebrook, Kevin. *The Paradox of Revolution: Labor, the State, and Authoritarianism in Mexico*. John Hopkins University Press, 1995.
Mijangos, Pablo. *The Lawyer of the Church: Bishop Clemente de Jesús Munguía and the Clerical Response to the Mexican Liberal Reforma*. University of Nebraska, 2015.
Mitchell, Stephanie, and Patience A. Schell. *The Women's Revolution in Mexico, 1910–1953*. Lanham, MD: Rowman & Littlefield, 2007.
Mokyr, Joel. *A Culture of Growth: The Origins of the Modern Economy*. Princeton University Press, 2018.
Molinar Horcasitas, Juan. *El tiempo de la legitimidad. Elecciones, autoritarismo y democracia in México*. Cal y Arena, 1991.
Monsiváis, Carlos. *Dias de Guardar*. Ediciones Era, 1970.
Monsiváis, Carlos. "La solidaridad de la población en realidad fue toma de poder." *Proceso*, 23 September, 1985.
Montaño, Diana J. *Electrifying Mexico: Technology and the Transformation of a Modern City*. University of Texas Press, 2021.
Mora Forero, Jorge. "Los maestros y la práctica de la educación socialista." *Historia Mexicana* 29, no. 1 (July–September, 1979).
Moreno-Brid & Ros, Juan Carlos. *Development and Growth in the Mexican Economy*. Oxford University Press, 2009.
Morris, Melissa. "Cultivating Colonies: Tobacco and the Upstart Empires, 1580–1640." Unpublished Ph.D. dissertation, Columbia University, 2017.
Morris, Nathaniel. *Soldiers, Saints, and Shamans: Indigenous Communities and the Revolutionary State in Mexico's Gran Nayar, 1910–1940*. University of Arizona Press, 2020.
Morris, Stephen D. *Corruption and Politics in Contemporary Mexico*. University of Alabama Press, 1991.
Motolinía, Toribio de Benavente. *Historia de los indios de la Nueva España*. Castalia, 1985.
Mottier, Nicole. "Drug Gangs and Politics in Ciudad Juárez: 1928–1936." *Mexican studies/estudios mexicanos* 25, no. 1 (Winter 2009).
Mundy, Barbara E. *The Death of Aztec Tenochtitlan, the Life of Mexico City*. University of Texas Press, 2015.
Myrna Santiago, Isela. "Huasteca Crude: Indians, Ecology, and Labor in the Mexican Oil Industry, Northern Veracruz, 1900–1938." PhD diss., University of California, Berkeley 1997.
Nesvig, Martin Austin. *Promiscuous Power: An Unorthodox History of New Spain*. University of Texas Press, 2018.
Newcomer, Daniel. *Reconciling Modernity: Urban State Formation in 1940s León, Mexico*. University of Nebraska Press, 2004.
Obregón, Alvaro. *Ocho mil kilómetros en campaña*. La vda. de C. Bouret, 1917.
O'Gorman, Edmundo. *El proceso de la invención de América*. Fondo de Cultura Económica, 1998.
Oikión Solano, Verónica, and Marta Eugenia García Ugarte, eds. *Movimientos armados en México, siglo XX*. 3 vols. Colegio de Michoacán, 2008.
Olivera de Bonfil, Alicia. *La literatura cristera: antología*. Instituto Nacional de Antropología e Historia, 1994.
Olcott, Jocelyn. *Revolutionary Women in Postrevolutionary Mexico*. Duke University Press, 2005.
Orozco y Berra, Manuel, ed. *Códice Ramírez: relación del origen de los indios que habitan esta Nueva España según sus historias*. Editorial Innovación, 1979.

Ortíz Monasterio, José. *Historia y Ficción: los dramas y novelas de Vicente Riva Palacio*. Instituto Mora, 1993.

Ortíz Monasterio, José. *"Patria", tu ronca voz me repetía . . . biografía de Vicente Riva Palacio y Guerrero*. Instituto Mora, 1999.

Osten, Sarah. *The Mexican Revolution's Wake: The Making of a Political System, 1920–1929*. Cambridge University Press, 2018.

Otte, Enrique. "Mercaderes burgaleses en los inicios del comercio con México." *Historia Mexicana* 18, no. 2 (Oct.–Dec. 1968).

Overmyer-Velásquez, Mark, ed. *Beyond la Frontera: The History of Mexico–U.S. Migration*. Oxford University Press, 2011.

de la Cruz Pacheco Rojas, José. *Durango, historia breve*. Colegio de México, 2016.

Padilla, Tanalís. *Rural Resistance in the Land of Zapata: The Jaramillista Movement and the Myth of the Pax Priista, 1940–1962*. Duke University Press, 2008.

Padilla, Tanalís. *Unintended Lessons of Revolution: Student Teachers and Political Radicalism in Twentieth-Century Mexico*. Duke University Press, 2021.

Pagden, Anthony. *Spanish Imperialism and the Political Imagination: Studies in European and Spanish-American Social and Political Theory 1513–1830*. Yale University Press, 1990.

Palacios, Marco, ed. *Negocios, empresarios y entornos políticos, 1827–1958*. Colegio de México, 2015.

Pani, Alberto J. *El retroceso democrático del nuevo regimen*. A. J. Pani, 1947.

Pani, Erika. "La 'Innombrable': Monarquismo y cultura política en el México decimonónico." In *Prácticas populares, cultura política y poder en México, siglo XIX*, edited by Brian F. Connaughton. Universidad Autónoma Metropolitana, 2008.

Pani, Erika. *Para mexicanizar el segundo imperio: el imaginario político de los imperialistas*. Colegio de México, 2001.

Pansters, Wil G., and Benjamin T. Smith. *Histories of Drug Trafficking in Twentieth-Century Mexico*. University of New Mexico Press, 2022.

Pasztor, Suzanne B. *The Spirit of Hidalgo: The Mexican Revolution in Coahuila*. Michigan State University, 2002.

Paxman, Andrew. *Jenkins of Mexico: How a Southern Farm Boy Became a Mexican Magnate*. Oxford University Press, 2017.

de la Peña, Moisés T. *Veracruz económico* vol. 1. México DF, 1946.

Pensado, Jaime M. *Rebel Mexico: Student Unrest and Authoritarian Political Culture During the Long Sixties*. Stanford University Press, 2013.

Pensado, Jaime M. *Love and Despair: How Catholic Activism Shaped Politics and the Counterculture in Modern Mexico*. University of California Press, 2023.

Peralta Sandoval, Sergio H. *Hotel Regis: Historia de una época*. Editorial Diana, 1997.

Pérez Ricart, Carlos, and Jack Pannell. "The Guadalajara Cartel Never Existed." Noria Research, 2021. https://noria-research.com/the-guadalajara-cartel-never-existed/

Petrovsky-Shtern, Yohanan. *Jews in the Russian Army, 1827–1917*. Cambridge Univeristy Press, 2009.

Piccato, Pablo. *City of Suspects: Crime in Mexico City, 1900–1931*. Duke University Press, 2001.

Piccato, Pablo. *Historia mínima de la violencia en México*. Colegio de México, 2022.

Piccato, Pablo. *The Tyranny of Opinion: Honor in the Construction of the Mexican Public Sphere*. Duke University Press, 2010.

Pierce, Gretchen. *Alcohol in Latin America: A Social and Cultural History*. University of Arizona Press, 2014.

Pilcher, Jeffrey M. *Cantinflas and the Chaos of Mexican Modernity*. Scholarly Resources Inc., 2001.

Pillsbury, Joanne, Timothy Potts, and Kim N. Richter, eds. *Golden Kingdoms: Luxury Arts in the Ancient Americas*. J. Paul Getty Museum, 2017.

Pletcher, David M. *Rails, Mines, and Progress: Seven American Promoters in Mexico, 1867–1911*. American Historical Association, 1958.

Poblett Miranda, Martha, ed. *Cien viajeros en Veracruz: Crónicas y relatos*, vol. 9. Gobierno del Estado de Veracruz, 1992.

Poniatowska, Elena. *La noche de Tlatelolco. Testimonios de historia oral*. Biblioteca Era, 1999. Originally published in 1971.

Poppa, Terrence E. *Drug Lord: The Life and Death of a Mexican Kingpin: A True Story* (1990).

Porter, Roy. *The Greatest Benefit to Mankind: A Medical History of Humanity*. Norton & Company, 1999.

Porter, Jayson Maurice. "Making the Coast Pacific: Oilseeds and Environmental Violence and Justice in Guerrero and Sinaloa, 1900–1960." Unpublished PhD diss., Northwestern University, 2022.

Preston, Julia, and Samuel Dillon. *Opening Mexico: The Making of a Democracy*. Farrar, Straus and Giroux, 2004.

Prieto, Guillermo. *Memorias de mis tiempos*. Vda. De C. Bouret, 1906.

Prieto Laurens, Jorge. *Cincuenta Años de Política Mexicana: Memorias Políticas*. Editora Mexicana de Periódicos, Libros y Revistas, 1968.

Pureco Ornelas, Alfredo. *Empresarios lombardos en Michoacán. La familia Cusi entre el porfiriato y la posrevolución (1884–1938)*. Colegio de Michoacán/Instituto Mora, 2010.

Quinones, Sam. *True Tales From Another Mexico: The Lynch Mob, the Popsicle Kings, Chalino and the Bronx*. University of New Mexico Press, 2001.

Radding, Cynthia. *Landscapes of Power and Identity: Comparative Histories in the Sonoran Desert and the Forests of Amazonia from Colony to Republic*. Duke University Press, 2006.

Ramírez, Paul. *Enlightened Immunity: Mexico's Experiments with Disease Prevention in the Age of Reason*. Stanford, 2018.

Rath, Thomas. *Myths of Demilitarization in Postrevolutionary Mexico, 1920–1960*. University of North Carolina Press, 2013.

Recio, Gabriela. "Drugs and Alcohol: US Prohibition and the Origins of the Drug Trade in Mexico, 1910–1930." *Journal of Latin American Studies* 34, no. 1 (February 2002).

Reed, John. *Insurgent Mexico*. International Publishers, 1969.

Reséndez, Andrés. *The Other Slavery: The Uncovered Story of Indian Enslavement in America*. First Mariner, 2016.

Reséndez, Andrés. *Conquering the Pacific: An Unknown Mariner and the Final Great Voyage of the Age of Discovery*. Houghton Mifflin Harcourt, 2021.

Restall, Matthew. *When Montezuma Met Cortés*. Harper Collins, 2018.

Restall, Matthew, ed. *Beyond Black and Red: African-Native Relations in Colonial Latin America*. University of New Mexico Press, 2005.

Restall, Matthew, Lisa Sousa, and Kevin Terraciano. *Mesoamerican Voices: Native Language Writings from Colonial Mexico, Yucatán and Guatemala*. Cambridge University Press, 2005.

Ricard, Robert. *The Spiritual Conquest of Mexico*. Duke University Press, 1974.

Riva Palacio, Vicente. *Martín Garatuza*. México DF, 1945.

Roa Bárcena, José María. *Recuerdos de la invasión norteamericana (1846–1848) Por un joven de entonces tomo I*. CONACULTA, 1991.

Rodríguez O., Jaime E. *"We Are Now the True Spaniards": Sovereignty, Revolution, Independence, and the Emergence of the Federal Republic of Mexico, 1808–1824*. Stanford University Press, 2012.

Rodríguez Centeno, Mabel M. "El espejo de la vida: crédito al consumo y cotidianidad en la hancienda de Charco de Araujo (1796–1799)." In *Historia de la vida cotidiana*, edited by Gonzalbo Aizpuru, vol. III. Fondo de Cultura Económica, 2014.

Rodríguez Kuri, Ariel. *Historia del desasosiego. La revolución en la ciudad de México, 1911–1922*. Colegio de México, 2010.

Rodríguez Kuri, Ariel. *Historia mínima de las izquierdas en México*. Colegio de México, 2021.

Rodríguez Kuri, Ariel. *La experiencia olvidada: el ayuntamiento de México: política y gobierno, 1876–1912*. Colegio de México, 1996.

Rodríguez Lorenzo, Sergio M. "El contrato de pasaje en la carrera de Indias (1561–1622)." *Historia Mexicana* 66, no. 3. (Jan.–Mar. 2017).

Rodríguez Munguía, Jacinto, and José Reveles. "Cinco años de vuelos de la muerte." *Proceso*, 11 March 2024.

Rodríguez Piña, Javier, ed. *La Guerra de castas: Testimonios de Justo Sierra O'Reilly y Juan Suárez y Navarro*. CONACULTA, 1993.

Rogers, Woodes. *A Cruising Voyage Round the World*. CreateSpace Independent Publishing Platform, 2018.

Ross, Stanley R. *Francisco I. Madero: Apostle of Democracy*. Columbia University Press, 1955.

Rubenstein, Anne. *Bad Language, Naked Ladies and Other Threats to the Nation*. Duke University Press, 1998.

Ruiz Aguilar, Armando, ed. *Nosotros los ignorantes hombres que hacemos la guerra*. Consejo Nacional para la Cultura y las Artes, 2010.

Rugeley, Terry. *Alone in Mexico: The Astonishing Travels of Karl Heller, 1845–1848*. University of Alabama Press, 2007.

Rugeley, Terry. *Rebellion Now and Forever: Mayas, Hispanics, and Caste War Violence in Yucatán, 1800–1880*. Stanford University Press, 2009.

Rugeley, Terry. *The River People in Flood Time: The Civil Wars in Tabasco, Spoiler of Empires*. Stanford University Press, 2014.

de Sahagún, Bernardino. *Historia general de las cosas de la Nueva España. Primera versión integra del texto castellano del manuscrito conocido como Códice Florentino,* edited by Alfedeo López Austin and Josefina García Quintana. Fondo Cultural Banamex, 1982.

Salvucci, Ricardo. *Politics, markets, and Mexico's "London Debt," 1823–1887*. Cambridge University Press, 2009.

Samaniego López, Marco Antonio. "La revolución mexicana en Baja California: maderismo, magonismo, filibusterismo y la pequeña revuelta local." *Historia Mexicana* 56, no. 4 (Apr.–Jun. 2007).

de San Antón Muñon Chimalpahín Cuauhtlehuanitzin, Francisco. *Relaciones Originales de Chalco Amaquemecan*; anon., *Codex Ramírez, Codex Moctezuma, Lienzo de Tlaxcala*.

Santos, Gonzalo N. *Memorias*. Grijalbo, 1984.

Santoyo, Antonio. *La Mano Negra: poder regional y Estado en México (Veracruz, 1928–1943)*. Consejo Nacional para la Cultura y las Artes, 1995.

Saucedo Zarco, Carmen, and José Manuel Villalpando César. *Fray Antón de Montesinos*. Universidad Nacional Autónoma de México, 1982.

Scherer, Julio. "En la guarida del Mayo Zambada." *Proceso*, 4 April 2010.

Schmidt, Arthur P. *The Social and Economic Effects of the Railroad in Puebla and Veracruz, Mexico, 1867–1911*. Garland, 1987.

Schryer, Frans. *The Rancheros of Pisaflores: The History of a Peasant Bourgeoisie in Twentieth-Century Mexico*. University of Toronto Press, 1980.

Schwartz, Stuart B. *All Can Be Saved: Religious Tolerance and Salvation in the Iberian Atlantic World*. Yale University Press, 2008.

Seijas, Tatiana. *Asian Slaves in Colonial Mexico: From Chinos to Indians*. Cambridge University Press, 2014.

Semo, Enrique. *The History of Capitalism in Mexico: Its Origins, 1521–1763*. University of Texas Press, 1993.

Serrano, Mónica. "The Armed Branch of the State: Civil-Military Relations in Mexico." *Journal of Latin American Studies* 27, no. 2. May 1995.

Servín, Elisa. *Del nacionalismo al neoliberalismo, 1940–1994*. Fondo de Cultura Económica, 2010.

Sigüenza y Góngora, Carlos. *Obras Históricas*. Porrua, 1944.

Shawcross, Edward. *The Last Emperor of Mexico: The Dramatic Story of the Hapsburg Archduke Who Created a Kingdom in the New World*. Basic Books, 2021.

Sheridan, Thomas E. *Lanscapes of Fraud: Mission Tumacácori, the Baca Float, and the Betrayal of the O'odham*. University of Arizona Press, 2006.

Sloan, Kathryn A. *Death in the City: Suicide and the Social Imaginary in Modern Mexico*. University of California Press, 2017.

Soler Alonso, Pedro. *Biblioteca Enciclopedica Popular. 63. Virreyes de la Nueva España*.

Sordo Cedeño, Reynaldo. "Territorio, recursos naturales y población hacia 1858." In *1910, 1958, 1910: México en tres etapas de su historia*, edited by Gisela von Wobeser. Fondo de Cultura Económica, 2022.

Solís Gutiérrez, Patricio. "Social Mobility in Mexico Trends, Recent Findings and Research Challenges." Colegio de México, 2012.

Starr, Frederick. *In Indian Mexico: A Narrative of Travel and Labor*. Forbes & Co., 1908.

Stearns, Peter N. "The Columbian Exchange in the Early Modern Period," in *Documents in World History Vol. 2: The Modern Centuries—From 1500 to the Present*. Longman, 2008.

Stein, Stanley J., and Barbara H. Stein. *Silver, Trade, and War: Spain and America in the Making of Early Modern Europe*. Johns Hopkins University Press, 2000.

Stephens, John L. *Incidents of Travel in Yucatan*. Dover Publications, 1963.

Smith, Benjamin T. *Pistoleros and Popular Movements: The Politics of State Formation in Post-revolutionary Oaxaca*. University of Nebraska Press, 2009.

Smith, Benjamin T. *The Dope: The Real History of the Mexican Drug Trade*. W. W. Norton & Company, 2021.

Smith, Benjamin T. *The Mexican Press and Civil Society, 1940–1976: Stories from the Newsroom, Stories from the Street*. University of North Carolina Press, 2018.

Smith, Benjamin T. *The Roots of Conservatism in Mexico: Catholicism, Society, and Politics in the Mixteca Baja, 1750–1962*. University of New Mexico Press, 2012.

Smith, Benjamin T. "Who Governed? Grassroots Politics in Mexico under the Partido Revolucionario Institucional, 1958–1970." In *Past and Present* 225 (Nov. 2014).

Sousa, Lisa. *The Woman Who Turned Into a Jaguar and Other Narratives of Native Women in Archives of Colonial Mexico*. Stanford University Press, 2017.

Tannenbaum, Frank. *Peace by Revolution: Mexico After 1910*. Columbia University Press, 1966.

Taylor, William B. *Drinking, Homicide, and Rebellion in Colonial Mexican Villages*. Stanford University Press, 1979.

Taylor, William B. *Fugitive Freedom: The Improbable Lives of Two Impostors in Late Colonial Mexico*. University of California Press, 2021.

Tanck de Estrada, Dorothy. *Atlas Ilustrado de los Pueblos de Indios*. Colegio de México, 2005.

Tenorio-Trillo, Mauricio. *"Hablo de la ciudad". Los principios del siglo XX desde la Ciudad de México*. Fondo de Cultura Económica, 2017.
Tenorio-Trillo, Mauricio. *La historia en ruinas: El culto a los monumentos y a su destrucción*. Alianza Editorial, 2023.
Tenorio-Trillo, Mauricio. *Mexico at the World's Fairs: Crafting a Modern Nation*. University of California Press, 1996.
Terry, T. Philip. *Terry's Mexico Handbook for Travellers*. Gay & Hancock, 1911.
Thomas, Hugh. *The Conquest of Mexico*. London, 1993.
Thornton, Christy. *Revolution in Development: Mexico and the Governance of the Global Economy*. University of California, 2021.
Tilly, Charles. *War Making and State Making as Organized Crime*. Cambridge University Press, 1985.
Tischendorf, Alfred. *Great Britain and Mexico in the Time of Porfirio Díaz*. Duke University Press, 1961.
Topik, Steven, Carlos Marichal, and Zephyr Frank. *From Silver to Cocaine: Latin American Commodity Chains and the Building of the World Economy, 1500–2000*. Duke University Press, 2006.
Torres, Blanca. *Hacia la utopía industrial*. México DF, 1984.
Torres Puga, Gabriel. "La ciudad novohispana. Ensayo sobre su vida política." In *Historia política de la Ciudad de México (Desde su fundación hasta el año 2000)* by Ariel Rodriguez Kuri. Colegio de México, 2013.
de Torquemada, Juan. *Monarquía Indiana*. Universidad Nacional Autónoma de México, 1975.
Toribio Medina, José. *Biblioteca hispano-americana (1493–1810)*. Brown University Press, 2020.
Tourliere, Mathieu. "La red militar que controla la inteligencia del estado." *Proceso*, 23 April 2023.
Townsend, Camilla. *Malintzin's Choices: An Indian Woman in the Conquest of Mexico*. University of New Mexico, 2006.
Townsend, Camilla. *Annals of Native America: How the Nahuas of Colonial Mexico Kept Their History Alive*. Oxford University Press, 2017.
Townsend, Camilla. *Fifth Sun: A New History of the Aztecs*. Oxford University Press, 2019.
Traven, B., *Government*. Wilson & Day Ltd, 1994.
Trejo Rivera, Flor. "El barco como una ciudad flotante." In *Historia de la vida cotidiana en México*. Fondo de Cultura Económica, 2006.
Turner, J. K. *Barbarous Mexico*. Charles H. Kerr & Co., 1911.
Turrent, Lourdes. *La conquista musical de México*. Fondo de Cultura Económica, 2016.
Tutino, John. *Making a New World: Founding Capitalism in the Bajío and Spanish America*. Duke University Press, 2010.
Tweedie, Ethel. *Mexico as I Saw It*. Hurst and Blackett, 1902.
Twinam, Ann. *Purchasing Whiteness: Pardos, Mulattos, and the Quest for Social Mobility in the Spanish Indies*. Stanford University Press, 2015.
Urquizo, Rafael L. *Carranza: El Hombre. El Político. El Caudillo. El Patriota*. Instituto de Estudios Históricos de las Revoluciones de México, 2020.
Usigli, Rodolfo. "El caso de "El Gesticulador." In *Teatro Completo*. 4 vols. Fondo de Cultura Económica, 1996–1997.
Uslenghi, Alejandra. *Latin America at fin-de-siècle Universal Exhibitions: Modern Cultures of Visuality*. Palgrave Macmillan, 2016.
Van Young, Eric. *A Life Together: Lucas Alamán and Mexico, 1792–1853*. Yale University Press, 2021.
Van Young, Eric. *The Other Rebellion: Popular Violence, Ideology, and the Mexican Struggle for Independence, 1810–1821*. Stanford University Press, 2001.

Vanderwood, Paul J. *Disorder and Progress: Bandits, Police, and Mexican Development*. Scholarly Resources, 2009.

Vanderwood, Paul J. *Satan's Playground: Mobsters and Movie Stars at America's Greatest Gaming Resort*. Duke University Press, 2009.

Vanderwood, Paul J. *The Power of God Against the Guns of Government: Religious Upheaval in Mexico at the Turn of the Nineteenth Century*. Stanford University Press, 1998.

Various authors. *Diccionario biográfico español*. Real Academia de la Historia, 2009–13.

Various authors. *Historia Documental del Partido de la Revolución, tomo V: PRM-PRI, 1945–1950*. Partido Revolucionario Institucional, 1982.

Vasconcelos, José. *La raza cósmica*. Buenos Aires, 1948. Originally published in 1925 in Mexico.

Vasconcelos, José. *Obras completas*. Libreros Mexicanos Unidos, 1957.

Vásquez Meléndez, Miguel Ángel. *Los patriotas en escena (1862–1869)*. Colegio de México, 2018.

Vaughan, Mary Kay. *The State, Education, and Social Class in Mexico, 1880–1928*. Northern Illinois University Press, 1982.

Velasco Ávila, Cuauhtémoc. *La frontera étnica en el noreste mexicano. Los comanches entre 1800–1841*. CIESAS, 2012.

Velasco Murillo, Dana. *Urban Indians in a Silver City: Zacatecas, Mexico, 1546–1810*. Stanford University Press, 2016.

Vinson III, Ben. *Before Mestizaje: The Frontiers of Race and Caste in Colonial Mexico*. Cambridge University Press, 2018.

Villanueva, Carlos I., and Aleida García Aguirre, eds. *Memorias inquietas: De estudiantes rurales a guerrilleros urbanos*. Colectivo Memorias Subalternas, 2019.

Villoro, Juan. *El vértigo horizontal: una ciudad llamada México*. Almadia, 2018.

Villoro, Luis. "La Revolución de Independencia." In *Historia general de México* by Cosío Villegas et al. Colegio de México, 1977.

Villoro, Luis. *Los grandes momentos del indigenismo en México*. México DF, 1997.

Viquiera, Juan Pedro. "Reflexiones contra la noción histórica de mestizaje." *Nexos*. May 1, 2010.

Vitz, Matthew. *A City on a Lake: Urban Political Ecology and the Growth of Mexico City*. Duke University Press, 2018.

Voekel, Pamela. *For God and Liberty: Catholicism and Revolution in the Atlantic World, 1790–1861*. Oxford University Press, 2023.

Von Germeten, Nicole. *Profit and Passion: Transactional Sex in Colonial Mexico*. University of California Press, 2018.

de Vos, Jan. *Oro verde: La conquista de la Selva Lacandona por los madereros tabasqueños, 1822–1949*. Fondo de Cultura Económica, 1996.

Wagner, Henry Raup, and Helen Rand Parish. *The Life and Writings of Bartolomé de Las Casas*. University of New Mexico Press, 1967.

Walker, Louise E. *Waking from the Dream: Mexico's Middle Classes after 1968*. Stanford University Press, 2013.

Warman, Arturo. "The Political Project of Zapatismo." In *Riot, Rebellion and Revolution: Rural Social Conflict in Mexico*, edited by Friedrich Katz. Princeton University Press, 1988.

Warman, Arturo. *Venimos a contradecir: Los campesinos de Morelos y el estado nacional*. México: ediciones de la Casa Chata, 1978.

Wasserman, Mark. *Capitalists, Caciques, and Revolution: The Native Elite and Foreign Enterprise in Chihuahua, Mexico, 1854–1911*. University of North Carolina Press, 1984.

Wasserman, Mark. *Persistent Oligarchs: Elites and Politics in Chihuahua, Mexico, 1910–1940*. Duke University Press, 1993.

Weckmann, Luis. *La herencia medieval de México – II*. Colegio de México, 1984.
Wilkie, J. W. *The Mexican Revolution: Federal Expenditure and Social Change since 1910*. Berkeley, 1967.
Wislizenus, Dr. A. *Memoir of a Tour of Northern Mexico, connected with Col. Doniphan's expedition, in 1846 and 1847*. Tippin and Streeper, 1848.
Woldenberg, José. *Violencia y política*. Cal y arena, 1995.
Wolf, Eric. *Sons of the Shaking Earth*. University of Chicago Press, 1959.
Wolfe, Mikael D. *Watering the Revolution*. Duke University Press, 2017.
Womack Jr., John. *Zapata and the Mexican Revolution*. Thames & Hudson, 1968.
Wood, Stephanie. *Transcending Conquest: Nahua Views of Spanish Colonial Mexico*. University of Oklahoma Press, 2003.
Wright-Rios, Edward. *Revolutions in Catholicism: Reform and Revelation in Oaxaca, 1887–1934*. Duke University Press, 2009.
Yankelevich, Pablo. *Los otros: raza, normas y corrupción en la gestión de la extranjería en México, 1900–1950*. Bonilla Artigas Editores, 2019.
Young, Julia G. *Mexican Exodus: Emigrants, Exiles, and Refugees of the Cristero War*. Oxford University Press, 2015.
Zavala, Silvio *El mundo americano en la época colonial*. Porrua, 1967.
Zavala, Silvio. *Los esclavos indios en Nueva España*. Colegio Nacional, 1967.
Zeltsman, Corinna. *Ink Under the Fingernails: Printing Politics in Nineteenth-Century Mexico*. University of California Press, 2021.
Zogbaum, Heidi. *B. Traven: A Vision of Mexico*. Rowman & Littlefield, 1992.
Zoraida Vázquez, Josefina. "Los primeros tropiezos." Colegio de México, 1994.
Zoraida Vázquez y Meyer, Josefina. *México frente a Estados Unidos*. Colegio de México, 1982.
Zúñiga, Luis. *Carrasco en la revolución: En homenaje merecido a sus méritos revolucionarios*. Talleres gráficos del Gobierno, 1941.

Illustration Credits

In-text images

14. Courtesy of the Biblioteca Nacional, Madrid.
51. https://commons.wikimedia.org/wiki/File:FlorentineCodex_BK12_F54_smallpox.jpg
57. https://commons.wikimedia.org/wiki/File:Print,_Massacre_of_the_Innocents_(CH_18099823).jpg
70. Courtesy of the Rare Book Division, The New York Public Library.
95. https://commons.wikimedia.org/wiki/File:Loutherbourg-Spanish_Armada.jpg
102. https://commons.wikimedia.org/wiki/File:Flemish_School_(c._1515)_-_Emperor_Charles_V_(1500-58)_-_RCIN_403439_-_Royal_Collection.jpg
121. Courtesy of the Kislak Collection of the Rare Book Division of the Library of Congress
155. Richard Hakluyt, The Voyages (1582). Courtesy of the Library of Congress.
157. Relaciones Geográficas of Mexico and Guatemala, 1577-1585, Joaquín García Icazbalceta Manuscript Collection.
191. British Museum.
204. Museo de América, Madrid. Photograph Joaquín Otero.
221. https://commons.wikimedia.org/wiki/File:Arrietatertulia1.jpg
260. https://commons.wikimedia.org/wiki/File:Vicente_Guerrero.png
292. https://commons.wikimedia.org/wiki/File:Recinto_homenaje_a_Benito_Juárez_XVI.jpg
323. *El Mundo* (1899)
334. Courtesy of DeGolyer Library, Southern Methodist University.
337. https://commons.wikimedia.org/wiki/File:Yaqui_Indians_lynched_by_Mexicans_LCCN2014688840.jpg
395. Agustín Víctor Casasola, Niño Soldado (1914). Courtesy of The Museum of Fine Arts, Houston, Gift of Mike and Mickey Marvins, 2015.607. Photograph © The Museum of Fine Arts, Houston; Will Michels
398. https://commons.wikimedia.org/wiki/File:Urbina,_Villa_y_Zapata_en_Palacio,_Museo_de_la_Ciudad_de_México,_México_D.F.,_México,_2013-10-16,_DD_138.JPG
402. Bain News Service. Courtesy of the Library of Congress.
459. Courtesy of Benjamin T. Smith
489. Courtesy of Olivia Constantino
496. Anonymous, author's collection.
527. https://en.m.wikipedia.org/wiki/File:1985_Mexico_Earthquake_-_Pina_Suarez_Apartment_Complex.jpg
567. Courtesy of UCLA Library Special Collections.
601. Courtesy of Benjamin T. Smith

Insert 1

1. Newberry Library, Chicago.
2 i). Internet Archive. https://archive.org/details/volume-10_202404/001/
2 ii). Courtesy of Butler Library, Columbia University.
2 iii). Alamy, Inc.
3 i). Kislak Collection of the Rare Book Division of the Library of Congress.
3 ii). The Metropolitan Museum of Art, New York, Harris Brisbane Dick Fund, 1928.
4. Musée des Amériques – Auch.
5. https://commons.wikimedia.org/wiki/File:Virgen_de_guadalupe1.jpg
6 i). https://commons.wikimedia.org/wiki/File:Felipe_II_de_España_(Alcázar_de_Segovia).jpg
6 ii). https://commons.wikimedia.org/wiki/File:DelasCasasParraDF.JPG
6 iii). https://commons.wikimedia.org/wiki/File:Retrato_de_Sor_Juana_Inés_de_la_Cruz_(Miguel_Cabrera).jpg
7. https://commons.wikimedia.org/wiki/File:Casta_Painting_by_Luis_de_Mena.jpg
8 i). Courtesy of the Metropolitan Museum of Art, New York.
8 ii). https://commons.wikimedia.org/wiki/File:Batalla_de_la_Alhóndiga_de_Granaditas.jpg

Insert 2

1 i). https://commons.wikimedia.org/wiki/File:Antonio_López_de_Santa_Anna,_siglo_XIX,_óleo_sobre_tela.png
1 ii). United States Library of Congress, Prints and Photographs division.
2 i). https://en.wikipedia.org/wiki/The_Execution_of_Emperor_Maximilian#/media/File:Edouard_Manet_022.jpg
2 ii). https://commons.wikimedia.org/wiki/File:Recinto_homenaje_a_Benito_Juárez_XVI.jpg
3 i). The Miriam and Ira D. Wallach Division of Art, Prints and Photographs: Print Collection, The New York Public Library.
3 ii). Augustus and Alice Dixon Le Plongeon Photographs of Chichén Itza, Uxmal and Yucatán, The Getty Research Institute, Los Angeles.
3 iii). United States Library of Congress, Prints and Photographs division.
4 i). The Art Institute of Chicago.
4 ii). United States Library of Congress, Prints and Photographs division.
4 iii). United States Library of Congress, Prints and Photographs division
5 i). Colección Archivo Casasola - Fototeca Nacional, Instituto Nacional de Antropología e Historia, México.
5 ii). Author's Collection.
5 iii). Unknown author, Archivo Casasola, Hidalgo, Mexico, Public Domain, https://commons.wikimedia.org/w/index.php?curid=327762
6 i). © 2025 Banco de México Diego Rivera Frida Kahlo Museums Trust, Mexico, CDMX / Artists Rights Society (ARS), New York.
6 ii). Colección Archivo Casasola - Fototeca Nacional, Instituto Nacional de Antropología e Historia, México.
6 iii). Courtesy of Skinner, Inc., www.skinnerinc.com
7 i). Fondation Henri Cartier-Bresson
7 ii). https://en.wikipedia.org/wiki/Mexican_Movement_of_1968#/media/File:Exèrcit_al_Zócalo-28_d'agost.jpg
8. http://retablos.ru/en/artists/alfredo-vilchis/

Notes

Introduction

1. Inga Clendinnen, *Ambivalent Conquests: Maya and Spaniard in Yucatan, 1517–1570* (Cambridge University Press, 1987), 18; Friar Diego de Landa, *Yucatán Before and After the Conquest* (Mérida: San Fernando, 1991), 26; Bernal Díaz del Castillo, *Historia verdadera de la conquista de la Nueva España* (Madrid: Instituto Gonzalo Fernández de Oviedo, 1982), 54.
2. Landa, *Yucatán*, 26; Hugh Thomas, *The Conquest of Mexico* (Hutchinson, 1993), 163–164.
3. Thomas, *The Conquest*, 164.
4. Landa, *Yucatán*, 26.
5. Díaz, *Historia verdadera*, 53.
6. Clendinnen, *Ambivalent Conquests*, 22.
7. Gerard McNamara, trans., *The Voyage of Saint Brendan: The Navigator* (CreateSpace Independent Publishing Platform, 2013); Ahmad Ibn Fadlān, *Ibn Fadlān and the Land of Darkness: Arab Travellers in the Far North* (Penguin, 2011), 65–67; Erik Wahlgren, *The Vikings and America* (Thames and Hudson, 1986), 120–133; Louise Levathes, *When China Ruled the Sea: The Treasure Fleet of the Dragon Throne* (Oxford University Press, 1996), 75–136; Serge Gruzinski, *El águila y el dragón. Desmesura europea y mundialización en el siglo XVI* (Fondo de Cultura Económica, 2018), 54.
8. Andrés Reséndez, *Conquering the Pacific: An Unknown Mariner and the Final Great Voyage of the Age of Discovery* (Boston: Houghton Mifflin Harcourt, 2021), 11.
9. For a summary of the reasoning for using this ideologically freighted colonizers' term, see Charles G. Mann, *1491: New Revelations of the Americas Before Columbus* (Vintage Books, 2011), 393–396. To sum up, best practice is to use specific peoples' emic names, such as the Purépecha, when talking about a single people. The term "Indian" as applied to more than one Latin American ethnic group (a) is the collective noun historically used by many indigenous people in Latin America themselves when generalizing, eschewing "Native American" as US-centric (and so colonialist in itself); (b) is a better analytical bet than "Native American," which if generalized beyond the continental United States lumps together an even greater human diversity, including peoples like the Inuit or Aleutians who are of very different ancestry; and (c) can be used in a cultural and geographical, not racial, sense, an equivalent to "European" rather than "white."
10. Henry Kamen, *Empire: How Spain Became a World Power, 1492–1763* (HarperCollins, 2003), 3; Solange Alberro, *El águila y la cruz. Orígenes religiosos de la conciencia criolla. México, siglos XVI*-XVII, (Colegio de México, 1999), 87–88.

11. Pablo Yankelevich, *Los otros. Raza, normas y corrupción en la gestión de la extranjería en México, 1900–1950* (Bonilla Artigas Editores, 2019), 24–68, 100–104.
12. Guillermo Bonfil Batalla, *México profundo. Una civilización negada* (Grijalbo, 1987), 9–17.
13. Lawrence Durrell, *The Alexandria Quartet* (Faber & Faber, 1968), 338.
14. "Enormous condescension" comes from E. P. Thompson, *The Making of the English Working Class* (Penguin, 1968), 13.

Chapter One

1. Caesar, *The Conquest of Gaul* (Penguin Classics), 189–200, 210–212; Michael Herr, *Dispatches* (Picador, 1978), 81, 141.
2. Felipe Fernández-Armesto, *Our America: A Hispanic History of the United States* (W. W. Norton, 2014), 48.
3. Bernal Díaz del Castillo, *Historia verdadera de la conquista de la Nueva España* (Madrid, 1982), 34.
4. Ross Hassig, *Aztec Warfare: Imperial Expansion and Political Control* (University of Oklahoma Press, 1988), 186.
5. Charles G. Mann, *1491: New Revelations of the Americas Before Columbus* (Vintage Books, 2011), 278–280.
6. Michael P. Smyth et al., "The Perfect Storm: Climate Change and Ancient Maya Response in the Puuc Hills Region of Yucatán," *Antiquity* 91 no. 356 (April 2017): 490–509.
7. For the concept "mafia state," see Charles Tilly, *War Making and State Making as Organized Crime* (Cambridge University Press, 1985).
8. Francisco de Gómara, cited in Matthew Restall, *When Montezuma Met Cortés* (Harper Collins, 2018), 165.
9. *Diccionario biográfico de la Real Academia de la Historia*, "Hernán Cortés," https://dbe.rah.es/biografias/5138/hernan-cortes.
10. Bartolomé de las Casas. For Cortés as mediocrity, see Eulalia Guzmán, *Una visión crítica de la historia de la conquista de México-Tenochtitlán* (Universidad Nacional Autónoma de México, 1989), 135.
11. John H. Elliott, *Empires of the Atlantic World: Britain and Spain in America, 1492–1830* (Yale University Press, 2006), 26.
12. José Luis Martínez, *Hernán Cortés* (Fondo de Cultura Económica, 1990), 131.
13. Camilla Townsend, *Malintzin's Choices: An Indian Woman in the Conquest of Mexico* (University of New Mexico Press, 2006), 5, 16–22, 133, 134, 155.
14. Rodrigo Martínez Baracs, *Convivencia y utopía. El gobierno indio y español de la "ciudad de Mechuacan," 1521–1580* (Fondo de Cultura Económica, 2005), 109; Inga Clendinnen, *Ambivalent Conquests: Maya and Spaniard in Yucatan, 1517–1570* (Cambridge University Press, 2003), 3–4; Serge Gruzinski, *El águila y el dragón. Desmesura europea y mundialización en el siglo XVI* (Fondo de Cultura Económica, 2018), 95–98.
15. Cortés's private letter to Charles V, October 15, 1524, José Luis Martínez, *Documentos Cortesianos* (Fondo de Cultura Económica, 1991), 285–295.
16. Hugh Thomas, *The Conquest of Mexico* (Hutchinson, 1993), 149.
17. Díaz, *Historia verdadera*, 127.
18. Ibid., 36.
19. Bernardino de Sahagún, *Historia general de las cosas de la Nueva España. Primera versión integra del texto castellano del manuscrito conocido como Códice Florentino*, ed., Alfredo López Austin, Josefina García Quintana (Fondo Cultural Banamex, 1982), 2:495–502, 821, 834.

20. Stephanie Wood, *Transcending Conquest: Nahua Views of Spanish Colonial Mexico* (University of Oklahoma Press, 2003), 137.
21. Camilla Townsend, *Annals of Native America: How the Nahuas of Colonial Mexico Kept Their History Alive* (Oxford University Press, 2017), 37; Restall, *When Montezuma Met Cortés*, 41.
22. Wood, *Transcending Conquest*, 136.
23. Alan Knight, *Mexico: From the Beginning to the Spanish Conquest* (Cambridge University Press, 2002), 233.
24. Jorge Gurría Lacroix, *Hernán Cortés y Diego Rivera* (Instituto de Investigaciones Historicas, 1971), 29–45.
25. Díaz, *Historia verdadera*, 36; Francisco de Aguilar, *Relación breve de la conquista de la Nueva España*, ed. Jorge Gurría Lacroix (Universidad Autónoma de México, 1977), introduction. Restall, *When Montezuma Met Cortés*, 153.
26. Townsend, *Annals*, 145–146, 159–174.
27. Jorge Cañizares-Esguerra, *How to Write the History of the New World: Histories, Epistemologies, and Identities in the Eighteenth-Century Atlantic World* (Stanford University Press, 2001), 60, 65.
28. Sahagún, *Historia general*, 2:821, 827.
29. Toribio de Benavente Motolinía, *Historia de los indios de la Nueva España*, ed. Giuseppe Bellini (Alianza Editorial, 1988), 241–242.
30. Jerónimo López to Charles V, cited in Thomas, *The Conquest*, 40.
31. Andrea Martínez Baracs, *Un gobierno de indios. Tlaxcala, 1519–1750* (Fondo de Cultura Económica, 2014), 24–25.
32. Cortés second letter to Charles V, October 30 1520, in Hernán Cortés, *Cartas de relación de la conquista de Méjico* (Madrid: Espasa-Calpe, 1940), 1:49.
33. José Eduardo Contreras Martínez, "La confrontación tlaxcalteca ante la Conquista," *Dimensión antropológica* 61 (2014), 55–60.
34. Restall, *When Montezuma Met Cortés*, 207–210.
35. Sahagún, *Historia general*, 2:826, 831–832; Restall, *When Montezuma Met Cortés*, 222.
36. José Luis Arce et. al., "Geology and Stratigraphy of the Mexico Basin (Mexico City), Central Trans-Mexican Volcanic Belt," *Journal of Maps* 15, no. 2 (2019): 320–332.
37. Un compañero de Hernán Cortés, *El conquistador anónimo. Relación de algunas cosas de la Nueva España y de la gran ciudad de Temestitan Mexico* (Mexico City: Editorial América, 1941), 38.
38. Díaz, *Historia verdadera*, 165.
39. José Luis Martínez, *Hernán Cortés* (Fondo de Cultura Económica, 1990), 229.
40. Díaz, *Historia verdadera*, 176–177, 186–192.
41. Aguilar, *Relación breve de la Conquista*, 66.
42. David M. Carballo, *Collision of Worlds: A Deep History of the Fall of Aztec Mexico and the Forging of New Spain* (Oxford University Press, 2020), xiii–xiv.
43. Martínez, *Cortés*, 66; John H. Elliott, *Imperial Spain 1469–1716* (Penguin, 1981), 52–53.
44. Sahagún, *Historia general*, 2:833.
45. Díaz, *Historia verdadera*, 163.
46. Juan de Torquemada, *Monarquía Indiana*, 3 vols. (Universidad Nacional Autónoma de México, 1975), 2:174–175.
47. Díaz, *Historia verdadera*, 208–209.
48. Letter, Hernando de Castro to Alonso de Nebreda, August 1520, in James Lockhart and Enrique Otte, *Letters and People of the Spanish Indies, Sixteenth Century* (Cambridge University Press, 1976), 27–38.

49. Knight, *Mexico*, 234.
50. Florentine Codex book 12, quoted in Camilla Townsend et al., *Fifth Sun: A New History of the Aztecs* (Oxford University Press, 2021), 114.
51. Fernando de Alva Xitlilxochitl, *Obras históricas*, ed., Alfredo Chavero (Oficina tip. del Secretaría de Fomento, 1891), 2 vol., 1:340; Díaz, *Historia verdadera*, 294; Torquemada, *Monarquía Indiana*, 2:214–215; Fernando Alvarado Tezozómoc, *Crónica Mexicáyotl* (Universidad Autónoma de México, 1975), 151; Francisco de San Antón Muñon Chimalpahín Cuauhtlehuanitzin, *Relaciones Originales de Chalco Amaquemecan* (Fondo de Cultura Económica, 1965), 236; Manuel Orozco y Berra, ed., *Códice Ramírez: relación del origen de los indios que habitan esta Nueva España según sus historias* (Mexico: Editorial Innovación, 1979), 119.
52. Cortés's second letter to Charles V, *Cartas de relación*, 1:166.
53. Díaz says 870. William Prescott, *History of the Conquest of Mexico and the History of the Conquest of Peru*, (Random House, 1936), 452; Díaz, *Historia verdadera*, 289; Cortés, *Cartas de relación*, 1:173.
54. Ixtlilxóchitl, *Obras Históricas*, 1:397.
55. Motolinía, *Historia de los indios*, 54.
56. Sahagún, *Historia general*, 338.
57. Díaz, *Historia verdadera*, 330; Diego Durán, *Historia de las Indias de Nueva España e Islas de Tierra Firme* (México DF, 1967), 2:561.
58. Cortés, *Cartas de relación*, 1:4.
59. Inga Clendinnen, "'Fierce and Unnatural Cruelty': Cortés and the Conquest of Mexico," *Representations* 33 (Winter 1991): 79.
60. El conquistador anónimo, *Relación de algunas cosas*, 24.
61. Héctor de Mauleón, *La ciudad que nos inventa. Crónicas de seis siglos* (Cal y Arena, 2015), 26–27.
62. Díaz, *Historia verdadera*, 45–46.
63. Cortés, *Cartas de relación*, 1:228.
64. H. Berlin and R. Barlow, eds. *Anales de Tlatelolco* (Porrúa, 1948), 65–66.
65. Cortés, *Cartas de relación*, 1:207, 2:2, 40.
66. Ms. Anónimo de Tlatelolco, quoted in Miguel León-Portilla, *Visión de los vencidos. Relaciones indígenas de la conquista* (Universidad Autónoma de México, 1992), 166.
67. Díaz, *Historia verdadera*, 409.
68. Ibid., 410.
69. Ibid., 443.
70. Hernán Cortés to Martín Cortés, Tesuxtitan, September 26, 1526, Martínez, *Documentos Cortesianos*, 416–422.
71. Donald Chipman, "Isabel Moctezuma: Pioneer of Mestizaje," in Lewis Hanke and Jane M. Rausch, eds., *People and Issues in Latin American History, the Colonial Experience* (Princeton University Press, 2000).
72. *Diccionario biográfico de la Real Academia de la Historia*, "Álvar Núñez Cabeza de Vaca," https://dbe.rah.es/biografias/7081/alvar-nunez-cabeza-de-vaca.
73. Stafford Poole, "'War by Fire and Blood': The Church and the Chichimecas 1585," *The Americas* 74, no. 2 (2017): 126.
74. Andrés Reséndez, *The Other Slavery: The Uncovered Story of Indian Enslavement in America* (First Mariner, 2016), 70.
75. Martínez Baracs, *Convivencia y utopía*, 7, 124.

76. Jesús Gómez Serrano and Francisco Javier Delgado Aguilar, *Aguascalientes. Historia breve* (Colegio de México, 2012), 48.
77. Pedro Cieza de León, *The Discovery and Conquest of Peru*, trans. Noble David Cook and Alexandra Parma Cook (Duke University Press, 1998), 302.
78. Melissa Macauley, *Distant Shores: Colonial Encounters on China's Maritime Frontier* (Princeton University Press, 2021), 31.
79. Herbert E. Bolton, "The Mission as a Frontier Institution in the Spanish-American Colonies," *American Historical Review* 23, no. 12 (October 1917): 55.
80. Raquel E. Güereca Durán, "Las milicias tlaxcaltecas en Saltillo y Colotlán," *Estudios de Historia Novohispana* 54 (2016), 55–59.
81. Yanna Yannakis, "Allies or Servants? The Journey of Indian Conquistadors in the *Lienzo of Analco*," *Ethnohistory* 58, no. 4 (Fall 2011): 667.
82. Díaz, *Historia verdadera*, 695–696.
83. Barbara E. Mundy, *The Death of Aztec Tenochtitlan, the Life of Mexico City* (University of Texas Press, 2015), 73–86; Bradley Benton, *The Lords of Texcoco: The Transformation of Indigenous Rule in Postconquest Central Mexico* (Cambridge University Press, 2017), 49–78; Benjamin T. Smith, *The Roots of Conservatism in Mexico: Catholicism, Society, and Politics in the Mixteca Baja, 1750–1962* (University of New Mexico Press, 2012), 40.
84. Eric Wolf, *Sons of the Shaking Earth* (University of Chicago Press, 1959), 149.
85. Nathaniel Morris, *Soldiers, Saints, and Shamans: Indigenous Communities and the Revolutionary State in Mexico's Gran Nayar, 1910–1940* (University of Arizona Press, 2020), 26.
86. Edna Lucía García Rivera, "La rebelión yaqui en la frontera con Estados Unidos: 1926–1929," *Historia Mexicana* 74:1 (July–September 2024), 144.

Chapter Two

1. John H. Elliott, *The Old World and the New: 1492–1650* (Cambridge University Press, 1992), 13–14.
2. Carrie Gibson, *El Norte: The Epic and Forgotten Story of Hispanic North America* (Atlantic Monthly Press, 2019), 60–61.
3. Hugh Thomas, *The Conquest of Mexico*, (Hutchinson, 1993), 583; Letter from Francisco de Herrera to Hernando de Castro, September 20, 1522, reproduced in Enrique Otte, "Mercaderes burgaleses en los inicios del comercio con México," *Historia Mexicana* 18, no. 2 (October–December, 1968): 275.
4. Inga Clendinnen, *Ambivalent Conquests: Maya and Spaniard in Yucatan, 1517–1570* (Cambridge University Press, 1987), 21–24.
5. Antonio de Herrera y Tordesillas, quoted in Magali M. Carrera, *Traveling from New Spain to Mexico: Mapping Practices of Nineteenth-Century Mexico* (Duke University Press, 2011), 46.
6. Serge Gruzinski, *What Time Is It There? America and Islam at the Dawn of Modern Times* (Polity Press, 2010), 130–132.
7. Francisco López de Gómara, *Historia general de las Indias* (Barcelona: Memoria, 2014), 42–43.
8. Clendinnen, *Ambivalent Conquests*, 174; Gibson, *El Norte*, 59; Jacques Lafaye, *Quetzalcóatl y Guadalupe. La formación de la conciencia nacional en México* (Fondo de Cultura Económica, 1995), 89–91; John H. Elliott, *Empires of the Atlantic World: Britain and Spain in America, 1492–1830* (Yale University Press, 2006), digital ed. 3355.

9. *The Title of Totonicapán*, 1554, in Matthew Restall et al., *Mesoamerican Voices: Native Language Writings from Colonial Mexico, Yucatán, and Guatemala* (Cambridge University Press, 2005), 180.
10. Jorge Cañizares-Esguerra, *How to Write the History of the New World: Histories, Epistemologies, and Identities in the Eighteenth-Century Atlantic World* (Stanford University Press, 2001), 96–97.
11. Hampton Sides, "This Is Not the Place," in David Quamman, ed., *Best American Science and Nature Writing 2000* (Houghton Mifflin, 2000), 209–211, 222; Lawrence Gustave Desmond, *Yucatán Through Her Eyes: Alice Dixon Le Plongeon, Writer and Expeditionary Photographer* (University of New Mexico Press, 2009), 245.
12. Anthony Pagden, *Spanish Imperialism and the Political Imagination: Studies in European and Spanish-American Social and Political Theory 1513–1830* (Yale University Press, 1990), 28; Jill Lepore, *These Truths: A History of the United States* (Norton, 2018), 48.
13. Las Casas 1550 response, Apología contra Ginés de Sepúlveda, X.
14. Juan de Torquemada, *Monarquía Indiana*, 3 vols. (Universidad Nacional Autónoma de México, 1975), 2:257–258.
15. David Brading, *The Origins of Mexican Nationalism* (Cambridge University Press, 1985), 24–47; Alan Knight, *Mexico: From the Beginning to the Spanish Conquest* (Cambridge University Press, 2002), 160.
16. Quoted in Cañizares-Esguerra, *History of the New World*, 36.
17. Cañizares-Esguerra, *History of the New World*, 60, 64–67, 87.
18. Edwin G. Burrows and Mike Wallace, *Gotham: A History of New York City to 1898* (Oxford University Press, 1999), 5; Robert McCaa, "Spanish and Nahuatl Views on Smallpox and Demographic Catastrophe in Mexico," *Journal of Interdisciplinary History* 25, no. 3 (Winter 1995): 397–431.
19. Dana Velasco Murillo, *Urban Indians in a Silver City: Zacatecas, Mexico, 1546–1810* (Stanford University Press, 2016), 25; Luis Aboites Aguilar, *Chihuahua. Historia breve* (Colegio de México, 2016), 15; Clendinnen, *Ambivalent Conquests*, 36.
20. Alexander von Humboldt, *Political Essay on the Kingdom of New Spain*, trans. John Black (Longman, 1814), 1:118.
21. McCaa, "Spanish and Nahuatl Views on Smallpox," 430; Terry Rugeley, *The River People in Flood Time: The Civil Wars in Tabasco, Spoiler of Empires* (Stanford University Press, 2014), 31; Clendinnen, *Ambivalent Conquests*, 36; Alicia Hernández Chávez, *Morelos. Historia breve* (Colegio de México, 2011), 70.
22. Alfred W. Crosby, *The Columbian Exchange: Biological and Cultural Consequences of 1492* (Praeger, 1972), 44.
23. John H. Elliott, *Imperial Spain 1469–1716* (London: Edward Arnold, 1981), 324.
24. Roy Porter, *The Greatest Benefit to Mankind: A Medical History of Humanity* (W. W. Norton, 1999), 443.
25. Licenciado Diego Delgadillo, judge of the Royal Audiencia of New Spain, in Mexico City, to Juan de la Torre, merchant, in Seville, 1529, in James Lockhart and Enrique Otte, *Letters and People of the Spanish Indies, Sixteenth Century* (Cambridge University Press, 1976), 195.
26. Paul Ramírez, *Enlightened Immunity: Mexico's Experiments with Disease Prevention in the Age of Reason* (Stanford University Press, 2018), 29.
27. Virginia García Acosta et al,, *Desastres agrícolas en México. Catálogo histórico* (Fondo de Cultura Económica, 2014), 96, 98, 106, 113, 119, 131.

28. Åshild Vågene et al., "*Salmonella Enterica* Genomes from Victims of a Major Sixteenth-Century Epidemic in Mexico," *Nature Ecology & Evolution* 2, no. 3 (2018): 520–528.
29. Ramírez, *Enlightened Immunity*, 29.
30. Toribio de Benavente Motolinía, *Historia de los indios de la Nueva España* (Alianza, 1988), 54.
31. Clendinnen, *Ambivalent Conquests*, 18; Crosby, *The Columbian Exchange*, 52; David Grann, *The Lost City of Z: A Tale of Deadly Obsession in the Amazon* (Vintage Books, 2010).
32. Motolinía, *Historia de los indios*, 54.
33. McCaa, "Views on Smallpox," 419.
34. Sahagún, *Historia general*, 2:846.
35. McCaa, "Views on Smallpox," 428; Alan Knight, *Mexico: The Colonial Era* (Cambridge University Press, 2002), 96.
36. Robert Ricard, *The Spiritual Conquest of Mexico: An Essay on the Apostolate and the Evangelizing Methods of the Mendicant Orders in New Spain: 1523–1572* (University of California Press, 1966), 155.
37. "Relación geográfica de Coatepec, 1577," in René Acuña, *Relaciones geográficas del siglo XVI*. México tomo primero (Universidad Nacional Autónoma de México, 1985), 162.
38. Elinor G. K. Melville, *A Plague of Sheep* (Cambridge University Press, 1997), 134.
39. Lisa Sousa, *The Woman Who Turned into a Jaguar and Other Narratives of Native Women in Archives of Colonial Mexico* (Stanford University Press, 2017), 198–203.
40. Motolinía, *La Nueva España*, 180.
41. Ramírez, *Enlightened Immunity*, 62–66.
42. Ricard, *The Spiritual Conquest*, 155.
43. Georges Baudot, "El concepto de la muerte en la predicación de los primeros evangelizadores de México," *Caravelle* 74 (2000): 27.
44. Claudio Lomnitz, *Death and the Idea of Mexico* (Zone Books, 2005), 75.
45. Clendinnen, *Ambivalent Conquests*, 88–89.
46. *Mixtec Codex Sierra*, in Restall et al., *Mesoamerican Voices*, 89.
47. Florentine Codex, book 12, ch. 29, Restall et al., *Mesoamerican Voices*, 38.
48. Motolinía, *La Nueva España*, 69.
49. García Acosta et al., *Desastres agrícolas*, 74.
50. Lomnitz, *Death and the Idea of* Mexico, 73.
51. Motolinía, *La Nueva España*, 54.
52. Ibid., 54–61.
53. Melville, *A Plague of Sheep*, 119–122.
54. "Peasant" in some colonial and modern texts is pejorative, but unless otherwise suggested is used in this book as a sociological category for low-status farmers who control some of their labor while producing for themselves and the market. As a term it is vague, politically charged (in both positive and negative ways) and hard to replace. For questions of definition see Henry A. Landsberger, "The Role of Peasant Movements and Revolts in Development," in Landsberger, ed., Latin American Peasant Movements, (Ithaca, 1969), 1–5.
55. Inga Clendinnen, "'Fierce and Unnatural Cruelty': Cortés and the Conquest of Mexico," *Representations* 33 (Winter 1991): 74; Bartolomé de las Casas, *A Short Account of the Destruction of the Indies* (Penguin, 1999), 45.
56. Barbara E. Mundy, *The Death of Aztec Tenochtitlan, the Life of Mexico City* (University of Texas Press, 2015), 72.
57. Friar Diego de Landa, *Yucatán Before and After the Conquest* (Mérida: San Fernando, 1991), 47.

58. Andrés Reséndez, *The Other Slavery: The Uncovered Story of Indian Enslavement in America* (First Mariner, 2016), 60.
59. Bradley Benton, *The Lords of Tetzcoco: The Transformation of Indigenous Rule in Postconquest Central Mexico* (Cambridge University Press, 2017), 44.
60. Lomnitz, *Death and the Idea of Mexico,* 184; David E. Stannard, *American Holocaust: The Conquest of the New World* (Oxford University Press, 1993).
61. United Nations, "Definition of Genocide and Related Crimes," https://www.un.org/en/genocide-prevention/definition.
62. Reséndez, *The Other Slavery*, 28.
63. Edmundo O'Gorman, *El proceso de la invención de América* (Fondo de Cultura Económica, 1998), 34.
64. Elliott, *The Old World and the New*, 21.
65. Serge Gruzinski, *El águila y el dragón. Desmesura europea y mundialización en el siglo XVI* (Fondo de Cultura Económica, 2018), 64.
66. *Florentine Codex*, book 12, ch. 12, in Restall et al., *Mesoamerican Voices*, 29.
67. Thomas, *The Conquest*, 15–17.
68. Gruzinski, *El águila y el dragón*, 43; Joanne Pillsbury et al., eds., *Golden Kingdoms: Luxury Arts in the Ancient Americas* (J. Paul Getty Museum, 2017), xiv, 4.
69. *Florentine Codex*, 41.
70. Thomas, *The Conquest*, 577.
71. Elliott, *Empires*, 23–24.
72. Henry Kamen, *Empire: How Spain Became a World Power, 1492–1763* (Harper Collins, 2003), 493.
73. José Luis Martínez, *Pasajeros de Indias. Viajes trasatlánticos en el siglo XVI* (Fondo de Cultura Económica, 1999), 24–25; Thomas, *The Conquest*, 154; Díaz, *Historia verdadera*, 666–672.
74. Héctor de Mauleón, *La ciudad que nos inventa. Crónicas de seis siglos* (Cal y Arena, 2015), 35.
75. Las Casas, *Short Account of the Destruction of the Indies*, 43.
76. Kamen, *Empire*, 21, 490.
77. Thomas, *The Conquest*, 556–558.
78. Mario Contreras Valdez, *Nayarit. Historia breve* (Colegio de México, 2016), 35.
79. Ida Altman, *The War for Mexico's West: Indians and Spaniards in New Galicia, 1524–1550* (University of New Mexico Press, 2010), 46–47.
80. Laura E. Matthew, *Memories of Conquest: Becoming Mexican in Colonial Guatemala* (University of North Carolina Press, 2012), 84.
81. José Luis Martínez, *Hernán Cortés* (Fondo de Cultura Económica, 1990), 362–367.
82. Thomas, *The Conquest*, 596.
83. Matthew Restall, *When Montezuma Met Cortés* (Harper Collins, 2018), 271–276.
84. Rugeley, *The River People in Flood Time*, 26; Clendinnen, *Ambivalent Conquests*, 20.
85. Martínez, *Cortés*, 753–756; Mauleón, *La ciudad*, 308; Restall, *When Montezuma Met Cortés*, 179, 461–462.

Chapter Three

1. Barbara E. Mundy, *The Death of Aztec Tenochtitlan, the Life of Mexico City* (University of Texas Press, 2015), 73–86; Bradley Benton, *The Lords of Texcoco: The Transformation of Indigenous Rule in Postconquest Central Mexico* (Cambridge University Press, 2017), 49–78; Andrea Martínez Baracs, *Un gobierno de indios. Tlaxcala, 1519–1750* (Fondo de Cultura Económica, 2014), 178–182; Anne C. Collins, "The Maestros Cantores in Yucatán," in

Grant D. Jones, ed., *Anthropology and History in Yucatán* (University of Texas Press, 1977), 233–247; Elinor G. K. Melville, *A Plague of Sheep* (Cambridge University Press, 1997), 47–58; Alonso de la Mota y Escobar, "Descripción de la ciudad de nuestra señora de los Zacatecas," in Miguel León-Portilla, ed., *Historia Documental de México* (Universidad Nacional Autónoma de México, 1964), 1:227.

2. Alan Knight, *Mexico: The Colonial Era* (Cambridge University Press, 2002), 11.
3. Inga Clendinnen, *Ambivalent Conquests: Maya and Spaniard in Yucatan, 1517–1570* (Cambridge University Press, 1987), 43.
4. Dana Velasco Murillo, *Urban Indians in a Silver City: Zacatecas, Mexico, 1546–1810* (Stanford University Press, 2016), 46.
5. Carrie Gibson, *El Norte: The Epic and Forgotten Story of Hispanic North America* (Atlantic Monthly Press, 2019), 69.
6. Knight, *Mexico: The Colonial Era*, 9.
7. John H. Elliott, *Empires of the Atlantic World: Britain and Spain in America, 1492–1830* (Yale University Press, 2006), digital ed. 848.
8. Melville, *A Plague of Sheep*, 46; R. Douglas Cope, *The Limits of Racial Domination: Plebeian Society in Colonial Mexico City, 1660–1720* (University of Wisconsin Press, 1994), 10, 14.
9. Martínez Baracs, *Un gobierno de indios*, 78–80; Cope, *The Limits of Racial Domination*, 14–16.
10. James Lockhart, *The Nahuas After the Conquest: A Social and Cultural History of the Indians of Central Mexico, Sixteenth Through Eighteenth Centuries* (Stanford University Press, 1992), 429.
11. Antonio Mendoza, Virrey de Nueva España, para Luis de Velasco, "Relación, apuntamientos y aviso," 1550/1551, in *Instrucciones y memorias de los virreyes Novohispanos*, ed., Ernesto de la Torre Villar (Porrua, 1991), 99.
12. Joanne Pillsbury et al., eds., *Golden Kingdoms: Luxury Arts in the Ancient Americas* (J. Paul Getty Museum, 2017), 224.
13. Claudio Lomnitz, *Death and the Idea of Mexico* (Zone Books, 2005), 163.
14. Cited in Martínez Baracs, *Un gobierno de indios*, 165.
15. Jorge Cañizares-Esguerra, *How to Write the History of the New World: Histories, Epistemologies, and Identities in the Eighteenth-Century Atlantic World* (Stanford University Press, 2001), 90.
16. Gibson, *El Norte*, 71.
17. Miguel León-Portilla, *Los franciscanos vistos por el hombre Nahuatl. Testimonios indígenas del siglo XVI* (Universidad Nacional Autónoma de México, 1985), 32.
18. Stuart B. Schwartz, *All Can Be Saved: Religious Tolerance and Salvation in the Iberian Atlantic World* (Yale University Press, 2008), 279.
19. Elliott, *Empires*, 3345–3346.
20. Richard E. Greenleaf, *La inquisición en Nueva España, siglo XVI* (Fondo de Cultura Económica, 2015), 64.
21. Robert Ricard, *The Spiritual Conquest of Mexico: An Essay on the Apostolate and the Evangelizing Methods of the Mendicant Orders in New Spain: 1523–1572* (University of California Press, 1966), 117; Toribio de Benavente Motolinía, *Historia de los indios de la Nueva España* (Alianza, 1988), 153; Martínez Baracs, *Un gobierno de indios*, 123.
22. Informe referente al Colegio de Santa Cruz de Tlatelolco (1570), *Códice franciscano*, in León-Portilla, ed., *Historia Documental de México*, 1:285.
23. Thomas, *The Conquest*, 156; Díaz, *Historia verdadera*, 148.
24. Inga Clendinnen, "'Fierce and Unnatural Cruelty': Cortés and the Conquest of Mexico," *Representations* 33 (Winter 1991): 78.

25. León-Portilla, *Los franciscanos vistos por el hombre Nahuatl*, 27.
26. Ricard, *The Spiritual Conquest*, 203.
27. Landa, *Yucatán*, 58.
28. Max Harris, "'Indigenismo y Catolicidad': Folk Dramatizations of Evangelism and Conquest in Central Mexico," *Journal of the American Academy of Religion* 58, no. 1 (Spring 1990): 55; Ricard, *The Spiritual Conquest*, 197–198.
29. Motolinía, *La Nueva España*, quoted in León-Portilla, ed., *Historia Documental de México*, 1:153–155.
30. Ricard, *The Spiritual Conquest*, 47–49.
31. José Luis Martínez, *Pasajeros de Indias. Viajes trasatlánticos en el siglo XVI* (Fondo de Cultura Económica, 1999), 115–116.
32. Mauleón, *La ciudad*, 66; Miguel de Cervantes Saavedra, trans. J. M. Cohen, *The Adventures of Don Quixote* (Penguin, 1952), 55.
33. Schwartz, *All Can Be Saved*, 147; Martínez, *Pasajeros de Indias*, 115–116.
34. Ricard, *The Spiritual Conquest*, 201–202.
35. Elliott, *Empires*, 3738.
36. Ricard, *The Spiritual Conquest*, 213; Lockhart, *The Nahuas After the Conquest*, 283.
37. Martínez Baracs, *Un gobierno de indios*, 122.
38. Knight, *Mexico: The Colonial Era*, 46.
39. Nancy L. Kelker and Karen O. Bruhns, *Faking Ancient Mesoamerica* (Left Coast Press, 2010), 82–84; Clendinnen, *Ambivalent Conquests*, 70.
40. Landa, *Yucatán*, 161.
41. Ricard, *The Spiritual Conquest*, 20–23; Archbishop Petrus Moya de Contreras to Philip II, March 30, 1578, Archivum Romanum Societatis Iesu Monumenta Missionum (Monumenta Mexicana) 1:374.
42. Ramón A. Gutiérrez, *When Jesus Came, the Corn Mothers Went Away: Marriage, Sexuality, and Power in New Mexico, 1500–1846* (Stanford University Press, 1991), 5–6; Luis Aboites Aguilar, *Chihuahua. Historia breve* (Colegio de México, 2016), 47–48; Thomas E. Sheridan, *Landscapes of Fraud: Mission Tumacácori, the Baca Float, and the Betrayal of the O'odham* (University of Arizona Press, 2006), 30; Gibson, *El Norte*, 65.
43. Royal *cédula* of March 4, 1561, quoted in Ricard, *The Spiritual Conquest*, 81.
44. Motolinía, *La Nueva España*, 147.
45. Lockhart, *The Nahuas After the Conquest*, 204.
46. "Informe referente al Colegio de Santa Cruz de Tlatelolco," in León-Portilla, ed., *Historia Documental de México*, 1:285.
47. Gutiérrez, *When Jesus Came*, 92–94; Martínez Baracs, *Un gobierno de indios*, 117–119.
48. Fray Andrés Olmos, *Siete sermonos principales sobre los siete pecados capitales y las circunstancias en fin de cada uno por modo de pláticas,* quoted in Georges Baudot, "El concepto de la muerte en la predicación de los primeros evangelizadores de México," *Caravelle* 74 (2000): 26.
49. Lomnitz, *Death and the Idea of Mexico*, 126.
50. Lisa Sousa, *The Woman Who Turned into a Jaguar and Other Narratives of Native Women in Archives of Colonial Mexico* (Stanford University Press, 2017), 51, 61–63, 300.
51. Ricard, *The Spiritual Conquest*, 115.
52. Juan de Torquemada, *Monarquía Indiana*, 3 vols. (Universidad Nacional Autónoma de México, 1975), 3:101–102.
53. Camilla Townsend et al., *Fifth Sun: A New History of the Aztecs* (Oxford University Press, 2021), 210.

54. Lomnitz, *Death and the Idea of Mexico*, x.
55. Clendinnen, *Ambivalent Conquests*, 186–191; Gibson, *El Norte*, 70, 139.
56. Bede, *Ecclesiastical History of the English People*, ed. D. H. Farmer (Penguin, 1990), 92.
57. Emily Umberger, "The *Monarchía Indiana* in Seventeenth-Century Spain," in Diane Fane, ed., *Converging Cultures: Art & Identity in Spanish America* (Brooklyn Museum and Harry N. Abrams, Inc., 1996), 52–53.
58. Lomnitz, *Death and the Idea of Mexico*, 134, 495; Lockhart, *The Nahuas After the Conquest*, 257–258.
59. Edmundo O'Gorman, *El proceso de la invención de América* (Fondo de Cultura Económica, 1998), 84–85.
60. Book of Revelations, 20:2, 6:8 AV.
61. Lomnitz, *Death and the Idea of Mexico*, 123; Richard F. Townsend, "Moctezuma and the Renewal of Nature," in Colin MacEwan and Alejandro López Luján, eds., *Moctezuma: Aztec Ruler* (British Museum Press 2009), 140–143.
62. Revelation 21:1, 6:12, 16:18, 16:10.
63. Nancy Farriss, *Maya Society Under Colonial Rule: The Collective Enterprise of Survival* (Princeton University Press, 1984), 321–324.
64. Lockhart, *The Nahuas After the Conquest*, 236.
65. For the making of the actual relic, see Jeanette Favrot Peterson, "Creating the Virgin of Guadalupe: The Cloth, the Artist, and Sources in Sixteenth-Century New Spain," *The Americas* 61 (2005): 571–610; for skepticism, see William B. Taylor, "The Virgin of Guadalupe in New Spain: An Inquiry into the Social History of Marian Devotion," *American Ethnologist* 14, no 1 (February 1987): 9–33; Stafford Poole, *Our Lady of Guadalupe: The Origins and Sources of a Mexican National Symbol, 1531–1797* (University of Arizona Press, 1996), especially 26–39, 63–64; for a Tlaxcalan parallel, see Martínez Baracs, *Un gobierno de indios*, 125; for linguistic evidence for her early power, but confined to the Valley of Mexico, see Lockhart, *The Nahuas After the Conquest*, 246–251.
66. Pillsbury et al., *Golden Kingdoms*, 217.
67. Díaz, *Historia verdadera*, 99.
68. Gutiérrez, *When Jesus Came*, 67–69.
69. Baudot, "El concepto de la muerte," 30.
70. Lomnitz, *Death and the Idea of Mexico*, 248; Antonio de Robles, *Diario de sucesos notables (1665–1703)* (Porrúa, 1946), 1:116.
71. Lomnitz, *Death and the Idea of Mexico*, 247, 151.
72. Sahagún, *Historia general*, 31–32.
73. Sahagún, quoted in Enrique Florescano, *Etnia, estado y nación* (Fondo de Cultura Económica, 1997), 216–218; Diana Magaloni Kerpel, *Albores de la Conquista* (Artes de México, 2016), 33.
74. Magaloni, *Albores de la Conquista*, 30–32, 18–22, 16–18.
75. Camilla Townsend, *Annals of Native America: How the Nahuas of Colonial Mexico Kept Their History Alive* (Oxford University Press, 2017), 28.
76. Nahuatl decree against dancing with feathers around the Crucifix, issued by the cabildo of Tlaxcala in 1550, in Matthew Restall et al., *Mesoamerican Voices: Native Language Writings from Colonial Mexico, Yucatán, and Guatemala* (Cambridge University Press, 2005), 186.
77. Lockhart, *The Nahuas After the Conquest*, 236; Ricard, *The Spiritual Conquest*, 38; Mauleón, *La ciudad*, 41.
78. Barbara E. Mundy, *The Mapping of New Spain: Indigenous Cartography and the Maps of the Relaciones Geográficas* (University of Chicago Press, 1996), 56.

79. Fray Diego Valadés, *Rhetórica Cristiana*, in León-Portilla, ed., *Historia Documental de México*, 1:156–159.
80. The original phrase is from Chuck Colson, President Nixon's White House counsel. For the act, see Knight, *Mexico: The Colonial Era*, 33–35.
81. Sousa, *The Woman Who Turned into a Jaguar*, 59–61.
82. Townsend, *Annals*, 27.
83. Clendinnen, *Ambivalent Conquests*, 68–71.
84. Claire Gilbert, "A Grammar of Conquest: The Spanish and Arabic Reorganization of Granada after 1492," *Past & Present* 239, no. 1 (May 2018): 23, 35.
85. Inga Clendinnen, "Reading the Inquisitorial Record in Yucatán: Fact or Fantasy?," *The Americas* 38, no. 3 (January 1982): 338–345.
86. Sonia Corcuera de Mancera, *De pícaros y malqueridos. Huellas de su paso por la Inquisición de Zumárraga* (Fondo de Cultura Económica, 2009), 33.
87. "Informe referente al Colegio de Santa Cruz de Tlatelolco," in León-Portilla, ed., *Historia Documental de México*, 1:285.
88. Rodrigo de la Cruz to Charles V, May 4, 1550, Luis de Anguís to Philip II, February 20, 1561, in José Iturriaga de la Fuente, *Anecdotario de viajeros extranjeros en México. Siglos XVI–XX* (Fondo de Cultura Económica, 1993), 62, 71.
89. Thomas Gage, *Thomas Gage's Travels in the New World*, ed. J. Eric S. Thompson (University of Oklahoma Press, 1958), 44–45.
90. Fray Juan Bautista, *Advertencia para los confesores de los naturales* (Mexico City: El Convento de Santiago Tlatilolco, 1600), http://catarina.udlap.mx/xmLibris/projects/primeros_libros/xml/myBook.jsp?key=book_d01230.xml&id=pl&objects=/ximg&db=/db/xmlibris/system/metadata/.
91. Martin Austin Nesvig, *Promiscuous Power: An Unorthodox History of New Spain* (University of Texas Press, 2018), 80, 92–95.
92. Greenleaf, *La inquisición en Nueva España*, 84–92.
93. David Tavárez, *Rethinking Zapotec Time: Cosmology, Ritual, and Resistance in Colonial Mexico* (University of Texas Press, 2022), 9–10.
94. Farriss, *Maya Society*, 292.
95. Henry Mayr-Harting, *The Coming of Christianity to Anglo-Saxon England* (B. T. Batsford, 1991), 29.
96. For a fuller treatment, see Mundy, *The Death of Aztec Tenochtitlan*, 103–107.

Chapter Four

1. Stanley J. Stein and Barbara H. Stein, *Silver, Trade, and War: Spain and America in the Making of Early Modern Europe* (Johns Hopkins University Press, 2000), 53.
2. John H. Elliott, *Imperial Spain 1469–1716* (Penguin, 1963), 283, 321.
3. Stephanie Mawson, "Convicts or Conquistadores: Spanish Soldiers in the Seventeenth-Century Pacific," *Past & Present* 232, no. 1 (June 2016): 102.
4. D. A. Brading, *Miners and Merchants in Bourbon Mexico, 1763–1810* (Cambridge University Press, 1971), 11. Informal imperialism comes from Stein and Stein, *Silver, Trade, and War*, 18, 33, 38, 65–69, 73.
5. Casans, an eye witness, *The Tears of the Indians: Being An Historical and True Account of the Cruel Massacres and Slaughters of above Twenty Millions of Innocent People* (London: Nath Brook, 1656), title page.

6. Memorandum, Thomas Gage to Oliver Cromwell, 1654, quoted in J. Eric S. Thompson's introduction to Thomas Gage, *Travels in the New World*, ed. J. Eric S. Thompson (University of Oklahoma Press, 1958), xviii.
7. Alexander von Humboldt, *Political Essay on the Kingdom of New Spain*, trans. John Black (Longman, 1814), II:69.
8. Melissa N. Morris, "Cultivating Colonies: Tobacco and the Upstart Empires, 1580–1640" (PhD diss., Columbia University, 2017), 7–8.
9. Melissa Macauley, *Distant Shores: Colonial Encounters on China's Maritime Frontier* (Princeton University Press, 2021), 24–28.
10. Michael Kwass, "The Global Underground: Smuggling, Rebellion, and the Origins of the French Revolution," in Suzanne Desan et al., eds., *The French Revolution in Global Perspective* (Cornell University Press, 2013), 15–31.
11. John H. Elliott, *Empires of the Atlantic World: Britain and Spain in America, 1492–1830* (Yale University Press, 2006), digital ed. 2376, 2487.
12. Donald Thomas, *Cochrane: Britannia's Sea Wolf* (Cassell, 1978), 44.
13. Mauricio Drelichman and Hans-Joachim Voth, *Lending to the Borrower from Hell: Debt, Taxes, and Default in the Age of Philip II* (Princeton University Press, 2014), 33–35, 271–280.
14. Joel Mokyr, *A Culture of Growth: The Origins of the Modern Economy* (Princeton University Press, 2018), 58–60.
15. Bank of England, "Public Sector Debt Outstanding in the United Kingdom," https://fred.stlouisfed.org/series/PSDOTUKA.
16. Neil Cummins, "Lifespans of the European Elite, 800–1800," *Journal of Economic History* 77, no. 2 (June 2017): 431.
17. Elliott, *Imperial Spain*, 19.
18. Henry Kamen, *Empire: How Spain Became a World Power, 1492–1763* (Harper Collins, 2003), 16–17.
19. Peter Martyr, *De Orbe Novo* (New York: Knickerbocker Press, 1912), 2:3, 246, 403–404.
20. Earl Rosenthal, "Ultra, Non plus Ultra, and the Columnar Device of Emperor Charles V," *Journal of the Warburg and Courtauld Institutes* 34 (1971): 204–228.
21. Kamen, *Empire*, 17, 24–32, 83.
22. Elliott, *Imperial Spain*, 16.
23. Kamen, *Empire*, 68.
24. John Lynch, *Spain 1516–1598: From Nation State to World Empire* (Blackwell, 1991), 435–436; Stein and Stein, *Silver, Trade, and War*, 108.
25. Anthony Pagden, *Spanish Imperialism and the Political Imagination: Studies in European and Spanish-American Social and Political Theory 1513–1830* (Yale University Press, 1990), 91.
26. Kamen, *Empire*, 41.
27. Lynch, *Spain*, 55–59; quote is from Elliott, *Imperial Spain*, 143.
28. Fernand Braudel, *The Mediterranean and the Mediterranean World in the Age of Philip II*, 3 vols. (London: Collins, 1973), 2:785–787.
29. Don Juan of Austria to Rui Gómez, November 5, 1570, quoted in Kamen, *Empire*, 182.
30. Andrew C. Hess, "The Moriscos: An Ottoman Fifth Column in Sixteenth-Century Spain," *American Historical Review* 74, no. 1 (1968), 5–6, 15–16.
31. Jerry Brotton, *The Sultan and the Queen: The Untold Story of Elizabeth and Islam* (Penguin, 2017), 1–2, 263, 271.
32. John H. Elliott, *The Old World and the New: 1492–1650* (Cambridge University Press, 1992), 100.

33. Henry Barnby, "The Algerian Attack on Baltimore 1631," *Mariner's Mirror* 56, no. 1 (1970): 27–31.
34. Edmundo O'Gorman, *El proceso de la invención de América* (Fondo de Cultura Económica, 1998), 13–14, 33, 80–85.
35. Carrie Gibson, *Empire's Crossroads: A History of the Caribbean from Columbus to the Present Day* (Atlantic Monthly Press, 2014), 81.
36. Alfred W. Crosby, *The Columbian Exchange: Biological and Cultural Consequences of 1492* (Praeger, 1972), 87, 69.
37. Martyr, *De Orbe Novo*, x; Gibson, *Empire's Crossroads*, 83.
38. Hernán Cortés, *Cartas de relación de la conquista de Méjico* (Madrid: Espasa-Calpe, 1940), 1.
39. Daniela Bleichmar, *Visual Voyages: Images of Latin American Nature from Columbus to Darwin* (Yale University Press, 2017), 1.
40. F. Mateos, "Ecos de América en Trento," *Revista de Indias* 6, no. 22 (January 1, 1945): 601.
41. Juan de Zumárraga, "Carta a Su Majestad sobre Nueva España," August 27, 1529, General Archives of the Ordo Fratrum Minorum Nueva España M/33, 261–316.
42. Don Luis de Velasco, Mexico City, to Charles V, May 4, 1553, in James Lockhart and Enrique Otte, *Letters and People of the Spanish Indies, Sixteenth Century* (Cambridge University Press, 1976), 187–194.
43. Robert Thorne to Doctour Ley, Seville, 1527, in Richard Hakluyt, *Voyages*, 8 vols. (London: J. M. Dent, 1939), 1:218.
44. The metaphor is Braudel's. Fernand Braudel, *Civilization and Capitalism 15th–18th Century*, vol. 1, *The Structures of Everyday Life*, trans. Siân Reynold, (Fontana, 1981), 409.

Chapter Five

1. José Luis Martínez, *Hernán Cortés* (Fondo de Cultura Económica, 1990), 410.
2. Carlos V, Carta a Hernán Cortés, Valladolid, June 26, 1523, in José Luis Martínez, *Documentos Cortesianos* (Fondo de Cultura Económica, 1991), 269.
3. José Luis Martínez, *Pasajeros de Indias: Viajes trasatlánticos en el siglo XVI* (Fondo de Cultura Económica, 1999), 26.
4. Martínez, *Pasajeros de Indias*, 51.
5. Héctor de Mauleón, *La ciudad que nos inventa. Crónicas de seis siglos* (Cal y Arena, 2015), 33; Barbara E. Mundy, *The Death of Aztec Tenochtitlan, the Life of Mexico City* (University of Texas Press, 2015), 93.
6. *Ordenanzas de buen gobierno dadas por Hernán Cortés para los vecinos y moradores de la Nueva España*, Temistitlan, 20 de marzo de 1524, in Martínez, *Documentos Cortesianos*, 277–283.
7. Quoted in Martínez, *Hernán Cortés*, 410.
8. *Ordenanzas de buen gobierno*, in Martínez, *Documentos Cortesianos*, 277–283.
9. Martínez, *Hernán Cortés*, 396.
10. Ibid., 387–398; Toribio de Benavente Motolinía, *Historia de los indios de la Nueva España* (Castalia, 1985), 121.
11. Luis Weckmann, *La herencia medieval de México*, 2nd ed. (Colegio de México, 1984), 692–695.
12. Carta reservada de Hernán Cortés al emperador Carlos V, Tenochtitlán 15 de octubre de 1524, in Martínez, *Documentos Cortesianos*, 286.
13. Mundy, *The Death of Aztec Tenochtitlan*, 72–81, 193–199; Carta del Consejo de las Indias a Su Majestad, October 23, 1552, reproduced in Francis V. Scholes, "The Colegio de San Juan de Letrán in 1552, *The Americas* 2, no. 1 (July 1945): 106.

14. Motolinía, *La Nueva España*, 238.
15. Francisco Cervantes de Salazar, *México en 1554* (Universidad Nacional Autónoma de México, 2001), 153–167.
16. Mauleón, *La ciudad*, 48; Bernardo de Balbuena, *Grandeza mexicana* (Universidad Nacional Autónoma de México, 1941), 9.
17. Matthew Restall, *When Montezuma Met Cortés* (Harper Collins, 2018), 365; Thomas, *Cortés*, 556, 582; Martínez, *Hernán Cortés*, 359, 371; Bernal Díaz del Castillo, *Historia verdadera de la conquista de la Nueva España* (Madrid: Instituto Gonzalo Fernández de Oviedo, 1982), 569, 575; Richard Greenleaf, *La inquisición en Nueva España, siglo XVI* (Fondo de Cultura Económica, 2015), 38–39; Martínez, *Hernán Cortés*, 430, 461.
18. Martínez, *Hernán Cortés*, 413, 449–457, 471–478, 897–905; John H. Elliott, *Imperial Spain 1469–1716* (Penguin, 1963), 1806.
19. María Elena Martínez, *Genealogical Fictions: Limpieza de Sangre, Religion, and Gender in Colonial Mexico* (Stanford University Press, 2008), 125.
20. Gabriel Torres Puga, "La ciudad novohispana. Ensayo sobre su vida política," in Ariel Rodríguez Kuri, *Historia política de la Ciudad de México (Desde su fundación hasta el año 2000)* (El Colegio de México, 2013), 76–85; José Luis Martínez, *Hernán Cortés*, 900–902.
21. Deborah Cohen, *Family Secrets: Shame and Privacy in Modern Britain* (Oxford University Press, 2017), 27.
22. José Joaquín Fernández de Lizardi, *El Periquillo Sarniento* (México City: Alexandro Valdés, 1816), 32.
23. Camilla Townsend et al., *Fifth Sun: A New History of the Aztecs* (Oxford University Press, 2021), 155–179; Stafford Poole, "'War by Fire and Blood': The Church and the Chichimecas 1585," *The Americas* 74, no. 2 (2017): 123.
24. Bernardo García Martínez, *El Desarrollo regional y la organización del espacio, siglos XVI al XX* (Universidad Autónoma de México, 2004), 32–34.
25. Stephanie Wood, *Transcending Conquest: Nahua Views of Spanish Colonial Mexico* (University of Oklahoma Press, 2003), 121–122; Bernardo García Martínez, "Encomenderos españoles y British residents. El sistema de dominio indirecto desde la perspectiva novohispana," *Historia Mexicana* 60, no. 4 (April–June 2011): 1915–1978.
26. Thomas Calvo, "Soberano, plebe y cadalso bajo una misma luz en Nueva España," in Pilar Gonzalbo Aizpuru, ed., *Historia de la vida cotidiana en México* (México: Fondo de Cultura Económica, 2014), 3:279.
27. Dorothy Tanck de Estrada, *Atlas Ilustrado de los Pueblos de Indios* (El Colegio de México, 2005), 52–53.
28. James Lockhart, *The Nahuas After the Conquest: A Social and Cultural History of the Indians of Central Mexico, Sixteenth Through Eighteenth Centuries* (Stanford University Press, 1992), 261; Ramón A. Gutiérrez, *When Jesus Came, the Corn Mothers Went Away: Marriage, Sexuality, and Power in New Mexico, 1500–1846* (Stanford University Press, 1991), 66–75; Elliott, *Empires of the Atlantic*, 1599; Matthew Restall et al., *Mesoamerican Voices: Native Language Writings from Colonial Mexico, Yucatán, and Guatemala* (Cambridge University Press, 2005), 62; Camilla Townsend, *Annals of Native America: How the Nahuas of Colonial Mexico Kept Their History Alive* (Oxford University Press, 2017), 1–11.
29. Antonio de Robles, *Diario de sucesos notables (1665–1703)* (Porrúa, 1946), 2:260–261.
30. Bradley Benton, *The Lords of Tetzcoco: The Transformation of Indigenous Rule in Postconquest Central Mexico* (Cambridge University Press, 2017), 11, 21–39, 46–47, 68–78, 137–138.
31. Nancy Farriss, *Maya Society Under Colonial Rule: The Collective Enterprise of Survival* (Princeton University Press, 1984), 22–24.

32. Mundy, *The Death of Aztec Tenochtitlan*, 71–86, 211.
33. Townsend, *Annals*, 181; Wood, *Transcending Conquest*, 95, 136.
34. Greenleaf, *La Inquisición*, 20; Torres Puga, "La ciudad novohispana," 86, 90–91.
35. Poole, "War by Fire and Blood," 116.
36. José Luis Martínez, *Pasajeros*, 189; Serge Gruzinski, *El águila y el dragón. Desmesura europea y mundialización en el siglo XVI* (Fondo de Cultura Económica, 2018), 309.
37. "Informe referente al colegio de Santa Cruz de Tlatelolco," in Miguel León-Portilla, ed., *Historia Documental de México* (Universidad Nacional Autónoma de México, 1964), 1:285.
38. Francisco Fernández del Castillo, *Libros y libreros en el siglo XVI* (Fondo de Cultura Económica, 2017), 1–3.
39. Henry Raup Wagner and Helen Rand Parish, *The Life and Writings of Bartolomé de Las Casas* (University of New Mexico Press, 1967), 98–100, 171, 190.
40. Thomas Gage, *Travels in the New World*, ed. J. Eric S. Thompson (University of Oklahoma Press, 1958), 17.
41. Ciudad de México to Philip II, 1570, Philip II to Francis Borgia, Padre General del Orden de Jesús, Archivum Romanum Societatis Iesu, Monumenta Missionum (Monumenta Mexicana) 1:1–5.
42. François Chevalier, *Land and Society in Colonial Mexico: The Great Hacienda* (University of California Press, 1966), 107; Enrique Florescano and Margarita Menegus, "La época de las reformas borbónicas y el crecimiento económico (1750–1808), in various authors, *Historia general de México, Versión 2000* (Colegio de México, 2017), 535.
43. Acta Congregationis Provincialis Novae Hispaniae, Archivum Romanum Societatis Iesu Monumenta Missionum (Monumenta Mexicana) 1:298–299, Frederick P. Bowser, "Africans in Spanish American Colonial Society," in Leslie Bethell, ed., *Cambridge History of Latin America*, vol. 2, *Colonial Latin America* (Cambridge University Press, 1985), 371.
44. Pedro Moya de Contreras to Philip II, March 30, 1578, Archivum Romanum Societatis Iesu Monumenta Missionum (Monumenta Mexicana) 1:374–376.
45. Martin Austin Nesvig, *Promiscuous Power: An Unorthodox History of New Spain* (University of Texas Press, 2018), 68–75; Luis de Anguis to Philip II, February 20, 1561, in José Iturriaga de la Fuente, *Anecdotario de* viajeros *extranjeros en México. Siglos XVI–XX* (Fondo de Cultura Económica, 1993), 68–73.
46. Gage, *Travels in the New World*, 113.
47. D. A. Brading, *Miners and Merchants in Bourbon Mexico, 1763–1810* (Cambridge University Press, 1971), 210, 218.
48. Fernández de Lizardi, *El Periquillo Sarniento*, 129.
49. Lisa Sousa, *The Woman Who Turned into a Jaguar and Other Narratives of Native Women in Archives of Colonial Mexico* (Stanford University Press, 2017), 171; Nicole von Germeten, *Profit and Passion: Transactional Sex in Colonial Mexico* (University of California Press, 2018), 41–43; Sonya Lipsett-Rivera, "De Obra Y Palabra: Patterns of Insults in Mexico, 1750–1856," *The Americas* 54, no. 4 (April 1998), 537.
50. William B. Taylor, *Fugitive Freedom: The Improbable Lives of Two Impostors in Late Colonial Mexico* (University of California Press, 2021), 20; Stuart B. Schwartz, *All Can Be Saved: Religious Tolerance and Salvation in the Iberian Atlantic World* (Yale University Press, 2008), 129.
51. Restall et al., *Mesoamerican Voices*, 169.
52. See, for example, the novels of the politician-writer Vicente Riva Palacio, such as *Martín Garatuza* or *Monja y casada, virgen y mártir*; for problems answering the mail, see Alan Knight, *Mexico: The Colonial Era* (Cambridge University Press, 2002), 60.

53. Schwartz, *All Can Be Saved*, 125–129.
54. Nesvig, *Promiscuous Power*, 104.
55. "Soberano, plebe y cadalso bajo una misma luz en Nueva España," 305–306; Lynch, *Spain*, 32.
56. Taylor, *Fugitive Freedom*, 52.
57. Antonio de Robles, *Diario de sucesos notables (1665–1703)* (Porrúa, 1946), 2:252–253.
58. Elliott, *Imperial Spain*, 90–91.
59. Romain Bertrand, "Where the Devil Stands: A Microhistorical Reading of Empires as Multiple Moral Worlds (Manila–Mexico, 1577–1580)," *Past & Present* 242 (November 2019): 98.
60. Andrés Reséndez, *Conquering the Pacific: An Unknown Mariner and the Final Great Voyage of the Age of Discovery* (Houghton Mifflin Harcourt, 2021), 123–127, 158.
61. Instrucción del Rey Felipe II al Virrey de Nueva España, Gastón de Peralta, Marqués de Falces, 10 de marzo de 1566, in Pedro Soler Alonso, *Biblioteca Enciclopedica Popular. 63. Virreyes de la Nueva España*, (Secretaría de Educación Pública, 1945), 32.
62. "Demanda por pago de unas vigas que promueve Nicolás Raya de Palos contra José Gómez de Santiago," Aguascalientes sin fecha 1690. Archivo Histórico de Aguascalientes, Fondo judicial civil general, caja 1, exp. 2, 183 f–v.
63. Velasco, Mexico City, to Charles V, May 4, 1553, in James Lockhart and Enrique Otte, *Letters and People of the Spanish Indies, Sixteenth Century* (Cambridge University Press, 1976), 185–187.
64. John Lynch, *Spain 1516–1598: From Nation State to World Empire* (Blackwell, 1991), 270.
65. Lynch, *Spain*, 267–268.
66. Alberto Portera-Sanchez et al., "Spanish-Speaking Countries," in Stephen Lock et al., eds., *The Oxford Companion to Medicine* (Oxford University Press, 2006); Kamen, *Empire*, 494–503.
67. Claire Gilbert, "A Grammar of Conquest: The Spanish and Arabic Reorganization of Granada after 1492," *Past & Present* 239, no. 1 (May 2018): 3.
68. William J. McCarthy, "Gambling on Empire: The Economic Cost of Shipwrecks in the Age of Discovery," *International Journal of Maritime History* 23, no. 2 (December 2011): 70; José Luis Martínez, *Pasajeros*, 80.
69. "Tripulación del barco *Nuestra Señora del Pilar*, 1631, in Flor Trejo Rivera, "El barco como una ciudad flotante," in Gonzalbo Aizpuru, *Historia de la vida cotidiana en México*, 2:143.
70. Andrés Reséndez, *The Other Slavery: The Uncovered Story of Indian Enslavement in America* (First Mariner, 2016), 96–97; "Relación del mineral de Real del Monte (Finales siglo XVI)," in León-Portilla, ed., *Historia Documental de México*, 1:225.
71. Von Germeten, *Profit and Passion*, 38.
72. R. Douglas Cope, *The Limits of Racial Domination: Plebeian Society in Colonial Mexico City, 1660–1720* (University of Wisconsin Press, 1994), 21.
73. Elinor G. K. Melville, "Land Use and the Transformation of the Environment," in Victor Bulmer-Thomas et al., eds., *The Cambridge Economic History of Latin America*, vol 1, *The Colonial Era and the Short Nineteenth Century* (Cambridge University Press, 2006), 129.
74. José Luis Martínez, *Pasajeros*, 52; Sergio M. Rodríguez Lorenzo, "El contrato de pasaje en la carrera de Indias (1561–1622)," *Historia Mexicana* 66, no. 3 (January–March, 2017): 1515–1517; Carlos Marichal, "The Spanish-American Silver Peso: Export Commodity and Global Money of the Ancien Regime, 1550–1800," in Steven Topik et al., eds, *From Silver to Cocaine: Latin American Commodity Chains and the Building of the World Economy, 1500–2000* (Duke University Press, 2006), 38.

75. Viceroy Antonio de Mendoza, "Cédula y Ordenanzas para la Nueva España, que manda la orden que se ha de tener en la Casa de la Moneda de ella en la labor de la dicha moneda, 1535," in León-Portilla, ed., *Historia Documental de México*, 1:232; Stanley J. Stein and Barbara H. Stein, *Silver, Trade, and War: Spain and America in the Making of Early Modern Europe* (Johns Hopkins University Press, 2000), 92.
76. Ida Altman, *The War for Mexico's West: Indians and Spaniards in New Galicia, 1524–1550* (University of New Mexico Press, 2010), 128.
77. Robles, *Diario*, 1:18.
78. Elizabeth Harper, "The Early Modern European (Non) Reception of the Zhuangzi Text," *Journal of East-West Thought* 9, no. 4 (Winter 2019): 23–37.
79. Lao Tzu, *Tao Te Ching*, ed. D. C. Lau (Penguin, 1963), 73, 87, 129.

Chapter Six

1. Cited in David Brading, *The First America: The Spanish Monarchy, Creole Patriots and the Liberal State, 1492–1867* (Cambridge University Press, 1991), 9.
2. Fernand Braudel, *Civilization and Capitalism 15th–18th Century*, vol. 1, *The Structures of Everyday Life*, trans. Siân Reynold, (Fontana, 1981), 407; Sea-Distances.org, https://sea-distances.org/.
3. All voyage times unless specified otherwise are from the period 1550–1650, analysed in the Chaunus' classic work. José Luis Martínez, *Pasajeros de Indias: Viajes trasatlánticos en el siglo XVI* (Fondo de Cultura Económica, 1999), 14; Pierre Chaunu, with the assistance of Huguette Chaunu, *Séville et l'Amérique, XVIe–XVIIe siècle* (Flammarion, 1977), 235.
4. José Luis Martínez, *Pasajeros*, 160–161.
5. Woodes Rogers, *A Cruising Voyage Round the World* (CreateSpace Independent Publishing Platform, 2018), 289.
6. Tatiana Seijas, *Asian Slaves in Colonial Mexico: From Chinos to Indians* (Cambridge University Press, 2014), 76–78.
7. Clemente Guillén, *Explorer of the South: Diaries of the Overland Expeditions to Bahía Magdalena and La Paz, 1719, 1720–21*, trans. and ed. W. Michael Mathes (Los Angeles: Dawson's Bookshop, 1979), 23–25.
8. Andrés Reséndez, *Conquering the Pacific: An Unknown Mariner and the Final Great Voyage of the Age of Discovery* (Houghton Mifflin Harcourt, 2021), 145.
9. Fernand Braudel, *The Mediterranean and the Mediterranean World in the Age of Philip II*, 3 vols. (London: Collins, 1973), 1:359.
10. José Luis Martínez, *Pasajeros*, 58–69; John Masefield, introduction to *Voyages*, by Richard Hakluyt, 8 vols. (London: J. M. Dent, 1939), 1:xxii.
11. Thomas Gage, *Travels in the New World*, ed. J. Eric S. Thompson (University of Oklahoma Press, 1958), 12.
12. María Carranza to Hernando de Soto, 1589, in James Lockhart and Enrique Otte, *Letters and People of the Spanish Indies, Sixteenth Century* (Cambridge University Press, 1976), 135–136.
13. Sergio M. Rodríguez Lorenzo, "El contrato de pasaje en la carrera de Indias (1561–1622)," *Historia Mexicana* 66, no. 3 (January to March, 2017): 1501–1502, 1513–1514.
14. Letter, Eugenio Salazar to Licenciado Miranda, in Flor Trejo Rivera, "El barco como una ciudad flotante," in Pilar Gonzalbo Aizpuru, ed., *Historia de la vida cotidiana en México*, 3 vols. (Fondo de Cultura Económica, 2014), 153.

15. Edward J. Sullivan, "European Painting and the Art of the New World," in Diane Fane, ed., *Converging Cultures: Art & Identity in Spanish America* (Brooklyn Museum and Harry N. Abrams, Inc., 1996), 30.
16. Francisco de Ajofrín, *Diario de viaje que hicimos a México Fray Francisco de Ajofrín y Fray Fermín de Olite, Capuchinos, con una introducción por Génaro Estrada* (Porrúa, 1936), 26.
17. Letter, Eugenio de Salazar to Lic. Miranda de Ron, 1573, reproduced in José Luis Martínez, *Pasajeros*, 296–297.
18. Braudel, *The Mediterranean*, 1:xxx.
19. José Luis Martínez, *Pasajeros*, 69.
20. Romain Bertrand, "Where the Devil Stands: A Microhistorical Reading of Empires as Multiple Moral Worlds (Manila–Mexico, 1577–1580)," *Past & Present* 242 (November 2019): 88.
21. William J. McCarthy, "Gambling on Empire: The Economic Cost of Shipwrecks in the Age of Discovery," *International Journal of Maritime History* 23, no. 2 (December 2011): 69.
22. José Luis Martínez, *Pasajeros*, 161; Henry Kamen, *Empire: How Spain Became a World Power, 1492–1763* (Harper Collins, 2003), 511.
23. Only 119 thousand disembarked out of 168 thousand who set out. Slave Voyages Database, https://www.slavevoyages.org.
24. Seijas, *Asian Slaves*, 80.
25. Peter McCandless, review of *Scurvy: The Disease of Discovery*, by Jonathan Lamb, *Journal of the History of Medicine and Allied Sciences* 73, no. 1 (January 2018): 98–100.
26. Reséndez, *Conquering the Pacific*, 374–376, digital ed.; Guillén, *Explorer of the South*, 46.
27. Chaunu, *Séville et l'Amérique*, 232, 323, 254.
28. Barbara E. Mundy, *The Mapping of New Spain: Indigenous Cartography and the Maps of the Relaciones Geográficas* (University of Chicago Press, 1996), 15; Magali M. Carrera *Traveling from New Spain to Mexico: Mapping Practices of Nineteenth-Century Mexico* (Duke University Press, 2011), 28, 41.
29. Stanley J. Stein and Barbara H. Stein, *Silver, Trade, and War: Spain and America in the Making of Early Modern Europe* (Johns Hopkins University Press, 2000), 73.
30. Chaunu, *Séville et l'Amérique*, 130–131, 234.
31. Dava Sobel, *Longitude: The True Story of a Lone Genius Who Solved the Greatest Problem of His Time* (Fourth Estate, 1995), 15, 24–27.
32. "Ship Types: Milestones in the Hisory of European Shipbuilding," Deutsches Historishes Museum Media Library, https://www.dhm.de/mediathek/en/ship-types/milestones-in-the-history-of-european-shipbuilding/09-fluyt/; Chaunu, *Séville et l'Amérique*, 223.
33. Matthew Restall, *When Montezuma Met Cortés* (Harper Collins, 2018), 128.
34. Robert C. Ritchie, "Piracy"; James Kelly, "Buccaneers and Buccaneering"; David J. Starkey, "Privateering," all in *The Oxford Encyclopedia of Maritime History* online (Oxford University Press, 2007).
35. Clearly under the influence of Captain Blood. Gage, *Travels in the New World*, 317.
36. Carlos Justo Sierra et al., *Campeche. Breve historia* (Fondo de Cultura Económica, 2011), 259–261.
37. David McCreery, "Indigo Commodity Chains in the Spanish and British Empires, 1560–1860," in Steven Topik et al., eds. *From Silver to Cocaine: Latin American Commodity Chains and the Building of the World Economy, 1500–2000* (Duke University Press, 2006), 53–56.

38. 1552–1553 and 1562–1563 stood out as catastrophic. Chaunu, *Séville et l'Amérique*, 282, 284, 331.
39. Francisco de Escobar to Diego Ribera, Seville, November 25, 1553, in Lockhart and Otte, *Letters and People*, 94–95.
40. Stein and Stein, *Silver, Trade, and War*, 13–14.
41. Carta al Rey, del Arzobispo de México, tratando de las relaciones que tenía con los religiosos de todas las órdenes, de la provisión de beneficios eclesiásticos, de lo que ocurría en el convento de monjas de Santa Clara y de otras cosas, 25 de septiembre de 1575; Real cédula disponiendo que los monasterios de frailes y monjas no tengan bienes propios, haciendas, rentas ni granjerías y ordenando la confección de un catastro, El Pardo, 24 de octubre, 1576; Real cédula prohibiendo que los laicos, como interpósitas personas, traten y contraten en nombre de clérigos y religiosos, El Pardo, 27 de septiembre, 1576; Real cédula al virrey de la Nueva España para que se envíe relación de los bienes, rentas y haciendas que poseen los monasterios y los religiosos en todo el virreinato, Aranjuez, 17 de mayo, 1579. Francisco de Solano, ed., *Cedularo de tierras: Legislación agraria colonial (1497–1820)*, (Universidad Autónoma de México, 1991), 249, 237, 238, 253.
42. A term popularized by Geoffrey Blainey in Blainey, *The Tyranny of Distance: How Distance Shaped Australia's History* (Sun Books, 1966).
43. Norman Hammond, *The Maya* (The Folio Society, 1988), 227.
44. John H. Elliott, *The Old World and the New: 1492–1650* (Cambridge University Press, 1992), 37.
45. Gage, *Travels in the New World*, 224.
46. Nancy Farriss, *Maya Society Under Colonial Rule: The Collective Enterprise of Survival* (Princeton University Press, 1984), 325.
47. Miruna Achim, "Making Lizards into Drugs: The Debates on the Medical Uses of Lizards in Late Eighteenth-Century Mexico," *Journal of Spanish Cultural Studies* 8, no. 2 (July 2007): 169–191.
48. Robert Thorne to Doctour Ley, Seville 1527, reproduced in Hakluyt, *Voyages*, 1:218.
49. Mundy, *The Mapping of New Spain*, ch. 2.
50. Carrera, *Traveling from New Spain*, 28, 41.
51. Alexander von Humboldt, *Political Essay on the Kingdom of New Spain*, trans. John Black, 3 vols. (London: 1814), 1:lvi–lvii, lxxi.
52. "Instrucción y memoria de las relaciones que se han de hacer para la descripción de las Indias . . . 1577," José Toribio Medina, *Biblioteca hispano-americana (1493–1810)*, (Brown University Press, 2020), 245.
53. *Relación geográfica de Coatepec*, in René Acuña, *Relaciones geográficas del siglo XVI: México tomo primero* (Universidad Autónoma de México, 1985), 148–220, 174, 167.
54. Quoted in Mundy, *The Mapping of New Spain*, 34.
55. Mundy, *The Mapping of New Spain*, ch. 3.
56. "Map of Property from Will of Juan de la Cruz, Teocaltitlan, Mexico City," 1678, Newberry Library Ayer Collection: Ayer MS 1477 folder 1.
57. Yanna Yannakis, "Allies or Servants? The Journey of Indian Conquistadors in the *Lienzo of Analco*," *Ethnohistory* 58, no. 4 (Fall 2011): 660.
58. Jan de Vos, *Oro verde. La conquista de la Selva Lacandona por los madereros tabasqueños, 1822–1949* (Fondo de Cultura Económica, 1996), 38, 47.
59. Carrie Gibson, *El Norte: The Epic and Forgotten Story of Hispanic North America* (Atlantic Monthly Press, 2019), 223–228; Humboldt, *New Spain*, 1:iii.

60. Elliott, *The Old World and the New*, 53.
61. Héctor de Mauleón, *La ciudad que nos inventa. Crónicas de seis siglos* (Cal y Arena, 2015), 85.
62. Nelson Fernando González Martínez, "Communicating an Empire and Its Many Worlds: Spanish American Mail, Logistics, and Postal Agents, 1492–1620," *Hispanic American Historical Review* 101, no. 4 (November 2021): 567–596.
63. Jesús Gómez Serrano and Francisco Javier Delgado Aguilar, *Aguascalientes. Historia breve* (Colegio de México, 2012), 63.
64. José Luis Martínez, *Pasajeros*, 144.
65. Fray Juan de Mora to family, March 29, 1574, in Lockhart and Otte, *Letters and People*, 114–115.
66. Elliott, *The Old World and the New*, 47–48.
67. Martin Austin Nesvig, *Ideology and Inquisition: The World of the Censors in Early Mexico* (Yale University Press, 2009), 5, 245.
68. Patrick Karl O'Brien, "The Global Economic History of European Expansion Overseas," in Victor Bulmer-Thomas et al., eds., *The Cambridge Economic History of Latin America*, vol 1, *The Colonial Era and the Short Nineteenth Century* (Cambridge University Press, 2006), 33–34; Elliott, *Imperial Spain*, digital ed.2957; Stein and Stein, *Silver, Trade, and War*, 113; Carlos Marichal, "The Spanish-American Silver Peso: Export Commodity and Global Money of the Ancien Regime, 1550–1800," in Topik et al., eds, *From Silver to Cocaine* (Duke University Press, 2006), 25–52; "The Columbian Exchange in the Early Modern Period," in Peter N. Stearns et al, *Documents in World History, Volume II: From 1500 to the Present* (Pearson, 2002), 111.
69. Elliott, *The Old World and the New*, 85.
70. Alonso de la Mota y Escobar, *Descripción geográfica de los reinos de Nueva Galicia, Nueva Vizcaya y Nuevo León*, in Miguel León-Portilla, ed., *Historia Documental de México* (Universidad Nacional Autónoma de México, 1964), 1:227.
71. Dana Velasco Murrillo, *Urban Indians in a Silver City: Zacatecas, Mexico, 1546–1810* (Stanford University Press, 2016), 45–47, 84.
72. Enrique Tandeter, "The Mining Industry," in Victor Bulmer-Thomas et al., eds., *The Cambridge Economic History of Latin America*, vol. 1, *The Colonial Era and the Short Nineteenth Century* (Cambridge University Press, 2006), 320; Marichal, "The Spanish-American Silver Peso," 27–28.
73. Mota y Escobar, *Descripción geográfica*, 227.
74. Tandeter, "The Mining Industry," 318–321; Brading, *Miners and Merchants*, 11; Marichal, "The Spanish-American Silver Peso," 28–29.
75. Marichal, "The Spanish-American Silver Peso," 30.
76. Stein and Stein, *Silver, Trade, and War*, 24, 84.
77. O'Brien, "The Global Economic History of European Expansion Overseas," 32–35.
78. Stein and Stein, *Silver, Trade, and War*, 83.
79. Fernand Braudel, *Civilization and Capitalism 15th–18th Century*, vol. 2, *The Wheels of CommerceI*, trans. Siân Reynold (Fontana Press, 1981), 406.
80. Chaunu, *Séville et l'Amérique*, 136.
81. Marichal, "The Spanish-American Silver Peso," 40–43.
82. O'Brien, "The Global Economic History of European Expansion Overseas," 11, 35.
83. Christopher Ebert, "Early Modern Atlantic Trade and the Development of Maritime Insurance to 1630," *Past & Present* 213, no. 1 (November 2011): 88.

84. For John Tutino, capitalism began in Mexico's Bajío: "A globally linked, commercially driven, ethnically mixed, patriarchally integrated, and religiously justified—and debated—society began in Querétaro and the Bajío in the sixteenth century," a "complex commercial society [that constituted] an early and original salient of capitalism," which is "the dynamic commercial ordering of production and society that concentrates power and orders the modern world." John Tutino, *Making a New World: Founding Capitalism in the Bajío and Spanish America* (Duke University Press, 2011), 6–8. For criticism of this proposal, see (among others) the reviews of Eric Van Young, *Hispanic American Historical Review* 93, no. 2 (May 2013): 273–275, and Juliette Levy, *Journal of Economic History* 73, no. 2 (June 2013): 620–621.
85. For a critical review of concepts of capitalism, see Andrew David Edwards et al., "Capitalism in Global History," *Past & Present* 249, no. 1 (November 2020): 1–32.
86. Enrique Semo, *The History of Capitalism in Mexico: Its Origins, 1521–1763* (University of Texas Press, 1993), x–xiii.
87. Marichal, "The Spanish-American Silver Peso," 43–44; Enrique Florescano and Margarita Menegus, "La época de las reformas borbónicas y el crecimiento económico (1750–1808), in various authors, *Historia general de México, Versión 2000* (Colegio de México, 2017), 510.
88. Mauricio Drelichman and Hans-Joachim Voth, *Lending to the Borrower from Hell: Debt, Taxes, and Default in the Age of Philip II* (Princeton University Press, 2014), 33, 35, 36; Braudel, *The Wheels of Commerce*, 100–101; Ebert, "The Development of Maritime Insurance," 102.
89. Stein and Stein, *Silver, Trade, and War*, 46.
90. Enrique Florescano, "La formación de los trabajadores en la época colonial, 1521–1750," in Enrique Florescano and Pablo González Casanova, eds., *La clase obrera en la historia de México*, vol. 1, *De la colonia al imperio* (Siglo XXI, 1996), 63–64.
91. Aurora Gómez-Galvarriato, "Premodern Manufacturing," in Victor Bulmer-Thomas et al., *The Cambridge Economic History of Latin America*, vol. 1, *The Colonial Era and the Short Nineteenth Century*), 377–381.
92. On the idea of ship as machine, see Marcus Rediker, *Between the Devil and the Deep Blue Sea: Merchant Seamen, Pirates, and the Anglo-American Maritime World, 1700–1750* (Cambridge University Press, 1987), 290.
93. "Padre comerciante, hijo caballero, nieto pordiosero." Alan Knight, *Mexico: The Colonial Era* (Cambridge University Press, 2002), 163.
94. Resendez, *The Other Slavery*, 106.
95. Velasco Murrillo, *Urban Indians*, 51; "Relación del mineral de Real del Monte (Finales siglo XVI)," in Miguel León-Portilla, ed., *Historia Documental de México* (Universidad Nacional Autónoma de México, 1964), 1:225; Brading, *Miners and Merchants*, 223.
96. Brading, *Miners and Merchants*, 7.
97. *Diccionario biográfico de la Real Academia de la Historia*, "Pedro Romero de Terreros," https://dbe.rah.es/biografias/22371/pedro-romero-de-terreros.
98. Quoted in Brading, *Miners and Merchants*, 12.
99. *Diccionario biográfico de la Real Academia de la Historia*, "Gonzalo Gómez de Cervantes," https://dbe.rah.es/biografias/19446/gonzalo-gomez-de-cervantes; María Elena Martínez, *Genealogical Fictions: Limpieza de Sangre, Religion, and Gender in Colonial Mexico* (Stanford University Press, 2008), 127–128.
100. Brading, *Miners and Merchants*, 13; Stein and Stein, *Silver, Trade, and War*, 187–188; Drelichman and Voth, *Lending to the Borrower from Hell*, 265.

101. Brading, *Miners and Merchants*, 98.
102. Gage, *Travels in the New World*, 73.
103. Sullivan, "European Painting and the Art of the New World," 37.
104. Melville, *A Plague of Sheep*, 156; Gómez Serrano and Delgado Aguilar, *Aguascalientes*, 33–37; Luis Aboites Aguilar, *Chihuahua. Historia breve* (Colegio de México, 2016), 77; Martha Rodríguez et al., *Coahuila. Historia breve* (Colegio de México, 2010), 72.
105. Brading, *Miners and Merchants*, 16; François Chevalier, *Land and Society in Colonial Mexico: The Great Hacienda* (University of California Press, 1966), 107.
106. Rodríguez et al., *Coahuila*, 78: Knight, *Mexico: The Colonial Era*, 159–167; Eric Van Young, "Beyond the Hacienda: Agrarian Relations and Socioeconomic Change in Rural Mesoamerica," *Ethnohistory* 50, no. 1 (Winter 2003): 242.
107. "Peon," like peasant, might be used as a pejorative but was until the twentieth century a technical designation for a salaried agricultural worker.
108. Carlos Marichal, "Mexican Cochineal and the European Demand for American Dyes, 1550–1850," in Topik et al., *From Silver to Cocaine* (Duke University Press, 2006), 76–92.
109. Brading, *Miners and Merchants*, 18.
110. Enriqueta Quiroz, "Del mercado a la cocina. La alimentación en la Ciudad de México," in Gonzalbo Aizpuru, *Historia de la vida cotidiana*, 3:33.
111. Alfred W. Crosby, *The Columbian Exchange: Biological and Cultural Consequences of 1492* (Praeger, 1972), 98; Thomas E. Sheridan, *Landscapes of Fraud: Mission Tumacácori, the Baca Float, and the Betrayal of the O'odham* (University of Arizona Press, 2006), 40; Guillén, *Explorer of the South*, 47; José Iturriaga de la Fuente, *Anecdotario de viajeros extranjeros en México. Siglos XVI–XX* (Fondo de Cultura Económica, 1993), 59, 79.
112. Joel Mokyr, *Culture of Growth: The Origins of the Modern Economy* (Princeton University Press, 2018), 37 et passim.

Chapter Seven

1. For the complexity, relevance, and variation over time of racial categories see Solange Alberro and Pilar Gonzalbo Aizpuru, *La sociedad novohispana: esterotipos y realidades* (El Colegio de México, 2013), 17–43.
2. Nicole von Germeten, *Profit and Passion: Transactional Sex in Colonial Mexico* (University of California Press, 2018), 20–23; Stuart B. Schwartz, *All Can Be Saved: Religious Tolerance and Salvation in the Iberian Atlantic World* (Yale University Press, 2008), 130.
3. Zumárraga to Prince Philip, December 4, 1547, in José Iturriaga de la Fuente, *Anecdotario de viajeros extranjeros en México. Siglos XVI–XX* (Fondo de Cultura Económica, 1993), 3:59.
4. For the integration of some mixed-race nabob children into British society see Deborah Cohen, *Family Secrets: Shame and Privacy in Modern Britain* (Oxford University Press, 2017), 13–46; Ann Hyde, "'Tinker, Tailor, Soldier, Sailor, Rich Woman, Poor Woman, Beggar Man, Thief': The Fortunes of Half-Breed Life in the U.S. West," paper given at the Chabraja Center for Historical Studies, Northwestern University, January 11, 2018.
5. Jorge Cañizares Esguerra, *How to Write the History of the New World: Histories, Epistemologies, and Identities in the Eighteenth-Century Atlantic World* (Stanford University Press, 2001), 136.
6. Albeit by marriage—he was José Sarmiento de Valladeres, the widower of María Jerónima Moctezuma y Jofre de Loaiza, third Countess of Moctezuma. Cañizares Esguerra, *How to Write the History of the New World*, 136, 233; Diane Fane, ed., *Converging Cultures: Art & Identity in Spanish America* (Brooklyn Museum and Harry N. Abrams, Inc., 1996), 72.

7. Archivo Histórico de la Secretaría de Hacienda (AHSH)-1/28/40, AHSH-113/1159/23, AHSH-113/1178/100, AHSH-113/1187/57, AHSH-S/N/3085/12.
8. Relación del Virrey de Nueva España, Antonio Mendoza, a Luis del Velasco al término de su gobierno, 1550–1551, paragraph 12; Maria Elena Martínez, *Genealogical Fictions: Limpieza de Sangre, Religion, and Gender in Colonial Mexico* (Stanford University Press, 2008), 144; John H. Elliott, *Empires of the Atlantic World: Britain and Spain in America, 1492–1830* (Yale University Press, 2006), 1539–1559; Ben Vinson III, *Before Mestizaje: The Frontiers of Race and Caste in Colonial Mexico* (Cambridge University Press, 2018), 83, 108.
9. Andrés Reséndez, *Conquering the Pacific: An Unknown Mariner and the Final Great Voyage of the Age of Discovery* (Houghton Mifflin Harcourt, 2021), 47.
10. Asunción Lavrín, "Women in Spanish American colonial society," in Leslie Bethell, ed., *The Cambridge History of Latin America* (Cambridge, 1989) 2:322–323.
11. "The Mayflower Story," 1620–2020: Mayflower 400, https://www.mayflower400uk.org/education/the-mayflower-story/.
12. Martín Fernández Cubero to Pedro Fernández Cubero, 1572, in James Lockhart and Enrique Otte, *Letters and People of the Spanish Indies, Sixteenth Century* (Cambridge University Press, 1976), 130–131.
13. Nicolás Sánchez-Albornoz, "The Population of Colonial Spanish America," in Leslie Bethell, ed., *Cambridge History of Latin America* (Cambridge University Press, 1985), 2:16.
14. Matthew Restall, *Seven Myths of the Spanish Conquest* (Oxford University Press, 2004), 148.
15. Vinson, *Before Mestizaje*, 5–7, 12–13; Frederick P. Bowser, "Africans in Spanish American Colonial Society," in Leslie Bethell, *Cambridge History of Latin America*, vol. 2, *Colonial Latin America*, 361; Bartolomé de las Casas, *The History of the Indies* (Harper & Row, 1971), 257.
16. Bowser, "Africans in Spanish American Colonial Society," 361; Tatiana Seijas, *Asian Slaves in Colonial Mexico: From Chinos to Indians* (Cambridge University Press, 2014), 253; Andrés Reséndez, *The Other Slavery: The Uncovered Story of Indian Enslavement in America* (First Mariner, 2016), 110; Pierre Chaunu, *Séville et l'Amérique, XVIe–XVIIe siècle* (Flammarion, 1977), 130–131.
17. Seijas, *Asian Slaves*, 84, 32.
18. Archivo Histórico de Aguascalientes, Fondo judicial civil general, caja 1, exp 2 47f–v.
19. Héctor de Mauleón, *La ciudad que nos inventa. Crónicas de seis siglos* (Cal y Arena, 2015), 79.
20. Elliott, *Imperial Spain*, 22.
21. John Tutino, *Making a New World: Founding Capitalism in the Bajío and Spanish America* (Duke University Press, 2011), 102.
22. Caterina Pizzigoni, "'Como frágil y miserable': Las mujeres Nahuas del Valle de Toluca," Gonzalbo Aizpuru, ed., *Historia de la vida cotidiana en México* 3:514–517.
23. Taylor, *Fugitive Freedom*, 15.
24. Carlos Sigüenza y Góngora, *Obras Históricas* (Porrua, 1944), 196.
25. Sor Juana Inés de la Cruz, *Poems, Protest, and a Dream: Selected Writings* trans. Margaret Sayers Peden, introduction by Ilan Stavans (Penguin, 1997), xi-xliii; Octavio Paz, *Sor Juana, Or, The Traps of Faith* (Belknap, 1990), 216–219.
26. "One of Five Burlesque Sonnets," Sor Juana Inés de la Cruz, *Poems, Protest, and a Dream*, 179.
27. "A Philosophical Satire," Sor Juana Inés de la Cruz, *Poems, Protest, and a Dream*, 150–151.
28. Sor Juana Inés de la Cruz, *Poems, Protest, and a Dream*, xi-xliii, 38.
29. Pizzigoni, "'Como frágil y miserable,'" 517.

30. Asunción Lavrín, "La sexualidad y las normas de la moral sexual," in Gonzalbo Aizpuru, ed., *Historia de la vida cotidiana en México*, 2:511–513.
31. Seijas, *Asian Slaves*, 112–113; Agustín Grajales Porras, "Structure et comportement démographique différentiel d'une population citadine du Mexique colonial, La paroisse d'Analco, à Puebla de los Ángeles, en 1792," *Annales de démographie historique* 119, no. 1 (December 2010): 43; Tutino, *Making a New World*, 175–177; Fray Antonio Vázquez de Espinosa, *Compendio y Descripción de las Indias Occidentales* (MS early seventeenth century), in Miguel León-Portilla, ed., *Historia Documental de México* (Universidad Nacional Autónoma de México, 1964), 2:246; Camilla Townsend et al., *Fifth Sun: A New History of the Aztecs* (Oxford University Press, 2021), 278.
32. Elliott, *Empires of the Atlantic World*, 1904; Vinson, *Before Mestizaje*, 83.
33. Maria Elena Martínez, *Genealogical Fictions*, 138; Jorge Cañizares Esguerra, "New World, New Stars: Patriotic Astrology and the Invention of Indian and Creole Bodies in Colonial Spanish America, 1600–1650," *American Historical Review* 104, no. 1 (February 1999): 33–68; Nancy Appelbaum, "Blood, Nation, Science, and Language: Essentializing Race from the Sixteenth Century to the Present," *Latin American Research Review* 55, no. 2 (2020): 353.
34. Richard M. Morse, "The Urban Development of Colonial Spanish America," in Leslie Bethell, ed., *Cambridge History of Latin America*, vol. 2, *Colonial Latin America* (Cambridge University Press, 1985), 87; Jesús Gómez Serrano and Francisco Javier Delgado, *Aguascalientes. Historia breve* (Colegio de México, 2012), 21–26.
35. Toribio de Benavente Motolinía, *Historia de los indios de la Nueva España* (Castalia, 1985), 58–62.
36. Reséndez, *The Other Slavery*, 62–65.
37. "Los sermones de fray Antón de Montesinos en la transcripción resumida y comentada que hizo fray Bartolomé de la Casas," in Carmen Saucedo Zarco and José Manuel Villalpando César, *Fray Antón de Montesinos* (Universidad Nacional Autónoma de México, 1982), 24.
38. Lawrence A. Clayton, *Bartolomé de las Casas and the Conquest of the Americas* (Wiley & Blackwell, 2011), 5, 11, 17, 49–51, 61, 133.
39. Nigel Davies, *The Aztecs* (The Folio Society, 2000), 322.
40. Reséndez, *The Other Slavery*, 46.
41. Reséndez, *The Other Slavery*, 46–47, 60, 126–130; Nancy E. van Deusen, *Global Indios: The Indigenous Struggle for Justice in Sixteenth-Century Spain* (Duke University Press, 2015), xi–xiii.
42. Motolinía, *Historia de los indios*, 58.
43. Colin MacEwan and Alejandro López Luján, eds., *Moctezuma: Aztec Ruler* (British Museum Press 2009), 277–278.
44. Woodrow Borah, *Justice by Insurance: The Great Indian Court of Colonial Mexico and the Legal Aides of the Half-Real* (University of California Press, 1983), 34, 47.
45. R. Douglas Cope, *The Limits of Racial Domination: Plebeian Society in Colonial Mexico City, 1660–1720* (University of Wisconsin Press, 1994), 10.
46. "Ordenanzas sobre el buen tratamiento que se debe dar a los negros," in León-Portilla, ed., *Historia Documental de México*, 1:237–240.
47. Velasco to Charles V, 1553, in Lockhart and Otte, *Letters and People*, 187.
48. Minutes of the cabildo, January 26, 1598, *Actas de Cabildo de la ciudad de México* (México: Imprenta de Aguilar e Hijos, 1898), 13:115.

49. Camilla Townsend, *Annals of Native America: How the Nahuas of Colonial Mexico Kept Their History Alive* (Oxford University Press, 2017), 156.
50. Mauleón, *La ciudad*, 60.
51. Cope, *The Limits of Racial Domination*, 16–19.
52. Lavrín, "Women in Spanish American Colonial Society," 350; Bowser, "Africans in Spanish American Colonial Society," 375.
53. Borah, *Justice by Insurance*, 40–42.
54. Reséndez, *The Other Slavery*, 60–61.
55. James Lockhart, *The Nahuas After the Conquest: A Social and Cultural History of the Indians of Central Mexico, Sixteenth Through Eighteenth Centuries* (Stanford University Press, 1992), 413–415.
56. Borah, *Justice by Insurance*, 93.
57. William B. Taylor, *Drinking, Homicide, and Rebellion in Colonial Mexican Villages* (Stanford University Press, 1979), 17.
58. Borah, *Justice by Insurance*, 53.
59. Cañizares Esguerra, "New World, New Stars."
60. Thanks are due to Caterina Pizzigoni for helping decipher the judge's hit-and-miss writing. Aguascalientes, December 10, 1669. Capitán Juan Fco Ruíz, "Averiguación contra quien resulte responsable por las heridas hechas a una mulata esclava, no especifica el nombre," Archivo Histórico del Estado de Aguascalientes, Fondo judicial civil general, caja 1, exp 2 158f–v.
61. Ruíz, "Averiguación contra quien resulte responsable por las heridas hechas a una mulata esclava."
62. "Ordenanzas sobre el buen tratamiento que se debe dar a los negros," in León-Portilla, ed., *Historia Documental de México*, 1:237–240.
63. Reséndez, *Conquering the Pacific*, 69, 198.
64. Cope, *The Limits of Racial Domination*, 17–22.
65. Elliott, *Empires of the Atlantic World*, digital ed. 3067.
66. Cope, *The Limits of Racial Domination*, 24.
67. Peter Guardino, The *Time of Liberty: Popular Political Culture in Oaxaca, 1750–1850* (Duke University Press, 2005), 137.
68. Maria Elena Martínez, *Genealogical Fictions*, 256–257.
69. Vinson, *Before Mestizaje*, 108.
70. Mabel M. Rodríguez Centeno, "El espejo de la vida. Crédito al consumo y cotidianidad en la hancienda de Charco de Araujo (1796–1799)," in Pilar Gonzalbo Aizpuru, ed., *Historia de la vida cotidiana*, 3 vols. (Fondo de Cultura Económica, 2014), 123–154.
71. Borah, *Justice by Insurance*, 49–51; Stafford Poole, "'War by Fire and Blood': The Church and the Chichimecas 1585," *The Americas* 74, no. 2 (2017); Reséndez, *The Other Slavery*, 73.
72. Reséndez, *The Other Slavery*, 92–99.
73. Poole, "War by Fire and Blood," 115–137.
74. Elliott, *Empires of the Atlantic World*, 1842.
75. Tutino, *Making a New World*, 111–112; Alonso de la Mota y Escobar, "Descripción geográfica de los reinos de Nueva Galicia, Nueva Vizcaya y Nuevo León," in Miguel León-Portilla, ed., *Historia Documental de México* (Universidad Nacional Autónoma de México, 1964), 1:230.
76. Woodes Rogers, *A Cruising Voyage Round the World* (CreateSpace Independent Publishing Platform, 2018), 241.

77. Elinor G. K. Melville, "Land Use and the Transformation of the Environment," in Victor Bulmer-Thomas et al., eds., *The Cambridge Economic History of Latin America*, vol. 1, *The Colonial Era and the Short Nineteenth Century* (Cambridge University Press, 2006), 109–142.
78. Chaunu, *Séville et l'Amérique*, 143; Maria Elena Martínez, *Genealogical Fictions*.
79. Edward J. Sullivan, "European Painting and the Art of the New World," in Diane Fane, ed., *Converging Cultures: Art & Identity in Spanish America* (Brooklyn Museum and Harry N. Abrams, Inc., 1996), 36.
80. Minutes of the cabildo, January 26, 1598, *Actas de Cabildo*, 1:115; Rogers, *A Cruising Voyage Round the World*, 240; Thomas Gage, *Travels in the New World*, ed. J. Eric S. Thompson (University of Oklahoma Press, 1958), 67.
81. Andrés de Islas, "De español y negra, mulata," Mexico, 1774, Museo de América, Madrid.
82. Giovanni F. Gemelli Careri, cited in Rogers, *A Cruising Voyage Round the World*, 239.
83. Antonio de Robles, *Diario de sucesos notables (1665–1703)* (Porrúa, 1946), 1:152.
84. Townsend, *Annals*, 177.
85. Cope, *The Limits of Racial Domination*, 17–18, 125–160.
86. Josefina Muriel, "Una nueva version del motín de 1692," *Estudios de historia novohispana*, 18 (1998) 110–111; Robles, *Diario*, 2:258, 261.
87. Joseph Carlos de Colmenares, *Ordenanzas del Baratillo de México*, ed., Guillermo Espinosa Estrada and Éric Ibarra Monterroso (Universidad Autónoma de Nuevo León, 2022).
88. Jane Landers, "African and Native Americans on the Spanish Florida Frontier," in Matthew Restall, ed., *Beyond Black and Red: African-Native Relations in Colonial Latin America* (University of New Mexico Press, 2005), 54–55; Cope, *The Limits of Racial Domination*, 17.
89. For this influential concept see Gonzalo Aguirre Beltrán, *Regiones de refugio. El desarrollo de la comunidad y el proceso dominical en Mestizo América* (Mexico: Instituto Indigenista Interamericano, 1967).
90. Nathaniel Morris, *Soldiers, Saints, and Shamans: Indigenous Communities and the Revolutionary State in Mexico's Gran Nayar, 1910–1940* (University of Arizona Press, 2020), 26; Nancy Farriss, "Persistent Maya Resistance and Cultural Retention in Yucatán," in John Kicza, ed., *The Indian in Latin American History: Resistance, Resilience, and Acculturation* (Delaware: Scholarly Resources, 1993), 56.
91. Townsend, *Fifth Sun*, 184.
92. Alan Knight, *Mexico: The Colonial Era* (Cambridge University Press, 2002), 169–171.
93. Vera Candiani, "The Desagüe Reconsidered: Environmental Dimensions of Class Conflict in Colonial Mexico," *Hispanic American Historical Review* 92, no. 1 (January 2012); 10–17.
94. Townsend, *Fifth Sun*, 183–188, 193–194.
95. Robles, *Diario*, 2:258–264.
96. Real Cédula de Carlos II, dada en Madrid, a 22 de marzo de 1697, in Alberro and Gonzalbo, *La sociedad novohispana*, 158.
97. Ann Twinam, *Purchasing Whiteness: Pardos, Mulattos, and the Quest for Social Mobility in the Spanish Indies* (Stanford University Press, 2015), 27–32.
98. Stephanie Wood, *Transcending Conquest: Nahua Views of Spanish Colonial Mexico* (University of Oklahoma Press, 2003), 133–134; Bradley Benton, *The Lords of Tetzcoco: The Transformation of Indigenous Rule in Postconquest Central Mexico* (Cambridge University Press, 2017), 78, 110; Gómez Serrano and Delgado Aguilar, *Aguascalientes*, 38.
99. Gage, *Travels in the New World*, 76, 363.

100. Thiago Henrique Mota, "Muslims, Moriscos, and Arabic-Speaking Migrants in the New World," *Latin American Research Review* 55, no. 4 (2020): 822.
101. Corcuera de Mancera, *De pícaros y malqueridos*, 241; Gruzinski, *El águila y el dragón*, 300; Ilona Katzew, "The Radiating Image: The Mobility of Painting in Eighteenth-Century Mexico" in Ilona Katzew, ed., *Painted in Mexico, 1700–1790: Pinxit Mexici* (New York: Prestel, 2017), 79.
102. Antonio de Herrera, quoted in José Luis Martínez, *Hernán Cortés* (Fondo de Cultura Económica, 1990), 401.

Chapter Eight

1. Paul Ramírez, *Enlightened Immunity: Mexico's Experiments with Disease Prevention in the Age of Reason* (Stanford University Press, 2018).
2. For the largely unexplored chronology of clean undies, see María Elena Santoscoy Flores, "Estampas de Saltillo a fines del virreinato," in Pilar Gonzalbo Aizpuru, ed., *Historia de la vida cotidiana en México*, 3 vols. (Fondo de Cultura Económica, 2014), 3:407.
3. Juan Carlos Moreno-Brid and Jaime Ros, *Development and Growth in the Mexican Economy: An Historical Perspective* (Oxford University Press, 2009), 35.
4. Hipólito Villaroel, *Enfermedades políticas que padece la capital de esta Nueva España, 1787*, ed. Genaro Estrada (Porrúa, 1979), 373.
5. Enrique Florescano and Margarita Menegus, "La época de las reformas borbónicas y el crecimiento económico (1750–1808), in various authors, *Historia general de México, Versión 2000* (Colegio de México, 2017), 525.
6. *Diccionario biográfico de la Real Academia de la Historia*, "Pedro Romero de Terreros," https://dbe.rah.es/biografias/22371/pedro-romero-de-terreros.
7. Leticia Arroyo Abad et al., "Between Conquest and Independence: Real Wages and Demographic Change in Spanish America, 1530–1820," *Explorations in Economic History* 49 (2012): 158.
8. Virginia García Acosta et al., *Desastres agrícolas en México. Catálogo histórico* (Fondo de Cultura Económica, 2014), 420–424.
9. John Tutino, *Mexico City, 1808: Power, Sovereignty, and Silver in an Age of War and Revolution* (University of New Mexico Press, 2018), 104.
10. Eric Van Young, *The Other Rebellion: Popular Violence, Ideology, and the Mexican Struggle for Independence, 1810–1821* (Stanford University Press, 2001), 75.
11. Ignacio Bernal, *Arqueología ilustrada y mexicanista en el siglo XVIII* (Centro de Estudios de Historia de México, 1975), 16.
12. Florescano, *memoria mexicana*, 264–265, Bernal, *Arqueología ilustrada*, 22, Rebecca Earle, *The Return of the Native: Indians and Myth-making in Spanish America, 1810–1930* (Duke University Press, 2007), 137.
13. Alexander von Humboldt, *Political Essay on the Kingdom of New Spain*, trans. John Black, 3 vols. (London: 1814), 1:xl–xlii.
14. Paul F. Ramírez, *Enlightened Immunity: Mexico's Experiments with Disease Prevention in the Age of Reason* (Stanford University Press, 2018), 135–212.
15. Nicole von Germeten, *Profit and Passion: Transactional Sex in Colonial Mexico* (University of California Press, 2018), 103.
16. Humboldt estimated between twenty and thirty thousand. Alexander von Humboldt, *Political Essay on the Kingdom of New Spain*, trans. John Black, 3 vols. (London: 1814), 1:235; Tutino, *Mexico City, 1808*, 97.

17. Pamela Voekel, *For God and Liberty: Catholicism and Revolution in the Atlantic World, 1790–1861* (Oxford University Press, 2023), 232.
18. William B. Taylor, *Fugitive Freedom: The Improbable Lives of Two Impostors in Late Colonial Mexico* (University of California Press, 2021), 10.
19. Juan Ortiz Escamilla, "Política y poder en una época revolucionaria: Ciudad de México (1800–1824)," in Ariel Rodríguez Kuri, *Historia política de la Ciudad de México (Desde su fundación hasta el año 2000)* (Colegio de México, 2013), 175.
20. Alan Knight, *Mexico: The Colonial Era* (Cambridge University Press, 2002), 261.
21. José Joaquín Fernández de Lizardi, *El Periquillo Sarniento* (México City: Alexandro Valdés, 1816), 126.
22. Taylor, *Fugitive Freedom*, 24–57.
23. Thomas Calvo, "Soberano, plebe y cadalso bajo una misma luz en Nueva España," in Gonzalbo Aizpuru, *Historia de la vida cotidiana*, 307; Ortiz Escamilla, "Política y poder," 181.
24. Humboldt, *New Spain*, 2:184, 1:iv.
25. Taylor, *Fugitive Freedom*, 39.
26. Florescano and Menegus, "La época de las reformas borbónicas," 476; D. A. Brading, *Miners and Merchants in Bourbon Mexico, 1763–1810* (Cambridge University Press, 1971, 180.
27. José Joaquín Fernández de Lizardi, *El Periquillo Sarniento* (México City: Alexandro Valdés, 1816), digital ed. 4048, 5862, 10225.
28. William B. Taylor, *Drinking, Homicide, and Rebellion in Colonial Mexican Villages* (Stanford University Press, 1979), 38–39.
29. Florescano and Menegus, "La época de las reformas borbónicas," 489.
30. Quoted in Miguel Ángel Vásquez Meléndez, "Las pulquerías en la vida diaria de los habitantes de la Ciudad de México," in Gonzalbo Aizpuru, *Historia de la vida cotidiana*, 3:91.
31. Arnaud Exbalin, "Riot in Mexico City: A Challenge to the Colonial Order?," *Urban History* 43, no. 2 (May 2016): 215–231.
32. Josefina Muriel, "Una nueva versión del 8 de junio motín de 1692," *Estudios de Historia Nuevahispana* 18 (1998): 114–115.
33. Taylor, *Drinking, Homicide, and Rebellion*, 115–120.
34. Ibid., 114.
35. Paul Ramírez, *Enlightened Immunity: Mexico's Experiments with Disease Prevention in the Age of Reason* (Stanford University Press, 2018), 102–125.
36. Ryan Dominic Crewe, "Brave New Spain: An Irishman's Independence Plot in Seventeenth-Century Mexico," *Past & Present* 207, no. 1 (May 2010): 53–87.
37. Taylor, *Drinking, Homicide, and Rebellion*, 124–125; Enrique Florescano, *Memoria mexicana* (Fondo de Cultura Económica, 1988), 215–217; Declaración del rey Joseph Jacinto Uc de los Santos Canek, Mérida a 8 y 9 de diciembre de 1761, AGI, México 3050, ff. 542r–549r, 180r–187r.
38. John H. Elliott, *Empires of the Atlantic World: Britain and Spain in America, 1492–1830* (Yale University Press, 2006), loc 3135; Christoph Rosenmüller, "Mexico in Spain's Oceanic Empire, 1519–1821," *Oxford Research Encyclopedia of Latin American History* (Oxford University Press, 2018), 15; Jaime Cuadriello, "The Politicization and Sociability of the Public Image: The King and His Representatives, 1700–1790," *Pinxit Mexici*, 112–120.
39. Elliott, *Empires of the Atlantic World*, digital ed. 5293.
40. For total numbers built, see David Brading, "Bourbon Spain and Its American Empire," in Leslie Bethell, ed., *The Cambridge History of Latin America*, vol. 1, *Colonial Latin America* (Cambridge University Press, 1985), 396.

41. Brading, "Bourbon Spain," 400–401.
42. Von Germeten, *Profit and Passion*, 19; "Instrucción reservada al Marqués de Branciforte," in José Iturriaga de la Fuente, *Anecdotario de viajeros extranjeros en México. Siglos XVI–XX* (Fondo de Cultura Económica, 1993), 3:136–138.
43. Knight, *Mexico: The Colonial Era*, 244.
44. Taylor, *Drinking, Homicide, and Rebellion*, 127; Knight, *Mexico: The Colonial Era*, 259.
45. Tutino, *Making a New World*, 179–182.
46. Crewe, "Brave New Spain," 78; David Brading, *The First America: The Spanish Monarchy, Creole Patriots and the Liberal State, 1492–1867* (Cambridge University Press, 1991), 502, 499.
47. Letter, Pope Clement XIII to Miguel Anselmo Alvarez Abreu, Bishop of Oaxaca, April 9, 1766, in Mariano Cuevas and Peter P. Forrestal, "Expulsion of the Jesuits from Mexico," *Records of the American Catholic Historical Society of Philadelphia* 43, no. 2 (June 1932): 142–143.
48. "Papel sacrílego" aparecido en San Luis de la Paz"; Felipe Cleere to Marqués de la Croix, July 1767, both in José de Gálvez, *Informe sobre las rebeliones populares de 1767*, ed. Felipe Castro Gutiérrez (Universidad Nacional Autónoma de México, 1990), 87–91.
49. Cleere to de la Croix, July 1767, in Gálvez, *Informe*, 89.
50. Brading, *The First America*, 498; Knight, *Mexico: The Colonial Era*, 247; *Diccionario biográfico de la Real Academia de la Historia*, "Felipe Cleere" and "José de Gálvez y Gallardo," https://dbe.rah.es/biografias/60422/felipe-cleere; https://dbe.rah.es/biografias/10139/jose-de-galvez-y-gallardo.
51. Jaime E. Rodríguez O., *"We Are Now the True Spaniards": Sovereignty, Revolution, Independence, and the Emergence of the Federal Republic of Mexico, 1808–1824* (Stanford University Press, 2012), 26.
52. Gálvez, *Informe*, 86; Taylor, *Drinking, Homicide, and Rebellion*, 122.
53. *Diccionario biográfico español*, "Juan Vicente de Güemes Pacheco de Padilla y Horcasitas, Conde de Revillagigedo," https://dbe.rah.es/biografias/11393/juan-vicente-de-guemes-pacheco-de-padilla-y-horcasitas.
54. Gabriel Torres Puga, "La ciudad novohispana. Ensayo sobre su vida política," in Ariel Rodríguez Kuri, *Historia política de la Ciudad de México (Desde su fundación hasta el año 2000)* (Colegio de México, 2013), 139–140; Tutino, *Mexico City, 1808*, 141–147; Florescano, *Memoria mexicana*, 281–287; Tutino, *Making a New World*, 481.
55. Robert Sidney Smith, "Shipping in the Port of Veracruz, 1790–1821," *Hispanic American Historical Review* 23, no. 1 (February 1943): 17–19; Rodríguez, *True Spaniards*, 37.
56. Ortiz Escamilla, "Política y poder en una época revolucionaria," 170.
57. Rodríguez, *True Spaniards*, 34–67.

Chapter Nine

1. Enrique Krauze, *Mexico, Biography of Power: A History of Modern Mexico, 1810–1996* (Harper Collins, 1997), 93.
2. Carlos Herrejón Peredo, *Hidalgo antes del Grito de Dolores* (Universidad Michoacana, 1992), 10–11, 133–135.
3. Hidalgo quoted in Pamela Voekel, *For God and Liberty: Catholicism and Revolution in the Atlantic World, 1790–1861* (Oxford University Press, 2023), 158, 50.
4. *Diario de México*, November 4, 1809.
5. Krauze, *Mexico*, 92–93.
6. Lucas Alamán, *Semblanzas e ideario* (Universidad Autónoma de México, 2010), 40–41.

7. For this and the ensuing narrative, Eric Van Young, *The Other Rebellion: Popular Violence, Ideology, and the Mexican Struggle for Independence, 1810–1821* (Stanford University Press, 2001), 39–65; Jaime E. Rodríguez O., *"We Are Now the True Spaniards": Sovereignty, Revolution, Independence, and the Emergence of the Federal Republic of Mexico, 1808–1824* (Stanford University Press, 2012), 97–148; Luis Villoro, "La Revolución de Independencia," in Daniel Cosío Villegas et al., eds. *Historia general de México* (Colegio de México, 1994), 624–669.
8. Eric Van Young, *A Life Together: Lucas Alamán and Mexico, 1792–1853* (Yale University Press, 2021), 47–48.
9. Alamán quoted in Gilbert M. Joseph and Timothy Henderson, *The Mexico Reader: History, Culture, and Politics* (Duke University Press, 2002), 185.
10. Alamán, *Semblanzas e ideario*, 51.
11. Rodríguez, *True Spaniards*, 137–141, 146–148.
12. América Molina del Villar, "Los vecinos de los pueblos y haciendas ante los cataclismos de principios del siglo XIX: El caso de Santa María Guadalupe, Atlacomulco, 1810–1814," in Pilar Gonzalbo Aizpuru and Andrés Lira González, eds., *México, 1808–1821: Las ideas y los hombres* (Colegio de México, 2014), 383.
13. Christon I. Archer, "Los patriotas del rey. El impacto militar y político de los criollos novohispanos en la guerra de independencia, 1810–1821," in Gonzalbo Aizpuru and Lira González, *México, 1808–1821*, 429–430.
14. Alamán, *Semblanzas e ideario*, 45, 46, 53.
15. Carlos A. Forment, *Democracy in Latin America, 1760–1900*, vol. 1, *Civic Selfhood and Public Life in Mexico and Peru* (University of Chicago Press, 2003), 74.
16. Krauze, *Mexico*, 103–110.
17. Villoro, "La Revolución de Independencia," 660.
18. Jefferson to Germaine de Staël-Holstein, September 6, 1816, *Thomas Jefferson Encyclopedia*, https://www.monticello.org/research-education/thomas-jefferson-encyclopedia/mexico/#fn-7.
19. Forment, *Democracy in Latin America*, 72–73.
20. David Brading, *The Origins of Mexican Nationalism* (Cambridge University Press, 1985), 51–52, 83; Enrique Florescano, *Memoria mexicana* (Fondo de Cultura Económica, 1988), 305–306.
21. Rodríguez, *True Spaniards*, 149–194.
22. Ibid., 102–103, 191.
23. Arturo Arnáiz y Freg, prologue to *Semblanzas e ideario*, by Lucas Alamán, vi.
24. Krauze, *Mexico*, 108.
25. Corinna Zeltsman, *Ink Under the Fingernails: Printing Politics in Nineteenth-Century Mexico* (University of California Press, 2021), 54–55.
26. Archer, "Los patriotas del rey," 430.
27. Miguel Salinas, Fábulas del *pensador mexicano. Corregidas, explicadas y anotadas* (México: José Ballesca, 1918), 41–42.
28. Hans-Joachim König, "El Indigenismo Criollo. ¿Proyectos vital y político realizables, o instrumento político?," *Historia Mexicana* 46, no. 4 (April–June 1997): 758.
29. Virginia García Acosta et al., *Desastres agrícolas en México. Catálogo histórico* (Fondo de Cultura Económica, 2014), 448–453; Archer, "Los patriotas del rey," 410; Forment, *Democracy in Latin America*, 75.
30. Christon I. Archer, "Royalist Scourge or Liberator of the Patria? Agustín de Iturbide and Mexico's War of Independence, 1810–1821," *Mexican Studies/Estudios Mexicanos* 24, no. 2 (Summer 2008): 325–261.

31. Ivana Frasquet and Manuel Chust, "Agustín de Iturbide: From the Pronunciamiento of Iguala to the Coup of 1822," in Will Fowler, ed., *Forceful Negotiations: The Origins of the* Pronunciamiento *in Nineteenth-Century Mexico* (University of Nebraska Press, 2010), 1–21.
32. Timothy E. Anna, "Iguala: The Prototype," in Fowler, ed., *Forceful Negotiations*, 1–21.
33. GDP per capita went from 14 percent above average to 23 percent below. Juan Carlos Moreno-Brid and Jaime Ros, *Development and Growth in the Mexican Economy: An Historical Perspective* (Oxford University Press, 2009), 19.
34. Peter F. Guardino, *Peasants, Politics, and the Formation of Mexico's National State: Guerrero, 1800–1857* (Stanford University Press, 1996), 90.
35. Zeltsman, *Ink Under the Fingernails*, 81–111.
36. Guillermo Prieto, *Memorias de mis tiempos* (Paris: Vda. De C. Bouret, 1906), 189.
37. Prieto, *Memorias*, 192.
38. Fanny Calderón de la Barca, *Life in Mexico* (Oakland: University of California Press, 1982), 125, 420.
39. Will Fowler, introduction to *Forceful Negotiations*, xv–xxxix.
40. Carlos María de Bustamante 1981 104 quoted in Thomas Calvo, "Soberano, plebe y cadalso bajo una misma luz en Nueva España," in in Pilar Gonzalbo Aizpuru, ed., *Historia de la vida cotidiana en México* (México: Fondo de Cultura Económica, 2014), vol. III 279.
41. Voekel, *For God and Liberty*, 227.
42. Timothy E. Anna, *Forging Mexico, 1821–1835* (University of Nebraska Press, 1998), 258.
43. García López to Santa Anna, February 23, 1845, in *Correspondencia entre el Supremo Gobierno y el General D. Antonio López de Santa Anna* (México: Imprenta de Vicente García Torres, 1845), 46.
44. Alan Knight, "The Several Legs of Santa Anna: A Saga of Secular Relics," *Past & Present* (2010): Supplement 3, 227–255.
45. Prieto, *Memorias*, 83.
46. Calderón, *Life in Mexico*, 45–46.
47. Florencia Mallon, "Los campesinos y la formación del Estado en el México del siglo XIX: Morelos, 1848–1858," *Secuencia* 15 (1989): 54.
48. Cited in Enrique Florescano, *Etnia, estado y nación* (Fondo de Cultura Económica, 1997), 369; Luis Villoro, *Los grandes momentos del indigenismo en México* (Ediciones de la Casa Chata, 1979), 176.
49. Paul J. Vanderwood, *Disorder and Progress: Bandits, Police, and Mexican Development* (Scholarly Resources, 1992), xx, 7.
50. Calderón, *Life in Mexico*, 352.
51. Forment, *Democracy in Latin America*, 79.
52. Rodríguez, *True Spaniards*, 291; Peter Guardino, *The Time of Liberty: Popular Political Culture in Oaxaca, 1750–1850* (Duke University Press, 2005), 182.
53. Fernando Díaz Díaz, *Caudillos y caciques: Antonio López de Santa Anna y Juan Álvarez* (El Colegio de México, 1972), 138–139.
54. John L. Stephens, *Incidents of Travel in Yucatan*, 2 vols. (Dover Publications, 1963), 1:42–43.
55. Josefina Zoraida Vázquez, "Los primeros tropiezos," in Cosío Villegas et al., *Historia general de México*, 697.
56. Florescano, *Etnia, estado y nación*, 355.
57. Fernand Braudel, *Civilization and Capitalism 15th–18th Century*, vol. 2, *The Wheels of Commerce*, trans. Siân Reynold (Fontana, 1981), 303.

58. Luis Jáuregui, "Los orígenes de un malestar crónico: Los ingresos y los gastos públicos de México, 1821–1855," in Luis Aboites Aguilar and Luis Jáuregui, eds., *Penuria sin fin. Historia de los impuestos en México siglos VVIII–XX* (Instituto Mora, 2005), 78–114; Ricardo Salvucci, *Politics, Markets, and Mexico's "London Debt," 1823–1887* (Cambridge University Press, 2009), 79.
59. Felipe Cole, "When Debt Made Sovereignty, 1820–1933" (PhD diss., Northwestern University, 2023), 100.
60. Cole, "When Debt Made Sovereignty," 101; Zoraida Vázquez, "Los primeros tropiezos," 705–706; Michael P. Costeloe, "The British and an Early Pronunciamiento, 1833–1834," in Fowler, ed., *Forceful Negotiations*, 125–142.
61. Calderón, *Life in Mexico*, 48; Stephens, *Incidents of Travel in Yucatan*, 156; Karl Bartolomeus Heller, *Alone in Mexico: The Astonishing Travels of Karl Heller, 1845–1848*, trans. Terry Rugeley (University of Alabama Press, 2007), 119–121.
62. Rodríguez, *True Spaniards*, 157.
63. Forment, *Democracy in Latin America*, 74.
64. Guardino, *The Time of Liberty*, 179.
65. Rodríguez, *True Spaniards*, 158.
66. The law of 14 February 1822, in Manuel Dublán and José María Lozano, *Legislación Mexicana o colección complete de las disposiciones desde la independence de la república* (Imprenta del Comercio), 1:597.
67. Prieto, *Memorias*, 32–33, 62–69; Krauze, *Mexico*, 130.
68. Calderón, *Life in Mexico*, 45–46; Miguel Ángel Vásquez Meléndez, *Los patriotas en escena (1862–1869)* (Colegio de México, 2018), 31.
69. Rosalina Ríos Zúñiga, "Una retórica para la movilización popular. El Cometa, periódico político-literario de Zacatecas, 1832," *Historia Mexicana* 2 (2008): 756–757.
70. Zeltsman, *Ink Under the Fingernails*, 85, 102.
71. Pablo Piccato, *The Tyranny of Opinion: Honor in the Construction of the Mexican Public Sphere* (Duke University Press, 2010), 34–38.
72. *La Abeja Poblana*, February 28, 1841.
73. Michael P. Costeloe, "Generals versus Politicians: Santa Anna and the 1842 Congressional Elections in Mexico," *Bulletin of Latin American Research* 8, no. 2 (1989): 257–274.
74. Luis Aboites Aguilar, *Chihuahua. Historia breve* (Colegio de México, 2016), 122.
75. Guardino, *The Time of Liberty*, 156–222.
76. Quoted in Pablo Mijangos, *The Lawyer of the Church: Bishop Clemente de Jesús Munguía and the Clerical Response to the Mexican Liberal Reforma* (University of Nebraska Press, 2015), introduction.
77. Michael T. Ducey, *A Nation of Villages: Riot and Rebellion in the Mexican Huasteca, 1750–1850* (University of Arizona Press, 2004), 109.
78. Erika Pani, "La 'Innombrable': Monarquismo y cultura política en el México decimonónico," in Brian F. Connaughton, ed., *Prácticas populares, cultura política y poder en México, siglo XIX* (Universidad Autónoma Metropolitana, 2008), 388–389.
79. Enrique Florescano, "Mexico in the Nineteenth Century: A Fragmented Political Culture," paper given at Oxford University Latin American Center, May 1997.
80. Benjamin T. Smith, *The Roots of Conservatism in Mexico: Catholicism, Society, and Politics in the Mixteca Baja, 1750–1962* (University of New Mexico Press, 2012), 12.
81. Raymond Buve, "Ayuntamientos and Pronunciamientos during the Nineteenth Century," in Will Fowler, ed., *Malcontents, Rebels, and Pronunciados: The Politics of Insurrection in Nineteenth-Century Mexico* (University of Nebraska Press, 2012), 137.

82. Guardino, *Peasants, Politics, and the Formation of Mexico's National State*, 94–101; Ducey, *Nation of Villages*.
83. Alan Knight, "Peasants into Patriots: Thoughts on the Making of the Mexican Nation," *Mexican Studies/Estudios Mexicanos* 10, no. 1 (1994): 135–161; Stephens, *Incidents of Travel in Yucatan*, 204–205.

Chapter Ten

1. Katherine Manthorne, ed., *California Mexicana: Missions to Murals, 1820–1930* (Laguna Art Museum, 2017), 36, 197–199; George P. Taylor, "Spanish-Russian Rivalry in the Pacific, 1769–1820," *The Americas* 15, no. 2 (October 1958): 116–127; Inocente García, *Hechos históricos de California, as told to Thomas Savage, 1878* (University of California Press, 1974), 15; Ukase of 1799, reproduced in HM Stationery Office, "Behring Sea Arbitration," 1893, 25–27.
2. Steven Hahn, *A Nation Without Borders: The United States and Its World in an Age of Civil Wars, 1830–1910* (Viking, 2016), 117.
3. Alexander von Humboldt, *Political Essay on the Kingdom of New Spain*, trans. John Black, 3 vols. (London: 1814), 3:310.
4. Christon I. Archer, "Independence and the Generation of the Generals, 1810–1848," in William H. Beezley, ed., *A Companion to Mexican History and Culture* (Wiley-Blackwell, 2011), 256.
5. Luis González y González, *El indio en la era liberal* (Colegio de México, 1996), 33.
6. Gregory A. Barton, *Informal Empire and the Rise of One World Culture* (Cambridge University Press, 2014), 113.
7. Carlos Marichal, *A Century of Debt Crises in Latin America: From Independence to the Great Depression, 1820–1930* (Princeton University Press, 1998), 13–14.
8. Josefina Zoraida Vázquez, "Los primeros tropiezos," in Daniel Cosío Villegas et al., eds., *Historia general de México* (Colegio de México, 1994), 682, 705, 707, 713, 714, 720.
9. Octavia Herrera Pérez, *Tamaulipas. Historia breve* (Colegio de México, 2010), 106–108; Michael T. Ducey, *A Nation of Villages: Riot and Rebellion in the Mexican Huasteca, 1750–1850* (University of Arizona Press, 2004), 94.
10. Ducey, *A Nation of Villages*, 94–96.
11. Timothy E. Anna, *Forging Mexico, 1821–1835* (University of Nebraska Press, 1998), 225–226.
12. Terry Rugeley, *The River People in Flood Time: The Civil Wars in Tabasco, Spoiler of Empires* (Stanford University Press, 2014), 109–148, 153–153.
13. Felipe Fernández-Armesto, *Our America: A Hispanic History of the United States* (W. W. Norton, 2014), 77; Hahn, *A Nation Without Borders*, 29.
14. Fernández-Armesto, *Our America*, 63.
15. James H. Shaw, "Neither Stable nor Pristine: American Bison Populations Were Long Influenced by Humans," *Therya* 12, no. 2 (2021): 171–175.
16. Brian DeLay, *War of a Thousand Deserts: Indian Raids and the U.S.-Mexican War* (Yale University Press, 2008), 9–17, 44–48; Pekka Hämäläinen, *The Comanche Empire* (Yale University Press, 2008); Gerald Betty review of same, *American Historical Review*, December 2008, 1470–1472.
17. Fernández-Armesto, *Our America*, 63–68.
18. A. Wislizenus, *Memoir of a Tour of Northern Mexico, connected with Col. Doniphan's expedition, in 1846 and 1847* (Washington: Tippin and Streeper, 1848), 28.

19. DeLay, *War of a Thousand Deserts*, 159, 243; Fernández-Armesto, *Our America*, 182.
20. Luis Aboites Aguilar, *Chihuahua. Historia breve* (Colegio de México, 2016), 210.
21. DeLay, *War of a Thousand Deserts*, 317–318, 114–115; José de la Cruz Pacheco Rojas, *Durango. Historia breve* (Colegio de México, 2016), 114.
22. DeLay, *War of a Thousand Deserts*, 12–20, 50–69, 317; González, *El indio en la era liberal*, 192; Andrés Reséndez, *The Other Slavery: The Uncovered Story of Indian Enslavement in America* (First Mariner, 2016), 221; Aboites Aguilar, *Chihuahua*, 120.
23. Aboites Aguilar, *Chihuahua*, 118.
24. Jürgen Buchenau, "Small Numbers, Great Impact: Mexico and Its Immigrants, 1821–1973," *Journal of American Ethnic History* 20, no. 3 (Spring 2001): 26.
25. Zoraida Vázquez, "Los primeros tropiezos," 730–731.
26. Josefina Zoraida Vázquez and Lorenzo Meyer, *México frente a Estados Unidos. Un ensayo histórico, 1776–2020* (Fondo de Cultura Económico, 2022), 36–44.
27. Eric Van Young, *A Life Together: Lucas Alamán and Mexico, 1792–1853* (Yale University Press, 2021), 105.
28. John A. Cochran, *Money, Banking, and the Economy* (Macmillan, 1967), 42; Richard J. Salvucci, *Politics, Markets, and Mexico's "London Debt," 1823–1887* (Cambridge University Press, 2009), 191–192.
29. Hahn, *A Nation Without Borders*, 116.
30. Both quoted in Fernández-Armesto, *Our America*, 146–147.
31. John O'Sullivan, "Annexation," *United States Magazine and Democratic Review*, July–August 1845, 5–10.
32. For the narrative of the war, unless otherwise noted see Peter Guardino, *The Dead March: A History of the Mexican-American War* (Harvard University Press, 2017); Zoraida Vázquez, "Los primeros tropiezos," 737–745.
33. José María Roa Bárcena, *Recuerdos de la invasión norteamericana (1846–1848), Por un joven de entonces*, vol. 1 (Conaculta, 1991), 89–112; *El Republicano*, April 14, 1847.
34. James Polk, "State of the Union Address," Presidential Rhetoric.com, http://www.presidentialrhetoric.com/historicspeeches/polk/stateoftheunion1846.html.
35. Roa Bárcena, *Recuerdos*, 1:208–240.
36. Carlos María de Bustamante, *El nuevo Bernal: Memorias de la Guerra México-Estados Unidos* (Fondo de Cultura Económica, 1997), 37.
37. Guillermo Prieto, *Memorias de mis tiempos* (Paris: Vda. De C. Bouret, 1906), 250.
38. *Daily American*, January 1, 1848.
39. Miguel Angel Fernández Delgado, "Muerte de Carlos María Bustamante, el historiador insurgente," 5, https://www.inehrm.gob.mx/en/inehrm/Muerte_de_Carlos_Maria_de_Bustamante_el_historiador_insurgente, accessed March 1, 2025.
40. William H. Beezley, "Juan O'Gorman, Daniel Cosío Villegas, and the Mexican Historical Profession: An Interview with Josefina Zoraida Vázquez," *The Americas* 67, no. 2 (October 2010): 262–263.
41. Lincoln speech to the House of Representatives, January 12, 1848 https://www.loc.gov/resource/mal.0007400/?st=text, accessed March 1, 2025.
42. Guardino, *The Dead March*, 1.
43. Bustamante, *El nuevo Bernal*, 35.
44. Ibid., 23; General Orders no. 372, December 12, 1847.
45. Wislizenus, *Memoir*, 78.
46. DeLay, *War of a Thousand Deserts*, 268.

47. Guardino, *The Dead March*, 151–152, 248.
48. Samuel E. Chamberlain, *Recollections of a Rogue* (London: Museum Press Limited, 1957), 94–95.
49. Guardino, *The Dead March*, 131.
50. Chamberlain, *Recollections*, 30–31.
51. Guardino, *The Dead March*, 123–158.
52. Hahn, *A Nation Without Borders*, 136.
53. Guardino, *The Dead March*, 259.
54. Ibid., 250–263.
55. Bustamante, *El nuevo Bernal*, 33.
56. Guardino, *The Dead March*, 243–246.
57. Zoraida Vázquez, "Los primeros tropiezos," 700–702.
58. Prieto, *Memorias*, 234.
59. Karl Jacoby, *Shadows at Dawn: An Apache Massacre and the Violence of History* (Penguin, 2000), 62.
60. Roa Bárcena, *Recuerdos*, 1:191.
61. DeLay, *War of a Thousand Deserts*, 264.
62. For the Caste War, unless otherwise indicated, see Terry Rugeley, *Rebellion Now and Forever: Mayas, Hispanics, and Caste War Violence in Yucatán, 1800–1880* (Stanford University Press, 2009).
63. John L. Stephens, *Incidents of Travel in Yucatan*, 2 vols. (Dover Publications, 1963), 1:231.
64. Javier Rodríguez Piña, ed., *La Guerra de castas. Testimonios de Justo Sierra O'Reilly y Juan Suárez y Navarro* (Conaculta, 1993), 156.
65. González, *El indio en la era liberal*, 73–74.
66. Rodríguez Piña, ed., *La Guerra de castas*, 164.
67. Rodríguez, *True Spaniards*, 108–109, 229.
68. Humboldt, *New Spain*, 1:v-vi; Cynthia Radding, *Landscapes of Power and Identity: Comparative Histories in the Sonoran Desert and the Forests of Amazonia from Colony to Republic* (Duke University Press, 2006), 2.
69. O'Sullivan, "Annexation," 5.
70. González, *El indio en la era liberal*, 20.
71. Richard Henry Dana, *Two Years Before the Mast* (Penguin, 1948), 218–219, 115.
72. Cuauhtémoc Velasco Ávila, *La frontera étnica en el noreste mexicano. Los comanches entre 1800–1841* (México: CIESAS, 2012), 274–279, 364.
73. Fernández-Armesto, *Our America*, 154–164; Jacoby, *Shadows at Dawn*, 63; Carrie Gibson, *El Norte: The Epic and Forgotten Story of Hispanic North America* (Atlantic Monthly Press, 2019), 226.
74. Thomas E. Sheridan, *Landscapes of Fraud: Mission Tumacácori, the Baca Float, and the Betrayal of the O'odham* (University of Arizona Press, 2006), 140–143.
75. Dana, *Two Years Before the Mast*, 357–358.

Chapter Eleven

1. Carlos María de Bustamante, *El nuevo Bernal: Memorias de la Guerra México-Estados Unidos* (Fondo de Cultura Económica, 1997), 44.
2. Guillermo Prieto, *Memorias de mis tiempos* (Paris: Vda. De C. Bouret, 1906), 217.
3. Felipe Fernández-Armesto, *Our America: A Hispanic History of the United States* (W. W. Norton, 2014), 235.

4. Will Fowler, *The Grammar of Civil War: A Mexican Case Study, 1857–1861* (University of Nebraska, 2022), 136.
5. Paul Gillingham, *Cuauhtémoc's Bones: Forging National Identity in Modern Mexico* (University of New Mexico Press, 2012), 151.
6. Reynaldo Sordo Cedeño, "Territorio, recursos naturales y población hacia 1858," in Gisela von Wobeser, ed., *1810, 1858, 1910: México en tres etapas de su historia* (Fondo de Cultura Económica, 2022), 42–44.
7. Miguel Ángel Vásquez Meléndez, *Los patriotas en escena (1862–1869)* (Colegio de México, 2018), 41–57; José Ortíz Monasterio, *Historia y Ficción. Los dramas y novelas de Vicente Riva Palacio* (Instituto Mora, 1993).
8. Quoted in Clementina Díaz y de Ovando, *Vicente Riva Palacio y la identidad nacional* (Universidad Nacional Autónoma de México, 1985), 22.
9. Luis González y González, "El liberalismo triunfante," in Daniel Cosío Villegas et al., *Historia general de México* (Colegio de México, 1994), 814–819.
10. Porfirio Díaz, prólogo Moisés González Navarro, *Memorias de Porfirio Díaz* (Conaculta, 1994), 1:38.
11. Andrés Lira, "Gobierno, justicia y administración hacia 1858," in Gisela von Wobeser, ed., *1810, 1858, 1910: México en tres etapas*, 105.
12. Benito Juárez, libreta, Archivo General de la Nación, AGN/CL03/SB01/FO088BJU10001UC022.
13. Erika Pani, *Para mexicanizar el segundo imperio. El imaginario político de los imperialistas* (Colegio de México, 2001), 64.
14. Lilia Díaz, "El liberalismo militante," in Cosío Villegas et al., *Historia general de México*, vol. 2 (Colegio de México, 1996), 760; Enrique Krauze, *Mexico, Biography of Power: A History of Modern Mexico, 1810–1996* (Harper Collins, 1997), 169.
15. Prieto, *Memorias*, 93.
16. Terry Rugeley, *The River People in Flood Time: The Civil Wars in Tabasco, Spoiler of Empires* (Stanford University Press, 2014), 247.
17. Josefina Zoraida Vázquez, "Los primeros tropiezos," in Cosío Villegas et al., *Historia general de México*, 717.
18. François Achille Bazaine, "Cartas," in José Iturriaga de la Fuente, *Anecdotario de* viajeros *extranjeros en México. Siglos XVI–XX* (Fondo de Cultura Económica, 1993), 3:149.
19. Díaz, "El liberalismo militante," 756.
20. Preamble quoted in Díaz, "El liberalismo militante," 760
21. Bishop Munguía protest, April 8, 1857, in Miguel León-Portilla, ed., *Historia Documental de México* (Universidad Nacional Autónoma de México, 1964), 1:292–293.
22. Díaz, "El liberalismo militante," 763.
23. "Manifesto of the Supreme Executive Power of the Nation," June 24, 1863, reproduced in Henry M. Flint, Esq., *Mexico Under Maximilian* (Philadelphia: National Publishing Company, 1867), 43.
24. Frédéric Johansson, "La Constitución de 1857: Un texto renegado convertido en el símbolo del liberalismo," in Catherine Andrews, ed., *La tradición constitucional en México (1808–1940)* (México: CIDE, 2017), 2:127.
25. Fowler, *Grammar of Civil War*, 46.
26. Bishop Munguía protest, April 8, 1857, in León-Portilla, *Historia Documental de México*, 1:292–293.
27. Pani, *El segundo imperio*, 200; González, "El liberalismo triunfante," 814.
28. Vanderwood, *Disorder and Progress*, 53–62.

29. Cited in José Ortiz Monasterio, *"Patria", tu ronca voz me repetía . . . Biografía de Vicente Riva Palacio y Guerrero* (Instituto Mora, 1999), 233–234.
30. Peter F. Guardino, *Peasants, Politics, and the Formation of Mexico's National State: Guerrero, 1800–1857* (Stanford University Press, 1996), 113.
31. Fowler, *Grammar of Civil War*, 121.
32. Andrés Lira González, *Comunidades indígenas frente a la Ciudad de México. Tenochtitlán y Tlatelolco, sus pueblos y barrios, 1812–1919* (Colegio de México, 1995), 213.
33. Angélica Castillo, "Lessons from a 'Pequeña República': Lancasterian Education, State-Making, and the Crisis of Patriarchal Authority in Early Post-Independence Mexico" (master's thesis, University of North Carolina, 2012), 7.
34. Carlos A. Forment, *Democracy in Latin America, 1760–1900*, vol. 1, *Civic Selfhood and Public Life in Mexico and Peru* (University of Chicago Press, 2003), 99–129.
35. Ortíz Monasterio, *Historia y Ficción*, 183–188, 139–140; Corinna Zeltsman, *Ink Under the Fingernails: Printing Politics in Nineteenth-Century Mexico* (University of California Press, 2021), 125–140.
36. Patrick J. McNamara, *Sons of the Sierra: Juárez, Díaz, and the People of Ixtlán, Oaxaca, 1855–1920* (University of North Carolina Press, 2007), 33–34.
37. Josefina García Quintana, *Cuauhtémoc en el siglo XIX* (Universidad Nacional Autónoma de México, 1977), 56; Ortíz Monasterio, *Historia y Ficción*, 313.
38. Zeltsman, *Ink Under the Fingernails*, 137; Fowler, *Grammar of Civil War*, 120–129.
39. For this and the following narrative see, unless otherwise noted, Fowler, *Grammar of Civil War*, 43–88.
40. Guy P. C. Thompson, "Bulwarks of Patriotic Liberalism: The National Guard, Philharmonic Corps and Patriotic Juntas in Mexico, 1847–1888," *Journal of Latin American Studies* 22 (1990): 31–68.
41. Daniela Trafano, "De cómo el católico fiel resolvió ser ciudadano. Indígenas, iglesia y estado en Oaxaca, 1857–1890" in Ariadna Acevedo Rodrigo and Paula López Caballero, eds., *Ciudadanos inesperados. Espacios de formación de la ciudadanía ayer y hoy* (Colegio de México, 2012), 81.
42. Nathaniel Morris, *Soldiers, Saints, and Shamans: Indigenous Communities and the Revolutionary State in Mexico's Gran Nayar, 1910–1940* (University of Arizona Press, 2020), 32; Evelyn Hu-Dehart, *Yaqui Resistance and Survival: The Struggle for Land and Autonomy, 1821–1910* (University of Wisconsin Press, 1984), 74–83; Luis González y González, *El indio en la era liberal* (Colegio de México, 1996), 249; Arturo Arnáiz y Freg et al., *Los Hallazgos de Ichcateopan: Actas y dictámenes de la Comisión Investigadora* (Mexico City: Comisión Investigadora de los hallazgos de Ichcateopan, 1962), 313.
43. Pani, *El segundo imperio*, 225–226.
44. Pamela Voekel, *For God and Liberty: Catholicism and Revolution in the Atlantic World, 1790–1861* (Oxford University Press, 2023), 247–248.
45. Josefina Zoraida Vázquez and Lorenzo Meyer, *México frente a Estados Unidos. Un ensayo histórico, 1776–2020* (Fondo de Cultura Económico, 2022), 68.
46. Richard J. Salvucci, *Politics, Markets, and Mexico's "London Debt," 1823–1887* (Cambridge University Press, 2009), 231, 238–239, 242–243.
47. "Projet politique sur les moyens les plus surs de recouvrir le payment de l'ultimatus demande par la France au Mexique dans l'année 1831," Newberry Library Ayer Collection, Ayer_MS_1269_FL014_00001_02.
48. Steven Hahn, *A Nation Without Borders: The United States and Its World in an Age of Civil Wars, 1830–1910* (Viking, 2016), 235.

49. Salvucci, *Politics, Markets, and Mexico's "London Debt,"* 241.
50. Edward Shawcross, *The Last Emperor of Mexico: The Dramatic Story of the Habsburg Archduke Who Created a Kingdom in the New World* (Basic Books, 2021), 26–30, 59–62.
51. "Carte de la défense de Mexico contre l'attaque du Major Géneral Scott en 1847: pour server l'intelligence des operations militaires de l'armée française en 1863," Newberry Library Ayer Collection, Ayer_MS_1269_FL014_00001_02.
52. Shawcross, *The Last Emperor*, 79.
53. Ibid., 71; Díaz, "El liberalismo militante," 785–787.
54. Shawcross, *The Last Emperor*, 95, 123, 54–55; Karl Marx, *The Eighteenth Brumaire of Louis Napoleon* (Marx/Engels Internet Archive 1995 [1852]), 16, 42.
55. Shawcross, *The Last Emperor*, 61, 74.
56. Zeltsman, *Ink Under the Fingernails*, 92–111; Shawcross, *The Last Emperor*, 66.
57. Díaz, "El liberalismo militante," 786.
58. Pani, *El segundo imperio*, 189.
59. Shawcross, *The Last Emperor*, 24–26, 130–131.
60. Pani, *El segundo imperio*, 203, 221–233.
61. Émile de Keratry, *La contraguerrilla francesa en México. Recuerdos de Tierra Caliente*, in Iturriaga, *Anecdotario*, 4:190.
62. Matthew Butler, *Popular Piety and Political Identity in Mexico's Cristero Rebellion* (Oxford University Press, 2004), 32.
63. Díaz, "El liberalismo militante," 799–800.
64. Shawcross, *The Last Emperor*, 125–130, 164–165; Vásquez Meléndez, *Los patriotas en escena*, 64.
65. Albert Hans, *Querétaro. Memorias de un official del Emperador Maximiliano*, in Iturriaga, *Anecdotario*, 3:166.
66. *El Diario del Imperio*, January 1, 1865.
67. Adolfo Schmidtlein, *Un médico alemán en el México de Maximilian*, in Iturriaga, *Anecdotario*, 2:157.
68. Amparo Gómez Tepexicuapan, "Los decretos en náhuatl del emperador Maximiliano," in Rodrigo Martínez Baracs and Salvador Rueda Smithers, eds., *De la A a la Z: El conocimiento de las lenguas en México* (México: Instituto Nacional de Antropología y Historia, 2015); González, *El indio en la era liberal*, 318.
69. *El Diario del Imperio*, January 1, 1865.
70. Lira González, *Comunidades indígenas*, 224–225.
71. Shawcross, *The Last Emperor*, 145.
72. Héctor de Mauleón, *La ciudad que nos inventa. Crónicas de seis siglos* (Cal y Arena, 2015), 196.
73. McNamara, *Sons of the Sierra*, 59–60.
74. Salvucci, *Politics, Markets, and Mexico's "London Debt,"* 248–253.
75. Zoraida Vázquez and Lorenzo Meyer, *México frente a Estados Unidos*, 74.
76. Shawcross, *The Last Emperor*, 191–202, 233–262.
77. *El Diario del Imperio*, June 19, 1867.
78. Princess Félix Salm-Salm, *Ten Years of My Life* in Iturriaga, *Anecdotario*, 3:159–163.
79. Claudio Lomnitz, *Death and the Idea of Mexico* (Zone Books, 2005), 32.
80. Krauze, *Mexico*, 227.
81. González, "El liberalismo triunfante," 827.
82. Carlos Marichal, *A Century of Debt Crises in Latin America: From Independence to the Great Depression, 1820–1930* (Princeton University Press, 1998), 249.

Chapter Twelve

1. "Civilized" and all other contemporary compliments are textual quotes from a paper and a guidebook. For Switzerland see *Two Republics*, December 21, 1884, cited in Alfred Tischendorf, *Great Britain and Mexico in the Time of Porfirio Díaz* (Duke University Press, 1961), 41; all else, T. Philip Terry, *Terry's Mexico Handbook for Travellers* (London: Gay & Hancock, 1911), lxii–lxix, lxvii. For "civilized" vs. "barbaric" see Ethel Alec-Tweedie, *Mexico As I Saw It* (London: Hurst and Blackett, 1902), 1.
2. Edison film catalogue, quoted in Katherine Manthorne, ed., *California Mexicana: Missions to Murals, 1820–1930* (Laguna Art Museum: University of California Press, 2017), 147.
3. *Terry's Mexico Handbook*, xxiii; Héctor de Mauleón, *La ciudad que nos inventa. Crónicas de seis siglos* (Cal y Arena, 2015), 233.
4. Manthorne, *California Mexicana*, 146.
5. Alejandra Uslenghi, *Latin America at Fin-de-Siècle Universal Exhibitions: Modern Cultures of Visuality* (Palgrave Macmillan, 2016), 86–89.
6. Jeffrey M. Pilcher, "Mexico City, 1891," in *Victorian Review* 36, no. 1 (Spring 2010): 43; Paul J. Vanderwood, *Satan's Playground: Mobsters and Movie Stars at America's Greatest Gaming Resort* (Duke University Press, 2009), 109; *Terry's Mexico Handbook*, lii, 236.
7. Alec-Tweedie, *Mexico As I Saw It*, 460.
8. B. Traven, *Government* (Wilson & Day, 1994), 98–99.
9. Frederick Starr, *In Indian Mexico: A Narrative of Travel and Labor* (Chicago: Forbes & Co., 1908), 299–303.
10. Lawrence Gustave Desmond, *Yucatán Through Her Eyes: Alice Dixon Le Plongeon, Writer and Expeditionary Photographer* (University of New Mexico Press, 2009), 178.
11. *Terry's Mexico Handbook*, 581–582, 566–567.
12. Christina Bueno, "*Forjando Patrimonio*: The Making of Archaeological Patrimony in Porfirian Mexico," *Hispanic American Historical Review* 90, no. 2 (2010): 215–216, 227; *Terry's Mexico Handbook*, 534–537.
13. William H. Beezley, *Judas at the Jockey Club and Other Episodes of Porfirian Mexico* (University of Nebraska Press, 2004), 37.
14. *Terry's Mexico Handbook*, 477, xxiv, 580.
15. Harry L. Foster, *A Gringo in Mañana-Land* (Dood, Meade and Co., 1925).
16. Manthorne, *California Mexicana*, 263; Vanderwood, *Satan's Playground*, 109; Mauleón, *La ciudad*, 395.
17. Eric Hobsbawm, *The Age of Capital: 1848–1875* (Vintage Books, 1996); Clementina Díaz y de Ovando, *Los cafés en México en el siglo XIX* (Universidad Nacional Autónoma de México, 2000), 92.
18. Reid Samuel Yalom, *Colonial Noir: Photographs from Mexico* (Stanford University Press, 2004), 76; Jacqulyn Ann Sumner, *Indigenous Autocracy: Power, Race, and Resources in Porfirian Tlaxcala, Mexico* (Stanford University Press, 2023), 171.
19. Beezley, *Judas at the Jockey Club*, 63.
20. Claudia del Palacio Montiel, *Indice del fondo hemerográfico veracruzano del IEHS* (Universidad Veracruzana, 1999), 65.
21. Diana J. Montaño, *Electrifying Mexico: Technology and the Transformation of a Modern City* (University of Texas Press, 2021), 109, 111, 135, 124.
22. Mauleón, *La ciudad*, 96; Matthew Vitz, *A City on a Lake: Urban Political Ecology and the Growth of Mexico City* (Duke University Press, 2018), 24.

23. Beezley, *Judas at the Jockey Club*, 50–51; Robert Buffington, *A Sentimental Education for the Working Man: The Mexico City Penny Press, 1900–1910* (Duke University Press, 2015), 155; Carlos G. Halaburda, "La fragilidad de la piel: El melodrama y los futuros reproductivos de la blanquitud en América Latina, 1880–1910," (PhD diss., Northwestern University, 2021), 244–274; Michael Matthews, "De Viaje: Elite Views of Modernity and the Porfirian Railway Boom," *Mexican Studies/Estudios Mexicanos* 26, no. 2 (Summer 2010): 283–287.
24. Beezley, *Judas at the Jockey Club*, 13–66; Mauleón, *La ciudad*, 217; Sergio H. Peralta Sandoval, *Hotel Regis: Historia de una época* (Editorial Diana, 1997), 20.
25. *El Siglo XIX*, January 24, 1891.
26. Montaño, *Electrifying Mexico*, 36–38, 48, 98, 100.
27. Luis González y González, *Pueblo en vilo. Una microhistoria de San José de Gracia* (Colegio de México, 1995), 81.
28. Guy P. C. Thompson, "Bulwarks of Patriotic Liberalism: The National Guard, Philharmonic Corps and Patriotic Juntas in Mexico, 1847–1888," *Journal of Latin American Studies* 22 (1990): 31–68.
29. On the grounds of language registered in the 1900 census, a deeply flawed but irreplaceable quantitative indicator. "Población de 5 años y mas que habla español o lengua indígena 1895–1995," INEGI.
30. Quoted in Mary Kay Vaughan, *The State, Education, and Social Class in Mexico, 1880–1928* (Northern Illinois University Press, 1982), 22–39.
31. Vicente Riva Palacio, *Martín Garatuza* (Porrúa, 1945), 175.
32. Prospectus, cited in José Ortiz Monasterio, *"Patria", tu ronca voz me repetía . . . Biografía de Vicente Riva Palacio y Guerrero* (Instituto Mora, 1999), 233–234.
33. Miguel Angel Aviles-Galan, "Measuring Skulls: Race and Science in Vicente Riva Palacio's *México a través de los siglos*," *Bulletin of Latin American Research* 29, no. 1 (January 2010): 90–98.
34. José Ortiz Monasterio, *Historia y Ficción. Los dramas y novelas de Vicente Riva Palacio* (Instituto Mora, 1993), 93.
35. Sumner, *Indigenous Autocracy*, ch. 2.
36. Alec-Tweedie, *Mexico As I Saw It*, 331–332.
37. Bueno, "Forjando Patrimonio," 242–245.
38. *Periódico Oficial del Estado de Guerrero*, November 20, 1903.
39. Matthew Esposito, *Funerals, Festivals, and Cultural Politics in Porfirian Mexico* (University of New Mexico Press, 2010), 53–82.
40. James Creelman, "President Díaz: Hero of the Americas," *Pearson's Magazine* 19, no. 3 (March 1908).
41. Porfirio Díaz to Nicolasa Díaz, May 10, 1862, quoted in Patrick J. McNamara, *Sons of the Sierra: Juárez, Díaz, and the People of Ixtlán, Oaxaca, 1855–1920* (University of North Carolina Press, 2007), 55.
42. Mauricio Tenorio-Trillo, *Mexico at the World's Fairs: Crafting a Modern Nation* (University of California Press, 1996), 54.
43. Traven, *Government*, 28, 44.
44. Leonardo Weller, "Government versus Bankers: Sovereign Debt Negotiations in Porfirian Mexico, 1888–1910," *Journal of Economic History* 75, no. 4 (December 2015): 1035.
45. Memoria presentada a la H. Legislatura del Estado Libre y Soberano de Veracruz, September 16, 1894.

46. Weller, "Government versus Bankers," 1032; Felipe Cole, "When Debt Made Sovereignty, 1820–1933," (PhD diss., Northwestern University, 2023), 130–135, 183–195.
47. María Angeles Cortés Basurto, "Cimientos del impero de la familia Guggenheim en México, 1890–1905," in Marco Palacios, ed., *Negocios, empresarios y entornos políticos, 1827–1958* (Colegio de México, 2015), 105–148.
48. Arthur P. Schmidt, *The Social and Economic Effects of the Railroad in Puebla and Veracruz, Mexico, 1867–1911* (New York: Garland, 1987), 134.
49. Vitz, *A City on a Lake*, 36.
50. Quoted in Karl Jacoby, *The Strange Career of William Ellis: The Texas Slave Who Became a Mexican Millionaire* (W. W. Norton, 2017), 102.
51. Theresa Alfaro-Velcamp, *So Far from Allah, So Close to Mexico* (University of Texas Press, 2007), 54–55; Jacoby, *The Strange Career of William Ellis*, 58–64, 131, 126–129, 105–119.
52. David M. Pletcher, *Rails, Mines, and Progress: Seven American Promoters in Mexico, 1867–1911* (American Historical Association, 1958), 106.
53. For the Barcelonettes see Leticia Gamboa Ojeda, ed., *Los Barcelonettes en México, miradas regionales* (Benemérita Universidad Autónoma de Puebla, 2008).
54. Alfredo Pureco Ornelas, *Empresarios lombardos en Michoacán. La familia Cusi entre el porfiriato y la posrevolución (1884–1938)* (Colegio de Michoacán/Instituto Mora, 2010), 251–265; *Terry's Mexico Handbook*, xlvi–xlvii.
55. J. K. Turner, *Barbarous Mexico* (Chicago: Charles H. Kerr, 1911), 91.
56. Friedrich Katz, *The Life and Times of Pancho Villa* (Stanford University Press, 1998), 468.
57. Turner, *Barbarous Mexico*, 83–92.
58. Thomas Benjamin, *A Rich Land, a Poor People: Politics and Society in Modern Chiapas* (University of New Mexico Press, 1989), 33–90.
59. Turner, *Barbarous Mexico*, 12–36, 58–59.
60. Turner, *Barbarous Mexico*, 47–48; Evelyn Hu-Dehart, "Development and Rural Rebellion: Pacification of the Yaqui in the late Porfiriato," *Hispanic American Historical Review* 54 (1974): 72–94.
61. Jan de Vos, *Oro verde. La conquista de la Selva Lacandona por los madereros tabasqueños, 1822–1949* (Fondo de Cultura Económica, 1996), 194–201.
62. Friedrich Katz, *The Secret War in Mexico: Europe, the United States, and the Mexican Revolution* (University of Chicago Press, 1981), 9–10.
63. Paul Vanderwood, *The Power of God Against the Guns of Government: Religious Upheaval in Mexico at the Turn of the Nineteenth Century* (Stanford University Press, 1998), 269; 2ª zona militar Brigada expedicionaria, 4 November 1892, Relación que manifiesta las municiones ed Artilleria, Infanteria y Caballeria, etc; Resumen general de los muertos que tuvo el enemigo; Relación que manifiesta las familias procedentes de Tomochic. SEDENA–XI/481.4/12733.
64. Heriberto Frías, *Tomóchic* (Porrua, 2015), 205.
65. Raymond B. Craib, *Cartographic Mexico: A History of State Fixations and Fugitive Landscapes* (Duke University Press, 2004), 107; Alan Knight, *The Mexican Revolution: Porfirians, Liberals, and Peasants* (University of Nebraska Press, 1990), 96; Arturo Warman, *Venimos a contradecir: Los campesinos de Morelos y el estado nacional* (Ediciones de la Casa Chata, 1978), 55.
66. Isela Myrna Santiago, "Huasteca Crude: Indians, Ecology, and Labor in the Mexican Oil Industry, Northern Veracruz, 1900–1938" (PhD diss., University of California, Berkeley 1997), 51–113.

67. Petition of naturales of San Juan de Tequesquitengo to the King, AGN Fondo Indios, vol 7, exp 485; John Womack Jr., *Zapata and the Mexican Revolution* (Thames & Hudson, 1968), 45–46.
68. Paul Friedrich, *The Princes of Naranja: An Essay in Anthrohistorical Method* (University of Texas Press, 1986), 4–20.
69. Luis Cabrera, quoted in Vitz, *A City on a Lake*, 61; for the Noriegas elsewhere see Vitz, *A City on a Lake*, 32–33, 25; for the story of Naranja see Paul Friedrich, *Agrarian Revolt in a Mexican Village* (University of Chicago Press, 1970).

Chapter Thirteen

1. J. Edgar Mendoza García, "De condueñazgo a municipio. El caso de Tlactopec Plumas, Oaxaca, 1863–1901," in Antonio Escobar Ohmstede et al., *Agua y tierra en México, siglos XIX y XX* (Colegio de Michacán/Colegio de San Luis, 2008), 1:187–208.
2. "Plano topográfico y mercantil de la ciudad de San Andrés Tuxtla, 1906," Papeles Personales Manuel Turrent.
3. José González Sierra, *Monopolio del Humo (elementos para la historia del tabaco en México y algunos conflictos de tabaqueros veracruzanos: 1915–1930)* (Universidad Veracruzana, 1987), 110–112.
4. González, *Pueblo en vilo*, 110.
5. *El Siglo XIX*, January 24, 1891; Claudia Agostoni, *Monuments of Progress: Modernization and Public Health in Mexico City, 1876–1910* (University of Calgary Press, 2003), 24.
6. Assorted documents, 1908–1911, Archivo Histórico del Distrito Federal Obras Públicas, vol. 1380 A, tomo II.
7. Oscar Castañeda Batres, "Revolución Mexicana y Constitución de 1917," in Ernesto Lemoines et al., eds. *Documentos para la historia del México independiente* (Porrúa, 2010), 653.
8. For child labor, Aurora Gómez-Galvarriato, *Industry and Revolution: Social and Economic Change in the Orizaba Valley, Mexico* (Harvard University Press, 2013), 72; for mine collapse, Castañeda Batres, "Revolución Mexicana y Constitución de 1917," 656.
9. Rodney D. Anderson, "Mexican Workers and the Politics of Revolution, 1906–1911," *Hispanic American Historical Review* 54, no. 1 (February 1974): 95; author's translation.
10. Rodney D. Anderson, *Outcasts in Their Own Land: Mexican Industrial Workers, 1906–1911* (Cornell University Press, 1976), 168–169.
11. For strikes in Veracruz and Mexico City, see Moisés González Navarro, *El Porfiriato: La vida social* (Fondo de Cultura Económica, 1957), 299; Heather Fowler-Salamini, *Working Women, Entrepreneurs, and the Mexican Revolution: The Coffee Culture of Córdoba, Veracruz* (University of Nebraska Press, 2013), 11; Gómez-Galvarriato, *Industry and Revolution*, 77, 81, 71.
12. Corinna Zeltsman, *Ink Under the Fingernails: Printing Politics in Nineteenth-Century Mexico* (University of California Press, 2021), 172; Robert Buffington, *A Sentimental Education for the Working Man: The Mexico City Penny Press, 1900–1910* (Duke University Press, 2015), 23, 9.
13. Bernardo García Díaz, *Un pueblo fabril del Porfiriato. Santa Rosa, Veracruz* (Fondo de Cultura Económica, 1981), 44–48; Gómez-Galvarriato, *Industry and Revolution*, 85.
14. Manchester Statistical Society report on life expectancy laborers, 1837, https://www.scienceandindustrymuseum.org.uk/objects-and-stories/water-and-sanitation.
15. Gómez-Galvarriato, *Industry and Revolution*, 73–74.

16. Mauricio Tenorio-Trillo, *"Hablo de la ciudad". Los principios del siglo XX desde la Ciudad de México* (Fondo de Cultura Económica, 2017), 47.
17. Héctor de Mauleón, *La ciudad que nos inventa. Crónicas de seis siglos* (Cal y Arena, 2015), 139–142.
18. Agostoni, *Monuments of Progress*, 110, 146; Matthew Vitz, *A City on a Lake: Urban Political Ecology and the Growth of Mexico City* (Duke University Press, 2018), 27–39.
19. Mauleón, *La ciudad*, 220–221; Vitz, *A City on a Lake*, 27; Agostoni, *Monuments of Progress*, 132, 134, 144; Henry Howard Harper, *A Journey in Southeastern Mexico* (New York: DeVinne Press), 9–12; Jayson Maurice Porter, "Making the Coast Pacific: Oilseeds and Environmental Violence and Justice in Guerrero and Sinaloa, 1900–1960" (PhD diss., Northwestern University, 2022), 57.
20. Paul Garner, *Porfirio Díaz* (Longman, 2001), 105.
21. Guerrero, for example. Romana Falcón, "Force and the Search for Consent: The Role of the Jefaturas Políticas of Coahuila in National State Formation," in Gilbert M. Joseph and Daniel Nugent, eds., *Everyday Forms of State Formation* (Duke University Press, 1994), 107–134; Charles M. Flandrau, *¡Viva México!* (Eland Books, 1985); Ana María Serna Rodríguez, "Journalists on Trial: The Press, Censorship, and the Law, 1898–1920," in Paul Gillingham et al., eds. *Journalism, Satire, and Censorship in Mexico* (University of New Mexico Press, 2017), 66.
22. Cited in Daniel Cosío Villegas, "El Porfiriato, era de consolidación," *Historia* 13, no. 1 (July 1963): 76–87.
23. José Vasconcelos, *Ulises criollo* in *Obras completas*, vol. 1 (Libreros Mexicanos Unidos, 1957), 583.
24. James Creelman, "President Díaz: Hero of the Americas," *Pearsons Magazine* 19, no. 3 (March 1908).
25. Flyer *Gaceta Callejera* May 15 1892.
26. Ariel Rodríguez Kuri, *La experiencia olvidada. El ayuntamiento de México. Política y gobierno, 1876–1912* (Colegio de México, 1996), 73.
27. W. S. Langslan, "Coahuila: Centralisation Against State Autonomy," in Thomas Benjamin and William McNellie, *Other Mexicos: Essays on Regional Mexican History, 1876–1911* (University of New Mexico Press, 1984), 55–72.
28. Instituto Nacional de Antropología e Historia, Archivo Sónoro PHO/CUAUH/5/15, 36.
29. Daniel Cosío Villegas, *El Porfiriato. La vida política interior* (México: Hermes, 1972), 2:425; Jacqulyn Ann Sumner, *Indigenous Autocracy: Power, Race, and Resources in Porfirian Tlaxcala, Mexico* (Stanford University Press, 2023), 27.
30. Friedrich Katz, "Restored Republic and Porfiriato," in Leslie Bethell, ed., The *Cambridge History of Latin America*, vol. 5, *c. 1870 to 1930* (Cambridge University Press, 1985), 1–78.
31. Ulises Íñiguez Mendoza, "Los religioneros contra la Républica Restaurada: '¡Viva la religión y mueran los *protestantes!*'," *Historia mexicana* 72, no. 4 (2023): 1703–1736.
32. Jean Meyer, *The Cristero Rebellion: The Mexican People Between Church and State, 1926–1929* (Cambridge Latin American Studies, 1976), 9; Garner, *Porfirio Díaz*, 102.
33. Edward Wright-Rios, *Revolutions in Catholicism: Reform and Revelation in Oaxaca, 1887–1934* (Duke University Press, 2009), 63, 296; Alan Knight, *The Mexican Revolution: Porfirians, Liberals, and Peasants* (University of Nebraska Press, 1990), 1:44.
34. Buffington, *A Sentimental Education*, 2–3.
35. Pablo Piccato, *City of Suspects: Crime in Mexico City, 1900–1931* (Duke University Press, 2001), 5, 212–213, 231; Kathryn A. Sloan, *Death in the City: Suicide and the Social Imaginary in Modern Mexico* (University of California Press, 2017), 164.

36. *El Diario del Hogar*, October 16, 1885, October 28, 1892; in Gillingham et al., *Journalism, Satire, and Censorship*, 5–6.
37. Sumner, *Indigenous Autocracy*, ch. 2, 92–94; John Womack, *Zapata and the Mexican Revolution* (Thames & Hudson, 1968), 13–15.
38. Patricia Romero Lankao, "Coatzacoalcos-Minatitlán: El proceso histórico de transformación de la región y sus consecuencias socio-ambientales" (bachelor's thesis, Universidad Nacional Autónoma de México, 1986), 22; Knight, *The Mexican Revolution*, 1:118.
39. Knight, *The Mexican Revolution*, 1:41, 119.
40. The Sonoran revolutionary Benjamin Hill, in *La Voz de Juárez*, 1908, cited in Héctor Aguilar Camín, *La frontera nomada. Sonora y la Revolución Mexicana* (Fondo de Cultura Económica, 2017).
41. Creelman, "President Díaz: Hero of the Americas."
42. Author's translation of cartoon attributed to José Guadalupe Posada "El regaño de Mama," *El Diablito Rojo*, March 16, 1908, reproduced in Buffington, *A Sentimental Education*, 120.
43. Barbara Weinstein, *The Amazon Rubber Boom: 1850–1920* (Stanford University Press, 1983), 210.
44. Mark Wasserman, *Capitalists, Caciques, and Revolution: The Native Elite and Foreign Enterprise in Chihuahua, Mexico, 1854–1911* (University of North Carolina Press, 1984); Steven Haber, *Industry and Underdevelopment: The Industrialization of Mexico, 1890–1940* (Stanford University Press, 1989), 68.
45. Alfonso de Maria y Campos, "Porfirianos prominentes. Orígenes y años de juventud de ocho integrantes del grupo de los Científicos, 1846–1876," *Historia Mexicana*, 34, no. 4 (April–June, 1985): 610–661.
46. John Reed, *Insurgent Mexico* (International Publishers, 1969), 183.
47. Luis A. V. Catão, "Mexico and Export-Led Growth: The Porfirian Period Revisited," *Cambridge Journal of Economics* 22, no. 1 (January 1998): 59.
48. Carlo Levi, *Christ Stopped at Eboli: The Story of a Year* (Picador, 2020), 1–10; Robert A. Caro, *The Years of Lyndon Johnson*, vol. 1, *The Path to Power* (Vintage Books, 1990), 115.
49. Quoted in Karl Marx, *Capital*, vol. 1 (Penguin, 1990), 886–887; for overall analysis, see "The Expropriation of the Agricultural Population," 877–895.
50. Joaquín Costa, *Oligarquía y caciquismo como la forma actual de gobernar en España: Urgencia y modo de cambiarla* (Madrid: Imprenta de los hijos de M.G. Hernández, 1902), 107, 89, 131.
51. Enrique Krauze, *Mexico, Biography of Power: A History of Modern Mexico, 1810–1996* (Harper Collins, 1997), 254.

Chapter Fourteen

1. For the below biography see Enrique Krauze, *Francisco I. Madero: Místico de la libertad* (Fondo de Cultura Económica, 1987); for the politics of 1908–1910, Alan Knight, *The Mexican Revolution: Porfirians, Liberals, and Peasants* (University of Nebraska Press, 1990), 37–77.
2. Francisco I. Madero, "Los diarios espiritistas de Francisco I. Madero," *Letras libres*, February 28, 1999.
3. https://archivomagon.net/en/obras-completas/
4. John Womack, *Zapata and the Mexican Revolution* (Thames & Hudson, 1968), 55.
5. Friedrich Katz, *The Life and Times of Pancho Villa* (Stanford University Press, 1998), 2–8.

6. John Reed, *Insurgent Mexico* (International Publishers, 1969), 138; Alvaro Obregón, *Ocho mil kilómetros en campaña* (Paris: La vda. de C. Bouret, 1917), 266.
7. Katz, *Villa*, 243–244.
8. José María Jaurrieta, *Seis años con el general Francisco Villa* (Fondo de Cultura Económica, 2023), 195.
9. Katz, *Villa*, 101.
10. Vladimir Lenin, *What Is to Be Done?* (Marxists Internet Archive, 1999 [1902]), 63–64, 76–81; Robert Service, *Lenin: A Biography* (Macmillan, 2000), 136.
11. Mariano Azuela, *Los de abajo* (Fondo de Cultura Económica, 1994), 13.
12. Bernardo Ibarrola, "La rebelión de la Ciudadela hiere de muerte al gobierno de Madero. La historia militar por contar de la Decena Trágica," *Estudios de historia moderna y contemporánea de México* 58 (2019): 159–194.
13. Porfirio Díaz, *Memorias de Porfirio Díaz con un prólogo de Moisés González Navvro* (Conaculta, 1994), 1:68.
14. Womack, *Zapata*, 72–78.
15. Letter, Vázquez Gómez to Gustavo Madero, February 1912, Ignacio Solares, ed., *Gustavo Madero: epistolario* (Editorial Diana, 1991).
16. Carta abierta a Don Francisco I. Madero, April 27, 1911, in Luis Cabrera, *La revolución es la revolución: antología* (Comisión Nacional Editorial del C.E.N., Partido Revolucionario Institucional, 1985), 69.
17. Rafael L. Urquizo, *Carranza: El Hombre. El Político. El Caudillo. El Patriota* (Instituto de Estudios Históricos de la Revolución Mexicana, 2020), 24–25.
18. Jaurrieta, *Seis años con el general Francisco Villa*, 195.
19. Stanley R. Ross, *Francisco I. Madero: Apostle of Democracy* (Columbia University Press, 1955), 158.
20. Knight, *The Mexican Revolution*, 1:202–246; Ross, *Madero*, 150–174.
21. Ross, *Madero*, 172–173.
22. Katz, *Villa*, 137; Knight, *The Mexican Revolution*, 1:269; Paul Gillingham, "Suzanne B. Pasztor, *The Spirit of Hidalgo: The Mexican Revolution in Coahuila*," *Journal of Latin American Studies* 36 (2004), 818–820.
23. The Plan de Ayala, November 28, 1911, Oscar Castañeda Batres, "Revolución Mexicana y Constitución de 1917," in Ernesto Lemoines et al., *Documentos para la historia del México independiente* (Porrúa, 2010), 834, 836.
24. Adrián Aguirre Benavides, *Errores de Madero* (Editorial JUS, 1980), 108.
25. Womack, *Zapata*, 3–9, 61–75, 85–88, 97–129.
26. Plan de Ayala; Knight, *The Mexican Revolution*, 1:374–377.
27. Katz, *Villa*, 139–178.
28. Enrique Krauze, *Mexico, Biography of Power: A History of Modern Mexico, 1810–1996* (Harper Collins, 1997), 265.
29. Félix Díaz manifesto, printed in *El Imparcial*, October 17, 1912.
30. *El País* March 17, 1911; Letter, Íñigo Noriega to Porfirio Díaz, March 6, 1911, Universidad Iberoamericana. Archivo Porfirio Díaz leg. 36, caja 11, doc. 5375 y 5367–5371.
31. Knight, *The Mexican Revolution*, 1:456–457.
32. Letter, Gustavo to Francisco Madero, November 8, 1911 Archivo General de la Nación, Colección Revolución: c. 1, carp. 10, expediente 241.
33. Ariel Rodríguez Kuri, *Historia del desasosiego. La revolución en la ciudad de México, 1911–1922* (Colegio de México, 2010), 87–88.
34. Ibid., 17.

35. Ibid., 92; Héctor de Mauleón, *La ciudad que nos inventa. Crónicas de seis siglos* (Cal y Arena, 2015), 256.
36. Ibarrola, "La rebelión de la Ciudadela, 180–183.
37. Knight, *The Mexican Revolution*, 1:481.
38. *El Imparcial*, July 20, 1912, quoted in Rodríguez Kuri, *Historia del desasosiego*, 51.
39. Knight, *The Mexican Revolution*, 1:455.
40. Ana María Serna Rodríguez, "Journalists on Trial: The Press, Censorship, and the Law, 1898–1920," in Gillingham et al., *Journalism, Satire, and Censorship*, 71.
41. Jean Meyer, *The Cristero Rebellion: The Mexican People Between Church and State, 1926–1929* (Cambridge University Press, 1976), 11.
42. Arturo Warman, "The Political Project of Zapatismo," in Friedrich Katz, ed., *Riot, Rebellion, and Revolution: Rural Social Conflict in Mexico* (Princeton University Press, 1988), ch. 11. For Swiss comparison, see Womack, *Zapata*, 320.
43. Manuel Ceballos Ramírez, "La enciclica Rerum Novarum y los trabajadores catolicos en la Ciudad de Mexico (1891–1913)," *Historia Mexicana* 33, no. 1 (July–September 1983): 3–38.
44. Where according to Jean Meyer they won one hundred seats and were adjudicated. Meyer, *The Cristero Rebellion*, 23.
45. "Necesitamos gobierno," *El País*, January 24, 1913.
46. Knight, *The Mexican Revolution*, 2:64.
47. Marco Antonio Samaniego López, "La revolución mexicana en Baja California. Maderismo, magonismo, filibusterismo y la pequeña revuelta local," *Historia Mexicana* 56, no. 4 (April–June 2007): 1201–1262.
48. The epithets in the original are "*mariconería*" and "*pelados*." Carlos Fuentes, *La muerte de Artemio Cruz* (Fondo de Cultura Económica, 1962), 195.
49. Azuela, *Los de abajo*, 21, 44–45.
50. Reed, *Insurgent Mexico*, ch. 4.
51. Luis González y González, *Pueblo en vilo. Una microhistoria de San José de Gracia* (Colegio de México, 1995), 118–122.
52. Paul Gillingham, *Cuauhtémoc's Bones: Forging National Identity in Modern Mexico* (University of New Mexico Press, 2012), 141–142.

Chapter Fifteen

1. Robert McCaa, "Missing Millions: The Demographic Costs of the Mexican Revolution," *Mexican Studies/Estudios Mexicanos* 19, no. 2 (Summer 2003): 396.
2. Mariano Azuela, *Los de abajo* (Fondo de Cultura Económica, 1994), 63, 128; Anita Brenner, *The Wind That Swept Mexico: The History of the Mexican Revolution 1910–1942* (Harper & Brothers, 1943), caption plate 58; Manuel Gamio, *Forjando Patria (Pro-Nacionalismo)* (Porrua Hermanos, 1916), 303.
3. Luis Cabrera, "La Revolución es la Revolución," in Luis Cabrera, *El Pensamiento de Luis Cabrera. Selección y prólogo de Eduardo Luquín* (Instituto Nacional de Estudios Históricos de las Revoluciones de México, 1960), 178.
4. Luis Zúñiga, *Carrasco en la revolución. En homenaje merecido a sus méritos revolucionarios* (Culiacán: Talleres gráficos del Gobierno, 1941).
5. Ariel Rodríguez Kuri, *Historia del desasosiego. La revolución en la ciudad de México, 1911–1922* (Colegio de México, 2010), 94–95.
6. Alan Knight, *The Mexican Revolution*, vol. 2, *Counter-revolution and Reconstruction* (University of Nebraska Press, 1990), 2:9–10, 66–67, 74–75.

7. Knight, *The Mexican Revolution* 2:14–17.
8. Martín Luis Guzmán, *El águila y la serpiente* (Editorial Anahuac, 1949), 346–347, 62, 69.
9. Knight, *The Mexican Revolution* 2:15–25; Héctor Aguilar Camín, *La frontera nómada. Sonora y la Revolución Mexicana* (Fondo de Cultura Económica, 2017), 4.
10. Friedrich Katz, *The Life and Times of Pancho Villa* (Stanford University Press, 1998), 206.
11. Hector Aguilar Camín, "The Relevant Tradition: Sonoran Leaders in the Revolution," in David Brading, ed., *Caudillo and Peasant in the Mexican Revolution* (Cambridge University Press, 1980), 92–123.
12. Gonzalo N. Santos, *Memorias* (Grijalbo, 1984), 167.
13. Jürgen Buchenau, *The Last Caudillo: Alvaro Obregón and the Mexican Revolution* (Wiley-Blackwell, 2011), 30–56, 60.
14. Knight, *The Mexican Revolution*, 2:78, 30–32l, 150–158.
15. Vicente Blasco Ibañez, *El militarismo mejicano: estudios publicados en los principales diarios de los Estados Unidos* (Madrid: 1920), 105.
16. The comparison is that of Alan Knight. Knight, *The Mexican Revolution*, 2:165.
17. Rodríguez Kuri, *Historia del desasosiego*, 138–139; Héctor de Mauleón, *La ciudad que nos inventa. Crónicas de seis siglos* (Cal y Arena, 2015), 254–257.
18. De la Barra (international mediator, involved in Versailles), Mondragón (crony arms consultant), and Limantour (French with ear of Americans) all got one.
19. Guzmán, *El águila y la serpiente*, 11–12, 237, 232.
20. Villa to Zapata, April 17, 1915, in Armando Ruiz Aguilar, ed., *Nosotros los ignorantes hombres que hacemos la guerra* (Consejo Nacional para la Cultura y las Artes, 2010), 157–158.
21. José María Jaurrieta, *Seis años con el general Francisco Villa* (Fondo de Cultura Económica, 2023), 91.
22. Obregón's official report to Carranza on the second Battle of Celaya, April 15, 1915, reproduced in Alvaro Obregón, *Ocho mil kilómetros en campaña* (Paris: La vda. de C. Bouret, 1917), 499–501; Katz, *Villa*, 488–495.
23. Jaurrieta, *Seis años con el general Francisco Villa*, 62, 25–27.
24. Zapata to Villa, January 11, 1915, reproduced in Ruiz Aguilar, *Nosotros los ignorantes hombres*, 144, 205.
25. Arturo Warman, *Venimos a contradecir: Los campesinos de Morelos y el estado nacional* (Ediciones de la Casa Chata, 1978), 116–118, 128.
26. Ian Jacobs, "Rancheros of Guerrero," in Brading, ed. *Caudillo and Peasant*, 76–91.
27. Edwin Lieuwen, *Mexican Militarism: The Political Rise and Fall of the Revolutionary Army, 1910–1940* (University of New Mexico Press, 1968), 35.
28. *El Pueblo*, February 24, 1917.
29. Jaurrieta, *Seis años con el general Francisco Villa*, 225–240; Knight, *The Mexican Revolution*, 2:375–392.
30. Knight, *The Mexican Revolution*, 2:460; Katz, *Villa*, 637, 649.
31. Katz, *Villa*, 550–566, 612, 662. For the morphine addict slur, see *El Tucsonense*, March 11, 1916.
32. George S. Patton, *George S. Patton Papers: Diaries, -1945; Original; 1914 , 1916 , and 1917*. 1914. Manuscript/Mixed Material. https://www.loc.gov/item/mss35634002.
33. Mitchell Yockelson, "The United States Armed Forces and the Mexican Punitive Expedition: Part 2," *Prologue Magazine* 29:4 (Winter, 1997), https://www.archives.gov/publications/prologue/1997/winter/mexican-punitive-expedition-2.html#T10
34. Katz, *Villa*, 566–595; Jaurrieta, *Seis años con el general Francisco Villa*, 30.
35. Katz, *Villa*, 650–653.

36. Knight, *The Mexican Revolution*, 2:470–477; Lieuwen, *Mexican Militarism*, 153.
37. Guzmán, *El águila y la serpiente*, 276.
38. Nathaniel Morris, *Soldiers, Saints, and Shamans: Indigenous Communities and the Revolutionary State in Mexico's Gran Nayar, 1910–1940* (University of Arizona Press, 2020), 67.
39. Santos, *Memorias*, 314.
40. Buchenau, *The Last Caudillo*, 94–105.
41. Katz, *Villa*, 609; Jaurrieta, *Seis años con el general Francisco Villa*, 119–135.
42. Womack, *Zapata*, 322–326, 331–357.
43. Adolfo de la Huerta, *Memorias de Don Adolfo de la Huerta según su propio dictado* (Instituto Nacional de Estudios Históricos de las Revoluciones de México, 2020), 365.
44. Katz, *Villa*, 765–782; John W. F. Dulles, *Yesterday in Mexico: A Chronicle of the Revolution, 1919–1936* (University of Texas Press, 1961), 367–369; Mario Gill, "Los Escudero, de Acapulco," *Historia Mexicana* 3, no. 4 (October–December 1953): 299–303; Sarah Osten, *The Mexican Revolution's Wake: The Making of a Political System, 1920–1929* (Cambridge University Press, 2018), 118.
45. Buchenau, *The Last Caudillo*, 104.
46. Ibid., 126–127.
47. De la Huerta, *Memorias*, 245–247. Jorge Prieto Laurens, *Cincuenta años de política mexicana. Memorias políticas* (Editora Mexicana de Periódicos, Libros y Revistas, 1968), 151.
48. Dudley Ankerson, *Agrarian Warlord: Saturnino Cedillo and the Mexican Revolution in San Luis Potosí* (Northern Illinois University Press, 1984), 108.
49. Lorenzo Meyer, "La institucionalición del nuevo régimen," in Daniel Cosío Villegas et al., eds. *Historia general de México* (Colegio de México, 1994), 1061; De la Huerta, *Memorias*, 249.
50. Meyer, "La institucionalición del nuevo régimen," 1085.
51. Overy, Mexico City, to Chamberlain, February 14, 1929, March 13, 1929, National Archives, London, Public Record Office, Foreign Office (hereafter PRO FO), FO 371/13488/1533/39/26.
52. Osten, *The Mexican Revolution's Wake*, 99–131.
53. De la Huerta, *Memorias*, 335; José Vasconcelos, *Obras completas*, vol. 8 (Libreros Mexicanos Unidos, 1957), 1452; Osten, *The Mexican Revolution's Wake*, MS 179.
54. For singing, PRO FO371 AN1816/1656/26, 5.
55. Ogilvie Forbes, Mexico City, to Henderson, September 25, 1929, PRO FO371/13490/A6821/39/26.
56. Lieuwen, *Mexican Militarism*, 153.
57. Dulles, *Yesterday in Mexico*, 332–354.
58. Overy, Mexico City, to Craigie, January 11, 1929, PRO FO371/13501/A11/682; Overy, Mexico City, to Chamberlain, "Mexico: Annual Report, 1928," June 12, 1929, PRO FO371/13502/A4391/26.
59. Dulles, *Yesterday in Mexico*, 436–458.
60. Memo, Department of Overseas Trade, Foreign Office, May 14,1929, PRO FO371/13502/A3326.
61. Julia G. Young, *Mexican Exodus: Emigrants, Exiles, and Refugees of the Cristero War* (Oxford University Press, 2015), 5–8, 45.
62. Matthew Butler, *Mexico's Spiritual Reconquest: Indigenous Catholics and Father Pérez's Revolutionary Church* (University of New Mexico Press, 2023), 5–6, 45, 76.
63. Butler, *Mexico's Spiritual Reconquest*, 40–68.
64. Carlos Martínez Assad, *El laboratorio de la Revolución. El Tabasco garridista* (Siglo Veintiuno, 2004), 37.

65. Dulles, *Yesterday in Mexico*, 303–304; *El Informador de Guadalajara*, July 30 and 31, 1926.
66. Cosío Villegas et al., *Historia general de México*, 1063.
67. Luis González y González, *Pueblo en vilo. Una microhistoria de San José de Gracia* (Colegio de México, 1995), 148–149.
68. Alicia Olivera de Bonfil, "Victoriano Ramírez, el catorce," in Carlos Martínez Assad, ed., *Estadistas, caciques y caudillos* (Universidad Nacional Autónoma de México, 1988), 284.
69. Jean Meyer, *The Cristero Rebellion: The Mexican People Between Church and State 1926–1929* (Cambridge University Press, 2008), 79.
70. Graham Greene, *The Lawless Roads* (Penguin, 1982 [1939]), 44.
71. Meyer, *The Cristero Rebellion*, 41–42; for its endurance beyond the Cristiada see Gema Kloppe–Santamaría, "Martyrs, Fanatics, and Pious Militants: Religious Violence and the Secular State in 1930s Mexico," *The Americas* 79, no. 2 (April 2022): 197–227.
72. Meyer, *The Cristero Rebellion*, 74; González, *Pueblo en vilo*, 150.
73. Morris, *Soldiers, Saints, and Shamans*, 3–6.
74. Olivera de Bonfil, "Victoriano Ramírez, el catorce," 281–289.
75. Matthew Butler, "The 'Liberal' Cristero: Ladislao Molina and the Cristero Rebellion in Michoacán, 1927–9," *Journal of Latin American Studies* 31, no. 3 (October 1999): 645–671.
76. Jean Meyer, *La Cristiada* (Siglo Vientiuno, 1970), 3 vols., 3:51.
77. "Corrido de Ramón Aguilar," quoted in Alicia Olivera de Bonfil, *La literatura cristera. Antología* (Instituto Nacional de Antropología e Historia, 1994), 70–71.
78. Matthew Butler, *Popular Piety and Political Identity in Mexico's Cristero Rebellion* (Oxford University Press, 2004), 213–221; Morris, *Soldiers, Saints, and Shamans*, 121–175.
79. Meyer, *The Cristero Rebellion*, 17–32.
80. Moisés González Navarro, *Cristeros y agraristas en Jalisco* (Colegio de México, 2001), 2:395.
81. An average over the years 1927–1929. Lieuwen, *Mexican Militarism*, 153; Leslie Bethell, ed., *The Cambridge History of Latin America*, vol. 5, *c. 1870 to 1930* (Cambridge University Press, 1985), 221.
82. Tzvi Medin, *El minimato presidencial. Historia politica del Maximato* (Colegio de México, 1982), 37, 30.
83. Young, *Mexican Exodus*, 85–86.
84. Lorenzo Meyer, "La revolución mexicana y sus elecciones presidenciales," in Pablo González Casanova, ed., *Las elecciones en México. Evolución y perspectiva* (Siglo XXI, 1985), 88; Dulles, *Yesterday in Mexico*, 422; Vasconcelos, *Obras Completas*, 2:80, 70, 87, 7:104, 143.
85. Meyer, *The Cristero Rebellion*, 67–82.
86. Presidential address, September 1, 1928, quoted in Medin, *El minimato presidencial*, 35.

Chapter Sixteen

1. *New York Times*, December 7, 1930.
2. In Article 27, alongside the better-known provisions for expropriation and nationalization of natural resources. Mikael D. Wolfe, *Watering the Revolution: An Environmental and Technological History of Agrarian Reform in Mexico* (Duke University Press, 2017), 15.
3. Mark Wasserman, *Persistent Oligarchs: Elites and Politics in Chihuahua, Mexico, 1910–1940* (Duke University Press, 1993), 74–83; Alberto J. Olvera R., "La estructura económica y social de Veracruz hacía 1930. Un análisis inicial," *Anuario* 3, 1983, 17–19.
4. Victor Alejandro Sorell, "Orozco and American Muralism: Re/viewing an Enduring Artistic Legacy," in Renato González Mello and Diane Miliotes, eds., *José Clemente Orozco in the United States, 1927–1934* (W. W. Norton, 2002), 266, 267.

5. Ariadna Acevedo Rodrigo, "Las apariencias importan: Indumentaria e higiene personal como marcas de civilización y ciudadanía en la educación para campesinos e indígenas, México ca. 1921–1943," in Ariadna Acevedo Rodrigo and Paula López Caballero, eds., *Ciudadanos inesperados: Espacios de formación de la ciudadanía ayer y hoy* (Colegio de México, 2012), 133–134.
6. Patrick Marnham, *Dreaming with His Eyes Open: A Life of Diego Rivera* (Alfred Knopf, 1998), 83.
7. Héctor Aguilar Camín, "Nociones presidenciales de la cultura nacional de Alvaro Obregón a Gustavo Díaz Ordaz, 1920–1968," in José Emilio Pacheco, *En torno a la cultura nacional* (Secretaría de Educación Pública, 1976), 127.
8. Brenner cited in Marnham, *Dreaming with His Eyes Open*, 183; John Lear, *Workers, Neighbors, and Citizens: The Revolution in Mexico City* (University of Nebraska Press, 2001), 287.
9. José Vasconcelos, *Obras completas* (Libreros Mexicanos Unidos, 1957), 2:772, 3:1215–1395.
10. Jesús Guzmán Urióstegui, *Evila Franco Nájera, a pesar del olvido* (Instituto Nacional de Estudios Históricos de las Revoluciones de México, 1995), 43–44, 61, 65.
11. Mary Kay Vaughan, *The State, Education, and Social Class in Mexico 1880–1928* (University of Illinois Press, 1982), 214–238.
12. Elsie Rockwell, "Schools of the Revolution: Enacting and Contesting State Forms in Tlaxcala, 1910–1930," in Gilbert M. Joseph and Daniel Nugent, eds., *Everyday Forms of State Formation: Revolution and the Negotiation of Rule in Modern Mexico* (Duke University Press, 1992), 191–192.
13. Tomás Bustamante, "La reforma agraria en Guerrero durante el gobierno de Lázaro Cárdenas," in Jaime Salazar Adame et al., eds., *Historia de la cuestión agraria mexicana. Estado de Guerrero, 1867–1940* (Chilpancingo: Gobierno del Estado de Guerrero, 1987), 404.
14. Director de Educación Federal Guerrero annual report 1932, SEP DGEP caja 1365 ant. 226 exp. 15–6–8–165.
15. "El Grito de Guadalajara," July 20, 1934, quoted in Enrique Krauze, *Mexico, Biography of Power: A History of Modern Mexico, 1810–1996* (Harper Collins, 1997), 433.
16. Robert Service, *Lenin: A Biography* (Macmillan, 2000), 314–317; William Hinton, *Fanshen: A Documentary of Revolution in a Chinese Village* (Monthly Review Press, 2008).
17. Jean Meyer, "Mexico: Revolution and Reconstruction in the 1920s," in Leslie Bethell, ed., *Mexico Since Independence* (Cambridge University Press, 1991), 220–224.
18. Between 1929 and 1933. Fernando Saúl Alanís Enciso, *They Should Stay There: The Story of Mexican Migration and Repatriation During the Great Depression*, trans. Russ Davidson (University of North Carolina Press, 2017), 16.
19. Steven Haber, *Industry and Underdevelopment: The Industrialization of Mexico, 1890–1940* (Stanford University Press, 1989), 152–153.
20. Josefina Zoraida Vázquez and Lorenzo Meyer, *México frente a Estados Unidos. Un ensayo histórico, 1776–2020* (Fondo de Cultura Económico, 2022), 149–150; John J. Dwyer, *The Agrarian Dispute: The Expropriation of American-Owned Rural Land in Revolutionary Mexico* (Duke University Press, 2008), 190–191.
21. Alan Knight, *The Mexican Revolution*, vol. 2, *Counter-revolution and Reconstruction* (University of Nebraska Press, 1990), 2:13; Tzvi Medin, *El minimato presidencial. Historia politica del Maximato* (Colegio de México, 1982), 96.
22. Ernest Gruening, *Mexico and Its Heritage* (D. Appleton-Century, 1936), 416–417; Martha Rodríguez et al., *Coahuila. Historia breve* (Colegio de México, 2010), 293–295.
23. Lázaro Cárdenas, *Obras I – Apuntes 1913/1940* (Universidad Nacional Autónoma de México, 1972), 5–20; Krauze, *Mexico*, 438–380.

24. John Gunther notes on 1940 interview with Cárdenas, University of Chicago Library Special Collections, The John Gunther papers, 1935–1967, Box 17, Folder 12; Anita Brenner, *The Wind That Swept Mexico: The History of the Mexican Revolution 1910–1942* (Harper & Brothers, 1943), 84.
25. R. H. K. Marett, *An Eye-Witness of Mexico* (Oxford University Press, 1939), 141, 256.
26. "Leading personalities in Mexico," Confidential Print of the Foreign Office, 1950.
27. Gonzalo N. Santos, *Memorias* (Grijalbo, 1984), 511, 714–716.
28. Dudley Ankerson, *Agrarian Warlord: Saturnino Cedillo and the Mexican Revolution in San Luis Potosí* (Northern Illinois University Press, 1984), 143–144; Cárdenas, *Apuntes 1913/1940*, 233–238.
29. Medin, *El minimato presidencial*, 141.
30. Cárdenas, *Apuntes 1913/1940*, 12, 230.
31. Frans Schryer, *The Rancheros of Pisaflores: The History of a Peasant Bourgeoisie in Twentieth-Century Mexico* (University of Toronto Press, 1980), 77–90.
32. Paul Gillingham, *Unrevolutionary Mexico: The Birth of a Strange Dictatorship* (Yale University Press, 2021), 178–179.
33. Héctor Ceballos Garibay, *Francisco J. Múgica: Crónica política de un rebelde* (Ediciones Coyoacán, 2002), 149.
34. John W. F. Dulles, *Yesterday in Mexico: A Chronicle of the Revolution, 1919–1936* (University of Texas Press, 1961), 634–646, 659–681.
35. Enrique Cárdenas, *La hacienda pública y la política económica 1929–1958* (Colegio de México, 1994), 45–69; INEGI *Estadisticas históricas de México.*
36. Romana Falcón, *El agrarismo en Veracruz. La etapa radical (1928–1935)* (Colegio de México, 1977), 32, 48–49; Paul Friedrich, *Agrarian Revolt in a Mexican Village* (University of Chicago Press, 1970), 66–69; Andrew Paxman, *Jenkins of Mexico: How a Southern Farm Boy Became a Mexican Magnate* (Oxford University Press, 2017),153.
37. Frank Tannenbaum, *Peace by Revolution: Mexico after 1910* (Columbia University Press, 1966), 206–212; Benjamin T. Smith, *Pistoleros and Popular Movements: The Politics of State Formation in Postrevolutionary Oaxaca* (University of Nebraska Press, 2009), 59.
38. Friedrich, *Agrarian Revolt*, 130, 140.
39. Falcón, *El agrarismo en Veracruz*, 22.
40. Instituto Nacional de Estadística y Geografía, "Beneficiados con dotación de tierras por periodos presidenciales según entidad federativa 1900–1992," http://datos.cide.edu/
41. Instituto Nacional de Estadística y Geografía, "Dotación de tierras y beneficiarios por tipo de tierra según periodos presidenciales 1900–1992," http://datos.cide.edu/
42. Tannenbaum, *Peace by Revolution*, 211–214; Patricia San Pedro López, "Élites regionales, política local y reparto agrario en Huejutla, Hidalgo, 1920–1940," in Nicolás Cárdenas García and Enrique Guerra Manzo, eds., *Integrados y marginados en el México posrevolucionario. Los juegos del poder local y sus nexos con la política nacional* (Universidad Autónoma Metropolitana, 2009), 184.
43. Ben Fallaw, *Cárdenas Compromised: The Failure of Reform in Postrevolutionary Yucatán* (Duke University Press, 2001), 12.
44. Cárdenas, *Apuntes 1913/1940*, 272.
45. Wolfe, *Watering the Revolution*, 96.
46. Fallaw, *Cárdenas Compromised*, 97–157.
47. Brenner, *The Wind That Swept Mexico*, 88.
48. Alan Knight, "The Rise and Fall of Cardeniso, c.1930–c.1946" in Bethell, ed., *Mexico Since Independence*, 256–272.

49. Roger J. Bergeret Muñoz et al., "Evolución y mutación del modelo turístico de Guerrero. Caso Acapulco 1945–2000," in Tomás Bustamante Alvarez and Sergio Sarmiento Silva, eds., *El sur en movimiento. La reinvención de Guerrero del siglo XXI* (Consejo de Ciencia y Tecnología del Estado de Guerrero, 2001), 495.
50. Marett, *An Eye-Witness of* Mexico, 152.
51. Manuel Gamio, *Arqueología e indigenismo* (Secretaría de Educación Pública, 1972), 123; Gamio, *Forjando Patria*, 33, 170, 6
52. Rick A. López, *Crafting Mexico: Intellectuals, Artisans, and the State after the Revolution* (Duke University Press, 2010), 100; Heidi Zogbaum, *B. Traven: A Vision of Mexico* (Rowman & Littlefield, 1992), 116.
53. Carleton Beals, *Mexican Maze* (J. B. Lippincott, 1931), 118–119.
54. Rick A. López, "The India Bonita Contest of 1921 and the Ethnicization of Mexican National Culture," *Hispanic American Historical Review* 82, no. 2 (2002), 291–328.
55. Guillermo Bonfil Batalla, "Del indigenismo de la revolución a la antropología crítica," in *Obras escogidas* (Instituto Nacional de Antropología e Historia: 1995 [1970]), 296–297, 519.
56. Gamio, *Forjando Patria*, 12–20; Pablo Yankelevich, *Los otros. Raza, normas y corrupción en la gestión de la extranjería en México, 1900–1950* (Bonilla Artigas Editores), 100–117.
57. Gamio, *Forjando patria*, 28, 325; José Vasconcelos, *La raza cósmica* (Buenos Aires: 1948 [1925]), 25, 28, 32, 53.
58. Guillermo de la Peña, "The End of Revolutionary Anthropology: Notes on *indigenismo*," in Paul Gillingham and Benjamin T. Smith, eds., *Dictablanda: Politics, Work, and Culture in Mexico, 1938–1968* (Duke University Press, 2014), 280–283.
59. "Normas dadas por el Excmo. Sr. Arzobispo de México," 1935, Secretaría de Educación Pública DGEP caja 1394 ant. 255 exp. 7.
60. Jorge Mora Forero, "Los maestros y la práctica de la educación socialista," *Historia Mexicana* 29, no. 1 (July–September, 1979): 133–139.
61. Luis González y González, *Pueblo en vilo. Una microhistoria de San José de Gracia* (Colegio de México, 1995).
62. Paul Gillingham, "Ambiguous Missionaries: Rural Teachers and State Façades in Guerrero, 1930–1950," *Mexican Studies/Estudios Mexicanos* 22, no. 2 (Summer 2006): 340.
63. Anne Rubenstein, *Bad Language, Naked Ladies and Other Threats to the Nation* (Duke University Press, 1998), 87; Samuel Brunk, "Remembering Emiliano Zapata: Three Moments in the Posthumous Career of the Martyr of Chinameca," *Hispanic American Historical Review* 78, no. 3 (August 1998): 471–472.
64. Gema Kloppe-Santamaría, *In the Vortex of Violence: Lynching, Extralegal Justice, and the State in Post-Revolutionary Mexico* (University of California Press, 2020), 129, 50–55; Judith Friedlander, *Being Indian in Hueyapan: A Study of Forced Identity in Modern Mexico* (St. Martin's Press, 1975), 145–146.
65. Friedlander, *Being Indian*, 7; Stephen E. Lewis, *The Ambivalent Revolution: Forging State and Nation in Chiapas, 1910–1945* (University of New Mexico Press, 2005), 108.
66. Manuel Hidalgo to Bonilla, May 15, 1935, SEP DGEP caja 1336 ant. 196 exp. 9.
67. Aguayo, *La charola*, digital ed. 386; Gabriela Cano, "Unconcealable Realities of Desire: Amelio Robles's (Transgender) Masculinity," in Jocelyn Olcott et al., eds., *Sex in Revolution: Gender, Politics, and Power in Modern Mexico* (Duke University Press, 2006), 35–56; Ríos Thivol to Gobernación, September 26, 1947, AGN/DGIPS-84/MRT.
68. Katz, *Villa*, 628.
69. Rockwell, "Schools of the Revolution," 203.

70. Paxman, *Jenkins of Mexico*, 142; Andrew Grant Wood, "'The Proletarian Women Will Make the Social Revolution': Female Participation in the Veracruz Rent Strike, 1922–1927"; Stephanie Schell, "Por la liberación de la mujer: Women and the Anti-Alcohol Campaign," both in Stephanie Mitchell and Patience A. Schell, eds., *The Women's Revolution in Mexico, 1910–1953* (Rowman & Littlefield, 2007), 151–164, 169.
71. Jocelyn Olcott, *Revolutionary Women in Postrevolutionary Mexico* (Duke University Press, 2005), 237–238.
72. Schell, "Por la liberación de la mujer," 181; Tasas de criminalidad por 100,000 habitantes, fuero común y federal, EUM 1926–2001, http://www.columbia.edu/~pp143/estadisticascrimen/EstadisticasSigloXX.htm; Edgar Pavía Guzmán, in discussion with the author, Chilpancingo, April 4 and 5, 2002.
73. Dulles, *Yesterday in Mexico*, 620–621.
74. Olcott, *Revolutionary Women*, 166–169.
75. Carmen Ramos Escandón, "Women and Power in Mexico: The Forgotten Heritage, 1880–1954," in Victoria E. Rodríguez, ed., *Women's Participation in Mexican Political Life* (University of Texas Press, 1998), 87–102.
76. María Teresa Fernández Aceves, "Advocate or Cacica? Guadalupe Urzua Flores: Modernizer and Peasant Political Leader in Jalisco," in Gillingham and Smith, *Dictablanda*, 253.
77. Gillingham "Ambiguous Missionaries," 332.
78. Gruening, *Mexico and Its Heritage*, 349–350.
79. Aurora Gómez-Galvarriato, *Industry and Revolution: Social and Economic Change in the Orizaba Valley, Mexico* (Harvard University Press, 2013), 198–199; Pablo Piccato, *City of Suspects: Crime in Mexico City, 1900–1931* (Duke University Press, 2001, 206–207.
80. Barry Carr, *La izquierda mexicana a través del siglo XX* (Ediciones Era, 1996), 56–59.
81. J. W. Wilkie, *The Mexican Revolution: Federal Expenditure and Social Change since 1910* (University of California Press, 1967); Alan Knight, "Cardenismo: Juggernaut or Jalopy?," *Journal of Latin American Studies* 26, no. 1 (February 1994): 86.
82. Arnaldo Córdova, *La política de masas del cardenismo* (Serie Popular Era, 1974), 84–90.
83. Robert F. Alegre, *Railroad Radicals in Cold War Mexico: Gender, Class, and Memory* (University of Nebraska Press, 2014), 36; Córdova, *La política de masas*, 84.
84. Carr, *La izquierda mexicana*, 108–113.
85. Jeffrey Bortz, *Los salaries industriales en la Ciudad de México, 1939–1975* (Fondo de Cultura Económica, 1988), 270.
86. Mary R. Goldsmith Connelly, "Espacios laborales y sindicalización de las mujeres en los márgenes del poder. Las trabajadoras domésticas en Tampico y Ciudad Madero, 1929–1944," in Cárdenas García and Guerra Manzo, *Integrados y marginados*, 262–263.
87. The ensuing narrative is based on Ivonne Carillo Dewar, *Industria Petrolera y Desarrollo Capitalista en el Norte de Veracruz, 1900–1990* (Universidad Veracruzana, 1993), 21–35; Isela Myrna Santiago, "Huasteca Crude: Indians, Ecology, and Labor in the Mexican Oil Industry, Northern Veracruz, 1900–1938" (PhD diss., University of California, Berkeley 1997), 51–113.
88. Knight, "Cardenismo: Juggernaut or Jalopy?," 91.
89. Ceballos Garibay, *Francisco J. Múgica*, 197.
90. Knight, "The Rise and Fall of Cardenismo, c.1930 – c.1946," 279–282.
91. Cárdenas, *Apuntes 1913/1940*, 390–391.
92. Quoted in Alan Knight, "The Politics of the Expropriation," in Jonathan C. Brown & Alan Knight, *The Mexican Petroleum Industry in the Twentieth Century* (Austin: University of Texas Press, 1992), 104.

93. Marett, *An Eye-Witness of Mexico*, 187, 225–229.
94. Ibid., 250.
95. Cárdenas, *Apuntes 1913/1940*, 390.
96. *El Nacional*, March 20, 1938.
97. Graham Greene, *The Lawless Roads* (Penguin, 1982 [1939]), 58.
98. Elena Jackson Albarrán, *Seen and Heard in Mexico: Children and Revolutionary Cultural Nationalism* (University of Nebraska Press, 2014), 319–320.
99. Christy Thornton, *Revolution in Development: Mexico and the Governance of the Global Economy* (University of California, 2021), 40–41, 56–60; Jean Meyer, "Mexico: Revolution and Reconstruction," 212; Amelia Kiddle, *Mexico's Relations with Latin America during the Cárdenas Era* (University of New Mexico Press, 2016), 16; Zoraida Vázquez and Meyer, *México frente a Estados Unidos*, 162.
100. Kiddle, *Mexico's Relations with Latin America*, 3, 77, 99; Robert Whitney, "The Architect of the Modern State: Fulgencio Batista and Populism in Cuba, 1937–1940," *Journal of Latin American Studies* 32, no. 2 (May 2000): 454.
101. Confidential Documents of the State Department Relating to Mexico: Internal Affairs, 1930–1939, microfilm roll 32, 812.113/10948.
102. John Gunther, "Notes on Fifth Column," University of Chicago Library Special Collections, The John Gunther papers, 1935–1967, Box 17, Folder 15.
103. Inspector PS-1 to Gobernación, 8 May 1939, AGN/DGIPS-127/2–1/266.7(727.1)1
104. Tanalís Padilla, "Rural Education, Political Radicalism, and *Normalista* Identity in Mexico after 1940," in Gillingham and Smith, *Dictablanda*, 343.
105. Alan Knight, "The End of the Mexican Revolution? From Cárdenas to Avila Camacho, 1937–1941," in Gillingham and Smith, *Dictablanda*, 63.
106. James Dunkerley, "The Bolivian Revolution at 60: Politics and Historiography," *Journal of Latin American Studies* 45, no. 2 (May 2013): 325–350

Chapter Seventeen

1. Massimo Livi–Bacci, *A Concise History of World Population* (Oxford University Press, 2007), 102.
2. Paul Gillingham, "Mexican Elections, 1910–1994: Voters, Violence, and Veto Power," in Roderic Ai Camp, ed., *The Oxford Handbook of Mexican Politics* (Oxford University Press, 2011), 54.
3. US State Department, "Comments Upon the Report of the OSS Concerning the Sinarquista Movement in Mexico," August 15, 1943, NARG–812.00/32185.
4. Gonzalo N. Santos, *Memorias* (Grijalbo, 1984), 647; Bateman to Attlee, "Leading Personalities in Mexico, 1946": National Archives, London, Public Record Office, Foreign Office (hereafter PRO FO), FO 371/60955.
5. PS-10 to Gobernación, 18/07/1940, AGN/DGIPS-173/311(7.2)1; PS-2 to Gobernación, 03/03/1940, AGN/DGIPS-78/5; PS-50 Orizaba to Gobernación, 10/03/1940, AGN /DGIPS-140/9; Santos, *Memorias*, 723.
6. Paul Gillingham, "Maximino's Bulls: Popular Protest after the Mexican Revolution," *Past & Present* 206 (February 2010), 145, 151–155.
7. Halbert Jones, *The War Has Brought Peace to Mexico: World War II and the Consolidation of the Post-Revolutionary State* (University of New Mexico Press, 2014), 62–81; Juan Alberto Cedillo, *Los Nazis en México* (De Bolsillo, 2017), 14–15, 35–39.
8. Quoted in Alberto J. Pani, *El retroceso democrático del nuevo regimen* (A. J. Pani, 1947), 10.

9. US State Department, "Comments Upon the Report of the OSS"; Gunther, "Notes on Fifth Column," University of Chicago Library Special Collections, The John Gunther papers, 1935–1967, Box 17, Folder 15.
10. Gillingham, "Maximino's Bulls," 145–181.
11. Paul Friedrich, *Princes of Naranja: An Essay in Anthrohistorical Method* (University of Texas Press, 1986), 23.
12. Susana Glantz, *El ejido colectivo de Nueva Italia* (Instituto Nacional de Antropología e Historia, 1974), 121; Moisés T. de la Peña, *Veracruz Económico*, 2 vols., (Gobierno del Estado de Veracruz, 1946), 1:317–318.
13. Kevin Middlebrook, *The Paradox of Revolution: Labor, the State, and Authoritarianism in Mexico* (Johns Hopkins University Press, 1995), 171.
14. Annual report for Mexico 1944, January 22, 1945, FO371/44478; Daniel Newcomer, *Reconciling Modernity: Urban State Formation in 1940s León, Mexico* (University of Nebraska Press, 2004), 143.
15. Declaration of Principles, in various authors, *Historia Documental del Partido de la Revolución*, vol. 5: *PRM–PRI, 1945–1950* (Partido Revolucionario Institucional, 1982), 254; *El Nacional*, January 21, 1946.
16. Ashley Black, "The Politics of Asylum: Caribbean Revolutionaries, Humanitarianism, and Foreign Policy in Mexico, 1944–1961" (PhD diss., Stony Brook University, 2018), 60.
17. Enrique Krauze, *La presidencia imperial. Ascenso y caida del sistema político mexicano (1940–1996)* (Tusquets Editores, 1997), 88.
18. Santos, *Memorias*, 650; Erasmo Hernández Garcia, "Redes políticas y sociales. Consolidación y permanencia del régimen posrevolucionario in Veracruz, 1920–1970" (Ph.D. diss., Universidad Veracruzana, 2010), 150–151.
19. *Diario de Xalapa*, August 15, 1948.
20. Washington to State Department, June 7, 1948, NARG–812.00/6–748.
21. Rodolfo Usigli, "El caso de 'El Gesticulador,'" in Rodolfo Usigli, *Teatro Completo*, 4 vols. (Fondo de Cultura Económica, 1996–1997), 2:54; "Gaceta de Clausura sobre 'EI Gesticulador,'" 3:552.
22. Benjamin T. Smith, *The Mexican Press and Civil Society, 1940–1976: Stories from the Newsroom, Stories from the Street* (University of North Carolina Press, 2018), 110–111.
23. Ibid., 109–111; *El Universal*, July 4, 1950.
24. Paul Gillingham, "'We Don't Have Arms, but We Do Have Balls': Fraud, Violence, and Popular Agency in Elections," in Paul Gillingham and Benjamin T. Smith, eds., *Dictablanda: Politics, Work, and Culture in Mexico, 1938–1968* (Duke University Press, 2014), 149–172.
25. Gillingham, *Unrevolutionary Mexico*, 134–160.
26. Carlos Martínez Assad, *El henriquismo, una piedra en el camino*, Colección Memoria y olvido (Martín Casillas Editores, 1982), 19, 58–60.
27. Mizayawa to De la Fuente, January 18, 1952, Archivo General de la Nación, México DF, DFS–Guerrero–100—10–14–51H219L4; *El Universal*, July 8, 1952; Assorted reports, November 16, 1952, Archivo General de la Nación, México DF, DGIPS–104/2–1/131/1062; Salvador Novo, "Poza Rica," in Martha Poblett Miranda, ed., *Cien viajeros en Veracruz. Crónicas y relatos* (Gobierno del Estado de Veracruz, 1992), 11:194; Joy Langston, "Breaking Out Is Hard to Do: Exit, Voice, and Loyalty in Mexico's One-Party Hegemonic Regime," *Latin American Politics and Society* 44, no. 3 (2002): 71.
28. Garran to Foreign Office, January 25, 1963, FCO371/AM1915/13.

29. Gabriel A. Almond and Sidney Verba, *The Civic Culture: Political Attitude and Democracy in Five Nations* (SAGE Publications, 1989), 54.
30. Benjamin T. Smith, "Who Governed? Grassroots Politics in Mexico under the Partido Revolucionario Institucional, 1958–1970" in Past and Present 225 (Nov., 2014), 241, 253.
31. Gillingham, *Unrevolutionary Mexico*, 151–152.
32. Enrique Krauze, *Mexico, Biography of Power: A History of Modern Mexico, 1810–1996* (HarperCollins, 1997), 606.
33. Taylor to Foreign Office, October 25, 1951, FO 371/90820/AM1015/8.
34. Gillingham, *Unrevolutionary Mexico*, 245–273.
35. Ibid., 262–266.
36. Inspector no. 37 to Ortega Peregrino, August 5, 1948, AGN/DGIPS–111/2–1/260/82.
37. Carlos Alatorre Blanco et al., "Proclama a la Nación," September 1, 1948, AGN/DGIPS –115/2–1/263.6/7.
38. Gillingham, *Unrevolutionary Mexico*, 267–269; Report, December 11, 1952, AGN/DGIPS –104/2–1/131/1062.
39. *Diario de Xalapa*, April 9–15, 1950.
40. http://www.columbia.edu/~pp143/estadisticascrimen/EstadisticasSigloXX.htm
41. Christy Thornton, *Revolution in Development: Mexico and the Governance of the Global Economy* (University of California Press, 2021), 222–226.
42. María Antonia Martínez, *El despegue constructivo de la Revolución. Sociedad y política en el alemanismo* (México: CIESAS, Porrúa, 2004), 50–52, 57, 89.
43. Inflation-adjusted. *Montevideo-Oxford Latin American Economic History Database* (MOXLAD), http://moxlad.cienciassociales.edu.uy/.
44. GE advertisement, *Impacto*, August 5, 1950.
45. Oscar Lewis, *The Children of Sánchez: Autobiography of a Mexican Family* (Vintage Books, 1963), 93–95.
46. Andrew Paxman, *Jenkins of Mexico: How a Southern Farm Boy Became a Mexican Magnate* (Oxford University Press, 2017), 272, 298, 250.
47. María Félix, *Todas mis guerras* (Editorial Clío, 1993), 199.
48. *El Nacional*, October 3, 1950.
49. Bateman to Bevin, January 21, 1947, PRO FO371/60940.
50. *Novedades*, September 2, 1952.
51. Michael Snodgrass, "The Golden Age of Charrismo: Workers, Braceros, and the Political Machinery of Post-Revolutionary Mexico," in Gillingham and Smith, *Dictablanda*, 176–177.
52. *Novedades*, April 20, 1951.
53. *Excélsior*, September 2, 1952.
54. Frank Cancian, *The Decline of Community in Zinacantán: Economy, Public Life, and Social Stratification, 1960–1987* (Stanford University Press, 1992), 171–210.
55. Luis González y González, *Pueblo en vilo. Una microhistoria de San José de Gracia*, 257–292.
56. Jocelyn Olcott, *Revolutionary Women in Postrevolutionary Mexico* (Duke University Press, 2005), 120, 225; *Estadísticas Históricas de México* (Instituto Nacional de Estadística y Geografía, 2000), 58.
57. Gillingham, *Unrevolutionary Mexico*, 204–211.
58. Jefe del depto de control de comunicaciones SCOP to presidency, wire transcript, Sra. María to General Robles, December 10, 1945, Fundación Miguel Alemán Velasco Exp. 632.

59. Benjamin T. Smith, "The Rise and Fall of Narcopopulism: Drugs, Politics, and Society in Sinaloa, 1930–1980," *Jounral for the Study of Radicalism* 7, no. 2 (2013): 137–138.
60. Ricardo de la Garza y Garza, Memorandum, April 23, 1953, AGN / DFS–VP Eucario León.
61. Guzmán Carriles to Avila Camacho, December 12, 1942, AGN / DGG–2 / 311P(26)2 / 107; *La Verdad*, 06 / 10 / 1949.
62. Statement of Manuel Vázquez, May 23, 1940, AGN / DGG–2 / 380(9) / 20 / 35; "Salario medio pagado a la semana," *Estadísticas históricas de México*, 180–181.
63. Susan Gauss, *Made in Mexico: Regions, Nation, and the State in the Rise of Mexican Industrialism, 1920s–1940s* (Penn State University Press, 2010), 199, 204.
64. Foreign Office, "Further correspondence respecting Mexico Part 6, January to December 1952," 13, 17.
65. *Excélsior*, August 5, 1959.
66. Luis Barrón "La construcción del cargo público," symposium paper, CIDE / University of Warwick / AHRC, November 2017.
67. Almond and Verba, *The Civic Culture*, 39; raw data for the same study, revised ICPR edition, available online, https: / / escholarship.org / uc / item / 4mm1285j, accessed February 1, 2024.
68. 4,400,000 of 7,400,000. Susana Sosenski Correa, "El niño consumidor. Una construcción publicitaria de la prensa mexicana en la década de 1950," in Ariadna Acevedo Rodrigo and Paul López Caballero, eds., *Ciudadanos inesperados: espacios de formación de la ciudadanía ayer y hoy* (Colegio de México, 2012), 195.
69. "'Cooling to Cinema and Warming to Television': State Mass Media Policy, 1940–1964" in Gillingham & Smith, *Dictablanda*, 313–314; Paxman, *Jenkins of Mexico*, 272, 296; *Proceso* 15 May 1982.
70. *Novedades* April 20, 1951.
71. Rath, *Myths of Demilitarization*, 84–85.
72. Gillingham, *Unrevolutionary Mexico*, ch. 9.
73. Ibid., 239–240.
74. Laurence Whitehead, "On Presidential Graft: The Latin American Evidence," in Michael Clarke, ed., *Corruption: Causes, Consequences and Control* (Pinter, 1983), 150.
75. Krauze, *Mexico*, 601–605; Eric Zolov, *The Last Good Neighbor: Mexico in the Global Sixties* (Duke University Press, 2020), 25.
76. Abel Quezada in *Ovaciones*, January 26, 1953.
77. *Información sobre información. En este número: minimos de bienestar salud y seguridad social* (Secretaría de programación y presupuesto, 1978), 16.
78. Various authors, *Historia Documental del Partido de la Revolución*, vol. 7, *PRM–PRI, 1945–1950* (Partido Revolucionario Institucional, 1982), 61–67.
79. Private secretary to Secretario de Defensa Nacional, quoted in Rath, *Myths of Demilitarization*, 117.
80. Jaime M. Pensado, *Rebel Mexico: Student Unrest and Authoritarian Political Culture During the Long Sixties* (Stanford University Press, 2013), 106–115.
81. Memorandum, Dir. DFS Castillo Venegas, August 19, 1955, AGN / DFS–VP Alemán Velasco, Miguel, tomo 1 11.
82. Krauze, *Mexico*, 628–629, 664.
83. Almond and Verba, *The Civic Culture*, 39.
84. Christy Thornton, *Revolution in Development: Mexico and the Governance of the Global Economy* (University of California Press, 2021), 124–142.

85. Lewis, *The Children of Sánchez*, 338.
86. Oscar Altamirano, in discusión with the author, Mexico City, March 1998.
87. Rosemary Thorp, *Progress, Poverty and Exclusion: An Economic History of Latin America in the 20th Century* (Baltimore, MD: John Hopkins University Press, 1998), 28, 352.
88. Lewis, *The Children of Sánchez*, 77, 119, 343.
89. Tanalís Padilla, *Rural Resistance in the Land of Zapata: The Jaramillista Movement and the Myth of the Pax Prïsta, 1940–1962* (Duke University Press, 2008), ch. 2.
90. Guillermo de la Peña, "'The End of Revolutionary Anthropology?' Notes on *Indigenismo*," in Gillingham and Smith, *Dictablanda*, 279–298.
91. Warman, *Venimos a contradecir*, 172; Daniel Cosío Villegas, *Memorias* (J. Moritz, 1976), 199.
92. Across the course of the twentieth century. Daniel Immerwahr, *Thinking Small: The United States and the Lure of Community Development* (Harvard University Press, 2015), 41.
93. INEGI *Estadísticas Históricas de México* CD-ROM.
94. Michael Snodgrass, "The Golden Age of Charrismo: Workers, Braceros, and the Political Machinery of Post-Revolutionary Mexico," in Gillingham and Smith, *Dictablanda*, 182; Mexlight employees got 100 kwh per month free. Camilo Ruiz Tassinari, in discussion with the author, Chicago 2024.
95. Foreign and Commonwealth Office, further correspondence respecting Mexico, Part 6, January to December 1952, 13, 17.
96. Egon Kisch, "Los indios de la vainilla," in Poblett Miranda, *Cien viajeros en Veracruz*, 9:251.
97. Renata Keller, *Mexico's Cold War: Cuba, the United States, and the Legacy of the Mexican Revolution* (Cambridge University Press, 2015), 73–74, 156–165, 192–195; Stephen G. Rabe, *The Killing Zone: The United States Wages Cold War in Latin America* (Oxford University Press, 2016), 116; Rafael Bernal, *El Complot Mongol* (Grupo Planeta, 2013), 195–142; Zolov, *The Last Good Neighbor*, 63–79.
98. Dwyer, Mérida, to State, February 28, 1963, NARG microfilm 63–66, reel 3.
99. For critical memoirs of former CIA officers re Latin America, see Victor Marchetti and John D. Marks, *The CIA and the Cult of Intelligence* (Alfred A. Knopf, 1974); William Colby, *Honorable Men: My Life in the CIA* (Simon & Schuster, 1978); Philip Agee, *Inside the Company: CIA Diary* (Farrar, Straus and Giroux, 1975). The genre also extends to Asia and Africa. In 1975 the Senate's Church Committee on Intelligence eviscerated the CIA's record in Latin America; in 1995 Daniel Patrick Moynihan introduced a Senate bill called the Abolition of the Central Intelligence Agency Act, arguing that the agency repeatedly failed due to its cult of secrecy and that the State Department was better at the job of intelligence-gathering.
100. State Department to Embassy Mexico, October 7, 1968, National Archives, RG 59, 1967–69, Politics 13–2 Mexico, Box 2340.
101. José Luis Piñeyro, "Las fuerzas armadas y la guerrilla rural en México. Pasado y presente," in Verónica Oikión Solano and Marta Eugenia García Ugarte, eds., *Movimientos armados en México, siglo XX* (Colegio de Michoacán, 2008), 1:71.
102. American Embassy Mexico to State, September 2 1966, NARG microfilm 63–66, reel 1.
103. Mónica Serrano, "The Armed Branch of the State: Civil-Military Relations in Mexico," *Journal of Latin American Studies* 27, no. 2 (May 1995): 422–448.
104. Dwyer, Mérida, to State, February 28, 1963, NARG microfilm 63–66, reel 3.
105. Christopher Andrew and Vasili Mitrokhin, *The World Was Going Our Way: The KGB and the Battle for the Third World* (Basic Books, 2006), 27, xxvi, 4–5, 9–11, 41–43, 53.

106. Anne Rubenstein, "Bodies, Cities, Cinema: Pedro Infante's Death as Political Spectacle," in Gilbert M. Joseph et al., eds, *Fragments of a Golden Age: The Politics of Culture in Mexico Since 1940* (Duke University Press, 2001), 206–207.
107. The Beatles Bible, https://www.beatlesbible.com/discography/mexico/.
108. Poster for *5 de chocolate y 1 de fresa*, directed by Carlos Velo, (AM Libra, 1968), kindly provided by Olivia Consentino.
109. Elena Poniatowska, *La noche de Tlatelolco. Testimonios de historia oral* (Biblioteca Era, 1999 [1971]), 23.
110. Héctor de Mauleón, *La ciudad que nos inventa. Crónicas de seis siglos* (Cal y Arena, 2015), 332.
111. Gabriel García Márquez, *Vivir para Contarla* (Pamplona: Ediciones Leer-e, 2015), 258–259.
112. Claudia Fernández and Andrew Paxman, *El Tigre: Emilio Azcárraga y su imperio de Televisa* (Grijalbo, 2000), 21.
113. Juan Orbe, "An Intellectual Biography of Octavio Paz: Conversation with Enrico Mario Santí," *Centennial Review* 36, no. 3 (Fall 1992): 548.
114. Patrick Iber, *Neither Peace nor Freedom: The Cultural Cold War in Latin America* (Harvard University Press, 2015), 111–114, 186–188.
115. Carlos Fuentes, "Un día en la tierra de Zapata," *La Cultura en México. Suplemento de Siempre!* July 11 1962.
116. *Excélsior*, November 19, 1965.
117. Poniatowska, *La Noche de Tlatelolco*, 68.

Chapter Eighteen

1. Cuarto Informe de Gobierno del Presidente Luis Echeverría, September 1 1974, https://cede.izt.uam.mx/index.php/informes-presidenciales/
2. Gustavo A. Hirales Morán, *México, ajustando cuentas con la historia (justicia transicional fallida)* (México: Comisión Nacional de los Derechos Humanos, 2017), 145, 147, 151.
3. Jacinto Rodríguez Munguía, "The Invisible Tyranny, or, The Origin of the Perfect Dictatorship," in Paul Gillingham, et al., *Journalism, Satire, and Censorship in Mexico* (University of New Mexico Press, 2017), 191–192.
4. Cuenca Díaz to Comdte. 35ª zona militar, 1971, reproduced in *El Universal*, August 16, 2015.
5. Jorge Luis Sierra, "Fuerzas armadas y contrainsurgencia (1965–1982)," in Verónica Oikión Solano and Marta Eugenia García Ugarte, eds., *Movimientos armados en México, siglo XX* (Colegio de Michoacán, 2008), 380.
6. Memo, Capt. Fernando Gutiérrez Barrios, DFS, AGN/DGIPS–1280/119.
7. Jaime M. Pensado, *Rebel Mexico: Student Unrest and Authoritarian Political Culture During the Long Sixties* (Stanford University Press, 2013), 100–128; Sergio Aguayo, *La Charola. Una historia de los servicios de inteligencia en México* (Raya en el agua, 2001), digital ed. 1890.
8. Elena Poniatowska, *La noche de Tlatelolco. Testimonios de historia oral* (Biblioteca Era, 1999 [1971]), 27.
9. "Les évènements du mai 1968," in Encyclopédie Larousse online, https://www.larousse.fr/encyclopedie/divers/ percentc3 percenta9v percentc3 percenta9nements_de_mai_1968/131140, accessed March 2, 2024.
10. Poniatowska, *La noche de Tlatelolco*, 21.
11. Fiscalía Especial para Movimientos Sociales y Políticos del Pasado (FEMOSPP), *Informe Histórico a la Sociedad Mexicana* (México: Comisión Nacional de los Derechos Humanos, 2006), 119–120.

12. Alfonso Corona del Rosa, *Mis memorias políticas* (Grijalbo, 1995), 270–273.
13. Aguayo, *La Charola*, digital ed. 2154, 1467.
14. FEMOSPP, *Informe Histórico*, 123.
15. Aguayo, *La Charola*, digital ed. 2188. An overreaching court case against Echeverría was launched in 2006; in 2009 he was absolved.
16. FEMOSPP, *Informe Histórico*, 119–139; Poniatowska, *La noche de Tlatelolco*, 168.
17. Eyewitness reports of night in general, see Poniatowska, *La noche de Tlatelolco*, 160–274; on bayonets, 225; students and vecinos shooting back, 231–214; quote, José Luis Mejías, "Mítin trágico," *Diario de la Tarde*, October 5, 1968, 201.
18. Poniatowska, *La noche de Tlatelolco*, 171, 190.
19. FEMOSPP, *Informe Histórico*, 144, 139–140.
20. Jaime M. Pensado, *Love and Despair: How Catholic Activism Shaped Politics and the Counterculture in Modern Mexico* (University of California Press, 2023), 108–127.
21. Louise E. Walker, *Waking from the Dream: Mexico's Middle Classes after 1968* (Stanford University Press, 2013), 29; Enrique Krauze, *Mexico, Biography of Power: A History of Modern Mexico, 1810–1996* (Harper Collins, 1997), 752.
22. Alexander Aviña, *Spectres of Revolution: Peasant Guerrillas in the Mexican Cold War Countryside* (University of Oxford Press, 2014), 108.
23. Poniatowska, *La noche de Tlatelolco*, 42, 46, 48.
24. "La foto de Ernesto Zedillo durante el Movimiento de 68," *El Universal*, July 26, 2018.
25. Poniatowska, *La noche de Tlatelolco*, 236, 247–8, 199, 185–187, 256, 142, 16.
26. Sandra C. Mendiola García, *Street Democracy: Vendors, Violence and Public Space in Late Twentieth-Century Mexico* (University of Nebraska Press, 2017), 77–78.
27. Rogelio Hernández Rodríguez, *La formación del político mexicano. El caso de Carlos A. Madrazo* (Colegio de México, 1991), 28–129.
28. Rogelio Ramos Oranday, "Oposición y abstencionismo en las elecciones presidenciales, 1964–1982," in Pablo González Casanova, ed., *Las elecciones en México. Evolución y perspectiva* (Siglo XXI, 1985), 148–161, 163–194.
29. Hernández Rodríguez, *La formación del político mexicano*, 135–150; memo, DGIPS to Gobernación, March 11, 1965; Bustamante Díaz and De la Peña Hernández to DFS, March 11, 1965, AGN/DGIPS–1303/1.
30. *Excélsior*, November 19, 1965; Hernández Rodríguez, *La formación del político mexicano*, 175–199.
31. Jon Lee Anderson, *Che Guevara: A Revolutionary Life* (Grove Press, 1997), 198–200.
32. Lázaro Cárdenas, *Obras I – Apuntes 1957/1966 tomo III* (UNAM Nueva Biblioteca Mexicana, 1973), 252–258.
33. https://politicaldictionary.com/words/art-of-the-possible/
34. Cárdenas, *Obras I – Apuntes 1957/1966*, 292.
35. Renata Keller, *Mexico's Cold War: Cuba, the United States, and the Legacy of the Mexican Revolution* (Cambridge University Press, 2015), 1–2; Eric Zolov, *The Last Good Neighbor: Mexico in the Global Sixties* (Duke University Press, 2020), 187, 255–257, 259, 264–265; Hernández Rodríguez, *La formación del político mexicano*, 121.
36. Lázaro Cárdenas, *Obras I – Apuntes 1967/1970*, 100–102; Zolov, *The Last Good Neighbor*, 265.
37. José Luis Piñeyro, "Las fuerzas armadas y la guerrilla rural en México: pasado y presente," in Oikión Solano and García Ugarte, *Movimientos armados en México*, 1:74.
38. Aguayo, *La Charola*, digital ed. 202, 1029, 1917, 3934, 3945.
39. David Mares, "The National Security State" in Thomas H. Holloway, ed., *A Companion to Latin American History* (Blackwell, 2011), 399.

40. Patrick Iber, *Neither Peace nor Freedom: The Cultural Cold War in Latin America* (Harvard University Press, 2015), 189.
41. Laura Castellanos, *México armado 1943–1981* (Biblioteca Era, 2007), 67; Elizabeth Henson, "Madera 1965: Primeros Vientos," in Fernando Herrera Calderón and Adela Cedillo, eds., *Challenging Authoritarianism in Mexico: Revolutionary Struggles and the Dirty War, 1964–1982* (Routledge, 2012), 19–39.
42. Aviña, *Spectres of Revolution*, 100–101, 140–147.
43. Ibid., 50–51, 92, 113–118.
44. Armando Batra, ed., *Crónicas del sur. Utopías campesinas en Guerrero* (Ediciones Era, 2000), 60.
45. Liga Acapulco to Cárdenas, February 21, 1940, AGN/DGG–2.012.2(9)/19/31; Gustavo A. Hirales Morán, *México, ajustando cuentas con la historia (justicia transicional fallida)* (México: Comisión Nacional de los Derechos Humanos, 2017), 149.
46. Aviña, *Spectres of Revolution*, 140–141.
47. Castellanos, *México armado*, 93–94.
48. Aviña, *Spectres of Revolution*, 110.
49. Fernando Herrera Calderón and Adela Cedillo, introduction to *Challenging Authoritarianism in Mexico: Revolutionary Struggles and the Dirty War, 1964–1982*, edited by Fernando Herrera Calderón and Adela Cedillo (New York: Routledge, 2012), 7.
50. Dení Prieto Stock, quoted in Macrina Cárdenas Montaño, "La participación de las mujeres en los movimientos armados," in Oikión Solano and García Ugarte, *Movimientos armados*, 2:615.
51. Pablo Piccato, *Historia minima de la violencia en México* (Colegio de México, 2022), 195–196; Aviña, *Spectres of Revolution*, 158; Aguayo, *La Charola*, digital ed. 3338–3359.
52. Lillian Guerra, *Visions of Power in Cuba: Revolution, Redemption, and Resistance, 1959–1971* (University of North Carolina Press, 2012), 37–74.
53. Karl Marx, *The Eighteenth Brumaire of Louis Bonaparte* (New York, 1926), 133.
54. Verónica Oikión Solano, "El Movimiento de Acción Revolucionaria. Una historia de radicalización política," in Oikión Solano and García Ugarte, *Movimientos armados*, 2:434–437.
55. Governor of Chihuahua General Práxedes Gíner Durán, quoted in Victor Orozco Orozco, "La guerrilla chihuahuense de los sesenta," in Oikión Solano and García Ugarte, *Movimientos armados*, 2:369; Castellanos, *México armado*, 92–94.
56. Orozco Orozco, "La guerrilla chihuahuense," 382.
57. Carlos Antonio Flores Pérez, *El Estado en crisis. Crimen organizado y política. Desafíos para la consolidación democrática* (México: CIESAS, 2009), 174–176.
58. Aguayo, *La Charola*, digital ed. 1470.
59. Hirales Morán, *México, ajustando cuentas con la historia*, 148–159.
60. Jacinto Rodríguez Munguía and José Reveles, "Cinco años de vuelos de la muerte," *Proceso*, March 11, 2024.
61. James P. Brennan, *Argentina's Missing Bones: Revisiting the History of the Dirty War* (Oakland: University of California Press, 2018), 123–146; Piccato, *Historia mínima de la violencia*, 208.
62. Partido Agrarista de Guerrero to Gobernación, July 18, 1940, PS–10 to Gobernación, July 18, 1940, AGN/DGIPS–173/311(7.2)1.
63. Quoted in Hirales Morán, *México, ajustando cuentas con la historia*, 162.
64. Piccato, *Historia mínima de la violencia*, 178.
65. Carlos I. Villanueva and Aleida García Aguirre, eds., *Memorias inquietas. De estudiantes rurales a guerrilleros urbanos* (Mexico City: Colectivo Memorias Subalternas, 2019), 41–43; Aguayo, *La Charola*, digital ed. 82–103.

66. Cárdenas Montaño, "La participación de las mujeres en los movimientos armados," 610.
67. Aviña, *Spectres of Revolution*, 79, 119; Piccato, *Historia minima de la violencia*, 174, 179.
68. Oikión Solano, "El Movimiento de Acción Revolucionaria," 437.
69. Aviña, *Spectres of Revolution*, 114.
70. Abel Quezada, "Crimen contra Todos," reproduced in Roderic Ai Camp, "The Cartoons of Abel Quezada," in Gillingham et al., *Journalism, Satire, and Censorship in Mexico*, 215.

Chapter Nineteen

1. Louise E. Walker, *Waking from the Dream: Mexico's Middle Classes after 1968* (Stanford University Press, 2013), 3, 209–216, 46, 53, 67.
2. Susan Eckstein, *The Poverty of Revolution: The State and the Urban Poor in Mexico* (Princeton University Press, 1988), 219.
3. Francisco Alba, Joseph E. Potter, "Population and Development in Mexico since 1940: An Interpretation" in *Population and Development Review*, vol. 12, No. 1 (Wiley-Blackwell, 1986), 47, 56–57.
4. Viviane Brachet Marquez, "Poverty and Social Programs in Mexico, 1970–1980: The Legacy of a Decade," *Latin American Research Review* 23, no. 1 (1988): 220–222.
5. Tanalís Padilla, *Unintended Lessons of Revolution: Student Teachers and Political Radicalism in Twentieth-Century Mexico* (Duke University Press, 2021), 205.
6. Brachet Marquez, "Poverty and Social Programs in Mexico," 221.
7. Luis Echeverría Álvarez, *Cuauhtémoc es la luminaria sin ocaso que señala el camino de México en su marcha permanente hacia horizontes de superación* (Chilpancingo: Comité Directivo Estatal del PRI, 1970), 3–8.
8. Elizabeth Henson, "Madera 1965: Primeros Vientos," in Fernando Herrera Calderón and Adela Cedillo, eds., *Challenging Authoritarianism in Mexico: Revolutionary Struggles and the Dirty War, 1964–1982* (Routledge, 2012), 19.
9. Claudia E. G. Rangel and Evangelista Sánchez Serrano, "Las guerrillas de Genaro Vázquez y Lucio Cabañas en Guerrero," in Verónica Oikión Solano and Marta Eugenia García Ugarte, eds., *Movimientos armados en México, siglo XX* (Colegio de Michoacán, 2008), 2:521–522.
10. Octavio Paz, introduction to *Quetzalcóatl y Guadalupe. La formación de la conciencia nacional en México*, by Jacques Lafaye (Fondo de Cultura Económica, 2005), 13.
11. Note in this and subsequent uses, "a billion" is short scale, i.e., a thousand million, 10 to the nine, and "a trillion" is a thousand billion, i.e., 10 to the 12. "Presupuesto de egresos del gobierno federal por ramos administrativos," Tim Merill, Ramón Miró, *Mexico: A Country Study*, (Library of Congress, 1997), 57.
12. Benjamin T. Smith, "Building a State on the Cheap: Taxation, Social Movements, and Politics," in Paul Gillingham and Benjamin T. Smith, eds., *Dictablanda: Politics, Work, and Culture in Mexico, 1938–1968* (Duke University Press, 2014), 255–275.
13. Wayne A. Cornelius, *Politics and the Urban Poor in Mexico City* (Stanford University Press, 1975), 201–234; Beatriz García Peralta, "Vivienda social en México (1940–1999): Actores públicos, económicos y sociales," *Cuadernos de Vivienda y Urbanismo* 3, no. 5 (2010): 34–49; María L. Olin Muñoz, "¡De Pie y en Lucha! Indigenous Mobilizations After 1940," in William H. Beezley, ed., *A Companion to Mexican History and Culture* (Wiley-Blackwell, 2011), 595–597; Guillermo de la Peña, "The End of Revolutionary Anthropology? Notes on Indigenismo," in Gillingham and Smith, *Dictablanda*, 290–291.

14. Francisco Alba and Joseph E. Potter, "Population and Development in Mexico since 1940: An Interpretation," *Population and Development Review* 12:1 (March 1986), 57.
15. Isabelle Rousseau, "Las nuevas élites y su Proyecto modernizador," in Elisa Servín, *Del nacionalismo al neoliberalismo, 1940–1994* (Fondo de Cultura Económica, 2010), 247–249.
16. Walker, *Waking from the Dream*, 23–24.
17. Presupuesto de egresos del gobierno federal por ramo administrativo, 1925–1979 http://datos.cide.edu/discover?scope=%2F&query=presupuesto+por+ramo&submit=
18. Agent's report to Director DFS, Jaunary 16, 1970, AGN/DFS–Scherer García Julio VP1/47/L–16.
19. Enrique Krauze, *Mexico, Biography of Power: A History of Modern Mexico, 1810–1996* (Harper Collins, 1997), 746, 742–743.
20. *Excélsior*, July 9, 2022.
21. *Excélsior*, March 24, 1973.
22. Vanessa Freije, "Censorship in the Headlines: National News and the Contradictions of Mexico City's Press Opening in the 1970s," in Paul Gillingham, et al., eds., *Journalism, Satire, and Censorship in Mexico* (University of New Mexico Press, 2017), 237–262.
23. Rogelio Hernández Rodríguez, *Historia mínima del Partido Revolucionario Institucional* (Colegio de México, 2016), 146–149.
24. Paoli Bolio, "Legislación electoral y proceso político," in Pablo González Casanova, ed., *Las elecciones en México. Revolución y perspectiva* (Siglo XXI, 1985), 152–156; Rogelio Ramos Oranday, "Oposición y abstencionismo en las elecciones presidenciales, 1964–1982," in González Casanova, *Las elecciones en México*, 163.
25. Eric Zolov, *The Last Good Neighbor: Mexico in the Global Sixties* (Duke University Press, 2020), 292–295.
26. Gabriela Soto Laveaga, "'Let's Become Fewer': Soap Operas, Contraception, and Nationalizing the Mexican Family in an Overpopulated World," in *Sexuality Research and Social Policy* 4, no. 3 (September 2007): 28; Krauze, *Mexico*, 747.
27. Felipe Cole, "When Debt Made Sovereignty, 1820–1933," (PhD diss., Northwestern University, 2023), 162–170.
28. Christy Thornton, *Revolution in Development: Mexico and the Governance of the Global Economy* (University of California Press, 2021), 267.
29. Ibid., 264–289.
30. Walker, *Waking from the Dream*, 49.
31. James M. Boughton, *The Silent Revolution: The International Monetary Fund, 1979–1989* (International Monetary Fund, 2001), 282–283.
32. Rachel Harker, *NHS Funding and Expenditure* (London: House of Commons Library, 2019), 14.
33. Sergio Aguayo, *La Charola. Una historia de los servicios de inteligencia en México* (Raya en el agua, 2001), digital ed. 3179, 3357; Instituto Nacional de Estadística y Geografía, "Presupuesto de egresos del gobierno federal por ramos administrativos," http://datos.cide.edu/
34. Benjamin T. Smith, *The Dope: The Real History of the Mexican Drug Trade* (W. W. Norton, 2021), 308–309, 320; Vanessa Freije, *Citizens of Scandal: Journalism, Secrecy, and the Politics of Reckoning* (Duke University Press, 2020), 118.
35. Krauze, *Mexico*, 758.
36. Stephen D. Morris, *Corruption and Politics in Contemporary Mexico* (University of Alabama Press, 1991), xvi.

37. Walker, *Waking from the Dream*, 77–81; Rousseau, "Las nuevas élites," 250–253; "Presupuesto de egresos del gobierno federal por ramos administrativos," Merill et al, *Mexico: A Country Study*, 57–59.
38. Rousseau, "Las nuevas élites," 250–253.
39. Rogelio Hernández Rodríguez, *El oficio político. La élite gobernante en México, (1946–2020)* (Colegio de México, 2021), 96–105.
40. Freije, *Citizens of Scandal*, 104–105; Walker, *Waking from the Dream*, 144–145.
41. Boughton, *The Silent Revolution*, 6–7.
42. Ariel Rodríguez Kuri, "Challenges, Political Opposition, Economic Disaster, Natural Disaster and Democratization," in Beezley, *A Companion to Mexican History*, 498.
43. Marlise Simons, "Mexico Turns Sleepy Port Into Industrial Boom Town," *Washington Post*, October 22, 1979.
44. Rodríguez Kuri, "Challenges," 499.
45. Quoted in Walker, *Waking from the Dream*, 79–80.
46. Boughton, *The Silent Revolution*, 282.
47. Instituto Nacional de Estadística y Geografía, "Capacidad instalada nacional para la generación de energía eléctrica 1900–1996"; "Areas beneficiadas con obras de irrigación"; "Principales características de las viviendas"; "Población derechohabiente de las instituciones de seguridad social"; "Tasas específicas de mortalidad infantil"; "Servicios de medicina preventiva otorgados por el IMSS"; "Unidades médicas y número de camas de las instituciones de seguridad social," http://datos.cide.edu/
48. Boughton, *The Silent Revolution*, 306.
49. Instituto Nacional de Estadística y Geografía, "Presupuesto en educación, 1868–1996," http://datos.cide.edu/
50. Eckstein, *The Poverty of Revolution*, 222–223.
51. Sandra C. Mendiola García, *Street Democracy: Vendors, Violence, and Public Space in Late Twentieth-Century Mexico* (University of Nebraska Press, 2017), 147–164.
52. Eckstein, *The Poverty of Revolution*.
53. Walker, *Waking from the Dream*, 111.
54. Adolfo Aguilar Zinser, "Mexico: The Presidential Problem," in *Foreign Policy* 69 (Winter 1987–1988): 44.
55. Abel Quezada, *Novedades*, June 18, 1985.
56. James L. Rowe, "IMF Cuts Off Lending to Mexico," *Washington Post*, September 20, 1985.
57. In Spanish-language accounts, *La Jornada* and *Proceso* stand out; in English, *The New York Times*. For a good recent summary of events and memories, see Eugenia Allier Montaño, "Memorias imbricadas: terremotos en México, 1985 y 2017," *Revista Mexicana de Sociología* 80, núm. especial (September 2018): 9–40.
58. Últimas Noticias de Excélsior, September 19, 1985, *Ovaciones*, September 19, 1985; Héctor de Mauleón, *La ciudad que nos inventa. Crónicas de seis siglos* (Cal y Arena, 2015), 356–359.
59. Julia Preston and Samuel Dillon, *Opening Mexico: The Making of a Democracy* (Farrar, Straus and Giroux, 2004), 95–115; Freije, *Citizens of Scandal*, 138–141.
60. Freije, *Citizens of Scandal*, 144–158.
61. Carlos Monsiváis, "La solidaridad de la población en realidad fue toma de poder," *Proceso*, September 23, 2017, 6–15; Marcos Rascón quote in Walker, *Waking from the Dream*, 195.
62. Eckstein, *The Poverty of Revolution*, 231; Walker, *Waking from the Dream*, 184–195.
63. Carlos Martínez Assad, "Las elecciones legislativas y la ilusión democrática," in González Casanova, *Las elecciones en México*, 237.

64. Eckstein, *The Poverty of Revolution*, 225.
65. Carlos Monsiváis, *Dias de Guardar* (Ediciones Era, 1970), 16.
66. Classic chilango middle-class descriptors: *precioso* (so pretty), *hermoso* (beautiful), *chido* (cool).
67. Guillermo de la Peña, "Civil Society and Popular Resistance: Mexico at the End of the Twentieth Century," in Elisa Servín et al., eds., *Cycles of Conflict, Centuries of Change: Crisis, Reform, and Revolution in Mexico* (Duke University Press, 2007), 328–329.
68. Preston and Dillon, *Opening Mexico*, 138–139.
69. Barry Carr, *La izquierda mexicana a través del siglo XX* (Ediciones Era, 1996), 308–312.
70. Hernández Rodríguez, *Historia mínima del Partido Revolucionario Institucional*, 176–179.
71. Juan Villoro, *El vértigo horizontal. Una ciudad llamada México* (Almadia, 2018), 324–331.
72. Rogelio Hernández Rodríguez, *El centro dividido. La nueva autonomía de los gobernadores* (Colegio de México, 2008), 151.
73. Alvaro Arreola Ayala, "Elecciones municipales," in González Casanova, *Las elecciones en México*, 337; Victoria Malkin, "Narcotrafficking, Migration, and Modernity in Rural Mexico," *Latin American Perspectives* 28, no. 4 (July 2001): 119.
74. Joy Langston, "Why Rules Matter: Changes in Candidate Selection in Mexico's PRI, 1988–2000," *Journal of Latin American Studies* 33, no. 3 (August 2001): 497.
75. Roderic Ai Camp, *Politics in Mexico: The Democratic Consolidation* (Oxford University Press, 1993), 149.
76. Caroline C. Beer, *Electoral Competition and Institutional Change in Mexico* (University of Notre Dame Press, 2003), 95–117.
77. Preston and Dillon, *Opening Mexico*, 114–115, 181–182.
78. José Carreño Carlón, *Excélsior* January 16, 2013.
79. Javier Garza Ramos, "Democratization and the Regional Press," in Gillingham et al., *Journalism, Satire, and Censorship in Mexico*, 268, 272–274.
80. Preston and Dillon, *Opening Mexico*, 149–180.
81. Beatriz Magaloni, *Voting for Autocracy: Hegemonic Party Survival and Its Demise in Mexico* (Cambridge University Press, 2006), 5.
82. Carr, *La izquierda mexicana*, 312; Juan Molinar Horcasitas, *El tiempo de la legitimidad. Elecciones, autoritarismo y democracia in México* (Cal y Arena, 1991), 219, 245; Jorge I. Domínguez and James A. McCann, "Shaping Mexico's Electoral Arena: The Construction of Partisan Cleavages in the 1988 and 1991 National Elections," *American Political Science Review* 89, no. 1 (1995): 34–48; Franz A. Von Sauer, "Measuring Legitimacy in Mexico: An Analysis of Public Opinion during the 1988 Presidential Campaign," *Mexican Studies/Estudios Mexicanos* 8, no. 2 (1992): 259–280.
83. Julio Labastida Martín del Campo and Martín Armando López Leyva, "México: una transición prolongada (1988–1996/7)," *Revista Mexicana de Sociología* 66, no. 4 (October–December 2004): 763.
84. Preston and Dillon, *Opening Mexico*, 171–173.
85. Labastaida Martín del Campo and López Leyva, "México: una transición prolongada," 761–766.
86. Hélène Combes, "Matar candidatos en México: El PRD en los años 90," Noria Research, June 3, 2021, https://noria-research.com/mxac/es/matar-candidatos-en-mexico-el-prd-en-los-90/#noria-3865.
87. Hernández Rodríguez, *El centro dividido*, 173–191, 121.
88. Freije, *Citizens of Scandal*, 194–195.

89. Organization for Economic Co-Operation and Development, *Economic Survey of Mexico* (Paris: OECD, 2002), 81–82.
90. Stephen Haber et al., *Mexico Since 1980* (Cambridge University Press, 2008), 96.
91. Wikipedia, "Volkswagen Tipo 1," *https://es.wikipedia.org/wiki/Volkswagen_Tipo_1#R percentC3 percentA9cord_de_producci percentC3 percentB3n*, accessed March 25, 2024.
92. "Vehículos registrados 1924–1997," http://datos.cide.edu/handle/10089/17742
93. El Fisgón and Helguera, *El sexenio me da risa* (Grijalbo, 1994), 105, 21.
94. Ibid., 108–113.
95. Haber et al., *Mexico Since 1980*, 67, 79, 92–93.
96. Barbara Bush, *Barbara Bush: A Memoir* (Simon & Schuster, 1994), 290–291.
97. El Fisgón y Helguera, *El sexenio me da risa*, 166.
98. *Washington Post*, January 2, 1994.
99. Nick Henck, *Subcommander Marcos: The Man and the Mask* (Duke University Press, 2007), 13–56.
100. Ibid., 249.
101. Marta Durán de Huerta, ed., *Yo, Marcos* (Ediciones del Milenio, 1994), 14; Subcomandante Marcos, *Shadows of Tender Fury: The Letters and Communiqués of Subcomandante Marcos and the Zapatista Army of National Liberation* (Monthly Review Press, 1995), 191–193.
102. Jan Rus, "The 'Comunidad Revolucionaria Institucional': The Subversion of Native Government in Highland Chiapas, 1936–1968," in Gilbert M. Joseph and Daniel Nugent, eds., *Everyday Forms of State Formation: Revolution and the Negotiation of Rule in Modern Mexico* (Duke University Press, 1994), 265–300.
103. As estimated by the 1990 census results for bilingual and monolingual speakers of indigenous languages. Instituto Nacional de Estadística y Geografía, "Población de 5 años y más que habla español o lengua indígena"; "Población de 10 años y más alfabeta y analfabeta por sexo y entidad federativa, 1895–1995," http://datos.cide.edu/
104. Edgardo Bermejo Mora, *Marcos Fashion: O de cómo sobrevivir al derrumbe de las ideologías sin perder el estilo* (Editorial Oceano, 1996).
105. Ana Paula Morales, "Unsolved Murder of Cardinal Posadas Is 'an Open Wound,' Mexican Bishops Say," Catholic News Agency, May 26, 2023, https://www.catholicnewsagency.com/news/254432/unsolved-murder-of-cardinal-posadas-is-an-open-wound-mexican-bishops-say, accessed March 25, 2024.
106. Fausto Salcedo, "Así fue el asesinato del Cardenal Posadas Ocampo, a 30 años de la tragedia," Informador.mx, May 24, 2023, https://www.informador.mx/jalisco/Posadas-Ocampo-Asi-fue-el-asesinato-del-Cardenal-de-Guadalajara-a-30-anos-de-la-tragedia-20230522-0077.html.
107. *La Jornada*, March 26, 1994.
108. "Discurso íntegro de Luis Donaldo Colosio aquel 6 de marzo de 1994," https://www.excelsior.com.mx/nacional/discurso-integro-colosio-6-marzo-1994/1639582, accessed March 6, 2024.
109. For a concise view of the killing and subsequent investigations see Jesús Zamora Pierce, *Ciudadano Cero: El asesinato de Luis Donaldo Colosio* (CreateSpace Independent Publishing Platform, 2014).
110. Rafael Loret de Mola, *Manos sucias. Crónicas verdaderas del poder* (Editorial Océano, 1996), 15–16.
111. José Woldenberg, *Violencia y política* (Cal y Arena, 1995), 7–8.
112. Haber et. al., *Mexico Since 1980*, 139–141.

113. Preston and Dillon, *Opening Mexico*, 301–322; *Proceso*, August 7, 1996.
114. For a good summary, see Alma Guillermoprieto, "The Riddle of Raúl," *New Yorker*, June 2, 1997, 36–47; for Paulina Castañon arrest, "Narcotráfico ronda al Clan Salinas," *Tiempo* 25 November 1995; for relationship with Alfredo Díaz Ordaz, https://www.univision.com/famosos/hija-de-alfredo-diaz-ordaz-thalia-murio-relacion; for grandfather's 1948 coup-plotting, see memoranda, 08/17/1948–08/19/1948, AGD/DGIPS-24/"militares políticos"-1948-se"; Agent 35 to Dirección Federal de Seguridad, 08/26/1948, AGN/DFS-VP Amaro, Gral Joaquín; Memorandum, 08/31/1948, AGN/DGIPS-24/3; for Citibank's lack of due diligence, breach of its own know-your-customer policy, and creation of Cayman Islands shell companies that "facilitated" money laundering, see the Government Accounting Office publication "Raúl Salinas, Citibank, and Alleged Money Laundering" (October 1998), *Washington Post*, January 21, 1999.
115. Labastida Martín del Campo and *López Leyva, "México: una transición prolongada,"* 787–798.
116. The author was in the crowd behind the parrot.
117. Hernández Rodríguez, *El centro dividido*, 151, 320.
118. *New York Times*, September 13, 1999.
119. *El Financiero*, September 11, 2017.
120. *New York Times*, June 11, 2000.
121. Haber et. al., *Mexico Since 1980*, 115–116.
122. Loret de Mola, *Manos sucias*, 15–16, 181.
123. https://mexicoaeroespacial.com.mx/2017/05/14/escoltando-al-tp-01/
124. Haber et. al., *Mexico Since 1980*, 161–200.
125. Labastida Martín del Campo and *López Leyva, "México: una transición prolongada,"* 787–798.

Chapter Twenty

1. "Statistical Portrait of the Foreign-Born Population in the United States, 2007," Pew Hispanic Center Report, March 5, 2009.
2. XII Censo General de Población y Vivienda 2000, https://www.inegi.org.mx/programas/ccpv/2000/.
3. Robert McCaa, "Missing Millions: The Demographic Costs of the Mexican Revolution," *Mexican Studies/Estudios Mexicanos* 19, no. 2 (Summer 2003): 396.
4. Moisés González Navarro, *Población y Sociedad en México (1900–1970)*, 2 vols. (Universidad Nacional Autónoma de México, 1974), 1:120–142; Miguel de la Madrid, "Miguel de la Madrid on Population Policy in Mexico," *Population and Development Review* 8, no. 2 (June 1982): 436.
5. Once this path is chosen as state policy. Only Colombia, Indonesia, and China achieved anything like Mexico's rapid fertility reduction in the last quarter of the twentieth century. Carlos Brambila, "Mexico's Population Policy and Demographic Dynamics: The Record of Three Decades," in Anrudh Jain, ed., *Do Population Policies Matter? Fertility and Politics in Egypt, India, Kenya, and Mexico* (New York: Population Council, 1998), 157; Francisco Alba and Joseph E. Potter, "Population and Development in Mexico Since 1940: An Interpretation," *Population and Development Review* 12, no. 1 (March 1988): 48.
6. Alexander von Humboldt, *Political Essay on the Kingdom of New Spain*, 2:98–110; José Gustavo González Flores, "Consecuencias demográficas de las epidemias en la Parroquia de Santa María de las Parras (1762–1815)," *Letras históricas* 18 (October 2018–January 2019): 85–88.

7. Virginia Garcí Acosta et al., *Desastres agrícolas en México. Catálogo histórico* (Fondo de Cultura Económica, 2014), 368.
8. Karl Bartolomeus Heller, *Alone in Mexico: The Astonishing Travels of Karl Heller, 1845–1848*, trans. and ed. Terry Rugeley (University of Alabama Press, 2007), 35.
9. J. K. Turner, *Barbarous Mexico* (Chicago: Charles H. Kerr, 1911).
10. León Medel y Alvarado, *Historia de San Andrés Tuxtla (1525–1975)*, 3 vols. (Xalapa, 1993–1994), 1:188–191.
11. Alan Knight and Lidia Lozano, "Guerra total: México y Europa, 1914," *Historia Mexicana*, 64, no. 4 (April–June 2015): 1591.
12. I have preferred Robert McCaa's revisionist estimates, which sharply increase mortality estimates, due to their use of (mutually reinforcing) inverse projection and cohort analysis methods, and their input of previously unavailable evidence such as US census microdata. McCaa, "Missing Millions," 368–369, 384–385, 388, 393–395.
13. José María Jaurrieta, *Seis años con el general Francisco Villa* (Fondo de Cultura Económica, 2023), 112; Martín Luis Guzmán, *El Águila y la serpiente* (Editorial Anahuac, 1949), 201–213.
14. Knight and Lozano, "Guerra total," 1605–1606.
15. Ariel Rodríguez Kurí, *Historia del desasosiego. La revolución en la ciudad de México, 1911–1922* (Colegio de México, 2010), 141–177.
16. McCaa, "Missing Millions," 379–380; Rodríguez Kurí, *Historia del desasosiego*, 140.
17. Alan Knight, *The Mexican Revolution*, vol. 2, *Counter-revolution and Reconstruction* (University of Nebraska Press, 1990), 2:20.
18. David Luke Robichaux, "Determinants of a 20th-Century Population Explosion in the Malinche Region of Tlaxcala, Mexico," *Medical Anthropology Quarterly* 6, no. 3 (September 1992): 200–201.
19. J. Guzmán Urióstegui, *Evila Franco Nájera, a pesar del olvido* (Instituto Nacional de Estudios Históricos de las Revoluciones de México, 1995), 46.
20. John Womack, *Zapata and the Mexican Revolution* (Thames & Hudson, 1968), 311; Knight, *The Mexican Revolution*, 2:422; Ryan M. Alexander, "The Spanish Flu and the Sanitary Dictatorship: Mexico's Response to the 1918 Influenza Pandemic," *The Americas* 76, no. 3 (July 2019): 444.
21. 9.2 percent of prewar population compared to 3.7 percent for Germany.
22. McCaa, "Missing Millions," 373, 397.
23. 1930–2000. Massimo Livi-Bacci, *A Concise History of World Population* (Oxford University Press, 2007), 102.
24. "Población por entidad federal" Instituto Nacional de Estadística y Geografía, *Estadísticas Históricas de México* CD-ROM (Instituto Nacional de Estadística y Geografía, 2000), cuadro 1.2.6.
25. Isela Myrna Santiago, "Huasteca Crude: Indians, Ecology, and Labor in the Mexican Oil Industry, Northern Veracruz, 1900–1938" (PhD diss., University of California, Berkeley 1997), 51–113; Paul Friedrich, *Agrarian Revolt in a Mexican Village* (University of Chicago Press, 1970), 45–46; Bernardo García Díaz, *Un pueblo fabril del Porfiriato. Santa Rosa, Veracruz* (Fondo de Cultura Económica, 1981), 28–29, 156–161.
26. The 1942 outbreak killed eight thousand people. Instituto Nacional de Estadística y Geografía, *125 años de la Dirección General de Estadística: 1882–2007* (Colección Memoria, 2010), 120; Claudia Agostoni, *Médicos, Campañas y Vacunas: La viruela y la cultura de su prevención en México, 1870–1952* (UNAM / Instituto Mora, 2016), 172.
27. Carleton Beals, *Mexican Maze* (J. B. Lippincott, 1931), 151.

28. Gabriela Recio, "Drugs and Alcohol: Prohibition and the Origins of the Drug Trade in Mexico, 1910–1930," *Journal of Latin American Studies* 34, no. 1 (February 2002): 33.
29. Marcel Anduiza, "From Pacific Gateway to Tourist City: Mobility, Revolution, and the Development of the Mexican Seaside, Acapulco, Mexico, 1849–1970," (Phd diss., University of Chicago, 2019), 472–477.
30. "Mexico: Pineapple Pioneer," *Time*, March 24, 1952.
31. Moisés González Navarro, *Población y Sociedad en México (1900–1970)*, 2 vols. (Universidad Nacional Autónoma de México, 1974), 1:49–50, 73.
32. Guillermo Bonfil Batalla, "Del indigenismo de la revolución a la antropología crítica," in *Obras escogidas* (Instituto Nacional de Antropología e Historia: 1995 [1970]), 519.
33. Dorothy Tanck de Estrada, *Atlas Ilustrado de los Pueblos de Indios* (El Colegio de México, 2005), 67; Juan Pedro Viquiera, "Reflexiones contra la noción histórica de mestizaje," *Nexos* May 1, 2010, 80.
34. Zadia M. Feliciano, "Mexico's Demographic Transition," in Michael R. Haines and Richard H. Steckel, eds., *A Population History of North America* (Cambridge University Press, 2000), 621–622; Kendra McSweeney and Shahna Arps, "A 'Demographic Turnaround': The Rapid Growth of the Indigenous Populations in Lowland Latin America," *Latin American Research Review* 40, no. 1 (2005): 3–29.
35. "First Declaration from the Lacandon Jungle, Today We Say 'Enough is Enough!' (Ya Basta!)," EZLN Command (1993), https://www.struggle.ws/mexico/ezln/ezlnwa.html.
36. González Navarro, *Población y Sociedad*, 1:74.
37. Instituto Nacional de Estadística y Geografía, *125 años de la Dirección General de Estadística: 1882–2007* (Colección Memoria, 2010), 236–237; INEGI, "Resultados preliminares del XII Censo General de Población y Vivienda 2000," press release, July 20, 2000.
38. Oscar Lewis, *The Children of Sánchez: Autobiography of a Mexican Family* (Knopf Doubleday, 1963), xvi–xvii.
39. Blanca Torres, *Hacia la utopía industrial* (Colegio de México, 1984), 44; INEGI, *Estadísticas Históricas de México* CD-ROM; Robichaux, "Determinants of a 20th-Century Population Explosion," 198.
40. Across the century more women than men migrated to Mexico City. González Navarro, *Población y sociedad*, 1:57.
41. Gabriela Soto Laveaga, "'Let's Become Fewer': Soap Operas, Contraception, and Nationalizing the Mexican Family in an Overpopulated World," *Sexuality Research and Social Policy* 4, no. 3 (September 2007): 24.
42. Alberto González, *Doña Loba, Una historia de cacicazgo y poder* (México: Penguin Random House, 2013).
43. The classic work is Wayne Cornelius, *Politics and the Migrant Poor in Mexico City* (Stanford University Press, 1975).
44. Lewis, *The Children of Sánchez*, xvi–xvii, Moisés T. de la Peña, *Veracruz económico*, 2 vols. (Gobierno del Estado de Veracruz, 1946), 1:311.
45. I.e., *cantinfleando*. Jeffrey M. Pilcher, *Cantinflas and the Chaos of Mexican Modernity* (Scholarly Resources Inc., 2001), 143.
46. Jeffrey Bortz and Marcos Aguila, "Earning a Living: A History of Real Wage Studies in Twentieth-Century Mexico," *Latin American Research Review* 41, no. 2 (2006).
47. De la Peña, *Veracruz Económico*, 1:317–318.
48. Luis Aboites Aguilar, "The Illusion of National Power: Water Infrastructure in Mexican Cities, 1930–1990," in Christopher R. Boyer, ed., *A Land Between Waters: Environmental Histories of Modern Mexico* (University of Arizona Press, 2012), 228.

49. Miguel Alemán Velasco, *Miguel Alemán contesta. Ensayos* (Austin, TX: Institute of Latin American Studies, 1975), 9.
50. Blanca Torres, *Hacia la utopía industrial*, 28, 41.
51. Adjusted for inflation. INEGI, *Estadísticas históricas de México* CD-ROM; Jeffrey H. Cohen, "Transnational Migration in Rural Oaxaca, Mexico: Dependency, Development, and the Household," *American Anthropologist* 103, no. 4 (December 2001): 957.
52. Acta, comisario municipal Severiano Ocampo, Pachivia, September 24, 1947, Archivo Municipal de Ixcateopan, AMI–1947.
53. André Burguière, "Demography," in Jacques Le Goff & Pierre Nora, (eds.), *Constructing the Past: Essays in Historical Methodology* (Cambridge University Press, 1984), 104.
54. They survived, he judged, thanks to the oft unmeasured labor of women and children. Cited in Tanalís Padilla, *Rural Resistance in the Land of Zapata: The Jaramillista Movement and the Myth of the Pax Prïsta, 1940–1962* (Duke University Press, 2008), 166.
55. Klaus Deininger and Lyn Squire, "A New Data Set Measuring Income Inequality," *World Bank Economic Review*, 10, no. 3 (September 1996): 565–591.
56. Fernando Saúl Alanís Enciso, *They Should Stay There: The Story of Mexican Migration and Repatriation During the Great Depression*, trans. Russ Davidson (University of North Carolina Press, 2017), 13.
57. Friedrich Katz, *The Life and Times of Pancho Villa* (Stanford University Press, 1998), 521.
58. Julia G. Young, *Mexican Exodus: Emigrants, Exiles, and Refugees of the Cristero War* (Oxford University Press, 2015), 42–43, 126, 50–51.
59. T. Wilson Longmore and Homer L. Hitt, "A Demographic Analysis of First and Second Generation Mexican Population of the United States: 1930," *Southwestern Social Science Quarterly* 24, no. 2 (September 1943): 138–149.
60. Robert A. Caro, *The Years of Lyndon Johnson: The Path to Power* (Vintage, 1990), 166–173.
61. Jefe del Departamiento de Migración flyer discouraging Mexicans from migrating to the United States, Mexico City, May 1929, author's collection.
62. Alanís Enciso, *They Should Stay There*, 15–16, 25–26, 169–170, 186.
63. For rural hunger, see "Report of Conditions in Mexico from August 1 to September 15, 1943," NARG–812.00/32198.
64. Poster, "Aviso a los aspirants a braceros," March 1948, AHEG ramo ejecutivo caja 53 exp sin número; report, Grupos Alemanistas' exploitation of braceros in Mexico City, September 26, 1949, AGN/DGIPS–93/2.1/131/802 Alfredo García.
65. Michael Snodgrass, "The Bracero Program, 1942–1964," in Mark Overmyer-Velásquez, ed., *Beyond la Frontera: The History of Mexico-U.S. Migration* (Oxford University Press, 2011), 79–102; "National Shame" from *Excélsior* February 1, 1954, cited 92.
66. In 1964–65, the year the program ended. INEGI, *Estadísticas Históricas de México* CD-ROM.
67. Alberto García, *Abandoning Their Beloved Land: The Politics of Bracero Migration in Mexico* (University of California Press, 2023), 121–122.
68. Ibid., 32–37.
69. Secretario de gobierno Guerrero to *presidentes municipales*, September 3, 1952, AMI 1952.
70. Cohen, "Transnational Migration in Rural Oaxaca," 957–959.
71. Lewis, *The Children of Sánchez*, 328.
72. Snodgrass, "The Bracero Program, 1942–1964," 84.
73. García, *Abandoning Their Beloved Land*, 34.
74. Lewis, *The Children of Sánchez*, 338.
75. Luis González, *Pueblo en vilo, Una microhistoria de San José de Gracia*, 280–286.

76. Cohen, "Transnational Migration in Rural Oaxaca," 957; Modesto Jaimes, in discussion with the author, Ixcateopan, Guerrero, June 2, 2002.
77. Cohen, "Transnational Migration in Rural Oaxaca," 959; Sam Quinones, *True Tales from Another Mexico: The Lynch Mob, the Popsicle Kings, Chalino and the Bronx* (University of New Mexico Press, 2001), 117–136.
78. *New York Times*, August 4, 2006.
79. Cohen, "Transnational Migration in Rural Oaxaca," 964.
80. Snodgrass, "The Bracero Program, 1942–1964," 89.
81. Proceeds went to women's health services. Gustavo Cabrera, "Demographic Dynamics and Development: The Role of Population Policy in Mexico," in *Population and Development Review* 20:Supplement, 109; Michael A. Ervin, "Marte R. Gómez of Tamaulipas: Governing Agrarian Revolution," in Jürgen Buchenau and William Beezley, eds., *State Governors of the Mexican Revolution, 1910–1952: Portraits in Conflict, Corruption, and Courage* (Rowman & Littlefield, 2009), 127–128.
82. González Navarro, *Población y sociedad*, 1:120–121.
83. In the schematic terms in which the IWY has been represented, delegates from the North were concerned with issues of sex workers, sexual identity, and reproductive freedom, while delegates from the South were more concerned with economic issues. Jocelyn Olcott, "Cold War Conflicts and Cheap Cabaret: Sexual Politics at the 1975 UN International Women's Year Conference" (paper delivered at the New York City Latin American History Workshop, 2010); Joseph E. Potter and Axel I. Mundigo, "Fertility Planning," in Dudley L. Poston and Michael Micklin, eds., *Handbook of Population* (Springer 2005), 750–751.
84. Gabriela Soto Laveaga, "'Let's Become Fewer': Soap Operas, Contraception, and Nationalizing the Mexican Family in an Overpopulated World," *Sexuality Research and Social Policy* 4, no. 3 (September 2007): 19, 22, 28, 30.
85. González Navarro, *Población y sociedad*, 1:142.
86. Robert Buffington, *A Sentimental Education for the Working Man: The Mexico City Penny Press, 1900–1910* (Duke University Press, 2015), 155.
87. Soto Laveaga, "Let's Become Fewer," 9.
88. González y González, *Pueblo en vilo*, 311–312.
89. Brambila, "Mexico's Population Policy and Demographic Dynamics," 157.
90. Soto Laveaga, "Let's Become Fewer," 27.
91. Cited in Alfred W. Crosby, *The Columbian Exchange: Biological and Cultural Consequences of 1492* (Praeger, 1972), 53.
92. Roy Porter, *The Greatest Benefit to Mankind: A Medical History of Humanity* (W. W. Norton, 1999), 434–443, 454–472; death records from the *registros civiles* of Ixcateopan and Ometepec, Guerrero.
93. INEGI, *Estadísticas Históricas de México* CD-ROM.
94. Robichaux, "Determinants of a 20th-Century Population Explosion," 195–196.
95. Anne-Emmanuelle Birn, "A Revolution in Rural Health? The Struggle Over Local Health Units in Mexico, 1928–1940," *Journal of the History of Medicine* 53 (January 1998): 46; Marcos Cueto, "Appropriation and Resistance: Local Responses to Malaria Eradication in Mexico, 1955–1970," *Journal of Latin American Studies* 37, no. 3 (August 2005): 533–559.
96. Thomas Rath, *The Dread Plague and the Cow Killers: The Politics of Animal Disease in Mexico and the World* (Cambridge University Press, 2022), 3.
97. Porter, *The Greatest Benefit to Mankind*, 426–427.

98. Letter, jefe del centro de salubridad to presidente municipal Ixcateopan, February 16, 1952, AMI–1952 exp. 131.
99. Governor of Veracruz annual reports 1945, 1947, in Carmen Blázquez Domínguez, *Estado de Veracruz: informes de sus gobernadores, 1826–1986*, 20 vols. (Universidad Veracruzana, 1986), 13:7352, 14:7554.
100. Birn, "A Revolution in Rural Health?," 58.
101. INEGI, *Estadísticas Históricas de México* CD-ROM.
102. US Government Spending website, https://www.usgovernmentspending.com/healthcare_spending.
103. Compared with the shorter school careers and higher infant mortality found in India, Egypt, and Kenya. Arundh Jain, "Population Policies That Matter," in Jain, ed., *Do Population Policies Matter?*, 6; Feliciano, "Mexico's Demographic Transition," 621, 616.
104. Jocelyn Olcott, *Revolutionary Women in Postrevolutionary Mexico* (Duke University Press, 2005), 120, 155, 215.
105. González Navarro, *Población y sociedad*, 139.
106. Brambila, "Mexico's Population Policy and Demographic Dynamics," 157; World Bank dataset, "Contraceptive prevalence, any method (percent of married women ages 15–49), https://data.worldbank.org/indicator/SP.DYN.CONU.ZS?end=1995&start=1961, accessed January 9, 2024.
107. Alba and Potter, "Population and Development in Mexico Since 1940," 62; Brambila, "Mexico's Population Policy and Demographic Dynamics," 157.
108. Soto Laveaga, "Let's Become Fewer," 28.
109. Birn, "A Revolution in Rural Health?," 63.
110. Brambila, "Mexico's Population Policy and Demographic Dynamics," 173.
111. Jain, "Population Policies That Matter," 9; Soto Laveaga, "Let's Become Fewer," 27; Potter and Mundigo, "Fertility Planning," 747–753.
112. James W. McGuire, "Social Policy and Mortality Decline in East Asia and Latin America," *World Development* 29, no. 10 (2001): 1673–1697.

Chapter Twenty-One

1. Subcomandante Marcos, interview by Julio Scherer, March 10, 2001, https://aristeguinoticias.com/3012/mexico/la–entrevista–insolita–marcos–julio–scherer–en–2001/.
2. Mathew C. Gutmann, *The Romance of Democracy: Compliant Defiance in Contemporary Mexico* (University of California Press, 2002), 1–25.
3. "En el 2000," by Natalia Lafourcade, Sony Music Entertainment Mexico, 2002.
4. Juan Villoro, *El vértigo horizontal. Una ciudad llamada México* (Almadia, 2018), 18.
5. The obvious example comes from the Familia Michoacana, a cartel that dominated Michoacán in the early 2010s, whose communiqués stressed their concern for traditional family values, as opposed to the winner-takes-all approach of their neoliberal rivals.
6. The bar went topless after intense DEA patronage fell off under the eyes of the FBI, who aspired to take over the agency. *New York Times*, October 31, 1981.
7. Adriana Malvido, "Reporteros asesinados," *Milenio*; Committee to Protect Journalists, "111 Journalists and Media Workers Killed in Mexico between 2006 and 2020," https://cpj.org/data/killed/?status=Killed&motiveConfirmed percent5B percent5D=Confirmed&motiveUnconfirme d percent5B percent5D=Unconfirmed&type percent5B percent5D=Journalist&type percent5B percent5D=Media percent20Worker&cc_fips

percent5B percent5D=MX&start_year=2006&end_year=2020&group_by=year, accessed December 11, 2023.

8. Genaro García Luna, "García Luna: Todos sabían," *Proceso*, January 22, 2023, https://www.proceso.com.mx/reportajes/2023/1/22/garcia-luna-todos-sabian-300783.html.
9. Judith Matloff, "Killing the Messenger: The Perils of Committing Journalism"; Everard Meade, "The Plaza Is for the Populacho, the Desert Is for Deep-Sea Fish," both in Paul Gillingham et al., *Journalism, Satire, and Censorship in Mexico* (University of New Mexico Press, 2017), xiv, 309–310.
10. "Víctimas anuales del crimen organizado," Latina Intelligence, https://lantiaintelligence.com/, accessed December 11, 2023.
11. Human Rights Watch World Country report 2023. https://www.hrw.org/world-report/2023/country-chapters/mexico.
12. United Nations High Commission for Refugees, "Desplazamiento Interno en México Junio 2022."
13. United Nations Office on Drugs and Crime (UNODC), *World Drug Report 2020* (United Nations publication, Sales No. E.20.XI.6), 2:20, 26–27.
14. In 2010 8.9 percent of the US population were habitual users, "2010 National Survey on Drug Use and Health," Office of National Drug Control Policy, https://obamawhitehouse.archives.gov/ondcp/ondcp-fact-sheets/2010-national-survey-on-drug-use-and-health; in 2020 it was 13.5 percent, National Center for Drug Abuse Statistics, https://drugabusestatistics.org/ https://drugabusestatistics.org/heroin-statistics/ https://www.statista.com/statistics/611697/methamphetamine-use-during-past-year-in-the-us/.
15. Merianne Rose Spencer et al., "Drug Overdose Deaths in the United States, 2001–2021," NCHS Data Brief no. 457, December 2022, 4–5.
16. Rubén Fosso, "Aumenta a 193 los muertos por matanza en San Fernando, Tamaulipas: PGR," *Milenio*, June 9, 2011.
17. "Liberan a 'El Ponchis,' niño sicario, y lo repatrian a EU," Aristegui, https://aristeguinoticias.com/2611/mexico/liberan-a-el-ponchis-nino-sicario-y-lo-repatrian-a-eu/.
18. Estimates vary widely; this is a comparatively conservative figure, drawn from the NGO Reinserta; Sandra Berenice et al., "Niñas, niños y adolescentes reclutados por la delincuencia organizada," *Reinserta.org* (2022), 7.
19. Ingo W. Schröder and Bettina E. Schmidt, "Introduction: Violent Imaginaries and Violent Practices," in Bettina E. Schmidt and Ingo W. Schröder, *Anthropology of Violence and Conflict* (Routledge, 2001), 2–6.
20. Benjamin T. Smith, *The Dope: The Real History of the Mexican Drug Trade* (W. W. Norton, 2021), 386–387, 397.
21. México Evalua/CIPE/UCSD/Global Initiative Against Transnational Crime joint policy brief 007, September 2022.
22. Anonymous, Blog del Narco, https://www.blogdelnarcomexico.com/2022/02/grupo-x-del-cjng-amenaza-comerciantes.html, accessed October 3 2022; eloquently now shut down.
23. Terrence E. Poppa, *Drug Lord: The Life and Death of a Mexican Kingpin: A True Story* (Pharos Books, 1990), 235.
24. Ruth G. Ornelas, "Organized Crime in Michoacán: Rent-Seeking Activities in the Avocado Market," *Politics & Policy* 52, no. 4 (August 2024): 785; Secretaría de Finanzas y Administración del Gobierno del Estado de Michoacán, "Análisis de Ingresos," 2009.
25. Alexander Curry, "Violence and Avocado Capitalism in Michoacán, Mexico," Noria Research, March 17, 2021, https://noria-research.com/violence-and-avocado-capitalism-in-mexico/.

26. *Informe de la Presidencia de la Comisión para la Verdad y Acceso a la Justicia del Caso Ayotzinapa*, August 2022, 88–94.
27. Miguel Fernando Valle, "Criminales atacaron tres aeronaves," *Milenio*, January 5, 2023, https://www.milenio.com/politica/tres-helicopteros-fueron-averiados-durante-detencion-de-ovidio-guzman.
28. Vanda Felbab-Brown, "How the Sinaloa Cartel Rules," Brookings Institution, April 4, 2022.
29. Julio Scherer, "En la guarida del Mayo Zambada," *Proceso*, April 4, 2010; Sean Penn, "El Chapo Speaks," *Rolling Stone* January 10, 2016.
30. Azam Ahmed, *Fear Is Just a Word: A Missing Daughter, a Violent Cartel, and a Mother's Quest for Vengeance* (Random House, 2023), xxviii–xxx.
31. *Proceso*, December 2023.
32. *New York Times*, May 18, 2012.
33. Vanda Felbab-Brown, "Cienfuegos and the US-Mexico Firestorm," Brookings Institute, November 23, 2020, https://www.brookings.edu/articles/cienfuegos-and-the-us-mexico-firestorm/.
34. Mathieu Tourliere, "La red militar que controla la inteligencia del estado," *Proceso*, April 23, 2023, 12–14.
35. Rubén Aguilar and Jorge G. Castañeda, *El narco. La guerra fallida* (Punto de Lectura, 2009), 20–22; UNODC, *World Drug Report 2006*, 2:383.
36. Isaac Campos, *Home Grown: Marijuana and the Origins of Mexico's War on Drugs* (University of North Carolina Press, 2012), 39–40, 56–58, 89, 161.
37. "Sears Once Sold Heroin," *The Atlantic* March 2019, https://www.theatlantic.com/magazine/archive/2019/03/sears-roebuck-bayer-heroin/580441/.
38. Gabriela Recio, "Drugs and Alcohol: US Prohibition and the Origins of the Drug Trade in Mexico, 1910–1930," *Journal of Latin American Studies* 32:1 (February 2002), 23–24.
39. Recio, "Drugs and Alcohol," 32.
40. Alan Knight, *The Mexican Revolution*, vol. 2, *Counter-revolution and Reconstruction* (University of Nebraska Press, 1990), 502.
41. Isaac Campos, "'Pressure-Response' and the Origins of Mexican Drug Prohibition, 1912–1920," in Wil G. Pansters and Benjamin T. Smith, *Histories of Drug Trafficking in Twentieth-Century Mexico* (University of New Mexico Press, 2022), 56–57.
42. Campos, *Home Grown*, 124.
43. Nicole Mottier, "Drug Gangs and Politics in Ciudad Juárez: 1928–1936," *Mexican Studies/Estudios Mexicanos* 25, no. 1 (Winter 2009): 24.
44. Smith, *The Dope*, 63–70; Mottier, "Drug Gangs and Politics," 25–26; José López to US Ambassador Daniels, March 5, 1934, NARG–812.114 narcotics/370.
45. Recio, "Drugs and Alcohol," 41; Smith, *The Dope*, 68.
46. Consul Smale, Ensenada, to State Department, January 29, 1932, NARG–812.114 narcotics/222.
47. Consul Macy, Tampico, to Secretary of State, September 4, 1931, NARG–812.114 narcotics/188.
48. Nathaniel Morris, "Heroin, the Herreras, and the 'Chicago Connection': The Drug Trade in Durango, 150–1985," in Pansters and Smith, *Histories of Drug Trafficking*, 293.
49. Ibid., 292.
50. Benjamin T. Smith and Wil G. Pansters, "Highs and Lows: Drug Trafficking in Baja California, 1930–1960," in Pansters and Smith, *Histories of Drug Trafficking*, 138; Smith, *The Dope*, 146–147, 164.

51. Elaine Carey, *Women Drug Traffickers: Mules, Bosses, and Organized Crime* (University of New Mexico Press, 2014), 91–157; Ambassador Josephus Daniels to Secretary of State, September 1, 1936, NARG–812.114 narcotics/571.
52. Luis Astorga, "Cocaine in Mexico: A Prelude to 'los Narcos,'" in Paul Gootenberg, *Cocaine: Global Histories* (Routledge, 1999), 182–190.
53. Douglas Clark Kinder and William O. Walker III, "Stable Force in a Storm: Harry J. Anslinger and United States Narcotics Foreign Policy, 1930–1962," *Journal of American History* 72, no. 4 (March 1986): 919.
54. Smith, *The Dope*, 92–110.
55. María Celia Toro, *Mexico's "War" on Drugs: Causes and Consequences* (Lynne Rienner Publishers, 1995), 12–14.
56. Smith, *The Dope*, 62.
57. Smith and Pansters, "Highs and Lows," 138.
58. Smith, *The Dope*, 234; UNODC, *Report of the International Narcotics Control Board 1970*, 39–42.
59. Harry J. Anslinger, "Marijuana: Assassin of Youth," *American Magazine* 124 (July 1937): 18–19, 150.
60. Smith, *The Dope*, 215.
61. Toro, *Mexico's "War" on Drugs*, 15.
62. Jack Kerouac, *On the Road* (Viking, 1959), 168, 134.
63. "Special Presidential Task Force Report: Narcotics, Marijuana and Dangerous Drugs," June 6, 1969, 23, 25, https://nsarchive2.gwu.edu/NSAEBB/NSAEBB86/.
64. Carlos Antonio Flores Pérez, "With a Little Help from His Friends: Juan N. Guerra, Smuggling, and Drug Trafficking in Tamaulipas and Nuevo León, 1940s–1960s"; Morris, "Heroin, the Herreras, and the 'Chicago Connection,'" both in Pansters and Smith, *Histories of Drug Trafficking*, 193–214, 294–295.
65. *The United Nations Single Convention on Narcotic Drugs, 1961*, 14, 23. For the full story of Coca-Cola's exception, see Paul Gootenberg, "Secret Ingredients: The Politics of Coca in US-Peruvian Relations, 1915–1965," *Journal of Latin American Studies* 36, no. 2 (May 2004): 233–265.
66. Smith, *The Dope*, 215, 231.
67. https://www.usip.org/publications/2022/01/addressing-harmful-legacy-agent-orange-vietnam.
68. Toro, *Mexico's "War" on Drugs*, 64, 27; Richard Craig, "Operation Condor: Mexico's Anti-Drug Campaign Enters a New Era," *Journal of Interamerican Studies and World Affairs* 22, no. 2 (August 1980): 346–347; Adela Cedillo, "The War on Drugs, Counterinsurgency, and the State of Siege in the Golden Triangle, 1977–1982," in Pansters and Smith, *Histories of Drug Trafficking*, 252.
69. Wil G. Pansters and Benjamin T. Smith, "Writing Twentieth-Century Mexico's Drug Histories," in Pansters and Smith, *Histories of Drug Trafficking*, 18.
70. Craig, "Operation Condor," 355, 349.
71. Smith, *The Dope*, 285–301.
72. Paul Gootenberg, *Andean Cocaine: The Making of a Global Drug* (University of North Carolina Press, 2008), 291–324.
73. Toro, *Mexico's "War" on Drugs*, 52.
74. Flores Pérez, "With a Little Help from His Friends," 210.

75. Toro, *Mexico's "War" on Drugs*, 58.
76. Julia Preston and Samuel Dillon, *Opening Mexico: The Making of a Democracy* (Farrar, Strauss and Giroux, 2005), 343.
77. Smith, *The Dope*, 37.
78. *El País*, November 6, 1997.
79. Garciá Luna was promoted yet higher under the next presidency, becoming Secretario de Seguridad Pública between 2006 and 2012. In October 2024 a court in New York sentenced him to 38 years in jail for his links to the Sinaloa Cartel. For a full treatment see Peniley Ramírez, *Los millonarios de la Guerra: El expediente inédito de García Luna y sus socios* (Grijalbo, 2020); https://www.justice.gov/es/usao-edny/pr/ex-secretario-de-seguridad-publica-mexicana-genaro-garcia-luna-condenado-mas-de-38 accessed March 2 2025.
80. The laundry cart story is the most widely accepted version; the out-the-front-door explanation is explored in Anabel Hernández, *Narcoland: The Mexican Drug Lords and their Godfathers* (Verso, 2013), 137–160.
81. Israel Cervantes Porrúa, "El drama de Felipe Calderón en la guerra en contra del narcotráfico," *Andamios* 14:34 (May-Aug 2017), 309–310.
82. A conclusion understandably undocumented but endorsed by some of Mexico's premier investigative journalists, including Sergio Aguayo and Carmen Artistegui; leading election specialist Silvia Gómez Tagle; and key operator in the Fox government, foreign minister Jorge Castañeda. Aguilar and Castañeda, *El narco*, 13.
83. The DEA and FBI systematically hyphenate Spanish last names and omit accents.
84. Ioan Grillo, *El Narco: Inside Mexico's Criminal Insurgency* (Bloomsbury Press, 2011), 76.
85. Richard C. Bonner, "The New Cocaine Cowboys: How to Defeat Mexico's Drug Cartels," *Foreign Affairs* 89, no. 4 (July/August 2010): 35–48.
86. George Jung, quoted in Grillo, *El Narco*, 97–98.
87. Romain Le Cour Grandmaison et al., "The Last Harvest? From the US Fentanyl Boom to the Mexican Opium Crisis," *Journal of Illicit Economies and Development* 1, no. 3 (2019): 313.
88. *Latin American Weekly Report*, June 25, 2009.
89. Joseph A. Schumpeter, *Capitalism, Socialism and Democracy* (Harper and Bros., 1942), 83–84.
90. Carlos Pérez Ricart and Jack Pannell, "The Guadalajara Cartel Never Existed," Noria Research, November 25, 2021, https://noria–research.com/the–guadalajara–cartel–never–existed/.
91. Grillo, *El Narco*, 371.
92. Pérez Ricart and Pannell, "The Guadalajara Cartel Never Existed".
93. Ibid.
94. Luis Chaparro, "A New DEA Map Shows Where Cartels Have Influence in the US," *Business Insider*, April 2, 2021, https://www.businessinsider.com/cartel–operatives–criticize–dea–map–of–cartel–influence–in–us–2021–4.
95. Patrick Corcoran, "US Report: Takedowns of Mexico Capos Don't Stop Drug Flow," Insight Crime, July 22, 2011, https://insightcrime.org/news/analysis/us–report–takedowns–of–mexico–capos–dont–stop–drug–flow/.
96. Quoted in Scherer, "En la guarida del Mayo Zambada," https://proceso.hn/proceso-en-la-guarida-de-el-mayo-zambada/
97. DEA paper, "A Potential for a Forward Strategy Against Heroin in Mexico," August 15, 1975, quoted in Smith, *The Dope*, 234.

98. Quoted in Smith, *The Dope*, 368.
99. *Los Angeles Times* 3 February 1990; Smith, *The Dope*, 259–260.
100. Smith, *The Dope*, 258–260, 273–275.
101. Office of the Inspector General, US Department of Justice, "Review of the Department's Oversight of Cash Seizures and Forfeiture Activities," March 2017, 10–30.
102. Morris, "Heroin, the Herreras, and the 'Chicago Connection,'" 302.
103. Bonner, "The New Cocaine Cowboys," 36.

Epilogue

1. Pablo Yankelevich, *Los otros. Raza, normas y corrupción en la gestión de la extranjería en México, 1900–1950* (Bonilla Artigas Editores), 100–117.
2. https://www.thecanadianencyclopedia.ca/en/timeline/the-indian-act; LePore, *These Truths*, 120.
3. Bernardo García Martínez and Gustavo Martínez Mendoza, *Señorios, pueblos y municipios* (Colegio de México, 2012), 40.
4. Luis Gabriel Ferrer Ortega, *La pena de muerte en el Sistema Interamericano: aproximación jurídica-filosófica* (México: Comisión Nacional de los Derechos Humano, 2015), 16.
5. According to CDC data, between 1999 and 2012 prescription opioid overdoses killed 159,819 Americans, while heroin killed 37,801. Across the period the Sacklers held as much as 30 percent market share by volume of prescription opioids. Assuming a close correlation between supply and deaths, that gives forty-eight thousand deaths. Even had the Sinaloa cartel held an absolute monopoly over heroin—which they did not, high estimates running at c. 60 percent—this is still a substantially higher number. https://www.cdc.gov/nchs/data/hestat/drug_poisoning/drug_poisoning.htm, accessed March 1, 2025; Radden Keefe, "The Family that Built an Empire of Pain," *The New Yorker*, October 23, 2017. For Sinaloa cartel market share estimates of 40 to 60 percent of opioids see J. Beittel, "Mexico: Organized Crime and Drug Trafficking Organizations" (Congressional Research Service, 2019). Pierre Gaussens, "La otra montaña roja: el cultivo de la amapola en Guerrero" Economía y Políticas Públicas 2018, registers c. 60 percent of poppy production destroyed from 2007–2015 coming from Sinaloa Cartel-controlled regions.
6. Mark Stevenson, "Mexico City's First Day of the Dead Parade Inspired by James Bond Film 'Spectre,'" *The Hollywood Reporter* November 1, 2016.
7. Over 50 percent of political articles in *El Informador de Guadalajara* and *El Norte* between 1951 and 1980 were coded as critical; by contrast a 1974 study of 94 US papers found only 31 percent of front-page articles to be critical, and inside those articles 89 percent of criticism was attributed to sources rather than the journalists themselves. Louise Falls Montgomery, "Stress on Government and Mexican Newspapers' Commentary on Government Officials: 1951–1980" (PhD diss., University of Texas at Austin, 1983), 82; Arthur H. Miller et al., "Type-Set Politics: The Impact of Newspapers on Public Confidence," *American Political Science Review* 73, no. 1 (March 1979): 68–69.
8. Gabriela Cano, "Unconcealable Realities of Desire: Amelio Robles's (Transgender) Masculinity," in Jocelyn Olcott et al., eds., *Sex in Revolution: Gender, Politics, and Power in Modern Mexico* (Duke University Press, 2006), 35–56.
9. Robert Buffington, *A Sentimental Education for the Working Man: The Mexico City Penny Press, 1900–1910* (Duke University Press, 2015), 173, 201–204; Carmen Ramos Escandón,

"Genaro García, historiador feminista del fin del siglo," *Signos históricos* 3, no. 5, 87–107. I thank L. Amari Ramírez for introducing me to Genaro García in her excellent honors thesis.

10. Drawing on Salo Baron. Yohanan Petrovsky Stern, *Jews in the Russian Army, 1827–1917* (Cambridge University Press, 2009), 4.
11. Mauricio Tenorio-Trillo, *La historia en ruinas. El culto a los monumentos y a su destrucción* (Alianza, 2023), 140.

INDEX

(*continued*)